PROTESTANT NONCONFORMIST TEXTS
VOLUME 1

Like the other volumes in the four-volume series of which it is a part, this book breaks new ground in gathering and introducing texts relating to the origins of English and Welsh Dissent. Through contemporary writings it provides a lively insight into the life and thought of early Presbyterians, Congregationalists, Baptists and Quakers, as well as of smaller groups no longer extant.

PROTESTANT NONCONFORMIST TEXTS

Series editor: Alan P. F. Sell

This series of four substantial volumes is designed to demonstrate the range of interests of the several Protestant Nonconformist traditions from the time of their Separatist harbingers in the sixteenth century to the end of the twentieth century. It represents a major project of the Association of Denominational Historical Societies and Cognate Libraries. Each volume comprises a General Introduction followed by texts illustrative of such topics as theology, philosophy, worship and socio-political concerns. This work has never before been drawn together for publication in this way. Prepared by a team of twelve editors, all of whom are expert in their areas and drawn from a number of the relevant traditions, it provides a much-needed comprehensive view of Nonconformity told largely in the words of those whose story it is. The works will prove to be an invaluable resource to scholars, students, academics and specialist and public libraries, as well as to a wider range of church, intellectual and general historians.

Other titles in the series:

Protestant Nonconformist Texts Volume 2
The Eighteenth Century
Edited by Alan P. F. Sell
with David J. Hall and Ian Sellers

Protestant Nonconformist Texts Volume 3
The Nineteenth Century
Edited by David Bebbington
with Kenneth Dix and Alan Ruston

Protestant Nonconformist Texts Volume 4
The Twentieth Century
Edited by David M. Thompson
with J. H. Y. Briggs and John Munsey Turner

Protestant Nonconformist Texts
Volume 1
1550 to 1700

Edited by
R. TUDUR JONES

with
ARTHUR LONG
and
ROSEMARY MOORE

WIPF & STOCK · Eugene, Oregon

Wipf and Stock Publishers
199 W 8th Ave, Suite 3
Eugene, OR 97401

Protestant Nonconformist Texts Volume 1
1550 - 1700
By Jones, R. Tudur and Long, Arthur
Copyright©2007 by Jones, R. Tudur
ISBN 13: 978-1-4982-1915-0
Publication date 01/20/2015
Previously published by Ashgate, 2007

Contents

Series Editor's Preface ix
Preface xi
Abbreviations xiii

Introduction 1

Part I: The Beginnings, 1550–1603

I.1	Early Separatism in London	19
I.2	The Vestiarian Controversy	20
I.3	Parker's *Advertisements*, 1566	22
I.4	London Separatists	22
I.5	The Plumbers' Hall Congregation	23
I.6	Richard Fitz's Church	33
I.7	The Admonition to the Parliament, 1572	37
I.8	Edmund Grindal Defends Prophesyings, 1576	45
I.9	The Queen Suppresses Prophesyings, 1577	53
I.10	Robert Browne: *A True and Short Declaration*	55
I.11	Robert Browne: *A Treatise of Reformation without Tarying for Anie*	63
I.12	Henry Barrow: A True Description	67
I.13	A Barrowist Declaration	72
I.14	Henry Barrow: *A Brief Discoverie of the False Church*	73
I.15	Martin Marprelate	87
I.16	John Penry: The Case for Wales	91
I.17	John Penry before the High Commission	97

Part II: Perseverance, 1604–1642

II.1	The Millenary Petition and the Hampton Court Conference	103
II.2	William Bradshaw: English Puritanism	109
II.3	Henry Jacob: The Nature of the Church	113
II.4	John Smyth: Short Confession of Faith in XX Articles	116
II.5	John Robinson: Private and Public Communion	118
II.6	The King's Declaration of Sports, 1633	125
II.7	'The New England Way'	128
II.8	The Norwich Covenant, 1643	130
II.9	The Last Will of William Wroth	131
II.10	Thomas Helwys: *The Mistery of Iniquity*	132
II.11	John Milton: *Areopagitica*	135

Part III: Facets of Freedom, 1640–1660

III.1	John Milton: Of Reformation	149
III.2	The 'Five Brethren': *An Apologeticall Narration*	151
III.3	The Westminster Confession of Faith, 1646	165
III.4	Anabaptists	190
III.5	A Fifth Monarchist Protest	192
III.6	The Ranters	198
III.7	'The Children of the Light'	201
III.8	The Earliest Account of Quakerism	202
III.9	George Fox and the Parish Ministry	205
III.10	George Fox Refutes Charges of Blasphemy	209
III.11	The Arrival of the Quaker Preachers John Camm and John Audland in Bristol, September 1654	211
III.12	A Woman's Ministry: Margaret Fell and the Kendal Fund	213
III.13	Women Preachers	215
III.14	The Case of James Nayler	216
III.15	The Savoy Declaration, 1658	221

Part IV: Persecution, 1660–1689

IV.1	Early Persecution of Quakers	229
IV.2	Consolation in Prison	230
IV.3	The Quaker Peace Testimony	232
IV.4	The Ejected Ministers Bid Farewell, 1662	235
IV.5	Philip Henry's Diary	243
IV.6	Robert Collins: Prepare for Suffering	248
IV.7	Joseph Alleine: Be Resolute!	250
IV.8	Calamy's Sufferers	251
IV.9	Persecution and Toleration	256
IV.10	The Declaration of Indulgence, 1672	259
IV.11	1672 Indulgence: Petition and Licence	261
IV.12	John Milton: True Religion and Toleration	262
IV.13	The Bristol Baptists	266
IV.14	Richard Baxter Rebuts Slanders	270
IV.15	Doing Penance	272
IV.16	Episcopal Attitudes	274
IV.17	The Trial of Richard Baxter	278

Part V: Aspects of Nonconformist Experience

V.1	Preaching	285
V.2	John Cotton: Conversion	287
V.3	John Bunyan: Temptations and Conversion	288
V.4	Morgan Llwyd: Conversion	290
V.5	Quaker Convincements	292
V.6	The Joy of the Spiritual Marriage	298
V.7	John Owen: Union with Christ	299
V.8	George Fox: 'According to the Spirit I Am the Son of God'	300
V.9	James Nayler: Union with Christ	302
V.10	A Puritan Soldier at Home	304
V.11	Thomas Goodwin: *The Heart of Christ*	305
V.12	John Owen: The Presence of Christ	309
V.13	The Glory of Silent Meetings	310
V.14	Jeremiah Burroughs: The Principles of Worship	312
V.15	Bedford Church Book	314
V.16	Richard Baxter: Faith and Love	316
V.17	Samuel Fisher: A Prophetic Call	317
V.18	George Fox: The Care of Souls	319
V.19	Morgan Llwyd: True Justice	322
V.20	John Bunyan: The Final Triumph	323

Part VI: A Theological Miscellany

VI.1	The Baptist Confession of Faith, 1677, 1688	329
VI.2	William Dell: Church, Holy Spirit and Learning	334
VI.3	Morgan Llwyd: Be Nonconformists!	340
VI.4	Regeneration	341
VI.5	Faith and Justification	342
VI.6	Sanctification	343
VI.7	Heaven	344
VI.8	Hell	346
VI.9	Walter Cradock: Gospel Liberty	348
VI.10	John Biddle: Against the Trinity	351
VI.11	Stephen Nye: Unitarianism	353
VI.12	Henry Hedworth v. William Penn	356
VI.13	The Quakers' Gospel Order	360
VI.14	Early Quaker Theology	367
VI.15	The Baptists and Total Immersion	370
VI.16	Walter Cradock: The Simplicity of the Gospel	371
VI.17	William Penn: Quaker Theology for the Non-Quaker	372
VI.18	Robert Barclay: *The Possibility and Necessity of ... Immediate Revelation*	374

Contents

Part VII: Poetry

VII.1	John Milton: On the New Forcers of Conscience	385
VII.2	John Milton: Sonnet XV, On the Late Massacre in Piedmont	386
VII.3	John Milton: 'Lycidas'	387
VII.4	John Milton: Psalm LXXXIV and Psalm VIII	388
VII.5	Morgan Llwyd: A Hymn	391
VII.6	A Fifth Monarchy Hymn	392
VII.7	Two Quaker Poems	393

Part VIII: The Dawn of Toleration

VIII.1	The Toleration Act, 1689	397
VIII.2	The Happy Union, 1691	400
VIII.3	Quakers and the Trinity	404

Select Bibliography   407
Index of Persons   415

Series Editor's Preface

I had long felt the need of a series which would present texts from the history and thought of Protestant Nonconformity in England and Wales in such a way that the breadth of the Nonconformists' interests, the extent and variety of their activities, and the depth of their devotion from the days of the sixteenth-century Separatists onwards would become plain. When the Association of Denominational Historical Societies and Cognate Libraries was formally constituted on 23 October 1993, with the objective of sharing intelligence and facilitating co-operative scholarly activity across the several denominational boundaries, I formally proposed the preparation of a series of Protestant Nonconformist Texts to the membership.

There was unanimous agreement that a need existed which could, and should, be met. It was determined that the series should comprise four volumes covering the periods 1550–1700, the eighteenth century, the nineteenth century and the twentieth century; and that each volume should be in the hands of a co-ordinating editor assisted by two co-operating editors drawn from different church traditions. The secretaries of the member societies, with the guidance of their respective committees, nominated scholars who might be approached to serve as editors. I am pleased to say that within a month the twelve editors were mustered, and I am most appreciative of their enthusiasm for the task, and of the expeditious way in which they have carried it out. It is proper to make special and grateful mention of the late Reverend Professor R. Tudur Jones who, in addition to serving as the co-ordinating editor of the first volume – a task he completed within days of his sudden and much-lamented death on 23 July 1998 – also cordially agreed to act as consultant on Welsh matters to the editors of all four volumes. The sudden death of the Reverend Dr Ian Sellers, a contributing editor of Volume II, has left a further significant gap in the ranks of scholars of English Nonconformity, as has the passing of the Reverend Dr Arthur Long, a contributing editor to this volume, whose death was announced as Volumes I and IV were in the press.

The editors were given a fairly free hand in the organisation of their volumes: indeed, the nature of the materials has been permitted to suggest the layout of the several volumes. It is claimed that the order of each volume is clear and justifiable, even if in format one may differ slightly from another.

It is hoped that the series will prove helpful to students and interested readers, and that scholars may find it useful to have a checklist of sources which, though necessarily limited by considerations of space, is intended as an appetiser and a stimulus to further quarrying.

Above all, it is hoped that worthy tribute is here paid to those who, often at great personal cost, and in face of socio-political obstacles of various kinds, declared their faith and bore their witness. Indeed (to advert to realities, not to utter a lament), in a time of general apologetic caution, widespread doctrinal ignorance

Series Editor's Preface

and apathy, fitful ecumenism, queried national institutions and overall numerical decline among the Protestant Nonconformists of England and Wales, it may even be that forebears have something to teach those who inherit their mantle – and any others who may care to listen.

On behalf of my editorial colleagues I should like to thank Sarah Lloyd, Liz Pearce and all at Ashgate Publishing for their commitment to this project and for the care they have lavished upon it.

Alan P. F. Sell

Preface

This collection of documents is the first in a series which is intended to illustrate the development of Protestant Nonconformity in England and Wales. This volume is inevitably highly selective but the extensive bibliography should make it possible for readers to explore this aspect of Christian history in greater detail. We have depended upon the advice and assistance of many people. We have drawn upon the resources of The National Library of Wales, Aberystwyth, and of Dr Williams's Library, London. At the University of Wales, Bangor, the Welsh Librarian, Mr Rheon Pritchard, has been most helpful, as well as Dr Densil Morgan and Dr Geraint Tudur of the School of Theology and Religious Studies. The expenses incurred by Dr Rosemary Moore in preparing the Quaker material were largely met by a grant from the Edith Ellis Trust and she has drawn heavily on the advice and assistance of Mr Malcolm Thomas, the Friends House Librarian and his staff at the Friends House Library, London. Dr Hugh Pyper proposed and most kindly edited the extract from Robert Barclay's writings. Mr Cecil Sharman advised on Isaac Penington and Professor Edwin B. Bronner on William Penn. Ms Elisa Glines helped with the transcription of Margaret Fell's letter from the Thirnbeck MSS. Valuable comments and advice were also received from Dr Hugh Barbour, Dr Daniel Christopher, Professor J. William Frost, Dr Douglas Gwyn, Dr H. Larry Ingle, Dr Phyllis Mack, Dr Geoffrey F. Nuttall, Mr Joseph Pickvance and Mr John Punshon. None of these scholars is in any way responsible for the use that has been made of their contributions. The general editor of the series, Professor Alan P. F. Sell, has monitored our progress with unfailing sympathy and generosity.

To all these, we extend our warmest gratitude. But any errors or faults in the volume are the responsibility of the editors.

R. Tudur Jones

Abbreviations

BQ	W. C. Braithwaite, *The Beginnings of Quakerism*
CHST	*Congregational Historical Society Transactions*
CJ	*The Journal of George Fox* (ed. N. Penney, Cambridge edition)
CR	*Calamy Revised* (ed. A. G. Matthews)
DNB	*Dictionary of National Biography*
DQB	*Dictionary of Quaker Biography*, Friends House, London
DWB	*Dictionary of Welsh Biography*
EED	Champlin Burrage, *Early English Dissenters*
EQL	Early Quaker Letters, 1952 (ed. G. F. Nuttall: unpublished but available in the main libraries)
EQW	Barbour and Roberts, *Early Quaker Writings*
JFHS	*Journal of the Friends Historical Society*
LEF	*Letters of Early Friends* (ed. A. R. Barclay)
NIDCC	*The new International Dictionary of the Christian Church* (ed. J. D. Douglas)
NJ	*The Journal of George Fox* (ed. J. L. Nickalls)
ODDC	*The Oxford Dictionary of the Christian Church* (ed. F. L. Cross)
QPE	H. Barbour, *Quakers in Puritan England*
SPQ	W. C. Braithwaite, *The Second Period of Quakerism*
VCH	Victoria County History

Introduction

According to the *Oxford English Dictionary*, the word 'Nonconformist' was first used in 1619 and it meant 'one who, while adhering to the doctrine of the Church of England, refused to conform to its discipline and practice (chiefly in the matter of certain ceremonies)'. Thus the authors of *An Apologeticall Narration* (1644) refer to Thomas Cartwright and his colleagues in the age of Elizabeth as the 'good old Nonconformists'. But, continues the *Oxford Dictionary*, 'after the passing of the Act of Uniformity of 1662 and the consequent ejection from their livings of those ministers who refused to conform' the word was used to refer to 'a member of a religious body which is separated from the Church of England' and so became synonymous with 'Protestant Dissenter'. In fact the word 'Dissenter' began to be used in a general sense as early as the 1640s. Thus we find Dr John Owen in the appendix, 'On Toleration', to his sermon before the House of Commons, 31 January 1648, referring to 'those dissenters who are known by the names of Presbyterians and Independents'.[1] After the passing of the Toleration Act in 1689, 'Dissenters' came into common use to signify those whose limited freedom to worship was assured by that Act.

In selecting documents for inclusion in this collection we have used the word 'Nonconformist' in a more inclusive way than its history, strictly interpreted, would permit. Thus we have included quotations referring to Elizabethan 'Separatists' although their contemporaries would not have called them 'Nonconformists', as well as those in the period before 1662 considered by our contemporary historians to be the precursors of modern Nonconformist denominations.

The history of Nonconformity moves through five closely interconnected stages. First was the period coinciding with the reign of Elizabeth when the main principles of protest were being developed in defiance of official oppression. The second stage, beginning with the accession of James I and extending to about 1640, was characterised by gradual growth whose consequences became evident in the third stage. At the same time these were years of increasing frustration when hundreds of Nonconformists emigrated to seek a wider freedom in the Netherlands and New England. The third stage was the period of ascendancy extending from 1640 to 1660 in which Presbyterians and Independents secured access to the centres of power. At the same time there emerged at this time a new type of vigorous sectarian Nonconformity. With the restoration of the monarchy and the Church of England in 1660 came a long period of persecution which failed to uproot Nonconformity and which in many ways brought out the best elements in it. This stage continued up to the Glorious Revolution of 1688 and the subsequent accession of William and Mary. And so the last ten years of the period covered in this book ushered in the age of toleration.

When interpreted in a broad sense, Nonconformity is seen as a very complex movement. The amount of material available to illustrate its many facets is enormous. A selection of documents restricted to one volume therefore can hope to do no more than illustrate some of the various aspects of the movement as it developed in the period up to 1700. A parallel selection could easily be made consisting of quite different documents.

The government, liturgy and theology of the Church of England were 'by law defined'. To be a Nonconformist meant disobeying the laws of the land. So it could be said, albeit in a negative way, that Nonconformity was defined by law. That is why a selection of relevant portions of the laws that had a bearing on the actions and beliefs of Nonconformists are included. The implementation of the laws and their administration involved the use of several modes of discipline. The ecclesiastical courts were still active in the period between 1559 and 1700 although their authority was diminishing. Their records, where they have survived, often cast a vivid light on the treatment meted out to Nonconformists.[2] Much the same is true of the civil courts particularly in the period after 1662 when Nonconformists were accused of infringing the Penal Code. The Court of High Commission, although originally an ad hoc commission, had become by 1580 a permanent institution and under the guidance of John Whitgift, who became archbishop of Canterbury in 1583, it proved an efficient instrument for eliminating overt Puritanism amongst the clergy.[3] Cases involving Nonconformists inevitably took up much of its time. Now and again cases involving them were tried in the Court of Star Chamber, whose existence as an institution separate from the Privy Council can be dated from about 1540.[4] The implementation of the laws relating to religion involved also pronouncements by archbishops. Examples of such are Matthew Parker's *Advertisements* of 1566 or the articles which John Whitgift formulated in 1583 in which preaching, catechising or reading in private houses were prohibited while no one was to exercise ecclesiastical functions unless he had subscribed to the royal supremacy and promised to abide strictly by the Book of Common Prayer and the Thirty-nine Articles. Equally demanding were the detailed visitation articles produced by William Laud in the 1630s. The monarch was, of course, the 'Supreme Governor' of the Church of England and as such could intervene in religious matters. Elizabeth had no qualms about doing this as when she instructed Archbishop Grindal to prohibit the holding of prophesyings. The *Book of Sports*, first issued by James I in 1617 and reissued in 1633 by Charles I, described what recreations were permissible on Sundays. But the most dramatic example of royal intervention was the promulgation by Charles II of the Declaration of Indulgence in 1672.

Naturally the Puritans in general were compelled to seek relief from the legal restraints upon them by parliamentary action. An early example of such action was the *Admonition to the Parliament* of 1572 which expressed the views of those like Thomas Cartwright (1535–1603), John Field (1545–88) and Thomas Wilcox (1549?–1608) who hoped that the support they had among members of parliament would lead to further reformation of the Church of England and bring about amongst other things the replacement of its episcopal structure by some form of Presbyterianism. They were disappointed in their hopes and the movement had collapsed by 1591. Its hopes revived with the accession of James I in 1603 and they found expression in the Millenary Petition which was presented to him on his way south. These hopes, however, did not find favour with the King.

Official representations to the authorities were not the only means of protest open to Nonconformists. A constant flow of books and pamphlets promulgated their views. Most of these were contributions to the learned debate about the various points of difference between the parties. Such were the tomes produced by the likes of Thomas Cartwright, William Ames (1576–1633) and John Cotton (1584–1652). The more radical agitators, however, dared to defy censorship by producing pamphlets on illegal printing presses. The most notorious of these productions was the series of seven pamphlets known as the Martin Marprelate Tracts, the first of which appeared about October 1588 and the last in September 1589. Not all Nonconformists were satisfied with printed declarations of their views. The more moderate amongst this group felt that practical action was necessary. One such activity was to organise a 'prophesying'. A group of ministers would meet every Saturday morning to expound scripture, each one taking it in turn to address the meeting. The public were invited to be present and were permitted to ask questions. But this experiment in adult education was prohibited when the Queen in May 1577 ordered them to be suppressed, a step she took on her own account when Archbishop Edmund Grindal (1519?–83) refused to obey the order. After a meeting of some sixty leaders at Cockfield in Suffolk an attempt was made to organise groups of parishes into voluntary presbyteries. This 'Classis Movement' blossomed mainly in the Midlands and East Anglia and its best-known centre was at Dedham in Essex. These attempts to graft a nascent form of Presbyterianism on the Church of England were short-lived and succumbed under the pressure brought upon their instigators by John Whitgift (c. 1530–1604) and Richard Bancroft (1544–1610), bishop of London from 1597 and Whitgift's successor at Canterbury from 1604.

These activities took place within the Church of England but there were more impatient spirits who raised fundamental questions about the doctrine and the administration of the Established Church. For them the logical course to take was to leave it and establish new churches. These were the Separatists. Such groups existed early on in the reign of Elizabeth. The congregation associated with the name of Richard Fitz is an example. They caused some anxiety to the authorities and the members were arrested and closely examined. Soon the case for separation from the Church of England was argued with greater consistency and vigour. The pioneer in this activity was Robert Browne (c. 1553–1633) who together with his friend Robert Harrison (d. 1585), established a Separatist Church at Norwich about 1580. Browne expounded his views on the nature of the church in *A Treatise of Reformation without Tarying for Anie* (1582). Separatism in London moved in the same direction. The leaders, Henry Barrow and John Greenwood, both of whom were executed in 1593, were arrested in 1586 and after May 1587 were imprisoned together at the Fleet Prison. They were able to acquire writing materials and to provide the public with accounts of the treatment to which they were subjected as well as to publicise their views. Barrow's book *A Brief Discoverie of the False Church* is an unsparing indictment of the Church of England and, together with his other writings, expounds his understanding of the nature of the Christian Church. Towards the end of 1592 John Penry, who had been deeply implicated in the printing of the Marprelate Tracts, became a member of the London Separatist Church. He too was executed in 1593. It is true that the Separatists formed a minute proportion of the population but their significance lies not in the undoubted bitterness of their writing but in the fundamental challenge they made to conceptions of the nature of the Christian Church and of its relationship with the secular power which had dominated European culture ever since the reign of the Emperor Constantine the Great.

Despite the fact that some fifty-two of its members were in prison by 1590, the London Separatist congregation organised itself into a gathered church in September 1592 and elected Francis Johnson (1562–1618) to be its pastor and the learned John Greenwood (d. 1609) as its teacher. In April 1593 the 'Act to retain the Queen's subjects in obedience' was passed and decreed banishment for incorrigible Nonconformists. Harsh as its wording was, it prompted the Separatists to seek a safe haven in Amsterdam. Soon Separatism was to gain support in the neighbourhood of Gainsborough, where John Smyth (c. 1565–1612) was the leading light, and Scrooby, where the church was organised by John Robinson (c. 1575–1625). Following the example of the London Separatists they too emigrated. Smyth and his flock settled at Amsterdam where he adopted Baptist principles about 1609 and embraced an Arminian theology. He and his supporters were admitted into the Mennonite Church. Those members of the congregation who disagreed with his disavowal of his own baptism supported Thomas Helwys in his opposition to Smyth and returned to England in 1612, thus pioneering the tradition of the General Baptists. Because these differences led to animated controversy in Amsterdam, John Robinson and his people moved to Leyden where he became a much respected figure in the life of the university and town. They were not entirely happy there and sought a new home. With this end in view many of them emigrated to New England and found fame as the 'Pilgrim Fathers'. Robinson did not share the bitterness of the earlier Separatists. In his book *Of Religious Communion Private and Public* (1614) he had argued that to refuse to participate in the official church actions of the Church of England did not entail a refusal to join in personal religious acts with individual godly members of the church. By 1617 he had taken a further step in *A Treatise of the Lawfulness of Hearing of the Ministers of the Church of England*, published posthumously in 1634, and argued that Separatists could attend parish services in order to hear ministers whose sermons were edifying and scriptural without compromising their opposition to the pattern of government in the church. This 'semi-Separatism', as it has been called, found support on English soil when Robinson's friend Henry Jacob (1563–1624) founded the Independent Church at Southwark in 1616.

The objections of these early Nonconformists to the religion by law established centred on four topics. First, there was intense disquiet amongst all Nonconformists about the Book of Common Prayer. They asked themselves whether it conformed with the prescriptions of the New Testament and decided that it did not. The central concern of Christianity is the relationship between people and God.

Introduction

Never has that concern been expressed more succinctly and more memorably than in the opening words of the Shorter Westminster Catechism, 'What is the chief end of man? To glorify God and enjoy Him for ever.' Amongst the many implications of this conviction was the desire to ensure that fellowship with God was maintained and enriched in ways pleasing to God and in consonance with his revealed will in Holy Scripture. It was therefore little wonder that such an animated discussion about Christian worship should have exercised the minds of religious leaders in the sixteenth and seventeenth centuries. Early in the reign of Elizabeth controversy began about the vestments which clergy were instructed to wear in accordance with the ornaments rubric of the 1559 Book of Common Prayer. The 1552 book had merely required priests and deacons to wear a surplice but in the 1559 book they were commanded to wear alb and vestment or cope. The protesters would not wear them. Archbishop Matthew Parker at the behest of the Queen sought to preserve compliance with the rubric by issuing his *Advertisements* in 1566 and threatening suspension upon all clergymen who did not wear the required vestments. But the disobedience continued despite the punishment meted out from time to time by the authorities. Dissatisfaction with the Book of Common Prayer was not confined to the question of vestments. Richard Hooker (c. 1554–1600), the foremost apologist for the Anglican Church in the reign of Elizabeth, summarised what Puritans said about the Prayer Book in these words: 'it is not orderly read, nor gestured as beseemeth, ... it hath a number of short cuts or shreddings, which may be better called wishes than Prayers: it useth the Lord's Prayer too often; ... it craveth earthly things too much; ... some things it asketh unseasonably, when they need not be prayed for, as deliverance from thunder and tempest, when no danger is nigh'.[5] These and many other detailed criticisms sound petty and niggling but the fundamental objections were serious enough such as the objection to kneeling when receiving Communion because it smacked of adoring the elements and the objection to making the sign of the Cross over a child at baptism because it suggested that it produced a miraculous transformation such as immediate regeneration. And the Baptists, of course, objected to the baptism of infants. Unless the New Testament stipulated what a minister must wear and do in the conduct of divine service, then the secular authority could not make them compulsory.

The second topic which made many Nonconformists dissatisfied with the Church of England was episcopacy. Here much of their thinking was conditioned by the fact that the Reformed churches on the Continent of Europe had rejected episcopacy. As with worship, so with church government, the crucial question was what kind of ministry was authorised by the New Testament. There was no unanimity amongst Nonconformists on this topic. In fact, there were those who combined objections to the stipulations of the Prayer Book about worship with acceptance of episcopacy, although not necessarily the precise type of episcopacy to be found in the Church of England. Then there were those who wished to substitute some form of presbyterianism for episcopacy and this group was to become very influential by the time the Long Parliament met. Then there were the more radical Nonconformists who argued for a congregational form of church polity.

The third point of protest had to do with the church courts and their Canon Law. Naturally, people who had suffered at the hands of these institutions had very strong feelings about them. Again, they felt that there was no warrant in Scripture for them and that discipline in the church should be in accordance with biblical principles and not in accordance with a system of law that had persisted since the Middle Ages.

A fourth point of disagreement concerned the relationship between church and state. This was a difficult and dangerous topic in the period because to criticise the integration between the Established Church and the state could only too easily be construed as treason. Here again there was a diversity of opinion amongst Nonconformists. Some merely wanted a revision of the relationship in order to ensure that the church was not oppressed by political considerations. But the more radical protesters, and the Separatists particularly, did raise questions that in a later era would imply the disestablishment of the church. But the time for such a demand lay in the future.

Thus by 1620 Nonconformity had found expression in a variety of forms. There were ministers within the Church of England who deviated from the strict stipulations of the laws of religion and the orders of archbishops and bishops. There were also those outside the Church who adopted the views of John Robinson and appreciated the piety and theology of these Puritan ministers but felt bound in conscience to form churches separate from the Church of England. Alongside them were those Separatists or Brownists who rejected any kind of communion public or private with the Established Church.

The harassment suffered by Nonconformists of all kinds reached a new pitch with the advent to power of William Laud (1573–1645). His election to the see of London in 1628, followed by his elevation to Canterbury in 1633, provided him with the authority to attack Puritanism by a rigorous application of his High Church principles. The Separatists and the Pilgrim Fathers were not the only ones who sought freedom from his attentions by emigrating. Many thousands went to New England or to the Netherlands. Despite losing many able leaders, Nonconformity was by no means entirely uprooted. That it had been quietly spreading in the kingdom became obvious in a dramatic way after the Long Parliament began its work in 1640.

Thus all Nonconformists were dissatisfied with the Elizabethan religious settlement but they were not all dissatisfied for the same reasons nor to the same extent. In addition people's attitudes were affected by powerful economic, social and political influences at work during the period with which we are concerned. The state was seeking to maintain stability in a volatile society where brutality and disorder were never far from erupting into something much more serious. There was a prolonged crisis in the economy. The late sixteenth and early seventeenth centuries experienced a distressing escalation of inflation which continued from about 1510 up to the outbreak of the Civil Wars. In the 1590s domestic prices rose alarmingly because of bad harvests and government expenditure on wars. Conditions in this respect grew even worse in the 1630s. If the price index be put at 158 in 1540, by 1638 it had reached 707. The price of grain, for example, rose from 154 points in 1540 to 569 in 1639. It is true that the wages of agricultural labourers had risen threefold between 1509 and 1640 but their purchasing power had halved.[6] Obviously such a severe economic crisis bore hard upon the workers of the land and fuelled a desperation that was to find expression amongst the radical sects of the Interregnum. But it also deeply affected the professional classes, the people who were not closely attached to the soil and could not produce their own food. Naturally, they became increasingly uneasy. There was deep dissatisfaction with government administration and it found a focus in growing criticism of the central institutions of state and the monarchy in particular. The condition of the poor was often desperate. Many of the well-to-do found their wealth being eroded while those who had the means could buy them out. In addition, the immense increase in internal trade from 1570 onwards brought into being a mobile class of people who were wanderers and wayfarers. They were a challenge to any settled order, mercantile pilgrims whose spiritual equivalent was John Bunyan's Christian who had no settled home this side of the Eternal City. The very foundations of the patriarchal, feudal society were cracking. The ferment was strongly affected also by the influence of the Renaissance and the Protestant Reformation upon the attitudes of the intellectuals. No longer could cultured people be expected to be governed by principles elaborated by a handful of leaders at the behest of a monarch. There was a growing conviction that personal independence was a right to be treasured. The doctrine of the Priesthood of all Believers might emerge initially as a spiritual and theological principle but it could very easily be transformed into a political demand for equality of opportunity. The protagonists of the ecclesiological convictions of Presbyterians, Separatists and Independents might insist stridently that these were no threat to social order. In practice, however, they did confer on all the members of their respective congregations a real local self-government in the religious sphere which could without difficulty be transformed into democratic political programmes. It was little wonder that their activities prompted the sharp disapproval of Queen Elizabeth, Charles I and William Laud. It is therefore possible to argue that the defenders of the Church of England were inspired by a frequently unacknowledged anxiety about preserving social order while their Nonconformist opponents were motivated by a desire for social change.

Whatever measure of truth there is in these possibilities they should not be allowed to justify cynicism about the sincerity of the theological concerns of the participants. No economic and social crisis is without its spiritual repercussions in the minds and hearts of those who are caught up in it. It was an age when people took the wrath of God seriously. As John Penry put it:

> We feel the Lords hand many waies against vs at this time in regard of the scarcity of all thinges, and especially of victuals, and great number of poor ... The vnseasonable haruest 1585 yealded very little Corne ... The winter 1585 destroied al their cattle wel near, so that now the very sinowe of their mainteinance is gone ... This famine is for our sinnes, the Lord without our repetaunce saith it shal continue.[7]

The lengthy and tortuous theological controversies that erupted in the reign of Elizabeth and subsequently might seem highly academic to a more secular age but in the sixteenth and seventeenth centuries they were intensely relevant precisely because famine, poverty and oppression were closely connected with God's displeasure with a disobedient people. All these controversial topics were matters of intense seriousness for the Christians of that age and it behoves us to consider with patience and understanding the theological disquisitions that they produced in such abundance. And so in our selection of documents we have sought to give examples, if no more, of this side of the Nonconformist experience.

The period between 1603 and 1640 was a frustrating time for Nonconformists of all kinds. Those who found it possible to continue in the ministry of the Church of England were reconciled to biding their time, concentrating on the educational, spiritual and moral aspects of their work and eschewing for the time being any thought of parliamentary agitation. Others withdrew to New England or the Netherlands, many of them looking forward to a time when they could return and continue the struggle to reform the Church of England. Then in 1640 with the convening of the Long Parliament a remarkable opportunity was offered them. As early as 11 December 1640 the citizens of the City of London expressed their criticisms of the Church in the Root and Branch Petition submitted to the House of Commons demanding that the existing ecclesiastical government 'with all its dependencies, roots and branches, may be abolished' and enumerating in detail twenty-four objections. Reforms followed one another rapidly. On 5 July 1641 the Court of Star Chamber was abolished as well as the High Commission. Then on 1 December 1641 the House of Commons presented to the King its Grand Remonstrance on the state of the kingdom, enumerating complaints about most aspects of government policy. But the King's Proclamation on Religion on 10 December demonstrated that he was quite unmoved by this agitation and commanded that the services of the Church of England should be conducted in accordance with the laws of the land. The tensions between King and Parliament intensified and at last the King decided to take the field against Parliament. On 22 August 1642 he raised his banner at Nottingham and declared the Commons and their soldiers to be traitors. So the first Civil War began.

It soon became obvious to Parliament that it could not effectively prosecute the war without help from Scotland. That help was secured by signing the Solemn League and Covenant. The signatories undertook, amongst other things, 'the reformation of religion in the kingdoms of England and Ireland, in doctrine, worship, discipline and government, according to the Word of God, and the example of the best reformed Churches'. In the preceding negotiations, the Scots had wanted the covenant to include a specific commitment to establishing Presbyterianism. Two of the parliamentary commissioners, Henry Vane and Philip Nye, who were Independents, objected and it was they who insisted on the words 'according to the Word of God'. In order to fulfil its promise, Parliament convened 'an Assembly of learned, godly and judicious Divines' to advise it how best to bring the Church of England 'into a nearer conformity with the Church of Scotland and other Reformed Churches abroad'. This was the Westminster Assembly which held its sittings from 1 July 1643 until 22 February 1649. It was to make a very significant contribution to Calvinistic theology that was to influence not only the Nonconformists but many thousands of Christians in many countries over the next three centuries. Its Confession of Faith was completed on 4 December 1646 and approved by Parliament on 20 June 1648. It also produced two catechisms which were completed in the autumn of 1647. The Shorter Catechism became exceptionally popular and for several generations was used as an educational tool in the Nonconformist churches. The Savoy Declaration, produced by the delegates of the Independent churches in England and Wales in 1658 hardly differs in its dogmatic sections from the Westminster Confession and the same is true of the Baptist Confession of 1677. If there was agreement on dogmatic theology in the Westminster Assembly, there were acute differences on the point of church government. A small group of Independents, usually referred to as the 'Dissenting Brethren', objected to the proposals of the majority to institute a thoroughly presbyterian system on the Scottish model. The leaders of this dissenting group were Philip Nye (1596?–1672), Thomas Goodwin (1800–80), William Bridge (1600?–1670), Jeremiah Burroughes (1599–1646) and Sidrach Simpson (1600?–55) and they were supported by others from time to time. They expounded their main principles in *An Apologeticall Narration* (1643). The debates in the Assembly provoked a fierce pamphlet warfare in the country. But the Presbyterians carried the day and drew up plans to reform the Church of England in ways consonant with their own convictions.

Calvinism was the theology favoured by the majority of Nonconformists and it had some able expositors in men like John Owen (1616–83), Thomas Goodwin and John Bunyan (1628–88). There were those who were critical of the Westminster Standards. The Independent John Goodwin (1594?–1665), for example, was a vociferous Arminian and Richard Baxter (1615–91), the most prolific of all Puritan authors, insisted on modifying the accepted Calvinism. The Quakers also were vigorous and trenchant critics of Calvinism.

During the turbulent years between 1640 and 1650 virtually every group of Christians was at one time or another Nonconformist. The Roman Catholic recusants had, of course, been Nonconformists from the Church by law established ever since the accession of Elizabeth. Their faith was still proscribed but Oliver Cromwell himself showed a moderation towards them that was quite exceptional at the time. He desired to assist those among them who abided by the law. English Catholics (in contrast to Irish Catholics) had no real reason to feel bitter towards the Protector.[8]

The Anglicans experienced mixed fortunes. It is difficult if not impossible to compute the exact number of incumbents who were ejected between 1643 and 1660. John Walker in his book *The Sufferings of the Clergy* (1714) sought to provide as full a picture as he could but A. G. Matthews in his *Walker Revised* (1948, 1988) showed that Walker had underestimated the number. Matthews counted 2,425 sequestered benefices, about a thousand more than those listed by Walker but with the prevalence of pluralism it is not possible to estimate accurately how many incumbents suffered as a result. In the case of Wales (with which

Matthews was not concerned) we can be fairly certain that under The Propagation Act (1650) 271 clergymen were ejected with an added 81 in the previous years.[9] Walker was quite justified in writing about 'the sufferings of the clergy' for suffer they did, many hundreds of them. It is true that Anglicans were still able to maintain clandestine services and many priests succeeded in continuing their ministrations unmolested and hundreds were ordained secretly. But the Church of England suffered permanent disruption as a result and, as A. G. Matthews put it, 'Nonconformity had become inevitable'.[10] It would have been possible for us to include documents to illustrate what the experience of refusing to conform meant to Anglicans and Catholics but we have chosen not to do so.

The 1640s saw a remarkable outburst of intellectual energy. Publication of books and pamphlets overwhelmed the official machinery for controlling the press. Ever since Elizabeth's Injunctions of 1559, the government had sought to protect the public from offensive, heretical and seditious ideas. Printers and booksellers were required to seek permission to publish and sell books through the Stationers' Company. Censorship was exercised under the Crown by the Bishop of London and the Archbishop of Canterbury. It became impossible to maintain this system as the attack on episcopacy intensified. A parliamentary ordinance on 14 June 1643 sought to reimpose control over the press by appointing licensers to act as censors while the Stationers' Company and the officers of the two Houses were authorised to search for unlicensed presses and to break them up as well as to search for unlicensed books, to confiscate them and apprehend the offenders. But in vain. Not only were illicit books being published but an increasing number of them were arguing openly for toleration. No wonder a Presbyterian like Matthew Newcomen (1610?–69), in his sermon before Parliament on 12 September 1644, insisted that the opinion 'that every man is to be left to the Liberty of his own Religion' which 'if encouraged, (& they are encouraged, if connived at) will open a door to *Turcisme, Judaisme, Atheisme, Polytheisme*, any monster of opinion'.[11] November 1644 saw the publication of the most powerful plea for liberty of printing and freedom in general, namely John Milton's *Areopagitica*. In practice the failure of censorship let loose a flood of books and pamphlets upon the public. George Thomason (d. 1666), the London bookseller, made a hobby of collecting every possible publication issued between 1642 and 1662, by which time he had amassed a collection of no less than 23,000 items. Every conceivable aspect of religion, morality and politics found expression in these publications. The Presbyterian Thomas Edwards (1599–1647) was appalled and on 16 February 1646 the first part of his three-volume *Gangraena* was published, in which he produced a massive list of heresies and of heretics. Similarly Ephraim Pagit (1575?–1647) treated every divergence from Calvinistic orthodoxy as pernicious heresy in his *Heresiography* (1645). Such virulent protests did nothing to stem the expression of divergent and alarming views. It was a time of intense excitement amongst Puritans. There was a feeling that history was moving towards a dramatic climax. The victories of Cromwell and the execution of Charles I on 30 January 1649 intensified the conviction that these events had a profound eschatological significance. The Fifth Monarchy Men were not the only ones who believed that a new age was dawning.

Introduction

Dr John Owen, for example, in his sermon on 19 April 1650, *The Shaking and Translating of Heaven and Earth* based on Hebrews 12.2, said:

> The Lord Jesus Christ, by his mighty power, in these latter days, as anti-christian tyranny draws to its period will so far shake and translate the political heights, governments and strength of the nations, as shall serve for the full bringing in of his own peaceable kingdom – the nations so shaken become thereby a quiet habitation for the people of the Most High.[12]

Owen was not himself a Fifth Monarchist but he was one of those who contributed towards the creation of that feverish atmosphere in which fantastic speculation about God's intervention in worldly matters jostled with sober exposition of the Bible. The clash of ideas led to the formation of groups and parties which caused the authorities, both religious and secular, no little anxiety. Such were William Walwyn (*fl.* 1600–51) and John Lilburne (1614?–57), the leaders of the Levellers; Gerard Winstanley (*fl.*1648–52) and the Diggers; Ludovicke Muggleton (1609–80) and John Reeve (1608–58), the founders of the Muggletonians, men who, like William Erbury, believed that the Age of the Spirit, the Third Dispensation, had dawned; Vavasor Powell (1617–70) and the Fifth Monarchy Men; Laurence Clarkson (1615–67) who at various times belonged to almost every possible sect, together with Abiezer Coppe (1619–72) are linked with the Antinomian group usually called the Ranters. Then there were such free spirits as John Saltmarsh (d. 1647) and William Dell (d. 1664) whose emphasis on free grace and criticism of legalism laid them also open to the charge of Antinomianism. Several sectarians were critical of the orthodox doctrine of the Trinity and agreed with the Unitarianism of John Biddle (1615–62). Amidst all this John Durie (1596–1680) worked diligently but unsuccessfully to promote Christian unity.

These groups were short-lived although many of their ideas were to persist and to reappear in varying contexts in later generations. But there was one notable exception. Amongst all these fascinating personalities none was more impressive than George Fox (1624–91). In his youth he had known what it was to seek the truth amidst the conflicting voices of his religious contemporaries. At last he found rest in 1647 when he was 'convinced' by profoundly moving experiences of the 'infinite love of God', as he put it in his *Journal*, and the reality of the guidance provided by the 'Light Within'. In 1649 he began his mission to proclaim the truth that had been revealed to him. It was a mission which took him through large areas of Britain at the cost of incessant harassment, persecution, insult and imprisonment. His was a heroic career which resulted in the formation of the Religious Society of Friends. Unlike the other groups and sects that flourished during the Interregnum, the Quakers survived to make their unique contribution to modern Christianity.

This was a highly articulate age in religious matters. Nonconformists shared the faith of their contemporaries in the influence of the press. But that enthusiasm was not confined to the printed word. This was one of the most striking periods in the history of preaching, more so in England than in Wales. Preaching was seen as the foremost means of grace. Thomas Goodwin made the point in a poetical metaphor when he said:

> When en ointment box is once opened, then it casts its savour about; and when the juice of the medicinal herb is once strained out and applied, then it heals. And so, it is the spiritual meaning of the word let into the heart which converts it and turns it to God.[13]

It was this conviction that inspired the passing on 22 February 1650 of the Act for the Better Propagation of the Gospel in Wales and of a similar act for the northern counties of England a week later. Naturally, preachers varied considerably in their abilities as communicators. John Owen, for example, admitted that he was envious of John Bunyan's gifts as a preacher. King Charles II once asked Owen why he listened to an uneducated tinker. He replied, 'Could I possess the tinker's abilities for preaching, please your majesty, I would gladly relinquish all my learning'.[14] Owen was rather too modest. He himself was an impressive preacher, as was his colleague, Thomas Goodwin, although doubtless their appeal was to a rather different audience from that which crowded to hear Bunyan on his visits to London. There is no doubt about people's readiness to listen to sermons at least up to the Restoration. Inevitably the Nonconformist congregations diminished during the age of persecution. Alongside the sermon was the lecture although the distinction between them was a very thin one. Some series of lectures were exceptionally long. Joseph Caryl (1602–73) spent twenty-three years expounding the book of Job while William Gouge (1578–1653) lectured on Hebrews for thirty-three years. Preaching or lecturing was usually in the context of a leisurely service. Thus John Howe (1630–1705) on a fast day would begin the day at nine o'clock and continue with prayers, bible readings and sermon until four o'clock with only a brief break for a snack.[15] The willingness of people to listen to sermons and the fact that such large numbers of the sermons were published means that what was said from the pulpits was felt to be relevant to the concerns, hopes and anxieties of the listeners.

The enthusiasm and excitement of the Interregnum came to an abrupt end. On 3 September 1658 Oliver Cromwell died and the Puritan ascendancy ended. When the news was conveyed to the small company that had been praying for the Protector's recovery, Thomas Goodwin expressed his grief in the words of Jeremiah 20.7, 'O Lord, thou hast deceived me, and I was deceived'. The death of Cromwell and the events that followed were more than a political disappointment for Nonconformists. They created a profound spiritual crisis. They meant the shattering of those apocalyptic hopes that had been the focus of so many prayers and sermons over the previous years. In view of the increasing turmoil and uncertainty of 1659, both Parliament and the army concluded that the only solution was to invite the exiled king to return to his throne. Charles II landed at Dover on 25 May 1660. Those who had participated in the struggle against the Church of England took heart from the Declaration he had made at Breda on 4 April which promised that there would be 'a liberty to tender consciences, and that no man shall be disquieted or called in question for differences of opinion in matter of religion ... excepting only such persons as shall hereafter be excepted by Parliament'.[16] The Presbyterians hoped that a settlement could be achieved which would make it possible for the Church of England to accommodate them. The King did issue a declaration promising to institute limited episcopacy and relaxing conformity with the Book of Common Prayer,[17] but a further suggestion by the King that an addition to the declaration could admit Anabaptists and Independents provoked the opposition of Richard Baxter.[18] When the original document was laid before the Commons on 28 November, the motion to accept it was lost by 157 votes to 183.

It was becoming obvious that the leaders of the restored Anglican Church had no intention of making any compromises. The new Archbishop of Canterbury, William Juxon (1582–1663), although he had a reputation for tolerance, was a close friend of William Laud and committed to his principles as was his successor, Gilbert Sheldon (1598–1677). The new Archbishop of York was Accepted Frewen (1588–1664) who, although considered by Richard Baxter to be a mild and peaceable man, was well known as the man who had introduced Laudian High Church practices into the college chapel when he was President of Magdalen, Oxford. Discussions between the Presbyterians and the Anglican leaders proved fruitless. On 15 April 1661 the Savoy Conference brought them together but to no purpose. The culmination of the process of restoration came on 19 May 1662 when the royal assent was given to the Act for the Uniformity of Public Prayers, and Administration of the Sacraments. Every minister was required on some Lord's day before the feast of St Bartholomew (24 August 1662) to declare publicly his 'unfeigned Assent and Consent to all and everything contained ... in ... the ... Book of Common Prayer'. All who failed to do so would be automatically deprived. The total number deprived was 1,909 in England,[19] and 120 in Wales.[20] That makes a total of 2,029.

In this way modern Nonconformity emerged in England and Wales. The long struggle to achieve a more comprehensive Established Church was over. Nor was the Act of Uniformity the end of the story. Like Louis XVIII's courtiers the Cavaliers 'had forgotten nothing and learnt nothing'.[21] A series of repressive acts, commonly known as the Clarendon Code, was passed in order to prohibit dissenting religious meetings and to exile ministers from the parishes where they had previously served.

A long period of persecution followed. Persecution was an element in the Nonconformist experience which had far-reaching consequences. Memories of those years of suffering lasted long and it took many generations for them to be extinguished. Persecution engenders fear, suspicion and bitterness but one of the remarkable things about the Nonconformists of the sixteenth and seventeenth centuries is the way in which they produced a theology which transformed persecution into a creative experience. They drew inspiration from the account of Stephen's martyrdom in Acts 6 and 7, from Eusebius's history of the persecutions of the early church and not least from John Foxe's *Acts and Monuments*. Of course, Foxe's martyrs suffered in defence of the Reformed Church of England against Roman Catholic repression but Nonconformist protesters against their Anglican successors cast themselves, not without some subtle manipulation of the evidence, in the role of witnesses to the same fundamental truths. In consequence, they were enabled to explain their own sufferings as an integral part of their Christian testimony. So the sufferers were seen as saints and heroes. Their example was to be kept alive from generation to generation. In this way we see them marshalled and extolled on the pages of Edmund Calamy's *Account*. Their deeds of spiritual valour were to be recounted and celebrated down to the end of the nineteenth century and beyond.[22] This very powerful body of thinking led to both a realistic and idealised understanding of persecution. Even before the Restoration, Walter Cradock had summed up the theme in a telling phrase, 'All a Christian's life is spent either in believing, or in doing, or in suffering'.[23]

People who suffer persecution learn the value of liberty. It is one thing to demand freedom for one's own convictions but it takes time to embrace a philosophy or a theology that encourages the promotion of general toleration. That was true of the Nonconformists. Throughout the ages it has been assumed that since Christianity is the true religion, it had a duty to suppress the untruth which was embraced by others. In Elizabethan England, this principle was embraced in the policy that the state should support one form of religion and that its monopoly should be made secure by penal statutes to punish those that advocated other religious forms. Nonconformists did make a substantial contribution to the achievement of toleration, partly by their suffering but partly also by the dissemination of considered arguments. It was no fault of theirs that the aim was not fully achieved in the seventeenth century.

The persecution was intermittent and varied in intensity in different parts of the kingdom. There were examples of friendly co-operation between Anglican clergy and nonconforming ministers. Thus Calamy writes of the Congregationalist Stephen Hughes (1622–88), 'his Moderation and Lively Preaching, recommended him to the Esteem of the sober Part of the Gentry, by whose Connivances he often preach'd in the publick Churches ...'.[24] Such examples were rare. Even when due allowance is made for them, there is little justification for minimising the anxiety, fear and suffering caused by the persecution. Nevertheless it was a period which brought out some of the finest elements in the Nonconformist character. Gone were the days of compromise and of surrendering to the temptations of political and military power. It was now a time to display courage and perseverance. There was the discomfort of making clandestine journeys to inaccessible places such as caves or remote valleys. In towns there was the constant danger that a service would be betrayed by spies and broken up by order of magistrates. And above all there was the peril of imprisonment. It was now a time to concentrate upon the spiritual consolations of their faith and to meditate upon the significance of their failure to consolidate that spiritual and social revolution in which so many of them had participated. Out of the bitterness of these experiences came some of the most memorable products of Nonconformist culture – John Milton's *Paradise Lost* (1667), *Paradise Regained* and *Samson Agonistes*, both in 1671. John Bunyan produced a remarkable autobiography in his *Grace Abounding to the Chief of Sinners* (1666) and his literary work reached a brilliant climax in his *Pilgrim's*

Progress (1678, 1684) and *The Holy War* (1682). In theology the period was no less fruitful with the appearance of many substantial books by the likes of John Owen, Thomas Goodwin, Richard Baxter, John Howe and many others.

Despite the repression, the Nonconformist congregations continued to meet. The extent of their success in maintaining their work became obvious as their leaders sought licences for themselves and their meeting-places under Charles II's Declaration of Indulgence in 1672–3. It became obvious that the elimination of Nonconformity was beyond the capabilities of the authorities. That did not prevent them from attempting even more repression in the years following 1673. But when James II sought to secure the support of Nonconformists for his own pro-Catholic policies by issuing his two Declarations of Indulgence, it became clear that their support was not forthcoming. It was clear also that his days as king were numbered. With the Glorious Revolution of 1688 and the accession of William and Mary, the future of Nonconformity seemed brighter. They greeted the passing of the Act of Toleration in 1689 with profound relief. It is true that it did not grant them the full freedom for which they had hoped and the Unitarians amongst them were not included in the terms of the act. But they were allowed to build their own places of freedom and were ensured of freedom from molestation as long as they licensed their places of worship and their ministers swore the necessary oaths that would secure for them a licence to preach. But the Test and Corporation Acts were still in force. That meant that Nonconformists were excluded from specified public offices and in practice were treated as second-class citizens. It would take several generations of effort to secure full equality with other citizens.

Notes

1. *Works*, ed. W. H. Goold (Edinburgh, 1862), VIII, 193.
2. For a lucid account of the procedures in the ecclesiastical courts, see W. T. Morgan, 'The Consistory Courts in the Diocese of St. David's, 1660–1858', *Journal of the Historical Society of the Church in Wales*, VII (1957), 5–24 as well as his articles in subsequent issues.
3. For its history, see G. R. Elton, *The Tudor Constitution* (Cambridge, 1968), 217–21 and R. G. Usher, *The Rise and Fall of the High Commission* (Oxford, 1913).
4. Elton, *The Tudor Constitution*, 158–61.
5. *The Laws of Ecclesiastical Polity*, V. xxvii. 1.
6. F. P. Braudel and F. Spooner, 'Prices in Europe from 1450 to 1750', *Cambridge Economic History of Europe*, 4 (1967), 378–486; Y. S. Brenner, 'The Inflation of Prices in Early Sixteenth-Century England', *Economic History Review*, II: 14 (1961), 225–39 and 'The Inflation of Prices in England, 1551–1650', ibid., 15 (1962), 266–84; E. H. Phelps Brown and S. V. Hopkins, 'Wage-rates and Prices', *Economica*, 24 (1957), 289–306.
7. *The Aequity of an Humble Supplication* (London, 1587), 58–9.
8. R. T. Petersson, *Sir Kenelm Digby: The Ornament of England* (London, 1956), 256 for Cromwell's close friendship with a well-known Catholic and ibid., 257, for Cromwell's abortive negotiations with the Pope. See also P. H. Hardacre, *The Royalists during the Puritan Revolution* (The Hague, 1956), 119.

9. T. Richards, *Puritan Movement in Wales, 1639 to 1653* (London, 1920), 115–33.
10. A. G. Matthews (ed.), *Calamy Revised* (Oxford, 1934), xvii.
11. *A Sermon, Tending to Set Forth the Right Use of the Disasters that Befall our Armies* (London, 1644), 31ff.
12. *Works*, VIII, 244ff.
13. *Works*, XI, 364.
14. J. Ivimey, *Life of Mr. John Bunyan* (London, 1809), 294.
15. Henry Rogers, *The Life ... of John Howe* (London, 1863), 32.
16. S. R. Gardiner, *The Constitutional Documents of the Puritan Revolution* (London, 1906), 465–7.
17. It is printed in George Gould (ed.), *Documents Relating to the Act of Uniformity* (London, n.d.), 63ff.
18. Matthew Sylvester, *Reliquiae Baxterianae* (London, 1696), I, 277.
19. A. G. Matthews (ed.), *Calamy Revised*, (Oxford, 1934), Introduction, xiii–xiv.
20. *Y Cofiadur* (1962), 8. These figures include all those excluded between 1660 and August 1662.
21. The phrase of Maréchal Dumouriez (1739–1823) – *n'ont rien oublié et n'ont rien appris*.
22. For a penetrating analysis of the Puritan understanding of heroic suffering, see John R. Knott, *Discourses of Martyrdom in English Literature, 1563–1694* (Cambridge, 1993).
23. *Gospel-holinesse* (1651), 363. He compares contemporary experiences of persecution with the martyrdom of Stephen on pp. 60–1.
24. E. Calamy, *Account* (London, 1713), II, 718.

PART I

THE BEGINNINGS, 1550–1603

Document I.1

Early Separatism in London: Letter of Thomas Lever to Henry Bullinger, 8 August 1559

The proclamation referred to, dated 27 December 1558, is in John Strype, *Annals of the Reformation in England*, 4 vols (3rd edn, London, 1735), I.ii.390. For Thomas Lever (1521–77), v., DNB. He was minister of the exiled English congregation at Aarau from September 1556 to January 1559. He arrived back in England the following month. Johann Heinrich Bullinger (1504–75) became Zwingli's successor at Zurich in December 1531. He supported the leaders of the Church of England in their opposition to the Presbyterianism advocated by Thomas Cartwright and others. John Whitgift made his collection of sermons, *The Decades*, required reading for Anglican clergymen. For a study of his extensive influence in England, v., D. Keep, *Henry Bullinger and the Elizabethan Church* (1970). See also G. W. Bromiley (ed.), *Zwingli and Bullinger* (London: Library of Christian Classics, 1953).

The letter is printed in H. Robinson (ed.), *The Zurich Letters* (second series, Cambridge: Parker Society, 1845), 28–30.

On returning from you towards England, in the course of my journey I saw at Strasburgh a proclamation,[1] that is, an edict published by the authority of queen Elizabeth, strictly prohibiting all preaching and exposition of holy scripture, or any change of religion throughout all England, until the ... Parliament, hereafter to be called together, shall have come to a decision respecting religion. When then I returned to England, I saw, according to the proclamation above mentioned, or rather, I shrunk from seeing, masses and all the follies and abominations of popery, everywhere sanctioned by the authority of the laws, and the gospel no where to be met with, except among some persons at London, who were either admitted to preach before the queen at court on a few stated days, only in the time of Lent, or else in a congregation that remained in concealment during the whole time of persecution, and then not venturing forth beyond such private houses as were open to them, on the cessation of persecution, they were permitted by queen Elizabeth in open private houses, but in no public churches. For there had been a congregation of faithful persons concealed in London during the time of Mary, among whom the gospel was always preached, with the pure administration of the sacraments; but during the rigour of the persecution under that queen they carefully concealed themselves, and on the cessation of it under Elizabeth they openly continued in the same congregation. But as their godly mode of worship was condemned by the laws of the realm, the magistrates, though they connived at their frequent assembling in private houses, would not allow them notwithstanding, to occupy the parish churches. In consequence of which, large numbers flocked to them not in the churches, but in private houses. And when the Lord's supper was administered among them, no strangers were admitted, except such as were kept pure from popery and even from the imputation of any evil conduct; or who, ingenuously acknowledging their backsliding and public offence, humbly sought pardon and reconciliation in presence of the whole assembly. I have frequently been present on such occasions, and have seen many returning with tears, and many too in like manner receiving such persons into communion; so that nothing could be more delightful than the mutual tears of all parties, on the one side lamenting their sins, and on the other congratulating them on their reconciliation and renewed communion in Christ Jesus ...

Document I.2

The Vestiarian Controversy

Thomas Sampson (1517?–89) was dean of Christ Church, Oxford, from 1561 until 1565 when he was ejected on the orders of the Queen for inconformity. Laurence Humphrey (1527?–1590), elected President of Magdalen College, Oxford, in 1561, had also written to Bullinger (see letter in *Zurich Letters* (first series), 151–2, dated 9 February 1566). Bullinger's reply to both men's questions is long but the excerpts in (b) give the essential parts of it.

Sampson's letter is in H. Robinson (ed.), *Zurich Letters 1558–1579* (first series, Cambridge: Parker Society, 1842), 153–5; Bullinger's in ibid., 345–55.

(a) Letter of Thomas Sampson to Henry Bullinger, London, 16 February 1566

that you may more readily understand the matter in controversy, I have thought it best to reduce it into certain questions, which are these:

I. Whether a peculiar habit, distinct from that of the laity, were ever assigned to the ministers of the gospel in better times, and whether it ought now to be assigned to them in the reformed church?

II. Whether the prescribing habits of this kind be consistent with ecclesiastical and christian liberty?

III. Whether the nature of things indifferent admits of coercion; and whether any violence should be offered to the consciences of the many who are yet not persuaded?

IV. Whether any new ceremonies may be instituted, or superadded to what is expressly commanded in the word?

V. Whether it be lawful to revive the Jewish ceremonies respecting the habit of the priesthood, and which were abolished by Christ?

VI. Whether it be expedient to borrow rites from idolaters or heretics, and to transfer such as are especially dedicated to their sect and religion to the use of the reformed church?

VII. Whether conformity and general agreement must of necessity be required in ceremonies of this kind?

VIII. Whether those ceremonies may be retained which occasion evident offence?

IX. Whether any ecclesiastical constitutions may be tolerated, which, though from their nature they are free from any thing impious, do not, nevertheless, tend to edification?

X. Whether any thing of a ceremonial nature may be prescribed to the church by the sovereign, without the assent and free concurrence of churchmen?

XI. Whether a man ought thus to obey the decrees of the church; or on account of non-compliance, supposing there is no alternative, to be cast out of the ministry?

XII. Whether good pastors, of unblemished life and doctrine, may rightfully be removed from the ministry on account of their non-compliance with such ceremonies? ...

(b) Henry Bullinger to Laurence Humphrey and Thomas Sampson, 1 May 1566

1. To the question, *whether laws respecting habits ought to be prescribed to ecclesiastics, that they may be distinguished by them from the laity*, I reply, that there is an ambiguity in the word *ought*. For if it is taken as implying what is necessary and appertaining to salvation, I do not think that even the authors of the laws themselves intend such an interpretation. But if it is asserted, that for the sake of decency, and comeliness of appearance, or dignity and order, some such regulation may be made ...

2. *Whether the ceremonial worship of the Levitical priesthood is to be reintroduced into the church?* I reply, if a cap and habit not unbecoming a minister, and free from superstition, are commanded to be used by the clergy, no one can reasonably assert that Judaism is revived ...

3. *Whether is it allowable to have a habit in common with papists?* I answer, it is not yet proved that the pope introduced a distinction of habits into the church; so far from it, that it is clear that such distinction is long anterior to popery. Nor do I see why it should be unlawful to use, in common with papists, a vestment not superstitious, but pertaining to civil regulation and good order ...

6. *Whether the dress of the clergy is a matter of indifference?* It certainly seems such, when it is a matter of *civil* ordinance, and has respect only to decency and order, in which things religious worship does not consist ...

[The latter part of the letter deals with Sampson's questions. They cover much the same ground as his answers to Laurence's questions but the following excerpt reveals Bullinger's views on active nonconformity.]

Whether it be more expedient to obey the church, or on account of disobedience to be cast out of the ministry? And *whether good pastors may lawfully be removed from the ministry on account of their non-compliance with such ceremonies?* I answer, if in these ceremonies there is no superstition, no impiety, but yet are imposed on godly pastors ... I will certainly allow ... that a burden and bondage is imposed upon them; but I will not allow ... that their station or ministry is on that account to be deserted, and place given to wolves ... or to ministers less qualified than themselves; especially, since there remains the liberty of preaching ...

Document I.3

Parker's *Advertisements*, 1566

The *Advertisements* were issued by Archbishop Matthew Parker, apparently on his own authority, in order to secure a measure of uniformity with regard to ecclesiastical dress in view of the Puritan protests against the traditional Catholic vestments. The following selection deals with this particular issue.
    Text in H. Gee and W. J. Hardy, *Documents Illustrative of English Church History* (London, 1896), 467–75. For Matthew Parker (1504–75), archbishop of Canterbury from 1559, v., J. Strype, *Life and Acts of Matthew Parker* (London, 1711) and modern life by V. J. K. Brook (*Matthew Parker* (Oxford, 1962)).
    The 'queen's majesty's Injunctions' are the Royal Injunctions of March 1559, v., Gee and Hardy, *Documents*, 417–42.

Item, in the ministration of the Holy Communion in cathedral and collegiate churches, the principal minister shall use a cope with gospeller and epistoler agreeably; and at all other prayers to be said at the Communion Table, to use no copes but surplices.
    Item, that the dean and prebendaries wear a surplice with a silk hood in the choir; and when they preach in the cathedral or collegiate church, to wear their hood.
    Item, that every minister saying any public prayers, or ministering the sacraments or other rites of the Church, shall wear a comely surplice with sleeves, to be provided at the charges of the parish; and that the parish provide a decent table standing on a frame for the Communion Table.
    Item, that they shall decently cover with carpet, silk, or other decent covering, and with a fair linen cloth (at the time of the ministration) the Communion Table, and to set the Ten Commandments upon the east wall over the said table.
    Item, that all communicants do receive kneeling, and as is appointed by the laws of the realm and the queen's majesty's Injunctions ...

Document I.4

London Separatists: Edmund Grindal to Henry Bullinger, 11 June 1568

Edmund Grindal became bishop of London, 1559; archbishop of York, 1570 and archbishop of Canterbury, 1575. For his career, v., P. Collinson, *Archbishop Grindal 1519–1583* (London, 1979). His letter is in *Zurich Letters 1558–1579* (first series), 201–2.

Some London citizens of the lowest order, together with four or five ministers, remarkable neither for their judgment nor learning, have openly separated from us; and sometimes in private houses, sometimes in the fields, and occasionally even in ships, they have held their meetings and administered the sacraments. Besides this, they have ordained ministers, elders, and deacons, after their own way, and have even excommunicated some who had seceded from their church. And because masters Laurence Humphrey, Sampson, Lever, and others, who have suffered so much to obtain liberty in respect of things indifferent, will not unite with them, they now regard them as semi-papists, and will not allow their followers to attend their preaching. The number of this sect (*hujus factionis*) is about two hundred, but consisting of more women than men. The privy council have lately committed the heads of this faction (*hujus factionis*) to prison, and are using every means to put a timely stop to this sect.

Document I.5

The Plumbers' Hall Congregation

On 19 June 1567 a company of about one hundred persons had gathered at Plumbers' Hall in London under pretence of celebrating a wedding. They were apprehended and fifteen of the leaders were arrested. The following day, 20 June, eight of them were examined by two Ecclesiastical Commissioners, Edmund Grindal, bishop of London, and Gabriel Goodman, dean of Westminster, the Lord Mayor of London and seven lay persons.[1]

In the 1593 edition of this document the printer added this information: 'Here they entered into a question of ministering the sacraments in a private house. And further is not come into my hands.'

The report is slightly abbreviated. It was first published in *A Parte of a Register* (Middelburgh, 1593) and in W. Nicholson (ed.), *The Remains of Edmund Grindal* (Cambridge: Parker Society, 1843), 201–16, and in part in H. C. Porter, *Puritanism in Elizabethan England* (History in Depth Series, Cambridge, 1970), 80–94. It is the earliest surviving Puritan document of this kind and is a rare example of how the High Commission conducted an examination. From this account it is clear that none of the usual judicial procedures of a court were observed. No oaths were tendered and no counsel were present either for the prosecution or the defence. Grindal conducted the proceedings and at this time his primary concern was pastoral. His attitude was to change later on. For the significance of this account in the history of ecclesiastical discipline, v., R. G. Usher, *The Rise and Fall of the High Commission* (Oxford, 1913), 56–8.

When we were come in, we did our obeisance, and they bade us come near, and the bishop's registrar called us by name: John Smith, William Nixon, William White, James Ireland, Robert Hawkins, Thomas Boweland, and Richard Morecraft. The bishop said, Is here all? One answered, No, there are ten or eleven in the Compter.[2]

Bishop Grindal:- I know that well enough.

The bishop said unto the mayor: My lord, will you begin?

The mayor said unto him, I pray you begin.

Bishop Grindal:- Well then, here you have showed yourselves disorderly, not only in absenting yourselves from your parish churches, and the assemblies of other Christians in this commonwealth, which do quietly obey the Queen's proceedings, and serve God in such good order, as the Queen's grace, and the rest having authority and wisdom, have set forth and established by Act of Parliament; but also you have gathered together, and made assemblies, using prayers and preachings, yea, and ministering the sacraments among yourselves; and thus you gather together to the number of an hundred; whereof there were about fourteen or fifteen of you sent to prison. And our being here is to will you to leave off, or else you shall see the Queen's letter,[3] and the council's hand at it. (Then he opened it, and showed it us, but would not read it. The effect of it, he said, was to move us to be conformable by gentleness, or else at the first we should lose our freedom of the city, and abide that would follow.) And moreover, you have hired the Plumbers' Hall, saying, you would have it for a wedding. Where is Boweland?

Thomas Boweland:- Here I am, and if it please you.

Bishop Grindal:- Did you hire the hall?

One of us said: 'In that we said to the sheriffs, it was for a wedding, we did it to save the woman harmless, and at her request.'

Bishop Grindal:- Yea, but you must not lie; that is against the admonition of the apostle: 'Let every man speak the truth to his neighbour.' And herein you have put the poor woman to great blame, and enough to lose her office: this is against the order of charity.

Here we would have answered, but he would not suffer us, but said, You shall be heard anon.

Bishop Grindal:- But to the matter. In this severing yourselves from the society of other Christians, you condemn not only us, but also the whole state of the church reformed in King Edward's days, which was well reformed according to the word of God, yea, and many good men have shed their blood for the same, which your doings condemn.

Robert Hawkins:- We condemn them not, in that we stand to the truth of God's word.

But he would not suffer us to answer to it.

Bishop Grindal:- But have you not the gospel truly preached, and the sacraments ministered accordingly, and good order kept, although we differ from other churches in ceremonies, and in indifferent things, which lie in the prince's power to command for order's sake? How say you, Smith? You seem to be the ancientest of them, answer you.

John Smith:- Indeed, my lord, we thank God for reformation; and that is it we desire, according to God's word. (And there he stayed.)

William White:- I beseech you, let me answer.

Bishop Grindal:- Nay, William White, hold your peace, you shall be heard anon.

William Nixon:- I beseech you, let me answer a word or two.

Bishop Grindal:- Nixon, you are a busy fellow, I know your words; you are full of talk. I know from whence you came.

Robert Hawkins:- I would be glad to answer.

Bishop Grindal:- Smith shall answer. Answer you, Smith.

John Smith:- Indeed, as you said even now, for preaching and ministering the sacraments, so long as we might have the word freely preached, and the sacraments administered without the preferring of idolatrous gear above it, we never assembled together in houses. But when it came to this point, that all our preachers were displaced by your law, that would not subscribe to your apparel and your law, so that we could not hear none of them in any church by the space of seven or eight weeks, except Father Coverdale,[4] of whom we have a good opinion; and yet (God knoweth) the man was so fearful, that he durst not be known unto us where he preached, though we sought it at his house. And then were we troubled and commanded to your courts from day to day, for not coming to our parish churches.

Then we bethought us what were best to do; and we remembered that there was a congregation of us in this city in Queen Mary's days;[5] and a congregation at Geneva, which used a book and order of preaching, ministering of the sacraments and discipline, most agreeable to the word of God; which book is allowed by that godly and well learned man, Master Calvin, and the preachers there; which book and order we now hold.[6] And if you can reprove this book, or anything that we hold, by the word of God, we will yield to you, and do open penance at Paul's Cross; if not, we will stand to it by the grace of God.

Bishop Grindal:- This is no answer.

William White:- You may be answered, if you give leave.

Bishop Grindal:- White, you shall speak anon; let the elder speak first.

John Smith:- Would you have me go back from the better, to such churches that I had as leave go to mass as go to them, they are so evil-favouredly used; as the parish church where I dwell is one. He is a very papist that is there, and yet he hath another place too.

Dean Goodman:- Lo, he counteth the service and reformation in King Edward's days as evil as the mass.

Bishop Grindal:- Lo, because he knoweth one that is evil, he findeth fault with all. But you may go to other places, as at St. Laurence.

William White:- You say we find fault with all, for one papist. If it were well tried, there should a great company of papists be found in this city, whom you do allow to be preachers and ministers, and thrust out the godly for your pleasure's sake ...

Roper:- I know one that in Queen Mary's time did persecute God's saints, and brought them forth to Bishop Bonner,[7] and now he is minister allowed of you, and never made recantation.

Bishop Grindal:- Can you accuse any of them of false doctrine, and show us of it?

William Nixon:- Yea, that I can, and he is even now in this house that I can accuse of false doctrine. Let him come forth and answer his doctrine that he preached upon the 10th of John. (And so I looked back upon Bedel, and Bedel hung down his head, and the bishop looked upon the dean, and one looked upon another.)[8]

Dean Goodman:- You would take away the authority of the prince, and liberty of a Christian man.

Bishop Grindal:- Yea, and therefore you suffer justly.

Robert Hawkins:- But it lieth not in the authority of the prince, and liberty of a Christian man, to use and to defend that appertaining to papistry and idolatry, and the pope's canon law, as we may plainly see in the 7th of Deuteronomy, and other places of the Scriptures.

Dean Goodman:- When do you hear us maintain such things in our preachings?

Robert Hawkins:- Though you do it not in your preachings, yet you do it in your deeds and by your laws.

William White:- The prophet saith, That the foolish say not with their mouths, there is no God, but in their hearts; their doings are corrupt and vain.

Robert Hawkins:- You preach Christ to be priest and prophet, but you preach him not to be king, neither will you suffer him to reign with the sceptre of his word in his church alone; but the pope's canon law and the will of the prince must have the first place, and be preferred before the word and ordinance of Christ.

Dean Goodman:- You speak unreverently here of the prince before the magistrates: you were not bidden to speak; you might hold your peace.

Robert Hawkins:- You will suffer us to make our purgation, seeing that you persecute us.

Bishop Grindal:- What is so preferred?

William Nixon:- Why, that which is upon your head and upon your back, your copes and your surplices, and your laws and ministers; because you will suffer none to preach nor minister, except he wear them, or subscribe to them.

Bishop Grindal:- No, how say you to Sampson and Lever,[9] and other: do not they preach?

William White:- Though they preach, you have deprived them and forbidden them, and the law standeth in force against them still, howsoever you suffer them now. And for what purpose you will not suffer other, whom you cannot reprove by the word of God, I know not.

Bishop Grindal:- They will not be preachers, nor meddle with you.

William White:- Your doings is the cause.

Robert Hawkins:- They will not join with you. I heard one of them say that he had rather be torn in a hundred pieces than to communicate with you. We hold nothing, nor allow any thing but that which is maintained by the word of God; the which word, saith Esau, 'shall come forth of Sion, and give sentence among the heathen, and reform the multitude'. And Christ saith, 'The word that I have spoken, shall judge in the last day', when both the prince, and you, and we, shall stand naked before the judgement-seat of Christ. And if you can prove that we hold not the truth, show it and we will leave it.

John Smith:- And if you cannot, we pray you, let us not be thus used.

Dean Goodman:- You are not obedient to the authority of the prince.

William White:- Yes, that we are; for we resist not, but suffer that the authority layeth upon us.

Bishop Grindal:- So do thieves suffer that the law layeth upon them.

William White:- What a comparison is this? They suffer for evil doing, and you punish us for seeking to serve God according to his word.

William Nixon:- Both the prince and we must be ruled by the word of God, as we read in the first book of Kings, the 12th chapter, that the king should teach only the word of God.

Bishop Grindal:- What, that the king should teach the word of God? Lie not.

William Nixon:- It is that both king and people should obey the word of God, or else they shall perish.

Bishop Grindal:- Indeed it is true in effect, that the prince should and must obey the word of God only. But I will show you this consisteth in three points. The first is, that which God commandeth may not be left undone. The second is, that which forbideth may not be done. And the third consisteth in things which God neither commandeth nor forbideth, and they are of the middle sort, and are things indifferent. And such things princes have authority to order or to command.

Prisoners:- Prove that, said one. Where find you that? said another.

Bishop Grindal:- I have talked with many men, and yet I never saw any behave themselves so unreverently before magistrates.

William White:- I beseech you, let me speak one word or two.

Bishop Grindal:- White, stay a little, you shall speak anon.

Robert Hawkins:- Kings have their rule and commandment in the 17th of Deuteronomy, not to decline neither to the right hand nor to the left from the word of God, howsoever you make your distinction.

John Smith:- How can you prove that indifferent, which is abominable?

Bishop Grindal:- What, you mean of our caps and tippets, which, you say, came from Rome?

James Ireland:- It belongeth to the papists; therefore throw it to them.

Canon Watts:- You would have us use nothing that the papists used; then should we use no churches, as the papists have used.

Robert Hawkins:- Churches be necessary to keep our bodies from the rain, but surplices and copes be superstitious and idolatrous.

William White:- Christ did cast out the buyers and sellers in the temple and their ware, and yet the temple was not overthrown for all that.

Bishop Grindal:- Things not forbidden of God may be used for order and obedience' sake: you shall hear the mind and judgement of a well learned man, whom you like of, namely, Master Bullinger: (then he read out of a book this in effect): 'It is not yet proved that these garments had their first origin from Rome. And though we use them not here in our ministry, yet we may lawfully use them as things that have not yet been removed away.'[10] These be Bullinger's words: therefore we desire and wish you to leave off and be conformable.

John Smith:- What if I can show you Bullinger against Bullinger in this thing?

Bishop Grindal:- I think not, Smith.

John Smith:- Yes, that I can.

Bishop Grindal:- Well, all reformed churches do differ in rites and ceremonies, and we agree with all reformed churches in substance of doctrine.

Canon Watts:- Yea, that we do.

Robert Hawkins:- Yea, but we should follow the trueth and best way. Christ saith, 'Go you forth and preach to all nations, baptizing them in the name of the

Father, of the Son and of the Holy Ghost, teaching them to observe all things that I have commanded you'. But you have brought the gospel and sacraments into bondage to the ceremonies of anti-Christ, and you defend idolatry and papistry. There is no ordinance of Christ but you have mingled your own inventions withal. How say you to godfathers and godmothers in baptism?

Canon Watts:- O! wise reason.

Bishop Grindal:- How say you to the church of Geneva? They communicate with wafer cakes, which you are so much against.

William Nixon:- Yea, but they do not compel to receive so, and with none other.

Bishop Grindal:- Yes, in their parish churches.

William White:- The English congregation did minister loaf bread there.

Bishop Grindal:- Because they were of another language.

William White:- It is good to follow the best example: but we must follow them as they follow Christ.

Dean Goodman:- All the learned men in Europe are against you.

Canon Watts:- Ye will believe no man.

John Smith:- Yes, we reverence the learned in Geneva, or in other places wheresoever they be; yet we build not on them our faith and religion.

Bishop Grindal:- Will you be judged by the learned in Geneva? They are against you.

Robert Hawkins:- We will be judged by the word of God, which shall judge us all at the last day, therefore sufficient to judge now. But how can they be against us, seeing they know not of our doings; also, holding of the same truth as they do (except they will be against the truth and against themselves)?

Bishop Grindal:- Here is the letter that came from Geneva, and they are against you and your doings and going from us, in these words. Then he turned to this place, which is: That against the prince's and bishops' wills they should exercise their office, we do so much the tremble at, because of these reasons, which of themselves are plain enough, albeit we do not utter them. Mark how that he saith he doth 'tremble' at your cause.

Robert Hawkins:- Why, the place is against you: for they do tremble at the prince's case and yours, because that you by such extremities, should drive us against our wills to that which of itself is plain enough, albeit they would not utter them.

Then the bishop wrong himself and said: See, ye enter into judgement against us.

Robert Hawkins:- Nay we judge not; but we know the letter well enough, for we have it in our houses; it maketh nothing against us.

Bishop Grindal:- We grant it doeth not. But yet they count this apparel indifferent, and not impious and wicked in their own nature; and therefore they counsel the preachers not to give over their function or flocks for these things.

Robert Hawkins:- But it followeth in the same letter that if they should be 'compelled to allow it by subscription' or silence, that they should give over the ministry.

William Nixon:- Let us answer to your first question.

Bishop Grindal:- Say on, Nixon.

William Nixon:- We do not refuse you for preaching the word of God, but because you have tied the ceremonies of Antichrist to it, and set them before it, so that no man may preach or minister the sacraments without them. For before you compelled them by law, all was quiet.

Bishop Grindal:- See how you be against indifferent things, which may be borne withal for order and obedience sake.

Mayor:- Well, good people, I would you would wisely consider these things, and be obedient to the Queen's Majesty's good laws, as I and other of the Queen's subjects are, that you may live quietly and have liberty, as my lord here and masters have said. And as for my part, I would you were at your heart's ease, and I am sorry that you are troubled; but I am an officer under my prince, and therefore blame not me. I cannot talk learnedly with you in celestial matters, but I have a mother wit, and I will persuade the best that I can. The Queen hath not established these garments and things for any holiness' sake or religion, but only for a civil order and comeliness; because she would have the ministers known from other men, as the aldermen are known by their tippets, and the judges by their red gowns, and sometimes they wear coifs; and likewise lords' servants are known by their badges. I will tell you an example. There was an alderman within this year, that went in the street, and a boisterous fellow met him, and went between him and the wall and put him towards the channel, and some that were about him said to him, 'Knowest thou not what thou doest? He is an alderman.' And he said, 'I knew him not, he might have worn his tippet.' Even so, when the ministers began to be despised, the Queen's grace did ordain this priests' apparel, but the people cannot be content and like it. Now what may the papists say? Some of them goeth to the court, whispering, saying that you cannot be content that the Queen should command anything in the church, not so much a cap or a tippet, whereupon the Queen may have occasion to say: 'Will they not be content that I should rule in the Church, I will restore that my forefathers have followed.' And therefore, masters, take heed.

Robert Hawkins:- I beseech you to let me answer your lordship before all your wisdoms. Philip Melancthon [sic], writing upon the 14th chapter of Romans, hath these words: 'When the opinion of holiness, of merit, or necessity, is put unto things indifferent, then they darken the light of the gospel, and ought by all means to be taken away.'

Bishop Grindal:- It is not commanded of necessity in the church, or of heavenly things.

Robert Hawkins:- You have made it a matter of necessity in the church, and that many a poor man doeth feel.

William Nixon:- Even so, my lord, as you do say that the alderman is known by his gown and tippet, even so by this apparel that these men do now wear were the papist mass-priests known from other men.

Dean Goodman:- What a great matter you make of it.

Robert Hawkins:- The apostle Paul would not be like the false apostles in anything, and therefore you have the apostle against you.

Bishop Grindal:- There be good men and good martyrs that did wear these things in King Edward's days; do you condemn them?

William Nixon:- We condemn them not: we would go forward to perfection, for we have had the gospel a long time amongst us. And the best of them that did maintain it did recant for it at their death, as did Ridley, sometime bishop of London, and Doctor Taylor.[11] Ridley did acknowledge his fault to Hooper, and when they would have put on the same apparel upon him, he said, they were abominable and too fond for a vice in a play.

Bishop Grindal:- Where find you that in the book of letters of the martyrs?

Robert Hawkins:- It may be showed in the book of the monuments of the church, that many which were burned in Queen Mary's time died for standing against popery, as we now do.

Bishop Grindal:- I have said mass: I am sorry for it.

James Ireland:- But you go like one of the mass-priests still.

Bishop Grindal:- You see me wear a cope or a surplice in Paul's. I had rather minister without these things, but for order's sake and obedience to the prince. ...

Dean Goodman:- Doth not St. Peter say, 'Be obedient to all manner ordinance of man?'

William White:- Yes, as they obey God.

William Nixon:- This hath always been the doings of popish bishops. When as they cannot maintain their doings by the scriptures, nor overcome them, then they make the mayor and the aldermen their servants and butchers, to punish them that they cannot overcome by scripture. But I trust that you, my lord, seeing you have heard and seen it, will take good advisement.

Mayor:- Good Lord, how unreverently do you speak here before my lords and us in comparing so.

Bishop Grindal:- Have we not a godly prince? Answer, is she evil?

William White:- What a question is that, the fruits do show.

Thomas Bowland:- No: but the servants of God are persecuted under her.

Bishop Grindal:- Yea, go to; mark this, my lord. (Reader, see Luke xix.7.)

Robert Hawkins:- Why, this question the prophet may answer in the psalm: 'How can they have understanding that work iniquity, spoiling my people, and that extol vanity?'

Dean Goodman:- Do we hold any heresy? Do we deny any article of the faith, as 'I believe in God the Father Almighty, and in Jesus Christ his Son?' Do we deny any of these articles? Do we maintain purgatory or pilgrimages? No, we hold the reformation that was in King Edward's days.

One of us said, No more did the papists in words.

William White:- You build much of King Edward's time. A very learned man as any is in the realm, (I think you cannot reprove him,) writeth these words of King Edward's time: 'I will let pass to speak of King Henry's time, but come to King Edward's time, which was the best time of reformation: all was driven to a prescript order of service, pieced and patched out of the popish portas of

The Beginnings, 1550–1603

matins,[12] mass, and evensong; so that when the minister had done his service, he thought his duty done. To be short, there might no discipline be brought into the church.'

William Nixon:- Yet they never came so far as ye have done, to make a law that none should preach or minister without these garments.

Bishop Grindal:- Saint Paul saith, that 'to the clean all things are clean': that which other have evilly abused we may use well, as not receiving them for any such purpose of holiness or religion.

William Nixon:- Howsoever you received them we now see you have exalted them, and brought the word of God in subjection and slavery to them.

Robert Hawkins:- It cannot be proved, that the ceremonies of Antichrist, works of darkness, and the pope's canon law, may be clean to a true Christian; for the apostle saith, 'There is no fellowship between Christ and Belial, light and darkness' 2 Cor.vi.14,15. ...

William White:- We will be tried by the word of God, which shall judge us all at the last day.

Dean Goodman:- But who will you have to be judge of the word of God?

Robert Hawkins:- Why, that was the saying of the papists in Queen Mary's time. I have heard it, when the truth was defended by the word of God, then they would say, 'Who shall judge of the word of God? The Catholic church must be judge'.

William White:- We will be tried by the best reformed churches. The Church of Scotland hath the word truly preached, the sacraments truly administered, and discipline according to the word of God; and these be the notes by which the true church is known.

Dean Goodman:- We have a gracious prince.

We said, 'God preserve her grace and the council.' ...

William White:- ... The sabbath is appointed to rest in, and to serve God. Exodus, xx.10.

Dean Goodman:- Why then you would have no sermons nor prayer all the week.

William White:- Who is not against that? I think him to be no Christian that does not pray and serve God every day before he begin his work.

William Nixon:- You can suffer bear-baiting and bowling and other games to be used on the sabbath day, and on your holy-days, and no trouble for it.

Dean Goodman:- Then you would have no holy sabbath days, because the papists used them.

William White:- We ought to do that God commandeth.

Dean Goodman:- Why then you must not use the Lord's prayer, because the papists used it, and many other prayers because the priests used them; you would have nothing but the word of God. Is all the psalms you sing the word of God? They are turned into metre.

William White:- Is every word that is preached in a good sermon the word of God?

Dean Goodman:- No.

William White:- But every word and thing agreeing with the word of God, is as the word of God.

Bishop Grindal:- There has been no heretic but that he hath challenged the word to defend him.

William White:- What is that to us? If you know any heresy we hold, charge us with it.

Bishop Grindal:- Holy-days may be well used.

Robert Hawkins:- Well, master Hooper saith in his commentary upon the commandments that holy-days are the leaven of Antichrist.

From hence to prison they went all, or most part of them.[13]

Notes

1. For Gabriel Goodman (1528–1601), dean of Westminster from 1560, v., DNB and DWB. He was considered for several bishoprics but never elected, most likely because, as Strype wrote of him, he was 'a grave, solid man, yet ... peradventure too severe', *The life ... of Matthew Parker* (London, 1711), II, 6. The Lord Mayor of London in 1567 was Sir Roger Martin, mercer. He had been sheriff in 1559 and died 1573 and was buried in the church of St Anthony, v., John Stow, *A Survey of London, Reprinted from the Text of 1603*, ed. C. L. Kingsford, 2 vols (Oxford, 1971), II, 183, 184, 252.
2. For William White, a baker, v., A.Peel, 'William White, an Elizabethan Puritan', *Trans. Congregational Hist. Soc.*, VI (1913–15), 4ff. and A. Peel, 'A Conscientious Objector of 1575 ...', *Trans. Baptist Hist. Soc.*, VII (1921), 71–128 and *The Seconde Parte of a Register* (Cambridge, 1915), I, 64–6. R. G. Usher discusses 'A note of my Examination and Answer as my weake memory could gather it, at my last being before the Worshipfull and honourable Commissioners, the 18th day of Januray 1573', a much more severe examination of White recorded in the Morrice MSS. A. fos. 581–4, v., Usher, *The Rise and Fall of the High Commission*, 58–60. There were present then the Lord Chief Justice, the Master of the Rolls, the Master of Requests, the Attorney-General, the Dean of Westminster (i.e., Gabriel Goodman) and the Sheriff of London.
3. For the Queen's letter, 25 January 1565, v., *Correspondence of Matthew Parker* (Cambridge: Parker Society, 1853), J. Bruce and T. T. Perowne (eds), 223–7, and R. W. Dixon, *The History of the Church of England* (Oxford, 1902), VI, 44–6.
4. For Miles Coverdale (1488–1569), v., DNB and J. F. Mozley, *Coverdale and His Bibles* (London, 1953) and P. Collinson, *The Elizabethan Puritan Movement* (London, 1967), 86–7, for Coverdale as one of the popular preachers at the Minories, where, according to John Stow, some 'who called themselves puritans or unspotted lambs of the Lord ... kept their church in the Minories without Aldgate'. This use of the word 'puritans' by Stow in 1567 is the earliest known example.
5. See B. R. White, *The English Separatist Tradition* (Oxford, 1971), 10–15, for the London congregation in Mary's time.
6. This was, *The Forme of Prayers and Ministrations of the Sacraments, etc., used in the English Congregation at Geneva: and approved by the famous and Godly learned man, Iohn Caluyn. Imprinted at Geneva by Iohn Crespin. MDLVI*. For description and analysis, v., Horton Davies, *The Worship of the English Puritans* (Westminster: Dacre Press, 1948), 28–34.
7. Edmund Bonner (c.1500–69) remained unyielding in his loyalty to the Catholic

Church. He was bishop of London during Mary's reign and his zeal in prosecuting Protestants made him a byword amongst them for cruelty.
8. It is just possible that this was Henry Bedell (dates unknown), the preacher who published *Sermon Exhorting to Pitie the Poor* (London, 1572), v., DNB and M. M. Knappen, *Tudor Puritanism* (3rd edn, London, 1970), 414, n. 39.
9. It is possible that when Grindal withdrew to the Continent in May 1554, Thomas Sampson travelled in the same company, v., P. Collinson, *Archbishop Grindal 1519–1583* (London, 1979), 71, a suggestion on the basis of J. Foxe, *The Acts and Monuments of the Church*, ed. J. Pratt, 8 vols (London, 1877), VIII, 597–8.
10. Bullinger made this point also in his letter of 1 May 1566 to Laurence Humphrey and Thomas Sampson, v., *Zurich Letters 1558–1579* (first series), 348.
11. Nicholas Ridley, bishop of London from 12 April 1550, was burnt at the stake, 16 October 1555. John Hooper, bishop of Gloucester from 1550, suffered the same fate, 9 February 1555, as did Rowland Taylor, LL.D, on the same date.
12. 'Porta' was the vulgarised form of the medieval Latin 'portiforium' which meant a portable breviary.
13. They were not in prison for long. On 4 March 1568, 77 persons (Burrage omitted the 5 wives listed) were taken prisoner. The list of 'Parsons fownde to gether within the parishe of St martens in the felde in the howse of Iames Tynne gooldsmythe ...' is given by C. Burrage, in *Early English Dissenters*, 2 vols (Cambridge, 1912), 9–11. It comes from *State Papers Domestic, Elizabeth*, XLVI, 46 and was discussed in F. J. Powicke, 'The Early Separatists', *Trans. Congregational Hist. Soc.*, II (1905–6), 11–12. The list includes those examined by Grindal in June 1567 except Hawkins and Roper. But on 22 April 1569, 24 men and 7 women were discharged from Bridewell, and the list includes 10 of those taken in James Tynne's house while all the leader's of the Plumbers' Hall group are mentioned except Morecraft, v., A. Peel, *The First Congregational Churches* (Cambridge, 1920), 10–11.

Document I.6

Richard Fitz's Church

The following extracts were printed in *State Papers Domestic, Elizabeth*, Addenda, XX, 107.1 and are reproduced in Champlin Burrage, *The Early English Dissenters* (Cambridge, 1912), II, 13–18. Burrage calls extract (d) 'Separatist Covenant' of the congregation. It lacks the usual characteristics of the early covenants and perhaps it is better to think of it as a declaration made by individual members.

As the reference in extract (c) to the thirteenth year of Elizabeth shows, this petition was composed in 1571. Michael R.Watts describes the people who prepared it as 'an organized Separatist church' (*The Dissenters* (Oxford, 1978), I, 23). It had a minister, Richard Fitz, and a deacon, Thomas Bowland, although both of them, together with two of its members, Giles Fowler and Randall Partridge, had died in prison and it exercised discipline. R. W. Dale went further and described it as the 'first regularly constituted English Congregational Church of which any record or tradition remains' (*History of English Congregationalism* (London, 1907), 95) and based this assessment partly on a statement made in 1593 and quoted by Waddington to the effect that Fitz's church 'professed and practised' Congregationalism before it was expounded by Robert Browne. Unfortunately John Waddington does not name the source of the quotation (*Congregational Martyrs* (London, 1861), 15–16). Champlin Burrage denied Dale's claim that Fitz's congregation was a regularly constituted Congregational church but admitted that it was both separatist and congregational. However, it did not seem to have all the characteristics of later Congregational churches (*Early English Dissenters* (Cambridge, 1912), I, 92–3). It belongs to the pre-history of Congrega-tionalism and Watts's decription of it as 'an organized Separatist church' seems justified. There has also been some discussion of the relationship between the Plumbers' Hall congregation and Fitz's church by the authors to which reference is made above.

(a) The order of the priuye churche in London, whiche by the malice of Satan is falslie slaundered, and euill spoken of

The myndes of them, that by the strengthe and workinge of the almighty, our Lorde Iesus Christe, haue set their hands and hartes, to the pure vnmingled and sincere worshippinge of God, accordinge to his blessed and glorious words in al things, onely abolishinge and abhorringe all tradicions and inuentions of man, what soeuer in the same Religion and Seruice of oure Lord God, knowinge this alwayes, that the trewe and afflicted churche of oure Lorde and sauyoure Iesus Christe, eyther hath, or else euer more continually vnder the crosse stryueth for to haue. Fyrste and formoste, the Glorious worde and Euangell preached, not in bondage and subiection, but freely, and purelye. Secondly, to haue the Sacraments mynistred purely, onely and all together accordinge to the institution and good worde of the Lorde Iesus, without any tradicion or inuention of man. And laste of all to haue, not the fylthye Cannon lawe, but dissiplyne onelye, and all together agreable to the same heauenlye and allmighty worde of our good Lorde, Iesus Chryste.

Richarde Fytz, Minister

(b) Separatist Declaration of Fitz's Congregation

Beyng throughly perswaded in my conscience, by the working and by the worde of the almightie, that these reliques of Antichriste be abominable before the Lorde our God.

And also for that by the power and mercie, strength and goodnes of the Lorde my God onelie, I am escaped from ye filthynes & pollution of these detestable traditions, through the knowledge of our Lorde and sauiour Iesus Christ:

And last of all, in asmuch as by the workyng also of the Lorde Iesus his holy spirite, I haue ioyned in prayer, and hearyng of Gods worde, with those that haue not yelded to this idolatrouse trash, notwithstandyng the danger for not commyng to my parysh church. &c,

Therfore I come not backe agayne to the preachynges. &c, of them that haue receaued those markes of the Romysh beast.

[Then follow nine reasons for separating the essence of which is that God's words must be obeyed and that true believers must not compromise themselves by participating in other men's disobedience and sin. It ends with the following words:]

God geue vs strength styl to stryue in suffryng vndre the crosse, that the blessed worde of our God may onely rule, and haue the highest place, to cast downe strong holdes, to destroy or ouerthrow policies or imaginations, and euery high thyng that is eralted [sic: exalted] against the knowledge of God, and to bryng in to captiuitie or subiection, euery thought to the obedience of Christ. &c. 2 Corinth. 10 verses .4. and .5. &c, that the name and worde of the eternall our Lorde God, may be exalted or magnified aboue all thynges. Psalm.138. verse .2.

(c) A Petition by Members of the Church

We the poore afflicted & your humble and obedient subiectes in the lorde most earnestly desyer, that the word of our god may be set to raygne, and haue the hiest place, to rule & reforme all estates and degrees [o]f men, to build and plante his holy sygnes and true markes, to cut downe, to roote out and vtterly destroy by the axe of the same his holy word, all monumentes of Idolatry, to wit, that wicked cannon law, which is the onely roote, out of the whiche these abhominable braunshes do growe, as forked cappes, & tipetes, surplices, copes, starche cakes, popishe holy days, forbidding of mariages and meates which the holy gost our almighty calleth doctrines of devills as in .1. timothie .4. verses .3 .4. more to destroy idol temples & chapels whiche the papistes or infideles haue builded to the sevice of their god. Our god hath straytly commaunded & charged his people Israell chiefly the governours as in dewteronomie .16. verse .20. with the note [*marginal note*: Dew.31.23. Iosua .1. verses .7.8.9.] & so in them ye maiestrates of our tyme, not to vse in his service, the manners, fashions, or customes of the papistes, but contrary wyse vtterly to destroy them, to consume them, and abhorr them dewte .7. verse .26. whiche holy commaundment of the almighty our god yf it be not executed spedely, the lordes wrathe will surely breake out vpon this whole reallme of england as in numbers .25. verse .3. .9. & for such abhominations our god will cause this land to spew vs out as in leviticus .20. verse .22. the allmightie our god will not allway suffer suche dishonour to his blessed evanell, whiche for the sinnes and tryall of his people he suffreth the papistes and newters, faulse brethren, and domesticall enemies to suppresse, to wrest, and abvse to serve their purposes, (as they perswade them selves) yet for all their policye and fyne pinnyng these abhominations aboue named with many other, are no more able to stand in presence before the word of our god having the power of discipline, then dagon was able to stand before the lord his holy arke the power wherof threw downe dagon twyse to the dust as in .1. samuell .5. verses .3 .4. Therefore according to the saying of the almighty our god mathew .18. verse .20. wher ii or iij are gathered in my name ther am I. so we a poore congregation whom god hath seperated from the churches of englande and from the mingled and faulse worshipping therin vsed, out of the which assemblies the lord our onely saviour hath called vs, and still calleth, saying cume out from among them, and seperate your selves from them & touche no vnclean thing, then will I receyue you, and I wilbe your god and you shalbe my sonnes and doughters sayth the lord. 2. corinth .6. verses .17. 18. so as god geveth strength at this day we do seruuue the lord every saboth day in houses, and on the fourth day in the weke we meet or cum together weekely to vse prayer & exercyse diciplyne on them whiche do deserve it, by the strength and sure warrant of the lordes good word as in mathew. 18 verses 15 . 16 . 17 . 18 ./ .1. corinth .5. / but wo be vnto this cursed cannon Lawe the gayne [?] whereof hath caused the byshopes and clargi of england to forsake the right way and haue gone astray, folowyng the way of balaam sonn of bosor, which haue throughe their pompe and covetousnesse broughte the gospell of our saviour Iesus christ into suche sclaunder and contempte, that men do thinke for the most part that the papists do vse and hold a better religion then those which call them selves christians, and ar not, but do lye revela. 3 verse .9. the holy gost sayth. I behold another beast cummyng vp out of the earthe which had ij hornes lyke the lame, so this secrete and disguysed antechrist to wit, this cannon l[a]w wth the braunshes and their maintayners thoughe not so openly, haue by lon[g]e inprisonment pyned & kylled the lords servantes (as our minister Rycherd fitz) thomas bowlande deacon / one partryge} & gyles fouler / & besydes them a great multitude, which no man could number of all nations and people and tounges as revela. 7. verse .9. whose good cause and faythfull testimony though we should cease to grone and crye vnto our god to redresse suche wronges & cruell handelyng of his pore memberes, the very walles of the prisons about this citye, as the gatehouse, brydewell, the counters, the kynges benche, the marcialsey, the whyte lyon, would testifye gods anger kyndlyde agynst this land for suche iniustyce and subtyll persecucion.

O Lord god almyghty graunte, for thy mercyes sake, that as Ieshosaphat, in the iijth yeare of his raygne destroyed the hye places and groves, out of Iudahe, and sent his prynces and priestes, and gaue them the boke of the lawe with them to reforme religion by, and so feare came vpon every citye that they made not ware agaynst Ieshosaphat So Lord we most humbly beseche thee to strengthen the quenes hi[g]hnesse with his holy spirit that in the .13th eare of her reygne, she may cast downe all hye places of Idolatrye with in her land, withe the popyshe cannon Lawe and all the supersticion and commaundmentes of men, and to plucke vp by the rootes all filthi ceremonies perteynyng to the same, and that her highnesse may send forth princes and ministers and geue them the booke of the Lord, that they may bryng home the people of god to the purity and truthe of the apostolycke churche, Then shall the feare of the Lord cume vpon every citye and cutnrye, that they shall not make warre agaynst her highnesse, no the very enemies that be with out, shalbe compelled to bring presentes to her grace, thus olord graunt that her highnes may not onely haue a blessed, longe, and prosperous reygne, with peace of conscience in this life, but also in the lyfe to cum, her highnesse may enIoye, by the merites and death of christ Iesus our onely saviour, lyfe everlastyng, to whome with the father and the holy gost be all honour and glory for ever and ever amen.

Ioane Abraham	Constance foxe	Annes Hall	Marg Race
Helene stokes	Eliz.Balfurth	Sara Cole	by me George Hares
Ihon Thomas	Annes. Evance	Elizabeth Leanordes	Ioane Ireland
Ihon Davy	Elizabeth Hill	Ioane havericke	Abraham foxe

Mary Mayer	Eliz. Rumney	Marten [?] tilmans [?]
Eliz slacke	by me Harry sparowe.	By me Iohn King.
by me Iames awbynes	by me Ihon Leonarde.	by me Iasper weston
edyee Burre [?]	Mary wever	

[The last eight signed their names, the rest made their mark.]

Document I.7

The Admonition to the Parliament, 1572

Since 1566 those Puritans who hoped to initiate further reformation in the Church of England had expected much from Parliament and the support of 'godly' bishops. By 1571 these hopes were fading. The bishops were insisting more forcibly on conformity with the Articles of Religion and the liturgical stipulations of the Book of Common Prayer. The attempt in May 1572 to secure the passing of a parliamentary bill to relax the terms of conformity was frustrated when the Queen confiscated the bill. The more ardent spirits in the Puritan party decided that the time had come to make an appeal to the country under the guise of an address to Parliament. This was the *Admonition to the Parliament* which was published some time before 27 June 1572.

The document is printed in its original form in W. H. Frere and C. E. Douglas (eds), *Puritan Manifestoes* (London, 1954). It includes a critical apparatus to show the differences between the first and second editions and an excellent introduction which describes the motives for its publication. In the selections from the document printed above the spelling has been modernised but capital letters and punctuation have been left unchanged. The numerous scripture references have been omitted.

The author of the first part, the *Admonition* proper, was John Field (died 1588), for whom, v., DNB, and A. Peel (ed.), *The Seconde Parte of a Register* (Cambridge, 1915), I, 14–15. The section on *Popish Abuses* was by Thomas Wilcox (1549?–1608) for whom v., DNB.

Seeing that nothing in this mortal life is more diligently to be sought for, and carefully to be looked unto than the restitution of true religion and reformation of God's church: it shall be your parts (dearly beloved) in this present Parliament assembled, as much as in you lieth to promote the same, and to employ your whole labour and study; not only in abandoning all popish remnants both in ceremonies and regiment, but also in bringing in and placing in God's church those things only, which the Lord himself in his word commandeth ...

May it therefore please your wisdoms to understand, we in England are so far off, from having a church rightly reformed, according to the prescript of God's word, that as yet we are not come to the outward face of the same. For to speak of that wherein all consent, & whereupon all writers accord. The outward marks whereby a true christian church is known, are preaching of the word purely, ministering of the sacraments sincerely, and ecclesiastical discipline which consisteth in admonition and correction of faults severally. Touching the first, namely the ministry of the word, although it must be confessed that the substance of doctrine by many delivered is sound and good, yet herein it faileth, that neither the ministers thereof are according to God's word proved, elected, called, or ordained: nor the function in such sort so narrowly looked unto, as of right it ought, and is of necessity required. For whereas in the old church a trial was had both of their ability to instruct, and of their godly conversation also: now, by the letters commendatory of some one man, noble or other, tag and rag, learned and unlearned, of the basest sort of the people (to the slander of the Gospel in the mouths of the adversaries) are freely received. In those days no idolatrous sacrificers or heathenish priests were appointed to be preachers of the Gospel: but we allow, and like well of popish mass mongers, men for all seasons, King Henry's priests, King Edward's priests, Queen Mary's priests, who of a truth (if God's word were precisely followed) should from the same be utterly removed. Then they taught others, now they must be instructed themselves, and therefore like young children they must learn catechisms. Then election was made by the common consent of the whole church: now every one picketh out for himself some notable good benefice, he obtaineth the next advowson, by money or by favour, and so thinketh himself to be sufficiently chosen. Then the congregation had authority to call ministers: instead thereof now, they run, they ride, and by unlawful suit & buying, prevent other suitors also. Then no minister placed in any congregation, but by the consent of the people, now, that authority is given into the hands of the bishop alone, who by his sole authority thrusteth upon them such, as they many times as well for unhonest life, as also for lack of learning, may & do justly dislike. Then, none admitted to the ministry, but a place was void beforehand, to which he should be called: but now, bishops (to whom the right of ordering ministers doth at no hand appertain) do make 60, 80, or a 100 at a clap, & send them abroad into the country like masterless man. Then, after just trial and vocation they were admitted to their function, by laying on of the hands of the company of the eldership only: now there is (neither of these being looked unto) required an alb, a surplice, a vestment, a pastoral staff, beside that ridiculous, and (as they use it to their new creatures) blasphemous saying, receive the holy ghost. Then every pastor had his flock, and every flock his shepherd, or else shepherds. Now they do not only run fisking [i.e., scampering about] from place to place (a miserable disorder in God's church) but covetously join living to living, making shipwrecks of their own consciences, and being but one shepherd (nay, would to God they were shepherds and not wolves) have many flocks. Then the ministers were preachers: now are bare readers. And if any be so well disposed to preach in their own charges, they may not, without my Lord's licence. In those days known by voice, learning and doctrine: now they must be discerned from other by popish and Antichristian apparel, as cap, gown, tippet, &c. Then, as God gave utterance they preached the words only: now they read homilies, articles, injunctions, &c. Then it was painful: now gainful. Then poor and ignominious: now rich & glorious. And therefore titles, livings, and offices by Antichrist devised are given to them, as Metropolitan, Archbishop, Lord's grace, Lord bishop, Suffragan, Dean, Archdeacon, Prelate of the garter, Earl, County Palatine, Honour, High commissioners, Justices of the peace and Quorum, etc. All which, together with their offices, as they are strange & unheard of in Christ's church, nay plainly in God's word forbidden: So are they utterly with speed out of the same to be removed. Then ministers were not tied to any form of prayers invented by man, but as the spirit moved them, so they powered forth hearty supplications to the Lord. Now they are bound of necessity to a prescript order of sevice, and book of common prayer in which a great number of things contrary to God's word are contained, as baptism by women, private Communions, Jewish purifyings, observing of holy days, etc, patched (if not altogether, yet the greatest piece) out of the Pope's portuis [i.e., portable breviary]. Then feeding the flock diligently: now teaching quarterly. Then preaching in season and out of season: now once in a month is thought sufficient, if twice, it is judged a work of supererogation. Then nothing taught but God's word, Now Princes' pleasures, men's devices, popish ceremonies, and Antichristian rites in public pulpits defended. Then they sought them, now they seek theirs ...

The way therefore to avoid these inconveniences, and to reform these deformities is this: Your wisdoms have to remove Advowsons, Patronages, Impropriations, and bishops' authority, claiming to themselves thereby right to ordain ministers, and to bring in that old and true election, which was accustomed to be made by the congregation. You must displace those ignorant and unable ministers, already placed, & in their rooms appoint such as both can, and will by God's assistance feed the flock. You must pluck down & utterly overthrow without hope of restitution, the court of Faculties, from whence not only licences to enjoy many benefices, are obtained, as Pluralities, Trialities, Totquots, etc, but all things for the most part, as in the court of Rome are set on sale, licences to marry, to eat flesh in times prohibited, to lie from benefices and charges, and a great number beside, of suchlike abominations. Appoint to every congregation a learned & diligent preacher. Remove homilies, articles, injunctions, a prescript order of service made out of the mass book. Take way the Lordship, the loitering, the pomp, the idleness, and livings of Bishops, but yet employ them to such ends as they were in the old church appointed for. Let a lawful and a godly Seignory look that they preach, not quarterly or monthly, but continually: not for filthy lucre sake, but of a ready mind. So God shall be glorified, your consciences discharged, and the flock of Christ (purchased with his own blood) edified.

Now to the second point, which concerneth ministration of the Sacraments. In the old time, the word was preached, before they were ministered: now it is supposed to be sufficient, if it be read. Then, they were ministered in public assemblies, now in private houses. Then by ministers only, now by midwives, and Deacons, equally. But because in treating of both the sacraments together, we should deal confusedly: we will therefore speak of them severally. And first for the Lord's supper, or holy communion.

They had no introit, for Celestinus a pope brought it in, about the year 430. But we have borrowed a piece of one out of the mass book. They read no fragments of the Epistle and Gospel: we use both. The Nicene creed was not read in their Communion: we have it in ours. There was then, accustomed to be an examination of the communicants, which now is neglected. Then they ministered the Sacrament with common and usual bread: now with wafer cakes, brought in by Pope Alexander, being in form, fashion and substance, like their god of the altar. They received it sitting: we kneeling, according to Honorius' Decree. Then it was delivered generally, & indefinitely, Take ye and eat ye: we particularly, and singularly, Take thou, and eat thou. They used no other words but such as Christ left: We borrow from papists, The body of our Lord Jesus Christ which was given for thee. &c. They had no Gloria in excelsis in the ministry of the Sacrament then, for it was put to afterward. We have now. They took it with conscience. We with custom. They shut men by reason of their sinnes, from the Lord's Supper. We thrust them in their sin to the Lord's Supper. They ministered the Sacrament plainly. We pompously, with singing, piping, surplice and cope wearing. They simply as they received it from the Lord. We, sinfully, mixed with man's inventions and devices. And as for Baptism, it was enough with them, if they had water, and the party to be baptised faith, and the minister to preach the word and minister the sacraments.

Now, we must have surplices devised by Pope Adrian, interrogatories ministered to the infant, godfathers and Godmothers, brought in by Higinus, holy fonts invented by Pope Pius, crossing and suchlike pieces of popery, which the church of God in the Apostles times never knew (and therefore not to be used) nay (which we are sure of) were and are man's devices, brought in long after the purity of the primitive church. To redress these, your wisdoms have to remove (as before) ignorant ministers, to take away private communions and baptisms, to enjoin Deacons and Midwives not to meddle in ministers' matters, if they do, to see them sharply punished. To join assistance of Elders, and other officers, that seeing men will not examine themselves, they may be examined, and brought to render a reason of their hope. That the statute against wafer cakes may more prevail than an Injunction. That people be appointed to receive the Sacrament, rather sitting, for avoiding of superstition, than kneeling, having in it the outward show of evil, from which we must abstain. That Excommunication be restored to his old former force. That papists nor other, neither constrainedly nor customably, communicate in the mysteries of salvation. That both the Sacrament of the Lord's supper and Baptism also, may be ministered according to the ancient purity & simplicity. That the parties to be baptised, if they be of the years of discretion, by themselves & in their own persons, or if they be infants, by their parents (in whose room if upon necessary occasions & businesses they be absent, some of the congregation knowing the good behaviour and sound faith of the parents) may both make rehearsal of their faith, And also if their faith be sound, and agreeable to holy scriptures, desire to be in the same baptised. And finally, that nothing be done in this or any other thing, but that which you have the express warrant of God's word for.

Let us come now to the third part, which concerneth ecclesiastical discipline. The officers that have to deal in this charge, are chiefly three ministers preachers or pastors of whom before. Seniors or Elders, and Deacons. Concerning Seniors, not only their office but their name also is out of this english church utterly removed. Their office was to govern the church with the rest of the ministers, to consult, to admonish, to correct, and to order all things appertaining to the state of the congregation. Instead of these Seniors in every church, the pope hath brought in and we yet maintain, the Lordship of one man over many churches, yea over sundry Shires. These Seniors then, because their charge was not overmuch, did execute their offices in their own persons without substitutes. Our Lord bishops have their under officers, as Suffragans, Chancellors, Archdeacons, Officials, Commissaries, and such like. Touching Deacons, though their names be remaining, yet is the office foully perverted and turned upside down, for their duty in the primitive church, was to gather the alms diligently, and to distribute it faithfully, also for the sick and impotent persons to provide painfully, having ever a diligent care, that the charity of godly men, were not wasted upon loiterers and idle vagabonds. Now it is the first step to the ministry, nay, rather a mere order of priesthood. For they may baptise in the presence of a bishop or priest, or in their absence (if necessity so require) minister the other Sacrament, likewise read the holy Scripture and homilies in the congregation, instruct the youth in the Catechism, and also preach, if he be commanded by the bishop. Again, in the old church every congregation had their Deacons. Now they are tied to athedral churches only, and what do they there? gather the alms and distribute to the poor? nay, that is the least piece or rather no part of their function. What then? to sing a gospel when the bishop ministreth the Communion. If this be not a perverting of this office and charge, let every one judge. And yet lest the reformers of our time should seem utterly to take out of God's Church this necessary function, they appoint somewhat to it concerning the poor, and that is, to search for the sick, needy, and impotent people of the parish, and to intimate their estates, names, and places where they dwell to the Curate, that by his exhortation they may be relieved by the parish, or other convenient alms. And this as you see, is the nighest part of his office, and yet you must understand it to be in such places where there is a Curate and a Deacon: every parish can not be at that cost to have both, nay, no parish so far as can be gathered, at this present hath. Now then, if you will restore the church to his ancient officers, this you must do. Instead of an Archbishop or Lord bishop, you must make equality of ministers. Instead of Chancellors, Archdeacons, Officials, Commissaries, Proctors, Doctors, Summoners, Churchwardens, and suchlike: you have to plant in every congregation a lawful and godly seignory. The deaconship must bot be confounded with the ministry, nor the Collectors for the poor, may not usurp the Deacons' office: But he that hath an office, must look to his office, and every man must keep himself within the bounds and limits of his own vocation. And to these three jointly, that is, the Ministers, Seniors, and deacons, is the whole regiment of the church to be committed. This regiment consisteth especially in ecclesiastical discipline, which is an order left by God unto his church, whereby men learn to frame their wills and doings according to the law of God, by instructing and admonishing one another, yea and by correcting and punishing all wilful persons, and contemners of the same. Of this discipline there is two kinds, one private, wherewith we will not deal because it is impertinent to our purpose, another public, which although it hath been long banished, yet if it might now at length be restored, would be very necessary and profitable for the building up of God's house. The final end of this discipline, is the reforming of the disordered, and to bring them to repentance, and to bridle such as would offend. The chiefest part and last punishment of this discipline is excommunication, by the consent of the church determined, if the offender be obstinate, which how miserably it hath been by the Popes proctors, and is by our new Canonists abused, who seeth not? In the primitive church it was in many men's hands: now one alone excommunicateth. In those days it was the last censure of the church, and never went forth but for notorious crimes: Now it is pronounced for every light trifle. Then excommunication was greatly regarded and feared. Now because it is a money matter, no whit at all esteemed. Then for great sins, severe punishment, and for small offences, little censures. Now great sins either not at all punished, as blaspheny, usury, etc, or else slightly passed over with pricking in a blanket, or pinning in a sheet, as adultery, whoredom, drunkenness, etc, Again, such as are no sins (as if a man conform not himself to popish orders and ceremonies, if he come not at the whistle of him, who hath by God's word no authority to call, we mean Chancellors, Officials, Doctors, and all that rabble) are grievously punished, not only by excommunication, suspension, deprivation and other (as they term it) spiritual coercion, but also by banishing, imprisoning, revelling, taunting, and what not? Then the sentence was tempered according to the notoriousness of the fact. Now on the one side either hatred against some persons, carrieth men headlong into rash and cruel judgement: or else favour, affection, or money, mitigateth the rigour of the same, and all this cometh to pass, because the regiment left of Christ to his church, is committed into one man's hands, whom alone it shall be more easy for the wicked by bribing to pervert, than to overthrow the faith and piety of a zealous and godly company, for such manner of men indeed should the Seigniors be ... And this is that order of ecclesiastical discipline which all godly wish to be restored, to the end that every one by the same, may be kept within the limits of his vocation, and a great number be brought to live in godly conversation. Not that we mean to take away the authority of the civil Magistrate and chief governor, to whom we wish all blessedness, and for the increase of whose godliness we daily pray: but that Christ being restored into his kingdom, to rule in the same by the sceptre of his word, and severe discipline: the Prince may be better obeyed, the realm more flourish in godliness and the Lord himself more sincerely and purely according to his revealed will served than heretofore he hath been, or yet at this present is ... Is a reformation good for France? and can it be evil for England? Is discipline meet for Scotland? and is it unprofitable for this Realm? Surely God hath set these examples before your eyes to encourage you to go forward to a thorough and a speedy reformation ...

> A View of the Popish Abuses yet remaining in the English Church,
> for the which godly Ministers have refused to subscribe.

Whereas immediately after the last Parliament, holden at Westminster, begun in Anno. 1570, and ended in Anno. 1571. the ministers of God's holy word and sacraments, were called before her Majesty's high commissioners, and enforced to subscribe unto the articles, if they would keep their places and livings, and some for refusing to subscribe, were unbrotherly and uncharitably intreated, and from

The Beginnings, 1550–1603

their offices and places removed: May it please therefore this honourable and high court of Parliament, in consideration of the premisses, to take a view of such causes, as then did withhold, & now doth the foresaid ministers from subscribing and consenting unto those foresaid articles, by way of purgation to discharge themselves of all disobedience towards the church of God and their sovereign, and by way of most humble intreaty, for the removing away and utter abolishing of all such corruptions and abuses as witheld them, through which this long time brethren have been at unnatural war and strife amongst themselves, to the hindrance of the gospel, to the joy of the wicked, and to the grief and dismay of all those that profess Christ's religion, & labour to attain Christian reformation.

The First Article

First, that the book commonly called the book of common prayers for the church of England, authorised by Parliament, and all and every the contents therein be such as are not repugnant to the word of God

[Twenty-one points of criticism follow. They contain the general Puritan objections to the Book of Common Prayer and also vivid examples of the persistence of Catholic folk practices in church worship.]

1. They should first prove, that a reading service by the word of God going before, and with the administration of the sacraments, is according to the word of God, that private Communion, private baptism, baptism ministered by women, holy days ascribed to saints, prescript services for them, kneeling at communion, wafer cakes for their bread when they minister it, surplice and cope to do it in; churching of women, coming in veils, abusing the psalm to her [i.e., Psalm cxx], I have lifted up mine eyes unto the hills, etc, and such other foolish things, are agreeable to the written word of the almighty ...

8. The public baptism, that also is full of childish & superstitious toys. First in their prayer they say that God by the baptism of his son Jesus Christ, did sanctify the flood of Jordan, and all other waters, to the mystical washing away of sin, attributing that to the sign which is proper to the work of God in the blood of Christ, as though virtue were in water, to wash away sins. Secondly, they require a promise of the godfathers and godmothers (as they term them) which is not in their power to perform. Thirdly, they profane holy baptism, in toying foolishly, for that they ask questions of an infant, which can not answer, and speak unto them, as was wont to be spoken unto men, and unto such as being converted, answered for themselves, & were baptized ...

9. As for matrimony, that also hath corruptions too many. It was wont to be counted a sacrament, and therefore they use yet a sacramental sign, to which they attribute the virtue of wedlock. I mean the wedding ring, which they foully abuse & dally withal, in taking it up, and laying it down: In putting it on, they abuse the name of the Trinity, they make the new married man, according to the Popish form, to make an idol of his wife, saying: with this ring I thee wed, with my body I thee

worship, etc. And because in Popery, no holy action might be done without a mass, they enjoin the married persons to receive the communion (as they do their bishops and priests when they are made, etc.) other petty things out of the book, we speak not of, as that women contrary to the rule of the Apostle, come, and are suffered to come bare headed, with bagpipes and fiddlers before them, to disturb the congregation, and that they must come in at the great door of the church, or else all is marred ...

11. They appoint a prescript kind of service to bury the dead ... We say nothing of the threefold peal because that is rather licensed by injunction, than commanded in their book, nor of their strange mourning bychanging their garments, which if it be not hypocritical, yet it is superstitious and heathenish ... As for the superstitions used both in Country and City, for the place of burial, which way they must lie, how they must be fetched to church, the minister meeting them at church style with surplice, with a company of greddy clerks, that a cross white or black, must be set upon the dead corpse, that bread must be given to the poor, and offerings in burial time used, and cakes sent abroad to friends, because these are rather used of custom and superstition, than by authority of the book ...

13. In their order of service there is no edification, according to the rule of the Apostle, but confusion, they toss the Psalms in most places like tennis balls. The people some standing, some walking, some talking, some reading, some praying by themselves, attend not to the minister. He again posteth over, as fast as he can gallop. For either he hath two places to serve, or else there are some games to be played in the afternoon, as lying for the whetstone, heathenish dancing for the ring, a bear or a bull to be baited, or else Jackan apes to ride on horseback, or an interlude to be played, and if no place else can be gotten, it must be done in the church, etc. Now the people sit and now they stand up. When the old Testament is read, or the lessons, they make no reverence, but when the gospel cometh, they all stand up. For why, they think that to be of greatest authority, and are ignorant that the scriptures came from one spirit. When Jesus is named, then off goeth the cap, and down goeth the knees, with such a scraping on the ground, that they cannot hear a good while after, so that the word is hindered, but when any other names of God are mentioned, they make no curtsey at all, as though the names of God were not equal, or as though all reverence ought to be given to the syllables ... As for organs and curious singing, though they be proper to popish dens, I mean to Cathedral churches, yet some others also must have them ...

The 2. Article

That the manner and order appointed by public authority about the administration of the Sacraments and common prayers, and that the apparel by sufficient authority appointed for the ministers within the church of England, be not wicked nor against the word of God, but tolerable, and being commanded for order and obedience sake, are to be used.

... And as for the apparel ... We marvel that they could espy in their last Synod, that a grey Amice, which is but a garment of dignity, should be a garment (as they say) defiled with superstition, and yet that copes, caps, surplices, tippets and suchlike baggage, the preaching signs of popish priesthood, the pope's creatures, kept in the same form to this end, to bring dignity and reverence to the Ministers and Sacraments, should be retained still, and not abolished. But they are as the garments of the Idol, to which we should say, avaunt and get thee hence. They are as the garments of Balaamites, of popish priests, enemies to God and all Christians ...

The 3. Article

That the articles of Religion which only concern the true christian faith, and the doctrine of the Sacraments, comprised in a book imprinted: Articles, whereupon it was agreed by both Archbishops, etc. and every one of them contain true and godly Christian doctrine.

For the Articles concerning that substance of doctrine using a godly interpretation in a point or two ... we were and are ready according to duty, to subscribe unto them. We would to God that as they hold the substance together with us, and we with them: so they would not deny the effect and virtue thereof. Then should not our words and works be divorced, but Christ should be suffered to reign, a true ministry according to the word instituted, Discipline exercised, Sacraments purely and sincerely ministered. This is what we strive for, and about which we have suffered not as evildoers, but for resisting Popery ...

Document I.8

Edmund Grindal Defends Prophesyings, 1576

The passing of parliamentary acts could give Protestantism a legal and official status in the kingdom but the personal faith of its citizens could not be transformed by such means. The task of Elizabeth and her bishops was to give spiritual substance to the prescriptions of the laws passed by Parliament. That was a daunting task. Even though the Catholic hierarchy of Mary's reign was soon removed and men of Protestant convictions occupied their dioceses, there were thousands of priests in the parishes who were still Catholic in their sympathies. They had only a hazy idea about the meaning of the changes that were being thrust upon them by the authorities. Those who had a firm grasp of Catholic teaching either withdrew to the Continent or practised their faith in secret. Those who remained at their posts in the parishes were often ill educated and ineffective in the discharge of their pastoral and liturgical duties. If Protestantism was to take root in the hearts of the public generally, an effective ministry was essential.

The Marian exiles had been impressed by the way this kind of challenge was met on the Continent – especially at Zurich – by arranging courses in the biblical languages and conducting group studies in theology for ministers. It was felt that some such method should be adopted in the reformed Church of England. They may well have been initiated soon after 1560 and gradually increased in their popularity as more and more bishops saw fit to patronise them. By about 1570 they were to be found in a large number of areas, in East Anglia, in the Midlands, in places like Shropshire and Devon, even in the diocese of St. David's in Wales. They never became an official part of the structure of the Church and so official records say very little about them. Most typically, they were the fruit of enthusiasm amongst the ministers themselves, particularly those who were imbued with the evangelistic zeal of the Puritans.

Grindal provides a succinct description of their methods of procedure in his letter to the Queen. He felt, as he explains, that they were to be encouraged. The Queen, however, did not agree. The trouble was that these 'prophesyings' or 'exercises' often developed into something more dynamic than staid extramural classes. One reason was that they were conducted in English rather than Latin and were open to the public. Most of them had a rule that the public could only listen to the discussions; it could not participate in them. But there is evidence that some people travelled substantial distances in order to hear their more learned ecclesiastical superiors debating sensitive questions not only about theology but about church order. And since men of a Puritan bent were staunch patrons of these exercises, it was inevitable that they should use them to propagate their particular convictions. For the Queen such activities savoured of a desire to modify, if not to overthrow, the established order. Moreover, when these activities were prohibited and branded as nonconformity, their legacy was transmitted to people who were to become dissenters from the Anglican Church. In that way they have a place in the pre-history of Nonconformity.

In W. Nicholson (ed.), *The Remains of Edmund Grindal* (Cambridge, 1843), 376–90, this celebrated letter marks a confrontation between queen and archbishop that was to have dramatic consequences in subsequent history. Elizabeth saw the prophesyings as a subversive activity that might well have ominous effects. Grindal saw them as a creative agency that would contribute substantially towards strengthening and enriching the ministry of the Church of England. Grindal in the first of his two 'short petitions' towards the end of his letter made a suggestion that could only enrage the Queen because asking her to entrust decisions on matters of doctrine and church discipline impinged upon the Royal Supremacy. She was too much the daughter of her father to countenance such a transfer of authority. But Grindal himself is revealed in the letter as a man whose concern for the promotion of an effective preaching ministry inspired a courageous stand. His plain speaking is indeed remarkable.

But for those who sought further reformation, the reaction of the Queen was a bitter disappointment. The policy of 'tarrying for the magistrate' had failed (so G. R. Elton, in *The Tudor Constitution* (Cambridge, 1968), 435). That meant that there were many of them driven towards nonconformity either clandestinely within the Church of England or outside it.

For a full treatment of the issue and its sad consequences for Grindal, v., Patrick Collinson, *The Elizabethan Puritan Movement* (London, 1982), Part 4, and his *Archbishop Grindal* (London, 1979), 232–52; and M. M. Knappen, *Tudor Puritanism* (Chicago and London, 1970), 253–5.

To the Queen, concerning suppressing the prophecies, and restraining the number of preachers, 20 December 1576

With most humble remembrance of my bounden duty to your Majesty: It may please the same to be advertised, that the speeches which it hath pleased you to deliver unto me, when I last attended on your Highness, concerning abridging the number of preachers, and the utter suppression of all learned exercises and conferences among the ministers of the church, allowed by their bishops and ordinaries, have exceedingly dismayed and discomforted me. Not so much for that the said speeches sounded very hardly against mine own person ... but most of all for that the same might both tend to the public harm of God's church, whereof your Highness ought to be *nutricia*,[1] and also to the heavy burdening of your own conscience before God, if they should be put in strict execution. It was not your Majesty's pleasure then, the time not serving thereto, to hear me at any length concerning the said two matters then propounded: I thought it therefore my duty by writing to declare some part of my mind unto your Highness; beseeching the same with patience to read over this that I now send, written with mine own rude scribbling hand; which seemeth to be of more length than it is indeed: for I say with Ambrose, *Scribo manu mea, quod sola legas*.[2]

MADAM,

First of all, I must and will, during my life, confess, that there is no earthly creature to whom I am so much bounden as to your Majesty; who, notwithstanding mine insufficiency ... hath bestowed upon me so many and so great benefits, as I could never hope for, much less deserve. I do therefore, according to my most bounden duty, with all thanksgiving, bear towards your Majesty a most humble, faithful, and thankful heart; and that knoweth He which knoweth all things. Neither do I ever intend to offend your Majesty in any thing, unless, in the cause of God or of his church, by necessity of office, and burden of conscience, I shall thereunto be enforced: and in those cases, (which I trust in God shall never be urged upon me,) if I should use dissembling or flattering silence, I should very evil requite your Majesty's so many and so great benefits; for in so doing, both you might fall into peril towards God, and I myself into endless perdition ...

[He adduces a number of scriptural examples of prophets reproving monarchs.]

[*Margin*: Prima Pars. Concerning suppressing preachers.] And so, to come to the present case; ... I cannot marvel enough, how this strange opinion should once enter into your mind, that it should be good for the church to have few preachers.

Alas, Madam! is the scripture more plain in any one thing, than that the gospel of Christ should be plentifully preached; and that plenty of labourers should be sent into the Lord's harvest; which, being great and large, standeth in need, not of a few, but many workmen? ...

Christ, when he sendeth forth his apostles, saith unto them, *Ite, praedicate evangelium omni creaturae*.³ But all God's creatures cannot be instructed in the gospel, unless all possible means be used, to have multitude of preachers and teachers to preach unto them.

Sermo Christi inhabitet in vobis opulente,⁴ saith St. Paul to the Colossians; and to Timothy, *Praedica sermonem, insta, tempestive, intempestive, argue, increpa, exhortare*.⁵ Which things cannot be done without often and much preaching.

To this agreeth the practice of Christ's apostles, *Qui constituebant per singulas ecclesias presbyteros*.⁶ St Paul likewise, writing to Titus, writeth thus, *Hujus rei gratia reliqui te in Creta, ut quae desunt pergas corrigere, et constituas oppidatim presbyteros*.⁷ And afterwards describeth, how the said *presbyteri* were to be qualified; not such as we are sometimes compelled to admit by mere necessity, (unless we should leave a great number of churches desolate,) but such indeed as were able to exhort *per sanem doctrinam, et contradicentes convincere*.⁸ And in this place I beseech your Majesty to note one thing necessary to be noted; which is this, If the Holy Ghost prescribe expressly that preachers should be placed *oppidatim*,⁹ how can it well be thought, that three or four preachers may affirm for a shire?¹⁰

Public and continual preaching of God's word is the ordinary mean and instrument of the salvation of mankind.¹¹ St. Paul calleth it the *ministry of reconciliation* of man unto God. By preaching of God's word the glory of God is enlarged, faith is nourished, and charity increased. By it the ignorant is instructed, the negligent exhorted and incited, the stubborn rebuked, the weak conscience comforted, and to all those that sin of malicious wickedness the wrath of God is threatened. By preaching also due obedience to Christian princes and magistrates is planted in the hearts of subjects: for obedience proceedeth of conscience; conscience is grounded in the word of God; the word of God worketh his effect by preaching. So as generally, where preaching wanteth, obedience faileth.

No prince ever had more lively experience hereof than your Majesty hath had in your time, and may have daily. If your Majesty come to the city of London never so often, what gratulation, what joy, what concourse of people is there to be seen! ... Whereof cometh this, Madam, but of the continual preaching of God's word in that city, whereby that people hath been plentifully instructed in their duty towards God and your Majesty? On the contrary, what bred the rebellion in the north? Was it not papistry, and ignorance of God's word, through want of often preaching? ...

Now, where it is thought, that the reading of the godly homilies, set forth by public authority, may suffice, I continue of the same mind I was when I attended last upon your Majesty. The reading of the homilies hath its commodity; but is nothing comparable to the office of preaching. The godly preacher is termed in the gospel *fidelis servus et prudens, qui novit famulitio Domini cibum demensum dare in tempore*;¹² who can apply his speech according to the diversity of times, places, and hearers, which cannot be done in homilies: exhortations, reprehensions, and persuasions, are uttered with more affection, to the moving of the hearers, in sermons than in homilies. Besides, homilies were devised by the godly bishops in your brother's time, only to supply necessity, for want of preachers; and are by the statute not to be preferred, but to give place to sermons, whensoever they may be had; and were never thought in themselves alone to contain sufficient instruction for the Church of England ...

[*Margin:* Secunda Pars. Concerning the exercises.] Now for the second point, which is concerning the learned exercise and conference amongst the ministers of the church: I have consulted with divers of my brethren, the bishops, by letters; who think the same as I do, viz. a thing profitable to the church, and therefore expedient to be continued. And I trust your Majesty will think the like, when your Highness shall have been informed of the manner and order thereof; what authority it hath of the scriptures; what commodity it bringeth with it; and what incommodities will follow, if it be clean taken away.

The authors of this exercise are the bishops of the diocese where the same is used; who both by the law of God, and by the canons and constitutions of the church now in force, have authority to appoint exercises to their inferior ministers, for increase of learning and knowledge in the scriptures, as to them seemeth most expedient: for that pertaineth *ad disciplinam clericalem*.[13] The times appointed for the assembly is once a month, or once in twelve or fifteen days, at the discretion of the ordinary. The time of the exercise is two hours: the place, the church of the town appointed for the assembly. The matter entreated of is as followeth. Some text of scripture, before appointed to be spoken of is interpreted in this order: First, the occasion of the place is shewed. Secondly, the end. Thirdly, the proper sense of the place. Fourthly, the propriety of the words: and those that be learned in the tongues shewing the diversities of interpretations. Fifthly, where the like phrases are used in the scriptures. Sixthly, places in the scriptures, seeming to repugn, are reconciled. Seventhly, the arguments of the text are opened. Eighthly, it is also declared, what virtues and what vices are there touched; and to which the commandments pertain. Ninthly, how the text hath been wrested by the adversaries, if occasion so require. Tenthly, and last of all, what doctrine of faith or manners the text doth contain. The conclusion is, with the prayer for your Majesty and all estates, as is appointed by the Book of Common Prayer, and a psalm.

[*Margin*: The orders of them] These orders following are also observed in the said exercise. First, two or three of the gravest and best learned pastors are appointed of the bishop to moderate in every assembly. No man may speak, unless he be first allowed by the bishop, with this *proviso*, that no layman be suffered to speak at any time. No controversy of this present time and state shall be moved or dealt withal. If any attempt is made to the contrary, he is put to silence by the moderator. None is suffered to glance openly or covertly at persons public or private; neither yet any one to confute another. If any man utter a wrong sense of the scripture, he is privately admonished thereof, and better instructed by the moderators, and other his fellow-ministers. If any man use immodest speech, or irreverent gesture or behaviour, or otherwise be suspected in life, he is likewise admonished, as before. If any wilfully do break these orders, he is presented to the bishop, to be by him corrected.

[Some Old Testament precedents are given on the basis of 1 Samuel 19, 1 Samuel 10 and 2 Kings 2.]

St. Paul also doth make express mention, that the like in effect was used in the primitive church; and giveth rules for the order of the same; as namely, that two or three should speak, and the rest should keep silence. [*Margin*: I Cor. 14]

That exercise of the church in those days St. Paul calleth *prophetiam* [*Margin*: Called prophecies in scripture] and the speakers *prophetas*: terms very odious to some, because they are not rightly understood. For indeed *prophetia*, in that and like places of St. Paul, doth not, as it doth sometimes, signify *prediction* of things to come, which gift is not now ordinary in the church of God; but signifieth there, by the consent of the best ancient writers, the interpretation and exposition of the scriptures. And therefore doth St. Paul attribute unto those that be called *prophetae* in that chapter, *doctrinam ad aedificationem, exhortationem, et consolationem*.[14]

This gift of expounding and interpreting the scriptures was, in St. Paul's time, given to many by special miracle, without study: so was also, by like miracle, the gift to speak with strange tongues, which they had never learned. But now, miracles ceasing, men must attain to the knowledge of the Hebrew, Greek, and Latin tongues, &c by travail and study, God giving the increase. So must men also attain by like means to the gift of expounding and interpreting the scriptures. And amongst other helps, nothing is so necessary as these above named exercises and conferences amongst the ministers of the church; which in effect are all one with the exercises of students in divinity in the universities; saving that the first is done in a tongue understood, to the more edifying of the unlearned hearers.

Howsoever report hath been made to your Majesty concerning these exercises, yet I and others of your bishops, whose names are noted in the margin hereof, as they have testified unto me by their letters, having found by experience, that these profits and commodities following have ensued of them:-

[*Margin*: Cantuar. London. Winton. Bathon. Litchfield. Glocestren. Lincoln. Cicestren. Exon. Menevensis, al. Davids., i.e., Canterbury, London, Winchester, Bath, Lichfield, Gloucester, Lincoln, Chichester, Exeter and St. David's]

1. The ministers of the church are more skilful and ready in the scriptures, and apter to teach their flocks.
2. It withdraweth them from idleness, wandering, gaming, &c.
3. Some, afore suspected in doctrine, are brought hereby to open confession of the truth.
4. Ignorant ministers are driven to study, if not for conscience, yet for shame and fear of discipline.
5. The opinion of laymen, touching the idleness of the clergy, is hereby removed.
6. Nothing by experience beateth down popery more than that ministers (as some of my brethren do certify) grow to such good knowledge, by means of these exercises, that where afore were not three able preachers, now are thirty, meet to preach at St. Paul's Cross; and forty or fifty besides, able to instruct their own cures.

The Beginnings, 1550–1603

So as it is found by experience the best means to increase knowledge in the simple, and to continue it in the learned. Only backward men in religion, and contemners of learning in the countries abroad, do fret against it; which in truth doth the more commend it. The dissolution of it would breed triumph to the adversaries, and great sorrow and grief unto the favourers of religion; contrary to the counsel of Ezekiel, who saith, *Cor justi non est contristandum*.[15] And although some few have abused this good and necessary exercise, there is no reason that the malice of a few should prejudice all. Abuses may be reformed, and that which is good may remain. Neither is there any just cause of offence to be taken, if divers men make divers senses of one sentence of scripture ... for otherwise we must needs condemn the ancient fathers and doctors of the church, who most commonly expound one and the same text of the scripture diversely, and yet all to the good of the church ...

I trust, when your Majesty hath considered and well weighed the premises, you will rest satisfied, and judge that no such inconveniences can grow of these exercises, as you have been informed, but rather the clean contrary. And for my own part, because I am very well assured, both by reasons and arguments taken out of the holy scriptures, and by experience, (the most certain seal of sure knowledge,) that the said exercises, for the interpretation and exposition of the scriptures, and for exhortation and comfort drawn out of the same, are both profitable to increase knowledge among ministers, and tendeth to the edifying of the hearers, – I am forced, with all humility, and yet plainly, to profess, that I cannot with safe conscience, and without the offence of the majesty of God, give my assent to the suppressing of the said exercises: much less can I send out any injunction for the utter and universal subversion of the same. I say with St. Paul, 'I have no power to destroy, but to only edify', and with the same apostle, 'I can do nothing against the truth, but for the truth.'

If it be your Majesty's pleasure, for this or any other cause, to remove me out of this place, I will with all humility yield thereunto, and render again to your Majesty that I received of the same. I consider with myself, *Quod horrendum est incidere in manus Dei viventis* ...'[16] And what should I win, if I gained' (I will not say a bishoprick, but) 'the whole world, and lose mine own soul?'

... And now being sorry, that I have been so long and tedious to your Majesty, I will draw to an end, most humbly praying the same well to consider these two short petitions following.

The first is, that you would refer all these ecclesiastical matters which touch religion, or the doctrine and discipline of the church, unto the bishops and divines of your realm; according to the example of all godly Christian emperors and princes of all ages. For indeed they are things to be judged, (as an ancient father writeth,) *in ecclesia, seu synodo, non in palatio*.[17] When your Majesty hath questions of the laws of your realm, you do not decide the same in your court, but send them to your judges to be determined. Likewise for doubts in matters of doctrine or discipline of the church, the ordinary way is to refer the decision of the same to the bishops, and other head ministers of the church.

[He quotes examples from the history of the early Christian emperors.]

The second petition I have to make to your Majesty is this: that, when you deal in matters of faith and religion, or matters that touch the church of Christ, which is his spouse, bought with so dear a price, you would not use to pronounce so resolutely and peremptorily ... as ye may do in civil and extern matters; but always remember, that in God's causes the will of God, and not the will of any earthly creature, is to take place ... In God's matters all princes ought to bow their sceptres to the Son of God, and to ask counsel of his mouth, what they ought to do ...

Remember, Madam, that you are a mortal creature. 'Look not only (as was said to Theodosius)[18] upon the purple and princely array, wherewith ye are apparelled; but consider withal, what is that that is covered therewith. Is it not flesh and blood? Is it not dust and ashes? Is it not a corruptible body, which must return to his earth again, God knoweth how soon?' Must not you also one day appear *ante tremendum tribunal Crucifixi, ut recipias ibi, prout gesseris in corpore, sive bonum sive malum*?[19]

And although you are a mighty prince, yet remember that He which dwelleth in heaven is mightier ...

Wherefore I do beseech you, Madam, *in visceribus Christi*,[20] when you deal in these religious causes, set the majesty of God before your eyes, laying all earthly majesty aside; determine with yourself to obey his voice, and with all humility, say unto him, *Non mea, sed tua voluntas fiat*.[21] God hath blessed you with great felicity in your reign, now many years; beware you do not impute the same to your own deserts or policy, but give God the glory ... Ye have done many things well; but except ye persevere to the end, ye cannot be blessed. For if ye turn from God, then God will turn away his merciful countenance from you. And what remaineth then to be looked for, but only a terrible expectation of God's judgments, and an heaping up of wrath against the day of wrath?

But I trust in God, your Majesty will always humble yourself under his mighty hand, and go forward in the zealous setting forth of God's true religion, always yielding due obedience and reverence to the word of God, the only rule of faith and religion. And if ye so do, although God hath just cause many ways to be angry with you and us for our unfaithfulness, yet I doubt nothing, but that for his own name's sake, and for his own glory's sake, he will still hold his merciful hand over us, shield and protect us under the shadow of his wings, as he hath done hitherto.

I beseech God, our heavenly Father, plentifully to pour his principal Spirit upon you, and always to direct your heart in his holy fear. Amen.

Notes

1. 'nursing mothers', Is. 49: 23.
2. 'I write with my own hand, that you alone may read it'.
3. 'Go, preach the gospel to every creature', Mk. 16: 15.
4. 'Let the word of Christ dwell in you richly', Col. 3: 16.

5. 'Preach the word; be instant in season, out of season; reprove, rebuke, exhort', 2 Tim. 4: 2.
6. 'who ordained elders in every church', Acts 14: 23.
7. 'For this cause left I thee in Crete, that thou shouldest set in order the things that are wanting, and ordain elders in every city', Tit. 1: 5.
8. 'by sound doctrine ... to convince the gainsayers', Tit. 1: 9.
9. 'in every city'.
10. This was suggested by Queen Elizabeth.
11. For a heated exchange on this topic see the examination of John Penry before the High Commission.
12. 'a faithful and wise servant, who knows how to give his Lord's family their meat in due season', Mt. 24: 45.
13. 'to the discipline of ministers'.
14. 'teaching unto edification, exhortation and comfort', 1 Cor. 14: 3.
15. 'the heart of the righteous is not to be made sad', Ezek. 13: 22.
16. 'That it is a fearful thing to fall into the hands of the living God', Heb. 10: 31.
17. 'in the church or synod, not in the palace'.
18. The reference is to Theodoret, *Ecclesiastical History*, V. 18, in B. Jackson (ed.), *Nicene and Post-Nicene Fathers* (Oxford, 1892), III, 143.
19. 'before the fearful judgment seat of the Crucified, to receive there the things done in the body, whether good or bad', 2 Cor. 5: 10.
20. 'in the bowels of Christ', Phil. 2: 1.
21. 'Not my will, but thine, be done', Lk. 22: 42.

Document I.9

The Queen Suppresses Prophesyings, 1577

Nothing that Grindal might say could persuade the Queen to moderate her objections to prophesyings. In the following letter of 7 May 1577 she gives her reasons.
In W. Nicholson (ed.), *The Remains of Edmund Grindal* (Cambridge, 1843), 467–9 and E. Cardwell, *Documentary Annals* (Oxford, 1839), I, 371 and partially in G. R. Elton, *The Tudor Constitution* (Cambridge, 1968), 443–4.

Right reverend father in God, we greet you well. We hear, to our great grief, that in sundry parts of our realm there are no small numbers of persons, presuming to be teachers and preachers of the church (though neither lawfully thereunto called nor yet fit for the same,) which, contrary to our laws established for the public divine service of Almighty God and the administration of his holy sacraments, within this Church of England, do daily devise, imagine, propound and put in execution, sundry new rites and forms in the church, as well by their preaching, reading and ministering the sacraments, as well by procuring unlawful assemblies of a great number of our people out of their ordinary parishes, and from place far distant, and that also some of good calling, (though therein not well advised) to be hearers of their disputations, and new devised opinions upon points of divinity, far and unmeet of unlearned people: which manner of invasions they in some places call *prophesying* and in some other places *exercises*. By which manner of assemblies great numbers of our people, especially the vulgar sort, meet to be otherwise occupied with honest labour for their living, are brought to idleness, and seduced; and in a manner schismatically divided amongst themselves into variety of dangerous opinions, not only in towns and parishes, but even in some families, and manifestly thereby encouraged to the violation of our laws, and to the breach of common order, and finally to the offence of all our quiet subjects, that desire to serve God according to the uniform orders established in the church: whereof the sequel cannot be but over dangerous to be suffered.

Wherefore, considering it should be the duty of the bishops being the principal ordinary officers in the church of God, as you are one, to see these dishonours against the honour of God and the quietness of the Church reformed; and that we see that by the increase of these through sufferance; great danger may ensue, even to the decay of the Christian faith, whereof we are by God appointed the defender; besides the other inconveniences, to the disturbance of our peaceable government. We therefore, according to the authority we have, do charge and command you ... to take order through your diocese ... that no manner of public and divine service, nor other form of administration of the holy sacraments, nor any other rites or ceremonies, be in any sort used in the church but directly according to the order established by our laws. Neither that any manner of person be suffered within your diocese to preach, teach, read, or anywise exercise any function in the church, but such as shall be lawfully approved and licensed, as persons able for their knowledge and conformable to the ministry in the rites and ceremonies of the church of England. And where there shall not be sufficient able persons for learning in any cures, to preach or instruct their cures, as were requisite, there shall you limit the curates to read the public homilies according to the injunctions heretofore by us given for like causes.

And furthermore, considering for the great abuses that have been in sundry places of our realm by reason of the foresaid assemblies, called exercises and for that the same are not, nor have been appointed or warranted by you. We will and straitly charge you, that you do cause the same forthwith to cease, and not to be used; but if any shall attempt, or continue, or renew the same, we will you not only to commit them unto prison, as maintainers of disorders, but also to advertise us, or our council, of the names and qualities of them, and of their maintainers and abettors; that thereupon, for better example, their punishment may be more sharp for their reformation.

And in these things we charge you to be so careful and vigilant, as by your negligence, if we should hear of any person attempting to offend in the premises without your correction or information to us, we be not forced to make some example in reformation of you, according to your deserts.

Given under our signet at our manor of Greenwich the 7th May, 1577.

Document I.10

Robert Browne: A True and Short Declaration, Both of the Gathering and Joining Together of Certain Persons; and also of the Lamentable Breach which Fell amongst Them

This document has no name, place, or date but the author was Robert Browne and he seems to have written it before he left Middelburg in 1583. It gives us a vivid picture of the inner turmoil of an unhappy man as well as glimpses of the origins of the separatist group at Norwich. The orthography has been modernised and that has been particularly necessary because the original is execrably printed, probably by an amateur. Personal names and punctuation are as in the original, but the division into paragraphs is slightly different. The printed text in A. Peel and L. H. Carlson (eds), *The Writings of Robert Harrison and Robert Browne* (London, 1953), 396–429, reproduces the original in all its vagaries.

There were certain persons in England, of which, some were brought up in schools, & in the University of Cambridge, & some in families & households, as is the manner of that country. Some of these which had lived & studied in Cambridge, were there known & counted forward in religion, & others also both there and in the country were more careful & zealous, than their froward enemies could suffer. They in Cambridge were scattered from thence, some to one trade of life, & some to another: as Robert Broune, Robert Harrison, William Harrison, Philip Broune, Robert Barker. Some of these applied themselves to teach scholars: to the which labour, R. Broune also gave himself, for the space of three years. He having a special care to teach religion with other learning, did thereby keep his scholars in such awe and good order, as all the Townsmen where he taught gave him witness.

Yet the world being so corrupt as it is, & the times so perilous he greatly misliked the wants & defaults, which he saw everywhere, & marked plainly that without redress, neither the parents could long rejoice in their children, nor the children profit so much in religion, as that their other studies & learning might be blessed thereby[.] Hereupon he fell into great care, & was sore grieved while he long considered many things amiss, & the cause of all, to be the woeful and lamentable state of the church. Wherefore he laboured much to know his duty in such things, & because the church of God is his Kingdom, & his name especially is thereby magnified; he wholly bent himself to search & find out the matters of the church: as how it was to be guided & ordered, & what abuses there were in the ecclesiastical government then used. These things, he had long before debated in himself, & with others, & suffered also some trouble about them at Cambridge. yet now on fresh he set his mind on these things, & night & day did consult with himself & others about them, lest he should be ignorant, or mistake any of those matters. Whatsoever things he found belonging to the church, & to his calling as a member of the church, he did put in practice. For even little children are of the church & kingdom of God yea of such saith Christ, doth his kingdom consist: &

therefore both in his school he laboured that the kingdom of God might appear, & also in those of the town with whom he kept company. So by word & practice he tried out all things, that he might be stayed both in judgment & counsel, & also in enterprising matters, as his duty should lead him. But this his dealing got him much envy of the preacher & some others where he taught, & much trouble also when he broke his mind more plainly unto them. Presently after this he was discharged of his school by the grudge of his enemies. Yet he taught still, with great good will & favour of the Townsmen, till such time as the plague increased in the Town, & he was sent far away by his friends ...

Then he gave warning to the Town, & departed to come home, as his father willed him. So might he have lived with his father, being a man of some countenance, & have wanted nothing,[1] if he had been so disposed but his care as always before, so then especially being set on the church of God, he asked leave of his father, & took his Journey to Cambridge, from whence a few years before he had departed. He there had dealing with M. Greenham of Drayton,[2] who of all others he heard say was most forward, and thought that with him & by him he should have some stay of his care & hope of his purpose. Wherefore, as those which in old time were called the prophets & children of the prophets & lived together, because of corruptions among others, so came he unto him. He was suffered, as others also in his his [sic] house, to speak of that part of scripture, which was used to be read after meals. And although he said, that without leave & special word from the bishop, he was to suffer none to teach openly in his parish, yet without any such leave he suffered R.B. Notwithstanding, when R.B. saw, that the bishops feet were too much set in every place, & that spiritual infection too much spread even to the best reformed places, he took that occasion which the Lord did first give him for redress, and when certain in Cambridge had both moved him, & also with consent of the Mayor, & Vice-chancellor, called him to preach among them, he dealt in this manner.

He first considered the state of Cambridge, how the church of God was planted therein. For he judged that the church was to call and receive him, if he should be there chosen and appointed to preach. Then did he think on this, who should be chiefest, or have charge before others, to look to such matters. For the bishops take upon them the chiefty, but to be called and authorised by them, he thought it unlawful. And why he was of this mind, he had these & such like warrants: namely, they should be chiefest, which partake unto us the chiefest graces, and use of their callings. And that doth Christ, as it is written, of his fulness have all we received, and grace for grace. Joh.1.16. And to him hath God made all things subject saith Paul, Ephes. 1.22. even under his feet, and hath appointed him over all things, to be head of the church, which is his body, even the fulness of him, which filleth all in all things. Now next under Christ, is not the bishop of the diocese, by whom so many mischiefs are wrought, neither any one which hath but single authority, but first they that have their authority together: as first the church, which Christ also teacheth, where he saith, If he will not vouchsafe to hear them tell it unto the church, & if he refuse to hear the church also, let him be unto thee as an heathen man & a publican, Mat.18.17. Therefore is the church called the pillar & ground of truth. I Tim.3.15. & the voice of the whole people, guided by the elders and forwardest, is said to be the voice of God ...

Therefore the meetings together of many churches, also of every whole church, & of the elders therein, is above the Apostle, above the Prophet, the Evangelist, the Pastor, the Teacher, & every particular Elder. For the joining & partaking of many churches together, & of the authority which many have, must needs be greater & more weighty, than the authority of any single person. And this also meant Paul where he saith, I Cor.2.22. We are yours, & you are Christ's, & Christ is God's. So that the Apostle is inferior to the church, & the church is inferior to Christ, & Christ concerning his manhood & office in the church, is inferior to God. This he judged, not only to be against the wickedness of the bishops, but also against their whole power and authority. For if the authority of the church, & of the forwardest brethren or elders therein, be above the bishops, how should it not follow, but that the bishops may be commanded, accused & charged by the church, yea also discharged & separated as is their desert?

[There follows an attack on the alleged tyranny of the bishops and their misrule in the church.]

While R.B. thought these things in himself he moved the matter divers times unto others. Some did gainsay & those of the forwardest, affirming that the bishops' authority is tolerable, & he might take licence & authority of them. Others of them said they would not counsel nor meddle for another man's conscience in that matter, but they themselves judged, that the bishops preached the word of God, & therefore ought not lightly to be rejected. Also they said, that seeing they had the word & sacraments, they must needs have withal the church & people of God: & seeing this was under the government of the bishops & by means of them, they could not wholly condemn the bishops, but rather judge them faulty in some part. Then did R.B. again & again discuss these matters, as he had often before, as whether the bishops could be said to preach the word of God & minister the sacraments or no. For if that were true, then also might they call & place ministers: & seeing they themselves did minister so great a thing as is the word & the sacraments, they might also minister their help in other things not so great.

Therefore to know whether they preached the word of God, he searched & found by the scriptures, what it is to preach the word: namely to do the Lord's message, as it is written in Jeremy 23.22. in teaching the people those things, whereby they might turn them from their evil ways & from the wickedness of their inventions ... For to make a sermon is not to preach the word of God, no, nor yet to make a true sermon. For the servant that telleth a true tale hath not done his master's message, nor the arraunt [i.e., errand] for the which he was sent, except he tell & speak that for which his master sent him. Therefore though the bishops teach the people, and give them laws, & make many injunctions, yea, though they be laws of Christ, yet if they abuse the obedience of the people, to hold and follow with some laws of Christ their own laws especially, what are they but antichrists? ... For example while they pervert the law of God in this, they can not be said to preach his law:

namely whereas God commandeth to plant & to build his church, by gathering the worthy and refusing the unworthy. Mat.10.11. Act. 19.9. Ezr. 6.21. they hook by their contrary laws both papists & careless worldlings, as crooked trees, to build the Lord's sanctuary, & force the wretched to their worshippings & service, as if dogs might be thrust upon God for sweet sacrifice ... Thus was he [i.e., R.B.] settled not to seek any approving or authorising of the bishops. But because he knew the trouble that would follow, if he so proceeded, he sought means of quietness so much as was lawful; & for dealing with the bishops, he was of this judgment, that men may now deal with them, as before they might with the pharisees: that is, so far as we neither sin against God, nor give offence unto men: Therefore if Christ did his Father's will, when he sat in the middle of the doctors, hearing them, & asking them questions. Luc.2.46 & if Paul did his duty, when he sat down in the synagogue, as it were offering himself, & seeking leave to speak to the people. Act. 13.14. if he also did lawfully apply himself to their ceremonies, Act.21.26. then thus far also is there meddling with the bishops, to try & prove them, or to be tried of them, as we see the like did fall out in Christ, also to yield to their power, so that, wherein we yield, it be not against the truth, & we do not establish it: as we know Paul did to the power of the priests, of the pharisees, & of the chief of the synagogue.

Therefore he thought it lawfull first to be tried of the bishops, then also to suffer their power, though it were unlawful, if in anything it did not hinder the truth. But to be authorised of them, to be sworn, to subscribe, to be ordained & to receive their licensing, he utterly misliked & kept himself clear in those matters.

Howbeit the bishop's seals were gotten him by his brother, which he both refused before the officers, & being written for him would not pay for them, & also being afterward paid for by his brother, he lost one, & burnt another in the fire & another being sent him to Cambridge, he kept it by him, till in his trouble it was delivered to a Justice of peace, & so from him, as is supposed, to the bishop of Norwich. Yet lest his dealing on this manner, should encourage others to deal in worse manner, he openly preached against the calling & authorising of preachers by bishops, & spake it often also openly in Cambridge ... And this his duty he said was, first to discharge his message before God, & deserve no reproof of them, & then also, either to find them worthie, or else, if they refused such reformation, as the Lord did now call for, to leave them, as his duty did bind him ... Therefore he finding the parishes too much addicted, & pliable to that lamentable state, he judged that the kingdom of God was not to be begun by whole parishes, but rather of the worthiest, were they never so few ... So he having tried about half a year, both by open preaching, & by daily exhortation in sundry houses, that either by bondage of the bishops in that diocese, or of the colleges, or of wicked ministers & readers of service, or by the proneness of the parishes to like of that bondage, no redress could be waited for, he knew that the Lord had appointed him there to be occupied, only to try & prepare him to a further, & more effectual message, & to be a witness of that woeful state of Cambridge, whereunto those wicked prelates and doctors of divinity have brought it. This he foresaw before he preached among them, & therefore when they gathered him a stipend, & would have had him take charge, he refused, and did both send back the money they would have given him, and also gave them warning of his departure. So he continued preaching a while, till he fell sore sick: and in his sickness while he ceased his labour, he was forbidden to preach by a letter shewed him from the council. For indeed he had dealt boldly in his duty, and provoked the enemies. The bishop's officer named Bancraft,[3] did read the letter before him, but he nothing moved therewith did answer, that if he had taken charge in that place, he would no whit less cease preaching for that, but as he was he took not on him he said, though the letter were not, to preach there any longer.

OF R.B. COMING TO NORWICH
& how the company there joined together

After these things, when he was recovered of his sickness, & had gotten his strength he took counsel still & had no rest, what he might do for the name & kingdom of God. He often complained of these evil days & with many tears sought where to find the righteous, which glorified God, with whom he might live & rejoice together, that they put away abominations.

While he thus was careful, & besought the Lord to show him more comfort of his kingdom & church, than he saw in Cambridge, he remembered some in Norfolk, whom he heard say were very forward. Therefore he examined the matter, & thought it his duty to take his voyage to them. First because he considered, that if there were not only faults but also open and abominable wickedness, in any parish or company, & they would not or could not redress them, but were held in bondage, by antichristian power, as were those parishes in Cambridge by the bishops, then every true christian was to leave such parishes, & to seek the church of God wheresoever. For where open wickedness is incurable, & popish prelates do reign upholding the same, there is not the church & Kingdom of God: as it is written, 2 Chro.15.4. for a long season, Israel hath been without the true God, & without priest to teach, & without law So that though there be a name of priests, & of preaching, and of God amongst any, yet if there be set over them idol shepherds, popish prelates, & hireling preachers worse than they, that uphold antichristian abominations, there God doth not reign in his kingdom, neither are they his church, neither is there his word of message ...

So while he thought on these things, and was purposed to try also in Norfolk the forwardness of the people, it fell out that R.H.[4] one whom he partly was acquainted with before, came to Cambridge. What was his purpose in coming, and how he thought to have entered the ministry, & did use some means to that end, it is needless to rehearse, only this I shew, that he seemed to be very careful in that matter, & though he leaned too much upon men for that matter, as upon M. Greneham, M. Robardes,[5] & others, & was careful amiss for the bishop's authorising, yet his mind and purpose might be judged to be good, & no otherwise but well did R.B. judge of him. When he had talked with R.B. and shewed him the matter whereabout he went, he received this answer at his hands, that it was unlawful to use either Master Greenham's help, or any man's else for the bishop's authorising. So he shewed him how before he had dealt concerning the bishop, & was now so far from seeking licence, ordaining or authorising at his hands, that though he never had them, yet for that he knew of them, he abhorred such trash & pollutions, as the marks and poison of Antichrist. Notwithstanding he said that if his conscience led him, to deal as before he had dealt, he would do for him what he might, for he had before requested his help. But R.H. either changing his mind, or disappointed of his purpose, returned to Norwich whither also a short time after R.B. took his journey. He came to R.H. house, who then was Master in the Hospital at Norwich. He there finding room enough, and R.H. willing enough that he should abide with him, agreed for his board, & kept in his house. They often had talk together, of the lamentable abuses, disorders, & sins which now reign everywhere. At the first they agreed well together, but yet so as that in some things R.H. doubted: notwithstanding he came on more and more, and at last wholly yielded to the truth, when he saw it began to prevail and prosper.

> There follows a section entitled 'The talk and Counsel which R.B. and R.H. had together, about matters of the church & Kingdom of God'. They discussed the role of preaching in conversion. Harrison, in opposition to Browne, defended the position that reading the Bible could be as effective as preaching. The next section bears the title, 'What good the Public Preaching doth nowadays in England'. In this Browne urges the view that even those preachers who are commendable in that they profess to favour further reformation of the Church are really hypocrites because they refrain from taking active measures to promote it. The theme is continued with even more asperity in the next section entitled, 'How and wherefore the Company left the preachers & their followers: and of the ignorance & sin in the preachers & people'. This section also has some sharp comments on Anglican worship, as follows.

Their stinted service is a popish beadrow full of vain repetitions as if seven paternosters did please the Lord better than six: & as if the chattering of a pie or a parrot were much more the better, because it is much more than enough. Their tossing to and fro of psalms & sentences, is like tennis play whereto God is called a Judge who can do best & be most gallant in his worship: as by organs, solfaing, pricksong, chanting, bussing & mumbling very roundly, on divers hands. Thus they have a shew of religion but indeed they turn it to gaming, & play mockholiday with the worship of God. For the minister & people are bridled like horses & everything appointed unto them like puppies: as to hear, read, answer, kneel, sit, stand, begin, break off, & that by number, measure, & course, & only after the order of antichrist. Their whole service is broken, disordered, patched, taken out of the massbook, & a dumb and idle ministry maintained thereby yea a vain worship without knowledge and feeling ...

THE ORDER AGREED ON FOR THE GUIDING & establishing of the company in all Godliness, & such like.

This doctrine before being shewed to the company, & openly preached among them many did agree thereto, & though much trouble & persecution did follow, yet some did cleave fast to the truth but some fell away: for when trial by pursuits losses, & imprisonment came, & further increased then Robert Barker, Nicholas Woedowes, Tatsel, Bond[6] & some others, forsook us also & held back, & were afraid at the first. There was a day appointed, and an order taken, for redress of the former abuses, and for cleaving to the Lord in greater obedience. so a covenant was made & their mutual consent was given to hold together. There were certain chief points proved unto them by the scriptures, all which being particularly rehearsed unto them with exhortation, they agreed upon them, & pronounced their agreement to each thing particularly, saying, to this we give our consent. First therefore they gave their consent, to join themselves to the Lord, in one covenant & fellowship together, & to keep and seek agreement under his laws & government: and therefore did utterly flee & avoid such like disorders & wickedness, as was mentioned before. Further they agreed of those which should teach them, and watch for the salvation of their souls, whom they allowed & did choose as able and meet for that charge. For they had sufficient trial & testimony thereof by that which they heard & saw of them, & had received of others. So they prayed for their watchfulness & diligence, & promised their obedience.

Likewise an order was agreed on for meetings together, for their exercises therein, as for prayer, thanksgiving, reading of the scriptures, for exhortation & edifying, either by all men which had the gift, or by those which had a special charge before others. And for the lawfulness of putting forth questions, to learn the truth, as if anything seemed doubtful & hard, to require some to shew it more plainly, or for any to shew it himself & to cause the rest to understand it. ... Again it was agreed that any might protest, appeal, complain, exhort, dispute, approve &c as he had occasion, but yet in due order, which was then also declared. Also that all should further the kingdom of God in themselves, & especially in their charge and household, if they had any, or in their friends & companions & whosoever was worthy. Furthermore they particularly agreed of the manner, how to watch to disorders, & reform abuses, & for assembling the company, for teaching privately, and for warning & rebuking both privately & openly, for appointing public humbling in more rare judgements, & public thanksgiving in stronger blessings, for gathering & testifying voices in debating matters, & propounding them in the name of the rest that agree, for an order of choosing teachers, guides, & relievers, when they want, for separating clean from unclean, for receiving any into fellowship, for presenting the daily success of the church, & the wants thereof, for seeking to other churches to have their help, being better reformed, or to bring them to reformation, for taking an order that none contend openly, nor persecute, nor trouble disorderedly, nor bring false doctrine, nor evil cause after once or twice warning or rebuke.

Thus all things were handled, set in order, & agreed on to the comfort of all, & so the matter wrought & prospered by the good hand of God. But last of all was this thing determined. Whether God did call them to leave their country, & to depart out of England.

Some had decreed it to be gone into Scotland, & by writing, sending, & riding to and fro, did labour in the matter, & seemed to be jealous lest their counsel should not take place. But R.B. being then held as prisoner at London, did send down his answer by writing to the contrary. For he judged that it was against duty, & so wrote unto them, if they first should agree to go into Scotland, whenas yet they had not sifted whether they were to leave England. Also he sent unto them, that they were to do that good in England, which possibly they might do before their departure, & that they ought not to remove, before they had yet further testified the truth, & the Lord had with strong hand delivered them from thence. And rather indeed would he have it to be a deliverance by the Lord, than a cowardly fleeing of their own devising. Further he gave them his reasons, why Scotland could not be meet for them, seeing it framed itself in those matters to please England too much. We knew also that we could not there be suffered, either because some corruption should come upon us from their parishes, which we ought to avoid, or because we there should have great trouble wrought us from England, as if we kept still in England. So when some were better advised they changed their minds for going into Scotland. Notwithstanding again they would be gone into Gersey [i.e., Jersey] or Garnsey [i.e., Guernsey] & had the consent, as they said of divers others, that thought it meet they should learn the state of those countries. R.B. said he was not against their going to that purpose[.] But yet he told them there was no such haste to be gone out of England, & that further delay & deliberation should be had in that matter. But at last, when divers of them were again imprisoned, & the rest in great trouble & bondage out of prison, they all agreed, & were fully persuaded that the Lord did call them out of England.

The final part of the Declaration is headed, 'Of the Breach and Division which fell amongst the company'. It describes (from Robert Browne's point of view) how the quarrel developed in the congregations. It started because Browne allegedly had 'condemned his Sister Allens as a reprobate' who had not repented of her 'abominations'. She was Alice Allen, Browne's wife. Browne denied the accusations. His critics were led by Robert Harrison who was supported by Charles Munneman, John Chandler, and 'W.H.' (?William Harrison). The document ends abruptly so that what more Browne had to say is unknown.

Notes

1. Robert Browne (c. 1550–1633) was the third child of Anthony Browne of Tolethorp, Rutland, and Dorothy, daughter of Sir Philip Boteler of Watton Woodhall, Herts., v., DNB; C. Burrage, *The True Story of Robert Browne* (London, 1906); A. Peel, *The Brownists of Norwich and Norfolk about 1580* (Cambridge, 1920); M. R. Watts, *The Dissenters* (Oxford, 1978), I, 26–34 and B. R. White, *The English Separatist Tradition* (Oxford, 1971), 44–66.
2. Richard Greenham (1535?–94?), rector of Dry Drayton, Cambs., 1570–91. For his character and ministry, v., M. M. Knappen, *Tudor Puritanism* (London, 1970), 305, 382–6, 388–91.
3. That is, Richard Bancroft (1544–1610), bishop of London, 1597–1604; archbishop of Canterbury, 1604–10. At the time of this incident he was chaplain to Richard Cox, bishop of Ely.

4. Robert Harrison, died probably in 1585. Very little information is available about the details of his career, v., A. Peel and L. H. Carlson, *The Writings of Robert Harrison and Robert Browne* (London, 1953), 1–3; DNB.
5. Thomas Roberts, archdeacon of Norwich, was one of the six Norwich ministers who signed a petition, dated 25 September 1576, possibly to the Lord Treasurer, protesting against the imposition of indifferent things that offended their (puritan) consciences. They say that they 'dare not yield to those ceremonies that be so far from edifying and building up the Church, that they have rent in sunder and miserably torn in pieces this our church to the miserable ruin of the same ...' and much more. See A. Peel, *The Seconde Parte of a Register* (Cambridge, 1915), I, 143–6.
6. The comma may be misplaced in 'Tatsel, Bond'. If so it is one name, Tatsel Bond.

Document I.11

Robert Browne: A Treatise of Reformation without Tarying for Anie, and of the Wickednesse of those Preachers which Will not Reforme till the Magistrate Commaunde or Compell Them

A full version of this treatise is printed in A. Peel and Leland H. Carlson (eds), *The Writings of Robert Harrison and Robert Browne* (London, 1953). In the present selection the orthography has been modernised but the punctuation and capitalisation have been left unchanged.

The treatise appeared originally in Middelburg in the Netherlands in 1582. For the bibliographical problems relating to it v., Peel and Carlson, *The Writings of ...*, 150–1. The author was Robert Browne (c. 1553–1633). For comments on Browne's standpoint, v., M. R. Watts, *The Dissenters* (Oxford, 1978), I, 26–34; R. W. Dale, *History of English Congregationalism* (London, 1907), 120–38; B. R. White, *The English Separatist Tradition* (Oxford, 1971), 44–66.

SEEING in this book we show the state of Christians, and have laboured also in good conscience to live as Christians, It is marvelled & often talked of among many, why we should be so reviled and troubled of many, & also leave our country. *Forsooth* (say the enemies) *there is some hidden thing in them more than plainly appeareth: for they bear evil will to their Princess Queen Elizabeth and to their country, yea they forsake the church of God, & condemn the same, and are condemned of all, and they also discredit & bring into contempt the Preachers of the Gospel*. To answer them, we say, That they are the men which trouble Israel, and seek evil to the Prince, and not we. And that they forsake and condemn the Church and not we.

... But for the Magistrate, how far by their authority or without it, the Church must be builded and reformation made, and whether any open wickedness must be tolerated in the Church because of them, let this be our answer. For chiefly in this point they have wrought us great trouble, and dismayed many weaklings from embracing the truth. We say therefore, and often have taught, concerning our Sovereign Queen Elizabeth, that neither the Pope, nor other Popeling, is to have any authority either over her, or over the Church of God, and that the Pope of Rome is Antichrist, whose kingdom ought utterly to be taken away. Again we say, that her Authority is civil, and that power she hath as highest under God within her Dominions, and that over all persons and causes. By that she may put to death all that deserve it by Law, either of the Church or common Wealth, and none may resist Her or the Magistrates under her by force or wicked speeches, when they execute the laws. Seeing we grant, and hold this much, how do they charge us as evil willers to the Queen? Surely, for that we hold all those Preachers and teachers accursed, which will not doe the duties of Pastors and teachers till the Magistrates do force them thereto. They say, the time is not yet come to build the Lord's House (Hag.1), they must tarry for the Magistrates and for Parliaments to do it. They want the civil sword forsooth, and the Magistrates do hinder the Lord's building and kingdom, and keep away his government. Are they not ashamed thus to slander the Magistrate? They have run their own swords upon the Wall and broken them, and now would they snatch unto them the Magistrates' sword.

Indeed can the Lord's spiritual government be no way executed but by the civil sword, or is this the judgement that is written, Such honour shall be to all his Saints? (Psal.149). Is this to bind the Kings in chains, and the Nobles with Fetters of Iron, by the high acts of GOD in their mouths, and a two edged sword in their hands? Those bands and chains, which is the spiritual power of the Church, they have broken from themselves, and yet would they have Magistrates bound with them, to begin Discipline. They would make the Magistrates more than Gods, and yet also worse than beasts. For they teach that a lawful Pastor must give over his charge at their discharging, and when they withhold the Church government, it ought for to cease, though the Church go to ruin thereby. Behold now, doth not the Lord's kingdom give place unto theirs? And do they not pull down the head Christ Jesus, to set up the hand of the Magistrate? yea and more than this, for they first proclaim the names and titles of wicked Bishops and popish officers, and the Lord's name after: Seeing also the Bishops must discharge the lawful Preachers, and stop their mouths, though the Lord God have given them a charge for to speak, and not to keep silence. The Lord hath exalted Christ Jesus. and given him a name above every name (Phil.2), that all things should bow and serve unto him, and yet have they exalted the power of wicked Bishops above him. Behold a great and most wholesome river, and yet their puddle water is preferred before it. Except the Magistrates will go into the tempest and rain, and be weather beaten with the hail of God's wrath, they must keep under the roof of God's government. They must be under a Pastorall charge. They must obey to the Sceptre of Christ, if they be Christians. How then should the Pastor, which hath the oversight of the Magistrate, if he be of his flock, be so overseen of the Magistrate, as to leave his flock, when the Magistrate shall unjustly and wrongfully discharge him. Yet these Preachers and teachers will not only do so, but even holding their charge and keeping with it, will not guide and reform it aright, because the Magistrates do forbid them forsooth. But they slander the Magistrate, and because they dare not charge them as forbidding them their duties, they have gotten this shift, that they do but tarry for the Magistrates' authority, and then they will guide and reform as they ought ...

For the Sceptre and kingdom of Christ is not of this world, to fight with dint of sword, but it is a right Sceptre, which subdueth the people under us, and the Nations under our feet (Psal.47; Psal. 45) ...

Now if the Magistrates be enemies unto the Lord's kingdom, why are not these men better warriors to uphold the same? For they give up the weapons of their warfare into the enemies' hands, and then say, they can not do withal. By their weapons I mean those whereof Paul doth speak (2 Cor.10), that they are not carnal, but mighty through God, to cast down holds, and so forth: These weapons have they given from them, for they have not the Keys of the Kingdom of heaven to bind and loose, and to retain or pronounce remitted the sins of men (Mat.18; John 20), seeing they grant much open wickedness incurable among them, and also avouch that it must needs be suffered. Yea they have given up these keys to the Magistrate or to the Spiritual Courts, and therefore have no right to call themselves the Church of God, or lawful Pastors hereof ... My kingdom, saith Christ, is not of this world, and they would shift in both Bishops and Magistrates into his spiritual throne to make it of this world; yea to stay the Church government on them, is not only to shift but to thrust them before Christ. Yet under him in his spiritual kingdom are first Apostles, secondly Prophets, thirdly, teachers &c. Also helpers and spiritual guides: But they put the Magistrates first, which in a common wealth are indeed first, and above Preachers, yet they have no ecclesiastical authority at all, but only as any other Christians, if so they be Christians ... Therefore hath God made these teachers fools, and these spiritual professors as mad men. For woe unto you, ye Priestly preachers and Doctors hypocrites, which are a snare to the people, and fill up their measure of iniquity, while ye pretend the Magistrates' authority ... For it is God's husbandry and not theirs. They are but members thereof if they be Christians, and are not any way to stay the building, neither is it to tarry or wait upon them ... They say, behold we have a Christian Prince, and a mother in Israel: but can they be Christians, when they make them to refuse, or withstand the government of Christ in his Church, or will not be subject unto it. If they therefore refuse and withstand, how should they be tarried for? If they be with them, there is no tarrying: and if they be against them, they are no christians, and therefore also there can be no tarrying. For the worthy may not tarry for the unworthy, but rather forsake them, as it is written, Save your selves from this froward generation (Acts 2): and cast not your pearls before Swine, nor holy things unto dogs ... He that will be saved, must not tarry for this man or that: and he that putteth his hand to the plough, and then looketh back, is not fit for the kingdom of God. Therefore woe unto you ye blind guides, which cast away all by tarrying for the Magistrates ... Therefore shall Christ be that rock of offence unto you, and ye shall stumble and fall, and shall be broken, and shall be snared, and shall be taken. You will be delivered from the yoke of Antichrist, to the which you do willingly give your necks, by bow, and by sword, and by battle, by horses and by horsemen, that is, by civil power and pomp of Magistrates: by their Proclamations and Parliaments: and the kingdom of God must come with observation, that men may say, Lo the Parliament, or lo the Bishops decrees: but the kingdom of God should be within you. The inward obedience to the outward preaching and government of the

Church, with newness of life, that is the Lord's kingdom. This ye despise. Therefore shall ye desire to see the kingdom of God, and shall not see it, and to enjoy one day of the Son of man, and ye shall not enjoy it. For ye set aloft man's authority above God's, and the Preacher must hang on his sleeve for the discharge of his calling.

... Therefore the Magistrate's commandment, must not be a rule unto me of this and that duty, but as I see it agree with the word of God. So then it is an abuse of my gift and calling, if I cease preaching for the Magistrate, when it is my calling to preach, yea & woe unto me, if I preach not, for necessity is laid upon me, and if I do it unwillingly, yet the dispensation is committed to me. And this dispensation did not the Magistrate give me, but God by consent and ratifying of the Church, and therefore as the Magistrate gave it not, so can he not take it away ... Be ashamed therefore ye foolish shepherds, and lay not a burden on the Magistrates, as though they should do that in building the Lord's kingdom, which the Apostles and Prophets could not do. They could not force Religion, as ye would have the Magistrate to do, and it was forbidden the Apostles to preach to the unworthy, or to force a planting or government of the Church. The Lord's kingdom is not by force, neither by an army or strength, as be the kingdoms of this world ...

For there is no end of their pride and cruelty which ascend up and sit in the Magistrates' chair and smite the people with a continual plague, and such of them as have not yet gotten the room, do cry for Discipline, Discipline, that is for a civil forcing, to imprison the people, or otherwise by violence to handle and beat them, if they will not obey them. But the Lord shall bring them down to the dust, and to the pit, as abominable carcasses, which would be above the clouds, yea which dare presume into the throne of Christ Jesus, and usurp that authority and calling to his Church, which is opposed and contrary to his kingdom and government. This shall appear afterwards: In the meantime let them know that the Lord's people is of the willing sort. They shall come unto Zion and inquire the way to Jerusalem, not by force nor compulsion, but with their faces thitherward (Jerem.50): yea as the he-goats shall they be before the flock, for the haste they have unto Zion, and they themselves shall call for the covenant, saying, Come and let us cleave fast unto the Lord in a perpetual covenant that shall never be forgotten. For it is the conscience and not the power of man that will drive us to seek the Lord's kingdom ... Yea and the Lord's people shall come willingly in the day of his assemblies, even his armies in holy beauty ...

We know that Moses might reform, and the Judges and Kings which followed him, and so may our Magistrates: yea they may reform the Church and command things expedient for the same. Yet may they do nothing concerning the Church, but only civilly, and as civil Magistrates, that is, they have not that authority over the Church, as to be Prophets or Priests, or spiritual Kings, as they are Magistrates over the same: but only to rule the common wealth in all outward Justice, to maintain the right, welfare, and honour thereof, with outward power, bodily punishment, & civil forcing of men. And therefore also because the church is in a commonwealth, it is of their charge: that is concerning the outward provision & outward justice, they are to look to it, but to compel religion, to plant churches by power, and to force a submission to Ecclesiastical government by laws & penalties belongeth not to them, as is proved before, neither yet to the Church. Let us not therefore tarry for the Magistrate: For if they be christians they give leave & gladly suffer & submit themselves to the church government. For he is a christian which is redeemed by Christ unto holiness and happiness for ever & professeth the same by submitting himself to his laws & government. And if they be not christians, should the welfare of the church or the salvation of men's souls, hang on their courtesy?

Document I.12

Henry Barrow: A True Description out of the Worde of God, of the Visible Church

This was the first Barrowist work to be published. There has been some argument about its authorship but the attribution to Henry Barrow is strongly attested. The first edition was printed at Dort in 1590. For further details, v., Leland H. Carlson, *The Writings of Henry Barrow 1587–1590* (Elizabethan Nonconformist Texts III) (1962), 208–13. The numerous scriptural references have been omitted.

As there is but one God and father of all, one Lorde over all, and one spirit: so is there but one trueth, one faith, one salvation, one church, called in one hope, joyned in one profession, guided by one rule, even the worde of the most high.

This church as it is universallie understood, conteyneth in it all the elect of God that have bin, are, or shalbe. But being considered more particularlie, as it is seene in this present worlde, it consisteth of a companie and fellowship of faithful and holie people gathered (togither) in the name of Christ Jesus, their only king, priest, and prophet, worshipping him aright, being peaceablie and quietlie governed by his officers and lawes, keeping the unitie of faith in the bonde of peace and love unfained.

Most joyfull, excellent, and glorious things are everie where in the Scriptures spoken of this church. It is called the citie, house, temple, and mountaine of the eternall God: the chosen generation, the holie nation, the peculiar people, the vineyarde, the garden enclosed, the spring shut up, the sealed fountaine, the orchyard of pomgranades with sweete fruites, the heritage, the kingdome of Christ: yea his sister, his love, his spouse, his queene, and his bodie, the joye of the whole earth. To this societie is the covenant and all the promises made of peace, of love, and of salvation, of the presense of God, of his graces, of his power, and of his protection.

And surelie if this church be considered in hir partes, it shall appeare most beautifull, yea most wonderfull, and even ravishing the senses to conceave, much more to beholde, what then to enjoy so blessed a communion. For behold[,] her king and Lord is the king of peace, and Lorde him selfe of all glorie. She enjoyeth most holy and heavenly lawes, most faithfull and vigilant pastours, most syncere and pure teachers, most carefull and upright governours, most diligent and trustie deacons, most lovinge and sober releevers, and a most humble, meeke, obedient, faithfull and loving people, everie stone living, elect and precious, every stone hath his beautie, his burden, and his order. All bound to edifie one another, exhort, reprove and comfort one another, lovinglie as to their owne members, faithefully as in the eyes of God.

No office here is ambitouslie affected, no law wrongfullie wrested or wilfully neglected, no trueth hid or perverted, everie one here hath freedome and power (not disturbing the peaceable order of the church) to utter his complaintes and griefes, and freely to reproove the transgressions and errours of any without exception of persons.

Here is no intrusion or climing up an other way into the sheepefolde, than by the holy and free election of the Lorde's holie and free people, and that according to the Lorde's ordinance, humbling them selves by fasting and prayer before the Lorde, craving the direction of his Holy Spirit, for the triall and approving of his giftes, etc.

Thus they orderlie proceede to ordination by fastinge and prayer, in which action the apostles used layinge on of handes. Thus hath everie one of the people interest in the election and ordination of their officers, as also in the administration of their offices upon transgression, offence, abuse, etc., having an especiall care unto the inviolable order of the church, as is aforesaid.

Likewise in this church they have holy lawes, as limites and bondes, whiche, it is lawful at no hande to transgresse. They have lawes to direct them in the choise of everie officer, what kinde of men the Lorde will have. Their pastour must be apte to teache, no yong scholer, able to divide the worde aright, holding faste that faithfull worde, according to doctrine, that he may be able also to exhorte, rebuke, improove, with wholesome doctrine, and to convince them that saye against it: he must be a man that loveth goodnes: he must be wise, righteous, holie, temperate: he must bee of life unreproveable, as God's stewarde: he must be generallie well reported of, and one that ruleth his owne housholde under obedience with all honestie: he must be modest, humble, meeke, gentle, and loving: he must be a man of great patience, compassion, labour and diligence: hee must alwaies be carefull and watchfull over the flock whereof the Lorde hath made him overseer, with all willingnes and chearefulnes, not holding his office in respect of persons, but doing his duetie to everie soule, as he will aunswer before the chief shephearde, etc.

Their doctor or teacher must be a man apte to teach, able to divide the worde of God aright, and to deliver sounde and wholesome doctrine from the same, still building upon that sounde groundworke; he must be mightie in the Scriptures, able to convince the gainsayers, and carefullie to deliver his doctrine pure, sounde and plaine, not with curiositie or affection [affectation], but so that it may edifie the most simple, approving it to everie man's conscience; he must be of life unreproveable, one that can governe his owne houshold, he must be of maners sober, temperate, modest, gentle and loving, etc.

Their elders must be of wisedome and judgement, endued with the spirit of God, able to discerne betweene cause and cause, betweene plea and plea, and accordinglie to prevent and redres evilles, alwayes vigilant and intending to see the statutes, ordinances and lawes of God kept in the church, and that not onely by the people in obedience, but to see the officers do their dueties. These men must bee of life likewise unreproveable, governing their owne families orderlie, they must be also of maners sober, gentle, modest, loving, temperate, etc.

Their deacons must be men of honest report, having the misterie of the faith in a pure conscience, endued with the Holy Ghost: they must be grave, temperate, not given to excesse, nor to filthie lucre.

Their releevers or widowes must bee women of sixty yeares of age at the least, for avoyding of inconveniences: they must be well reported of for good workes, such as have nourished their children, such as have bin harberous to straungers: diligent and serviceable to the saintes, compassionate and helpefull to them in adversitie, given to everie good worke, continuing in supplications and prayers night and daye.

These officers must firste be duelie proved, then if they be founde blameles, [let them] administer, etc.

Nowe as their persons, giftes, conditions, manners, life and proofe of these officers, is [are] set downe by the Holie Ghoste: so are their offices limited, severed, and divers [diverse].

The pastour's office is, to feede the sheepe of Christ in greene and wholesome pastures of his worde, and leade them to the still waters, even to the pure fountaine and river of life; hee must guyde and keepe those sheepe by that heavenlie sheepehooke and pastorall staffe of the worde, thereby drawing them to him, thereby lookinge into their soules, even into their most secrete thoughtes: thereby discerning their diseases, and thereby curinge them: applying to everie disease a fit and convenient medicine, according to the qualitie and malladie of the disease, and give warning to the church, that they may orderlie proceede to excommunication. Further, he must by this his sheepehooke watch over and defend his flock from ravenous beastes and the wolfe, and take the litle foxes, etc.

The doctour's office is alreadie sett downe in his description: His speciall care must bee, to builde uppon the onely true groundworke, golde, silver, and pretious stones, that his worke may endure the triall of the fire, and by the light of the same fire, reveale the tymber, hay, and stubble of false teachers: hee must take diligent heede to keepe the church from errours. And, further, hee must deliver his doctrine so playnlie, simplie, and purelie, that the church may increase with the increasing of God, and growe up into him which is the head, Christ Jesus.

The office of the auncientes is expressed in their description: Their especiall care must bee, to see the ordinaunces of God truely taught and practized, aswel by the officers in dooing their duetie uprightlie, as to see that the people obey willinglie and redilie. It is their duetie to see the congregation holilie and quietlie ordered, and no way disturbed, by the contentious and disobedient, frowarde and obstinate: not taking away the libertie of the least, but upholding the right of all, wiselie judginge of times and circumstances. They must bee readie assistauntes to the pastour and teachers, helpinge to beare their burden, but not intruding into their office.

The deacon's office is, faithfullie to gather, and collect by the ordinance of the church, the goodes and benevolence of the faithfull, and by the same direction, diligentlie and trustilie to distribute them according to the necessitie of the sainctes. Further, they must enquire and consider of the proportion of the wantes both of the officers and other poore, and accordinglie relate unto the church that provision may be made.

The reliever's and widowe's office is, to minister to the sicke, lame, wearie, and diseased, such helpfull comforts as they neede, by watching, tending and helping them: further, they must shewe good example to the yonger women, in sober, modest, and godlie conversation, avoyding idlenes, vaine talke, and light behaviour.

These officers, though they bee divers [diverse] and severall, yet are they not severed, least there should bee a division in the body, but they are as members of the body, having the same care one of another, joyntlie doing their severall dueties to the service of the sainctes, and to the edification of the bodie of Christ, till wee all meete togither in the perfect measure of the fulnes of Christe, by whom all the bodye being in the meane whyle thus coupled and knit togither by everie joynt for the furniture thereof, according to the effectuall power which is in the measure of everie part, receyveth increase of the bodie, unto the edifying of it selfe in love: neither can anie of these offices be wanting, without grievous lamenes, and apparent deformitie of the bodye, yea violent injurie to the head, Christ Jesus.

Thus, this holie armie of sainctes, is marshalled here in earth by these officers, under the conduct of their glorious emperour Christ, that victorious Michaell. Thus it marcheth in this most heavenlie order, and gratious araye, against all enimies both bodilie and ghostlie. Peaceable in it selfe as Jerusalem, terrible unto them as an armie with banners, triumphing over their tyrannie with patience, their crueltie with meekenes, and over death it selfe with dying. Thus through the blood of that spotles lambe, and that worde of their testimonie, they are more than conquerours, brusing the head of the serpent: yea, through the power of his worde, they have power to cast downe Sathan like lightning: to treade upon serpents and scorpions: to cast downe strong holds, and everie thing that exalteth it selfe against God. The gates of hell and all the principalities and powers of the worlde, shall not prevayle against it.

Further, he hath given them the keyes of the kingdome of heaven, that whatsoever they binde in earth by his worde, shalbe bounde in heaven: and whatsoever they loose on earth, shalbe loosed in heaven.

Nowe this power whiche Christe hath given unto his church, and to everie member of his church, to keepe it in order, hee hath not lefte it to their discretions and lustes to be used or neglected as they will, but in his last will and testament, he hath set downe both an order of proceeding, and an ende to whiche it is used.

And if the fault bee private, private [sic], holie and loving admonition and reproofe [is to be used], with an inwarde desire and earnest care to winne their brother: but if he will not heare thee, yet to take two or three other brethren with him, whom he knoweth most meete to that purpose, that by the mouth of two or three witnesses, everie worde may be confirmed: and if he refuse to heare them, then to declare the matter to the church, whiche ought severelie and sharp elie to reprehende, gravelie to admonishe, and lovinglie to perswade the partie offending:

shewing him the heynousnes of his offence, and the daunger of his obstinacie, and the fearefull judgements of the Lorde.

If this prevaile not to drawe him to repentance, then are they in the name and power of the Lorde Jesus, with the whole congregation, reverentlie in prayer to proceed to excommunication, casting him out of their congregation and fellowship, that is, out of the covenaunt and protection of the Lord, for his disobedience and obstinacie, and committing him to Sathan for the destruction of the fleshe, that the spirit may bee saved in the day of the Lord Jesus, if such bee his good will and pleasure.

Further, they are to warne the whole congregation and all other faithfull, to holde him as a heathen and a publicane, and to abstaine them selves from his societie, as not to eate or drinke with him, etc., unles it bee such as of necessitie must needes, as his wife, his children and familie: yet these (if they be members of the church) are not to joyne to him in any spirituall exercise.

All this notwithstanding the church is not to holde him as an enimie, but to admonish him and praye for him as a brother, prooving if at anie time the Lorde will give him repentaunce. For this power is not given them to the destruction of anie, but to the edification and preservation of all.

If the offence bee publike, the partie is publiquelie to bee reproved, and admonished: if he then repent not, to proceede to excommunication, *ut supra*.

The repentance of the partie must bee proportionable to the offence, viz., if the offence bee publique, [the repentance must be] publique: if private, [the repentance may be] private: humbled, submissive, sorrowfull, unfained, giving glorie to the Lord.

There must great care bee had of admonitions, that they bee not captious, or curious: finding faulte where none is; neither yet in bitternes or reproche, for that were to destroye and not to save our brother: but they must bee carefullie done, with prayer going before: they must bee seazoned with trueth, gravitie, love and peace.

Moreover, in this churche is an especiall care had by everie member thereof, of offences: the stronge ought not to offend the weake, nor the weake to judge the stronge: but all graces here are given to the service and edification of eache other in love and longe suffering.

In this church is the trueth purelie taught, and surelie kept: heere is the covenaunte, the sacramentes, and promisses, the graces, the glorie, the presens, the worship of God, etc.

Into this temple entreth no uncleane thinge, neither what so ever worketh abhominations or lyes, but they which are written in the lambe's booke of life.

But without this church shalbe dogges and enchaunters, and whoremongers, and murderers, and idolatours, and who so ever loveth and maketh lies.

FINIS

Document I.13

A Barrowist Declaration: A Breefe Sum of Our Profession

This document was probably produced in the summer of 1587 but first appeared in print in 1590 in George Gifford's *A Short Treatise*. The version printed in F. J. Powicke, *Henry Barrow, Separatist* (London, 1900), Appendix II, is reproduced from H. Barrow and J. Greenwood's *A Plaine Refutation of Mr. Giffard's Booke, intituled, A Short Treatise* ... ([Amsterdam?], 1605). The differences between the two versions are slight. A more recent edition, with explanatory comments, is to be found in Leland H. Carlson (ed.), *The Writings of Henry Barrow 1587–1590* (London, 1962), 81–5. The document concentrates on the four points of contention between the Separatists and their opponents, namely, worship, membership, ministry and discipline.

1. We seeke above all things the peace and protection of the most high, and the kingdome of Christ Jesus our Lord.

2. We seeke and fully purpose to worship God aright, as he hath commaunded in his holy worde.

3. We seeke the fellowship and communion of his faithfull and obedient servants, and together with them to enter covenant with the Lord. And by the direction of his holy spirite to proceed to a godly, free, and right choise of ministers and other officers by him ordained to the service of his church.

4. We seeke to establish and obey the ordinances and lawes of our saviour Christ, left by his last will and testament to the governing and guiding of his church, without altering, changing, innovating, wresting, or leaving out any of them, that the Lord shall give us sight of.

5. We purpose by the assistance of the Holy Ghost in this faith and order to leade our lives. And for this faith and order to leave our lives, if such be the good will and pleasure of our heavenly Father; to whom be all glory and praise for ever. Amen.

6. And now that our forsaking and utter abandoning these disordered assemblies, as they generally stand in England, may not seeme strange or offensive to any man, that will judge or be judged by the worde of God: we alledge and affirme them hainouslye faultie, and wilfullye obstinate, in these foure principall transgressions.

1. They worship the true God after a false manner, their worship being made of the invention of man, even of that man of sinne, erronious, and imposed upon them.

2. Then for that the prophane ungodly multitude without the exception of any one person, are with them received into, and retained in the bosome and body of their Church, etc.

3. Then for that they have a false and antichristian ministry imposed upon them, retained with them, and maintained by them.

4. Then for that their churches are ruled by, and remaine in subjection unto, an antichristian and ungodly government, cleane contrary to the institution of our Saviour Christ.

Document I.14

Henry Barrow: A Brief Discoverie of the False Church

Despite its title, *A Brief Discoverie of the False Church* is a substantial book of 263 pages. Henry Barrow wrote it in the Fleet Prison and it was published at Dordrecht in the Netherlands towards the end of 1590. An edition printed in 1707 was a severely mutilated version of the original owing to the numerous editorial changes. For Henry Barrow, v., F. J. Powicke, *Henry Barrow (?1550–1593) and the Exiled Church of Amsterdam* (London, 1900); pp. 91–129 deal with his doctrine of the Church. The full text is printed in Leland H. Carlson (ed.), *The Writings of Henry Barrow 1587–1590* (London, 1962), 261–672. The following selections preserve the original spelling but the marginal references to Scripture have been omitted. They seek to convey the essence of Barrow's uncompromising Separatism and his understanding of the doctrine of the Church. See also M. R. Watts, *The Dissenters* (Oxford, 1978), I, 35–40, 72–4, and R. T. Jones and Alan Tovey, *Some Separatists* (Evangelical Fellowship of Congregational Churches, 1993), 9–28. For an exhaustive study of Elizabethan Puritanism, v., S. Paas, *De Gemeenschap der Heiligen* (Zoetermeer: Uitgeverij Boekencentrum, 1995). The Separatists are discussed, with special attention to Barrow, on pp. 205–351.

The ministerie apointed unto the government and service of the church of Christ we find to be of two sortes, elders and deacons: the elders, some of them, to give attendance unto the publike ministerie of the word and sacramentes, as the pastor and teacher: the other elders together with them, to give attendance to the publike order and government of the church: the deacons, to attend the gathering and distributing the goodes of the church. Now these officers are first duly proved, examined, and compared by, and to these rules set downe in the testament of Christ, both in apparant graces, by the manifestation of the spirit; as also in al unreproveable conversation, witnessed, and wel aproved unto that flock, of which they are chosen to serve and attend. This done with praier and fasting, they are chosen and ordeined in the same congregation, by publike consent. They being thus chosen and ordeined by all, are now diligently and faithfully to execute their office unto all, not prejudicing the libertie of any, ambitiously assuming any inordinate authoritie, or abusing or neglecting their office, neither holding or executing it, in regard or in respect of person: but uprightly and indifferently performing it unto all men, as in the eies of God, whose word they purely and sincerely teach, faithfully and precisely observe, to their uttermost knowledg and power. If in any thing they transgresse or offend; they are, as well as any other members, liable to the censure of the church: which is, to reprove, depose, or excommunicate them, according to the qualitie of the sinne, and estate of the offenders, *etc*.

Now to come to the ministerie of the Church of England, which is so manifold and divers, as I know not how to begin to describe it. But let it first be divided into these three sorts: 1. *Reigning* or *Governing*. 2. *Serving* and 3. *Collegiate*. 1. Of the reigning and governing ministers, are arch-bishops, lord bishops, arch-deacons, chancellers, commissaries, all of the High Commission, as likewise such civil doctors, proctors, registers, scribes, pursuivantes, sumners as attend upon their Courtes of Faculties, Prerogative, Archies, Delegates, *etc.* 2. Of the serving sort, are parsons, vickars, curates, hireling lecturers, vagrant and mercenarie preachers, house priestes, chaplens, half-priestes or catechisers, church-wardens, sidemen, questmen, parish clarkes. 3. Of the ministerie collegiate, are lord bishops, deanes, sub-deanes, prebendaries, canons, petie channons, gospellers, pistellers, singing men, singing boies, vergiers, sextines. This division, I suppose, wil wel neere suffice for their officers. But now, how to divide or distinguish their offices, I know not; I am so unlearned and ignorant of such great secrets, and high misteries. Neither yet have I skil to marshial them in their degrees of honour, which (I have heard say) they have, both in the common welth, and in their schooles; as their primate, their metropolitane graces, their palatine lord bishops and their barony lordships: al which I weene be peeres of the realme, and estates of the land. Now there are also certayne doctors of divinitie, and bachelors of divinitie, which have many great privileges and pr[er]ogatives, of the cappe, the skarlet gowne, the hood, the habbite, the tippet, *etc.*, the ring, the chaire: the one of them, being a kinght's [knight's] fellow, the other an esquire's in any ground in England. Also how capable these are by statute of how many benefices, I cannot tell ...

... We find in the church of Christ no mention of these rufflers, they are not members of his bodie, they are neither pastors, teachers, elders nor deacons: but even of late before our eies, these self same officers, courses, attendantes, even from their primate arch-bishop to the parish priest, and so to the sumner [summoner], administred unto the whore of Rome, and had their originall from the apostatical seate of Antichrist. How then should they thus sodenly become the members of Christ, yea, rulers of his house whether he will or no? Who not only thrust in their parsons by intrusion, but these monstrous offices, courtes, and cannons, never read of, never heard of in the testament and church of Christ.

For there we find no mention of any other arch-bishop or lord bishop, than that chief shepheard and lord of life, Christ Jesus; unto whome everie knee ought to bowe, and everie tongue confesse. But these blasphemous beastes, or rather heades of that beast, are not ashamed to arrogate unto them Christe's names and titles, which are written upon them as names of blasphemie, that the Scripture might be fulfilled: which titles and honors, they blasphemously would defend with this Scripture which is spoken of the office and person of the civil magistrate: *I have saied, ye are goddes, and ye all are the children of the most high*, Psalms 82: 6, although our saviour Christ hath expresly, with his owne mouth, said to his apostles (than whome I am sure these are neither greater nor better): *the kinges of the Gentiles reigne over them, and they that beare rule over them are called bountifull, but be ye not so: but let the greatest among you, be as the least, and the chiefest, as he that serveth ...*

Now as we find their names and titles blasphemous, so if we looke wel into their offices, we shal find them no better. Of the ordinarie established permanent offices, pastour, teacher, elder, which are to oversee, and administer unto that flock, of which they are orderly chosen, *etc.*, these are not; who some of them standes a primate or pope unto the whole land, some other a metropolitane over half the land, the least of these Anakims over many hundreth steeples, churches (as they say). Therfore they have none of these ordinarie offices, which only now remaine. As for the extraordinarie offices of apostles, prophetes, evangelistes, which God at the first used to the cariing forth of his truth, the gathering together and setting in order of his saintes and we find them (apostles I meane and evangelistes) altogether ceased, and now needles; insomuch as the foundation is already fully and soundly layde, as also al ordinances and orders which the church is to receave, expressly set downe and manifested in the testament of Christ; to which al churches are now, for their direction in al thinges, wholy referred ...

... In the meane while, let us a litle goe back againe (as it were) that we may the more orderly proceed, and consider in a word or two, of these Rabbines' persons, education, learning, training, wherby they are made fit to these great offices; then of the offices themselves, and of their calling and entrance therunto; last of al, of their administration, how they behave themselves therin ...

... First, for their persons, we find them all generally the seed and offspring of the unbeleevers, of men without the faith, without the church, of these confuse idolatrous multitudes above spoken of, and as the unchristian education of these ympes maketh manifest; who, even from their cradles, are nourished in al maner of prophanenes, heathenisme, vaine and ungodly sciences and literature, ostentation, pride, more than monkish (that I say not) Sodomitish idlenes, superstition, idolatrie, *etc*. This, their ungodly nurture in their common scholes (where they must learne the Latine or Greeke tongue from lascivious poets and heathenish philosophers) sheweth evidently. With this liquor are their pitchers at the first seasoned: when they have beene well nouseled in these, and have orderly passed to the highest forme; then are they fit for one of the universities, where they being placed in some one colledg (as they tearme them) or other, after they have beene solemnely matriculate and sworne upon the proctor's booke to their mother the universitie, to conceale and keepe close her secretes and mysteries, as also to be obedient to her statutes and orders; there are they trained up in logick, rhetorick, and philosophy: which learning they draw from Aristotle and Cicero, and such like. There they learne to reason and speake by art, by sylogismes and tropes; which artes when they have gotten (or at the least, spent some apointed time in the universites), then they commence bachelors or maisters of art. Now if they continue still with their mother, and give their minde to the studie of divinitie (as they cal it), which is as much to say as the rearding [reading] of men's writinges, such as are best esteemed of in these times, with those feathers they flie, and with those eies they see: which bookes being taken from them, they are as mute as fishes, as blind as moles.

But when once they are growen skilful in this traditional divinitie, that they dare undertake upon some moneths' warning, to speake an howre upon some text, and that they dare trust their memories to deliver no worse stuffe than they have read in the commentaries and common places of these authors: then upon a litle practise they grow bould to set up their bylles of chalenge upon the schole dores, that they purpose to dispute for their degree, and to maintaine certaine hard pointes of divinitie, generally consented unto, and receaved of all men: which questions, as also the whole Scriptures, must in these their schooles and disputations, be unsufferably corrupted, abused, wrested, perverted, blasphemed according to the lustes of these philosophical and heathen disputers; which heer must handle, divide, utter and discusse, according to their vaine affected artes of logick and rhetorick ...

... I will only (or chiefly at the least) here meddle with their publike administration in their church, in their worship of God, *etc.* ... Unto this ministration, for their better instruction and direction in all thinges, as also that there might be found one uniforme order amongst them in all places, they have one service book, commonly called *The Book of Common Praier*: unto this are all the priestes of the land sworne, to use it in maner and forme prescribed. Now in this book is included the whole forme and substance of their ministerie. Heere are their prairs made to their hand, and prescribed what praiers to say in the morning, and likewise what at evensong: as also what psalmes, chapters, pistles and gospels to read in their due seasons, what in the winter, what in the sommer, what in the Lent, what in the Advent. Heere are set downe their praiers, chapters, *etc.*, for their fastes, their solemne feastes and saintes' daies, yea, and for everie other day of the yeare.

For the Sonday is a governing day, and is written in their calender with red letters, and ruleth all the daies of the week, save certaine unruly daies and their eaves, which will not be governed by it, but chalenge to themselves a peculiar worship also: they having their daies in the same calender written with great letters too, and that which more is, their eaves written with red letters. And because they are but strangers and come but once in the yeare, they looke for the more solemne intertainment, that the priest should diligently watch, and the people wait for their comming, and make preparation accordingly: if they come on a cluster, or at some solemne and double feast, then to intertaine them with new clothes, cleane houses, garnished with greene bowghes, or holly and ivye, with good cheàre and much pastime, al work on these their idol daies, laid aside. Yea, though they come but one alone, and that on the week day, yet that week is not S. [Saint] Sonday, Lord of the Ascendent, it is a part of his service to give warning unto the people of the others comming, that they keep his or her eave with fasting and praier; that upon their day they keep an holy feast, abstaine from labour, *etc*. Moreover, by this book are the priests to administer their sacramentes, by this book to church their women, by this book to marry, by this book to visit and housle the sick, by this book to burie the dead, by this book to keep their rogation, to say certaine psalmes and praiers over the corne and grasse, certayne gospels at crosswaies, *etc*. This booke is good at al assaies; it is the only book of the world. He that can but orderly and distinctly reade this booke, may get a living by it. It is no marvaile though they be sworne to and by this booke. Many great thinges might be said of this book, how it was made by certayne learned bishops, afterward godly martyres, and how some of the martyres used part of it (as the letany) the night before they suffered, *etc*. Well, who translated it we will not contend. For the thing it self, it is evident to be abstracted out of the pope's blasphemous masse-book, and how consonant it is unto the word of God, remaineth to be examined; and shall, through God's grace, by the discussing of some particular pointes, though not of everie singular error (for that were an endles labour) apeare: and so shall through God's grace, by the discussing of some particular pointes, though not of everie singular error (for that were an endless labour) apeare: and so shall neither the martyres' use commend, nor our dislike condemne, but God's word be judge of all

To let passe therefore what in times past this book hath beene, and how it hath beene used, either by the pope or those bishops; we find it now to be the very groundworcke of their faith, church and ministerie, in place to them of the word of God, as from whence they fetch all their direction for all thinges; yea herein above the word of God in that from hence they fetch not only their rules wherby to doe thinges but even the verie things themselves that they do, as their leitourgies, etc. So far is this book from being subject to the word of God, as it in al things overruleth the word of God, dismembreth, rendeth, corrupteth, perverteth, abuseth it to their stinted matters and evensong, to their idol dayes, fastes, feastes, etc. Yea, the word of God may not be taught, but where this book hath first beene read, and hath had the preeminence. This booke in their churches must have the soveraintie, it may not be gainsbut even the verie things themselves that they do, as their leitourgies, *etc*. So far is this book from being subject to the word of God, as it in al things overruleth the word of God, dismembreth, rendeth, corrupteth, perverteth, abuseth it to their stinted matters and evensong, to their idol dayes, fastes, feastes, *etc*. Yea, the word of God may not be taught, but where this book hath first beene read, and hath had the preeminence. This booke in their churches must have the soveraintie, it may not be gainsaied or controld, or if it be, the word of God must give place, that priest called *coram nobis*, lessoned, and scholed; if he wil not be conformable, deprived of his priestdome: if he be found stout or contumacious, then is he cast into prison to coole him, until his stomake come downe, that he make sute unto his grace or some other lord bishop his ordinarie, and enter bonde to be conformable, or silent.

Moreover this booke, in that it standeth a publike prescript continued leiturgy (not as yet to come to the particulars or meddle with the blasphemous contentes therof but to speake generally of it) as if it were the best that ever was devised by mortal man: yet in this place and use, being brought into the church, yea, or into any private house, it becometh a detestable idol, standing for that it is not in the church of God and consciences of men: namely, for holy, spirituall, and faithfull prayer, it being nothing lesse, but rather abhominable and lothsome sacrifice in the sight of God, even as a dead dogg ... Shall we think that God hath any time left these his servantes so singly furnished and. destitute of his grace, that they cannot find words according to their necessities and faith, to expresse their wantes and desires, but need thus to be taught line unto line, as children new weaned from the brestes, what and when to say, how much to say, and when to make an end; to say this collect at the beginning, that at the end, that before, the tother [sic] after, this in the morning, that at after noone, *etc*. How like children, or rather like masking fooles, are these great clarkes dressed? Shew they not hereby, that either they have no faith, or els are such infantes, as they have more need to be fed, than to divide the portion unto others? Know they, trow we, what praier or the spirit of God meaneth? Praier I take to be a confident demanding which faith maketh thorow the Holy Ghost, according to the wil of God, for their present wantes, estate, *etc*. How now? Can any read, prescript, stinted leitourgie, which was penned many yeares or daies before, be said a powring forth of the heart unto the Lord? ...

... May reading be said praying? ... Is not this presumptuously to undertake to teach the Spirit of God? And to take away his office, which (as hath beene said) instructeth al the children of God to pray, even with inward sighes and grones inexpressable, and giveth both wordes and utterance, yea, and (as the apostle Jhon saieth) we need no other teacher to these thinges, than that annointing which we have receaved, and dwelleth in us. Is not this (if they wil have their written stuffe to be held and used as praier) to bind the Holy Ghost to the froth and leaven of their lips, as it were to the holy word of God? Is not utterly to quench and extinguish the Spirit of God, both in the ministerie and people, whiles they tye both them and God to their stinted numbred praiers? ...

... For the apostles (I am sure), these maister builders, have left no such president [precedent] in, or commandement unto the churches, neither given them any such power to bring in or set up any such apocrypha lyturgie in the church of God. They alwaies used spiritual praiers according to their present wantes and occasions, and so taught all churches to pray, alwaies, with all maner of praier and supplication in the spirit, and therby to make knowen their wantes, and shew their requestes in al thinges unto God their heavenly Father. Our saviour Christ also, he taught his disciples, that God is a Spirit, and wil be worshipped in spirit and truth. He hath likewise set downe most excellent rules, and a most absolute forme for al praiers in that part of Scripture Mathew 6: 9, 10, 11, 12, 13, commonly (but falsly) called the Lord's Praier: wherin he hath most notably instructed, directed, and restrained our ignorant and inordinate desires, to those excellent heades. In which, whatsoever is needful for us to desire, or lawful for us to pray, is in some one or other of those branches included: everie one of them being a base and foundation, wherupon and wherby to frame many millions of several peticions, according to the several wantes and occasions, at such several times as the saintes have cause to pray ... Wherby it is evident, as also by the circumstances and maner of delivering the same by our saviour Christ; by his apostles', disciples' and churches' spiritual use of praier according to their present estate and wantes, that these prescript wordes were not given or injoyned as a prescript praier, so to be used by any, even the wisest, much lesse the simpler, unbroken up, unexpounded, *etc.*, so much as a compendious summarie of all necessarie knowledg, and rules for al praier, gathered (by the author of all wisdome) into a brief, for the direction and instruction of our weaknes and ignorance ...

But yet see how they abuse it [the Scripture] to more accursed idolatry and abhominacion, as to their idol feastes both Jewish and popish, their fastes of all sortes, their holy daies. All which, because they celebrate and solemnize in their church, it shall not be amisse a litle by the light of the word to examine what kind of stuffe they are.

First, therfore, I will begin with the Jewish feastes they stil retaine, as their

Easter and Pentecost. Of these solemnities and feastes we reade Exodus 12, Leviticus 23, Numbers 28, Deuteronomy 26, that they belonged and were injoined to the Jewes under the law, were meerly ceremonial and ritual, figuring Christ's person and belonging to the Levitical ministerie, such as appertaine not unto, neither are to be reteined in the church or ministerie of Christ, without the utter losse of Christ, and utter denial of him to be as yet come in the flesh, *etc.* ... Al these ceremonies the lawes and places above alledged, shew evidently to be derived from the Jewes. We find no such customes, no such commandements in the New Testament. We there reade, that if we observe or be brought in bondage of such feastes, daies, *etc.*, we turne from Christ, he profiteth us nothing ...

For the other feast of their Penticost, they have litle help from the second of the Acts: for the disciples assembling in that private maner, could not be to keep that publike feast of their first fruites, where they were to make publike and solemne offringes, according to the law, *etc.*, *so* much as according to the commandement of our saviour Christ, to wait for the promise of the Father, *etc* ...

For I am sure they cannot shew either commandement or example in the New Testament, that this or any such feastes have beene kept or are to be kept in the churches of Christ ...

... But see, these Phariseis not only reteine the day and the feast, but joine to the celebration of the one day a principal article of our faith, the resurrection of Christ from the dead: where have they learned (trow we) to make such a set and especial memorial of Christe's resurrection one day above all the daies in the yeare? But here their answere is ready, because forsooth Christ rose as that day of the yeare. Did he so? How shall we know that? ... Be it that Christ rose just as that day; yet would I faine know the mysterie of the matter, why we should more specially remember and celebrate Christe's resurrection that Lorde's day, than the next Lorde's day, yea, or than any day of the yeare? Or why they should keep such a solemne double feast that Lorde's day more than any other: unlesse peradventure it be, because the sunne daunceth that day when it riseth. I could never as yet find in Christ's Testament any such betternes of one day than another, neither that Christ's resurrection was to be celebrate with such a stagelike fleshly pompe, in superstition and idolatrie, in fles[h]ly lustes, riote and gluttony; that day making holy two other daies after it, and drawing the whole land both yonge and old, al these daies, to intermit their lawful callings, wherin they are placed of God (upon what necessitie or occasion soever) to give attendance to their popery and idolatrie, so spend the time in idlenes, follie, and vanitie. Is this to celebrate the resurrection of Christ from dead workes? and to be renewed in knowledg and holines, after the image of him that created them? ... For I would faine learne of them, where they can likewise shew any commandement or warrant for their solemne White Sonday and their feast of Pentecost, other than the Jewes' double Sabaths and feastes, *etc.* ... I now make hast to their popish feastes ...

... Of their double feastes are their Christmasse day, with the day of his circum[ci]sion and epiphanie, the Annunciation, and purification of their ladie, called *Candlemasse* day; their day of all the saintes together, called *Hallowmasse;* their *Michaelmasse* and all angels, besides their Easter and Whitsontide, wherof we have spoken, also their Assention day, and Trinitie Sonday. Now their single feastes and common holidaies are the saintes' daies in order as they come in their beadrolle, and their common Sundaies. Of which Sundaies, though they have commandement both in the law by the fourth commandement, and in the New Testament by the commandement and practise of the apostles, to keep in the church the first day of the weeke, an holy convocation unto the Lord, spending that day in praiers, hearing the word, and other holy exercises; yet seing they so miserablie profane it to idolatrie, both after the maner of the heathen and papistes, it becommeth an idol feast no lesse accursed than the others. After the maner of the heathen they abuse it, in dedicating it unto, and naming it after the chief idol of the pagans, the sonne, a creature, and in feasting that day after their maner in pride, gluttony, riot, idlenes, sport, play, *etc*. After the maner of the papistes they abuse it, in their stinted, superstitious, idolatrous service, their abuse of Scriptures, of praier at their meeting, which is not to any edifiing or leading forward in the waies of God, their course and direction being set downe both to priestes and people before hand, what they shall doe, say, pray, how much in the forenoone at Mattens, how litle at afternoone at Evensong ... the bare recital of these their trifling follies and vanities, is inough to scatter them into the wind: for what warrant, commandement, or proofe have these stage players in the word of God, in their maner to solemnize the birth, circumcision, epiphanie, resurrection and assention of Christ upon their several daies, with their set fastes, worship, and feastes? Why do not they celebrate as well his baptisme, temptation and victorie over Sathan in the wildernes, the calling of the woman of Samaria, the receaving the Syrophoenitian, his famous miracles, casting out devils, raising the dead, walking upon the sea, transfiguration upon the mountaine, giving the Holy Ghost unto his apostles, with his commission and mesage, *etc*. These are written in the New Testament, and were done of Him as wel as the other; for our learning and comfort as wel as the other. Why then should not they as well have their peculiar daies, fastes, worship, feastes, as the other? But where have they thus learned Christ, to worship Him by startes and stintes, by daies and eaves, by such idol fastes and feastes? Is not this to draw the worship of God (which is perpetual and spiritual) unto carnal commandementes, worldly ordinances and customes againe, and that after so superstitious and profane a maner? Superstititious, in that it is without commandement or president [precedent] in the testament of Christ, wil worship not required or accepted at their handes: prophane, in that they celebrate these feastes in al maner gluttonie, excesse, ryot, prodigalitie, pride, luxurie, vanitie, idle games, and heathen sportes. Thus they celebrate the nativitie, circumcision, epiphanie and resurrection of Christ, with gay clothes, cleane houses, good cheare, the viole in the feast to stir up lust in stead of devotion, eating and drinking and rising up to play and daunce, after the maner of Bacchus in his feastes, with their lords of misrule, commonly called Christmas lordes, games, enterludes, nummeries, Sodomitish maskes, wassal cuppes, with thowsandes of abhominations, which chast and christian heartes and eares abhor to heare or thinke of. This is the fruite of their idolatrie and idlenes: this they learned of their forefathers in the wildernes. Whiles Moses was on the mount, Exodus 32, their priest cast them a calfe of gold, made of their chiefe jewels that it might be of the more estimation. To this calfe they made an altar, the priest devoutly proclaimed a fast to al the people on the eave, a solemne feast and holy day unto the Lord, yea of the Lord Jehova ...

... But that their devotions may yet more appeare, they worship him even in his mother's belly, or rather before she was conceaved with him, they adore the wordes of salutation, even in the angel Gabriel his mouth, and give a solemne fast, worship, and feast day therunto, which they cal the Annunciation of their lady. And least she might be offended, they solemnise also with double feast her purification, comonly called Candlemasse. And heer in this feast I would know of these deep divines, what it is they worship and solemnize; whether this action she did, or the person of their Lady: for needes it must be the one or both of them, heere being nothing either in or joyned with this action besides, worthie of such special veneration and high solemnitie. If then it be the action of her purification; that was but a legal ceremonie, and not now to be brought into the church of Christ. If her person (as it is also like) how then wil they escape the breach of the first commandement; unlesse peradventure they hope through her mediation to be dispensed withal, and that she wil speake a good word unto her Sonne for them; and therfore they powre out unto her their drinke offringes, and burne incense to the queene of heaven ...

... Thus having summarily runne over the publike worship of the Church of England prescribed in their service booke, rather by way of discoverie than of discourse: I wil now ... addresse my self to speake a litle of these their holy synagogues or places of assemblie, commonly called their parish church, wherunto al this rabble of worshippers resort at their apointed seasons to heare this divine booke, together with their learned prieste's sermons, *etc.* ...

... These synagogues are built altogether to the forme of the old temple of the Jewes, in a long square east and west, with their holy court walled round about, commonly called the churchyard, which is holy ground, and serveth for christen burial, being altogether exempt for civil use: yet is it lawful for the yong men and maides to play there together upon their Sundaies and holydaies. But who so smiteth any in that holy ground, by statute is to have his hand cut off therfore. These synagogues have also their battlementes, and their porch adjoining to their church, not heer to speake of the solemne laying the foundation; where the first stone must be laid by the handes of the bishop or his suffragane, with certaine magical praiers, and holy water, and many other idolatrous rites. They have unto it their foulding dores and an especial Levite, the parish clerke, to keep the key. They have at the west end their hallowed belles, which are also baptised, sprinkled, *etc*. They have their isles, and their bodie of the church: they have also their selles [cells] to the sides of the walles, their vestery to keep the priestes' ministerial garmentes, where they are to attyre and dresse themselves before they goe to their service: they have their treasurie. Al the cathedral or mother churches also have their cloysters for their deane, prebendaries, cannons, petty cannons, singing men and singing boies, *etc.*, within their precinct and walles to abide and dwell, that they may keepe the watch of the temple, and their howers of orizons. Againe they have in the bodie of their church their hallowed fonte, to keepe the holy water wherwith they baptise, al other vessels and waters to the use of baptisme being by expresse law forbidden. They have also their holiest of al, or chauncel, which peculiarly belongeth to the priest and quire, which help the priest to say and sing his service. They have their roodloft as a partition betweene their holie and holiest of all. The priest also hath a peculiar dore into his chancel, through which none might passe but himself. Now this church thus reared up, is also throughly hallowed with their sprinkling water, and dedicate and baptised into the name of some especial saint or angel, as to the patrone and defendor therof, against al enemies, spirites, stormes, tempestes, *etc*. Yet hath it within also al the holy armie of saintes and angels in their windowes and walles, to keep it. Thus I think can be no doubt made, but that the verie erections of these synagogues (whether they were by the heathens or papistes) were idolatrous.

But ... they erred; in that they tooke the popish masse for God's service, and gave their landes for the maintenance and the celebration therof ... Let us then see in a word what kind of error it is, that the action may therby be discerned and judged. Is not this masse a most blasphemous and execrable idol, in that it is affirmed to be the verie body and flesh of Christ, and so is adored? Is it not an open and utter deniing of both the natures of Christ? His humanitie, in that they make that his body to be in many thowsand places at one instant, in that they make it now patible, manducable, to be digested and cast out, *etc*., his deity, in that they pluck him from the right hand of majestie, and now cast him into most filthy places by degestion, in that they offer him up againe, conjure and sacrifice him againe, and seperate his deity from his humanitie, both from his glorie: ...

... Be it they gave their lances *ad missae celebrationem*, to the celebration of the masse, and to these colledges to that end were they given: which necessarily presupposeth (if we had no other proof) that they were such sacrificing priestes as used to say masse, a colledg of these Sodomites, those locustes. Now then they erred in somwhat more, than in giving to that false worship, in that they gave to the maintenance of these idle bellies, these caterpillars, such an ungodly societe and fraternitie. And now, seing the same colleges and dennes remaine and consist of the same wicked idle priestes and their associates, in the same manner that they then did, only the Latine masse removed (and that in what manner, apeareth by that which hath beene above said concerning their service booke), how now can these colledges be said reformed, or these grauntes lawful? When the parties to whome such grauntes are made, are by all lawes, both God's and man's, uncapable of them, yea not to live or be suffred in a christian common welth. And the prince hath as good right to abolish these, as her auncestor hath their brethren the monkes and freeres, and to assume their landes into her handes, and employ them unto the benefite of the common welth: but utterly in like maner to dissolve these idle colleges and to desolate these idol synagogues, that (as it is said by the prophet) the ravens and owles may make their nestes there, as they doe in the other.

But heere peradventure it wilbe interjected, that these synagogues may be purged, or (as our learned priests say) reformed, and so stil used to the worship of God; seing al thinges are now made cleane unto us through the word of God and prayer.

Unto this I say: that idols cannot be clensed with the blood of Christ, neither by his word which utterly condemneth them, as oft hath bene said. Againe the idolatrous shape so cleaveth to everie stone, as it by no meanes can be severed from them whiles there is a stone left standing upon a stone. So that neither they can be used to the worship of God, nor we have any civil use of them, seing they are execrable and devote[d] to destruction: so that they that use such execrable and uncleane thinges, cannot be cleane, but must needs be defiled with the filthines of these idols. And heerin either the ignorance or wretchednes of these priestes appeareth, which thus plead for Baal and his temples, under colour of reformation: which you see appeareth to be no other thing, than to seeke to repair and daube that muddy wall (which the Lord so often commandeth to be utterly destroied) for their belly, that their portion may be made fat therby. ...

... But here pollicie maketh an other pollitike doubt: how these collegiate priestes and parsons should doe for livinges, and the people for places to assemble in, if these landes should be taken away, if the idolatrous temples should be puld downe. As to the first part, such unchristian colledges as these dennes of thieves and idle bellies are, ought to be dissolved; they deposed from their priesthood, and turned to some more honest trade of living in the commonwelth: and so is this doubt soone at an end; when their antichristian ministerie ceaseth and ungodly fraternities are dissolved, then there need not any longer landes for the maintenance of such abbey lubbers, and of such locustes.

As for the true ministrie of Christ, they look for no such lordly and setled provision, they depend upon the providence and blessing of God, upon that flock unto which they administer. They are content in the greatest plentie with sufficiencie to necessarie food and raiment for them and their families, as wives and children. ...

Now for places to assemble in: they have litle love to the gospell which build themselves such stately seeled houses, and allow not to the people of God a house to assemble and worship God in. There were synagogues built in Judea and Israel after the high places were destroied. Great were our blame, if we should suffer the idolaters so far to exceed and condemne us, which have built such magnificent and sumptuous aedifices to their idols; and we not afford a poore simple house to the Lord Jesus Christ, who now requireth not such sumptuous temples, his true temple being the soules and bodies of his chosen. But I doubt, this worldly pollicie which hath so long borne the sway and ruled religion, wil never in this world yeild her self prostrate as an humble handmaid, to take lawes at God, and suffer him to order and governe all things by his word: I doubt in this last age of the world, there are too many false prophets abrode, which are gone forth unto the kinges of the earth, rather to draw them into battel, against Christ and his saintes, than to bring Christ so generally and absolutely into their kingdomes. ...

... And now the publike worship of the Church of England being thus far discovered; me thinkes it due time, and most fit to examine the publike preaching of the gospell in the said church: seing that therwith, as with a goodly embroidered coverlet and fine sheets of Egipt they cover Jesabel's bed, and hide al their fornications: seing therwith, as with a sweet whistle they allure, as with a charme they retayne their auditory: ... what ought we in these our daies to do? Who find not only all the markes of false prophets which are recorded in the Scriptures upon them, but even Satan's uttermost deceites and effectual delusions amongst them, suborning and transforming them, as if they were ministers of righteousnes, taking unto them the names and titles of Christ's ministers, preachers of the gospel, seekers of reformation, wherby he deceaveth the world, draweth them into most heinous sinnes and high profanation of God's name, which can no other way be reformed or purged but by the utter dissolution of the whole frame, when this whole world shall be consumed with fire, unto the which day it hastneth and is reserved ...

But to returne to our present purpose, which is to shew after what maner these ministers of the Church of England preach the gospel. Here must be remembred after what order they stand priestes, how they entred, what they vowed by othe [oath] at their entrance ... how at the receaving this ministerie, they solemnly upon their knees (by othe) vowed their canonical obedience to these bishops and their substitutes their orders and decrees; and this not only to the observation of the things that are or shalbe by these their lordes and superintendents commanded them, but likewise by the same to be disciplined, censured and chasticed for anie thing offensive unto them, which in their ministerie they shal do or say, whither by mulct, suspension, deposition, or prison. Furthermore, from them they fetch their licence to preach, with their lawes of stint, limitation, and praescription, when to preach, what to preach, where and how long to preach, but especially by publike doctrine not to speake against any thing by publike authoritie injoined, or by the same authoritie hereafter to be injoined; as also, to exhort their parishioners unto the due obedience and observation of such injunctions ...

... I know our English priestes wil have many fine floorishes to hide this treacherie: as that they acknowledge him [Christ] their only priest and mediator, to have with that one oblation of his owne pretious bodie once offred fully satisfied the justice and appeased the wrath of his Father. Yea, they acknowledg him to be the verie first fruites, and sanctifier of the whole heape, clothing all his with his righteousnes, and that he is entered into the heavens into the verie throne of God, and there offreth up the praiers and maketh intercession for all them. Likewise, that he is heire and king over al both men and angels, that he hath in this his (or rather oure flesh) vanquished al our enemies, Satan, sin, death and hel, and triumphed over them in that his crosse, that he is ascended up on high and sitteth at the right hand of God, from whence he shal come to judge the quick and the dead. And for his prophecie, that he is the end of al prophecies to whome they were directed, the fulnes and fountaine of al wisdome whome we ought to heare; and how by that his heavenly word he begetteth us to life everlasting, *etc*.

These and many other comfortable and true doctrines they can and doe deliver touching the offices of Christ; but all these you must understand, and I pray you observe wel (for so shal you cleerly espie their error and deceit) are still but what Christ hath done in his owne person for his elect: here is not one word spoken what he doth in his elect: how he teacheth, sanctifieth and ruleth them by the scepter of his word, how he is a king, priest, a prophet heere on earth, and exerciseth the offices here in his church amongst his servantes the saints: how he is their pastour, their teacher, their king; how he feedeth and reigneth in Sion, yea, and maketh all his children kings, priests, and prophets. Kings, in that he hath given them his word into their hearts and mouthes, wherby as with a sharpe two edged sword they cut off sin, and fight against al errors; wherby they reigne over their owne affections, subdue the flesh, cast downe everie imagination that is exalted against the knowledg of God, and bring into captivitie everie thought to the obedience of Christ; wherby they unpartially censure, judge and cast out al maner of sin, as it ariseth and apeareth amongst them, binding their rulers in chaines and their nobles in fetters of yron, executing upon them the judgments that are written; yea, therby condemning everie weapon and tongue that shal arise in judgment against the truth. This is the heritage of the Lord's servants, this honor shalbe to al his saintes. Priestes he maketh them, in that he annointeth them with his owne Holy Spirit, wherby they both offer up their prayers and praises through him unto God, and their owne bodies and soules as living sacrifices unto him daily; which is their reasonable serving of God. Prophets he maketh them, in that he revealeth his truth unto them, and commandeth them to witnesse it and spread it forth in all places to his glorie.

One word of these heavenly effects in and amongst them of their dutie, obedience, love, and faithfulnes they owe and ought againe on their parts to performe unto him, they al this while shew not; and how without this there is no comfort or benefit to be expected or receaved by Christ; without this faith, love, and obedience, none can have him a king unto them to rule and defend them, none can have him a prophet to teach and instructe them, none can have him a priest to sanctifie and blesse them, none can have him a saviour. But al they that either acknowledge not the Lord Jesus Christ, or obey not unto his eternal gospel, but withhold the truth in unrighteousnes, shalbe punished with everlasting perdition from the presence of the Lord, and from the glorie of his power, when he shal come to be glorified in his saintes, and to be made mervailous in al them that beleeve. But alas, how is it possible that they should know or see this beautie of the king in Sion, whiles they remaine in Babilon? How is it possible that they should teach this submission and obedience unto Christ Jesus, when they themselves remaine the bondservants and sworne soldiours of antichrist in such maner as hath beene rehearsed? ...

... This maketh them [i.e., the clergy] thus ignorant and blind in all the lawes and ordinances of Christ, touching the true gathering, building, and governing the Church of Christ, that they know not the doctrines even of the beginnings of Christ, of repentance from dead workes, faith towardes God, of baptisme and laying on of handes. This maketh them not to know so much, as the stones wherof Christ's church must be built, nor the true foundation wherupon to build them, as you may see by that which hath beene said concerning their outward estate and practise; much lesse know they the true forme and fashion of the house, and least of all the true administration and ordinances therof; as apeareth evidently by their receaving of, and administring unto this monstrous confuse bodie of their profane rowtes of people; by their exercising this their false and antichristian ministerie, and that after such an idolatrous blasphemous symoniacal maner; as also by receaving antichrist's yoke, traditions, ordinances; wherby (as hath beene shewed) they deny Christ in the flesh, by deniing his offices, his annointing: they denie his ministerie, his ordinances, his whole Testament, by receaving an other ministerie, other lawes than such as he there hath prescribed. Or els they must affirme, that earthly men may admit into and make members of the church whome they please and wil; that they also may alter, add to, detract, yea, abrogate and disanul what part of Christ's Testament they list; that they may erect a new ministerie, a new forme of administration of sacraments, of worship, of government ...

... But for the people of Christ, they are all inlightened with that bright morning star, that sonne of righteousness. The eye of their faith is single, and the whole bodie is light. They are an humble, meek, obedient people, they will heare and follow the true shepheard, but a stranger they will not heare ... And therfore hath God amongst them bownd up the testimonie and sealed up the law. To them he hath committed the charge and keeping of his holy oracles: to them and everie one of them he hath given his holy sanctifying spirit, to open unto them and to lead them into al truth: to them he hath given his sonne to be their king, priest and prophet, who hath made them unto him kings and priests ... But if they should be debarred of this power, libertie, and dutie because they are not so learned as the priests, and have not beene at the universitie, *etc.*, by that popish reason were the word of God to be shut up from al lay men (as they cal them) that no man might reade or speake therof in his house or family, because they have not knowledg to understand it and open it after their schools maner, the word of God being such an abysme of wisdome and of so great dignitie and reverence, and that in al places alike ... As for these learned divines of our age. I refer them unto, or rather oppose unto them the wisdome and word of God, who you see hath given unto al his servantes this libertie and power; yea rather hath layd upon them this charge and duty, to reprove and censure any error or transgression which is committed by the whole church or any member of the church contrarie to the word of God, by the same word.

The apostle also in expresse wordes declareth, that this exercise [i.e., prophecy] belongeth to the whole church, verses 23, 24. [in 1 Corinthians 14]. If (saith he) 'when the whole church is come together unto the same, and all speake tongues, there come in also they that are ignorant or unbeleevers, wil they not say that ye are mad? But if al prophecie and there come in an infidel or idiote, he is convinced of all, he is judged of all,' *etc.* The 26 verse also: 'what is [it] then brethren? When ye come together everie one of you hath a psalme, hath doctrine,' *etc.* Likewise, verse 31. 'For you may all [one] by one, everie one of you, prophecie, that all may learne and all may be comforted.' What can be more manifest and direct than these places, that this exercise of prophecie belongeth to the whole church, and that everie faithful man hath here freedome and power both to be present and to speake also as need requireth, and God revealeth unto him?

Document I.15

Martin Marprelate

The identity of the brilliant satirist who hid behind the name 'Martin Marprelate' is still a matter of debate. In the latest stages of the discussion, Donald J. McGinn has argued strongly that Penry was the author in his *John Penry and the Marprelate Controversy* (Rutgers University, 1966). Glanmor Williams was not persuaded, see his article, 'John Penry and Martin Marprelate', *Welsh History Review*, 3 (1967), 361–80. Leland H.Carlson sought to prove that Job Throckmorton was Marprelate in his *Martin Marprelate, Gentleman: Master Job Throckmorton Laid Open in His Colors* (San Marino, 1981). A. L. Rowse in his *Ralegh and the Throckmortons* (London, 1962) had assumed that Throckmorton was Martin but in his review of McGinn's book in *English Historical Review*, 83 (1968), 69 he accepted that Penry was the author. See also David Williams (ed.), *John Penry: Three Treatises Concerning Wales* (Cardiff, 1960), Introduction.

The following quotations exemplify Marprelate's provocative treatment of leading figures in the Church of England. Some of his sharpest shafts were aimed at John Aylmer (1521–94), bishop of London from 24 March 1577, for whom v., John Strype, *Historical Collections of the Life and Acts of John Aylmer* (Oxford, 1701) and DNB.

The extracts are as follows:

(a) *The Epistle*, 8–9; reproduced in William Pierce, *The Marprelate Tracts, 1588, 1589* (London, 1911), 29. The 'Honourable Masterships' were the prelates of the Church of England. Pierce's edition is fully annotated and he quotes Aylmer's defence of himself against this and other allegations made by Marprelate.

(b) *The Epistle*, 20–1; reproduced in Pierce, *The Marprelate Tracts*, 47–9.

Stanhope was Dr Edward Stanhope (d. 16 March 1608). He was a civil lawyer who had held a variety of civil and ecclesiastical appointments and was MP for Marlborough, 1584–5, 1586–7, v., Pierce, *The Marprelate Tracts*, 32, n. 2. Aylmer's defence against the accusation that he had ordained his porter is given at length in Thomas Cooper's *Admonition* (London, 1589), 53–5 and reproduced in Pierce, *The Marprelate Tracts*, 46, n. 2. The allegation that he had felled trees at Fulham was a serious one. The matter was discussed by the Council in May 1579 and there was sufficient substance in the accusation for the Lord Treasurer to reprimand Aylmer. Finally, the Queen wrote to him that he should 'take down no more of his woods', Strype, *Aylmer*, 46–8. Bancroft, when he succeeded Aylmer, said that his predecessor had 'made £6,000 of his woods', ibid., 128. *The Epistle* was printed at the house of Mrs Crane at East Molesey, in mid-October 1588.

(c) *The Epitome*, 53; reproduced in W. Pierce, *The Marprelate Tracts*, 127–8.

The Epitome was printed at Fawsley House, Northamptonshire, the seat of Sir Richard Knightley, about the end of November 1588. It is Martin's rejoinder to the first of the sixteen books into which Dean John Bridges divided his long book, *A Defence of the Government Established in the Church of England for Ecclesiastical Matters* (London, 1587), the work which provoked Martin to launch his tracts. In the above quotation, he sets out, in serious vein, the central convictions of his 'brethren', the Puritans, about the nature of church government.

(d) This following quotation is part of a speech put into the mouth of Archbishop Whitgift by Marprelate. He is imagined addressing his pursuivants as they search for Martin and those responsible for the secret press on which his tracts are printed.

As William Pierce rightly says, 'It shows us, more vividly than any other document we possess, the situation created by the Marpelate writings: the popular excitement; the small result of the activities of the pursuivants; their vain and expensive expeditions ...' (*The Marprelate Tracts*, 338).

(e) The quotation is from *The Just Censure* in Pierce, *The Marprelate Tracts*, 352–9. It was printed at Wolston Priory, the house of Roger Wigston, 29 July 1589. The full title of the tract explains the reference to Martin's son. It reads, *The iust censure and reproofe of Martin Iunior. Wherein the rash and indiscreete headines of the foolish youth, is sharply mette with, and the boy hath his lesson taught him, I warrant you, by his reuerend and elderbrother, Martin Senior, sonne and heire vnto the renowned Marprelate. [t]he Great.*

For Robert Waldegrave (1554?–1604), v., DNB. For the parts played by Humphrey Newman and Henry Sharpe in printing the tracts, v., William Pierce, *An Historical Introduction to the Marprelate Tracts* (London, 1908). Anthony Munday (or Monday) was a registered stationer and a spy, v., J.Dover Wilson, 'Anthony Munday, Pamphleteer and Pursuivant', *Modern Language Review*, IV (July 1909), 484–90 and note in Pierce, *The Marprelate Tracts*, 353. It is not at all clear what motive prompted Martin to name his colleagues. It can hardly be believed that he was prepared to betray them.

(a)

Most pitifully complaineth Martin Marprelate unto your Honourable Masterships: That certain thieves, having stolen from dyers in Thames-street as much cloth as came to thirty pound, did hide the said cloth in Fulham, which is a place within the territories of the Lord Dumb John, who, by occupation, is Lord Bishop of London. The thieves were apprehended. The cloth came within your clutches, Don John of London; and all is fish that comes to the net, with your good Honour. The thieves being taken, the dyers came to challenge their cloth. John London, the Bishop, said it was his own, because it was taken within his own lordship. 'But', saith he, 'if the cloth be yours, let the law go upon the thieves, and then I'll talk farther with you'. Well, one or two of the thieves were executed, and at their deaths confessed that to be the cloth which the bishop had. But the dyers could not get their cloth, nor cannot to this day ...

(b)

Who made the porter of his gate a dumb minister? Dumb John of London. Who abuseth her Majesty's subjects in urging them to subscribe contrary to law? John of London. Who abuseth the High Commission, as much as any? John London (and Doctor Stanhope, too). Who bound an Essex minister in £200 to wear the surplice on Easter Day last? John London. Who is a carnal defender of the breach of the Sabbath in all places of his abode? John London. Who forbiddeth men to humble themselves in fasting and prayer before the Lord, and then can say unto the preachers, 'Now you were best tell the people that we forbid fasts'? John London. Who goeth to bowls upoin the Sabbath? Dumb, duncical John of good London, hath done all this.

I will ... tell your Venerable Masterdoms a tale worth the hearing ... The matter is this. A man dying in Fulham, made one of the Bishop of London's men his executor. The man had bequeathed certain legacies unto a poor shepherd in the town. The shepherd could get nothing of the Bishop's man, and therefore made his moan unto a gentleman of Fulham, that belongeth to the Court of Requests. The gentleman's name is Master Madox. The poor man's case came to be tried in the Court of Requests. The Bishop's man desired his master's help. Dumb John wrote to the Masters of Requests to this effect, and I think these were his words:

> My Masters of Requests, the bearer hereof, being my man, hath a cause before you. Inasmuch as I understand how the matter standeth, I pray you let my man be discharged the Court, and I will see an agreement made. Fare you well.

The letter came to Master Doctor Dale. He answered in this sort:

> My lord of London, this man delivered your letter. I pray you give him his dinner on Christmas day for his labour. And fare you well.

Dumb John not speeding this way, sent for the said Master Madox. He came; some rough words passed on both sides. Presbyter John said Master Madox was very saucy, especially seeing he knew before whom he spake; namely, the Lord of Fulham. Whereunto the gentleman answered that he had a poor freeholder in Fulham before Don John came to be lord there, hoping also to be so when he and all his brood, my Lady his daughter and all, should be gone. At the hearing of this speech, the wasp got my Brother by the nose, which made him in his rage to affirm that he would be Lord of Fulham as long as he lived, in despite of all England. 'Nay, soft there,' quoth Master Madox, 'Except her Majesty, I pray you.' 'That is my meaning,' quoth Dumb John. 'And I tell thee, Madox, thou art but a Jack to use me so.' Master Madox replying said that indeed his name was John, and if every John were a Jack he was content to be a Jack. (There he hit my Lord over the thumbs.) The Bishop growing in choler said that Master Madox's name did show what he was; 'for,' saith he, 'thy name is Mad-ox, which declareth thee to be an unruly and mad beast.' Master Madox answered again that the bishop's name, if it were descanted upon, did most significantly show his qualities. 'For,' said he, 'you are called Elmar; but you may be better called Mar-elm, for you have marred all the elms in Fulham, having cut them all down.'

(c)
Christ Jesus ordained that when there should be any ministers in His Church they should be able to gather together (a) the saints, and that these in their proper and limited places, should be either pastors or doctors. In like sort He ordained that some should (b) bear rule and oversee the flock with the minister [deacon] and they should be elders; that the oversight of the church treasury, and the care for the maintenance of the poor should be committed (c) unto deacons, under which, also, the widows and church servants are contained. He farther ordained, that before these officers should be instituted, and as it were invested into their offices, there should be had due examination of their (d) fitness to execute the same, and their unreproveable (e) life. And that their ordination should be by (f) imposition of

hands, with fasting and prayer. And by these four officers (say our brethren) Pastors, Doctors, Elders and Deacons, God hath appointed that all matters of the Church should be decided and determined. For these oficers only (and none else) must have to do with the preaching of the Word, administering the sacraments, making of ministers, excommunicating and administering of all other church censures and punishments; but, as for civil government, punishment, and censures, they must not meddle with them. Because these only belong to the civil magistrate, whose office is not to be usurped by any of the former ...

(d)
Now, sirs, is not her Majesty's High Commission and myself also, being the chief thereof, and one of her Majesty's Privy Council, well set up with a company of messengers, as long as we have you to go of our business? What think you? Have you been careful of us and our places, to find us out the press and letters wherewith these seditious 'Martins' are printed? Or have you diligently sought me out Waldegrave, the printer; Newman, the cobbler; Sharpe, the bookbinder of Northampton; and that seditious Welshman, Penry, who, you shall see, will prove the author of all these libels? I thank you Master Monday, you are a good gentleman of your word ... Didst thou not assure me, without all doubt, that thou wouldest bring me in Penry, Newman, Waldegrave, press, letters, and all, before St. Andrew's day last [30 November 1588]? And now thou seest we are as far to seek for them as ever we were. Nay, unless we have them now, they are like to trouble our Church more than ever they did ... Why truly it grieves me at the heart that I, by her Majesty's favour having more authority in mine hand to repress these Puritans than any bishop else hath had in England these thirty years, yet should be more troubled and molested by them these six years, than all my predecessors have been these six and twenty years. And all this cometh by reason of your unfaithfulness and negligence, whom we send for them ... Therefore look to it: for now every one of you shall have warrants both for himself, and as many as you will substitute under you besides. Bring us whomsoever you suspect, your warrants shall serve you to do it. And if you can find us either young or old Martin, Penry, or Waldegrave, so that you bring the press and letters, he shall have the forty pounds for his labour, whosoever will bring them: his charges and all borne clear ...

Well, if ever you mean to do any good in this matter, take me this course, which we here in Commission have thought meetest; let a six or seven of you, or your substitutes that stay here in London, watch me Paul's Churchyard, especially have an eye to Boyle's shop at The Rose. And let some one or two of you that are unknown go in thither, and if there be any strangers in the shop, fall in talk with them of Martin, commend him, and especially his son's last libel ... showing, that by great friendship you got one of them; saying also, that you understood a man might there help his friend to some, if he were acquainted with Master Boyle, and offer largely for it. Now, sir, if any shall either enter with you into any speeches against the State, and in defence of these libels; or else, if any man procure you the sight of the books, be sure to bring them before us ...

The Beginnings, 1550–1603

You that stay here in London must also be sure, if possibly you can, to have a watch at all common inns, to see what carriage of paper and other stuff either goes from, or comes to London. Thereby you may haply learn something. And mark if any Puritan receiveth anything. Open his pack, that you may be sure he hath no Martins sent him ...

As for you that go into the country, I would have ye especially go into Northampton and Warwick shires, and command the Mayor and Constables of Northampton to keep watch and ward for Sharpe and Penry, and if they can take them, let them bring them up, and we will be sure to content them for their pains. Others must go into Essex, Suffolk and Norfolk ...

These Martinists are all of them traitors and enemies unto her Majesty; they will overthrow the State; they are most rebellious and disobedient unto all good proceedings. No warning will serve them; they grow worse and worse ...

Document I.16

John Penry: The Case for Wales

This document shows how the general Puritan concern for the provision through parliamentary action of more adequate preaching was applied to Wales. That Penry's bleak analysis of the religious and social condition of Wales was not an idiosyncratic piece of polemic is confirmed by MS 12/1919 No. 17 in the Public Record Office. It opens with the heading, 'A briefe collection of the state of Brecnockshire, mense May, Anno dni 1586. Where Gods service is neglected, and his words not effectuallie preached, the Common wealth cannot prosper or be well governed'. It is tempting to speculate that there is some connection between it and Penry's *Aequity*.

The document consists of excerpts from John Penry, *The Aequity of an Humble Supplication* (Oxford, 1587). A facsimile reprint was published in London in 1905 by A. J. Grieve. It is also printed with an introduction in David Williams, *John Penry: Three Treatises Concerning Wales* (Cardiff, 1960). For Penry, v., W. Pierce, *John Penry, His Life, Times and Writings* (London, 1923); Champlin Burrage, *John Penry, the so-called Martyr of Congregationalism* (London, 1913) and R. Tudur Jones, 'Cyfraniad John Penri' (i.e., John Penry's Contribution') in *Y Cofiadur*, 58 (1993), 4–41. John Waddington's *John Penry* (London, 1855) was a pioneering work which first drew attention to the significance of Penry. Abraham Rees (1745–1825, v., DNB) claimed descent from the Penry family in his article on Penry in his *The New Cyclopaedia*, 39 vols (London, 1819).

Oh then what Christian, yea ingenious, humane, naturall heart will not be greeued to see any people in such a forlorne case, as not only to be bereaued of those vnspeakable blessings of the Lord, whereof al they shal be partakers that fear him, but also laid open vnto the weapons of his reuenging and consuming anger in this worlde, and in that to come, to his eternall and neuer ending wrath? And who would not strain himselfe to the vtmost of his ability, and beyond all his might, to make knowen the case of such a people vnto those who both can, and also would find a remedy therunto? For mine owne part, because I see the spirituall miserie wherein wee nowe liue in the country of WALES, for want of the preaching of the Gospel and the great plagues that are like vndoubtedly to fall vpon vs for the same; I cannot but be so affected toward these our calamities, as in respect of the Lords honor, the desire of the saluation of my breethren, my loyall obedience vnto her Maiesty, and the discharge of my own conscience, I doe alwaies from the bottome of mine heart wish and pray for the redresse heereof, & nowe by writing with all humility and submission in the feare of God, lay open our estate, first vnto the consideration of your excellent Maiesty my dread soueraigne Queene Elizabeth, vnto whom only of all the potentates of the earth, I owe all obedience and seruice in the Lord Iesus, and next vnto the viewe of your high court of Parliament, desiring you vpon my knees in the name of the great God the creator and preseruer of heauen and earth; whose honor is now in hand, that our petition may be so throughly waied, as our necessity requireth.

The summe whereof is, that it would please your Maiesty, & this honorable assembly, in a zealous and a godly compassion, to regard the lamentable and wofull estate of vs your poore subjects, and breethren, which liue at this day altogither without knowledge of a sauing God, because we haue not teaching Ministers among vs, & that some order may be taken by your Maiesty and the estate, whereby wee may bee freed from that destroieng grosse darckenesse of ignorance, wherein we nowe are bewrapped to the woe of our soules for euer: And so by our true conuersion vnto the Lorde, we may auoid euerlasting death, and preuent the fiercenesse of the wrath & indignation, which we see iustly to hang ouer vs in this life. The remedy of this our grieuous case, is only had (and no other way) by speedie prouiding vnto vs such pastors, as may feede vs with the food of life, the pure worde of God, and bring vs home vnto the only Lord of pastors, & sheepeheards, the Lord Iesus. This is the summe of al (my dread soueraigne) that I your base vassall haue emboldened my selfe to offer vnto you, and this your high court of Parliament; wherein I protest that in respect of my weakenesse al maner of waies; the basenesse of my condition, I intreated the Lorde to send vnto you by the hand of him whom hee should sende, that is by one endued with such giftes, and authority also, as whereby the suite might haue purchased some countenance, and so be found more auailable, and plausible ...

... I thought it most needefull in this briefe treatise to set downe some of the reasons whereupon our petition is grounded, that by the view of them, it may appeare how daungerous a thing it is in the sight of God and man to deny our suite ... Wee desire to haue the knowledge of our God, and the Lawes of his kingdome, (whose subiectes in name wee professe ourselues, and in deede ought to bee) made knowne and taught vnto vs. We desire that the tyranny of Sathan, who exerciseth a regencie in the hearts of all men (amongst whom Gods trueth hath not beene taught) may be ouerthrown by the powerfull arme of God the worde preached, who can saue our soules.

Now therefore ... we most earnestly and vehemently as in the cause of Iesus Christ, and in the cause of our soules, entreate and beseech you, cry and cal vpon you to do your endeuors, that Sathan may no longer keep vs in bondage ...

Moreouer you may be assured, dread soueraign, both that we and our children for euer wil blesse our God, that he hath enclined mercy vnto vs in your eies. And also our calling wil be testimony to our burning zeale vnto the truth among all the ages to come, euen to the enemies of your good name. Whereas on the other side the continuance of our blind ignorance wil be I fear me a blemish vnto your credit (in obedience I speak it) among our wofull posterities, and the enemies of God for euer. For what will our children that rise after vs and their children say, when they shal be brought vp in grosse superstition, but that it was not Queene Elizabethes will, that we their Parentes should haue that true religion she professed, made knowen vnto vs. Will not the enemies of Gods truth with vncleane mouthes auouch that shee had little regarde vnto true or false religion anie further than it belonged vnto hir profite? I would some of them did not slaunderously cast abroade amongst our people, that she careth not whether the gospel be preached or not preached. If she did wee also shoulde bee most sure to enjoy it after twenty yeares and vpward of most prosperous raigne. These thinges derogating from her Maiesties honor in a most villanous sort, must be withstoode thorough hir selfe and this whole assembly, by making prouision for vs betimes of the food of our soules. ...

It might greeue vs the lesse to be denied the gospel, vnlesse the same were the inheritance which our forefathers the Cymbrubrittons many hundred yeares agoe possessed in this lande. For although at this daie wee cannot cal true religion by the right name, yet are not our superstitious obseruations the blossoms of that auncient truth our forefathers professed and sealed with their blood. But the impes of that lifelesse and brutish stock of Rome, planted in England by Augustine that proud friar, whose tyranical proceedings our diuines in Wales resisted euen to the losse of their liues.[1] That these trash be but of small continuance among vs in respect of the antiquity the trueth hath had, I proue because the verie mother of them, the execrable Masse, was but yesterday, as it were, knowen vnto vs. Shewed by two reasons. First among the cartloades of oathes which wee haue, our people cannot tel for their liues how to sweare by the masse. Secondly we haue the masse at the end of none of our holy daies. For Christmasse, Candlemasse &c. wee name the day of the natiuity, the holie daie of Marie &c. Which things doe prooue the Masse to haue had but colde entertainement among vs, but within this later age wherin ignorance and idolatrie by the iust iudgement of God tooke such deepe roote in England, that it ran ouer our land also.

The equitie then of our petition appeareth also in that we aske nothing but the possession and inheritaunce of our fathers to be restored vnto vs, which they coulde not alienate from their children. This were a fitte place to stir vp my deare countrimen to bee earnest in obteining that iewell which is woorth all their riches besides, beeing their owne right: but their forwardnes in other causes persuadeth mee they wil not bee slacke in the matter of the soule ...

... Our case now is to bee especiallie pittied in respect of the inner man. For howe many souls doe daily starue and perish among vs for want of knowledge? And how many are like still to tread the same path? It grieueth me at the hart to consider how hel is enlarged to receaue us. And here the Lord knoweth and our soueraigne with this most honourable assembly shal know that I doe not complaine without cause. For our estate is such, that we haue not one in some score of our parishes, that hath a sauing knowledge. Thousands there be of our people that know Iesus Christ to be neither God nor man, king, priest nor prophet: o desolate and forlorne condition! yea almost that neuer heard of him. If anie by the great goodnesse of God be called, this came to passe not by the diligence of their pastours which are either dumme or greedy dogs that delight in sleeping, as saith the Prophet (a few honest men excepted) but either extraordinarily through reading, or by meanes of their resort and abode in some corner of the Church of England where the gospel is preached. And long may it be preached there, to the glory of God, the felicity of our soueraign, and the euerlasting good of that whole noblitiy and people, whose kindnes towards strangers the Lord wil not forget ... Theselatter aresome few gentlemen, or such like. The rest of our people are either such as neuer think of anie religion true or fasle, plainly meere Atheists or stark blinded with superstition.

The latter are of 2 sorts. The first crue is of obstinate idolaters that would fain be again in execrable Rome, and so hold for diuinity whatsoeuer hath bin hatched in that sacrilegious nest ... Hence flow our swarmes of southsaiers, and enchanters, such as will not stick openly, to professe that they walke, on Tuesdaies, and Thursdaies at nights, with the fairies, of whom they brag themselues to haue their knowledge. These sonnes of Belial, who shuld die the death, Leuit.20.6. haue stroken such an astonishing reuerence of the fairies into the hearts of our silly people, that they dare not name them without honor. We cal them *bendith û mamme*,[2] that is, such as haue deserued their mothers blessing. Now our people, wil neuer vtter, *bendith û mamme*, but they will saie, *bendith û mamme û dhûn*,[3] that is, their mothers blessing (which they account the greatest felicity that any creature can be capeable of) light vpon them, as though they were not to be named without reuerance. Hence proceed open defending of Purgatory & their Real presence, praying vnto images &c. with other infinit monsters.

The other sort is of good simple soules, that would full gladly learne the way vnto saluation, and spend their hart blood, for the safety of their godly Prince in whom they do claim more interest then the rest of hir subects whosoeuer. These poore soules, because the idol pastor can teach them nothing, entering more deeply with themselues into the consideration of things, find by the small light of religion we enjoy through the meanes of hir Maiestie, & by the instinct of nature, that there is a diuine essence who must be carefully and religiously served and praied vnto for al bleesinges that would be obtained. Which things they see vnperfourmed publikely, therefore priuatly they assay what they can doe.

But wofull estate, they being not taught out of the worde of God, what he is, that must be serued, & how he requireth this to be doone, inuent vnto themselues both their God and the maner of his seruice: concerning saluation they either thinke, that the Lorde is bound to saue all men, because they are his creatures, or that al shal be saued at the later day, at the intreaty of the virgin Mary, who shal desire her sonne, after iudgement giuen, to saue as many of the damned as may bee couered vnder her mantill: this being graunted al the damned souls shalbe there shrouded and so saued from hel fiar. This is the cause why our people make but a mocke of sinne. They thinke the soule only shal goe to heauen & not the body also, whence it commeth that they say, they care not what becommeth of their bodies, so their soules may bee saued. They ascribe sauadge cruelty vnto God the father, because he punished mans sinne so seuerely, euen in his son Christ; the Lord Iesus they commend. *Nû waeth genûf dhim am y tad y gwr craûlon hinnû onûd cydymmaith da ûwr mab*:[4] I care not saith one for the father, that cruel man, but the sonne is a good fellowe ... Because the poore creatures can hear nothing at the mouth of their minister, how their sinnes may be hidden & their iniquities couered, it is a common saying euen among those who care not for Rhomish Antichrist, that it was a good worlde then when a man might haue a pardon for his sins in such and such a place for one 4d. They see no felicity where mere ignorance of saluation is. A false perswasion thereof they thinke better than none at all. Man must haue religion, true or false.

Our people learn one of another most blasphemous paiers. This they doe so much the rather, because in them they commend them selues, families, &c vnto the tuition of some saint whom they think most fauourable vnto them and best able to grant their petitions. My hart bleedeth to think howe these villanies with other vngodly songs are learned of good painfull soules with greedines. I know masters of families that teach these vnto their housholds. If they meete with any who can write and read, they wil demand of him whether he can teach them euer a good praier against such a disease in man or beast. Vngodly welsh bookes are fraught with these Idolatries. If conscience would not keep me from vttering an vntruth before my soueraigne monarch, yet fear of punishment should containe me. But this I protest before Iesus Christ who shall iudge all euen according vnto their woordes, and in the presence of al the world, that the onely staffe & stay of al priuat religion among our people (the 2 sorts od men before named, I exempt) are latine praiers, praying vnto Saints, superstitious obseruations, with vngodlie welsh songs and books. If these things were not, meare Atheisme would ouer-grow vs. Surely the reading ministery hath not so much as wrought in the hearts of anie almost, the perswasion of one true God. It were folly to goe about to heale the disease and let the cause remaine. Concerning that which is reade, there is no man but thinketh very reuerently thereof. And we praise the Lorde that we haue so much publikely by meanes of her highnes, whereas in the daies of blindnes we had nothing but professed idolatry.

Take but a view of our liues, and you shal see also what effect reading hath brought to passe. There be many sinnes essential vnto our nation. Profaning the name of God in common talk is prodigious. 40 affirmations or negations will bring thirty oathes out of a greatmany. Some shires of South wales haue gotten them an ignominious name by this sin. I dare write that which I durst not vtter in words. They are called *gwûr cig Dûw*.[5] Looke the punishment of swearing Deut. 28.58, Leuit. 24. 15,16. This is the flieng book, Zach. 5.3. Look the Law of concealing an oath, Leu. 5.1. and you shall finde that the Parliament shoulde haue great regard to damme the springes of this sinne by the word preached. What a hand we haue had in adultery and fornication, the great number of illegitimate and base born among vs doe testify. I would our Princes and leuits had not beene chiefe in this trespasse. The punishment hereof in the Bishops court is derided by our people. For what is it to them to pay a litle money, or to run through the Church in a white sheete? They haue made rimes and songs of this vulgar penance. Neither justice of peace nor minister wil see the execution of the lawes prouided in this case. Though they did, seeing the Lords ordinance is not obserued, it would not peuaile. The seat of iudgement in our common courts is turned into wormwoode. A man cannot haue his right in a yeare or two, though his euidence be vnanswerable. They haue gotten many shifts, and when al failes, one wil stand viz. excommunication. The plaintife without al right maie be excommunicated in the Bishops court, and so not absolued in a whole yeare. Al which time hee is no person fit to prosecute his right in the common law. It is irksome to think how hardly a poor man can keepe any thing from theeues of great countenaunce. Though he seeth his own sheep or other cattel feed within two miles of him in some mens pastures, he dareth not aske them. Quaffing and surfeting is too too common. Al are become Ismaels. Euery mans hand against them, and theirs against all other. Church men and all will haue their right by the sword, for by the word they neuer seek it. These things I doe not set downe to disgrace my dear countrimen. I beare them another hart. My purpose is to shew that all the good politique lawes in the woorld cannot wash awaie these our stains. The nitre that washeth purely the word of the Lord must doe it. A conscience must be wrought in our people, else they wil neuer leaue their idolatry, swearing, adulterie, and theeuery. They that know the country know how little hold the straightest and seuerest laws in the world wil take on a great many. If it be the wil of the Parliament therfore we shal be bettered, let the word be preached among vs. We haue preaching. How often? Quarterly. It is not so. For to that one parish where there is one ordinary quarter sermon, we haue twenty that haue none. The number of fit preaching ministers in wales can easily proue the truth hereof. Wee paie tithes alwaies, and therefore we should haue preaching alway, for he that laboureth not must not eat. 2 Thess. 3.8, 10; continuall preaching is Gods ordinance, Eph. 4.12, therefore men must not dispence with it. Confer Rom. 8.9 with Eph. 1.3, 2 Tim. 4.2, Acts 20.18, 19, 20, 31, I Thess. 2.10, 11, Heb. 5.12, Acts 20.16, Colos. 3.16, I Pet. 1.23, Matt. 9.38. The seuerall reasons drawen out of these places of Scripture maie proue the necessity of continual preaching, either in respect that it is Gods decree, or that mans nature requireth it. They that denie this may learne their duty by Iacobs diligence in keeping of sheep Gen 31.40. So may they set others to take the ouersight of the Lords sanctuarie Ezec.44.8. and blush. Preaching is graunted conueniant, but so as reading wil serue the turne. I maruel the face of mortall man wil be so brasen as to affirtm this, the immortal word of God loudly gainsaying, 1 Cor. 1.21, Rom. 1.16, Iam. 1.21. I wil not light a candle before the sun …

Notes

1. This is an oblique reference to the 'Protestant Theory', espoused by William Salesbury and Bishop Richard Davies in their Welsh New Testament of 1567, namely the belief that the Elizabethan Reformation was a revival of the scriptural purity of the early Celtic Church. See Glanmor Williams, *Welsh Reformation Essays* (Cardiff, 1967), 183–5, 207–17.

2. The modern spelling is 'bendith y mamau', i.e., 'mothers' blessing', one of the Welsh names for 'fairies'.
3. The modern spelling is 'bendith eu mamau iddynt', i.e., 'mothers' blessing upon them'. It must be admitted that Penry's reasoning is obscure.
4. The modern spelling is 'Ni waeth gennyf am y Tad, y gŵr creulon hynny, ond cydymaith da yw'r Mab'. Penry translates the phrase in the following sentence.
5. The modern spelling is 'gwŷr cig Duw', i.e., 'God's meat men'. Again the allusion is obscure.

Document I.17

John Penry before the High Commission

The House of Commons was in session from 15 February to 23 March 1587. The debate on the *Aequity* took place on 28 February and was opened by Edward Donne Lee and he was supported by Job Throckmorton. Immediately afterwards the book was called in by order of John Whitgift, the archbishop of Canterbury. The wardens of the Stationers' Company, Bishop and Henry Denham, then seized Penry and 500 copies of the book. Penry was immediately examined by the High Commission. The first account of this examination appeared in Marprelate's *Epistle* which was issued on 15 October 1588. Penry's own account was published later, in *Th'Appellation of Iohn Penri vnto the Highe Court of Parliament* which was issued on 7 March 1589.

The extracts are as follows.

(a) *Epistle*, 29–30; reproduced in W. Pierce (ed.), *The Marprelate Tracts* (London, 1911), 65–6.

'His Grace' was John Whitgift, archbishop of Canterbury from 1583 until his death in 1604. 'Thomas of Winchester' was Thomas Cooper (1517?–94) who was translated from Lincoln to Winchester in 1584. He attacked Martin Marprelate in his *Admonition to the People of England* (London, 1589) and Martin replied in *Hay any Worke for Cooper* (n.p. [but Coventry], n.d. [but March 1589]). 'John of London' was the irascible and resentful John Aylmer (1521–94), bishop of London from 1567 until his death. He was the target for some of Marprelate's most vicious witticisms. For Cooper and Aylmer, v., DNB.

(b) *Th'Appellation of Iohn Penri* (1588), 3–6, 39–40, 42–3. This document reveals why the truculence and the arrogance of the High Commission aroused such hatred amongst the Puritans, as they did amongst many outside the ranks of the Puritans. The Long Parliament abolished it under the provisions of the Star Chamber Act of 1641. Critics of the High Commission refrained from attacking the High Commission itself because that would have meant questioning the authority of the queen and the statute and so they concentrated on its procedures, as Penry does here. The *ex officio* oath, which enabled certain stated officials to proceed without a specific indictment, was felt to be offensive because, as Penry says, it bound a defendant to answer any questions a tribunal chose to ask until he divulged some information that would incriminate him. If the defendant declined to take the oath, the proceedings were at a standstill and the only course left open to the court was to imprison him for contempt. For the constitutional implications, v., G. R. Elton, *The Tudor Constitution* (Cambridge, 1968), 217–27. See also, R. G. Usher, *The Rise and Fall of the High Commission* (Oxford, 1913) and M. R. Watts, *The Dissenters* (Oxford, 1978), I, 38–9.

(a)
John Penry, the Welshman – I think his Grace and my brother London would be better acquainted with him and they could tell how – about the beginning of Lent, 1587, offered a supplication and a book to the Parliament, entreating that some order might be taken for calling his country to the knowledge of God. For his bold attempt he was called before his Grace, with other of the High Commission – as Thomas of Winchester, John London, &c. After that his Grace has eased his stomach in calling him 'boy', 'knave', 'varlet', 'slanderer', 'libeller', 'lewd boy', 'lewd slanderer', &c. (this is *true*, for I have seen the notes of their conference), at the length, a point of his book began to be examined where nonresidents are thought intolerable. Here the Lord of good London asked Master Penry what he could say against that kind of cattle. Answer was made that they were odious in the sight of God and man, because as much as in them lie, they bereave people over whom they thrust themselves, of the ordinary means of salvation, which was the Word preached. John London demanded whether preaching was the only means to salvation. Penry answered, that it was the only ordinary means, although the Lord was not so tied unto it, but that He could extraordinarily use other means. That preaching was 'the only ordinary means; he confirmed it by those places of Scripture – Rom.10.14, I Cor.1.21, Ephes.1.18. This point being a long time canvassed, at the length his Worship of Winchester rose up and mildly, after his manner, brast [burst] forth into these words: 'I assure you, my Lords, it is an execrable heresy'. 'An heresy' quoth Penry, 'that I thank God that ever I knew that heresy. It is such an heresy, that I will, by the grace of God, sooner leave my life than I will leave it.' 'What, sir!' quoth the Archbishop. 'I tell thee it is an heresy, and thou shalt recant it as an heresy.' 'Nay,' quoth Penry, 'never so long as I live, God willing'.

(b)
And to the ende that I may truely acquaint you of the parliament with my troubles, and the true causes thereof, you are to vnderstand, that the beginning of these mens hatred towards me, did arise from the goodwill I beare vnto the glory of my God and the good of his church, and that the continuance thereof, is for the same cause. For vntill such time, as the Lord vouchsafed to vse me ... as an instrument to motion the parliament, holden by prorogation in the 29. yere of her Majesties raigne,[1] in the cause of Gods truth, I was a man altogether vnknowne vnto th'Archb. or any other of the high commission, by whome I am now persecuted. My suite then vnto the parliament was, that the gospell of Christ might in a sauing measure, be made knowen and published amongst the inhabitants of wales my deare and natiue countrimen. The equitie of this petition, I manifested in a published treatise allowed to be printed by publike authority.[2] The supplication, together with the printed treatise, were preferred by a worshipfull gentleman of my countrie, being himself a member of the howse, who shewed the equitie of the petition, and in effect auouched the truth of that which in the treatise was set downe.[3]

The suit I was perswaded, would haue beene verie plausible in a christian state, and the parliament shewed no dislyking thereof, though they sinned in the carelesse respect they had therevnto. Th'Archb. and his associates were contrarie minded, they thought the enterprise to be intollerable. And yet was there no alteration of the established gouernment of Bishops at that time sought for. The dislike of the petition they did not conceal, and therfore presently dispatched their warrants to call in the printed bookes, and to enquire for the author. The books in nomber about 500. togither with my selfe, were fastened vpon by the wardens of the Stacioners,[4] Master Bishop and Denham accompanied with Cole the Pursiuaunt, wherevpon being carried before the high commissioners, I was for enterprising the former action, charged by th'Archb. owne mouth, not onely to be a factious slaunderer of her Majesties gouernment: but also to haue published flat treason and heresie in my saide treatise. I was threatned very bloodily, and reuiled vpon in a most vnchristian sort, with earnest protestation, that they woondered how I durst sollicite the parliament in that petition ...

Well, mine offence in presuming to speake in the cause of God, oppugned by my betters, was accounted so haynous, as in close prison I must be kept 12. daies, at the keepers vttermost perill. Before my departure from the commision, vnderstanding their intent to commit me, I demanded the particuler cause why I was so hardlie dealt with. Answere was made, that they would examine me again and then I should know. After a moneths imprisonment I was deliuered without anie examination, or anye mention of the crimes of heresie and treason wherewith I had bene charged. And so vnto this daie, I remaine ignorant of anie expressed cause wherefore, they either tooke away my books, or debarred me of my libertie ...

What hath the high commission to doe, with men suspected of treason? Is the place at Lambeth now become the palor,[5] where traitors should be arraigned? The Archbishop of Canterbury, the bishops of London, Winchester, Doctor Cosin &c.,[6] now become judges in those causes? Whether they incurr not the danger of lawe, by entering into such matters, as are not within the compass of their commission, you of this honorable assembly[7] are best able to judge ... Tollerate this course, and what parloure or chamber may there be so priuate, wherein the Archbishop and his assistants wil not arraigne their seditious traitors as they faulsly account them ...

The injury which at that time they offered vnto the liberties of this honourable court,[8] (to commit their tiranny to me wards) had not bene so intollerable vnless they, who vsurped vnto them selues the deciding of my cause, had bene al of them members of this house. The persons then in commission were these. Th'Archb. of Cant. Bp. of London, Winchester and Lincoln: Doctor Lewine, Doctor Coosins,[9] all parliament men at that instant. Now judge whether it be not against all right, that some fewe of the inferiour members in that house ... should extort vnto their priuate censure, the judgement of a cause preferred publikely vnto the whole parliament ...

And yet all the justice that poore christians haue at Lambeth is this. 'You are now sent for by Lords grace here, and vs her Majesties commissioners, we grant indeed, that as yet we know nothing wherewith you may be charged ... And therefore you must here be deposed vpon your oath, to reueal whatsoeuer you know by your selfe, or any other of Gods children her Majesties subjects. Whereby it shall come to passe, that you shall escape vs narrowly, but ere you depart the court, we shall finde sufficient matter to imprison you, and if you refuse the oath, to prison you shall goe. For we administer it, Ex officio, and so vpon your refusall, we may imprison you.'

And will the high court of parliament suffer this bloodie and tirannous inquisition to be practized any longer within this kingdom? What can the murthering inquisitors of Spaine do more, then by this snare, inueigle mens consciences, and constraine them to spill their owne blood?

Notes

1. Strictly it was by adjournment from 15 February to 23 March 1587.
2. i.e., his *Aequity*.
3. This was Edward Donne Lee (d. 1598) of Abercynfor, Llandyfaelog, Carmarthenshire. His name is variously spelled, Downlee, Dounlee. He was the son of Ralph Lee of Saunderton, Bucks, by Frances, daughter of Sir Thomas Jones of Abermarlais. Edward entered Parliament in 1584 and represented the town of Carmarthen. He opened the debate on Penry's *Aequity* on 28 February 1587. His boldness led to his removal from the commission of the peace but it is noteworthy that the Privy Council in 1592 ordered Donne Lee and seven others to attempt the correction in Pembrokeshire of precisely the abuses that he had mentioned in his speech in the Commons, v., *Acts of the Privy Council*, XXII (HMSO, 1901), 544–5; also P. W. Hasler (ed.), *The History of Parliament: The House of Commons, 1558–1603*, (HMSO, 1981), II, Members, D-L, 48.
4. The Stationers' Company.
5. i.e., bar.
6. Richard Cosin (1549?–97) was a civil lawyer (LL.D., 1580); amongst the many positions he held were chancellor of the diocese of Worcester, 1583; Dean of Arches and vicar-general of the province of Canterbury, 1583; MP for various constituencies since October 1586, v., DNB.
7. i.e., Parliament.
8. i.e., Parliament.
9. i.e., Whitgift, Cooper and Wickham. William Wickham (1639–95) followed Cooper at the diocese of Lincoln in November 1584. He was one of Marprelate's targets, v., W. Pierce, *The Marprelate Tracts* (London, 1911), 23; 95 (a reference to his funeral sermon for Mary, Queen of Scots); 117, 230, 416. See DNB under Wykeham, William. William Lewin (d. 1598) was a civil lawyer with a high reputation for probity. He was Judge of the Prerogative Court of Canterbury from 1576 as well as chancellor of the diocese of Rochester and an MP from 1586, v., DNB.

PART II

PERSEVERANCE, 1604–1642

Document II.1

The Millenary Petition and the Hampton Court Conference

Thomas Fuller in *The Church History of Great Britain*, first published in 1655, provides a vivid account of the attempts of the Puritans to persuade King James I, on his accession to the English throne in 1603, to support their demands for changes in the liturgy, discipline and ceremonies of the Church of England. The first published account of the conference was *The Summe and Substance of the Conference at Hampton Court* (1604) by William Barlow, bishop of Lincoln. For Arthur Hildersham (1563–1632) and Stephen Egerton (1555?–1621?), v., DNB.

And now, because there was a general expectation of a parliament suddenly to succeed, the presbyterian party, that they might not be surprised before they had their tackling about them, went about to get hands of the ministers to a petition, which they intended seasonably to present to the king and parliament. Mr. Arthur Hildersham, and Mr. Stephen Egerton, with some others, were chosen, and chiefly intrusted to manage this important business. This was called 'the Millenary Petition', as *one of a thousand*; though indeed there were but seven hundred and fifty preachers' hands set thereunto; but those all collected only out of five-and-twenty counties. However, for the more rotundity of the number, and grace of the matter, it passeth for a full thousand; which, no doubt, the collectors of the names (if so pleased) might easily have completed. I dare not guess what made them desist before their number was finished; whether they thought that these were enough to do the deed, and more were rather for ostentation than use; or, because disheartened by the intervening of the Hampton Court Conference, they thought that these were even too many to petition for a denial. It is left as yet uncertain, whether this Conference was by the king's favour graciously tendered; or by the mediation of the lords of his Council, powerfully procured; or by the bishops, as confident of their cause, voluntarily proffered; or by the ministers' importunity, effectually obtained ...

The Millenary Petition

THE HUMBLE PETITION OF THE MINISTERS OF THE CHURCH OF ENGLAND, DESIRING REFORMATION OF CERTAIN CEREMONIES AND ABUSES OF THE CHURCH.

What is most striking about this petition is the absence of any reference to episcopacy. At the same time it provides a succinct presentation of the aspects of church life, ministry and liturgy which pressed most urgently on the consciences of those nonconforming ministers who wished to remain within the Church of England. The reforms suggested in the petition were moderate enough. King James, however, was in no mood to endorse their demands. This became obvious enough in the conference which the petitioners had asked for and which was held at Hampton Court Palace on 14, 16 and 18 January 1604. The defenders of conformity were a formidable group.

They were John Whitgift (1530?–1604), archbishop of Canterbury, Richard Bancroft (1544–1610), bishop of London, Tobie Matthew (1546–1628), bishop of Durham, Thomas Bilson (1547?–1616), bishop of Winchester, Henry Robinson (1553–1616), bishop of Carlisle, John Dove (1561–1618), bishop of Peterborough, Lancelot Andrews (1555–1626), dean of Westminster, John Overall (1560–1619), dean of St. Paul's, William Barlow (d. 1613), dean of Chester, John Bridges (d. 1618), dean of Salisbury, together with Dr. Richard Field (1561–1616) of Windsor, a royal chaplain, and Dr. John King (1559?–1621), later bishop of London. Those chosen by the King to present the case for changes were John Rainolds (or Reynolds, 1549–1607), President of Corpus Christi College, Oxford, Thomas Sparke (1548–1616), rector of Bletchley, Bucks. (who, according to Antony Wood did not speak a word at the conference), John Knewstubs (1544–1624), rector of Cockfield, Suffolk, and Laurence Chaderton (1536? 1640), Master of Emmanuel College, Cambridge (all these are in DNB). The Moderator of the Conference was King James. The chief spokesman for the Nonconformists was Rainolds, but he and his colleagues were not invited to take part in the first session. Extracts (a) to (f) provide a taste of the way in which the discussion was conducted. The Geneva Bible (extract b) was published in 1560 and was the work of a committee of exiles who had fled from the persecution under Mary Tudor. It was highly esteemed by Puritans of all kinds. The most significant outcome of the Hampton Court Conference was the preparation of the 'Authorised Version' of 1611, a version in the production of which Reynolds played a prominent part. The Regent of Scotland, 1554–59 (extract (f)), was Mary of Guise (1516–60), the mother of Mary Queen of Scots, King James's mother. For her, v., article in the *Dictionary of Scottish Church History and Theology* (Edinburgh, 1993) and the bibliography appended to it for the events to which King James alludes.

The text is in *The Church History of Great Britain* (London, 1868 edition), III, 215–17.

To the most Christian and excellent prince, our gracious and dread sovereign, James, by the grace of God &c. We, the ministers of the church of England that desire reformation, wish a long, prosperous, and happy reign over us in this life, and in the next everlasting salvation.

Most gracious and dread sovereign, seeing it hath pleased the Divine Majesty, to the great comfort of all good Christians, to advance your Highness, according to your just title, to the peaceable government of this church and commonwealth of England; we, the ministers of the gospel in this land, neither as factious men affecting a popular party in the church, nor as schismatics aiming at the dissolution of the state ecclesiastical; but as the faithful servants of Christ, and loyal subjects to your Majesty, desiring and longing for the redress of divers abuses of the church, could do no less, in our obedience to God, service to your Majesty, love to his church, than acquaint your princely Majesty with our particular griefs. For, as your princely pen writeth, 'The king, as a good physician, must first know what peccant humours his patient naturally is most subject unto, before he can begin his cure.' And, although divers of us that sue for reformation have formerly, in respect of the times, subscribed to the Book, some upon protestation, some upon exposition given them, some with condition, rather than the church should have been deprived of their labour and ministry; yet now, we, to the number of more than a thousand, of your Majesty's subjects and ministers, all groaning as under a common burden of human rites and ceremonies, do, with one joint consent, humble ourselves at your Majesty's feet to be eased and relieved in this behalf. Our humble suit, then, unto your Majesty is, that [of] these offences following, some may be removed, some amended, some qualified:-

I. *In the church-service.* – That the Cross in baptism, interrogatories ministered to infants, Confirmation, as superfluous, may be taken away: baptism not to be ministered by women, and so explained: the cap and surplice not urged; that examination may go before communion: that it be administered with a sermon; that divers terms of *priests* and *absolution*, and some other used, with the ring in marriage, and other such like in the Book, may be corrected: : the longsomeness of service abridged: church-songs and music moderated to better edification: that the Lord's day be not profaned, the rest upon holy-days not so strictly urged: that there may be uniformity of doctrine prescribed: no popish opinion to be any more taught or defended: no ministers charged to teach their people to bow at the name of Jesus: that the canonical scriptures only be read in the church.

II. *Concerning church-ministers.* – That none hereafter be admitted into the ministry but able and sufficient men; and those to preach diligently, and especially upon the Lord's day: that such as be already entered, and cannot preach, may either be removed, and some charitable course taken with them for their relief; or else to be forced, according to the value of their livings, to maintain preachers: and that non-residency be not permitted: that King Edward's statute for the lawfulness of ministers' marriage be revived: that ministers be not urged to subscribe but, according to the law, to the Articles of Religion, and the king's supremacy only.

III. *For church-livings and maintenance.* – That bishops leave their commendams; some holding prebends, some parsonages, some vacarages with their bishoprics: that double-beneficed men be not suffered to hold, some two, some three benefices with cure, and some two, three, or four dignities besides: that impropriations annexed to bishoprics and colleges be demised only to the preachers-incumbents, for the old rent: that the impropriations of laymen's fees may be charged with a sixth or seventh part of the worth, to the maintenance of the preaching minister.

IV. *For church-discipline.* – That the discipline and excommunication may be administered according to Christ's own institution; or, at the least, that enormities be redressed: as, namely, that excommunication come not forth under the name of lay persons, chancellors, officials &c.; that men be not excommunicated for trifles, and twelve-penny matters: that none be excommunicated without consent of his pastor: that the officers be not suffered to extort unreasonable fees: that none having jurisdiction, or registers' places, put out the same to farm; that divers popish canons (or for restraint of marriage at certain times) be reversed; that the longsomeness of suits in ecclesiastical courts, which hang sometimes two, three, four, five, six, or seven years, may be retrained: that the oath *ex officio*, whereby men are forced to accuse themselves, be more sparingly used: that licences for marriage, without bans asked, be more cautiously granted.

These, with such other abuses yet remaining, and practised in the church of

England, we are able to show not to be agreeable to the scriptures, if it shall please your Highness farther to hear us, or more at large by writing to be informed, or by conference among the learned to be resolved. And yet we doubt not but that, without any farther process, your Majesty, of whose Christian judgment we have received so good a taste already, is able of yourself to judge of the equity of this cause. God, we trust, hath appointed your Highness to heal these diseases. And we say with Mordecai to Esther, 'Who knoweth, whether you are come to the kingdom for such a time?' Thus your majesty shall do that which, we are persuaded, shall be acceptable to God; honourable to your Majesty in all succeeding ages; profitable to his church, which shall thereby be increased; comfortable to your ministers, who shall be no more suspended, silenced, disgraced, imprisoned for men's traditions; and prejudicial to none, but to those that seek their own quiet, credit, and profit in the world. Thus, with all dutiful submission, referring ourselves to your Majesty's pleasure for your gracious answer, as God shall direct you; we most humbly recommend your Highness to the Divine Majesty; whom we beseech for Christ's sake to dispose your royal heart to do herein what shall be to his glory, the good of his church, and your endless comfort.

Your Majesty's most humble subjects, the ministers of the gospel, that desire not a disorderly innovation, but a due and godly reformation.

(a) From the Second Day's Conference, 16 January

Bishop of London. – May your Majesty be pleased, that the ancient canon may be remembered, – *Schismatici contra episcopes non sunt audiendi*. And, there is another decree of a very ancient council, – that no man should be admitted to speak against that whereunto he hath formerly subscribed. And as for you Dr. Reynolds, and your sociates, how much are ye bound to his Majesty's clemency, permitting you, contrary to the statute *primo Elizabethae*, so freely to speak against the Liturgy and discipline established! Fain would I know the end you aim at, and whether you be not of Mr.Cartwright's mind, who affirmed, that we ought in ceremonies rather to conform to the Turks than to the papists. I doubt you approve his position, because here appearing before his Majesty in Turkey-gowns, not in your scholastic habits, according to the order of the universities.

[The Latin phrase means, 'Schismatics are not to be heard against bishops'. Thomas Cartwright (1535–1603) was the leading exponent of the Presbyterian form of church government.]

His Majesty. – Mt lord bishop, something in your passion I may excuse, and something I must mislike. I may excuse you thus far, – that I think you have just cause to be moved, in respect that they traduce the well-settled government, and also proceed in so indirect a course, contrary to their own pretence, and the intent of this meeting. I mislike your sudden interruption of Dr. Reynolds, who you should have suffered to have taken his liberty; for there is no order, nor can be any effectual issue, of disputation, if each party be not suffered, without chopping, to speak at large. Wherefore, either let the Doctor proceed, or frame your answer to his motion already made, although some of them are very needless.

(b) A New Translation of the Bible

Dr. Reynolds. – May your Majesty be pleased that the Bible be new translated, such as are extant not answering to the original ...

Bishop of London. – If every man's humour might be followed, there would be no end of translating.

His Majesty. – I profess I could never yet see a Bible well translated in English; but I think that, of all, that of Geneva is the worst. I wish some special pains were taken for a uniform translation; which should be done by the best-learned in both universities, then reviewed by the bishops, presented to the Privy Council, lastly, ratified by royal authority, to be read in the whole church, and no other.

Bishop of London. – But it is fit that no marginal notes should be added thereunto.

His Majesty. – That caveat is well put in; for in the Geneva translation, some notes are partial, untrue, seditious, and savouring of traitorous conceits: as when from Exodus i.19, disobedience to kings is allowed in a marginal note; and, 2 Chron. xv.16, King Asa taxed in the note for only *deposing* his mother for idolatry, and not *killing* her. To conclude this point: let errors in the matter of faith be amended, and indifferent things be interpreted, and a gloss added unto them ...

(c) Ecclesiastical Dress

Mr. Knewstubs. – I take exception to the wearing of the Surplice, a kind of garment used by the priests of Isis.

His Majesty. – I did not think until of late, it had been borrowed from the Heathen, because commonly called 'a rag of popery'. Seeing now we border not upon Heathens, neither are any of them conversant with or commorant amongst us, thereby to be confirmed in Paganism; I see no reason but for comeliness-sake it may be continued.

(d) Wedding Ceremony

Dr. Reynolds. – I take exception at these words in the marriage, 'With my body I thee worship.'

His Majesty. – I was made believe, the phrase imported no less than Divine adoration, but find it an usual English term; as when we say 'a gentleman of worship'; and it agreeth with the scriptures, 'giving honour to the wife'. As for you, Dr. Reynolds, (this the king spake smiling,) many men speak of Robin Hood, who never shot in his bow: If you had a good wife yourself, you would think all worship and honour you could do her were well bestowed on her.

Dean of Sarum. – Some take exception at the ring in marriage.

Dr. Reynolds. – I approve it well enough.

His Majesty. – I was married with a ring, and think others scarce well married without it.

(e) Clerical Meetings

Dr. Reynolds. – I desire, that, according to certain provincial constitutions, the clergy may have meetings every three weeks:-
(1) First, in rural deaneries, therein to have prophesyings, as Archbishop Grindal and other bishops desired of her late Majesty.
(2) That such things as could not be resolved on there, might be referred to the archdeacons' visitations.
(3) And so to the episcopal synod, to determine such points before not decided.

His Majesty. – If you aim at a Scottish presbytery, it agreeth as well with monarchy, as God and the devil. Then Jack, and Tom, and Will, and Dick shall meet and censure me and my Council. Therefore I reiterate my former speech, *Le roy s'avisera*. Stay, I pray, for one seven years, before you demand; and then if you find me grow pursy and fat, I may, perchance hearken unto you; for that government will keep me in breath, and give me work enough ...

[The French phrase means 'The King himself will see to it'.]

(f) The Royal Supremacy

His Majesty ... Dr. Reynolds, you have often spoken for my supremacy, and it is well. But know you any here or elsewhere, who like of the present government ecclesiastical, and dislike my supremacy?

Dr. Reynolds. – I know none.

His Majesty. – Why, then, I will tell you a tale: After that the religion restored by King Edward VI was soon overthrown by Queen Mary here in England, we in Scotland felt the effect of it. For, thereupon, Mr. Knox writes to the queen regent, a vituous and moderate lady; telling her, that she was the supreme head of the church, and charged her, as she would answer it at God's tribunal, to take care of Christ's Evangel, in suppressing the popish prelates, who withstood the same. But how long, trow you, did this continue? Even till, by her authority, the popish bishops were repressed, and Knox, with his adherents, being brought in, made strong enough.Then began they to make small account of her supremacy, when, according to that *more light* wherewith they were illuminated, they made a farther reformation of themselves. How they used the poor lady my mother, is not unknown, and how they dealt with me in my minority. I thus apply it: my lords the bishops, (this he said, putting his hand to his hat,) I may thank you that these men plead thus for my supremacy. They think they cannot make their party good against you, but by appealing unto it. But if once you were out and they in, I know what would become of my supremacy: for, 'No bishop, no king!' I have learnt of what cut they have been, who, preaching before me since my coming into England, passed over, with silence, my being supreme governor in causes ecclesiastical. Well, doctor, have you anything else to say?

Dr. Reynolds. – No more, if it please your Majesty.

His Majesty. – If this be all your party hath to say, I will make them conform themselves, or else I will harry them out of the land, or else do worse.

Document II.2

William Bradshaw: English Puritanism

English Pvritanisme was first published in 1605. It is from that edition that the following excerpts are taken. The author lists the convictions of those whom he describes as 'the rigidest sort of those that are called Puritanes'. This succinct and lively document is reproduced with all the printer's vagaries of spelling and punctuation. R. C. Simmons has produced a facsimile reprint of this tract and five others with a helpful introduction (Farnborough: Gregg International Publishers, 1972). That publication also includes the 1640 edition of *English Puritanisme* which was attributed (wrongly) to William Ames by the unknown editor who, as Simmons explains, made several changes, some of which are significant. William Bradshaw (1571–1618) is noticed at length by Alexander Gordon in DNB. In addition to the bibliography appended to that article, reference should be made to G. F. Nuttall's comments in *Visible Saints* (Oxford, 1957), 9–11, P. Collinson, *The Elizabethan Puritan Movement* (London, 1967), 433 and Perry Miller, *Orthodoxy in Massachusetts, 1630–50* (Cambridge, Mass., 1933), 81. Bradshaw was no Separatist although a pronounced Nonconformist on several points. He argued for the independence of each congregation and for the overthrow of the episcopal system. He was a close friend of Thomas Cartwright but only in his suggestions about the internal government of the congregation did he adopt any presbyterian principles. Not the least interesting section of his tract is his treatment of church censures where he enables us to understand why the ecclesiastical courts offended the Puritans.

Chap. 1 Concerning Religion or the worship of God in generall.

Imprimis, They hould and mainetaine that the word of God contained in the writings of the Prophets and Apostles, is of absolute perfection, giuen by Christ the head of the Churche, to bee vnto the same, the sole Canon and rule of all matters of Religion, and the worship and seruice of God whatsoeuer. And that whatsoeuer done in the same seruice and worship cannot bee iustified by the said word, is vnlawfull. And therfore that it is a sinne, to force any Christian to doe any act of religion or diuine seruice, that cannot evidently bee warranted by the same.

2 They hould that all Ecclesiasticall actions invented & deuised by man, are vtterlie to bee excluded out of the exercises of religion? Especially such actions as are famous and notorious mysteries of an Idolatrous Religion, and in doeing whereof, the true religion is conformed (whether in whol or in part) to Idolatrie and superstition ...

Chap. 2 Concernyng the Church.

1 They hould and maintaine that euery Companie, Congregation or Assemblie of men, ordinarlilie ioyneing together in the true worship of God, is a true visible church of Christ. and that the same title is improperlie attributed to any other Conuocations, Synods Societies, combinations, or assemblies whatsoeuer.

2 They hould that all such Churches or Congregations, communicating after that manner together, in diuine worship are in all Ecclesiasticall matters equall, and of the same power and authoritie, and that by the word and will of God they ought to haue the same spirituall priuilidges, prerogatius, officers, administrations, orders, and Formes of divine worship.

3 They hould that Christ Iesus hath not subiected any Church or Congregation of his, to any other superior Ecclesiasticall Iurisdiction, then vnto that which is within it self So that yf a wholl Churche or Congregation shall erre, in any matters of faith or religion, noe other Churches or Spirituall Church officers haue (by any warrant from the word of God) power to censure, punish, or controule the same: but are onely to counsell and aduise the same, and so to leaue their Soules to the immediate Iudgment of Christ, and their bodies to the sword & power of the Ciuill Magistrat, who alone vpon Earth hath power to punish a whol Church or Congregation ...

5 They hould that every established Church ought (as a speciall prerogative wherewith shee is endowed by Christ) to haue power and libertie to elect & chuse their owne Spirituall and Ecclesiasticall Officers, and that it is a greater wrong to haue any such forced vpon them against their wills, then if they should force vpon men wiues, or vpon weomen husbands against their will and likeing.

6 They hould that if in this choyse any perticular Churches shall erre, that none vpon Earth but the Civill Magistrate hath power to controule or correct them for it, And that though it be not lawfull for him to take away this power from them, Yet when they or any of them, shall apparently abuse the same, he stands bound by the Lawe of God, and by virtue of his Office (grounded vpon the same) to ounish them severely for it, & to force them vnder Civill mulcts to make better choyse.

7 They hould that the Ecclesiasticall Officers and Ministers of one Church, ought not to beare any Ecclesiasticall office in another, but ought to be tied vnto that Congregation of which they are members, and by which they are elected into Office ...

9 They hould that though one Church is not to differ from another in any Spirituall, Ecclesiasticall, or Religious matters whatsoever, but are to be equall and alike. Yet that they may differ and one excell another in outward Civill circumstaunces, of place, time, Person &c. So that although they hould that those Congregations of which Kings and Nobles make themselues members, ought to haue the same Ecclesiasticall Officers, Ministrie, worship, Sacraments, Ceremonies: and forme of worship, that the basest Congregation in the cuntry hath. And no other. Yet they hould also: That as their Persons in Ciuill respects excell, So in the exercises of religion in civill matters they may excel other assemblies.

Their Chappels, and Seats may be gorgeously sett forth with rich Arrace and Tapestrie, Their Fonts may be of Silver. Their Communion Tables of Ivorie & if they will covered with gould. The Cup out of which they drinke the Sacramentall blood of Christ may be of beaten gould sett about with Diamionds. Their Ministers may be clothed in silke & velvet, so themselues will maintaine them in that manner, other wise, they think it absurd and against commen reason, that other base and inferior Congregations muct by Ecclesiasticall Tithes, and Oblations maintaine, the silken and velvet suites & Lordly retinue of the Ministers and Ecclesiasticall Officers of Princes and Nobles ...

11 They hould and beleue that the equalitie in Ecclesiastical Iurisdiction & authoritie, of Churches and Church Ministers, is no more derogatorie and repugnaunt to the State and glorie of a Monarche, then the Paritie or equalitie of Schoolmasters, of severall Schooles, Captaines of severall Camps, Shepheards of severall stocks of Sheep, or Masters of severall Families ...

Chap. 3 Concerning the Ministers of the word.

1 They hould that the Pastors of particular Congregations are, or ought to be the highest Spirituall Officers in the Church, over whom, (by any Divine Ordinaunce) ther is noe superior Pastor but onely Iesus Christ, And that they are led by the spirit of Antichrist, that arrogate or take vpon themselues to be Pastors of Pastors.

2 They hould, that there are not by ant divine Institution in the word, any ordinarie Nationall, Provinciall, or Diocesan Pastors or Ministers vnder which the Pastors of perticular Congregation are to be suiect, as Inferior Officers. And that if ther were any such, that then the word of God would haue sett them downe more distinctly and precisly then any of the rest ...

5 They hould That no Pastor ought to exercise or accept of any Civilll publique Iurisdiction & authoritie, but ought to be wholly imployed in spirituall Offices & duties to that Congregation over which he is set ...

6 They hould that the highest and supreame office and authorities of the Pastor, is to preach the gospell solemnly and publickly to the Congregation, by interpreting the written word of God, and applying the same by exhortation and reproofe unto them ...

7 They hould that the Pastor or Minister of the word, is not to teach any Doctrine unto the church, grounded vpon his owne Iudgment or opinion, or upon the Iudgment or opinion of any or all the men in the world. But onely that truth, that he is able to demonstrate and proue evidently, and apparently, by the word of God soundly interpreted ...

9 They hould that the people of God ought not to acknowledge any such for their Pastors as are not able by preaching, to interpret and apply the word of God unto them ... And therfore that no ignorant, & sole reading Preists are to be reputed the ministers of Iesus Christ, who sendeth none into his ministrie and service, but such as he adorneth in some measure with spirituall guifts ...

13 They hould that by Gods Ordinance ther should be also in euery church a

Doctor whose spetiall office should be to instruct by way of Cathechizing the ignorant of the Congregation (& that perticularly) in the maine grounds & principles of Religion.

Chap. 4 Concerning the Elders.

1 For as much as through the mallice of Sathan, there are and wilbe in the best Churches many disorders and Scandalls committed, that redound to the reproch of the gospell & are a stumbling block to many both without & within the church, & sith they iudge it repugnant to the word of God, that any Minister should be a Sole Ruler and as it were a Pope so much as in one Parrish, (much more that he should be one ouer a wholl Diocess, Prouince or Nation) they hould that by Gods Ordinance the Congregaion should make choise of other officers, as Assistants vnto the Ministers in the spirituall regiment of the Congregation who are by Office iointly with the Ministers of the word to be as Monitors & Ouerseers of the manners & Conuersation of all the Congregation, & one of another ...

2 They hould that such only are to be chosen to this Office, as are the Grauest, Honestest, Discreetest, best grounded in Religion ... and such also (If it bee possible) as are of ciuill note and respect in the world, and able (with out any burden to the Church) to maintaine themselues, either by their Lands, or any other honest Ciuill Trade of life. nether doe they think it so much disgrace to the policie of the Church, that Tradsmen & artifficers, (indowed with such quallities as are above specified) should be admitted to bee Ouerseers of the Church ...

Chap. 5 Concerninge the Censures of the church.

1 They hould that the spirituall keyes of the Church are by Christ, committed to the aforesaid spirituall Officers and Gouernors, and vnto none other: which keyes they hould that they are not to be put to this vse, to lock vp the Crownes, Swords or Scepters, of Princes & ciuill States, or the ciuill Rightes prerogatiues, and immvnities, of ciuill subiects in the things of this Life, or to vse them as picklocks to open withall, mens Tresuries and Coffers, or as keyes of Prisons, to shut vp the bodies of men, for they think that such power & authority Ecclesiastical is fit for the Antichrist of Rome ...

2 They hould that by vertue of these Keyes, they are not to make any curious Inquisitions into the secreat or hidden vices or crimes of men, extorting from them a confession of those faults that are consealed from themselues and others: or to proceed to molest any man vpon secreat suggestions, priuat suspition, or vncertaine fame, or for such crimes as are in question whether they bee crimes or noe; But they are to proceed, only against evident and apparent crimes, such as are either graunted to be such of all civill honest men: or of all true Christians, or at least such, as they are able, by evidence of the word of God, to convince to bee sinnes, to the conscience of the offendor ...

3 They hould that when he that hath committed a scandalous crime commeth before them and is convinced of the same, they ought not (after the manner of our

ecclesiasticall Courtes) scorne, deride, taunt and revile him, with odious and contumelious speeches, Eye him with bigg and sterne lookes, procuer proctors to make Personall Invectiues against him, make him daunce attendance from Court day to Court day, and from terme to terms, frounyng at him in presence, & laughing at him behind his backe: but they are (though he be never so obstinate and perverse) to vse him brotherly, not giwuinge the least personall reproches, or threates, (but layinge open vnto him the nature of his sinne by the light of Gods word) are onely by denouncyng the iudgments of God against him, to terrifie him, and so to moue him to repentance.

4 They hould that if the partie offending be their civill Superior, that then they are to vse even throughout the whol cariadge of their censure, all civill complements Offices and Reverence due vnto him ... And if he be a King and Supreame Ruler, they are to kneele downe before him, and in the humblest manner to Censure his faults ...

Chap. 6 Concernyng the Civill Magistrate.

They hould that the Civill Magistrate as he is a Civill Magistrate hath and ought to haue Supreame power over all the Churches within his Dominions, in all causes whatsoever ...

6 They hould that all Arch Bishops, Bishops, Deanes, Officialls &c. have their Offices & Functions only by will & pleasure of the King and civill States of this Realme, and they hould that whosoever holdeth that the King may not without sinne remoue these Offices out of the Church, and dispose of their Temporalities and maintenaunce according to his pleasure, or that these Offices are Iure divino ... That all such deny a principall part of the Kings Supremacie.

Document II.3

Henry Jacob: The Nature of the Church

Henry Jacob, a native of Kent educated at Oxford, was born about 1563. He was ordained and served the parish of Cheriton, Kent, but in 1605 became minister at Middelburg. From 1610 to 1616 he was minister at Leyden but returned to England in 1616 to form a church at Southwark. In 1624 he emigrated to America and no more is known of him. His views changed over the years and the above extracts illustrate his mature views. He held a moderate view which acknowledged the self-government of individual congregations, while admitting that there were true Christians in the Church of England despite what he understood as the unscriptural features of the Church's government and he was supported in this respect by the likes of Robert Parker, William Bradshaw, Paul Baynes and William Ames. The most appropriate label for his position has been the subject of debate and for the details, v., M. R. Watts, *The Dissenters* (Oxford, 1978), I, 51–3 and G. F. Nuttall, *Visible Saints* (Oxford, 1957), 9–10 and the sources to which they refer. See also R. W. Dale, *History of English Congregationalism* (London, 1907), 213–18 and Christopher Damp, 'The

Development of Henry Jacob's Ecclesiology', *Congregational History Circle*, 3: 5 (Spring 1887), 15–32. The title of the 'little printed booke' to which Jacob refers on p. 8 of his preface was, *A Christian and Modest Offer of a most Indifferent Conference, or Disputation, about the maine and principall Controveries between the Prelats and the late silenced and deprived ministers to the Archbishops and Bishops, and all their adherents ... (1606).* He had been extremely active in promoting petitions to James I at his accession to protest against the oppression suffered by Puritans. The best-known of these was the Millenary Petition. The following extracts are taken from *The True Beginning and Institution of Christ's True Visible or Ministeriall Church ... Written by Henry Jacob, Imprinted at Leyden by Henry Hastings 1610.* The pages of the original were not numbered.

From the preface, 'To the Christian Reader'

[p. 6] I am not ignorant what will be excepted against this writing, & against my selfe. Many & divers there are, who will be not a little offended heere at ... By a great number this will be pronounced to be flatly *Schismaticall*. Whose hasty & rash censure I shall be exceedingly sory for. But yet I must tell them. First; that it is not the part of a *Schismatike* to labour ... to prove aginst all gainsayers ... the special honor of Iesus Christ our Mightie Lord & Saviour ...

[p. 7] Further more concerning *Schisme*, I must say to these Objectors, that in truth & indeed they are *Schismatiks* ... who wilfully divide themselves from, & possesse not the true & holy outward Ordinances of Christ Iesus, sufficient & duly ordered, given us in his unchangeable Testament, which only are the Ordinary assured meanes both of worshipping him & of saving our soules ...

[p. 8] Many wil avouch, that in England the Outward forme of the Visible Church, the Calling of the Ministers, the order of Church government & ceremoines [sic] are from Christ; & ought to be held his holy ordinances. To whom I answer; Why then did the chiefest *Prelats* [*in the margin*: 'Bp. of Canterb. London. Winchester. Lincolne &c'] in the land refuse openly the tryall hereof by a reasonable Conference or Disputation? I speake that I know; They expressly refused at *Lambeth* a most equall and unpartial tryall offered unto them, in the presence of sundry silenced & imporisoned Ministers being called about that little printed booke [*in the margin*: 'Offer of Disputation, 1606'] which was then newly published even for that purpose. They can not with any honest color reply, & say that the *Conference at Hampton Court* before was a sufficient deciding of these Controversies. For that objection of theirs is expressly confuted and taken away in the said printed treatise. Wherefore, till they accept that most equall and indifferent & Christian offer of trying these points now so much controverted in England; let them never say their Church state, Government & Ordinances are of God ...

[p. 12] Finally, they object that the profession of true Faith to Salvation is found in many Members of the visible Church of England. I answer; I willingly acknowledg this, that profession of true faith, yea and true faith indeed, is found in many 1000 among them. Gods ... extraordinary goodnes and mercy therein is excellently manifest towards the Land, notwithstanding the disordered Church estate there. But yet none may presume, nor rest themselves in assurance of this mercy ... The prevayling outward meanes in England, which should chiefly procure this grace to every one, are not only divers from, but also contrary to Christs owne appointed meanes in his word for [p. 13] this purpose ... It is objected againe heere withall, that this true Faith (acknowledged to be found in many in England) is the very Forme and essence of the Church. I answer: That is not so ... It is the forme of each true Christian a part &c of the Church Invisible Militant & Universall, The proper forme of Christs Visible church is *that Power of Spirituall Politic* before rehearsed.

[The preface is signed, 'From Leyden. Decemb. 20. An⁰ 1610. *Thine in Christ Iesus*. Henry Jacob'.]

[p. 15] Christ is the only Author, institutor, & framer of his Visible Ministeriall Church (touching the Constitution, Essence, Nature, and Forme thereof) every where and for ever. And in this respect we likewise affirme that he is the only Lord, & King & Lawgiver of the same.

[p. 16] [Jacob's definition of a church:] A true Visible & Ministeriall Church of Christ is a number of faithfull people joyned by their willing consent in a spirituall outward society or body politike, ordinarily comming together into one place, instituted by Christ in his New Testament & having the power to exercise Ecclesiasticall government and all Gods other spirituall ordinances (the meanes of salvation) in & for it selfe immediately from Christ.

[p. 18] Now the Christian Churches true and right government (in this regarde that the whole [p. 19] company of the people do give their free consent therein) is a certaine Democratie. The Diocesan, Provinciall and Catholike governments are monarchicall, or at the least they are Aristocraticall ...

[This popular government is no danger to civil government, first, because it is confined to 'one particular Congregation', and, second, because it may easily] yea with violence be resisted, and punished by any the meanest next dwelling officer of justice, if any person or persons in the Church become seditious and refractarie. Besides this government is to be informed, directed [p. 20] and guided by the Pastor chiefly, and also by the grave assistant Elders. And therefore indeed this government is not simply & plainly Democraticall, but firstly Aristocraticall, and partly Monarchicall. And so it is that mixt government which the learned do judge to be the best government of all.

[p. 21] [In making Christ the 'sole Author, institutor and framer' of the Church] Our purpose is not to intitle Christ to be the speciall Author & institutor allwayes & necessarily of things Accidentall and mutable in the Church [p. 22] but only of things concurring to the Essence, Nature, and constitution thereof, that is, of things which make the Matter and Forme of the same ...

[p. 32] Howbeit it [the visible church] is a spirituall Body politike, not a Civill Body politike: because it hath a speciall power from Christ to dispense spirituall things unto men heere on earth. That is to say, it hath power to dispense the Word of life, the holy Signes or Sacraments, to appoint meet Ministers for their uses, and to depose the unmeet, and also to receave into and cast forth the soules of men out of the Kingdom of heaven, as in the New Testament Christs true Visible and Ministeriall Church is called, and rightly believed to be.

[p. 34] [Referring to Mat. 18: 17 – 'Tell it to the Church'] Heere (*the Church*) signifieth a particular ordinary Congregation, or a Companie of Christians using to assemble in one place with authoritie for the managing of theire owne spirituall affaires.

Document II.4

John Smyth: Short Confession of Faith in XX Articles

John Smyth (c. 1565–1612) was the minister of the Separatist congregation at Gainsborough by 1608. About that time the church decided to emigrate to Amsterdam. Francis Johnson's 'Ancient Church' was already there but Smyth soon found himself in controversy with Johnson. The two subjects in dispute were, first, whether translations of the Bible should be used in worship if divine inspiration was confined to the text in the original languages, and, second, whether Johnson's presbyterian tendencies were sanctioned by Scripture. So Smyth's people separated from Johnson's. Smyth now became convinced that infant baptism was not permissible. He and his followers lived in property owned by a Waterlander Mennonite and so they became familiar with Mennonite beliefs. But Smyth, now that he had come to reject the validity of his own baptism, could not bring himself to accept the sacrament at the hands of the Mennonites because he disagreed with some aspects of their theology. So he baptized himself and then his colleague Thomas Helwys and the remainder of the congregation. As he became better acquainted with the Mennonites he came to believe that he had misjudged them and sought to be admitted into their communion. The above creed, which was not printed at the time, may well have accompanied his formal application for admission. The original manuscript is in the Mennonite Archives at Amsterdam. The above version is printed, with an introduction, in W. L. Lumpkin, *Baptist Confessions of Faith* (Philadelphia, 1959), 97–101. V., also M. R. Watts, *The Dissenters* (Oxford, 1978), I, 44–8 and W. T. Whitley, *The Works of John Smyth*, 2 vols (London, 1915), Introduction.

WE BELIEVE WITH THE HEART AND WITH THE MOUTH CONFESS:
(1) That there is one God, the best, the highest, and most glorious Creator and Preserver of all; who is Father, Son, and Holy Spirit.
(2) That God has created and redeemed the human race to his own image, and has ordained all men (no one being reprobated) to life.
(3) That God imposes no necessity of sinning in any one; but man freely, by Satanic instigation, departs from God.
(4) That the law of life was originally placed by God in the keeping of the law; then, by reason of the weakness of the flesh, was, by the good pleasure of God, through the redemption of Christ, changed into justification of faith; on which account, no one ought justly to blame God, but rather, with his inmost heart, to revere, adore, and praise his mercy, that God should have rendered that possible to man, by his grace, which before, since man had fallen, was impossible by nature.

(5) That there is no original sin, but all sin is actual and voluntary, viz., a word, a deed, or a design against the law of God; and therefore, infants are without sin.
(6) That Jesus Christ is true God and true man; viz., the Son of God taking to himself, in addition, the true and pure nature of a man, out of a true rational soul, and existing in a true human body.
(7) That Jesus Christ, as pertaining to the flesh, was conceived by the Holy Spirit in the womb of the Virgin Mary, afterwards was born, circumcised, baptized, tempted; also that he hungered, thirsted, ate, drank, increased both in stature and in knowledge; he was wearied, he slept, at last was crucified, dead, buried, he rose again, ascended into heaven; and that to himself as only King, Priest, and Prophet of the church, all power both in heaven and earth is given.
(8) That the grace of God, through the finished redemption of Christ, was to be prepared and offered to all without distinction, and that not feignedly but in good faith, partly by things made, which declare the invisible things of God, and partly by the preaching of the Gospel.
(9) That men, of the grace of God through the redemption of Christ, are able (the Holy Spirit, by grace, being before unto them, *grace prevemènt*) to repent, to believe, to turn to God, and to attain to eternal life; so on the other hand, they are able themselves to resist the Holy Spirit, to depart from God, and to perish for ever.
(10) That the justification of man before the Divine tribunal (which is both the throne of justice and of mercy), consists partly of the imputation of the righteousness of Christ apprehended by faith, and partly of inherent righteousness, in the holy themselves, by the operation of the Holy Spirit, which is called regeneration or sanctification; since any one is righteous, who doeth righteousness.
(11) That faith, destitute of good works, is vain; but true and living faith is distinguished by good works.
(12) That the church of Christ is a company of the faithful; baptized after confession of sin and of faith, endowed with the power of Christ.
(13) That the church of Christ has power delegated to themselves of announcing the word, administering the sacraments, appointing ministers, disclaiming them, and also excommunicating; but the last appeal is to the brethren or body of the church.
(14) That baptism is the external sign of the remission of sins, of dying and of being made alive, and therefore does not belong to infants.
(15) That the Lord's Supper is the external sign of the communion of Christ, and of the faithful amongst themselves by faith and love.
(16) That the ministers of the church are, not only bishops, to whom the power is given of dispensing both the word and the sacraments, but also deacons, men and widows, who attend to the affairs of the poor and sick brethren.
(17) That brethren who persevere in sins known to themselves, after the third admonition, are to be excluded from the fellowship of the saints by excommunication.
(18) That those who are excommunicated are not to be avoided in what pertains to worldly business.

(19) That the dead (the living being instantly changed) will rise again with the same bodies; not the substance but the qualities being changed.

(20) That after the resurrection, all will be borne to the tribunal of Christ, the Judge, to be judged according to their works; the pious, after sentence of absolution, will enjoy eternal life with Christ in heaven; the wicked, condemned, will be punished with eternal torments in hell with the devil and his angels.

Document II.5

John Robinson: Private and Public Communion

John Robinson's *Of Religious Communion, Public and Private* was printed and published, probably at Leyden, in 1614. The above selections are chosen to illustrate how Robinson sought to modify the more rigid Separatism of his predecessors whom Dr Geoffrey Nuttall describes as 'Hard in their judgments of their oppressors, vehement, offensive and extreme in the expression of their judgments'. Robinson's position was described by Robert Bailly (Baillie) in *The Diswasive ... Vindicated* (London, 1655), 8, as 'Semiseparatisme', a term of which Dr Nuttall approves in this connection, v., his *Visible Saints* (Oxford, 1957), 7, 10 n. 4. It is of interest that he claims to be developing concessions made by Barrow and Penry. How precisely he sought to justify his dissent from the Church of England with an acknowledgement that divine grace is not limited in its effects to those who agreed with this own ecclesiology is seen in the above excerpts.

Three of his suggestions have been made about the identity of the 'honorable Lady and Countesse Kindred' to whom Barrow addressed his letter. F. J. Powicke suggested Agnes, the wife of the Lord Keeper's eldest son, Sir Nicholas Bacon. Albert Peel suggested Lady Anne, the mother-in-law of the younger Sir Nicholas Bacon (and of Agnes). Leland Carlson's candidate is Anne Russell who on 11 November 1565 married Ambrose Dudley, earl of Warwick, the brother of Robert, earl of Leicester. Carlson discusses the matter in *The Writings of John Greenwood and Henry Barrow 1591–1593* (London, 1970), 238. The letter is to be seen also in C. Burrage, *Early English Dissenters* (Cambridge, 1912), II, 100–8 and a part of it in *Henry Barrow, Separatist* (London, 1900), 76–9.

For John Robinson (1575/6–1625), v., DNB; W. H. Burgess, *John Robinson* (London, 1920); E. Arber, *The Story of the Pilgrim Fathers* (London, 1897); H. M. Dexter and M. Dexter, *The England and Holland of the Pilgrims* (Boston, Mass., 1906); R. P. Stearns, *Congregationalism in the Dutch Netherlands* (Chicago, 1940); B. R. White, *The English Separatist Tradition* (Oxford, 1971); Timothy George, *John Robinson and the English Separatist Tradition* (1981); Daniel Plooij, *The Pilgrim Fathers from a Dutch Point of View* (New York, 1969); R. Tudur Jones, *John Robinson's Congregationalism* (London: The Congregational Lecture, 1987).

CHAPTER I. OF PRIVATE COMMUNION.

THE apostle writing to the church at Colosse with much joy for their stableness in the grace of God received, reduceth the whole matter of that his 'rejoicing' to two general heads: 'faith,' and 'order.' Col. ii. 5. Of which two, faith, though set after in place, is before, both in nature, time, and dignity: as making men in their persons severally fit for, and capable of that order, wherein they are jointly to be united.

Now from these two springheads, as it were, thus distinguished, do issue and arise two sorts of external religious actions, or exercises: which we may not unfitly, for distinction's sake, call, personal and church actions. By personal actions I do understand such as arise from, and are performed immediately by the personal faith, and other graces of God, in the hearts of holy men. Of which sort are, private prayer, thanksgiving, and singing of psalms, profession of faith, and confession of sins, reading or opening the Scriptures, and hearing them so read, or opened, either in the family, or elsewhere, without any church power, or ministry coming between. Of the second sort, are the receiving in, and casting out of members, the electing and deposing of officers, the use of a public ministry, and all communion therewith. For which works howsoever 'faith' and other personal graces be required that men in them may 'please God,' Heb. xi. 6: yet are not these graces sufficient for the doing of them, except withal there concur, and come between, a Church state, and order: in, and by which, they are to be exercised, as by their most immediate and proper cause: from which, by the rule of reason, they are to have their denomination, and so to be called church actions.

And that the actions of the first kind, and more particularly, private prayer, of which I am specially to speak, may, and ought to be performed by godly persons, though out of the order of a true visible church, both the Scriptures and common reason teach: and that not only by them severally, and one by one, but jointly, and together also, as there is occasion: they being joint members of the mystical body of Christ by faith, and jointly partakers of the same Spirit of adoption, and prayer; from which common faith, and union of the Spirit dwelling in them, this communion ariseth, they thereby being privileged jointly to say, 'Our Father:' as was also practised by Cornelius, and his holy family, though out of a true visible church. Matt. vi. 8–10, xv. 22, 23; Acts x. 1–3, 34, 35; Rom. viii. 26, x. 10; 1 Cor. xii. 7. Neither is it a matter worthy the proving lawful for a godly husband and wife jointly to sanctify their meat and drink by prayer, and thanksgiving, and so to beg together at God's hands, or to give thanks for other good things upon themselves, and theirs, though they be out of the order of a true church. Neither, indeed, do the members of the visible church perform private prayer, or the like exercises, whether severally, and by one and one, or jointly, by virtue of that their church state, or with any reference unto it, but merely as a duty of the Christian person, or family: (which must be before the Christian church, as parts whole:) and which they were also as well, and as much bound unto, though they were of no visible church at all: no more than was Cornelius, and his family, and friends, which, notwithstanding, was his, and their fault.

These things thus premised, I come to the thing I aim at in this whole discourse, which is, that we, who profess a separation from the English national, provincial, diocesan, and parochial church, and churches, in the whole formal state and order thereof, may notwithstanding lawfully communicate in private prayer, and other the like holy exercises (not performed in their church communion, nor by their church power and ministry,) with the godly amongst them, though remaining, of infirmity, members of the same church, or churches, except some other extraordinary bar come in the way, between them and us ...

And since the subject and ground of this communion is holy persons, and the same so discerned mutually, and on both sides, I think it needful, for the clearer passage of things, and better information of divers both adversaries and friends, having greatly misinterpreted our writings and testimony, here briefly to note down what our judgment hath always been of the sincere faith and holiness of many particular persons in the assemblies, notwithstanding our testimony against the body of the same assemblies, in their communion, order, and ordinances.

And first, our witnessing against the Church of England, so called, as Babylon, in her degree, both in respect of the confusion, as of persons good and bad, of all sorts, so of things Christian, and antichristian, covering all: as also of that spiritual bondage, wherein the Lord's people are kept under the spiritual lordship of the prelacy, there reigning, doth witness for us against all men, that we acknowledge the Lord's people, and godly persons there: out of which they are therefore called by the voice of the Lord fron heaven, to build up themselves 'as lively stones into a spiritual temple' for the Lord to dwell in, Rev. xviii. 4; 1 Pet. ii. 5: as were the Lord's people of old called out of Babylon civil, to build the material temple in Jerusalem, although as then was, so now is too slack obedience yielded to the Lord's call herein. Ezra i. and ii; Nehemiah ii.

More particularly, Mr. H. Barrowe in that his letter written a little before his death, and so the more advisedly, especially in that point, in which a snare was laid for his life, to an honourable lady yet living,[1] as he acknowledgeth her in her person, to have been educated and exercised in the faith and fear of God, so professeth he further, that he gladly embraceth, and believeth the common faith received, and professed in the land as good, and sound: that he had reverend estimation of sundry, and good hope of many hundred thousands in the land, though he utterly disliked the present constitution of the church, &c.

Unto which his testimony as the authors of the 'Apology' do assent,[2] so do they further profess their persuasion that of many the Lord's people in the realm, belonging to the Lord's election of grace, and partakers of his mercy to salvation in Christ, some are further called, and some still remain in defection: further instancing in sundry priests and friars, that have been martyrs of Jesus, witnessing the truth they saw against the Romish antichrist and yet retaining their popish functions, and communion with that church, which stands subject to the wrath of God: both Mr Barrowe, and they accordingly in another place, commending the faith ot the English martyrs, and deeming them saved notwithstanding the false offices and great corruptions in the worship they exercised: and so professing the same judgment of others in the realm, where the same precious faith in sincerity and simplicity is found, they neither neglecting to search out the truth, nor despising it, when they see it, the mercy of God through their sincere faith to Jesus Christ, extending, and superabounding above all their sins seen and unseen.

Lastly, Mr. Penry, a little before his execution, acknowledgeth in his

'Confession'[3] that both of the teachers and professors of the assemblies have so embraced the truth of doctrine in the land established, and professed, that the Lord in his infinite goodness hath granted them favour, to show out where, in regard of God's election, he judgeth them members of the body, whereof the Son of God Jesus Christ is the head: only herein praying the Lord to be merciful unto them, as unto himself in regard of his sins, that they are not ordered in that outward order which Christ Jesus left in his church, but instead thereof, &c.

All these, we see, as they rightly distinguish between faith and order, though even order also be a matter of faith, if it be not a matter of sin, and without warrant from God's Word, Rom. xiv. 23: so do they plainly acknowledge the personal faith, and grace unto salvation in many though remaining (of ignorance, and infirmity) members of that church against whose constitution, order, and ordinances, they witnessed, divers of them, unto death: and not only, that such people were there in the general, but also that they did so esteem and judge of many of them, in particular. And surely if the Lord's people be there, it is no difficult thing for the spiritual man, conversing with them, to discern and judge ordinarily, which they be. The Spirit of God in one of his people will own itself in another of them though disfigured with many failings especially in outward orders. and ordinances: and faith, if it be not dead. may be seen by works, of him that hath a spiritual eye through many infirmities. James ii. 17, 18. 'The tree,' saith Christ, 'is known by the fruits,' Luke vi. 44: so may the good trees truly planted by faith into Christ, and having in them the heavenly sap and juice of his Spirit, though growing for the present, out of the Lord's walled orchard, the true visible church, and in the wild wilderness of the profane assemblies, ordinarily be known by the good fruits of faith and of the Spirit evidently appearing in their persons, whom, whilst the world can in all places so far discern, as to hate, despise, and persecute them, as none of theirs, it were marvel if we should not discern them to be children of the same common Father with us, and so know and acknowledge one another, though the world, which knows not him know neither of both. 1 John iii. 1. And passing this judgment one upon another mutually, though not by the rule of certainty, which a man can have only of himself ordinarily, as only knowing his own heart, yet more than in hope, which extends itself to the apparently profane, for we are to hope that they who are not today, may be tomorrow, and even by that golden rule of love or charity, which 'thinketh not evil,' nor is suspicious, but 'believeth all things,' and taketh them in the best part: 1 Cor. xiii. 5, 7: 'covering,' especially under the graces of God's Spirit, where they appear, though in never so small a measure, 'a multitude of sins;' 1 Pet. iv. 8; we shall walk in love, after Christ's example, and fulfil the law of Christ by bearing one another's burden: thereby also procuring the like merciful measure to be meted out to us again both by God, and men, in respect of our infirmities Eph. v. 2, Gal. vi. 2; Mark iv. 24.

Lastly, if men were to judge us, even whilst we abode in the assemblies of ignorance, or infirmity, men fearing God, and sanctified in our persons, by the profession and appearance which we made: then are we also in equity to make the same estimate of the persons of others, though abiding in the assemblies, as we did making the same manifestation, and appearance, (and it may be greater than) the most of us have done. And, as we ourselves then having received of God the grace of sanctification, in our measure; and making manifestation thereof, according to that, we had received; and being to be judged by others according to the manifestation we made; did, and might justly look, that they should deem us truly faithful, and sanctified, though never so weakly: so are we to have again the like estimation of others, according to their measure received, and manifested: remembering always that most equal rule of Christ our Lord, that 'whatsoever we would men should do unto us, even so to do to them, which is the law, and the prophets.' Matt. vii. 12.

I will, therefore, conclude this point with a double exhortation: the former, respecting us ourselves, who have, by the mercy of God, with the faith of Christ, received his order, and ordinances; which is, that we please not ourselves therein too much, as if in them, piety and religion did chiefly consist: which was not the least calamity of the Lord's people of old, for which he also sharply reproved, and severely punished them; of which evil, and over valuation of these things, howsoever great in themselves, we are in the more danger, considering our persecutions, and sufferings for them: but that, as we believe these things are necessarily to be done, so we consider, that other things are not only not to be left undone, but to be done much more. The grace of faith in Christ, and the fear of God, the continual renewing of our repentance, with love, mercy, humility, and modesty, together with fervent prayer, and hearty thanksgiving unto God, for his unspeakable goodness, are the things wherein especially we must serve God: nourishing them in our own hearts, and so honouring them in others, wheresoever they appear to dwell. Psa. xl. 6–8; Heb. x. 3; Psa. xxxi. 16, 17; Jer. vii. 4, 21–23; Hos. vi. 6; Mic. vi. 6–8. And if God will be known, and honoured in all his creatures, yea, even, in the silliest worm that crawleth upon the earth, how much more in the holy graces of his Spirit vouchsafed to his elect, notwithstanding their failings of infirmity, especially in outward ordinances! Which personal graces whilst too many have undervalued in other men, and neglected in themselves, in comparison, God hath been provoked to suffer so many amongst us to fall, some, into such personal sins and evils, notwithstanding their advantage in the Lord's ordinances, as from which, without these helps many thousands of them have been preserved: and others, both from the conscience of God's ordinances, and of the personal duties of holiness, and honesty; as is generally to be seen in such as have made apostacy from their former profession with us.

The other exhortation, I direct unto them about whom I deal: which is, that they content not themselves with that faith and grace in their persons, which they have received, rejecting, or neglecting, under any pretext or excuse whatsoever, the order, ordinances, and institutions of the Lord Jesus; by the use whereof, their faith should be nourished in itself, and manifested unto others: much more, that they continue not their submission to the contrary, which is of antichrist; lest God, besides greater evils, punish them with yet greater confusion, and bondage therein: that, under which they are, being such already, as, I suppose, I may truly affirm, that never church in the world, in which so many excellent truths were taught, stood in such confusion both of persons and things, and under such a bondage spiritual, as that of England doth at this day.

Now before I come to prove the thing I aim at, I think it fit to satisfy the principal objections, which I have taken knowledge of against the thing I intend.

Objection 1.

And it will first be demanded of me, considering my judgment of the parish assemblies, as antichristian, and of sundry the practices there as idolatrous, and withal, what judgments the Scriptures denounce against such estates and practices, how I can deem any the members of such assemblies, and so practising, as truly Chlistian? or how I can, without pollution, communicate with them, who are by the touching of so many unclean, both persons and things, themselves made unclean ?

Reason.

For answer. First, it is true, that upon the true church the Scriptures do pronounce most excellent blessings, as they do also denounce fearful curses upon the false: as it is also true, that whatsoever is spoken of the whole body, the one or other, jointly, belongs to each member of either, severally: provided, that in both, things be in their right state and order: which is, that there be none but faithful and holy persons in the true church, and none but unholy and profane persons in the false: for none other should be, in the one or other. But, if now it come to pass otherwise, and that through the church's want of vigilance or zeal, and the party's hypocrisy, which hath been always, and is, too, too common, there be in the true church unfaithful and profane persons, shall we say, that those precious promises made to the true church in which they wrongfully are, do appertain unto them, and unto their persons? and that they are elect of God, saints by calling and sanctified in Christ, to the hope of life, &c.? So if on the contrary, it come to pass, through her craft and cruelty, and their own weakness, which is, too, too common also, that godly and faithful persons be in the false church, where they should not be, shall we now lay upon their persons all the curses, and condemnation, which the Scriptures denounce against the estate of the false church, and the superstitions thereof? Were not this to justify the wicked, because he is in the true church, where he should not be? ...

... Considering the many excellent truths taught in divers of the assemblies, and that with so great fruit in the knowledge, zeal, and other personal graces of many, the constant sufferings of divers martyrs for the truths there professed against that antichrist of Rome; the knowledge we had, of ourrselves, in that estate; together with the judgment of other churches abroad, touching the Church of England, as it is called, though indeed ignorant of her estate, save in such general heads of faith, wherein we also assent unto her; as also the manifold afflictions upon, and great offences, and those, many too just, at such as have made separation from that church; it is no marvel that so many (though otherwise learned and godly) by reason of the ignorance and infirmity yet cleaving to the best overmuch, are abused, by the times, for the succouring of antichrist in his declining age; for whose furtherance, in his rising, through the corruptions of times then so many, howsoever otherwise learned and godly, have, though unwittingly, put to their hands, as all men, soundly minded, if but a little exercised in their writings, and the stories of the times will confess.

Now for the second part of the objection, touching the idolatrous practices of the assemblies, I do answer, that every idolatry makes not an idolater, any more than every ignorance, or other sin of ignorance, an ignorant or wicked person. To make an idolater, there is required an idolatrous disposition, which we may not lay to their charge, of whom we speak. Besides, by this ground, we should challenge the reformed churches generally to be idolaters; for the most of them use a stint form of prayer, less or more, though they be not bound unto it: and so, consequently, should exclude them from God's kingdom, for no idolater hath any inheritance in the kingdom of heaven. Eph. iv. 3. And if any further object, that the Scriptures teach expressly, that they who partake of the sins of Babylon, shall receive of her plagues: and that every man worshipping that beast, and his image, and receiving his mark in his forehead or in his hand, shall drink of the wine of the wrath of God, &c., Rev. xviii. 4; xiv. 9, 10. I answer, as before, that that estate, and those practices are, indeed, under that curse in themselves; and further also, that every person so walking, as I am persuaded every member of the Church of England doth, is under that condemnation without repentance: which repentance, as it must be particular for sins known, so doth the Lord, in mercy, accept of the general repentance of his servants, for their sins unknown and secret, and which they discern not to be such: otherwise no flesh could be saved. Psa. xix. 12. Lastly, as I cannot excuse them, nor they themselves, from great sin in joining themselves with the profane parish assemblies, with which God hath not joined them; and that in the practice of their superstitions, especially, in such a bondage spiritual under the prelacy, as makes them cease to be the Lord's free people, and deprives them of all power for the reformation of public evils, either of persons, or things; so that being, as I hope, but their sins of infirmity, and by them unseen, though we discern them, as it may be, they also discern some evils in us, which we see not in ourselves, they no more dissolve the bond of the Spirit between their and our persons, than they destroy the work of the same Spirit in themselves: neither can these their sins pollute me, if by the default of my place or person I leave no means lawful unused, for their reformation: who, if they either purposely neglect to search out the truth, or unfaithfully withold it in unrighteousness, for any fleshly fear, or other corrupt regard, shall not, for our more respective judgment of them, or practice towards them, receive the more easy judgment at the hands of the Lord, in the day of the revelation of the secrets of all hearts.

Notes

1. 'Letter to an Honorable Lady and Countesse of his kin(d)red yet Living' is printed in Leland H. Carlson (ed.), *The Writings of John Greenwood and Henry Barrow 1591–1593* (London, 1970). The reference in the text is to p. 247.
2. Reference to [Henry Ainsworth and Francis Johnson], *An Apologie or Defence of such Christians as are Commonly (but Unjustly) Called Brownists* ([Amsterdam?] 1604).

The letter mentioned in the previous note appears on pp. 89–95.
3. Reference to *The Examinations of Henry Barrow John Greenwood and John Penrie before the High Commissioners and Lordes of the Counsel. Penned by the Prisoners Themselves before their Deathes* (no date), pp. [20]–[21].

Document II.6

The King's Declaration of Sports, 1633

'The King's Majesty's declaration to his subjects concerning lawful sports to be used was issued by Charles I on 18 October 1633. It caused no end of protest since Sabbatarianism had become one of the hallmarks of Puritanism inside and outside the Church of England. It was burnt by the Long Parliament in 1643. The conviction that the Christian Sunday should be observed as strictly as the Jewish Sabbath had begun to take root effectively in England with the publication of Nicholas Bownde's book, *Sabbathum Veteris et Novi Testamenti: or the True Doctrine of the Sabbath* (London, 1593). For further information, v., W. Whitaker, *Sunday in Tudor and Stuart Times* (1933); P. Collinson, 'The Origins of English Sabbatarianism', *Studies in Church History*, I (1964), 207–21 and W. Rordorf, *Sunday* (London, 1968).

Our dear father of blessed memory, in his return from Scotland, coming through Lancashire, found that his subjects were debarred from lawful recreations upon Sundays after evening prayers ended, and upon Holy-days; and he prudently considered that, if these times were taken from them, the meaner sort who labour hard all the week should have no recreations at all to refresh their spirits; and after his return, he further saw that his loyal subjects in all other parts of his kingdom did suffer in the same kind, though perhaps not in the same degree: and did therefore in his princely wisdom publish a Declaration to all his loving subjects concerning lawful sports to be used at such times, which was printed and published by his royal commandment in the year 1618, in the tenor which hereafter followeth:

Whereas upon our return the last year out of Scotland, we did publish our pleasure touching the recreations of our people in those parts under our hand; for some causes us thereunto moving, we have thought good to command those our directions then given in Lancashire, with a few words thereunto added, and most appliable to these parts of our realms, to be published to all our subjects.

Whereas we did justly in our progress through Lancashire rebuke some Puritans and precise people, and took order that the like unlawful carriages should not be used by any of them hereafter, in the prohibiting and unlawful punishing of our good people for using their lawful recreations and honest exercises upon Sundays, and other Holy-days, after the afternoon sermon or service, we now find that two sorts of people wherewith that country is much infected, we mean Papists and Puritans, have maliciously traduced and calumniated those our just and honourable proceedings: and therefore, lest our reputation might upon the one side (though innocently) have some aspersion laid upon it, and that upon the other part our good people in that country be misled by the mistaking and misinterpretation of our meaning, we have therefore thought good hereby to clear and make our pleasure to be manifested to all our good people in those parts.

It is true that at our first entry to this Crown and kingdom we were informed, and that too truly, that our county of Lancashire abounded more in Popish Recusants than any county of England, and thus hath continued since, to our great regret, with little amendment, save that, now of late, in our last riding through our said country, we find both by the report of the Judges, and of the Bishop of that Diocese, that there is some amendment now daily beginning, which is no small contentment to us.

The report of this growing amendment amongst them made us the more sorry, when with our own ears we heard the general complaint of our people, that they were barred from all lawful recreations and exercise upon the Sunday's afternoon, after the ending of all divine service, which cannot but produce two evils: the one the hindering of the conversion of many, whom their priests will take occasion hereby to vex, persuading them that no honest mirth or recreation is lawful or tolerable in our religion, which cannot but breed a great discontentment in our people's hearts, especially of such as are peradventure upon the point of turning: the other inconvenience is, that this prohibition barreth the common and meaner sort of people from using such exercises as may make their bodies more able for war, when his Majesty or his successors shall have occasion to use them; and in place thereof sets up filthy tippling and drunkenness, and breeds a number of idle and discontented speeches in their ale-houses. For when shall the common people have leave to exercise, if not upon the Sundays and Holy-days, seeing they must apply their labour and win their living in all working-days?

Our express pleasure therefore is, that the laws of our kingdom and canons of the Church be as well observed in that county, as in all other places of this our kingdom: and on the other part, that no lawful recreation shall be barred to our good people, which shall not tend to the breach of our aforesaid laws and canons of our Church: which to express more particularly, our pleasure is, that the Bishop, and all other inferior churchmen, and churchwardens, shall for their parts be careful and diligent, both to instruct the ignorant, and convince and reform them that are misled in religion, presenting them that will not conform themselves but obstinately stand out, to our Judges and Justices: whom we likewise command to put the law in due execution against them.

Our pleasure likewise is, that the Bishop of that Diocese take the like strait order with all the Puritans and Precisians within the same, either constraining them to conform themselves or to leave the county, according to the laws of our kingdom and canons of our Church, and so to strike equally on both hands against the contemners of our authority and adversaries of our Church; and as for our good people's lawful recreation, our pleasure likewise is, that after the end of divine service our good people be not disturbed, letted or discouraged from any lawful recreation, such as dancing, either men or women; archery for men, leaping, vaulting, or any other such harmless recreation, nor from having of May-games, Whitsun-ales, and Morris-dances; and the setting up of May-poles and other sports therewith used; so as the same be had in due and convenient time, without impediment or neglect of divine service; and that women shall have leave to carry rushes to the church for the decorating of it, according to their old custom; but withal we do here account still as prohibited all unlawful games to be used upon Sundays only, as bear and bull-baitings, interludes and at all times in the meaner sort of people by law prohibited, bowling.

And likewise we bar from this benefit and liberty all such known Recusants, either men or women, as will abstain from coming to church or divine service, being therefore unworthy of any lawful recreation after the said service, that will not first come to the church and serve God: prohibiting in like sort the said recreations to any that, though conform in religion, are not present in the church at the service of God, before their going to the said recreations. Our pleasure likewise is, that they to whom it belongeth, shall present and sharply punish all such, as in abuse of this our liberty, will use these exercises before the end of all divine services for that day: and we likewise straightly command that every person shall resort to his own parish church to hear divine service, and each parish by itself to use the said recreations after divine service: prohibiting likewise any offensive weapons to be carried or used in the said times of recreation: and our pleasure is, that this our Declaration shall be published by order from the Bishop of the Diocese, through all the parish churches, and that both our Judges of our circuit and our Justices of our Peace be informed thereof.

Given at our Manor of Greenwich the four and twentieth day of May, in the sixteenth year of our Reign, of England, France and Ireland; and of Scotland the one and fiftieth.

Now out of a like pious care for the service of God, and for suppressing of any humours that oppose truth, and for the ease, comfort and recreation of our well-deserving people, His Majesty doth ratify and publish this our blessed father's Declaration: the rather, because of late in some counties of our kingdom, we find that under pretence of taking away abuses, there hath been a general forbidding, not only of ordinary meetings, but of the Feasts of the Dedication of the Churches, commonly called Wakes. Now our express will and pleasure is, that these Feasts, with others, shall be observed, and that our Justices of the Peace, in their several divisions, shall look to it, both that all disorders there may be prevented or punished, and that all neighbourhood and freedom, with manlike and lawful exercises be used: and we further command all Justices of Assize in their several circuits to see that no man do trouble or molest any of our loyal and dutiful people, in or for their lawful recreations, having first done their duty to God, and continuing in obedience to us and our laws: and for this we command all our Judges, Justices of Peace, as well within liberties as without, Mayors, Bailiffs, Constables, and other officers, to take notice of, and to see observed, as they tender our displeasure. And we further will that publication of this our command be made by order from the Bishops, through all the parish churches of their several dioceses respectively.

Given at our Palace of Westminster, the eighteenth day of October, in the ninth year of our Reign. God save the King.

Document II.7

'The New England Way'

John Cotton (d. 1652), who after spending twenty-one years as vicar of Boston, Lincolnshire, emigrated to New Engand in 1633 to be minister of the Congregational Church at Boston, deeply influenced such Dissenting leaders as Thomas Goodwin and Philip Nye. The first Nonconformist Church on Welsh soil, which was organised at Llanfaches, Gwent, in November 1639, was formed 'according to the New England pattern' (William Erbury, *Apocrypha* (London, 1652), 8).

The following extracts come from Cotton's *The Way of the Churches of Christ in NEW ENGLAND* ... (London, 1645) and illustrate the nature of that pattern. (For the influence of Cotton, v., G. F. Nuttall, *Visible Saints* (Oxford, 1957), 15–17.)

It is the part of all Christians, who look for salvation by Christ Jesus, to joyn themselves (if God give them opportunity) to some one or other ... particular visible Church of Christ ...

[God joins faithful Christians together by means of a covenant.]

Neither is there any colour to conceive this way of entring into Church estate by Covenant, to be peculiar to the Paedagogy of the Old Testament, for it is evident by the light of nature, that all civill Relations are founded in Covenant. For, to passe by naturall Relations between Parents and Children, and violent Relations between Conquerors and Captives; there is no other way given whereby a people (sui juris) free from naturall and compulsory engagements, can be united or combined together into one visible body, to stand by mutuall Relations, fellow-members of the same body, but onely by mutuall Covenant; as appeared between husband and wife in the family, Magistrates and subjects in the Common-wealth, fellow Citizens in the same City: and therefore in the New Testament when a people whom the Apostles by their ministery had converted, were to be gathered by them into a Church estate, what did the Apostles else but combine them into one body, as one Spouse unto Christ ... [pp. 3–4]

To the erecting of a Church, as the presence of Christ is necessary for the acceptance of it, so the presence of neighbouring Churches and Brethren is requisite to cry Grace, Grace unto it ...

And seeing Christian Magistrates being also Brethren and members of Churches, are called of God to be Nursing Fathers unto the Church, *Isa.* 49. 23, it cannot but encourage them to take the more speciall notice and care of every Church, and to provide and assigne convenient allotments of land for the maintenance of each of them, when in times of peace they are made acquainted with the persons and proceedings of such as gather into Church-fellowship, under the wing of their Government: And yet seeing the Kingdome of Christ is not of this world, nor regulated by the wisedome of this world, wee doe not doubt but that a Church may be cleerly gathered, and rightl;y ordered though they want opportunity, or omit to acquaint the Magistrate with their proceedings, especially when Magistrates are not acquainted with the Laws of Christs Kingdome. [pp. 5–6]

How a Congregational Church is gathered

[First of all, they gather together to commend themselves to the Lord. Then they seek some minister to guide them in the work of church-formation. Spiritual conference and prayer gives them an opportunity of knowing one another. Then they]

doe acquaint the Governour, and some of the neerest Magistrates, and those Churches which are next adjoyning to them, with their intention to enter into Church fellowship ...

[The day appointed for gathering the Church having come,]

the whole day is kept as a day of humiliation, especially the former part of it, in seeking the face of God in prayer, and preaching the Word ...

[Then one of the brethren addresses himself to the task of giving expression to the faith and repentance of the congregation.]

This done with the silent approbation of the whole Assembly he propoundeth the Covenant of promise, *Eph.* 2. 12 ... they professe in the name of Christ their acceptance of the Lord for their God, and the Lord Iesus (the head and Saviour of his Church) to be their King, Priest, and Prophet; and give themselves in professed subjection unto all his holy ordinances, according to the Rules of the Gospel; withall they professe their full purpose of heart, to cleave one to another in Brotherly love, and mutuall subjection, according to God; not forsaking their Assembly, (but as the Lord shall call) and ministring one to another (as becometh good Stewards of the manyfold graces of God) till they grow up to the perfect man in Christ Jesus.

Having thus, or to the like purpose propounded the Covenant himselfe, with the rest of the Brethren, who are to joyn Church-estate, they declare their joynt consent in this Covenant, either by silence, or word of mouth, or writing ...

[Then the visiting representatives of other churches extend to them the right hand of fellowship (pp. 7–8).]

'Touching Church-Officers ...'

The Apostles, Prophets, and Evangelists, they still continue in their writings to be Master-builders of the Churches in all ages, and therefore the Church is said to be built upon their foundation ... *Eph.* 2. 20. It remaineth therefore, that the ordinary Officers of the Church which are to continue to the comming of Christ Iesus, are either Elders, (whom the Apostle calleth also Bishops, *Tit.* 1.5, 7. *Act.* 20.17, 28) or Deacons; of Elders he maketh two sorts, one sort he calleth them that rule, the other them that labour in the Word; whether of Exhortation, as the Pastors, or of Doctrine, as the Teachers, 2 *Tim.* 5.17. For the two sorts of ordinarie preaching Elders, the Apostle calleth *Pastors and Teachers Eph.* 4. 11 ... [pp. 10–11]

[He procedes to describe in detail the various aspects of church life, – the calling and ordaining of ministers, the extent and nature of their authority, the reception of new members, the administration of the sacraments and the exercising of discipline.]

Document II.8

The Norwich Covenant, 1643

The following minute (a), describing the formation of the church at Norwich, is copied from the Church book and printed in J. Browne, *History of Congregationalism in Norfolk and Suffolk* (London, 1877), 210. The date of the meeting was 23 November 1642. 'Mr Bridge' is William Bridge (d. 12 March 1671, aged 70), v., C. R. and DNB. The comment (b) is in Browne, *History of Congregationalism*, 211.

(a)
Hereupon, having first jointly offered themselves, Christopher Stygold freely offered himself to the work of the Lord in building a hiuse to His name, and made a motion to John Eyre to agree and to join with him in that service, who gladly embraced it, and agree with him. And they two moved [eight other named brethren] who all agreed in the same manner. Then it was moved to the rest of the brethren present by Mr. Bridge, whether they were all satisfied in what had been done; and they answered, they were satisfied. Then it was further moved to the sisters to come in and help in the work, who all agreed to do so; and after blessing God for success, they concluded the meeting for that time.

(b) The covenant, 28 June 1643, taken by William Bridge and the church members

First, That we will for ever acknowledge and avouch God to be our God in Jesus Christ.

Secondly, That we will always endeavour through the grace of God assisting us, to walk in His ways and ordinances according to His written word, which is the only sufficient rule of good life for every man.

Thirdly, Neither will we suffer ourselves to be polluted by any sinful ways, either public or private, but will abstain from the very appearance of evil, giving no offence to the Jew, or to the Gentile, or to the churches of Christ.

Fourthly, That we will, in all love, improve our communion as brethren, by watching over one another, and as need shall be, to counsel, admonish, reprove, comfort, relieve, assist, and bear with one another, humbly submitting ourselves to the government of Christ in His churches.

Lastly, we do not promise these things in our own, but Christ his strength, neither do we confine ourselves to the word of this covenant; but shall account it our duty at all times to embrace any further light or truth that shallbe revealed to us out of God's word.

Document II.9

The Last Will of William Wroth

The original is now in the National Library of Wales, Aberystwyth. It was first published in facsimile in the *Transactions of the Cardiff Naturalists' Society*, XXV (1892–3), ii. 6-7. Sir Joseph Bradney's treatment of Wroth and of his will in his *History of Monmouthshire* (London, 1932), IV, 189 has several slips that need to be corrected in the light of Thomas Richards' discussion in 'Eglwys Llanfaches', *Transactions of the Honourable Society of Cymmrodorion, 1941* (1943), 163–4. The will has also been published by Trefor Watts in *The Congregational History Magazine*, 2: 5 (1989), 69. It was proved on 23 April 1641. For Wroth (1570–1641), the pioneer of Welsh Nonconformity, see ibid., and *The Dictionary of Welsh Biography*. For Richard Blinman (1608–81), v., E. Stanley John's (Welsh) article in *Y Cofiadur* (1996), 14–20. Wroth Rogers was a Commissioner under the Act for the Better Propagation of the Gospel in Wales and Governor of Hereford.

In the name of Almighty God, Father of the Lord Jesus Christ, and in him my ever-gratious father, by whose precious blood I am redeemed, and have my Redemption sealed by his holy spirit of promise; which I believe, Lord helpe my unbeliefe; I say, In his blessed name, I William Wroth preacher of God's word being ready by age, to leave this present world, I put my poore house, & my Earthly talent in order, wherein I humbly beseech his ever-righteous direction, this seventeenth day of September Anno Domini 1638. I doe first commend my spirit into his All-powerful hands, not doubting of his gratious acceptance of me in Christ. And I leave my body to bee buried where ye Lord shall please to call for me; praying him to bring my hoarie-head into the grave in his peace which passeth all understanding. Item, I devize, give and bequeath unto Henry Walter of St Brides preacher of God's word, his heires and assignes, all that three Acres of Lands, bee it more or lesse, set, lying, and being in the parish of Magor (the which, of late, I purchased of Edmund Herbert of Penhow, and Blanch his wife) to the uses and limitations herein limited, and expressed, and to no other use of purpose; that is to say, The yearly rents, issues, and profits of ye said Lands to bee divided upon the first day of Aprill yearly for ever betweene twelve of the poorest people dwelling and living in the Parish of Llanfaches, chosen according to the discretion of the said Henry Walter, his heires and assignes for ever. Item, I do desire, and appoint, the said Henry Walter to dispose of all other worldly goods, which the Lord hath lent me, according to the note, which he shall receive herewithall. And I doe hereby nominate and appoint ye said henry Walter to bee my Executor of this my last will & Testament. In witness whereof, I have put here-unto my bond and seale, ye day and yeare above written.

Wm.Wroth

Sealed in ye presence of
William x Reece
John Thomas

A'ure Rogers
Richard Blinman
Minister of Gs word
Wroth Rogers.

Document II.10

Thomas Helwys: *The Mistery of Iniquity*

Thomas Helwys (c. 1550–c. 1616), a landed gentleman of Broxtowe Hall near Nottingham, had joined the Separatist congregation at Gainsborough of which John Smyth the 'Se-Baptist' was minister. They emigrated to Amsterdam in 1608. He, like Smyth, embraced the principle that infant baptism could not be justified from Scripture, and also rejected Calvinism in favour of Arminianism. But Helwys disagreed with Smyth's desire to join the Waterlanders. In 1612 he and a dozen others returned to England and established the first General Baptist Church on English soil. It was in 1612 also that he published *The Mistery of Iniquity*. It identifies the Church of Rome with the 'beast' of Revelation 13 whose oppressive actions make manifest the 'mystery of iniquity' mentioned in 2 Thes. 2: 7. The Anglican Church, insofar as it mimicked the Church of Rome, is seen as the 'second beast' of Revelation 13: 11ff. The book also criticises other Separatists, and especially John Robinson, for their inconsistency in maintaining that the Church of England was a false church and yet adhering to its practice of baptizing infants, which meant the compulsory baptism of those who are incapable of making a profession of faith. Robinson replied to these criticisms in his book, *Of Religious Communion*. *The Mistery of Iniquity* closes with a remarkable reproof of those Separatists who had chosen to withdraw to the Netherlands rather than face persecution at home – a dramatic change in his own attitude to that practice.

A facsimile edition of *The Mistery of Iniquity* was published in London in 1935 by The Baptist Historical Society in 1935. For further discussion of Helwys and his career, v., M. R. Watts, *The Dissenters* (Oxford, 1978), I, 47–50; C. Burrage, *Early English Dissenters* (Cambridge, 1912), I, 251–69; W. H. Burgess, *John Smith ... Thomas Helwys, and the First Baptist Church in England* (London, 1911), 107–296; B. R. White, *The English Separatist Tradition* (Oxford, 1971), chap. vi; W. K. Jordan, *The Development of Religious Toleration in England*, 4 vols (London, 1932, 1936, 1938, 1940), II, 274–84; O. P. Grell, J. I. Israel and H. Tyacke (eds), *From Persecution to Toleration* (Oxford, 1991), chap. 1.

(a) Plea for Toleration (The autographed dedication to the King in the Bodleian copy)

Heare o King, and dispise not ye counsell of ye poore, and let their complaints come before thee.

The King is a mortall man, & not God therefore hath no power over ye immortal soules of his subiects, to make lawes & ordinances for them, and so set spirituall Lords over them.

If the King have authority to make spirituall Lords & Lawes, then he is an immortal God and not a mortall man.

O King, be not seduced by deceivers to sin so against God whome thou oughtest to obey, nor against thy poore subiects who ought and will obey thee in all thinges with body and goods, or else let their lives be taken from ye earth.

God Save ye Kinge.

Spittlefield
neare London   Tho: Helwys

The Hyrarchie of Rome, expounds the scriptures: makes lawes, Canons, and decrees, and binds all mens consciences to obey, forceing them thereunto by excomunication, imprisonment, banishment, death, & none may examine the power, aucthority, or warrant thereof by the scriptures, but all must be received for holy and good, because the Hyrarchy of Rome, say in words they cannot err. And wee beseech our Lord the K[ing] to see that the Hyrarchy of Arch-B[ishop]s, and Lord B[ishop]s do all the same thinges; they expound the scriptures, make lawes, Canons, & decrees, & bindes all mens consciences to the obedience thereof, forceing the K[ing]s true & obedient subiects thereunto, by excomunication, imprisonment, banishment, (the K[ing] in mercy & justice restraning them of blood) & none may examine the power & aucthority of anie of their decrees by the scriptures, but all must be received for holy, & good ... [pp. 65–6]

... And will our lord the King be entised by evill men to enter upon the inheritance of the Sonne of God, in appointing and (by the Kings power) suffering to be appointed Lords and lawes in and over the house of God which are not according to the pattern? Which lords, because *Christ is not their buckler*, nor *faith their sheild*: nor *the sword of the spirit the weapon of their warfare*, they have deceitfully seduced our lord the King bringing themselves under his protection for their defence, and getting the K[ing]s sword into their hands to destroy all that speake or write against them, preferring their owne Kingdome before either Christs Kingdome, or the kingdom & State of our lord the King ... in that they with such loveing patience suffer and permitt so manie thousands of Romists, who by their profession, and the practices of some of them are dangerously opposite to the Kingdome of Christ, and to the King and State. But these Lords B[ishop]s Cannot in anie wise endure one, that doth faithfully seeke for reformation, because such are onely adversaries to their kingdome. Wee still pray our lord the King that wee may be free from suspect, for haveing anie thoughts of provoking evill against them of the Romish religion, in regard to their profession, if they be true & faithfull subiects to the King for wee do freely professe, that our lord the King hath no more power over their consciences then over ours, and that is none at all: for our lord the King is but an earthly King, and he hath no aucthority as a King but in earthly causes, and if the Kings people be obedient & true subiects, obeying all humane lawes made by the King, our lord the King can require no more; for mens religion to God, is betwixt God and themselves; the King shall not answere for it, neither may the King be iugd betweene God and man. Let them be heretikes, Turcks,

Jewes, or what soever apperteynes not to the earthly power to punish them in the least measure ... [pp. 68–9]

(b) Infant Baptism Condemned

... What words might we take to our selves to make your madnes, and the madnes of al the world, herein to appear, who pretend that al the seed of Christians and of the faithful are to bee Baptized onely, and under this pretence baptize, and approve of the baptizing of the seed of al the wicked and ungodly in these parts of the World, yea those that have beene wicked to the third and fowrth generation, and to the tenth generation enimies of God, and bloody persecutors of his truth, destroying the faith of Jesus, and advanceing the man of sinne: The seed of all these are baptized, and by reason of this Baptisme they are all held and accounted Christians by you, although they walke in the stepps of their fore-Fathers. Is there anie knowledg of God in these thinges?: Or do men thinke that now under the Gospel they may doe and approve off what they wil? ... Do you set downs a Law to your selves that the infants off the faithfull are to bee Baptized, and do you approve off the Baptizing of the infants of the enimies of God, that feight against the lambe and the infants of some also, that have not so much faith as Devils, who beleeve and tremble ... [p. 162]

(c) Flight to the Continent Condemned

Wee hold ourselves bound, to acknowledge, and that others be warned to manifest, how we have bene (through our great weakness) misled by deceitfull harted leaders, who have and do seeke to save their lives, and wil make sure not to loose them for Christ, and therefore they flee into foraine Countries and free States, and drawe people after them to support their kingdomes, first seeking their owne safeties, and there publishing (as they pretend)) the gospel, or seeking the Kingdome of heaven, as farr as they may with their safetie: and this they iustifie by perverting and misapplying the words of our saviour Christ, where he saith: *when they persecute you, or drive, or thrust you out off one city flee into another*, mat.10.23. these words have they picked out for their purpose casting away or leaving furth, divers rules of Christ goeing before ... [The] reason why our Saviour Christ bids them when they are persecuted in one Citie, go to another ... is this: *for verily I say vnto you, ye shal not go over al the Cities of Israel til the Sonne of man come.* This sheweth that our Saviour Christs meaning was, that when they were driven or expelled out of one Citie, they should go to another City in Israel to preach the gospel unto it: but these men flee to Cities to the which they cannot preach the gospel, being of a straing tongue, neither have they any intent or meaning to preach the gospel to those Cities, their fleeing is not to that end, but to save themselves ... [pp. 204–5]

Document II.11

Milton: *Areopagitica*

On 14 June 1643 Parliament passed the Order that 'no Book, Pamphlet, paper, nor part of any such Book, Pamphlet, or paper shall from henceforth be printed, bound, stitched or put to sale by any person or persons whatsoever, unlesse the same be first approved of and licensed under the hands of such person or persons, as both, or either of the said Houses shall appoint for the licensing of the same …'. It was against this Order that Milton wrote his *Areopagitica* which appeared in November 1644. For the background, the history of licensing, bibliographical details, summary of the argument and full annotation, see *Complete Prose Works of John Milton* (New Haven: Yale Univ. Press, 1959), II, the introduction by Ernest Sirluck together with his preface and notes to the text. The licensing Order of 1643 is reproduced in Appendix B.

    John Milton (1608–74), by common consent one of the greatest of the English poets, is also a figure of considerable importance in the history of Protestant Dissent. Firmly committed to the principles of radical Nonconformity and in particular to the tradition of Independency (which he saw as the inevitable corollary of the Protestant Reformation), he played an active part in all the religious and political controversies of his time. He has been rightly described as a 'vituperative polemicist, republican, defender of regicide, anti-clerical whether of old priest or new presbyter, with bishops almost as his anti-Christ' (Gordon S.Wakefield, *Expository Times*, 107: 10 (July 1996), 207–301, a useful and objective assessment of Milton and his significance). He was an unswerving supporter of the parliamentary cause in the Civil Wars. In 1649, after the establishment of the Commonwealth, he was appointed Latin Secretary to the Council of State and at the Restoration he only narrowly escaped execution. He was a man of immense learning. Much of his enormous literary output, in both prose and poetry, was in Latin. He was in many respects far in advance of his time as in his advocacy of divorce and his unflinching advocacy of toleration – but not for Roman Catholicism. His Latin treatise, *De Doctrina Christiana*, which was unknown and unpublished until 1825, reveals that his own personal theology was indeed heretical and anti-Trinitarian. But then several commentators had already detected Arian tendencies in *Paradise Lost*. In a sense he reflects a unique combination of the Renaissance and Puritanism. In particular, he is perhaps the supreme representative of the Puritan tradition at its best. See W. R. Parker, *Milton* (Oxford, 1968) for his biography.

    The full title reads, *Areopagitica; A Speech of Mr John Milton For the Liberty of Vnlicens'd Printing, To the Parlament of England* … (London, 1644). The page references are to the original edition.

[p. 11] As therefore the state of man now is; what wisdome can there be to choose, what continence to forbeare without the knowledge of evill? He that can apprehend and consider vice with all her baits and seeming pleasures, and yet abstain, and yet distinguish, and yet prefer that which is truly better, he is the true warfaring[1] Christian. I cannot praise a fugitive and cloister'd vertue, unexercis'd & unbreath'd, that never sallies out and sees her adversary, but slinks out of the race, where that immortall garland is to be run for, not without dust and heat. Assuredly we bring not innocence into the world, we bring impurity much rather; that which purifies us is triall, and triall is by what is contrary. That vertue therefore which is but a youngling in the contemplation of evill, and knows not the utmost [p. 12] that vice promises to her followers, and rejects it, is but a blank vertue, not a pure; her whitenesse is but an excrementall[2] whitenesse. Which was the reason why our sage and serious Poet *Spencer*, whom I dare be known to think a better teacher then *Scotus* or *Aquinas*, describing true temperance under the person of *Guion*,[3] brings him in with his palmer through the cave of Mammon, and the bower of earthly blisse, that he might see and know, and yet abstain. Since therefore the knowledge and survay of vice is in this world so necessary to the constituting of human vertue, and the scanning of error to the confirmation of truth, how can we more safely, and with less danger scout into the regions of sin and falsity then by reading all manner of tractats, and hearing all manner of reason? And this is the benefit which may be had of books promiscuously read. But of the harm that may result hence three kinds are usually reckn'd. First, is fear'd the infection that may spread; but then all human learning and controversie in religious points must remove out of the world, yea the Bible it selfe; for that oft times relates blasphemy not nicely, it describes the carnall sense of wicked men not unelegantly, it brings in holiest men passionately murmuring against providence through all the arguments of *Epicurus*: in other great disputes it answers dubiously and darkly to the common reader ... For these causes we all know the Bible it selfe put by the Papist into the first rank of prohibited books. The ancientest Fathers must be next remov'd, as *Clement* of *Alexandria*,[4] and that *Eusebian* book of Evangelick preparation,[5] transmitting our ears through a hoard of heathenish obscenities to receive the Gospel. Who finds not that *Irenaeus*, *Epiphanius*, *Jerom*,[6] and others discover more heresies then they well confute, and that oft for heresie which is the truer opinion. Nor boots it to say for these, and all the heathen Writers of greatest infection, if it must be thought so, with whom is bound up the life of human learning, that they writ in an unknown tongue, so long as we are sure those languages are known as well to the worst of men, who are both most able, and most diligent to instill the poison they suck, first into the Courts of Princes, acquainting them with the choisest delights, and criticisms of sin. As perhaps did that *Petronius*[7] whom *Nero* call'd his *Arbiter*, the Master of his revels; and that notorious ribald of *Arezzo*,[8] dreaded and yet dear to the Italian Courtiers. I name not him for posterities sake, whom Harry the 8. nam'd in merriment his Vicar of hell.[9] By which compendious way all the contagion that foreine books can infuse will finde a passage to the people farre easier and shorter than an Indian voyage, though it could be sail'd either by the north of *Cataio*[10] Eastward, or of *Canada* Westward, while our Spanish licencing gags the English Presse never so severely. But on the other side that infection which is from books of controversie in Religion is more doubtfull and dangerous to the learned then to the ignorant; and yet those books must be permitted untoucht by the licencer. It will be hard to instance where any ignorant man hath bin ever seduc't by Papisticall book in English, unlesse it were commended and expounded to him by some of that Clergy: and indeed all such tractats whether false or true are as the Prophecie of *Isaiah* was to the eunuch, not to be *understood without a guide*. But of our Priests and Doctors how many have bin corrupted by studying the comments of Jesuits and *Sorbonists*, and how fast they could transfuse that corruption into the people, our experience is both late and sad. It is not forgot, since the acute and distinct *Arminius*[11] was perverted meerly by the perusing of a namelesse discours written at Delf, which at first he took in hand to confute. Seeing therefore that those books, & those in great abundance, which are likeliest to taint both life and doctrine, cannot be suppress without the fall of learning and of all ability in disputation, and that these books of either sort are most and soonest catching to the learned, from whom to the common people whatever is hereticall or dissolute may quickly be convey'd, and that evill manners are as perfectly learnt without books a thousand other ways which cannot be stopt, and evill doctrine not with books can propagate, except a teacher guide, which he might also doe without writing, and so beyond prohibiting, I am not unable to unfold, how this cautelous enterprise of licencing can be exempted from the number of vain and impossible attempts. And he who were pleasantly dispos'd, could not well avoid to lik'n it to the exploit of that gallant man who thought to pound up the crows by shutting his parkgate. Besides another inconvenience, if learned men be the first receivers out of books & dispredders both of vice and error, how shall the licencers themselves be confided in, unlesse we can conferr upon them, or they assume to themselves above all others in the Land, the grace of infallibility, and uncorruptednesse? And again if it be true, that a wise man, like a good refiner can gather gold out of the drossiest volume, and that a fool will be a fool with [p. 14] the best book, yea or without a book, there is no reason that we should deprive a wise man of any advantage to his wisdome, while we seek to restrain from a fool, that which being restrain'd will be no hindrance to his folly ...

[p. 15] ... If we think to regulate Printing, thereby to rectifie manners, we must regulat all recreations and pastimes, all that is delightfull to man. No musick must be heard, no song be set or sung, but what is grave and *Dorick*.[12] There must be licencing dancers, that no gesture, motion, or deportment be taught our youth but what by their allowance shall be thought honest; for such *Plato* was provided of; It will ask more then the work of twenty licencers to examin all the lutes, the violins, and the ghittarrs in every house; they must not be suffer'd to prattle as they doe, but must be licenc'd what they may say. And who shall silence all the airs and madrigalls that whisper softnes in chambers? The Windows also, and the *Balcone's* must be thought on, there are shrewd books, with dangerous Frontispice's, set to sale; who shall prohibit them, shall twenty licencers? The villages also must have their visitors[13] to inquire what lectures the bagpipe and the rebbeck[14] reads, ev'n to the ballatry, and the gammuth of every *municipal* fidler for these are the Countrymans *Arcadia's*,[15] and his *Monte Mayors*.[16] Next, what more Nationall corruption, for which England hears ill abroad, then houshold gluttony: [p. 16] who shall be the rectors of our daily rioting? and what shall be done to inhibit the multitudes that frequent those houses where drunknes is sold and harbour'd? Our garments also should be referr'd to the licencing of some more sober work-masters to see them cut into a lesse wanton garb. Who shall regulat all the mixt conversation of our youth, male and female together, as is the fashion of this

Country, who shall still appoint what shall be discours'd, what presum'd, and no furder? Lastly, who shall forbid and separat all idle resort, all evill company? These things will be, and must be; but how they shall be lest hurtfull, how lest enticing, herein consists the grave and governing wisdom of a State ...

[p. 20] ... And how can a man teach with autority, which is the life of teaching, how can he be a Doctor in his book as he ought to be, or else had better be silent, whenas all he teaches, all he delivers, is but under the tuition, under the correction of his patriarchal licencer to blot or alter what precisely accords not with the hidebound humor which he calls his judgement? When every a [p. 21] cute reader upon the first sight of a pedantick licence, will be ready with these like words to ding the book a coits distance from him, I hate a pupil teacher, I endure not an instructor that comes to me under the wardship of an overseeing fist. I know nothing of the licencer, but that I have his own hand here for his arrogance; who shall warrant me his judgement? The State, Sir, replies the Stationer, but has a quick return: The State shall be my governours, but not my criticks; they may be mistak'n in the choice of a licencer, as easily as this licencer may be mistak'n in an author: this is some common stuffe; and he might adde from Sir *Francis Bacon*, That *such authorized books are but the language of the times*. For though a licencer should happ'n to be judicious more then ordinary, which will be a great jeopardy of the next succession, yet his very office, and his commission enjoyns him to let passe nothing but what is vulgarly receiv'd already.

Nay, which is more lamentable, if the work of any deceased author, though never so famous in his life time, and even to this day, come to their hands for licence to be Printed, or Reprinted, if there be found in his book one sentence of a ventrous edge, utter'd in the height of zeal, and who knows whether it might not be the dictat of a divine Spirit, yet not suiting with every low decrepit humor of their own, though it were *Knox* himself, the Reformer of a Kingdom, that spake it, they will not pardon him their dash: the sense of that great man shall to all posterity be lost, for the fearfulness or the presumptuous rashness of a perfunctory licencer. And to what an author this violence hath bin lately done, and in what book of greatest consequence to be faithfully publisht, I could now instance, but shall forbear till a more convenient season. Yet if these things be not resented seriously and timely by them who have the remedy in their power, but that such iron moulds as these shall have autority to knaw out the choisest periods of exquisitest books, and to commit such a treacherous fraud against the orphan remainders of worthiest men after death, the more sorrow will belong to that hapless race of men, whose misfortune it is to have understanding. Henceforth let no man care to learn, or care to be more than worldly wise; for certainly in higher matters to be ignorant and slothfull, to be a common stedfast dunce will be the only pleasant life, and only in request.

And as it is a particular disesteem of every knowing person alive, and most injurious to the writt'n labours and monuments of the dead, so to me it seems an undervaluing and vilifying of the whole Nation. I [p. 22] cannot set so light by all the invention, the art, the wit, the grave and solid judgement which is in England, as that it can be comprehended in any twenty capacities how good soever, much lesse that it should not passe except their superintendence be over it, except it be sifted and strain'd with their strainers, that it should be uncurrant without their manuall stamp. Truth and understanding are not such wares as to be monopoliz'd and traded in by tickets and statutes and standards. We must not think to make a staple commodity of all the knowledge in the Land, to mark and licence it like our broad cloath and our wooll packs. What is it but a servitude like that impos'd by the Philistim, not to be allow'd the sharpning of our own axes and coulters,[17] but we must repair from all quarters to twenty licencing forges. Had anyone writt'n and divulg'd erroneous things & scandalous to honest life, misusing and forfeiting the esteem had of his reason among men, if after conviction this only censure were adjudg'd him, that he should never henceforth write, but what were first examin'd by an appointed officer, whose hand should be annext to passe his credit for him, that now he might be safely read, it could not be apprehended lesse then a disgracefull punishment. Whence to include the whole Nation, and those that never yet thus offended, under such a diffident and suspectfull prohibition, may plainly be understood what a disparagement it is. So much the more, when as dettors and delinquents may walk abroad without a keeper, but unoffensive books must not stirre forth without a visible jaylor in their title. Nor is it to the common people lesse then a reproach; for if we be so jealous over them, as that we dare not trust them with an English pamphlet, what doe we but censure them for a giddy, vitious, and ungrounded people; in such a sick and weak state of faith and discretion, as to be able to take nothing down but through the pipe of a licencer. That this is care or love of them, we cannot pretend, whenas, in those Popish places where the Laity are most hated and despis'd, the same strictnes is used over them. Wisdom we cannot call it, because it stops but one breach of licence, nor that neither; whenas those corruptions which it seeks to prevent, break in faster at other dores which cannot be shut.

And in conclusion it reflects to the disrepute of our Ministers also, of whose labours we should hope better, and of the proficiencie which their flock reaps by them, then that after all this light of the Gospel which is, and is to be, and all this continuall preaching, they [p. 23] should still be frequented with such an unprincipl'd, unedify'd and laick rabble, as that the whiffe of every new pamphlet should stagger them out of their catechism, and Christian walking ...

[p. 24] ... I shall for neither friend nor foe conceal what the general murmur is, that if it come to inquisitioning again, and licencing, and that we are so timorous of our selvs, and so suspicious of all men, as to fear each book, and the shaking of every leaf, before we know what the contents are, if some who but of late were little better then silenc't, from preaching shall come now to silence us from reading, except what they please it cannot be gues't what is intended by som but a second tyranny over learning: and will soon put it out of controversie, that Bishops and Presbyters are the same to us both name and thing. That those evills of Prelaty which before from five or six and twenty Sees were distributivly charg'd upon the whole people, will now light wholly upon learning, is not obscure to us: whenas now the Pastor of a small unlearned Parish, on the sudden shall be exalted Archbishop over a large dioces of books, and yet not remove, but keep his other cure too, a mysticall pluralist. He who but of late cry'd down the sole ordination of every novice Bachelor of Art, and deny'd sole Jurisdiction over the simplest Parishioner, shall now at home in his privat chair assume both these over worthiest and excellentest books and ablest authors that write them. This is not, Yee Covenants[18] and Protestations[19] that we have made, this is not to put down Prelaty; this is but to chop an Episcopacy, this is but to translate the Palace *Metropolitan* from one kind of dominion into another, this is but an old canonicall slight of *commuting* our penance. To startle thus betimes at a mere unlicenc't pamphlet will after a while be afraid of every conventicle, and a while after will make a conventicle of every Christian meeting. But I am certain that a State govern'd by the rules of justice and fortitude, or a Church built and founded upon the rock of faith and true knowledge, cannot be so pusillanimous. While things are yet not constituted in Religion, that freedom of writing should be restrain'd by a discipline imitated from the Prelats, and learnt by them from the Inquisition, to shut us up all again into the breast of a licencer, must needs give cause of doubt and [p. 25] discouragement to all learned and religious men. Who cannot but discern the finenes of this politic drift, and who are the contrivers; that while Bishops were to be baited down, then all Presses might be open; it was the people's birthright and priviledge in time of Parlament, it was the breaking forth of light? But now, the Bishops abrogated and voided out of the Church, as if our Reformation sought no more, but to make room for others into their seats under another name, the Episcopall arts begin to bud again, the cruse of truth must run no more oyll,[20] liberty of Printing must be enthrall'd again under a Prelaticall commission of twenty, the privilege of the people nullify'd, and, which is wors, the freedom of learning must groan again, and to her old fetter; all this the Parlament yet sitting ...

[p. 27] For if we be sure we are in the right, and doe not hold the truth guiltily, which becomes not, if we our selves condemn not our own weak and frivolous teaching, and the people for an untaught and irreligious and gadding rout, what can be more fair, then when a man judicious, learned, and of a conscience, for aught we know, as good as theirs that taught us what we know, shall not privily from house to house, which is more dangerous, but openly by writing publish to the world what his opinion is, what his reasons, and wherefore that which is now thought cannot be sound. Christ urg'd it as wherewith to justifiee himself, that he preacht in publick; yet writing is more publick then preaching; and more easie to refutation, if need be, there being so many whose businesse and profession meerly it is, to be the champions of Truth; which if they neglect, what can be imputed but their sloth, or unability? ...

[p. 28] There is yet behind of what I purpos'd to lay open, the incredible losse and detriment that this plot of licencing puts us to, more then if som enemy at sea should stop up all our hav'ns and ports, and creeks, it hinders and retards the importation of our richest Merchandize, Truth; nay it was first establisht and put in practice by Antichristian malice and mystery on set purpose to extinguish, if it were possible, the light of Reformation, and to settle falshood; little differing from that policie wherewith the Turk upholds his *Alcoran*, by the prohibition of Printing. 'Tis not deny'd, but gladly confest, we are to send our thanks and vows to heav'n, louder then most of Nations, for that great measure of truth which we enjoy, especially in those main points between us and the Pope, with his appertenences the Prelats: but he who thinks we are to pitch our tent here, and have attain'd the utmost prospect of reformation, that the mortal glasse wherein we contemplate, can shew us, till we come to *beatific* vision, that man by this very opinion declares that he is yet farre short of Truth ... We boast our light; but if we look not wisely on the Sun it self, it smites us into darknes. Who can discern those [p. 29] planets that are oft *Combust*,[21] and those stars of brightest magnitude that rise and set with the Sun, until the opposite motion of their orbs bring them to such a place in the firmament, where they may be seen evning or morning. The light which we have gain'd, was giv'n us, not to be ever staring on, but by it to discover onward things more remote from our knowledge. It is not the unfrocking of a Priest, the unmitring of a Bishop, and the removing him from off the *Presbyterian* shoulders that will make us a happy Nation, no, if other things as great in the Church, and in the rule of life both economicall and politicall be not lookt into and reform'd, we have lookt so long upon the blaze that *Zuinglius*[22] and *Calvin* hath beacon'd up to us, that we are stark blind. There be who perpetually complain of schisms and sects, and make it such a calamity that any man dissents from their maxims. 'Tis their own pride and ignorance which causes the disturbing, who neither will hear with meeknes, nor can convince, yet all must be supprest which is not found in their *Syntagma*. They are the troublers, they are the dividers of unity, who neglect and permit not others to unite those dissever'd peeces which are yet wanting to the body of Truth. To be still searching what we know not, by what we know, still closing up truth to truth as we find it (for all her body is *homogeneal* and proportionall), this is the golden rule in *theology* as well as in Arithmetick, and makes up the best harmony in a Church; not the forc't and outward union of cold, and neutrall, and inwardly divided minds.

Lords and Commons of England, consider what Nation it is wherof ye are, and wherof ye are the governours: a Nation not slow and dull, but of a quick, ingenious and piercing spirit, acute to invent, suttle and sinewy to discours, not beneath the reach of any point the highest that human capacity can soar to. Therefore the studies of learning in her deepest Sciences have bin so ancient and so eminent among us, that Writers of good antiquity, and ablest judgement have bin perswaded that ev'n the school of *Pythagoras* and the *Persian* wisdom took beginning from the old Philosophy of this Iland. And that wise and civill Roman, *Julius Agricola*, who govern'd once here for *Caesar*, preferr'd the naturall wits of Britain, before the labour'd studies of the French. Nor is it for nothing that the grave and frugal *Transylvanian* sends out yearly from as farre as the mountanous borders of *Russia*, and beyond the *Hercynian* wildernes, not their youth, but their stay'd men, to learn our language and our *theologic* [p. 30] arts.[23] Yet that which is above all this, the favour and the love of heav'n we have great argument to think in a peculiar manner propitious and propending towards us. Why else was this Nation chos'n before any other, that out of her, as out of *Sion*, should be proclaim'd and sounded forth the first tidings and trumpet of Reformation to all *Europe*. And had it not bin the obstinat persevernes of our Prelats against the divine and admirable spirit of

Wicklef, to suppresse him as a schismatic and *innovator*, perhaps neither the *Bohemian Huss* and *Jerom*,[24] no nor the name of *Luther*, or of *Calvin* had bin ever known: the glory of reforming all our neighbours had bin completely ours. But now, as our obdurat Clergy have with violence demean'd the matter, we are become hitherto the latest and backwardest Schollers, of whom God offer'd to have made us the teachers. Now once again by all concurrence of signs, and by the general instinct of holy and devout men, as they daily and solemnly express their thoughts, God is decreeing to begin some new and great period in his Church, ev'n to the reforming of Reformation it self: what does he then but reveal Himself to his servants, and as his manner is, first to his English-men.[25] I say as his manner is, first to us, though we mark not the method of his counsels, and are unworthy. Behold now this vast City: a city of refuge, the mansion house of liberty, encompast and surrounded with his protection; the shop of warre hath not there more anvils and hammers waking, to fashion out the plates and instruments of armed Justice in defence of beleaguer'd Truth, then there be pens and heads there, sitting by their studious lamps, musing, searching, revolving new notions and ideas wherewith to present, as with their homage and their fealty, the approaching Reformation: others as fast reading, trying all things, assenting to the force of reason and convincement. What could a man require more from a Nation so pliant and so prone to seek after knowledge. What wants there to such a towardly and pregnant soyle, but wise and faithfull labourers, to make a knowing people, a Nation of Prophets, of Sages, and of Worthies ... Where there is much desire to learn, there of necessity will be much arguing, much writing, many opinions; for opinion in good men is but knowledge in the making. Under these fantastic terrors of [p. 31] sect and schism, we wrong the earnest and zealous thirst after knowledge and understanding which God hath stirr'd up in this City. What some lament of, we rather should rejoyce at, should rather praise this pious forwardnes among men, to reassume the ill deputed care of their Religion into their own hands again. A little generous prudence, a little forbearance of one another, and som grain of charity might win all these diligences to joyn, and unite in one generall and brotherly search after Truth; could we but foregoe this Prelaticall tradition of crowding free consciences and Christian liberties into canons and precepts of men ...

[p. 34] What would be best advis'd then, if it be found so hurtfull and so unequall to suppresse opinions for the newnes, or the unsutablenes to a customary acceptance, will not be my task to say; I only shall repeat what I have learnt from one of your own honourable number, a right noble and pious lord, who, had he not sacrific'd his life and fortunes to the Church and Commonwealth, we had not now mist and bewayl'd a worthy and undoubted patron of this argument. Ye know him, I am sure; yet I for honours sake, and may it be eternall to him, shall name him, the Lord *Brook*.[26] He writing of Episcopacy, and by the way treating of sects and schisms, left Ye his vote, or rather now the last words of his dying charge, which I know will ever be of dear and honoured regard with Ye, so full of meeknes and breathing charity, that next to his last testament, who bequeath'd love and peace to his Disciples, I cannot call to mind where I have read or heard words more mild and peaceful. He there exhorts us to hear with patience and humility those, however they be miscall'd, that desire to live purely, in such a use of Gods Ordinances, as the best guidance of their conscience gives them, and to tolerat them, though in some disconformity to our selves. The book it self will tell us more at large being publisht to the world, and dedicated to the Parlament by him who both for his life and for his death deserves, that what advice he left be not laid by without perusall.

And now the time in speciall is, by priviledge to write and speak what may help to the furder discussing of matters in agitation. The temple of *Janus*[27] with his two *controversal* faces might now not unsignificantly be set open. And though all the windes of doctrin were let loose to play upon the earth, so Truth be in the field, we do injuriously, by licencing and prohibiting to misdoubt her strength. Let her and Falshood grapple; who ever knew Truth put to the wors, in a free and open encounter. Her confuting is the best and surest suppressing. He who hears what praying there is for light and clearer knowledge to be sent down among us, would think of other matters to be constituted beyond the discipline of *Geneva*, fram'd and fabric't already to our hands. Yet when the [p. 35] new light which we beg for shines in upon us, there be who envy, and oppose, if it come not first in at their casements. What a collusion is this, whenas we are exhorted by the wise man to use diligence, *to seek for wisdom as for hidd'n treasures*[28] early and late, that another order shall enjoyn us to know nothing but by statute. When a man hath bin labouring the hardest labour in the deep mines of knowledge; hath furnisht out his findings in all their equipage, drawn forth his reasons as it were a battell raung'd; scatter'd and defeated all objections in his way, calls out his adversary into the plain, offers him the advantage of wind and sun, if he please; only that he may try the matter by dint of argument, for his opponents then to sculk, to lay ambushments, to keep a narrow bridge of licencing where the challenger should passe, though it be valour anough in shouldership, is but weaknes and cowardise in the wars of Truth. For who knows not that Truth is strong, next to the Almighty; she needs no policies, nor stratagems, nor licencings to make her victorious, those are the shifts and the defences that error uses against her power: give her but room, & do not bind her when she sleeps, for then she speaks not true, as the old *Proteus* did,[29] who spake oracles only when he was caught & bound, but then rather she turns herself into all shapes, except her own, and perhaps tunes her voice according to the time, as *Micaiah* did before *Ahab*, untill she be adjur'd into her own likenes. Yet is it not impossible that she may have more shapes than one. What else is all that rank of things indifferent, wherein Truth may be on this side, or on the other, without being unlike her self. What but a vain shadow else is the abolition of *those ordinances, that hand writing nayl'd to the cross*, what great purchase is this Christian liberty which *Paul* so often boasts of. His doctrine is, that he who eats or eats not, regards a day, or regards it not, may doe either to the Lord. How many other things might be tolerated in peace, and left to conscience, had we but charity, and were it not the chief strong hold of our hypocrisie to be ever judging one another. I fear yet this iron yoke of outward conformity hath left a slavish print upon our necks; the ghost of a linnen decency yet haunts us. We stumble and are impatient at the least dividing of one visible congregation from another, though it be not in fundamentalls; and through our forwardnes to suppresse, and our backwardnes to recover any [p. 36] enthrall'd peece of truth out of the gripe of custom, we care not to keep truth separated from truth, which is the fiercest rent and disunion of all. We doe not see that while we still affect by all means a rigid externall formality, we may as soon fall again into a grosse conforming stupidity, a stark and dead congealment of *wood and hay and stubble*, forc't and frozen together, which is more to the sudden degenerating of a Church than many *subdichotomies* of petty schisms.

Not that I can think well of every light separation, or that all in a Church is to be expected *gold and silver and precious stones*:[30] it is not possible for man to sever the wheat from the tares, the good fish from the other frie; that must be the Angels Ministery at the end of mortall things. Yet if all cannot be of one mind, as who looks they should be? this doubtles is more wholsome, more prudent, and more Christian that many be tolerated, rather than all compell'd. I mean not tolerated Popery, and open superstition, which, as it extirpats all religions and civill supremacies, so it self should be extirpat, provided first that all charitable and compassionat means be us'd to win and regain the weak and the misled: that also which is impious or evil absolutely either against faith or maners no law can possibly permit, that intends not to unlaw itself: but those neighbouring differences, or rather indifferences, are what I speak of, whether in some point of doctrine or of discipline, which though they may be many, yet need not interrupt *the unity of the Spirit*, if we could but find among us *the bond of peace* ...[31]

Notes

1. The 'wayfaring' of the printed text has been corrected to 'warfaring' because it is highly probable that the correction has Milton's authority.
2. The OED gives the meaning as 'of the nature of an outgrowth or excrescence'.
3. The reference to *Faerie Queene*, II, vii, 2; viii, 3.
4. For Clement (c. 150–c. 215), v., ODCC. Milton is probably thinking of his *Hortatory Address to the Greeks*.
5. Eusebius (c. 260–c. 340), bishop of Caesarea. The reference is to his *Praeparatio Evangelica*.
6. Irenaeus (c. 130–c. 200), bishop of Lyons; Epiphanius (c. 315–403), bishop of Salamis, whose *Panarion* attacks all the heresies known to him; Jerome (c. 342–420), biblical scholar. They, and Eusebius, are in ODCC.
7. The author of the *Satyricon*. He died in 66 AD.
8. Pietro Aretino (1492–1557), lewd poet.
9. Harris Fletcher has shown that the allusion is to Sir Francis Bryan (d. 1550), minor poet and cousin of Anne Boleyn, v., DNB and *Journal of English and Germanic Philology*, xlvii (1948), 387–9.
10. i.e., China.
11. Arminius (Jakob Hermandszoon, 1560–1609), professor of theology at Leyden and critic of some of the main tenets of Calvinism, v., C. Bangs, *Arminius: A Study of the Dutch Reformation* (Nashville, 1971). Later Milton embraced Arminianism.
12. A reference to Plato's discussion of music in *Republic*, III, 398–9.

13. A reference to the 'visitors' that bishops, under the Laudian regime, were to appoint to report on each parish, v., Daniel Neal, *The History of the Puritans* (London, 1754), I, 590–1.
14. or 'rebec'; a medieval three-stringed instrument played with a bow.
15. Sir Philip Sidney, *The Countesse of Pembrokes Arcadia* (London, 1590).
16. A reference to the extremely popular Spanish prose romanc by Jorge de Montemayer, *Diana* (c. 1559).
17. See 1 Samuel 13: 19–20.
18. The Scottish National Covenant of 23 Feb. 1638, the forerunner of the Solemn League and Covenant, ratified on 25 Sept. 1643, between England and Scotland.
19. Parliament's 'Protestation' of 3–4 May 1641 against the King's threat to coerce Parliament by force and which promised to defend 'the lawful rights and liberties of the subject' as well as Crown, Parliament and religion.
20. 1 Kings 17: 9–16.
21. i.e., planets whose orbits take them so near the sun that their influence is negated or 'burnt up'.
22. Huldrych Zwingli (1484-1531), Protestant reformer of Zurich.
23. Agricola (37-93 AD) was proconsul of Britain from 78 to 85 AD. Milton is referring to the alleged wisdom of the Druids. Hyrcania was Caesar's name for the forests of southern Germany. Transylvania in Milton's day was Protestant and sent scholars to study theology in western Europe.
24. Jerome of Prague (died 1416), follower of Wycliffe and Huss.
25. The conviction that England had a providential and messianic role in history is to be found also in *An Apologeticall Narration* (London, 1644), 22–3 and elsewhere.
26. Roberty Greville, Lord Brooke (1608–43), was a general in the parliamentary army, v., DNB.
27. The two-faced Roman god of beginnings. The two doors of his little temple in the forum at Rome were shut in times of peace and open in times of war.
28. Proverbs 2: 4–5.
29. *Odyssey*, IV, 384–93.
30. 1 Cor. 3: 10–13.
31. Ephes. 4: 3.

PART III

FACETS OF FREEDOM, 1640–1660

Document III.1

John Milton: Of Reformation

John Milton wrote five anti-prelatical tracts in 1641–2. Both quotations come from the first of them, *Of Reformation Touching Chvrch-Discipline in England and the Cavses that Hitherto Have Hindered It* (1641). It is divided into two 'books'. Extract (a) comes from the first and (b) from the second. The tract is printed in *The Complete Prose Works of John Milton* (New Haven: Yale Univ. Press, 1953), I (1624–42) with extensive annotations. The page references appended to the above paragraphs refer to this volume. It will be observed that Milton follows John Foxe, *Acts and Monuments*, 8 vols (London, 1877) in dating the origins of the English Reformation in the time of John Wycliffe. By 'Chanonies' Milton apparently means 'canonries'. The Puritan objections to ceremonies had just been rehearsed in the London Petition of 11 December 1640, v., H. Gee & W. J. Hardy, *Documents Illustrative of English Church History* (London, 1896), 537ff. There is a copious literature dealing with every aspect of Milton's career and work. Perhaps a beginning could be made with W. R. Parker, *Milton: A Biography*, 2 vols (Oxford, 1968).

(a)
When I call to mind at last, after so many darke Ages, wherein the huge overshadowing traine of *Error* had almost swept all the Starres out of the Firmament of the Church; how the bright and blissful *Reformation* (by Divine Power) strook through the black and settled Night of *Ignorance* and *Antichristian Tyranny*, me thinks a soveraigne and reviving joy must needs rush into the bosome of him that reads or heares; and the sweet Odour of the returning *Gospell* imbath his Soule with the fragrancy of Heaven. Then was the Sacred *Bible* sought out of the dusty corners where prophane Falshood and Neglect had throwne it, the *Schooles* opened, *Divine* and *Humane Learning* rak't out of the *embers* of *forgotten Tongues*, the *Princes* and *Cities* trooping apace to the new erected Banner of *Salvation*; the *Martyrs*, with the unresistable *might* of *weaknesse*, shaking the *Powers* of *Darknesse*, and scorning the *fiery rage* of the old *red Dragon*.

The pleasing pursuit of these thoughts hath oft-times led mee into a serious question and debatement with my selfe, how it should come to passe that *England* (having had this *grace* and *honour* from GOD, to bee the first that should set up a Standard for the recovery of *lost Truth*, and blow the first *Evangelick Trumpet* to the *Nations*, holding up, as from a Hill, the new Lampe of *saving light* to all Christendome) should now be last, and most unsettl'd in the enjoyment of the *Peace* whereof she taught the way to others?; although indeed our *Wicklefs* preaching at which all the succeding *Reformers* more effectually lighted their *Tapers*, was to his Countrey men but a short blaze soone dampt and stifl'd by the *Pope*, and *Prelates* for six or seven Kings Reignes; yet me thinkes that the *Precedencie* which GOD gave this *Iland*, to be the first *Restorer* of *buried Truth*, should have beene followed with more happy successe ... for, albeit in *purity* of *Doctrine* we agree with our Brethren; yet in Discipline, which is the *execution* and *applying* of *Doctrine* home, and laying the *salve* to the very *Orifice* of the *Wound*

... in this we are no better than a *Schisme* from all the *Reformation* and a score scandal to them; for while we hold *Ordination* to belong onely to *Bishops*, as our *Prelates* doe, wee must of necessity hold also their *Ministers* to be no *Ministers*, and shortly after their *Church* to be no *Church*. Not to speake of those senceless *Ceremonies* which wee onely retaine, as a dangerous earnest of sliding back to *Rome*, and serving meerely, either as mist to cover nakedness where true *grace* is extinguisht, or as an Enterlude to set out the *pompe* of *Prelatisme* ... [pp. 524–5, 527]

> Milton then analyses at considerable length and with impressive erudition, the 'mistakes' and 'errors' of the English Reformation which brought about this disastrous state of affairs. He ends his argument as follows:

If we will but purge with sovrain eyesalve that intellectual ray which *God* hath planted in us, then we would beleeve the Scriptures protesting their own plainnes, and perspicuity, calling to them to be instructed, not only the *wise* and *learned*, but the *simple*, the *poor*, the *babes*, foretelling an extraordinary effusion of *Gods* Spirit upon every age and sexe, attributing to all men, and requiring that which is good; and as the Scriptures themselves pronounce their own plainnes, so doe the Fathers testify of them. [p. 566]

(b)
... Seeing therfore the perillous and confused estate into which are faln, and that to the certain knowledge of all men, through the irreligious pride and hatefull Tyranny of Prelats, ... if we will now resolve to settle affairs either according to pure Religion, or sound Policy, we must first of all begin roundly to cashier, and cut away from the publick body the noysom, and diseased tumor of Prelacie, and come from Schisme to *unity* with our neighbour Reformed sister Churches, which with the blessing of *peace* and *pure doctrine* have now long time flourish'd; and doubtles with all hearty *joy* and *gratulation*, will meet, and welcome our Christian *union* with them, as they have bin all this while griev'd at our strangenes, and little better then separation from them ... [p. 598]

Let us not be so overcredulous, unlesse GOD hath blinded us, as to trust our deer Soules into the hands of men that beg so devoutly for the pride, and gluttony of their owne backs, and bellies, that sue and sollicit so eagerly, not for the saving of Soules, the consideration of which can have heer no place at all, but for their Bishoprickes, Deaneries, Prebends and Chanonies; how can these men not be corrupt, whose very cause is the bribe of their own pleading; whose mouths cannot open without the strong breath and loud stench of avarice, Simony, and Sacrilege, embezling the treasury of the Church on painted and guilded walles of Temples, wherein GOD hath testified to have no delight, warming their Palace Kitchins, and from thence their unctuous, and epicurean paunches, with the almes of the blind, the lame, the impotent, the aged, the orfan, the widow ... [pp. 609–11]

Document III.2

The 'Five Brethren':
An Apologeticall Narration

The imprimatur of the censor, facing the title-page, is that of Charles Herle (1598–1659), a Presbyterian and one of the twelve whom Parliament appointed in June 1643 to license religious books. In approving the book he praises its 'peaceablenesse, modesty, and candour' and says that it is in 'every way fit for the Presse'.

The full title was: *An Apologeticall Narration Hvmbly svbmitted to the Honourable Houses of Parliament. By Tho: Goodwin, Philip Nye, Sidrach Simpson, Jer: Burroughes, William Bridge. London, Printed for Robert Dawlman. M.DC. XLIII.* The five authors had all been in exile in the Netherlands during the 1630s and returned to England in 1640. Strictly speaking it is anachronistic to call them 'The Dissenting Brethren'. That term was originally used eleven months later, in November 1644, when the five, together with William Carter (d. 1658, aged 52) and William Greenhill (1591–1671), expressed their opposition to the type of church government which the Presbyterian majority in the Westminster Assembly then recommended to the House of Commons, v., M. R. Watts, *The Dissenters* (Oxford, 1978), I, 100–2. The *Apologeticall Narration* was composed to allay the fears of the Presbyterians that the unrestricted formation of gathered churches was producing ecclesiastical disorder and so undermining their resolve to secure uniformity in the reconstituted Church of England. Hence the harsh judgement on Brownists and Separatists. For the members of the Westminster Assembly, v., in addition to DNB, James Reid, *Memoirs of the Lives and Writings of those Eminent Divines who Convened in the ... Assembly at Westminster* (vol. I, 1811; vol. II, 1815 – both reprinted in one volume in London, 1982). See also on the significance of the *Apologeticall Narration*, W. Haller, *Liberty and Reformation in the Puritan Revolution* (3rd edn, London, 1967), 116–9; H. W. Clark, *History of English Nonconformity* (London, 1911), I, 326–7.

[p. 1] And now we shall begin to make some appearance into publique light, unto whose view and judgements should we (that have hitherto laine under so dark a cloud of manifold misapprehensions) at first present our selves, but the Supreame Judicatory of this Kingdome, which is and hath been in all times the most just and severe Tribunall for [p. 2] guiltinesse to appeare before, much more to dare to appeale unto; and yet withall the most sacred refuge and *Asylum* for mistaken and mis-judged innocence?

The most, if not all of us, had ten years since (some more, some lesse) severall setled Stations in the Ministery, in places of publique use in the Church, not unknown to many of your selves; but the sinfull evill of those corruptions in the publique worship and government of this Church, which all doe now so generally acknowledge and decrie, took hold upon our consciences long before some others of our brethren; And then how impossible it was to continue in those times our service and standings, all mens apprehensions will readily acquit us.

Neither at the first did we see or look further then the *dark part*, the evill of those superstitions adjoyned to the worship of God, which have been the common stumbling block and offence of many thousand tender consciences, both in our own and our neighbour Churches, ever since the first Reformation of Religion: which yet was enough to deprive us of the publique exercise of our Ministeries, and together therewith (as the watchfulnesse of those times grew) of our personall participation in some ordinances; and further exposed us either to personall violence and persecution, or an exile to avoid it: Which latter we did the rather choose, that so the use and exercise of our Ministeries (for which we were borne and live) might not be wholly lost, nor our selves remain [p. 3] debarred from the enjoyment of the Ordinances of Christ, which we account our birth-right, and best portion in this life.

This being our condition, we were cast upon a farther necessity of enquiring into and viewing the *light part*, the positive part of *Church worship* and Government; And to that end to search out what were the first Apostolique directions, pattern and examples of those Primitive Churches recorded in the New Testament, as that sacred pillar of fire to guide us. And in this enquirie, we lookt upon the word of Christ as impartially, and unprejudicedly, as men made of flesh and blood are like to doe in any juncture of time that may fall out; the places we went to, the condition we were in, the company we went forth with, affording no temptation to byas us any way, but leaving us as freely to be guided by that light and touch Gods Spirit should by the Word vouchsafe our consciences, as the Needle toucht with the Load-stone is in the Compasse: And we had (of all men) the greatest reason to be true to our own consciences in what we should embrace, seeing it was for our consciences that we were deprived at once of what ever was dear to us. We had no new Common-wealths to rear, to frame Church-government unto, whereof any one piece might stand in the others light, to cause the least variation by us from the Primitive pattern; We had no State-ends or Politicall interests to comply with; No Kingdoms in our eye to subdue unto our mould; (which yet will be coexistent with the peace of any form of Civil Govern [p. 4] ment on earth) No preferment or worldly respects to shape our opinions for: We had nothing else to doe but simply and singly to consider how to worship God acceptably, and so most according to his word.

We were not engaged by Education or otherwise to any other of the Reformed Churches; And although we consulted with reverence what they hold forth both in their writings and practice, yet we could not but suppose that they might not see into all things about worship and government, their intentions being most spent (as also of our first Reformers in *England*) upon the Reformation in Doctrine, in which they had a most happy hand: And we had with many others observed, that although the exercise of that Government had been accompanied with more peace, yet the Practicall part, *the power of godlinesse* and the profession thereof, with difference from carnall and formall Christians, had not been advanced and held forth among them, as in this our owne Island, as themselves have generally acknowledged. We had the advantage of all that light which the conflicts of our owne Divines (the good old Non-conformists) had struck forth in their times; And the draughts of Discipline which they had drawn; which we found not in all things the very same with the practises of the Reformed Churches; And what they had written came much more commended to us, not onely because they were our own, but because sealed with their manifold and bitter sufferings. We had likewise the fatall miscarriages and ship- [p. 5] wracks of the *Separation* (whom ye call *Brownists*) as Land-marks to fore-warn us of those rocks and shelves they ran upon; which also did put us upon an enquiry into the principles that might be the causes of their divisions. Last of all, we had the recent and later example of the wayes and practices (and those improved to a better Edition and greater refinement, by all the fore-mentioned helps) of those multitudes of godly men of our own Nation, almost to the number of another Nation, and among them some as holy and judicious Divines as this Kingdome hath bred; whose sincerity in their way hath been testified before all the world, and wil be unto all generations to come, by the greatest undertaking (but that of our father *Abraham* out of his own countrey, and his seed after him) a transplanting themselves many thousand miles distance, and that by sea, into a Wildernes, meerly to worship God more purely, whither to allure them there could be no other invitement. And yet we still stood as unengaged spectators, free to examine and consider what truth is to be found in and amongst all these, (all which we look upon as Reformed Churches) and this nakedly according to the word; We resolved not to take up our religion by or from any partie, and yet to approve and hold fast whatsoever is good in any, though never so much differing from us, yea opposite unto us.

And for our own congregations, we meane of *England* (in which thorough the grace of Christ we were converted, and exercised our Ministeries [p. 6] long, to the conversion of many others) We have this sincere profession to make before God and all the world, that all *that* conscience of the defilements we conceived to cleave to the true worship of God in them, or of the unwarranted power in Church Governours exercised therein, did never work in any of us any other thought, much lesse opinion, but that multitudes of the assemblies and parochiall congregations thereof, were *the true Churches and Body of Christ, and the Ministery thereof a true Ministery*: Much lesse did it ever enter into our hearts to judge them *Antichristian*; we saw and cannot but see that by the same reason the Churches abroad in *Scotland, Holland, &c.* (though more reformed) yet for their mixture must be in like manner judged no Churches also, which to imagine or conceive, is and hath ever been an horrour to our thoughts. Yea we always have professed, & that in these times when the Churches of *England* were the most, either actually overspread with defilements, or in the greatest danger thereof, and when our selves had least, yea no hopes of ever so much as visiting our own land again in peace and safety to our persons; that we both did and would hold a *communion* with them as the Churches of Christ. And besides this profession, as a reall testimony thereof, some of us after we, actually, were in this way of communion, baptized our children in Parishionall congregations, and (as we had occasion) did offer to receive into the communion of the Lords Supper with us, some (whom we knew godly that come to visit us when we were [p. 7] in our exile) upon that relation, fellowship, and commembership they held in their parish Churches in *England*, they professing themselves to be members thereof, and belonging thereunto. What we have since our returne publiquely and avowedly made declaration of to this purpose, many hundreds can witnesse, and some of our brethren in their printed bookes candidly do testify for us. [*Margin*: Mr. *Cheynell*, Rise & growth of Socinianisme.]

And as we alwayes held this respect unto our own Churches in this Kingdome, so we received and were entertained with the like from those reformed Churches abroad, among whom we were cast to live, we both mutually gave and received the right hand of fellowship, which they on their parts abundantly manifested by the very same characters and testimonies of difference which are proper to their own Orthodoxe Churches, and wherby they use to distinguish them from all those sects (which they tollerate, but not own) and all the assemblies of them (which yet now we are here some would needs ranke us with) granting to some of us their own Churches, or publique places for worship, to assemble in, where themselves met for the worship of God at differing houres the same day: As likewise the priviledge of ringing a publique Bell to call unto our meetings: which we mention because it is amongst them made the great signall of difference between their own allowed Churches and all other assemblies, unto whom it is strictly prohibited and forbidden, as *Guiciardine* hath long since observed: And others of us found such acceptance with them, that in testimony there- [p. 8] of they allowed a full and liberall maintenance annually for our Ministers, yea and constantly also Wine for our Communions. And then we again on our parts, not onely held brotherly correspondency with their Divines, but received also some of the members of their Churches (who desired to communicate with us) unto communion in the Sacraments and other ordinances, by virtue of their relation of membership retained in those Churches.

Now for the way & practices of our Churches, we give this briefe and generall account. Our *publique worship* was made up of no other parts then the worship of all other reformed Churches doth consist of. As, publique and solemne prayers *for Kings and all in authority, &c.* the reading the Scriptures of the Old and New Testament; Exposition of them as occasion was; and constant preaching of the word; the administration of the two Sacraments, Baptisme to infants, and the Lords Supper; singing of Psalmes; collections for the poor, &c. every Lords day. For *Officers* and publique Rulers in the Church, we set up no other but the very same which the reformed Churches judge necessary and sufficient, and as instituted by Christ and his Apostles for the perpetuall government of his Church, that is, *Pastors, Teachers, Ruling Elders,* (with us not lay but Ecclesiastique persons separated to that service) and *Deacons*. And for the matter *of governement and censures of the Church*, we had nor executed any other but what all ac- [p .9] knowledge, namely, *Admonition*, and *Excommunication* upon obstinacie and impenitencie, (which we blesse God we never exercised.) This latter we judged should be put in execution, for no other kind of sins then may evidently be presumed to be perpetrated against the parties known light; as whether it be a sin in manners and conversation, such as is committed against the light of nature, or the common received practices of Christianity, professed in all the Churches of Christ; or if in opinions, then such, as are likewise contrary to the received principles of Christianity, and the power of godlinesse, professed by the party himselfe, and universally acknowledged in all the rest of the churches, and no other sins to be the subject of such a dreadful sentence.

And for our directions in these or what ever else requisite to the management of them, we had these three Principles more especially in our eye, to guide and steere our practice by.

First, the supreame rule *without us*, was the Primitive patterne and example of the churches erected by the Apostles. Our consciences were possessed with that reverence and adoration of the fulnesse of the Scriptures, that there is therein a compleat sufficiencie, as to make the *man of God perfect*, so also to make the Churches of God perfect, (meere circumstances we except, or what rules the law of nature doth in common dictate) if the directions and examples therein delivered were fully known and followed. And although we cannot professe that sufficiencie of knowledge as to be [p. 10] able to lay forth all those rules therein which may meet with all cases and emergencies that may or sometimes did fal out amongst us, or that may give satisfaction unto all Queres possible to be put unto us; yet we found principles enough, not onely *fundamentall* and essential to the being of a Church, but *superstructory* also for the wel-being of it, and those to us cleare and certaine, and such as might well serve to preserve our Churches in peace and from offence, and would comfortably guide us to heaven in a safe way: And the observation of so many of those particulars to be laid forth in the Word, became to us a more certaine evidence and cleare confirmation that there were the like rules and ruled cases for all occasions whatsoever, if we were able to discerne them. And for all such cases wherein we saw not a cleare resolution from Scripture, example, or direction, wee stil professedly suspended, untill God should give us further light, not daring to eeke out what was defective in our light in matters Divine with humane prudence, (the fatall errour to Reformation) lest by *sowing* any *piece of the old garment* unto *the new*, we should make the *rent worse*; we having this promise of grace for our encouragement in this, which in our publique Assemblies was often for our comfort mentioned, that *in thus doing the will of God we should know more*.

A second Principle we carried along with us in all our resolutions, was, Not to make our present judgement and practice a binding law unto our selves for the future, which we in like manner made [p. 11] continuall profession of upon all occasions. We had too great an instance of our own frailty in the former way of our conformity; and therefore in a jealousie of our selves, we kept this reserve, (which we made open and constant professions of) to alter and retract (though not lightly) what ever should be discovered to be taken up out of a mis-understanding of the rule: Which Principle wee wish were (next to that most supreame, namely, to be in all things guided by the perfect wil of God) enacted as the most *sacred law* of all other, in the midst of all other Laws and Canons Ecclesiastical in Christian States and Churches throughout the world.

Thirdly, we are able to hold forth this true and just Apologie unto the world, That in the matters of greatest moment and controversie, we stil chose to practice safely, and so, as we had reason to judge that all sorts, or the most of all the Churches did acknowledge warrantable, although they make *additaments* thereunto.

For instance: Whereas one great controversie of these times is about the *qualification of the Members* of Churches, and the promiscuous receiving and mixture of good and bad; Therein we chose the better part, and to be sure, received in none but such as all the Churches in the world would by the balance of the Sanctuary acknowledge faithful. And yet in this we are able to make this true and just profession also, That the Rules which we gave up our judgements unto, to judge those we received in amongst us by, were of that la- [p. 12] titude as would take in any member of Christ, the meanest, in whom there may be supposed to be the *least of Christ*, and indeed such and no other as all the godly in this Kingdome carry in their bosomes to judge others by. We took measure of no mans holinesse by his opinion, whether concurring with us, or adverse unto us; And Churches made up of such, we were sure no Protestant could but approve of, (as touching the members of it) to be a true Church, with which communion might be held. Againe, concerning the great ordinance of *Publique Prayer* and the *Lyturgie* of the Church, whereas there is this great controversie upon it about the lawfulnesse of set formes prescribed; we practiced (without condemning others) what all sides doe allow, and themselves doe practice also, that the publique Prayers in our Assemblies should be framed by the meditations and study of our own Ministers, out of their own gifts, (the fruits of Christs Ascension) as well as their Sermons use to be. This we were sure all allowed of, though they superadded the other. So likewise for the government and discipline in the Churches, however the practice of the Reformed Churches is in greater matters to govern each particular congregation by a combined *Presbyterie* of the *Elders* of several congregations united in one for government; yet so, as in their judgements they allow, especially in some cases, a particular congregation, an entire and compleat power of jurisdiction to be exercised by the Elders thereof within it selfe; Yea and our own Master *Cartwright*, holy *Baynes*, and other old [p. 13] Non-conformists, place the power of Excommunication in the Eldership of each particular Church with the consent of the Church, untill they do miscarry, and then indeed they subject them to such Presbyterial and Provincial Assemblies as the proper refuge for appeales and for compounding of differences amongst Churches; which combination of Churches others of them therefore call *Ecclesiae ortae*, but particular congregations *Ecclesiae primae*, as wherein *firstly* the power and priviledg of a Church is to be exercised. And withall we could not but imagine, that the first Churches planted by the Apostles, were ordinarily of no more in one city at first then might make up one entire congregation, ruled by their own Elders, that also preached to them; for that in every city where they came, the number of converts did or should arise to such a multitude as to make several and sundry congregations, or that the Apostles should stay the setting up of any Churches at all, until they rose to such a numerous multiplication as might make such a Presbyterial combination, we did not imagine. We found also those *Non-conformists* (that wrote against the Episcopal Government) in their Answer to the Arguments used for Episcopal Government over many Churches, brought from the instances of the multitude of Beleevers at *Jerusalem* and other places and cities, mentioned in the New Testament, to assert that it could not be infallibly proved that any of those we reade of in the *Acts* and elsewhere, were yet so numerous, as necessarily to exceed the limits of one particular congre- [p. 14] gation in those first times. We found it also granted by them all, that there should be several Elders in every congregation, who had power over them in the Lord; and we judged that all those precepts, *obey your Elders*, and *them that are over you*, were (to be sure, and all grant it) meant of the Pastours and Teachers, and other Elders that were set over them in each particular congregation respectively, and to be as certainly the intendment of the holy Ghost, as in those like commands, *Wives obey your owne husbands, Servants your own governours*, to be meant of their several Families respectively.

We could not therefore but judge it a safe and an allowed way to retaine the government of our severall congregations for matter of discipline within themselves, to be exercised by their own Elders, whereof we had (for the most part of the time we were abroad) three at least in each congregation, whom we were subject to: yet not clayming to our selves an *independent power* in every congregation, to give account or be subject to none others, but onely a ful and entire power compleat within our selves, until we should be challenged to err grosly; such as *Corporations* enjoy, who have the power and priviledge to passe sentence for life & death within themselves, and yet are accountable to the State they live in. But that it should be the institution of Christ or his Apostles, that the combination of the Elders of many Churches should be the first compleat and entire seat of Church power over each congregation so combined; or that they could challenge and assume [p. 15] that authority over the Churches they feed and teach not ordinarily by virtue of those fore-mentioned Apostolicall precepts, was to us a question, and judged to be an *additament* unto the other, which therefore rested on those that allowed us what we practised, over and above, to make evident and demonstrate (and certainly of all other the challenge of all spiritual power from Christ had need have a cleare pattent to shew for it) ...

And whereas the common prejudice and exception laid into all mens thoughts against us and our opinions is, that in such congregationall governe- [p. 16] ment thus entire within it self, there is no allowed sufficient remedy for miscarriages, though never so grosse; no reliefe for wrongful sentences or persons injured thereby; no roome for complaints: no powerful or effectual means to reduce a Church or Churches that fal into heresie, schisme, &c. but every one is left and may take liberty without controule to do what is good in their own eyes; we have (through the good providence of God upon us) from the avowed declarations of our *judgements* among our Churches mutually during our exile, and that also confirmed by the most solemne instance of our *practice*, wherewith to vindicate our selves and way in this particular; which upon no other occasion we should ever have made thus publique.

God so ordered it that a scandall and offence fell out between those very Churches whilst living in this banishment (whereof we our selves, that write these things, were then the Ministers) one of our Churches having unhappily deposed one of their Ministers, the other judged it not onely as too suddaine an act (having proceeded in a matter of so great moment without consulting their sister Churches, as was publiquely professed we should have done in such cases of concernement) but also in the proceedings thereof as too severe, and not managed according to the rules laid down in the word. In this case our Churches did mutually and universally acknowledge and submit to this as a sacred and undoubted principle and supreame law to be observed among all Churches, that as by [p. 17] virtue of that Apostolical command, Churches as wel as particular men *are bound to give no offence neither to Iew nor Gentile, nor the Churches of God* they live amongst. So that in all cases of such offence or difference, by the obligation of the comon law of *comunion of Churches*, & for the *vindication of the glory of Christ*, which in comon they hold forth, the church or churches chalenged to *offend* or *differ*, are to submit themselves (upon the challenge of the offence or complaint of the person wronged) to the most full & open tryall & examination by other neighbour Churches offended thereat, of what ever hath given offence: And further, that by the virtue of the same and like law of *not partaking in other mens sins*, the Churches offended may & ought upon the impenitency of those Churches, persisting in their errour and miscarriage to pronounce that heavy sentence, against them, of with-drawing and renouncing all Christian communion with them until they do repent; And further to declare and protest this, with the causes thereof, to all other Churches of Christ, that they may do the like.

And what further *authority*, or proceedings purely *Ecclesiasticall*, of one, or many sister Churches towards another whole Church, or Churches offending, either the Scriptures doe hold forth, or can rationally be put in execution (without the Magistrate interposing a power of another nature, unto which we upon his particular cognisance, and examination of such causes, professe ever to submit, and also to be most willing to have recourse unto) for our parts we saw not then, nor do yet see. And [p. 18] likewise we did then suppose, and doe yet, that this principle of submission of Churches that miscarry unto other Churches offended, together with this other, that it is a command from Christ enjoyned to Churches that are finally offended to denounce such a sentence of *Non-communion* and *withdrawing* from them whilst impenitent, as unworthy to hold forth the name of Christ, (*these*) principles being received and generally acknowledged by the Churches of Christ to be a mutuall duty, as strictly enjoyned them by Christ as any other) that these would be as effectuall means (through the blessing of Christ) to awe and preserve Churches and their Elders in their duties, as that other of claime to an authoritative power Ecclesiastical to *Excommunicate* other Churches or their Elders offending, in a meere Ecclesiastial notion, *That* of Excommunication pretended hath but this more in it, That it is a *delivering* of whole Churches and their Elders offending *unto Satan*, (for which we know no warrant in the Scriptures, that Churches should have such a power over other Churches) And then as for the binding obligation both of the one way & the other, it can be supposed to lye but in these 2. things; First, in a warrant and injunction given by Christ to his Churches. to put either the one or the other into execution; and 2. that mens consciences be accordingly taken therewith, so as to subject themselves whether unto the one way or the other: For suppose that other principle of an *authoritative* power in the greater part of Churches [p. 19] combined to excommunicate other Churches, &c. to be the ordinance of God, yet unlesse it doe take hold of mens consciences, and be received amongst all Churches, the offending Churches will sleight all such *Excommunications* much, as they may be supposed to doe our way of protestation and sentence of *Non-communion*. On the other side, let this way of ours be but as strongly entertained, as that which is the way and command of Christ, and upon all occasions be heedfully put in execution, it will awe mens consciences as much, and produce the same effects. And if the Magistrates power (to which we give as much, and (as we think) more, then the principles of the Presbiteriall government will suffer them to yeeld) doe but assist and back the sentence of other Churches denouncing this *Non-communion* against Churches miscarrying, according to the nature of the crime, as they judge meet, and as they would the sentence of Churches excommunicating other Churches in such cases, upon their own particular judgement of the cause; then, without all controversie this our way of Church proceeding wil be every way as effectuall as their other can be supposed to be; and we are sure, more brotherly and more suited to that liberty and equality Christ hath endowed his Churches with. But without the Magistrates interposing their authority, their way of proceeding will be as ineffectuall as ours; and more lyable to contempt, by how much it is pretended to be more authoritative, and to inflict a more dreadul punishment, which carnall spirits are seldome sensible of. This for our judgements.

[p. 20] And for a *reall evidence* and *demonstration* both that this was then, our judgements, as likewise for an instance of the effectuall successe of such a course held by Churches in such cases, our own practice, and the blessing of God thereon, may plead and testifie for us to all the world. The manage of this transaction in briefe was this.

That Church which (with others) was most scandalized, did by letters declare their offence, requiring of the Church (supposed to be) offending, *in the name* and for the vindication of the honour of Christ, and the releeving the party wronged, to yeeld a full and publique hearing before all the Churches of our Nation, or any other whomsoever, offended, of what they could give in charge against their proceedings in that deposition of their Minister, and to subject themselves to an open tryall and review of all those forepassed carriages that concerned that particular; which they most cheerfully and readily (according to the fore-mentioned principles) submitted unto, in a *place*, and *state* where no outward violence or any other externall authority either civil or ecclesiasticall would have enforced them thereunto: And accordingly the Ministers of the Church offended with other two Gentlemen, of much worth, wisdom and piety, members thereof, were sent as *Messengers* from that Church; and at the introduction and entrance into that solemne assembly (the solemnity of which has left as deep an impression upon our hearts of Christs dreadfull presence as ever any we have been present at,) it was openly and publiquely pro- [p. 21] fessed in a speech that was the preface to that discussion, to this effect, 'That it was the most to be abhorred maxime that any Religion hath ever made profession of, and therefore of all other most contradictory and dishonourable unto that of Christianity, that a single and particular society of men professing the name of Christ, and pretending to be endowed with a power from Christ to judge them that are of the same body and society within themselves, should further arrogate unto themselves an exemption from giving account or being censurable by any other, either Christian Magistrate above them, or neighbour Churches about them.' So far were our judgements from that *independent* liberty that is imputed to us, then, when we had least dependency on this kingdom, or so much as hopes ever to abide therein in peace. And for the issue and successe of this *agitation* after there had been for many dayes as judiciary and full a charge, tryall, and deposition of witnesses openly afore all commers of all sorts, as can be expected in any Court where Authority enjoyns it, that Church, which had offended, did as publiquely acknowledge their sinfull aberration in it, restored their *Minister* to his place again, and ordered a solemn day of fasting to humble themselves afore God and men, for their sinfull carriage in it; and the party also which had been deposed did acknowledge to that Church wherein he had likewise sinned.

Thus we have rendred some smal account of those, the saddest days of our pilgrimage on earth, wherein [p. 22] although we enjoyed God, yet besides many other miseries (the companions of banishment) we lost some friends and companions, our fellow labourers in the Gospel, as precious men as this earth beares any, through the distemper of the place, and our selves came hardly off that service with our healths, yea lives.

When it pleased God to bring us his poor *Exiles* back again in these revolutions of the times, as also of the condition of this kingdom, into our own land, (the pouring forth of manifold prayers and teares for the prosperity whereof, had been no small part of that publique worship we offered up to God in a strange land;) we found the judgement of many of our godly learned brethren in the Ministery (that desired a general reformation) to differ from ours in some things, wherein we do professedly judge the *Calvinian* Reformed Churches of the first reformation from out of Popery, to stand in need of a further reformation themselves; And it may without prejudice to them, or the imputation of Schisme in us from them, be thought, that they comming new out of Popery (as well as *England*) and the founders of that reformation not having *Apostolique infallibility*, might not be fully perfect the first day. Yea and it may hopefully be conceived, that *God* in his secret, yet wise and gratious dispensation, had left *England* more unreformed as touching the outward form, both of worship & Church government, then the neighbour Churches were, having yet powerfully continued a constant conflict and con- [p. 23] tention for a further Reformation for these fourscore yeers; during which time he had likewise in stead thereof blessed them with the spiritual light (and that encreasing) of the power of Religion in the Practique part of it, shining brighter and clearer then in the neighbour Churches, as having in his infinite mercy on purpose reserved and *provided some better thing* for this Nation when it should come to be reformed, that the other Churches might not be made *perfect without it*, as the Apostle speaks.

We found also (which was as great an affliction to us as our former troubles and banishment) our opinions and wayes (wherein we might seem to differ) environed about with a cloud of mistakes and misapprehensions, and our persons with reproaches, Besides other calumnies, as of *schisme*, &c. (which yet must either relate to a differing from the former Ecclesiastical Government of this Church established, and then who is not involved in it as well as we? or to that constitution and government that is yet to come; and untill that be agreed on, established and declared, and actually exist, there can be no guilt or imputation of Schisme from it) *That* proud and insolent title of *Independencie* was affixed unto us, as our claime; the very sound of which conveys to all mens apprehensions the challenge of an exemption of all Churches from all subjection and dependance, or rather a trumpet of defiance against what ever *Power, Spirituall* or *Civill*; which we doe abhor and detest; Or else the odious name of *Brownisme*, together with all their opinions as they have stated and maintai- [p. 24] ned them, and must needs be owned by us: Although upon the very first declaring our judgements in the chief and fundamental point of all *Church discipline*, and likewise since, it hath been acknowledged that we differ much from them. And wee did then, and doe here publiquely professe, we beleeve the truth to lye and consist in a *middle way* betwixt that which is falsly charged on us, *Brownisme*; and that which is the contention of these times, the *authoritative Presbyteriall Government* in all the subordinations and proceedings of it.

And had we been led in our former wayes, and our removall out of this Kingdome by any such *spirit* of *faction* and division, or of *pride* and *singularity*, (which are the usual grounds of all Schisme) we had since our returns again during this intermisticall season, tentations, yea provocations enough to have drawn forth such a spirit; having manifold advantages to make and encrease a partie, which we have not in the least attempted. We found the spirits of the people of this Kingdome that professe or pretend to the power of godlinesse (they finding themselves to be so much at liberty, and new come out of bondage) ready to take any impressions, and to be cast into any mould that hath but the appearance of a stricter way. And we found that many of those mists that had gathered about us, or were rather cast upon our persons in our absence, began by our presence againe, and the blessing of God upon us, in a great measure to scatter and vanish, without speaking a word for our selves or Cause.

[p. 25] But through the grace of Christ, our spirits are and have been so remote from such dispositions & aymes, that on the contrary we call God and men to witnes our constant forbearance, either to publish our opinions by preaching (although we had the Pulpits free) or to print any thing of our owne or others for the vindication of our selves (although the Presses were more free then the Pulpits) or to act for our selves or way; although we have been from the first provoked unto all these all sorts of wayes, both by the common mis-understandings and mis-representations of our opinions and practises, together with incitements to this State not to allow us the peaceable practises of our *Consciences*, which the Reformed Churches abroad allowed us, and these edged with calumnies and reproaches cast upon out persons in print; and all these heightned with this further prejudice and provocation, that this our silence was interpreted, that we were either ashamed of our opinions, or able to say little for them; when as on the other side (besides all other advantages) Books have been written by men of much worth, learning, and authority, with moderation and strength, to prepossesse the peoples minds against what are supposed our Tenets. But we knew and considered that it was the *second blow that makes the quarrell*, and that the *beginning of strife* would have been as the *breaking in of waters*; and the sad and conscientious apprehension of the danger of rending and dividing the godly Protestant party in this Kingdome that were desirous of Reformation, and of making se- [p. 26] verall interests among them in a time when there was an absolute necessity of their neerest union and conjunction, and all little enough to effect that Reformation intended, and so long contended for, against a common adversary that had both present possession to plead for it selfe, power to support it, and had enjoyed a long continued settlement which had rooted it in the hearts of men; And this seconded by the instant and continuall advices and conjurements of many *Honourable*, wise, and godly *Personages* of both *Houses of Parliament*, to forbeare what might any way be like to occasion or augment this unhappy difference; They having also by their Declarations to His Majesty professed their endeavour and desire to unite the Protestant partie in this Kingdome, that agree in Fundamentall Truths against Popery and other Heresies, and to have that respect to tender consciences as might prevent oppressions and inconveniences which had formerly been; Together with that strict engagement willingly entred into by us for these common ends, with the rest of our brethren of the Ministery, (which though made to continue but *ad placitum*, yet hath been sacred to us.) And above all, the due respect we have had to the peaceable and orderly Reformation of this Church and State; and hopefull expectation we have been enterteined with of an happy *latitude* and agreement by means of this *Assembly*, and the wisdome of this *Parliament*; The conscience and consideration of all these, and the weight of each, have hitherto had more power with us to this deepe silence and forbearance, then [p. 27] all our own interests have any way prevailed with us to occasion the least disturbance amongst the people. We have and are yet resolved to beare all this with a quiet and a strong patience, (in the strength of which we now speak, or rather sigh forth this little) referring the vindication of our persons to God, and a further experience of us by men; and the declaration of our judgements, and what we conceive to be his truth therein, to the due and orderly agitation of this *Assembly* whereof *both Houses* were pleased to make us *Members*.

And whereas our silence upon all the forementioned grounds (for which we know we can never lose esteeme with good and wise men) hath been by the ill interpretation of some, imputed either to our consciousnesse of the badnesse and weaknesse of our Cause, or to our unability to maintain what we assert in difference from others, or answer what hath been written by others, wee shall (with all modesty) onely present this to all mens apprehensions in confutation of it. That what ever the truth and justnesse of our Cause may prove to be, or how slender our abilities to defend it, yet wee pretend at least to so much wisdome, that wee would never have reserved our selves for, but rather by all wayes have declined *this Theatre*, of all other, the most judicious and severe, an *Assembly* of so many able, learned, and grave *Divines*, where much of the piety, wisdome, and learning of two Kingdomes are met in one, honoured and assisted with the presence of the *Worthies* of both *Houses* at all debates (as often as they please to vouchsafe [p. 28] their presence) as the Stage whereon first wee would bring forth into publique view our Tenets (if false and counterfet) together with our own folly and weaknesse: We would much rather have chosen to have been venting them to the multitude, apt to be seduced, (which we have had these three yeers opportunity to have done.) But in a conscientious regard had to the orderly and peaceable way of searching out truths, and reforming the Churches of Christ, we have adventured our selves upon this way of God, wisely assumed by the prudence of the State; And therein also upon all sorts of disadvantages (which we could not but foresee) both of *number*, *abilities* of learning, *Authority*, the streame of *publique interest*; Trusting God both with our selves and his own truth, as he shall be pleased to manage it by us.

Moreover, if in all matters of *Doctrine*, we were not as *Orthodoxe* in our judgements as our brethren themselves, we would never have exposed our selves to this tryall and hazard of discovery in this Assembly, the mixture of whose spirits, the quicksightednes of whose judgements (intent enough upon us) and variety of debates about all sorts of controversies afoot in these times of contradiction, are such, as would be sure soon to find us out if we nourished any monsters or Serpents of opinions lurking in our bosomes. And if we had carryed it so, as that hitherto such errours were not *aforehand open* to the view and *judgement* of all, yet sitting here (unlesse we would be silent, which we have not been) *we could not long be hid*. But it is [p. 29] sufficiently known that in all *points of doctrine* (which hitherto in the review and examination of the *Articles* of our Church, or upon other occasions have been gone thorough) our judgements have still concurred with the greatest part of our brethren, neither do we know wherein we have dissented. And in matters of *Discipline* (which we are now upon) when our judgements cannot in all things concur with others (as indeed not others all, in all things amongst themselves) yet we are so farre from holding up the differences that occur, or making the breaches greater or wider, that we endeavour upon all such occasions to grant and yeeld (as all may see and cannot but testifie for us) to the utmost latitude of our light and consciences, professing it to be as high a point of Religion and conscience readily to own, yea fall down before whatsoever is *truth* in the hands of those that differ, yea though they should be enemies unto us, as much as earnestly to contend for & hold fast those truths wherein we should be found dissenting from them, and this as in relation to peace, so also as a just due to truth and goodnes, even to approve it & acknowledge it to the utmost graine of it, though mingled with what is opposite unto us. And further when matters of discussion are brought to the smallest dissent that may be, we have hitherto been found to be no *backward* urgers unto a temper (not onely in things that have concerned our own consciences, but when of others also) such as may suit and tend to union as well as searching out of truth; judging this to be as great and usefull an end of *Synods* [p. 30] and *Assemblies*, as a curious and exact discussion of all sorts of lesser differences with binding *Determinations* of truth one way.

And thus we have nakedly and with all simplicity rendred a cleare and true account of our wayes and spirits hitherto, Which we made choice of now at first to make our selves known by, rather then by a more exact and *Scholastique* relation of our judgements in the points of difference about *Church government*; reserving that unto the more proper season and opportunity of this *Assembly*, and that liberty given by both Honourable Houses in matters of dissent; or as necessity shall after require, to a more publique way of stating and asserting of them. In the meane time from this briefe historicall relation of our practices, there may a true estimate be taken of our opinions in difference, which being instanced in, and set out by practices, is the most reall and least collusive way, and carries its own evidence with it. All which we have taken the boldnes together with our selves humbly to lay at the feet of *your wisdom and piety*; Beseeching you to look upon us under no other Notion, or character, then as those, who if we cannot assume to have been no way furtherers of that reformation you intend, yet who have been no hinderers thereof, or disturbers of the publique peace; and who in our judgements about the present work of this age, the reformation of worship and discipline, do differ as little from the Reformed Churches, and our Brethren, yea far lesse, than they do from what themselves were three yeers past, or then the [p. 31] generallity of this kingdom from it self of late. And withall to consider us as those, who in these former times, for many yeers suffered even to exile, for what the kingdom it self now suffers in the endeavour to cast out; and who in these present times, and since the change of them, have endured (that which to our spirits is no lesse grievous) the opposition and reproach of good men, even to the threatning of another banishment, and have been through the grace of God upon us, the same men in both, in the midst of these varieties; And finally, as those that do pursue no other interest or designe but a subsistance (be it in the poorest and meanest) in our own land (where we have and may do further service, & which is our birth-right as we are men) with the enjoyment of the ordinances of Christ (which are our portion as we are Christians) with the allowance of a latitude to some lesser differences with peaceablenesse, as not knowing where else with safety, health, and livelyhood, to set our feet on earth.

        Tho: Goodwin   Jer: Burroughes
        Philip Nye
        Sidrach Simpson   William Bridge

FINIS

Document III.3

The Westminster Confession of Faith, 1646

The Westminster Confession of Faith was composed by an Assembly of 121 divines convened by the Long Parliament to formulate proposals for the reform of the Church of England in order to make it 'more agreeable to the Word of God'. It consisted of theologians and lay assessors nominated by the Parliament together with commissioners who represented the Church of Scotland. It met at Westminster Abbey from 1643 to 1648. It was commanded by Parliament to review the Thirty-nine Articles but it went beyond this and the fruit of its deliberations was the production of the so-called 'Westminster Standards', consisting of the above Confession of Faith, the Larger and Shorter Catechisms, the Directory for Public Worship and the Form of Church Government. The Confession was completed in 1646. It represents the precision and comprehensiveness of a fully developed theology. It presents a consensus of Reformed theology and draws upon a variety of traditions, Calvin, Bullinger, Zwingli, the Augustinianism of British Puritanism, the Reformed theology of the Rhineland, and the decrees of the Synod of Dort, which some members had attended. It expounds the principles of the Covenant Theology which was an innovation in contemporary Reformed thinking but sought to combine it with the emphasis on divine election. Throughout, the sovereignty of God is proclaimed and explained. The Confession and Catechisms were adopted by the Presbyterians of England and Scotland and became influential in many parts of the Protestant world. The Catechisms, particularly the Shorter Catechism, were to be prime instruments of religious education for generations.

The text printed here is taken from Philip Schaff, *Creeds of Christendom* (New York, 1877), III, 60–73 but corrected in the light of the first edition. The orthography has been modernised and the numerous scriptural 'proofs' have been omitted. For further information, v., J. H. Leith, *Assembly at Westminster* (Oxford, 1973); S. W. Carruthers, *The Everyday Work of the Westminster Assembly* (Philadelphia, 1943); S. W. Carruthers, *The Westminster Confession of Faith* (Manchester, 1937); W. M. Hetherington, *History of the Westminster Assembly of Divines* (Edinburgh, 1890); A. F. Mitchell and J. B. Struthers, *Minutes of the Sessions of the Westminster Assembly* (Edinburgh and London, 1874); R. S. Paul, *The Assembly of the Lord* (Edinburgh, 1985); A. F. Mitchell, *The Westminster Assembly; Its History and Standards* (London, 1883); B. B. Warfield, *The Westminster Assembly and Its Work* (New York, 1931); art. 'Westminster Assembly' and 'Westminster Confession of Faith' in D. K. McKim (ed.), *Encyclopedia of the Reformed Faith* (Edinburgh, 1992).

The five names which appear at the close of the document belong to the officials of the Assembly. Charles Herle (1598–1659) was elected Prolocutor after the death of William Twisse on 20 July 1646. Cornelius Burges (or Burgess, 1589–1665) and Herbert Palmer (1601–47) served as Assessors (or vice-presidents) while Henry Roborough (d. 1650) and Adoniram Byfield (d. 1660) served as scribes (or secretaries) to the Assembly. There are brief biographies of all five in James Reid, *Memoirs of the ... Divines, who convened in the ... Assembly at Westminster ...*, 2 vols (Paisley, 1811 and 1815; reprinted in one volume by The Banner of Truth Trust, Edinburgh in 1982). All except Roborough are in DNB. For Burgess, v., CR. All except Burgess are in Benjamin Brook, *The Lives of the Puritans*, 3 vols (London, 1813).

CHAPTER I.

Of the Holy Scripture.

I. Although the light of nature, and the works of creation and providence, do so far manifest the goodness, wisdom, and power of God, as to leave men inexcusable; yet are they not sufficient to give that knowledge of God, and of his will, which is necessary unto salvation; therefore it pleased the Lord, at sundry times, and in divers manners, to reveal himself, and to declare that his will unto his Church; and afterwards, for the better preserving and propagating of the truth, and for the more sure establishment and comfort of the Church against the corruption of the flesh, and the malice of Satan and of the world, to commit the same wholly unto writing; which maketh the holy Scripture to be most necessary; those former ways of God's revealing his will unto his people being now ceased.

II. Under the name of holy Scripture, or the Word of God written, are now contained all the Books of the Old and New Testament, which are these:

[Then follows a list of the books of the Bible.]

All which are given by inspiration of God, to be rule of faith and life.

III. The books commonly called Apocrypha, not being of divine inspiration, are no part of the Canon of the Scripture; and therefore are of no authority in the Church of God, nor to be any otherwise approved, or made use of, than other human writings.

IV. The authority of the holy Scripture, for which it ought to be believed and obeyed, dependeth not upon the testimony of any man or church, but wholly upon God (who is truth itself), the Author thereof; and therefore it is to be received, because it is the Word of God.

V. We may be moved and induced by the testimony of the Church to an high and reverent esteem of the holy Scripture; and the heavenliness of the matter, the efficacy of the doctrine, the majesty of the style, the consent of all the parts, the scope of the whole (which is to give glory to God), the full discovery it makes of the only way of man's salvation, the many other incomparable excellencies, and the entire perfection thereof, are arguments whereby it doth abundantly evidence itself to be the Word of God; yet, notwithstanding, our full persuasion and assurance of the infallible truth, and divine authority thereof, is from the inward work of the Holy Spirit, bearing witness by and with the Word in our hearts.

VI. The whole counsel of God, concerning all things necessary for his own glory, man's salvation, faith, and life, is either expressly set down in Scripture, or by good and necessary consequence may be deduced from Scripture: unto which nothing at any time is to be added, whether by new revelations of the Spirit, or traditions of men. Nevertheless we acknowledge the inward illumination of the Spirit of God to be necessary for the saving understanding of such things as are revealed in the Word; and that there are some circumstances concerning the worship of God, and government of the Church, common to human actions and societies, which are to be ordered by the light of nature and Christian prudence, according to the general rules of the Word, which are always to be observed.

VII. All things in Scripture are not alike plain in themselves, nor alike clear unto all; yet those things which are necessary to be known, believed, and observed, for salvation, are so clearly propounded and opened in some place of Scripture or other, that not only the learned, but the unlearned, in a due use of the ordinary means, may attain unto a sufficient understanding of them.

VIII. The Old Testament in Hebrew (which was the native language of the people of God of old), and the New Testament in Greek (which at the time of the writing of it was most generally known to the nations), being immediately inspired by God, and by his singular care and providence kept pure in all ages, are therefore authentical; so as in all controversies of religion the Church is finally to appeal unto them. But because these original tongues are not known to all the people of God who have right unto, and interest in the Scriptures, and are commanded, in the fear of God, to read and search them, therefore they are to be translated into the vulgar language of every nation unto which they come, that the Word of God dwelling plentifully in all, they may worship him in an acceptable manner, and, through patience and comfort of the Scriptures, may have hope.

IX. The infallible rule of interpretation of Scripture is the Scripture itself; and therefore, when there is a question about the true and full sense of any Scripture (which is not manifold, but one), it must be searched and known by other places that speak more clearly.

X. The Supreme Judge, by which all controversies of religion are to be determined, and all decrees of councils, opinions of ancient writers, doctrines of men, and private spirits, are to be examined, and in whose sentence we are to rest, can be no other but the Holy Spirit speaking in the Scripture.

CHAPTER II.

Of God, and of the Holy Trinity.

I. There is but one only living and true God, who is infinite in being and perfection, a most pure spirit, invisible, without body, parts, or passions, immutable, immense, eternal, incomprehensible, almighty, most wise, most holy, most free, most absolute, working all things according to the counsel of his own immutable and most righteous will, for his own glory; most loving, gracious, merciful, long-suffering, abundant in goodness and truth, forgiving iniquity, transgression, and sin; the rewarder of them that diligently seek him; and withal most just and terrible in his judgments; hating all sin, and who will by no means clear the guilty.

II. God hath all life, glory, goodness, blessedness, in and of himself; and is alone in and unto himself allsufficient, not standing in need of any creatures which he hath made, nor deriving any glory from them, but only manifesting his own glory in, by, unto, and upon them: he is the alone foundation of all being, of whom, through whom, and to whom are all things; and hath most sovereign dominion over them, to do by them, for them, or upon them whatsoever himself pleaseth. In his sight all things are open and manifest; his knowledge is infinite, infallible, and independent upon the creature; so as nothing is to him contingent or uncertain. He is most holy in all his counsels, in all his works, and in all his commands. To him is due from angels and men, and every other creature, whatsoever worship, service, or obedience, he is pleased to require of them.

III. In the unity of the Godhead there be three persons, of one substance, power, and eternity: God the Father, God the Son, and God the Holy Ghost. The Father is of none, neither begotten nor proceeding; the Son is eternally begotten of the Father; the Holy Ghost eternally proceeding from the Father and the Son.

CHAPTER III.

Of God's Eternal Decree.

I. God from all eternity did, by the most wise and holy counsel of his own will, freely and unchangeably ordain whatsoever comes to pass; yet so as thereby neither is God the author of sin, nor is violence offered to the will of the creatures, nor is the liberty or contingency of second causes taken away, but rather established.

II. Although God knows whatsoever may or can come to pass upon all supposed conditions, yet hath he not decreed any thing because he foresaw it as future, or as that which would come to pass upon such conditions.

III. By the decree of God, for the manifestation of his glory, some men and angels are predestinated unto everlasting life, and others foreordained to everlasting death.

IV. These angels and men, thus predestinated and foreordained, are particularly and unchangeably designed; and their number is so certain and definite that it can not be either increased or diminished.

V. Those of mankind that are predestinated unto life, God, before the foundation of the world was laid, according to his eternal and immutable purpose, and the secret counsel and good pleasure of his will, hath chosen in Christ, unto everlasting glory, out of his mere free grace and love, without any foresight of faith or good works, or perseverance in either of them, or any other thing in the creature, as conditions, or causes moving him thereunto; and all to the praise of his glorious grace.

VI. As God hath appointed the elect unto glory, so hath he, by the eternal and most free purpose of his will, foreordained all the means thereunto. Wherefore they who are elected, being fallen in Adam, are redeemed by Christ, are effectually called unto faith in Christ by his Spirit working in due season; are justified, adopted, sanctified, and kept by his power through faith unto salvation. Neither are any other redeemed by Christ, effectually called, justified, adopted, sanctified, and saved, but the elect only.

VII. The rest of mankind God was pleased, according to the unsearchable counsel of his own will whereby he extendeth or withholdeth mercy as he pleaseth, for the glory of his sovereign power over his creatures, to pass by, and to ordain them to dishonor and wrath for their sin, to the praise of his glorious justice.

VIII. The doctrine of this high mystery of predestination is to be handled with special prudence and care, that men attending the will of God revealed in his Word, and yielding obedience thereunto, may, from the certainty of their effectual vocation, be assured of their eternal election. So shall this doctrine afford matter of praise, reverence, and admiration of God; and of humility, diligence, and abundant consolation to all that sincerely obey the gospel.

CHAPTER IV.

Of Creation.

I. It pleased God the Father, Son, and Holy Ghost, for the manifestation of the glory of his eternal power, wisdom, and goodness, in the beginning, to create or make of nothing the world, and all things therein, whether visible or invisible, in the space of six days, and all very good.

II. After God had made all other creatures, he created man, male and female, with reasonable and immortal souls, endued with knowledge, righteousness, and true holiness, after his own image, having the law of God written in their hearts, and power to fulfill it; and yet under a possibility of transgressing, being left to the liberty of their own will, which was subject unto change. Beside this law written in their hearts, they received a command not to eat of the tree of the knowledge of good and evil; which while they kept they were happy in their communion with God, and had dominion over the creatures.

CHAPTER V.

Of Providence.

I. God, the great Creator of all things, doth uphold, direct, dispose, and govern all creatures, actions, and things, from the greatest even to the least, by his most wise and holy providence, according to his infallible foreknowledge and the free and immutable counsel of his own will, to the praise of the glory of his wisdom, power, justice, goodness, and mercy.

II. Although in relation to the foreknowledge and decree of God, the first cause, all things come to pass immutably and infallibly, yet by the same providence he ordereth them to fall out, according to the nature of second causes, either necessarily, freely, or contingently.

III. God, in his ordinary providence, maketh use of means, yet is free to work without, above, and against them, at his pleasure.

IV. The almighty power, unsearchable wisdom, and infinite goodness of God so far manifest themselves in his providence that it extendeth itself even to the first fall, and all other sins of angels and men, and that not by a bare permission, but such as hath joined with it a most wise and powerful bounding, and otherwise ordering and governing of them, in a manifold dispensation, to his own holy ends; yet so as the sinfulness thereof proceedeth only from the creature, and not from God; who, being most holy and righteous, neither is nor can be the author or approver of sin.

V. The most wise, righteous, and gracious God doth oftentimes leave for a season his own children to manifold temptations and the corruption of their own hearts, to chastise them for their former sins, or to discover unto them the hidden strength of corruption and deceitfulness of their hearts, that they may be humbled; and to raise them to a more close and constant dependence for their support unto himself, and to make them more watchful against all future occasions of sin, and for sundry other just and holy ends.

VI. As for those wicked and ungodly men whom God, as a righteous judge, for former sins, doth blind and harden, from them he not only withholdeth his grace, whereby they might have been enlightened in their understandings and wrought upon in their hearts, but sometimes also withdraweth the gifts which they had, and exposeth them to such objects as their corruption makes occasion of sin; and withal, gives them over to their own lusts, the temptations of the world, and the power of Satan; whereby it comes to pass that they harden themselves, even under those means which God useth for the softening of others.

VII. As the providence of God doth, in general, reach to all creatures, so, after a most special manner, it taketh care of his Church, and disposeth all things to the good thereof.

CHAPTER VI.

Of the Fall of Man, of Sin, and of the Punishment thereof.

I. Our first parents, being seduced by the subtilty and temptation of Satan, sinned in eating the forbidden fruit. This their sin God was pleased, according to his wise and holy counsel, to permit, having purposed to order it to his own glory.

II. By this sin they fell from their original righteousness and communion with God, and so became dead in sin, and wholly defiled in all the faculties and parts of soul and body.

III. They being the root of all mankind, the guilt of this sin was imputed, and the same death in sin and corrupted nature conveyed to all their posterity descending from them by ordinary generation.

IV. From this original corruption, whereby we are utterly indisposed, disabled, and made opposite to all good, and wholly inclined to all evil, do proceed all actual transgressions.

V. This corruption of nature, during this life, doth remain in those that are regenerated: and although it be through Christ pardoned and mortified, yet both itself and all the motions thereof are truly and properly sin.

VI. Every sin, both original and actual, being a transgression of the righteous law of God, and contrary thereunto, doth, in its own nature, bring guilt upon the sinner, whereby he is bound over to the wrath of God and curse of the law, and so made subject to death, with all miseries spiritual, temporal, and eternal.

CHAPTER VII.

Of God's Covenant with Man.

I. The distance between God and the creature is so great that although reasonable creatures do owe obedience unto him as their Creator, yet they could never have any fruition of him as their blessedness and reward but by some voluntary condescension on God's part, which he hath been pleased to express by way of covenant.

II. The first covenant made with man was a covenant of works, wherein life was promised to Adam, and in him to his posterity, upon condition of perfect and personal obedience.

III. Man by his fall having made himself incapable of life by that covenant, the Lord was pleased to make a second, commonly called the covenant of grace: wherein he freely offered unto sinners life and salvation by Jesus Christ, requiring of them faith in him that they may be saved, and promising to give unto all those that are ordained unto life his Holy Spirit, to make them willing and able to believe.

IV. This covenant of grace is frequently set forth in the Scripture by the name of a testament, in reference to the death of Jesus Christ the testator, and to the everlasting inheritance, with all things belonging to it, therein bequeathed.

V. This covenant was differently administered in the time of the law and in the time of the gospel: under the law it was administered by promises, prophecies, sacrifices, circumcision, the paschal lamb, and other types and ordinances delivered to the people of the Jews, all foresignifying Christ to come, which were for that time sufficient and efficacious, through the operation of the Spirit, to instruct and build up the elect in faith in the promised Messiah, by whom they had full remission of sins and eternal salvation; and is called the Old Testament.

VI. Under the gospel, when Christ the substance was exhibited, the ordinances in which this covenant is dispensed are the preaching of the word and the administration of the sacraments of Baptism and the Lord's Supper; which, though fewer in number, and administered with more simplicity and less outward glory, yet in them it is held forth in more fullness, evidence, and spiritual efficacy, to all nations, both Jews and Gentiles; and is called the New Testament. There are not, therefore, two covenants of grace differing in substance, but one and the same under various dispensations.

CHAPTER VIII.

Of Christ the Mediator.

I. It pleased God, in his eternal purpose, to choose and ordain the Lord Jesus, his only-begotten Son, to be the Mediator between God and man, the Prophet, Priest, and King; the Head and Saviour of his Church, the Heir of all things, and Judge of the world; unto whom he did, from all eternity, give a people to be his seed, and to be by him in time redeemed, called, justified, sanctified, and glorified.

II. The Son of God, the second person in the Trinity, being very and eternal God, of one substance, and equal with the Father, did, when the fullness of time was come, take upon him man's nature, with all the essential properties and common infirmities thereof, yet without sin: being conceived by the power of the Holy Ghost in the womb of the Virgin Mary, of her substance. So that two whole, perfect, and distinct natures, the Godhead and the manhood, were inseparably joined together in one person, without conversion, composition, or confusion. Which person is very God and very man, yet one Christ, the only mediator between God and man.

III. The Lord Jesus, in his human nature thus united to the divine, was sanctified and anointed with the Holy Spirit above measure; having in him all the treasures of wisdom and knowledge, in whom it pleased the Father that all fullness should dwell; to the end that, being holy, harmless, undefiled, and full of grace and truth, he might be thoroughly furnished to execute the office of a mediator and surety. Which office he took not unto himself, but was thereunto called by his Father, who put all power and judgment into his hand, and gave him commandment to execute the same.

IV. This office the Lord Jesus did most willingly undertake, which, that he might discharge, he was made under the law, and did perfectly fulfill it; endured most grievous torments immediately in his soul, and most painful sufferings in his body; was crucified, and died; was buried, and remained under the power of death, yet saw no corruption. On the third day he arose from the dead, with the same body in which he suffered; with which also he ascended into heaven, and there sitteth at the right hand of his Father, making intercession; and shall return to judge men and angels at the end of the world.

V. The Lord Jesus, by his perfect obedience and sacrifice of himself, which he through the eternal Spirit once offered up unto God, hath fully satisfied the justice of his Father, and purchased not only reconciliation, but an everlasting inheritance in the kingdom of heaven, for all those whom the Father hath given unto him.

VI. Although the work of redemption was not actually wrought by Christ till after his incarnation, yet the virtue, efficacy, and benefits thereof were communicated unto the elect, in all ages successively, from the beginning of the world, in and by those promises, types, and sacrifices, wherein he was revealed, and signified to be the seed of the woman which should bruise the serpent's head, and the lamb slain from the beginning of the world, being yesterday and to-day the same and forever.

VII. Christ, in the work of mediation, acteth according to both natures; by each nature doing that which is proper to itself; yet, by reason of the unity of the person, that which is proper to one nature is sometimes, in Scripture, attributed to the person denominated by the other nature.

VIII. To all those for whom Christ hath purchased redemption he doth certainly and effectually apply and communicate the same; making intercession for them, and revealing unto them, in and by the Word, the mysteries of salvation; effectually persuading them by his Spirit to believe and obey; and governing their hearts by his Word and Spirit; overcoming all their enemies by his almighty power and wisdom, in such manner and ways as are most consonant to his wonderful and unsearchable dispensation.

CHAPTER IX.

Of Free-will.

I. God hath endued the will of man with that natural liberty, that is neither forced nor by any absolute necessity of nature determined to good or evil.

II. Man, in his state of innocency, had freedom and power to will and to do that which is good and well-pleasing to God, but yet mutably, so that he might fall from it.

III. Man, by his fall into a state of sin, hath wholly lost all ability of will to any spiritual good accompanying salvation; so as, a natural man, being altogether averse from that good, and dead in sin, is not able, by his own strength, to convert himself, or to prepare himself thereunto.

IV. When God converts a sinner, and translates him into the state of grace, he freeth him from his natural bondage under sin, and by his grace alone, enables him freely to will, and to do that which is spiritually good; yet so, as that by reason of his remaining corruption, he doth not, perfectly, nor only, will that which is good, but doth also will that which is evil.

V. The will of man is made perfectly, and immutably free to good alone, in the state of glory only.

CHAPTER X.

Of Effectual Calling.

I. All those whom God hath predestinated unto life, and those only, he is pleased in his appointed and accepted time, effectually to call, by his Word and Spirit, out of that state of sin and death, in which they are by nature, to grace and salvation by Jesus Christ; enlightening their minds, spiritually and savingly, to understand the things of God; taking away their heart of stone, and giving unto them an heart of flesh; renewing their wills, and by his almighty power determining them to that which is good, and effectually drawing them to Jesus Christ; yet so as they come most freely, being made willing by his grace.

II. This effectual call is of God's free and special grace alone, not from any thing at all foreseen in man, who is altogether passive therein, until, being quickened and renewed by the Holy Spirit, he is thereby enabled to answer this call, and to embrace the grace offered and conveyed in it.

III. Elect infants, dying in infancy, are regenerated and saved by Christ through the Spirit, who worketh when, and where, and how he pleaseth. So also are all other elect persons, who are uncapable of being outwardly called by the ministry of the Word.

IV. Others, not elected, although they may be called by the ministry of the Word, and may have some common operations of the Spirit, yet they never truly come unto Christ, and therefore can not be saved: much less can men, not professing the Christian religion, be saved in any other way whatsoever, be they never so diligent to frame their lives according to the light of nature and the law of that religion they do profess; and to assert and maintain that they may is very pernicious, and to be detested.

CHAPTER XI.

Of Justification.

I. Those whom God effectually calleth, he also freely justifieth: not, by infusing righteousness into them, but by pardoning their sins, and by accounting and accepting their persons as righteous; not, for any thing wrought in them, or done by them, but for Christ's sake alone; nor, by imputing faith itself, the act of believing, or any other evangelical obedience, to them, as their righteousness; but by imputing the obedience and satisfaction of Christ unto them, they receiving, and resting on him and his righteousness by faith; which faith, they have, not of themselves, it is the gift of God.

II. Faith, thus receiving and resting on Christ, and his righteousness, is the alone instrument of justification; yet is it not alone in the person justified, but is ever accompanied with all other saving graces, and is no dead faith, but worketh by love.

III. Christ, by his obedience, and death, did fully discharge the debt of all those that are thus justified, and did make a proper, real, and full satisfaction to his Father's justice in their behalf. Yet, inasmuch as he was given by the Father, for them; and, his obedience and satisfaction accepted in their stead; and both freely, not for any thing in them; their justification is only of free grace; that both the exact justice, and rich grace of God, might be glorified in the justification of sinners.

IV. God did, from all eternity, decree to justify all the elect, and Christ did, in the fullness of time, die for their sins, and rise again for their justification:

nevertheless, they are not justified, until the Holy Spirit doth in due time, actually apply Christ unto them.

V. God doth continue to forgive the sins of those that are justified: and although they can never fall from the state of justification, yet they may by their sins fall under God's fatherly displeasure, and not have the light of his countenance restored unto them, until they humble themselves, confess their sins, beg pardon, and renew their faith and repentance.

VI. The justification of believers under the Old Testament, was in all these respects, one and the same with the justification of believers under the New Testament.

CHAPTER XII.

Of Adoption.

All those that are justified, God vouchsafeth, in and for his only Son Jesus Christ, to make partakers of the grace of adoption; by which they are taken into the number, and enjoy the liberties and privileges of the children of God; have his name put upon them, receive the spirit of Adoption; have access to the throne of grace with holiness; are enabled to cry, Abba, Father; are pitied, protected, provided for, and chastened by him, as by a father; yet never cast off, but sealed to the day of redemption, and inherit the promises, as heirs of everlasting salvation.

CHAPTER XIII.

Of Sanctification.

I. They who are effectually called, and regenerated, having a new heart, and a new spirit created in them; are further sanctified, really and personally through the virtue of Christ's death and resurrection, by his Word and Spirit dwelling in them; the dominion of the whole body of sin is destroyed, and the several lusts thereof are more and more weakened and mortified, and they more and more quickened and strengthened in all saving graces, to the practice of true holiness, without which no man shall see the Lord.

II. This sanctification is throughout, in the whole man; yet imperfect in this life, there abideth still some remnants of corruption in every part; whence ariseth a continual, and irreconcilable war, the flesh lusting against the spirit, and the spirit against the flesh.

III. In which war, although the remaining corruption, for a time, may much prevail, yet, through the continual supply of strength from the sanctifying Spirit of Christ, the regenerate part doth overcome; and so, the saints grow in grace, perfecting holiness in the fear of God.

CHAPTER XIV.

Of Saving Faith.

I. The grace of faith, whereby the elect are enabled to believe to the saving of their souls, is the work of the Spirit of Christ in their hearts, and is ordinarily wrought by the ministry of the Word: by which also, and by the administration of the sacraments, and prayer, it is increased and strengthened.

II. By this faith, a Christian believeth to be true, whatsoever is revealed in the Word, for the authority of God himself speaking therein; and acteth differently upon that which each particular passage thereof containeth; yielding obedience to the commands, trembling at the threatenings, and embracing the promises of God for this life, and that which is to come. But the principal acts of saving faith, are, accepting, receiving, and resting upon Christ alone for justification, sanctification, and eternal life, by virtue of the covenant of grace.

III. This faith is different in degrees, weak, or strong; may be often and many ways assailed, and weakened, but gets the victory; growing up in many to the attainment of a full assurance through Christ, who is both the author and finisher of our faith.

CHAPTER XV.

Of Repentance unto Life.

I. Repentance unto life, is an evangelical grace, the doctrine whereof is to be preached by every minister of the gospel, as well as that of faith in Christ.

II. By it a sinner, out of the sight and sense, not only of the danger, but also of the filthiness and odiousness of his sins, as contrary to the holy nature, and righteous law of God; and, upon the apprehension of his mercy in Christ to such as are penitent, so grieves for, and hates his sins, as to turn from them all unto God, purposing and endeavouring to walk with him in all the ways of his commandments.

III. Although repentance be not to be rested in as any satisfaction for sin, or any cause of the pardon thereof, which is the act of God's free grace in Christ; yet is it of such necessity to all sinners, that none may expect pardon without it.

IV. As there is no sin so small, but it deserves damnation; so there is no sin so great, that it can bring damnation upon those who truly repent.

V. Men ought not to content themselves with a general repentance, but it is every man's duty to endeavour to repent of his particular sins, particularly.

VI. As every man is bound to make private confession of his sins to God, praying for the pardon thereof; upon which, and the forsaking of them, he shall find mercy; so he that scandalizeth his brother, or the Church of Christ, ought to be willing, by a private or public confession, and sorrow for his sin, to declare his repentance to those that are offended, who are thereupon to be reconciled to him, and in love to receive him.

CHAPTER XVI.

Of Good Works.

I. Good works are only such as God hath commanded in his holy Word, and not such as, without the warrant thereof, are devised by men, out of blind zeal, or upon any pretence of good intention.

II. These good works, done in obedience to God's commandments, are the fruits and evidences of a true and lively faith: and by them believers manifest their thankfulness, strengthen their assurance, edify their brethren, adorn the profession of the gospel, stop the mouths of the adversaries, and glorify God, whose workmanship they are, created in Christ Jesus thereunto; that, having their fruit unto holiness, they may have the end, eternal life.

III. Their ability to do good works, is not at all of themselves, but wholly from the Spirit of Christ. And that they may be enabled thereunto, besides the graces they have already received, there is required an actual influence of the same Holy Spirit, to work in them to will and to do, of his good pleasure: yet are they not hereupon to grow negligent, as if they were not bound to perform any duty, unless, upon a special motion of the Spirit; but they ought to be diligent in stirring up the grace of God that is in them.

IV. They, who in their obedience, attain to the greatest height which is possible in this life, are so far from being able to supererogate, and to do more than God requires, as that they fall short of much which in duty they are bound to do.

V. We can not, by our best works, merit pardon of sin, or eternal life at the hand of God, by reason of the great disproportion that is between them and the glory to come, and, the infinite distance that is between us and God, whom, by them, we can neither profit, nor satisfy for the debt of our former sins, but when we have done all we can, we have done but our duty, and are unprofitable servants; and, because, as they are good, they proceed from his Spirit; and as they are wrought by us, they are defiled, and mixed with so much weakness and imperfection, that they can not endure the severity of God's judgment.

VI. Yet notwithstanding, the persons of believers being accepted through Christ, their good works also are accepted in him, not as though they were in this life wholly unblamable and unreprovable in God's sight; but that, he looking upon them in his Son, is pleased to accept, and reward that which is sincere, although accompanied with many weaknesses and imperfections.

VII. Works done by unregenerate men, although, for the matter of them, they may be things which God commands, and of good use both to themselves and others; yet, because they proceed not from an heart purified by faith; nor are done in a right manner, according to the Word; nor, to a right end, the glory of God; they are therefore sinful, and cannot please God, or make a man meet to receive grace from God. And yet their neglect of them is more sinful, and displeasing unto God.

CHAPTER XVII.

Of the Perseverance of the Saints.

I. They, whom God hath accepted in his Beloved, effectually called, and sanctified by his Spirit, can neither totally, nor finally, fall away from the state of grace: but shall certainly persevere therein to the end, and be eternally saved.

II. This perseverance of the saints depends, not upon their own free-will, but upon the immutability of the decree of election, flowing from the free and unchangeable love of God the Father; upon the efficacy of the merit, and intercession of Jesus Christ; the abiding of the Spirit, and of the seed of God within them; and the nature of the covenant of grace: from all which, ariseth also the certainty, and infallibility thereof.

III. Nevertheless, they may, through the temptations of Satan and of the world, the prevalency of corruption remaining in them, and the neglect of the means of their preservation, fall into grievous sins; and, for a time, continue therein: whereby they incur God's displeasure, and grieve his Holy Spirit; come to be deprived of some measure of their graces and comforts, have their hearts hardened, and their consciences wounded, hurt, and scandalize others, and bring temporal judgments upon themselves.

CHAPTER XVIII.

Of the Assurance of Grace and Salvation.

I. Although hypocrites and other unregenerate men may vainly deceive themselves with false hopes and carnal presumptions of being in the favour of God, and estate of salvation; which hope of theirs shall perish: yet such as truly believe in the Lord Jesus, and love him in sincerity, endeavouring to walk in all good conscience before him, may, in this life be certainly assured that they are in the state of grace, and may rejoice in the hope of the glory of God, which hope shall never make them ashamed.

II. This certainty is not a bare conjectural and probable persuasion, grounded upon a fallible hope; but an infallible assurance of faith, founded upon the divine truth of the promises of salvation, the inward evidence of those graces unto which these promises are made, the testimony of the Spirit of adoption witnessing with our spirits that we are the children of God: which Spirit is the earnest of our inheritance, whereby we are sealed to the day of redemption.

III. This infallible assurance doth not so belong to the essence of faith, but that a true believer may wait long, and conflict with many difficulties, before he be partaker of it: yea, being enabled by the Spirit to know the things which are freely given him of God, he may, without extraordinary revelation, in the right use of ordinary means, attain thereunto. And therefore it is the duty of every one, to give all diligence to make his calling and election sure; that thereby his heart may be enlarged in peace and joy in the Holy Ghost, in love and thankfulness to God, and in strength and cheerfulness in the duties of obedience, the proper fruits of this assurance: so far is it, from inclining men to looseness.

IV True believers may have the assurance of their salvation divers ways shaken, diminished, and intermitted, as, by negligence in preserving of it; by falling into some special sin, which woundeth the conscience, and grieveth the Spirit; by, some sudden, or vehement temptation, by God's withdrawing the light of his countenance, and suffering even such as fear him to walk in darkness and to have no light: yet are they never utterly destitute of that seed of God, and life of faith, that love of Christ and the brethren, that sincerity of heart, and conscience of duty, out of which, by the operation of the Spirit, this assurance may, in due time, be revived; and by the which, in the mean time, they are supported from utter despair.

CHAPTER XIX.

Of the Law of God.

I. God gave to Adam a law, as a covenant of works, by which he bound him and all his posterity, to personal, entire, exact, and perpetual obedience; promised life upon the fulfilling, and threatened death upon the breach of it: and endued him with power and ability to keep it.

II. This law, after his fall, continued to be a perfect rule of righteousness, and, as such, was delivered by God upon Mount Sinai in ten commandments, and written in two tables: the first four commandments containing our duty towards God, and the other six our duty to man.

III. Beside this law, commonly called moral, God was pleased to give to the people of Israel, as a Church under age, ceremonial laws, containing several typical ordinances, partly of worship, prefiguring Christ, his graces, actions, sufferings, and benefits; and partly, holding forth divers instructions of moral duties. All which ceremonial laws are now abrogated, under the New Testament.

IV. To them also, as a body politic, he gave sundry judicial laws, which expired together with the state of that people, not obliging any other now, further than the general equity thereof may require.

V. The moral law doth forever bind all, as well justified persons as others, to the obedience thereof; and that not only in regard of the matter contained in it, but also in respect of the authority of God the Creator, who gave it. Neither doth Christ in the gospel, any way dissolve, but much strengthen this obligation.

VI. Although true believers be not under the law, as a covenant of works, to be thereby justified, or condemned; yet is it of great use to them, as well as to others; in that, as a rule of life informing them of the will of God, and their duty, it directs,

& binds them to walk accordingly; discovering also the sinful pollutions of their nature, hearts and lives; so as, examining themselves thereby, they may come to further conviction of, humiliation for, and hatred against sin; together with a clearer sight of the need they have of Christ, and the perfection of his obedience. It is likewise of use to the regenerate, to restrain their corruptions, in that it forbids sin: and the threatenings of it serve to show, what, even their sins deserve; and, what afflictions, in this life, they may expect for them, although freed from the curse thereof threatened in the law. The promises of it, in like manner, show them God's approbation of obedience, and what blessings they may expect upon the performance thereof; although, not as due to them by the law, as a covenant of works. So as, a man's doing good, and refraining from evil, because the law encourageth to the one, and deterreth from the other, is no evidence of his being under the law; and, not under grace.

VII. Neither are the forementioned uses of the law contrary to the grace of the gospel, but do sweetly comply with it, the Spirit of Christ subduing and enabling the will of man to do that, freely and cheerfully, which the will of God, revealed in the law, requireth to be done.

CHAPTER XX.

Of Christian Liberty, and Liberty of Conscience.

I. The liberty which Christ hath purchased for believers under the gospel, consists in their freedom from the guilt of sin, the condemning wrath of God, the curse of the moral law, and in their being delivered from this present evil world, bondage to Satan, and dominion of sin; from the evil of afflictions, the sting of death, the victory of the grave, and everlasting damnation; as also in their free access to God, and their yielding obedience unto him, not out of slavish fear, but a child-like love and willing mind. All which were common also to believers under the law. But under the New Testament the liberty of Christians is further enlarged in their freedom from the yoke of the ceremonial law, to which the Jewish Church was subjected; and in greater boldness of access to the throne of grace, and in fuller communications of the free Spirit of God, than believers under the law did ordinarily partake of.

II. God alone is Lord of the conscience, and hath left it free from the doctrines and commandments of men which are in any thing contrary to his Word; or beside it, in matters of faith, or worship. So that, to believe such doctrines, or to obey such commands out of conscience, is to betray true liberty of conscience: and the requiring of an implicit faith, and an absolute and blind obedience, is to destroy liberty of conscience, and reason also.

III. They, who upon pretence of Christian liberty, do practise any sin, or cherish any lust, do thereby destroy the end of Christian liberty; which is, that, being delivered out of the hands of our enemies, we might serve the Lord without fear, in holiness and righteousness before him, all the days of our life.

IV. And because the power which God hath ordained, and the liberty which Christ hath purchased, are not intended by God, to destroy, but mutually to uphold and preserve one another; they, who upon pretense of Christian liberty, shall oppose any lawful power, or the lawful exercise of it, whether it be civil or ecclesiastical, resist the ordinance of God. And, for their publishing of such opinions, or maintaining of such practices, as are contrary to the light of nature, or to the known principles of Christianity; whether concerning faith, worship, or conversation; or to the power of godliness; or, such erroneous opinions or practices, as either in their own nature, or in the manner of publishing or maintaining them, are destructive to the external peace and order which Christ hath established in the Church; they may lawfully be called to account, and proceeded against by the censures of the Church, and by the power of the Civil Magistrate.

CHAPTER XXI.

Of Religious Worship and the Sabbath-day.

I. The light of nature showeth that there is a God, who hath lordship and sovereignty over all, is good, and doeth good unto all, and is therefore to be feared, loved, praised, called upon, trusted in, and served with all the heart, and with all the soul, and with all the might. But the acceptable way of worshipping the true God, is instituted by himself, and so limited to his own revealed will, that he may not be worshipped according to the imaginations and devices of men, or the suggestions of Satan, under any visible representations, or any other way not prescribed in the Holy Scripture.

II. Religious worship is to be given to God, the Father, Son, and Holy Ghost; and to him alone: not to angels, saints, or any other creature: and since the fall, not without a Mediator; nor in the mediation of any other, but of Christ alone.

III. Prayer, with thanksgiving, being one special part of religious worship, is by God required of all men; and that it may be accepted, it is to be made in the name of the Son, by the help of his Spirit, according to his will, with understanding, reverence, humility, fervency, faith, love, and perseverance; and, if vocal, in a known tongue.

IV. Prayer is to be made for things lawful, and for all sorts of men living, or that shall live hereafter; but not for the dead, nor for those of whom it may be known, that they have sinned the sin unto death.

V. The reading of the Scriptures with godly fear, the sound preaching; and conscionable hearing of the Word, in obedience unto God, with understanding, faith, and reverence; singing of psalms with grace in the heart; as also, the due administration, and worthy receiving of the sacraments instituted by Christ; are all, parts of the ordinary religious worship of God: besides religious oaths, vows, solemn fastings, and thanksgivings, upon several occasions, which are, in their several times and seasons, to be used in an holy and religious manner.

VI. Neither prayer, nor any other part of religious worship, is now under the gospel, either tied unto, or made more acceptable by any place in which it is performed, or towards which it is directed: but God is to be worshipped every where, in spirit and truth: as in private families, daily, and in secret, each one by himself; so, more solemnly, in the public assemblies, which are not carelessly, or willfully to be neglected, or forsaken, when God, by his Word or providence, calleth thereunto.

VII. As it is of the law of nature, that, in general, a due proportion of time be set apart for the worship of God; so, in his Word, by a positive, moral, and perpetual commandment, binding all men, in all ages, he hath particularly appointed one day in seven, for a Sabbath, to be kept holy unto him: which, from the beginning of the world to the resurrection of Christ, was the last day of the week; and, from the resurrection of Christ, was changed into the first day of the week, which, in Scripture, is called the Lord's day, and is to be continued to the end of the world, as the Christian Sabbath.

VIII. This Sabbath is then kept holy unto the Lord, when men, after a due preparing of their hearts, & ordering of their common affairs beforehand, do not only observe an holy rest all the day from their own works, words, & thoughts, about their worldly employments and recreations; but also are taken up the whole time, in the public and private exercises of his worship, and in the duties of necessity, and mercy.

CHAPTER XXII.

Of Lawful Oaths and Vows.

I. A lawful oath is a part of religious worship, wherein, upon just occasion, the person swearing solemnly, calleth God to witness what he asserteth, or promiseth; and to judge him according to the truth or falsehood of what he sweareth.

II. The name of God only, is that by which men ought to swear, and, therein it is to be used with all holy fear and reverence. Therefore to swear vainly, or rashly, by that glorious and dreadful Name, or to swear at all, by any other thing, is sinful, and to be abhorred. Yet, as in matters of weight and moment, an oath is warranted by the Word of God, under the New Testament, as well as under the Old; so, a lawful oath, being imposed by lawful authority, in such matters ought to be taken.

III. Whosoever taketh an oath, ought duly to consider the weightiness of so solemn an act; and therein to avouch nothing, but what he is fully persuaded is the truth. Neither may any man bind himself by oath to any thing, but what is good and just, and what he believeth so to be, and what he is able and resolved to perform. Yet it is a sin, to refuse an oath touching any thing that is good and just, being imposed by lawful authority.

IV. An oath is to be taken in the plain and common sense of the words, without equivocation, or mental reservation. It cannot oblige to sin: but, in any thing not sinful, being taken, it binds to performance, although to a man's own hurt. Nor is it to be violated, although made to heretics or infidels.

V. A vow is of the like nature with a promissory oath, and ought to be made with the like religious care, and to be performed with the like faithfulness.

VI. It is not to be made to any creature but to God alone: and, that it may be accepted, it is to be made voluntarily, out of faith, and conscience of duty, in way of thankfulness for mercy received, or for the obtaining of what we want; whereby we more strictly bind ourselves to necessary duties; or, to other things, so far, and so long, as they may fitly conduce thereunto.

VII. No man may vow to do any thing forbidden in the Word of God, or what would hinder any duty therein commanded, or which is not in his own power, and for the performance whereof he hath no promise or ability from God. In which respect, popish monastical vows of perpetual single life, professed poverty, and regular obedience, are so far from being degrees of higher perfection, that they are superstitious and sinful snares, in which no Christian may entangle himself.

CHAPTER XXIII.

Of the Civil Magistrate.

I. God the Supreme Lord and King of all the world, hath ordained civil magistrates to be under him over the people, for his own glory, and the public good; and to this end hath armed them with the power of the sword, for the defence and encouragement of them that are good, and for the punishment of evildoers.

II. It is lawful for Christians to accept and execute the office of a magistrate when called thereunto: in the managing whereof, as they ought especially to maintain piety, justice, and peace, according to the wholesome laws of each commonwealth: so, for that end, they may lawfully now under the New Testament, wage war upon just and necessary occasion.

III. The civil magistrate may not assume to himself the administration of the Word & Sacraments, or the power of the keys of the kingdom of heaven: yet he hath authority, and it is his duty to take order, that unity & peace be preserved in the Church, that the truth of God be kept pure & entire, that all blasphemies and heresies be suppressed, all corruptions and abuses in worship and discipline prevented or reformed; and all ordinances of God duly settled, administered, and observed. For the better effecting whereof he hath power to call synods, to be present at them, and to provide that whatsoever is transacted in them be according to the mind of God.

IV. It is the duty of people to pray for magistrates, to honour their persons, to pay them tribute and other dues, to obey their lawful commands, and to be subject to their authority, for conscience sake. Infidelity or difference in religion doth not make void the magistrate's just & legal authority, nor free the people from their due obedience to him: from which ecclesiastical persons are not exempted; much less hath the Pope any power or jurisdiction over them, in their dominions, or over any of their people; and least of all to deprive them of their dominions, or lives, if he shall judge them to be heretics, or upon any other pretence whatsoever.

CHAPTER XXIV.

Of Marriage and Divorce.

I. Marriage is to be between one man and one woman: neither is it lawful for any man to have more than one wife, nor for any woman to have more than one husband at the same time.

II. Marriage was ordained for the mutual help of husband and wife, for the increase of mankind with a legitimate issue, and of the church with an holy seed, and for preventing of uncleanness.

III. It is lawful for all sorts of people to marry who are able with judgment to give their consent. Yet it is the duty of Christians to marry only in the Lord: And therefore such as profess the true reformed religion should not marry with infidels, Papists, or other idolaters: Neither should such as are godly be unequally yoked, by marrying with such as are notoriously wicked in their life, or maintain damnable heresies.

IV. Marriage ought not to be within the degrees of consanguinity or affinity forbidden in the Word: Nor can such incestuous marriages ever be made lawful by any law of man, or consent of parties, so as those persons may live together as man and wife. The man may not marry one of his wife's kindred nearer in blood than he may of his own, nor the woman of her husband's kindred nearer in blood than of her own.

V. Adultery or fornication committed after a contract, being detected before marriage, giveth just occasion to the innocent party to dissolve that contract. In the case of adultery after marriage, it is lawful for the innocent party to sue out a divorce: and after the divorce to marry another, as if the offending party were dead.

VI. Although the corruption of man be such as is apt to study arguments, unduly to put asunder those whom God hath joined together in marriage; yet nothing but adultery, or such willful desertion as can no way be remedied by the Church, or civil magistrate, is cause sufficient of dissolving the bond of marriage: Wherein a public and orderly course of proceeding is to be observed; and the persons concerned in it, not left to their own wills and discretion in their own case.

CHAPTER XXV.

Of the Church.

I. The catholic or universal Church, which is invisible, consists of the whole number of the elect, that have been, are, or shall be gathered into one, under Christ the head thereof; and is the spouse, the body, the fullness of him that filleth all in all.

II. The visible Church, which is also catholic or universal under the gospel (not confined to one nation as before under the law) consists of all those, throughout the world, that profess the true religion; together with their children, and is the kingdom of the Lord Jesus Christ, the house and family of God, out of which there is no ordinary possibility of salvation.

III. Unto this catholic visible Church, Christ hath given the ministry, oracles, and ordinances of God, for the gathering and perfecting of the saints, in this life, to the end of the world: and doth by his own presence and Spirit, according to his promise, make them effectual thereunto.

IV. This catholic Church hath been sometimes more, sometimes less visible. And particular churches, which are members thereof, are more or less pure, according as the doctrine of the gospel is taught and embraced, ordinances administered, and public worship performed more or less purely in them.

V. The purest churches under heaven are subject both to mixture, and error: and some have so degenerated, as to become no churches of Christ, but synagogues of Satan. Nevertheless, there shall be always a Church on earth, to worship God according to his will.

VI. There is no other head of the Church, but the Lord Jesus Christ. Nor can the Pope of Rome in any sense be head thereof; but is that Antichrist, that man of sin and son of perdition, that exalteth himself, in the Church, against Christ, and all that is called God.

CHAPTER XXVI.

Of the Communion of Saints.

I. All saints, that are united to Jesus Christ their head, by his Spirit, and by faith, have fellowship with him in his graces, sufferings, death, resurrection, & glory: and being united to one another in love, they have communion in each other's gifts and graces, and are obliged to the performance of such duties, public and private, as do conduce to their mutual good, both in the inward and outward man.

II. Saints, by profession, are bound to maintain an holy fellowship and communion in the worship of God; and in performing such other spiritual services as tend to their mutual edification: as also in relieving each other in outward things, according to their several abilities, and necessities. Which communion, as God offereth opportunity, is to be extended unto all those, who, in every place, call upon the name of the Lord Jesus.

III. This communion which the saints have with Christ, doth not make them, in any wise partakers of the substance of his Godhead, or to be equal with Christ in any respect: either of which to affirm, is impious, and blasphemous. Nor doth their communion one with another, as saints, take away, or infringe the title or propriety which each man hath in his goods and possessions.

CHAPTER XXVII.

Of the Sacraments.

I. Sacraments are holy signs and seals of the covenant of grace, immediately instituted by God, to represent Christ and his benefits, & to confirm our interest in him: as also to put a visible difference between those that belong unto the Church, & the rest of the world: and solemnly to engage them to the service of God in Christ, according to his Word.

II. There is in every sacrament a spiritual relation, or sacramental union between the sign and the thing signified: whence it comes to pass, that the names and the effects of the one are attributed to the other.

III. The grace which is exhibited in, or by the sacraments rightly used, is not conferred by any power in them: neither doth the efficacy of a sacrament depend upon the piety or intention of him that doth administer it; but upon the work of the Spirit, and the word of institution; which contains, together with a precept authorizing the use thereof, a promise of benefit to worthy receivers.

IV. There be only two sacraments ordained by Christ our Lord in the gospel; that is to say, Baptism and the Supper of the Lord: neither of which may be dispensed by any, but by a minister of the Word lawfully ordained.

V. The sacraments of the Old Testament, in regard of the spiritual things thereby signified and exhibited, were for substance, the same with those of the New.

CHAPTER XXVIII.

Of Baptism.

I. Baptism is a sacrament of the New Testament, ordained by Jesus Christ, not only for the solemn admission of the party baptized into the visible Church, but also to be unto him a sign and seal of the covenant of grace, of his ingrafting into Christ, of regeneration, of remission of sins, and of his giving up unto God, through Jesus Christ, to walk in newness of life. Which sacrament is by Christ's own appointment to be continued in his Church until the end of the world.

II. The outward element to be used in this sacrament is water, wherewith the party is to be baptized, in the name of the Father, and of the Son, and of the Holy Ghost, by a minister of the gospel lawfully called thereunto.

III. Dipping of the person into the water is not necessary: but baptism is rightly administered by pouring or sprinkling water upon the person.

IV. Not only those that do actually profess faith in, and obedience unto Christ, but also the infants of one, or both believing parents, are to be baptized.

V. Although it be a great sin to contemn or neglect this ordinance, yet grace and salvation are not so inseparably annexed unto it, as that no person can be regenerated or saved without it: or, that all that are baptized are undoubtedly regenerated.

VI. The efficacy of baptism is not tied to that moment of time wherein it is administered: yet, notwithstanding by the right use of this ordinance, the grace promised is not only offered, but really exhibited and conferred by the Holy Ghost, to such (whether of age, or infants) as that grace belongeth unto, according to the counsel of God's own will, in his appointed time.

VII. The sacrament of baptism is but once to be administered to any person.

CHAPTER XXIX.

Of the Lord's Supper.

I. Our Lord Jesus, in the night wherein he was betrayed, instituted the sacrament of his body and blood, called the Lord's Supper, to be observed in his Church unto the end of the world, for the perpetual remembrance of the sacrifice of himself, in his death; the sealing all benefits thereof unto true believers, their spiritual nourishment and growth in him, their further engagement in, and to all duties which they owe unto him; and to be a bond, and pledge of their communion with him, and with each other, as members of his mystical body.

II. In this sacrament Christ is not offered up to his Father; nor any real sacrifice made at all, for remission of sin of the quick or dead, but only a commemoration of that one offering up of himself, by himself, upon the cross, once for all: and a spiritual oblation of all possible praise unto God, for the same: So that, the Popish sacrifice of the mass (as they call it), is most abominably injurious to Christ's one only sacrifice, the alone propitiation for all the sins of the elect.

III. The Lord Jesus hath, in this ordinance, appointed his ministers to declare his word of institution to the people; to pray, and bless the elements of bread and wine, and thereby to set them apart from a common to an holy use; and to take, and break the bread, to take the cup, and (they communicating also themselves) to give both to the communicants; but, to none who are not then present in the congregation.

IV. Private masses, or receiving this sacrament by a priest, or any other, alone, as likewise, the denial of the cup to the people, worshipping the elements, the lifting them up, or carrying them about for adoration, and the reserving them for any pretended religious use, are all contrary to the nature of this sacrament, and to the institution of Christ.

V. The outward elements in this sacrament, duly set apart, to the uses ordained by Christ, have such relation to him crucified, as that truly, yet sacramentally only, they are sometimes called by the name of the things they represent, to wit, the body, and blood of Christ, albeit in substance and nature, they still remain truly, and only, bread and wine, as they were before.

VI. That doctrine which maintains a change of the substance of bread and wine, into the substance of Christ, body and blood (commonly called transubstantiation) by consecration of a priest, or by any other way, is repugnant, not to Scripture alone, but even to common-sense and reason; overthroweth the nature of the sacrament; and hath been, and is the cause of manifold superstitions; yea, of gross idolatries.

VII. Worthy receivers outwardly partaking of the visible elements, in this sacrament, do then also inwardly by faith, really and indeed, yet not carnally and corporally, but spiritually receive, and feed upon Christ crucified, and all benefits of his death: the body and blood of Christ being then, not corporally or carnally, in, with, or under the bread and wine; yet as really, but spiritually, present to the faith of believers in that ordinance, as the elements themselves are to their outward senses.

VIII. Although ignorant and wicked men receive the outward elements in this sacrament; yet they receive not the thing signified thereby; but by their unworthy coming thereunto, are guilty of the body and blood of the Lord, to their own damnation. Wherefore, all ignorant and ungodly persons, as they are unfit to enjoy communion with him, so are they unworthy of the Lord's table; and cannot, without great sin against Christ, while they remain such, partake of these holy mysteries, or be admitted thereunto.

CHAPTER XXX.

Of Church Censures.

I. The Lord Jesus, as King and Head of his Church, hath therein appointed a government, in the hand of Church officers, distinct from the civil magistrate.

II. To these officers the keys of the Kingdom of Heaven are committed; by virtue whereof they have power respectively to retain, and remit sins; to shut that Kingdom against the impenitent, both by the Word and censures; and to open it unto penitent sinners by the ministry of the gospel, and by absolution from censures, as occasion shall require.

III. Church censures are necessary for the reclaiming & gaining of offending brethren, for deterring of others from the like offences; for purging out of that leaven which might infect the whole lump, for vindicating the honour of Christ, & the holy profession of the gospel, and for preventing the wrath of God, which might justly fall upon the Church, if they should suffer his covenant and the seals thereof to be profaned by notorious and obstinate offenders.

IV. For the better attaining of these ends, the officers of the Church are to proceed by admonition, suspension from the Sacrament of the Lord's Supper for a season; and by excommunication from the Church according to the nature of the crime and demerit of the person.

CHAPTER XXXI.

Of Synods and Councils.

I. For the better government, and further edification of the Church; there ought to be such assemblies as are commonly called synods or councils.

II. As magistrates may lawfully call a synod of ministers and other fit persons to consult and advise with, about matters of religion: So, if magistrates be open enemies to the Church, the ministers of Christ, of themselves, by virtue of their office; or they, with other fit persons, upon delegation from their churches, may meet together in such assemblies.

III. It belongeth to synods and councils ministerially to determine controversies of faith, and cases of conscience, to set down rules and directions for the better ordering of the public worship of God, and government of his Church; to receive complaints in cases of maladministration; and authoritatively to determine the same: which decrees and determinations, if consonant to the Word of God, are to be received with reverence & submission; not only for their agreement with the Word, but also for the power whereby they are made, as being an ordinance of God, appointed thereunto in his Word.

IV. All synods or councils since the apostles' times, whether general or particular, may err; & many have erred. Therefore they are not to be made the rule of faith or practice; but to be used as a help in both.

V. Synods and councils are to handle or conclude nothing but that which is ecclesiastical: and are not to intermeddle with civil affairs which concern the commonwealth, unless by way of humble petition in cases extraordinary; or by way of advice, for satisfaction of conscience, if they be thereunto required by the civil magistrate.

CHAPTER XXXII.

Of the State of Men after Death, and of the Resurrection of the Dead.

I. The bodies of men after death return to dust, & see corruption: but their souls (which neither die nor sleep) having an immortal subsistence, immediately return to God who gave them. The souls of the righteous, being then made perfect in holiness, are received into the highest heavens, where they behold the face of God in light and glory, waiting for the full redemption of their bodies: and the souls of the wicked are cast into hell, where they remain in torments and utter darkness, reserved to the judgment of the great day. Besides these two places for souls separated from their bodies, the Scripture acknowledgeth none.

II. At the last day such as are found alive shall not die, but be changed; and all the dead shall be raised up, with the self-same bodies, and none other, although with different qualities, which shall be united again to their souls forever.

III. The bodies of the unjust shall, by the power of Christ, be raised to dishonour: the bodies of the just by his Spirit, unto honour; and be made conformable to his own glorious body.

CHAPTER XXXIII.

Of the Last Judgment.

I. God hath appointed a day wherein he will judge the world in righteousness by Jesus Christ, to whom all power and judgment is given of the Father. In which day, not only the apostate angels shall be judged, but likewise all persons that have lived upon earth shall appear before the tribunal of Christ, to give an account of their thoughts, words, and deeds; and to receive according to what they have done in the body, whether good or evil.

II. The end of God's appointing this day, is for the manifestation of the glory of his mercy, in the eternal salvation of the elect; and of his justice, in the damnation of the reprobate, who are wicked and disobedient. For then shall the righteous go into everlasting life, and receive that fullness of joy and refreshing which shall come from the presence of the Lord: but the wicked, who know not God, and obey not the gospel of Jesus Christ, shall be cast into eternal torments, and be punished with everlasting destruction from the presence of the Lord, and from the glory of his power.

III. As Christ would have us to be certainly persuaded that there shall be a day of judgment, both to deter all men from sin, and for the greater consolation of the godly in their adversity: so will he have that day unknown to men, that they may shake off all carnal security, and be always watchful, because they know not at what hour the Lord will come; and may be ever prepared to say, Come, Lord Jesus, come quickly. Amen.

Charles Herle, Prolocutor.
Cornelius Burges, Assessor.
Herbert Palmer, Assessor.
Henry Robrough, Scriba.
Adoniram Byfield, Scriba.

Document III.4

Anabaptists

This quotation from a contemporary newsbook illustrates the kind of contempt with which Baptists were treated and how the word 'Anabaptist' was used as a term of abuse at the time. There was a general suspicion that 'Anabaptism' was a challenge to the social order, and the following account, which must be taken with a grain of salt, seeks to illustrate how the baptizing of women in a stream flouted the conventions of the day and the figure of the miller represents those who found it easy to make a mockery of the practice of adult Baptism by immersion.

For the significance of the newsbooks published between 1641 and 1660, v., Joad Raymond, *Making the News* (Moreton-in-Marsh: Windrush Press, 1993). The extract is from *Mercurius Civicus*, no. 177, 8–15 October 1646.

A Relation of the Rebaptizing of a Woman at Hempsted *in* Hartfordshire *in* September *last past,* 1646, *by one* James Brown *a Sawyer.*

In the parish of *Hempsted* in *Hartfordshire*, there liveth one *James Browne*, by trade, a Sawyer: by calling, a converter of holy Sisters; by person, of a very big and tall Stature; by Religion, formerly a good Protestant, diligent in hearing of Sermons, and always seeking to heare the best men: Now of late time, within these six or seven years, he hath quite left the Church: and instead of hearing Gods Ministers in publique, he is become a preacher and teacher of others, (especially of women) going about from house to house preaching and teaching, Instructing and Baptizing; (or Rebaptizing) doing good as they say, to so many as adhere to his kinde of Teaching: and he is either the second or third man of note for spirituall abilities (as the Brethren are pleased there to call them) in all that part of the Country.

About the middle of *September* now last past, 1646. This *James Browne*, having on a day Preached (or as they call it spoken) unto an assembly of Brethren, where he inveighed against Baptizing of Infants; affirming it to be a most damnable popishe sinne: and that all true Christians ought more to mourne and lament for that they were Baptized when they were Infants, then for all the sinnes that ever they committed in the whole course of their lives; and further shewing, how necessary and needfull it was to salvation (having attayned unto a sufficient measure of Faith) to be rebaptized. One *Mary Halsey*, wife of *William Halsey*, a holy woman of the company, desired to be Baptized anew: shewing her selfe to be very sorrowfull for the blindnesse of her Parents, that would have her Baptized in her Infancy, before she knew what it meant, and she (being then without Faith) unworthy of it. *Browne* having thoroughly examined this new convert, and found her to have attayned to a competent knowledge, the examination ended, This woman with *Browne* went into a River, neerehand to the house of that dayes exercise, called *Bourn End* River; and there neere unto *Bourne End* Mill, in a place of the River somewhat deeper then the ordinary Channell, where having joyned together they went down into the water: *Browne* went down in his leather Breeches, in which he used to go Sawing. And the woman went into the water in a paire of Linnen Drawers, onely to cover her shame; made of purpose for such like uses, the rest of her body being all quite naked.

In this water, *Browne* washed her body all over from top to toe, rubbing her with his hands, as men doe their sheep when they wash them; and so clensed her from all filthinesse, (as he saith both of body and spirit) and throwing water upon her, used the words of Baptisme, *I Baptize thee, in the name of the Father, and of the Sonne, and of the Holy Ghost*: thrusting her head three times into the water, because three persons in the Trinity: and in this water I wash and purge away all thy sinnes; sending them down the stream, together with this water that runneth off thy body: so that now thou art made as cleane againe from all sinne, and wickednesse, as ever thou wast in thy Infancy; nay, cleaner, for now thy originall sinne if thou hadst any, is quite taken away, and thou art now received into the number of Christs chosen Children: and made a member of his mysticall body, and mayest be fully assured of the Kingdome of Heaven.

This being done, they departed out of the water, and went to the place of that dayes exercise.

This was seene and heard by the Miller of *Bourn End*, and some others, who got behind a hedge to heare and see the action. As they were going out of the water, the Miller called to them, and wished *Brown* to rub her a little more: for there is (saith he) I doubt one spot that is not yet made white, and they departed making no answer, and a man with them, that the woman brought downe with her to looke to her apparell, which she put off neere the River side, when she went into the water: and had not that man kept her apparell, the Miller would have conveyed it out of the way, and made her go naked to the assembly, from whence she came.

Document III.5

A Fifth Monarchist Protest

Oliver Cromwell was installed as Lord Protector on 16 December 1653. On 19 December at St Anne's, Blackfriars, London, Christopher Feake (*fl.* 1645–60) and Vavasor Powell (1617-70), both Fifth Monarchists, launched a violent verbal attack on Cromwell. Powell prophesied the imminence of the Fifth Monarchy and the downfall of the Protectorate and said, 'let us go home and pray, and say, Lord, wilt thou have Oliver Cromwell or Jesus Christ to reign over us'. (*Calendar of State Papers, Domestic* (1653–4) (London, 1886), 304–7). He and Feake were arrested on 21 December but released on the 24th. On 10 February 1654 Powell opened his campaign against the Protectorate at Llanddewibrefi, Cardiganshire. He was seeking support for a petition to be sent to Cromwell and in April he, together with the signatories, was summoned to appear at the Montgomery sessions. The incident at Aberbechan, mentioned in the Postscript below, occurred in November 1655 when Powell was taken to Worcester to be interviewed by Major-General James Berry (for the interviews, v., *A Collection of the State Papers of John Thurloe Esq* ..., 7 vols (London, 174 and years following), IV, 211, 228). Berry did not take a very serious view of Powell's fulminations. *A Word for God* was published not later than 17 December 1655. For a detailed account of the events, v., Thomas Richards, *Religious Developments in Wales, 1654–1662* (London, 1923), 208ff. For the Fifth Monarchy movement v., L. F. Brown, *The Political Activities of the Baptists and Fifth Monarchy Men in England during the Interregnum* (London, 1912; New York, 1965), P. G. Rogers, *The Fifth Monarchy Men* (Oxford, 1966) and B. S. Capp, *The Fifth Monarchy Men* (London, 1972). For a Welsh study of Vavasor Powell v., R. Tudur Jones, *Vavasor Powell* (Swansea, 1971). The petition of Colonels Okey, Alured and Saunders, protesting against the Protectorate, was drawn up in November 1654. It had been drafted by the Leveller John Wildman. For John Okey, regicide, v., DNB. For Sir John Wildman (1621?–93) v., DNB and M. P. Ashley, *John Wildman, Plotter and Postmaster* (London, 1947). The 'Engagement', passed on 2 January 1650 was worded, 'I do declare and promise, that I will be true and faithful to the Commonwealth of England, as it is now established without a King or House of Lords'. For 'The Instrument of Government', 16 December 1653, instituting the Protectorate, v., S. R. Gardiner, *The Constitutional Documents of the Puritan Revolution* (Oxford, 1889 and 1968), 405–17.

A Word for God or a Testimony on Truths behalf; from several Churches, and diverse hundreds of Christians in Wales (and some adjacent) against Wickednesse in HIGH-PLACES. With a Letter to the Lord Generall CROMWELL. Both, first presented to his own hands, and now published for further Information. [Job 36: 1 and Esa. 44: 8, 9 quoted.]

To Oliver Cromwell Captain Generall of all Forces in England, Scotland and Ireland.

Sir,
Forasmuch as you have caused great searching of heart, and divisions among many of Gods People by a sudden, strange, and unexpected alteration of Government, and other actions to the great astonishment of those who knew your former publick Resolutions and Declarations; considering also, how (contrary to foregoing Acts and Engagements) you have taken upon you a Power by which you are utterly disinabled (if there were in you a heart) to prosecute the good things Covenanted and contended for, with so many great hazards, and the effucion of so much precious blood: and by reason whereof you are become justly suspected in your ends in time past, and actions for future to very many of those, of whose affections and faithfnll [sic] services, you have enjoyed no small share, in all [p. 2] the difficult passages and enterprizes of the late War. These things considered by us, (as we know they are by many Churches & Saints) and there being a deep sence upon our Spirits of the *Odium*, under which the name of Christ, his Cause, People and wayes do lye (as it were) buried; and also of the exceeding contempt which the wonderfull and excellent operations of God are brought into; even those eminent wonders, which the Nations have been Spectators and witnesses of, and wherein your hands have been partly engaged; We cannot after much serious consideration and seeking of the Lord, many of us, both together and a part, but present to your hands the ensuing testimony, w^{ch} (however you may look theron) is no more then necessity exacts from us, for the clearing of our own Souls from guilt and discharging of our duty to God & men. Therefore We earnestly wish you to peruse and weigh it, as in the sight of God, with a calm and Christian like Spirit, and harden not your neck against the truth as you will answer it to the great judge, before whose impartial Tribunal you (as well as we) shalbe very shortly cited to give an account of the things done in the body, whether good or evil. Where the true motives and ends of all your Actions will be evident, where no apologie will

be accepted of, your slighting and blaspheming of the Spirit of God, nor of the hard measure you give his people, by reproaches, imprisonment and other oppressions; and where Pride, Luxury, Lasciviousnesse, changing of Principles and forsaking the good wayes, justice and holinesse will not have the smallest rag of pretence to hide them from the eyes of the Judge: which things (whatsoever you say for your self) are (even at present) to be read in your Fore-head, and have produced most sad effects every where. Especially, first, The filling of the Saints hearts and faces with inexpressible grief and shame: And secondly, The stopping (at least) of the strong current of their Prayers, which was once for you; if not the turning thereof directly against you. To these we might adde (thirdly), The hardening of wicked men, yea the refreshing and justifying of them in their evill doings, and speaking against the Gospel, Name, and Spirit of our Lord Jesus Christ. And lastly, Gods signall withdrawing from you and your designes. Oh then! that you would ly down in the dust & acknowledge your iniquity, and return unto the Lord by unfeigned repentance, doing your first works, and that you would make hast to do so, least Gods fury break forth like fire upon you, and there be no quenching of it. This would rejoyce us much, as being reall welwishers to your souls everlasting happinesse, though we must declare with equall pity and destation against your designes and way.

[p. 3]

THE WORD for GOD

The wise God that teacheth the Fowls of Heaven to know their appointed times [*margin*: Ier.8.7.], who directs his peoples work in truth, hath we hope directed us (after a long time of silence and earnest seeking the Lord) to express and and [sic] declare what we find in our Consciences touching the transactions of this season; and though some may think (as we our selves have been tempted to think) that this is a time, wherein the prudent should hold his peace, it being such an evill time, that men are made offenders; yea, Traytors for words: Yet considering how the Lords remembrancers should not keep silence [*margin*: Isa 62.6.], and fearing that if we should altogether hold our peace at such a time as this (as *Mordecay* said to Hester) [*margin*: Hest.4.14.] deliverance would come another way, and we could expect no share in the enlargement of Gods people, or safety in the day of trouble: withall finding how self would prompt us (like *Issachar*) to see that rest is good, and outward prosperity pleasant [*margin*: Gen.49.15.], and how the same temptations (which we finde and fear many of our deare Brethren to be under) have set upon some of us, as to have mens persons in admiration because of advantage, and by good words, faire speeches and promises, to be deceived and drawn away in simplicity [*margin*: Iude 16.; Rom.16.8.; 2 Sam. 2.13.]; especially, by the example of some eminent men (like *Peter*) in so much that many *Barnabasses* are carried away with their dissimulation, [*margin*: Gal.2.13.; I Chron.4.23.] and as well Ministers as Military men willing to serve the King for his Work and Wages. However seeing every man must give an account unto God for himself; we have examined what particular duty was incumbent upon us, and how in faithfulnesse towards God and meeknesse towards men [*margin*: Rom.14.12.], we should perform the same: Moreover considering how the Saints did formerly bear their Testimony (not loving their lives unto the death) and by the blood of the Lamb, and their testimony did overcame [*margin*: Rev.12.7.]; and how God did heretofore stir up some of his people (both in *England* and *Scotland*) to bear witnesse (to the truth and wayes of God) against the wayes and wickednesse of men as a forelorn hope; though they were in comparison but a few; like *Joshuah* and *Caleb*, two of twelve [*margin*: Numb.14.6,7,8,9.]; or like the two Witnesses [*margin*: Rev.7.3.; 2 Pet.1.12.], a small but sufficient number. Observing also, that there are present Truths, and every work being beautifull in its season (as in the beginning of the late Wars) was the witnessing against the Book of *Common Prayer*, *Surplesse*, *Crosse* in Baptisme, and other Ceremonies (being superstitious things, imposed by the Bishops) and against Ship-money, Monopolyze, &c. (civill things) imposed formerly by the King. All which were afterwards Declared, Protested and Covenanted against; which Protestation and Covenant are fresh in the memories, and pressing upon the Consciences of some of us, even unto this day: Besides the Engagement, and the severall Acts of Parliament, made against Monarchy or Kingly government, all which now seem to be forgotten or neglected; and those that speak or write in defence of such things, as the Parliament, Army, and the Godly people in the Three Nations approved, asserted and purchased at a dear rate, are now accounted fanatick fools, disturbers of Civil States, and intermedlers in things that concern them not; under which notion many suffer imprisonment, and other tryals, as evill doers from those men, who now build what they did once destroy; and justifie what they did once condemn. Witnesse their own Writings, particularly the Declaration of the Officers and Souldiers of the English Army [*margin*: Aug. 1.1650, pag. 7,12.] (whereof [p. 4] the Lord Cromwell was General) the words whereof are as followeth.

We are perswaded in our Consciences that the late King and his Monarchy was one of the ten horns of the Beast spoken of, [margin: Rev.17 ver. 13, 14, 15.] *And that we were called forth by the Lord to be instrumentall to bring about that which was our continuall Prayers unto God, viz. The destruction of Antichrist, and the deliverance of his Church and people; and upon this single account we engaged, not knowing the deep Pollicies of worldly Statesmen, and have ever since hazarded our lives in the high places of the Field (where we have seen many wonders of the Lord) against all the opposers of the work of Jesus Christ, whom we have all along seen going with us, and making our way plain before us; and having these things singly in our eye, namely the destruction of Antichrist, the advancement of the Kingdome of Christ, the deliverance of his Church; and the establishment thereof, in the use of his Ordinances, in purity according to his word, and the just, civill, Liberties of Englishmen.*

These with many other expressions, both in the Declaration and severall other Papers of the Army, and Letters to the General, cited both in the Declaration of the members of severall Churches, and Petitions of the Three Colonels [*margin*: *Saunders*, *Okey* and *Allured*]; besides several other Papers which might be instanced in; which we leave to all unbyassed men to consider; and compare with actions done by the same men since that time: but in pursuance of our duty to God, our fellow members and Countrymen, as we are Christians, having a right to our native Priviledges: We do Declare our reall Apprehensions and consciences (which to the great grief of some of us) we have so long concealed, waiting if God might by his Providence alter our mindes.

First, That the sins and present condition of this Nation holds parallel in many things with the old Israelites after the mighty wonders of God, shewed unto them in their great deliverance out of Ægypt. For instance: They and we have soon forgotten God our Saviour [*margin*: Psal. 106.13], and the great works which he did; we have not set our hearts aright, and our spirits have not been stedfast with God, but have gone back, and dealt treacherously, and turned aside like a deceiptful bow; and not trusting to his salvation, have provoked the Lord to anger with our inventions; so that men have dominion over our bodies, and over our Cattle at their pleasure [*margin*: Psal. 78.2., 9.10.; Psal. 106.28,29; Neh. 9.3.7.] And we are in great distresse, for this is a day of trouble, and of Blasphemy, for the children are come to the Birth, and there is not strength to bring forth.

Secondly, That blessed Cause, and those noble Principles propounded, and prosecuted by the old Parliament, and the good People of this Nation (in the maintaining of which God did miraculously appear) are now altogether laid aside and lost; and another cause and interest (quite contrary as we conceive) espoused and maintained; For then the advancement of Christs Kingdome, the extirpation of Popery, and popish Innovations, the Priviledges of Parliament, the Liberty of the Subjects, and an equall distribution of Justice were Declared and fought for; and Tyranny, Oppression, Injustice, Arbitrarynesse; Destroying the Priviledges of Parliament, we Declared and Engaged against: But how far some men have now receded from, and acted contrarily to the dishonour of God, scandall of Religion, great grief of many faithfull men, and the strengthening of the wicked in their principles, and justifying their practices, we leave to the consideration of all those that are sober and wise.

[p. 5] Thirdly, Moreover the unadvised and unwarrantable changing of the Government and swearing threunto, doth (as we judge) put a necessity upon the chief undertaker thereof, to overthrow the very foundation of a Common-wealth: and to maintaine the things comprised in the said Instrument (whether right or wrong) and to turn the very edge and dint of his Sword against the faces and bowels of such as should or shall declare their consciences contrary thereunto.

Fourthly, As a consequence and fruit of this forbidden Tree, many of the choice servants of God and faithfull of the Nation, (some Noblemen, Gentlemen, Ministers of the Gospel, Souldiers, &c.) are imprisoned without knowing their accusers or having so much liberty as was granted by the Heathens to the Apostles, or the benefit of a fair and publique tryall, according to the fundamental laws of this Nation.

Fiftly, Under pretence of necessity still to continue the heavy burdens of Taxes, Customs, Excise, &c. upon the Nation, without (yea contrary to) the Consent of the People represented in Parliament, and contrary to their own INSTRUMENT.

Sixtly, Notwithstanding all the fair pretences and promises of Reformation, yet what abhominable and horrible Impieties, Injustice and Oppression are there couched and covered under this new Form, from the Head to the Taile (as the Prophet saith) treading in the very footsteps of their Predecessors [*margin*: Act. 27.30]: witnesse the receiving of the Honours, Profits, Customs, Benefits, Tenths, and First-fruits comming in formerly to the Crown: the exalting of Sons, Servants, Friends and Favourites (though some of them known to be wicked men) to the highest places and greatest preferment, which the good rulers of old, as *Gideon*, *Nehemiah* and others did not do; because of the fear of the Lord, and the Bondage that was heavy upon the people; Witnesse also the unreasonablenesse of the Army to have so many Officers, which might easily be reduced to a lesser number, and both Officers and Souldiers for many years to receive their pay (even in a time of peace) when the poore Peasants or Tenants (who pay but ten shilling rent *per Annum*) doe pay out of their penury to maintain them in pompe and luxury.

Seventhly, We cannot without grief mention the sad effects of the secret designe of *Hispaniola*, to be the losse of so many mens lives, the expence of so much blood and treasure, and the endangering of this Common-wealth by Invasion; as also thereby rendring us a scorn and snuffe to the Nations round about.

Lastly, We do declare and publish to all from our very hearts and souls, that those of us that had any hand in joyning with the Parliament and Army heretofore, had no other designe against the Late King and his Party, save as they were enemies of our Lord Christ, his Kingdome and people, hinderers of his work, and oppressors of the Nation, and that it never came into our hearts to think or intend the pulling down of one person to set up another; or, one unrighteous power to promote another: but we aymed as primarily at the glory of God: so likewise at the generall good of the Nation, and particular benefit and just liberty of every man; and it greives us, that any just cause is given them to stumble at Professors, or complain that they are deprived of their Freedome, and severall wayes more oppressed, then in the dayes of the wickedest Kings; we do also believe in our heart, that (though the worst things are not without Gods permission and providence) yet that this Government is not of Gods approbation, or taken up by his Counsell, or according to his word; And therefore, We do utterly Disclaime ha- [p. 6] ving any hand or heart in it, and for the Contrivers and undertakers thereof, we suspect and judge them to be great transgressors therein; and so much the more, because they are Professors of Religion, and Declarers, Engagers, and fighters against the very things they now practice: And it is most evident to us, that they thereby build again, what before they did destroy; and in so doing they render themselves and the Cause, Religion, Name and People of God abominable to Heathens, Papists and prophane Enemies, which is a grief to our Souls to consider. We doe also detest the practices of these men in imprisoning the Saints of God, for their Consciences and Testimony, and just men; who stand for morall and just principles, and the freedome of the Nation and People; and their breaking off Parliaments to effect their own Designe. We do also from our Souls Witnesse against their new Modelling of Ministers (as Antichristian) and keeping up parishes and Tythes (as Popish Innovations.) And we Disclaime all adherence to, owning of, or joyning with these men in their wayes. And do withdraw, and desire all the

Lords people to withdraw from these men, as those that are guilty of the sins of the later dayes [*margin*: 2 Tim. 3.5.]; and that have left following the Lord, and that Gods people should avoid their sin; least they partake with them in their plagues; Thus concluding our Testimony, We subscribe our Names hereunto.

[pp. 6–8, the names of the 322 subscribers are listed]

[p. 8]

A POSTSCRIPT

Reader,
This paper had sooner come into thy hands, if the Subscribers hereof (who are willing to do nothing rashly) had not waited for further Councel and direction from God herein then they had at their first intention of the publishing hereof, and withall it was deferred for a time, [*margin*: Rev. 2.21] hoping that God might some other way convince the Person chiefely concerned in it; and seeing God gave him time to repent, and yet repented not, we have published this our Testimony. To which you might have had many more Subscribers (who were willing to own this Paper) if conveniency and Providence had made way for it to come into their view: There hath been great endeavours to stifle it in the Birth; to that end, some of the Subscribers were threatnd with imprisonment, and Orders were issued out to imprison some (whereof one was secured) namely *Vavasor Powell*, who was taken by a company of Souldiers, from a day of Fasting and Prayer at *Aberbechan* in *Mountgomery* shire, where many Saints were gathered together, which caused much sadnesse, yea and much heart breakings to them all; and he remained for some time a prisoner on that account.

FINIS

Document III.6

The Ranters

Ranters, a name used to cover a wide variety of views and bizarre behaviour, proclaimed freedom from the moral law, pantheism and an extreme individualism often based on a belief in a divine Inner Light, as in Jacob Bauthumley's book, *The Light and Dark Sides of God* (London, 1650). See Christopher Hill, *The World Turned Upside Down* (London, 1972; Harmondsworth, 1975); A. L. Morton, *The World of the Ranters* (London, 1970); Nigel Smith, *A Collection of Ranter Writings from the 17th Century* (1983); J. F. McGregor and Barry Reay, *Radical Religion in the English Revolution* (Oxford, 1984). For the argument that there was 'no Ranter movement, no Ranter sect, no Ranter theology', v., J. C. Davis, *Fear, Myth and History: The Ranters and the Historians* (Cambridge, 1986) and his 'Fear, Myth and Furore: Reappraising the "Ranters"', *Past and Present*, 129 (1990), 79–103.

Extract (a) is from *A Perfect Account*, no. 21, 28 May–4 June 1651. Extract (b) is from *Mercurius Pragmaticus*, no. 22, 22–29 August 1648.

(a)
Munday. June 2 [1651]

Several persons called Ranters, were very lately apprehended in the Suburbs of London, and being carried before Justice *Hubbert*, their examinations were taken, a true copie of those that are more remarkable here follow.

The examination of *Elizabeth Haygood*, taken the 24 of *May* 1651, before *Thomas Hubbert* Esquire, one of the Justices of the Peace for the County of Middlesex, who being taken in the company of a blasphemous sort of people, commonly called Ranters, and examined, she confesseth and saith, That *Iohn Robbins* is her God Almighty, & that he is the eternal God & Father of our Lord Jesus Christ, and that Jesus Christ is now in the womb of *Ioan Robbins*, one of her society, and that he shall be born of her about five weeks hence, and she looks to be saved by none other God but her God *Iohn Robbins*. And further she saith, That the said *Iohn Robbins* is the Mediator between God and her, and that Christ is the mediator between *Iohn Robbins* and her. And further, she refuseth to set her name to this her examination, for she saith, She will not take the Divels pen into her hand, or acknowledg the Divels power.

Ioan Robins confesseth and saith, That she lived with *Ioshua Garment* (by the word of the Lord) as his wife 3 years; and that she hath lived with the above said *Iohn Robins* these three quarters of a year, as her Flesh and Bone; and that the said *Iohn Robins* is her Deliverer; and that the Lord told her about four years since, that she should conceive of a child that should be great in the work of the Lord, of which child she is now big, and that the said *Iohn Robins* begat it, and that about 5 weeks hence she expects to be delivered of it.

Ioshua Garment being examined confesseth and saith, That in the year 1631, as he was lying in his bed, the glory of the Lord did shine upon him, & the Angels of the Lord appeared unto him saying, fear not thou servant of the most high God, I am sent unto thee to declare unto thee things that shall be suddenly done in the world; which is the gathering and deliverance of the twelve scattered Tribes, but the religious men of the times must and shall oppose it; be thou silent untill thou art commanded to declare it to thy God. In the year 1647. the word of the Lord came to me to the ear, by the voice saying. Thou art within my new Covenant I will teach thee. The day following the Lord told him, I the Lord have appointed thee to salvation from eternity, thou shalt eat of the bread of life, and shalt live; and brought him some bread and he did eat. A voice came to him within few days following, saying *Iosherbah, Iosherbah*, the time draws near that the Jews must be gathered and delivered. Then he saw the man *John Robins* riding upon the wings of the wind in great glory and Majesty; the word of the Lord came unto him in great power saying: This is thy Lord, Israels King, Judge, & Law-giver: he it is that must deliver the scattered Hebrews; proclaim his day; but he shall be opposed by all men, but they shal be brought in subjection to him by the word of his mouth, he being so set by his Creator.

This Examinant confessseth and saith, That the said *Iohn Robins* is his Almighty God, so set by his Creator. And further saith, That *Ioan Robins* is the mother of the Church, both of Jews and Gentiles, to bring forth that seed which was promised to

Adam in the Garden; and the said *Iohn Robins* is the same *Adam* that was in the Garden. His several names written with his own hand.

> *Josherbah, Tangan, Tangarden, Pesautaviah, Phstanvah,*
> *Acher, Ahsha, Ba, Ha, Jah.*
> *Moses*, the servant of the Lord.
> *Joshua Garment.*

(b)

I received very memorable and sure *Intelligence*, concerning the *Examination* of one *William Harris*, taken before two *Iustices* of the *Peace* for the County of *Huntington*, upon the 29. of *July*. 1648. which being a *Rarity* I must needs publish. He avowes himself to bee *God*, and that there is no *God* besides him, with many other *Blasphemies*. There is likewise with him in prison a good *Sister* of his, one *Lockington's* wife of *Godmanchester*, committed for the like damnable expressions, whereof that the whole *Kingdome* may take notice, and also what this *Reformation* is come to, give me leave to set forth a *Copie* of the mans examination, *verbatim*.

Being demanded why he did lately commit Adultery upon the Lords day, with Lockington's *wife of* Godmanchester, *he confesseth she did come to his Bed's side and kisse him, and then did lie down upon the Bed by him, and that he did then kisse her, and that she stay'd above an houre with him. He further saith, she came to him by the will of God, and could not keep away, and that when God extends himself to any man, he must doe whatsoever he would have him, though it be to the committing of Adultery (as some call it) or killing of a man. And being demanded in particular, whether then he had the carnall knowledge of the said* Lockington's *wife, he saith he will not answer, but referreth himself to the witnesses, And he further saith, that which we call Adultery, or any other sin, is no sin, but that it is the suggestion of the Devill, he saith is a mistake of those that are not* Called, *there being no* Devill: *But* God *being in him, and he in* God, *all his Actions (how weak so ever seeming to us) are no sin, but his Commands.* Unto which *Examination* he set his *hand*; and both he and his *Adulteresse* lie now committed in *Huntington* Goale.

Document III.7

'The Children of the Light'

The charismatic movement that became Quakerism originated in the East Midlands, among Baptist and perhaps other religious groups, under the leadership of a young preacher named George Fox (1624–91), whose definitive religious experience took place about 1647. He wrote, 'But as I had forsaken the priests so I left the separate preachers also ... for I saw there was none among them all that could speak to my condition. And when my hopes in them and in all men were gone ... then, Oh then, I heard a voice which said, "There is one, even Christ Jesus, that can speak to thy condition", and when I heard it my heart did leap for joy.' (*The Journal of George Fox*, John L. Nickalls, ed. (Cambridge, 1952), 11 (NJ)). For Fox, v. Larry H. Ingle, *First among Friends: George Fox and the Creation of Quakerism* (New York and Oxford, 1994), and for early Quakerism v. William C. Braithwaite, *The Beginnings of Quakerism* (London, 1912; 2nd edn Cambridge 1955) and *The Second Period of Quakerism* (London, 1919; 2nd edn Cambridge, 1961); Rosemary Moore, *The Light in Their Consciences: Early Quakers in Britain 1644–1666* (University Park, PA, 2000). The first centre of the movement was at Skegby, in the house of Elizabeth Hooton (c. 1600–72), a Baptist who became a leading Quaker minister, NJ 9, 43 (Emily Manners, *Elizabeth Hooton* (London, 1914); Christine Trevett, *Women and Quakerism in the Seventeenth Century* (York, 1991), 16–22; Phyllis Mack, *Visionary Women: Ecstatic Prophecy in Seventeenth-Century England* (Berkeley, Calif., 1992), 127–30).

The following extract, from a lost 'History' written by Elizabeth Hooton's son Oliver, comes from a copy taken about 1686 by London Quakers who were seeking the origin of the old name for Quakers, 'the Children of Light'. It is now in the 'Children of Light Papers', Portfolio 10, Friends' House Library, London, and is the only evidence for Quaker beginnings independent of Fox. The 'mighty power of the Lord' was the 'quaking' which distinguished the 'Children of Light' from the other sects and groups of the time; 'Quaker' was a nickname first used by a judge when Fox was on trial for blasphemy in Derby in 1650. This shaking, the 'power of the Lord', appears to have started unexpectedly, and to explain it the Quakers searched their bibles for possible references. Ephraim Pagitt (1575?–1647) said that Quakers cited 'all the places in the Scripture which mention either trembling or shaking, never so impertinent [i.e. irrelevant] and far from the purpose', *Heresiography* (5th edn, London, 1662), 136. Quakers were asked, 'Where dost thou find that any Prophets, Apostles or Saints did ever quake or tremble in their bodies and yell and howl and roar?' (Richard Hubberthorne and John Lawson, *Trust Cleared and Made Manifest* (London, 1654), 8).

The phrase 'convinced of the truth' became the usual way to describe the experience of becoming a Quaker. 'Truth' was the favourite Quaker word for the Gospel experience, and later in the seventeenth century their preferred name for themselves became 'The Friends of Truth'. 'Doth Truth prosper?' was the usual formula used when enquiring about the well-being of Quaker meetings. The Quaker testimonies against oath-taking, 'pagan' names for months and days, and insincere forms of greeting, as well as their emphasis on complete honesty in business, all related to their use of the word 'Truth'.

'And my mother joined with the Baptists, but at some time, finding they were not upright-hearted to the Lord but did his work negligently, and she having testified against their deceit, left them, who in those parts soon all were scattered and gone. About the year 1647 George Fox came amongst them in Nottinghamshire, and then he went into Leicestershire where the mighty power of the Lord was manifest that startled their former separate meeting, and some came no more but most that were convinced of the truth stood, of which my mother was one, and embraced it.' [Oliver Hooton continued] So here you may see they were called Baptists and Separatists not Children of the Light until after George Fox preached the Gospel to them and they received it.

Document III.8

The Earliest Account of Quakerism

George Fox spent the year 1650–1 in a Derby prison for blasphemy and after his release moved north. In South-East Yorkshire he found groups of people who were seeking a new faith and whose experience was similar to his own. He travelled in East Yorkshire during the months following and in the early summer of 1652, accompanied by several of his new disciples, he set off westwards across the North of England. Here he found many more people who were ready for his message. Francis Howgill and John Audland, untrained ministers of Separated churches, joined him with members of their congregations. Meanwhile, others of his followers were active in the area of East Yorkshire where Fox had travelled the previous year. Quakers became, in the eyes of traditionalists, a serious threat. The next extract comes from a book published in 1653 by an unknown author who had experienced the Quaker activities in Yorkshire. Apparently somebody, alarmed by the Quakers, had made and published a list of thirty Queries, and somebody else, who described himself as 'a Seeker, but no profesed Quaker', had answered the Queries in a way very favourable to Quaker ideas. Inviting one's opponent to answer a set of queries was a common tactic in theological dispute. Opponent B would then answer the Queries and probably send back to Opponent A a further set of Antiqueries. At this point a third person sometimes joined the fray. The book, *The Querers and Quakers Cause at Second Hearing* was of this kind. The third author wrote a set of answers to the Antiqueries and added his own comments on Quaker activities in his locality. Together with Francis Higginson's anti-Quaker book, *A Brief Relation of the Irreligion of the Northern Quakers* (London, 1653), it is the earliest account of Quakerism. For extracts from Higginson, v., EQW, 63–78.

'Catabaptists' were those who rejected the sacrament of Baptism. 'Weigelianisme' refers to the views of Valentin Weigel (1533–88), a Lutheran mystical writer who greatly influenced Jakob Boehme (1575–1624) whose writings were of interest to the 'spiritual' writers of the period (v., ODCC). 'Zuenfieldianisme' is a rather clumsily spelt reference to the views of Kaspar von Schwenkfeld (1489–1561) who believed that God is the Father of Christ's humanity and divinity. The small community of Schwenkfelders in Pennsylvania is very similar to Quakers in belief and practice (NIDCC). 'Montanists' were the followers of Montanus (*fl.* c. 175–200), the leader of an apocalyptic, prophetic movement (v., ODCC). 'Carpocratians' are those who held the views of the second-century Gnostic teacher Carpocrates, who taught a licentious ethic, and the 'Valentinians' were an influential Gnostic sect founded by Valentinus in the second century (for both v., ODCC). The Adamites were a sect mentioned by St. Augustine. They sought to recover the primitive innocence of the human race by practising nudity amongst other things. Some Protestant radicals adopted the name in the Reformation period. 'Huttite Anabaptists' were the disciples of Jacob Hutter (d.1536) and Hutterite communities still exist in the United States, v., George H.Williams, *The Radical Reformation* (3rd edn, Kirksville, 1992).

[p. 1] To the Indifferent and Impartial Reader

By this be pleased to take notice, that some people all over Yorkshire being turned Seekers, having turned out prayer, preaching and the ordinances of God, and counting them too low things to follow, the Old Seeker, who goes about continually seeking whom he may devour, has fallen upon them, and drawn them into absurd and unreasonable practices, by running up and down the country to act in quakings and trancings, and drawing many after them.

> The first part of the book deals with Quaker practices, that Quakers break up families, that they are abusive to those who disagree with them, that they proclaim that the Son of God has already come, that they go around naked, and have caused particular disruption in the town of Malton, where it is known from Quaker correspondence that mercers had burnt their stock of ribbons rather than deal in what they now considered evil fripperies [see Swarthmore mss. i. 373; EQL 4).

[p. 47] They do hold themselves to be come into a state of perfection, when they are regenerate into their trancing way. You shall have for this, these words exactly according to one of their letters: 'You make the people believe that Christ hath but taken away part, and not all, (that is, of sin). Where he speaks of perfection in part, he speaks of the growing from faith to faith, but when he speaks of the New Man, he speaks of the Whole Man, redeemed wholly from the conversations of the world, the Old Man being crucified and dead, and cast out, and the New Man being raised, and reigning and ruling with power: then the acting of sinne is taken away, as well as the guilt and punishment: Here is a Perfectionist indeed, from whom the Acting of sinne is quite taken away.

2. Theirs [sic] letters tell us, that the Resurrection is past already. *Paul* [in 2 Tim. 2: 17] called this, in *Hymeneus* and *Philetus*, prophane and vaine babling, and that which tends to overthrow the Faith. It is a mad conceit of the Familists, when a man is converted and renewed, the Resurrection is past, the great Trumpet is already blowne. [*Margin*: 'Menandrians. Familists. Libertines']

3. It followes upon this, that the Resurrection being past, the day of Judgement may be in this life too. So in their letter to the Judges they write, that now is the Sonne come to Judgement, and the Saints shall judge the world. The Minister at *Malton* was opposed by one of them after Sermon before the Congregation, and accused of false Doctrine. Being asked how the charge arose, It was answered, he had taken away the Saints prerogative, and given it to God. For the Saints are to judge the world, and your Minister tells you, that God will judge the world. This is

Familisme, making Christ nothing without the Saints, and no Christ but in them. [*Margin*: 'Familists.']

4. They commend a community of goods, and practise a living upon one another too much, and too palpably, and urge it too far. [*Margin*: 'Catabaptists. Familists']

5. They make nothing of outward teaching of the word, Bread and Wine they call a Carnall Ordinance, Baptisme and Matrimonies they call Formalities, and tell of all these spiritually, onely to be looked after, and all inwardly onely to be taught, disgracing the word as a meere letter, and bidding hearken to that which is in them, though the light that is in them may be darknesse. [*Margin*: 'Weigelianisme. Familisme. Zuenfieldianisme. Enthusiasts.']

6. They Father all their bold and lewd speakings and doings upon the Spirit. One of them having a letter railed against a Minister and his preaching grievously, with very lewd tearmes, he writ in the bottome, from the Spirit of God in such a man. He might better have said, from the Spirit of Blasphemy and bitternesse, then have fathered revilings and clamors upon Gods spirit, whose wisdome and carriage is gentle, pure and peaceable, *James* 3. [*Margin*: 'Libertines.']

7. They looke for extraordinary raptures, inspirations, miracles, brag of miraculous healings, and promise the casting of Devills out of men and women, making all to have the Devill in them that are not their way. [*Margin*: 'Montanists']

8. They wait for new things every day, and seeke for strange things as ever were among Prophets or Apostles. [*Margin*: 'Seekers']

9. Applauded is by them the liberty of Prophesying, and what comes into their heads is all Spirit and Prophecy. Men, women, boyes and girles, may all turne into Prophets and Preachers by Quaking, and all other Preachers and Ministers are but deluders and without calling. [*Margin*: '*Iude*'s filthy dreamers, Socinians']

10. Too much are they addicted to conversing with women, and setting on them, to seduce them and teach them all pranks; as being fittest to draw on others, after the manner of them in Apostles times, leading Captives silly women, and after the manner of *Valentinians* drawing women from their husbands, having some kinde of *philtra & charitesia*, to that purpose, inticings to love and follow them. [*Margin*: 'Carpocratians. Valentinians. *Iren, I, cap.* 24'.]

11. Imaginations have they of great liberty and freedome, that none should say or doe any thing by way of Rule or Command. Hence are cryed down Magistrates & Ministers as unlawfull callings, that they may onely Magistrate it, and Minister all things themselves. [*Margin*: 'Monasterian Anabaptists. *Liberi*, the free Anabaptists'.]

12. Ministers to have no maintenance, not to preach upon Texts, though Scriptures tell us of both. [*Margin*: 'Anabaptists in Common. Antiscripturists'.]

13. If their supposed spirit stir them up to it, nakednesse and other obscenities may be used, and all good, by the will of the Father, and command of God upon them. [*Margin*: 'Tending to Adamites, Libertines, Enthusiasts'.]

14. A leaving all and running about to preach and cry out in Streets, Markets, House tops, every one that will, imagining he is called to it. [*Margin*: 'Apostolick Anabaptists.']

15. Thoughts that they onely are the people of God, and his *Israel*; and all others like *Canaanites* must be destroyed and rooted out by them. [*Margin*: 'Huttite Anabaptists.']

16. Regeneration and new birth is their Christ, justification, sanctification, perfection, all. All is confounded with and in this, Christ without them is little minded, this is that which states them in innocency of a sort, and being regenerate and denying themselves, they may do anything, for it is Christ in them, which is a kind of Popery, to be justified by grace in us. If they sin, it is not they but the flesh. As the Libertines said, it was their Ass that did it, their outward man. [*Margin*: 'Papists, Familists, Libertines.']

These all, and many more than these, may be drawn from their letters written, their speeches and principles, without straining of consequences. More might be mentioned, but their own writings and doings will in a short time lay them open.

Document III.9

George Fox and the Parish Ministry

The following extract comes from a virulent attack by Fox on the parish ministry. It bears the title, *A Paper sent forth into the World from them that are scornfully called Quakers* (London, 1655). It was published anonymously, probably first in 1653, and reprinted several times. The first three pages are reproduced in full, together with the paragraph introductions of most of the rest, and the ending.

There is much in this attack that is reminiscent of the complaints of such early Puritan writers as Henry Barrow and John Penry and it is somewhat ironic that Fox turns the force of that polemic against their successors. The document incidentally throws light on the primitive Quaker faith, the conviction that Christ had come, that He had freed them from sin and that they did not actually sin and that revelation did not cease after New Testament times.

[p. 1] A Paper Sent forth into the World from them that are scornfully called QUAKERS. Declaring the grounds and reasons why they deny the Teachers of the world (who profess themselves to be Ministers) and dissent from them

First, They are such Shepherds that seek for their gaine from their quarters, and can never have enough, which the Lord sent *Isaiah* to cry out against, who bid all *come freely, without money, and without price, and was not hired, but spake freely*; and these make merchandize and a trade of words, and therefore we cry out against them, and deny them, *Isai.* 56.11, & 54.1.

They are such Shepherds that seeke after the fleece, and cloath with the wool, and feed on the fat, which the Lord sent *Ezekiel* to cry wo against; who made a prey upon us; and the Lord said *he would gather his sheep from their mouthes, and that we should be a prey to them no longer*, and we do witness the promise of the Lord fulfilled: and therefore wee deny them, *Ezek* 14.34.

They are such Priests, as *beare rule by their means, which was a horrible and*

Filthy thing committed in the Land, which the Lord sent *Jeremiah* to cry out against; while we had eyes and did not see, we held up such Priests, but the Lord hath opened our eyes, and we see them now in the same estate that they were in which *Jeremiah* cryed out against, who did not beare rule by his means, and therefore we deny them, *Jer*. 5.31.

They are such Prophets and Priests that divine for money, and preach for hire, which the Lord sent *Micah* to cry against; and whilest we put into their mouths, they preached peace to us; but now we do not put into their mouths, they prepare war against us, and therefore we deny them, *Micah* 3.11.

They are such as are called of men Masters; and call men Masters, and have the chiefest place in the Assemblies, and stand praying in the Synagogues, and lay heavy burthens upon the people, which Jesus Christ cryed wo against, and bid his Disciples not be so, *Be ye not called of men Masters; for one is your Master, even Christ, and yee are all brethren*, so wee [p. 2] do witness Jesus Christ our Master, and see them to be in the steps of the *Pharisees*, and therefore we deny them, *Mat*. 3.10. *Mat*. 20.3.

They are such Teachers, that with feigned words, and through covetousness, made merchandize of us, and do upon the people; who by oppression, maintain themselves and wives in pride and idleness, in hoods, veils, and changeable suits of apparel; who go in the way of *Cain*, to envie, murder, and persecute; and after the error of *Balaam*, who loved the wages of unrighteousness, following after gifts and rewards, which the Apostle cryed against, and therefore we deny them, 2 *Pet*. 2. *Iude* 11.

They are such Teachers as have told us, the Steeple-house hath been the Church, when as the Scripture saith, the Church is in God, and therefore we deny them. I *Thes*.1.1.

They are such Teachers as have told us, the letter was the Word, when as the letter saith, *God is the word*, therefore we deny them, *Iohn* 1.1.

They are such Teachers as have told us, the letter was the light, when as the letter saith, *Christ is the light*, therefore we deny them, *Iohn* 1.19. and 2.12.

They are such Teachers as sprinkle Infants, calling it an Ordinance of Christ, and baptizing into the Faith, into the Church, when as the Scripture saith no such thing, and therefore we deny them: but the baptism by one Spirit into one body we own, I *Cor*. 12.13.

They are such Teachers as tell people of a Sacrament, for which there is not one Scripture, and so feed the people with their own inventions, and therefore we deny them, but the Table and Supper of the Lord we own, I *Cor*. 10.

They are such Teachers as tell people, that *Mathew*, *Marke*, *Luke*, and *Iohn*, is the Gospel, which are but the letter. The Lambe of God which takes away the sins of the world, is glad tydings to poor Captives: glad tydings were promised before the letter was written, *The seed of the Woman shall bruise the Serpents head*, and, *He shall be a light unto the Gentiles*: the letter is a Declaration of the Gospel, and many have the letter, but not Christ; but we having received the Gospel, know them to be no Ministers of it, and therefore do deny them. *Gen*. 3.15. *Luk*.1.1.

They are such Ministers as go to *Oxford* and *Cambridge*, and call them the Well-heads of Divinity, and so deny the Fountaine of living mercies, and there they study, and read books, and old Authors, and furnish themselves with Philosophy, and Fine words, and other mens matter; and when they come again, they sell it to poor people; when as the Apostle saith, *He was not made a Minister by the will of man*, and *that the Gospel which he preached was not of man, nor had he received it from man, neither was he taught it*, and denyed all his learning which he had got by the will of man at the feet of *Gamaliel*; and, so finding them in the will of man, preaching by the will of man, we cannot but deny them. *Gal.* 1.

They are such Teachers that tell people that *Hebrew* and *Greek* is the Originall, when as the Apostle spake in the *Hebrew* tongue to the *Hebrews* who heard him in their own language, and yet persecuted him; and the *Greeks*, who had the Gospel in their own tongues, said, *The Cross of Christ was foolishness*; these who had the Scripture, in their own languages were [p. 3] as ignorant of the life of them, as our naturall Priests, who spend so much time in learning a naturall language, to finde out what those meant that spoke forth the Scripture; who make poor people believe that to know a naturall tongue is the means to understand the Originall; the word which is the Original, was before all languages were, the word was in the beginning, which word was made manifest in all the children of God, who spake forth the Scriptures: holy men of God spake as they were moved by the holy Ghost. Now all ye learned ones, where is your Originall; here you and your original is razed out from the word, which is the original which the Apostles preached amongst the *Hebrews* and *Greeks*, which was before tongues were, and your originall, which will break all your tongues and original, to pieces. *Pilate* had your originall of *Hebrew*, *Greek*, and *Latine*, who crucified Christ: he that draws back into many languages, as into *Hebrew* and *Greek*, draws back into the naturalls, and so draws into confusion; but the Ministers of God who preach the everlasting Gospel which endures for ever, draw up into our language, and so the priests and all that trade in naturall languages we utterly deny, *Act*.22.1 *Cor*.1.13. *Iohn* 19.20.

They are such Teachers as have told us, that the Steeple-house is the Temple, when as the Apostle said, *Your bodies are the Temple of the holy Ghost*; and *Stephen* was stoned to death for witnessing against the Temple, who said, *God that made the World dwels not in Temples made with hands*; and here Finding them in the generation that hold up the Figures, and deny the substance, and to be ignorant of the Spirit that gaue forth the Scriptures, we cannot but deny them, 1 *Cor*. 6.19. *Act*.7.

They are such Priests that take Tythes, the tenth of mens labours and estates; and those that will not give them, they sue at the Law, and hale before Courts and Sessions; yea, even those they call their owne people, their own Parishioners: *Levi* according to the Law received Tythes, and he had a command to set open his gates, that the strangers and the fatherless should come within his gates, and be satisfied and filled, but we finde none more pitiless of the Fatherless and Widdows then they, and the strangers they complain against to Justices, and persecute, (though they neither seek to them nor others, for any outward thing) as wanderers; and here they walk contrary to the old Law: and the Apostle in his Epistle to the *Hebrews* said, *The Priesthood being changed, there must of necessity also be a change of the*

Law, and we witness both the Priesthood and the Law changed; but they that take Tythes, and they that pay Tythes, according to the old Covenant, deny Jesus Christ the everlasting Priest to be come in the flesh, and here these Priests shew themselves to be Antichrist, that are entred into the world, and oppress the Creation, when as Jesus Christ said, *Freely ye have received, freely give*: and the Apostle said, *Was there a wise man amongst them that went to Law one with another*: Here they are evill examples to the people, to sue, wrangle and contend, and walk out of the steps of Christ, and all the holy men of God; yea, they exceed all the false Prophets in wickedness, for we do not read that ever any of them sued men at the Law, and therefore we cannot but utterly deny them, *Deut*. 14.29. *Heb*.7.12.

They are such Priests as besides their Tythe of corn, hay, beast, sheep, hens, [p.4] pigs, geese, cherries, plums; take 10 shillings for preaching a funeral sermon more or less, as they can get it ...

They are such Preachers as take a text out of the Saints conditions, and take a week to study what they can raise out of it, adding their own Wisdom, Inventions, Imaginations and heathenish Authors, and then on the first day of the week they [p. 5] go among the people, having an hour-glass in their hand, and say, *Hear the Word of the Lord*, and for money they tell people what they have scraped together ...

['the Saints conditions' refers to the spiritual condition of the biblical authors. Quakers thought it wrong to apply these to oneself unless one was in the same spiritual condition. In particular, this applied to singing the psalms, which were 'David's conditions' – the next point he makes.]

They are such people as gave us, and give us, Davids conditions in metre, and when we had no understanding we sung after them ...

They are Teachers that deny the conditions that the Saints witnesses, viz., trembling and quaking ...

[p. 6] They are such Teachers as tell the people that Christ has not enlightened everyone that comes into the world ... and here they go about to make Christ a liar ... and we witness the light wherewith Christ has enlightened every one that comes into the world, and by obedience to that Light, he is become our Master, our Teacher ...

[John 1.9 was used so often in early Quaker writings that it became called 'the Quakers' text'.]

[p. 7] They are such Teachers as told us we should never be free from sin while we are upon the earth, when as the Apostle says; *They were made free from sin*, he thanks God, and had put off the body of sin ... (*Rom.* 6.6 and 8.3.)

And they are such Teachers that have told us, none shall ever be perfect while they are upon the earth, when as Christ says, *Be ye perfect, as your Father in heaven is perfect* ... (*Matt.* 5.48.)

[p. 8] They are such Teachers that say, Revelations are ceased, and deny Revelations, and so deny the Son, *For no man knows the Father, but he to whom the Son reveals him, and no man knows the things of God, but the Spirit of God, and he to whom the Spirit reveals them* ... And so he that denies Revelations, denies both the Father, and the Son, and the Spirit ...

Therefore all people, consider what you do, and hold up, and worship, for the worship is but one, and the word is but one, and the baptism is but one, and the Church is but one, and the way is but one, and the light is but one, and the power is but one; but they that are without, have many teachers, many wayes, many opinions and judgements, and many Sects; but we have but one Priest, which is over the household of God, and therefore are all of one heart and soule.

Moved of the Lord, written from the Spirit of the Lord, for the cleansing of the Land of all false teachers, seducers, and deceivers, and witches, who beguile the people, and inchanters, and diviners, and Sorcerers, and hirelings, and which is for the good of all people, that feare the Lord, and own Jesus Christ to be their teacher.

From them whom the world scornfully calls *Quakers*, but quaking and trembling we own, else we should deny the Scriptures, and the holy men of God; but the Scriptures we own, and the holy men of God; therefore wee deny all who deny quaking.

If you say, these things are frivolous things, which you have taught us, then we have been taught frivolous things all this while; but wee finde all these things frivolous things, wind and air, and therefore we deny them.

All people that read these things, never come ye more at the Steeple-house, nor pay your Priests more Tythes, till they have answered them; for if ye do, ye uphold them in their sins, and must partake of their plagues.

Document III.10

George Fox Refutes Charges of Blasphemy

Not surprisingly, opinions such as those expressed in Document V.8 led to charges under the Ordinance against Blasphemy (1648). Fox had been imprisoned for blasphemy at Derby in 1650. In 1652 he was again charged with the same offence and tried at Lancaster. His companion James Nayler (v. III.14) was similarly charged and tried at Appleby in January 1653. Both were acquitted and released early in 1653 and it is noticeable that after that date the Quakers were careful about the language they used in public, their pamphlets speaking less of unity with Christ and more of the 'Light Within'. Quakers had already realised the power of the press and, under the title *Sauls Errand to Damascus* (London, 1653), George Fox, James Nayler and John Lawson published an account of these trials, together with other documents relating to the petition to Cromwell which Lancaster church ministers drew up after the acquittal of Fox. The following extract is on p. 10 of *Sauls Errand* and gives Fox's answers to some of the charges mentioned in the petition. They indicate most of the chief points of contention between Quakers and mainstream Puritans. For a longer extract v., EQW 251–62.

Objections Against George Fox charged upon him by the contrivers of the aforesaid petition; and answered by him, as follows:-

Objection 1: That he did affirm that he had the Divinity essential in him.

Answer: For the word *essential*, it is an expression of their own; but that the saints are 'the temples of God' (II Cor. 6:1), and God doth 'dwell in them' (Eph.4:6), that the Scripture do witness. And if God dwell in them, then the Divinity dwells in them. And the Scripture says 'Ye shall be partakers of the Divine nature' (II Pet.1:4), and this I witness; but where this is not, they cannot witness it.

Objection 2: That both Baptism and the Lord's Supper are unlawful.

Answer: As for that word *unlawful*, it was not spoken by me: but the Baptism of infants I deny and there is no Scripture that speaks of a sacrament. But that Baptism that is into Christ, with 'one Spirit into one body', that I confess according to Scripture; and the Lord's Supper I confess; and that the bread the saints break is the body of Christ, And that cup that they drink is the blood of Christ, this I witness (Gal.3:27; John. 6: 53–58; II Cor. 10:16).

Objection 3: He did dissuade men from reading the Scriptures, telling them that it was carnal.

Answer: For dissuading men from reading the Scriptures, that is false, for they were given to be read as they are, but not to make a trade upon: the letter is carnal and killeth: but that which gave it forth is spiritual, eternal, and giveth life: and this I witness.

Objection 4: That he was equal with God.

Answer: That was not so spoken: but that 'He that sanctifieth, and they that are sanctified, are of one' (Heb.2:1), and the saints are all one in the Father and the Son, of his flesh and of his bone, this the Scripture doth witness: And 'Ye are sons of God;' and the Father and the Son are one; and 'they that are joined to the Lord are one Spirit, and they that are joined to an harlot are one flesh.' Eph.5.30.

Objection 5: That God taught deceit.

Answer. That is false, and was never spoken by me; God is pure.

Objection 6: That the Scriptures are Antichrist.

Answer: That is false, but that they which profess the Scriptures, and live not in the life and power of them, as they did that gave them forth, that I witness to be Antichrist.

Objection 7: That he was the judge of the world.

Answer: That 'the saints shall judge the world', the Scripture witness it; whereof I am one, and I witness the Scripture fulfilled. (I Cor.6:2,3.)

Objection 8: That he was as upright as Christ.

Answer: Those were not so spoken by me; but that 'as he is, so are we in this present world' (I John 4: 17): That the saints are made 'the righteousness of God' (I Cor. 5.21): That 'the saints are one with the Father and the Son', that 'we shall be like him'; (I John 3:2), and that all teaching which is given forth by Christ, is to bring the saints to perfection, even 'to the measure of the stature of the fulness of Christ:' This the Scripture doth witness. Where Christ dwells, must not he speak in his temple?

Facets of Freedom, 1640–1660

Document III.11

The Arrival of the Quaker Preachers John Camm and John Audland in Bristol, September 1654

During 1654 Quaker preachers spread over the whole country (BQ, 2nd edn, 153–76). No information survives about the preliminary planning. Fox in his *Journal* simply said that the Lord raised the ministers up (CJ I.141). The travelling ministers went out in pairs, generally an older person with somebody younger, and they were distributed to cover most of the country. More experienced and able ministers went to the major towns, London, Bristol and Norwich. In places their reception was hostile, the women being especially liable to abuse. However, the Quaker message was evidently meeting a need, so that before the end of the year there were Quaker groups in many places.

The Bristol mission is especially well documented. There are accounts of the early meetings from the point of view both of the travelling Quakers and of one of the recipients of their message, and also records of the opposition, from the Broadmead Baptist Church which lost many members to the Quakers, and from Ralph Farmer, a parish minister whose church was disturbed by Quakers and who also had a personal feud with the leading Quaker convert, one George Bishop, a member of a wealthy Bristol family who had made several enemies while serving in Cromwell's intelligence service.

On arrival at a new town, Quaker preachers often attended a local Separatist Church where they thought they would find a sympathetic hearing. Often it would be a Baptist Church, but at Bristol the visiting Quakers chose to attend a meeting of Seekers. The following extract is part of a letter from John Camm and John Audland, who became the leaders of the Quaker mission to Bristol, to Francis Howgill and Edward Burrough, two Quaker ministers who had visited Bristol a short time before. It is dated the 13th day of the 7th month (that is September), and addressed care of Giles Calvert, the radical printer who often assisted the Quakers by handling letters and money for them. The first part of the letter is by John Camm. Orthography and punctuation modernised.

On the Bristol mission, v., Charles Marshall, *Sions Travellers Comforted* (London, 1704), unpaginated introduction. He was a member of the Bristol Seeker congregation and his first experience of Quakerism was the meeting described above. Ralph Farmer was a Bristol parish minister and his *The Great Mysterie of Godlinesse and Ungodlinesse* (London, 1655), fo. 441 includes a letter to John Thurloe (1616–68), the Secretary of the Council of State, about the trouble in Bristol caused by 'morris-dancers from the North'. George Bishop, *The Cry of Blood* (London, 1656) has a full account of events. There was also a bitter dispute between leaders of the Broadmead Baptist Church and one of their members, Denys Hollister, who had converted to Quakerism. This is reported from the Quaker side in Hollister, *The Skirts of the Whore Discovered* (London, 1656) and *The Harlot's Veil Removed* (1658), and from the Baptist side in Ewens and others, *The Church of Christ in Bristol* (London, 1657).

The following text is in A. R. Barclay mss. 157, Friends' House, London.

This day the people in the city who are our friends met together to seek the Lord, as they call it. There were many with the glouriosest words in prayer I ever heard.

There was the trimmed harlot gloriously decked, and we were by, and heard them. At length we went in unto them. We bore them long till the power of the Lord took hold upon us both and I was forced to cry out amongst them. My life suffered and if I did not speak I should be an example amongst them, and in much tenderness I spoke unto them, and silence was amongst them all, and much tenderness and brokenness, and it is a glorious day and the Lord will do much good unto them by this days meeting together ... for now they are come to see the serpent which has beguiled them and robbed them of their simplicity ... They have many of them cast off their beautiful garments, which was without, but now the beautiful garments within is seen, the mystery of witchcraft is manifest to them, to be in them, and now their jewels of gold and silver they are casting to the moles and the bats, and shame does cover their faces for now they see themselves naked. There is a pure simplicity in them that would forgo all for the Truth, they are deeply in love with it, and do much breathe after it, and the Lord will work a short work on the earth, and we travail in pain until Christ be formed in them and we are with them in fear and trembling lest their faith should stand in wisdom of words and not in the power of God. For we are with them from 6 in the morning, they will come to us before we get up, and unto 11 or sometimes one at night they will never be from us; go into the fields they will follow us or go into any house, the house will be filled full, so that we cannot tell how we should get from them. The Lord has subjected them all under us and they are as fearful to offend us as a child is to offend its loving father. The mighty power of the Lord is seen, he doth open his voice before his camp, mountains do melt at his presence ... by his own right hand has he got himself the victory. Glory glory glory, joy for evermore: dear brethren our soul our heart our life, we are bundled up together in one, the eternal God of power keep us ... we are one with you in all conditions you may read us daily ...

[Personal messages follow. John Audland wrote his letter on the back of the same sheet of paper. He described Camm's ministry and continued:] The word of the Lord came to me, and when he had done, I stood up and all my bones smote together and I was like a drunken man ... and I was made to cry like a woman in travail and to proclaim war from the Lord with all inhabitants of the earth, and such a dreadful voice rang through me as I never felt before, and the terror of the Lord took hold upon many hearts and the trumpet sounded through the city. The afternoon we met at the fort where soldiers are, the greatest meeting I ever saw. It far exceeded the greatest when I was with you, and all was silent and not one dog moved his tongue.

Document III.12

A Woman's Ministry: Margaret Fell and the Kendal Fund

The growth of Quakerism would have been impossible without the organising ability of Margaret Fell (1614–1702), who was 'convinced' when George Fox visited her home at Swarthmoor Hall, near Ulverston, in June 1652. Margaret Fell was then the wife of Thomas Fell (1598–1658), a wealthy and influential landowner and country gentleman, Judge of Assize and Member of Parliament. He never became a Quaker, but gave the Quakers considerable support, assistance and protection.

Until recently, writers on Quakerism have underestimated Margaret Fell. The notion of a kindly 'nursing mother of Quakerism' pervaded the earlier literature, and although her efficiency and importance, particularly with regard to finance, were noted, her formidable nature has only recently been adequately recognised, in the first instance by Bonnelyn Kunze, *Margaret Fell and the Rise of Quakerism* (Stanford and London, 1993).

During the early years of Quakerism, Margaret Fell acted as the main troubleshooter for discipline and internal matters, dealing with difficult individuals, receiving reports from travelling Quaker ministers and organising their financial support. She took full advantage of her social position, and wrote a number of letters to local dignitaries concerning the treatment of Friends: a certain Justice John Sawrey ventured to complain to her husband about her, after which he received from her several lengthy appeals to repent (for Sawrey v. VCH *Lancashire*, VIII, 359). She was a great letter-writer, and her correspondence has been published (Elsa F. Glines, *Undaunted Zeal: the letters of Margaret Fell*. Richmond, Ind., 2003). After the Restoration she addressed Charles II several times on the subject of religious toleration, and she spent several years in prison for refusing to take the Oath of Allegiance to the King. She married George Fox in 1669, and together with her daughters was a powerful influence in the development of the Quaker women's business meetings (v. VI.13 (f)).

Despite her sometimes abrasive nature, Margaret Fell was perfectly capable of a tactful approach when necessary. The following document, with original syntax but with spelling and punctuation modified, is her well-crafted begging letter, written 1654, setting up a fund (now known as the Kendal Fund) for the support of the Quaker mission (Thirnbeck mss 1, Friends House, London. Exact transcription *Undaunted Zeal*, pp. 88–92). The subsequent operations of this fund are known from a number of surviving letters that passed between Margaret Fell and the fund's treasurers, Thomas Willan and George Taylor of Kendal. It was replaced by a national system of collections after 1657, as the administrative centre of Quakerism moved to London.

To all my dear brethren and sisters who be in the light, children of the light, who is obedient to the light, which is the eye of the whole body; in which light, every particular dwell and stand single, and you shall see the whole body full of light: for this leads into the unity and oneness, which is in the body, though many members; So my dear hearts, in that which is the light of the whole body, that eye which leads into the unity, to that be subject, and obedient, to be serviceable to the whole body; and give freely up to the service of the body which is one, and but one in all; and who is faithful, the one spirit makes subject: even so ye are called in one hope of your calling, where there is one Lord, one faith, one baptism, one God and father of all, who is above all, and through and in you all. So all my dear brethren and sisters, in this which is eternal, and leads into the eternal unity and oneness, be faithful and obedient; be of one mind, and live in peace, for the promise is but to one seed, and you are all one in Christ Jesus, are faithful in him, to whom all the promises are. Yea and Amen.

And now is the Lord's day made manifest, wherein he requires of you, in your particular measures, to be serviceable to the body in your particular places, for there is many members, and but one body; and the head cannot say to the feet, I have no need of you, for every one, in their measures, may be serviceable to the whole body, in what is called and required, and who dwells in the light, it makes subject to be serviceable to the body. And now, that nothing may be kept back, but as you have received freely, so freely you may administer, in obedience to the one eternal Light, you may be serviceable to the whole body. And as the Lord hath loved you, with his everlasting love, and visited you, and hath made manifest his eternal light in you, which is the way that leads to the father, and hath raised up the eternal witness in you, of his everlasting love, so let that love constrain you to love one another, and be serviceable to one another, and that every one may be made willing to suffer for the body's sake, and that there may be no rent in the body, but that the members have the same care one over another, and where one member suffers, all the members may suffer with it. And here is the unity of the Spirit, and the bond of peace.

And that you cannot be unmindful, nor is not ignorant of the present suffering and service of many members of the body in this our day, who are in bonds and imprisonment and hard persecution and tyranny, which is acted in the will of man, upon the righteous seed, which is of the body. And others there are that are sent forth into the service of the most high God, as Lambs among wolves, who is made willing and subject to give their backs to the smiter, yea to lay down their lives for the body's sake, and great and hard persecutions hath been suffered for the testimony of the Lord Jesus.

Now that every particular member of the body may be sensible of the hardship and sufferings of others and be willing and serviceable in their places, in what the Lord requires, and to remember those that are in bonds, as bound with them, and them that suffer adversity, as you being yourselves also in the body, and that you may bear one anothers burdens and be equally yoked in the sufferings. Our friends in Westmoreland hath borne the heat of the day, and many have been sent forth into the service from thence, and that hath caused the burden to lie heavy upon the rest of the friends there about, and most of all on our friends at Kendal. Our dear brethren, George Taylor and Thomas Willan, who have been very serviceable in their places to the truth to the whole body, to those that have been sent forth into the ministry, and to them that have suffered imprisonment, and for books, and several other things, that have been needful, wherein they have been serviceable to the truth, I bear them record, and have disbursed of their own moneys, when it hath been needful, until it was contributed among friends thereabouts. So I, knowing at this time that they are out of purse, I see in the eternal unchangeable light of God, that all and every member who are of the body, ought to be serviceable in their places, and to administer freely according to their ability, as they have received of the Lord freely, for Jerusalem which is above is free, which is the mother of us all, and who is here, is one. Therefore, that there may be some money in a stock, for disbursing according to necessity as the Lord requires, either to friends that go forth into service, or to prisoners necessity, I see it convenient and necessary in that which never changeth, and am moved of the Lord to acquaint you with it, that in your several meetings in this part of Lancashire, and Westmorland (excepting the town of Kendal) and at the several meetings in Cumberland, and so to be gathered, and sent to Thomas Willan and George Taylor to be disbursed according as the Lord requires, and that the burden may not lie upon them more than others, who have been very serviceable in this thing. So my dear brethren and sisters, let brotherly love continue, that every one as the Lord moves you and opens your heart, you may administer, that you may come into the oneness in all things, and in that abide which dwells in love and unity, which is one for evermore. And so you come to the fulfilling of the scriptures in your measures, and the practice of all the saints in the light that ever went before.

So God Almighty of life and power preserve and keep you in everlasting love and unity. Your dear sister in the everlasting unchangeable truth,

Margaret Fell

Document III.13

Women Preachers

George Fox and his followers believed in the complete spiritual equality of men and women, and the travelling Quaker women preachers scandalised many ordinary folk. Any Quaker preacher was liable to manhandling and arrest, but the women faced particular opposition. The Quakers justified the position that they gave to women by reference to the many prophetesses and religious leaders in the Bible, but 1 Corinthians 14:34–35, where St Paul said plainly that women should not speak in church, caused difficulties. See especially Margaret Fell, *Womens Speaking Justified* (1666 and 1667, also ed. Christine Trevett, London, 1989). There is now much literature on women in early Quakerism; see especially Phyllis Mack, *Visionary Women: Ecstatic Prophecy in Seventeenth Century England* (Berkeley, Los Angeles and Oxford, 1992) and Christine Trevett, *Women and Quakerism in the Seventeenth Century* (York, 1991) and *Quaker Women Prophets in England and Wales 1650–1700* (New York, 2000).

Some Quakers found an ingenious way round the traditional prohibition of women preachers, making use of a common idiom of the time, by which a weak and irresolute man would be called 'a woman'. The following extract illustrates what was probably the first use of this argument, and comes from a pamphlet called *To the Priests and People of England* which was written by two West Country women ministers, Priscilla Cotton and Mary Cole, during their imprisonment in Exeter gaol.

[p. 6] If a Son or a Daughter be moved from the Lord, to go into the Assembly of the people, in a message from the Lord God, thou canst not endure to hear them speak sound Doctrine, having a guilty conscience ... and in thy pride thou contemnest all others, thou tellest the people, Women must not speak in a Church, whereas it is not spoke onely of a Female, for we are all one both male and female in Christ Jesus, but it's weakness that is the woman by the Scriptures forbidden, for else thou puttest the Scriptures at a difference in themselves, as still its thy practice out of thy ignorance; for the Scriptures do say, that all [p. 7] the Church may prophesie one by one, and that women were in the Church, as well as men, do thou judge; and the Scripture saith, that a woman may not prophesie with her head uncovered, lest she dishonour her head: now thou wouldst know the meaning of that Head, let the Scripture answer, I *Cor*.11.3. *The head of every man is Christ*. Man in his best estate is altogether vanity, weakness, a lye. If therefore any speak in the Church, whether man or woman, and nothing appear in it but the wisdom of man, and Christ, who is the true head, be not uncovered, do not fully appear, Christ is then dishonoured. Now the woman or weakness, that is man, which in his best estate or greatest wisdom is altogether vanity, that must be covered with the covering of the Spirit, a garment of righteousness, that its nakedness may not appear, and dishonour thereby come. Here mayest thou see from the Scriptures, that the woman or weakness whether male or female, is forbidden to speak in the Church; but its very plain, *Paul*, nor *Apollo* [sic], nor the true Church of Christ, were not of that proud envious Spirit thou art of, for they owned Christ Jesus in man or woman; for *Paul* bid *Timothy* to help those women that laboured with him in the Gospel, and *Apollo* hearkened to a woman, and was instructed by her, and Christ Jesus appeared to the women first, and sent them to preach the Resurrection to the Apostles, and *Philip* had four Virgins that did prophesie. Now thou dost respect persons I know, and art partial in all things, and so judgest wickedly, but there is no respect of persons with God. Indeed, you your selves are the women, that are forbidden to speak in [p. 8] the Church, that are become women ... So leaving you to the light in all your consciences to judge of what we have writ, we remain, Prisoners in Exeter gaol for the word of God.

Priscilla Cotton
Mary Cole

Document III.14

The Case of James Nayler

James Nayler (1617?–1660) was a leader of the early Quaker movement second only to George Fox, indeed, some contemporaries considered him the Quakers' chief. He was a notable preacher, and gained considerable popularity in London during 1655 and 1656. In the summer of 1656 he had, possibly, some form of breakdown, and was taken into the house of Martha Simmons, a well-known London Quaker, wife to the Quaker printer Thomas Simmons and also sister to the radical printer Giles Calvert. (For printers, v. H. B. Plomer, *A Dictionary of the Booksellers and Printers ... in*

England, Scotland and Ireland from 1641–1667 (London, 1907). London Quakers arranged for him to be taken to see George Fox, then in prison in Exeter. Accounts of their meeting vary, but there was a complete breach between the two men. After this, Nayler, with Martha Simmons and others, travelled in the West Country, making an entry into Bristol in the style of Christ's entry into Jerusalem, after which he was arrested. After examination by local magistrates he was sent to London and tried for blasphemy by Parliament. Most leading Quakers distanced themselves from his actions, though a hard core of Nayler supporters persisted for some years. He survived his horrific punishment and was released in September 1659, and after an uncertain reconciliation with Fox, set out for the north and died after being attacked by robbers.

Quakers and their historians brushed Nayler fairly effectively out of their history, and it was well into the twentieth century before he was rehabilitated. It is salutary to compare the treatment of Nayler in W. C. Braithwaite, *The Beginnings of Quakerism* (Cambridge, 1912) with that in a modern history such as Rosemary Moore, *The Light in Their Consciences: Early Quakers in Britain 1644–1666* (University Park, Pa., 2000).

The best account of the political implications of the Nayler affair is William Bittle, *James Nayler, the Quaker Indicted by Parliament* (York and Richmond, Ind., 1986). The most insightful work on what may actually have been going on in Nayler's mind is Leo Damrosch, *The Sorrows of the Quaker Jesus: James Nayler and the Puritan Crackdown on the Free Spirit* (Harvard, 1996). The two main contemporary accounts are *Copies of Some Few of the Papers Given into the House of Parliament at the Time of James Naylers Trial there* (Fox and others, London 1656), and, from an anti-Quaker standpoint, John Deacon, *The Grand Imposter Examined* (London, 1656).

The following extracts come from contemporary news-sheets:

Extract (a) is from *Mercurius Politicus*, no. 340, 11–18 December 1656.

Extract (b) is from *Publick Intelligencer*, no. 63, 22–29 December 1656.

Extract (c) is from ibid., no. 345, 15–22 January 1657.

Notes on some of the persons mentioned in the texts:

Hannah Stranger was a London Quaker, one of the authors (Martha Simmons was another) of a collection of pro-Nayler papers, *O England thy time is come* (London, 1656).

Dorcas Erbury was the daughter of William Erbury (1604–54), a Seeker with affinities to Quakers (DNB).

Messrs Caryl, Manton, Nye and Griffith are in the DNB, and for Griffith v. Richard L. Greaves, '"A Notorious Independent", George Griffith and the survival of the Congregational Tradition' in *Saints and Rebels* (1985).

Robert Rich (d. 1679), was a wealthy Barbados merchant, for many years on the fringe of Quakers and much disliked by the leadership, who later re-opened the Nayler controversy by publishing his own account of these and other happenings as *Hidden Things Brought to Light* (London, 1678). See Moore, *Light in Their Consciences*, pp. 42, 255 n.34, 289 n.12.

(a) *A briefe Account concerning James Naylor the Quaker*

Having been released out of Excester Gaole, hee began immediately to play his Pranks at divers Places in the West; among the rest, he passed by Wells and

Glastenbury, through which Towns hee rod on horseback, a man going bare before him, and others walking a foot on each side of his Stirrup, and others strewing their garments in the way; from thence he took his way toward Bristol, and coming to a little Village called Bedminster, about a mile from Bristol, he rode through that place likewise, a young man bare-headed leading his horse by the Bridle, and another man before with his Hat on. There accompanied him two men, with each a woman behind him on horseback; which women alighted when they came to the Suburbs of Bristol, and footed it along on each side of Nailors horse, the man still bare-headed leading the horse; and as they advanced along, they sung, and entred Bristol singing, *Holy, Holy, Holy Lord God of Israel*, and then the Women led the horse with the Reins in their hands, up to the high Cross of Bristol, and from thence to the White-Hart-Inn in Broad-street. Then the Magistrates sending for Nailor ans his Companions, they came singing all the way Hosanna, and *Holy, Holy, Holy, &c.* His name that went bare before him is Timothie Wedlock, a Devonshire man. The one woman is named Martha Simons wife of Thomas Simonds Stationer of London; the other Hannah Stranger wife of Iohn Stranger of London Comb maker.

The Magistrates having convented Nailor and the rest, divers strange blasphemous Letters and other Papers were found about them, wherein it appeared, that the deceiver had so farr gained upon his Followers by his Impostures, that they ascribed to him divine Honors, and gave him in Scripture-Phrase the same Titles which are applicable to none but Christ himself.

In a Letter of one *Richard Fairman* from Dorcester-gaole to *Nailor*, are these horrid Expressions [*I am fild with joy & rejoycing when I behold thee in the eternal unity. O my Soul is melting within me, when I behold thy beauty and innocency, dear and precious son of Zion, whose Mother is a Virgin, and whose birth is immortal*] ...

... *Hannah Stranger* writing from London to *Nailor* in September last, begins her Letter most blasphemously thus: (*In the pure fear and power of God, my Soul salutes thee, thou everlasting son of Righteousness, and Prince of Peace. O how my Soul travelleth to see thy day, which Abraham did, and was glad.*) Then towards the latter end she useth these expressions ... (*The Lord shall not suffer his Holy one to see corruption, nor his soul to lie in Hell, but will cause the mountains to melt at his presence, and the little Hils to bring him peace.*)

The same woman, in another Letter to him, proceeds thus, [*O thou fairest of Ten Thousand, Thou only begotten Son of God, how my heart panteth after thee. O stay me with Flagons, and comfort me with wine. My well beloved thou art like a Roe, or young Hart, upon the Mountaines of Spices.* Then, by way of Post-Script her husband Thomas Stranger adds this, *Thy name is no more to be called Iames but Iesus.*]

Thus much of the Letters which were found about them.

Then being examined before the Magistrates of Bristol, Martha Simonds professed she ought to fall down and worship Nailor; also, that he is her Lord, Lord of righteousnes & Prince of Peace, and anointed King of Israel by a Prophet; but who that Prophet was, she would not tell.

Likewise, Hannah Stranger upon examination declared him to be the Prince of Peace, and his Name Jesus.

Also, a Maid names [?named] Dorcas Erbury, being examined, declared James Nailor to be the Holy one of Israel, the only begotten son of God, and that she pulled off his Stockins, and put her Clothes under his Feet, because he is the Holy Lord of Israel, and that she knew no other Saviour but him: affirming more over; That the Spirit of the Lord within her commanded her to call him Lord and Master, and to serve him; That in Excester-Gaole, he had raised her from the dead, after she had been dead two daies; And that James Nailor shall sit at the right hand of the Father, and judge the world.

Thus you see, how this wretched Impostor hath prevailed upon his Followers, to bewitch them to the committing of strange Absurdities, and uttering of many horrible Blasphemies, the like for all Circumstances, never heard of in any Age before ...

Wednesday, 17 Decemb.

This day *James Naylor* was according to the order made yesterday, brought to the Bar of the house, where being come, Mr. *Speaker* pronounced on him the Judgement of the House, for those high Crimes whereof he had been found guilty; which Judgment was as followeth.

That *Iames Nailor* be put on the Pillory, with his head in the Pillory, in the new Pallace, *Westminster*, during the space of two hours on Thursday next, and shall be whipped by the Hangman through thre streets from *Westminster*, to the *Old Exchange, London*; and there likewise set upon the Pillory with his head in the Pillory, for the space of two hours between the hours of eleven and one, on Saturday next; in each of the said places, wearing a Paper containing an Inscription of his Crimes: And that at the *Old Exchange* his Tongue shall be bored through with a hot Iron: and that he be there also stigmatised on the Forehead with the letter **B**. And that he be afterwards sent to *Bristol*, and conveyed into, and through the said City on a Horse bare ridged, with his face backward; and there also publickly whipped the next Market day after he comes thither.

That from thence he be committed to prison in *Bridewel, London*, and there restrained from the Society of all people and kept to hard labor, till he shall be released by parliament; and during that time, be debarred from the use of Pen, Ink, and Paper, and shall have no relief but what he earns by his daily labor.

(b)
Mr. *Caryl*, Mr. *Manton*, Mr. *Nye*, and Mr. *Griffith*, were ordered to repair to Newgate to *James Nailor*, to try if they could bring him to a Recantation of his Errors; but after divers Questions and Answers betwixt them, during the space of half an hour, or thereabouts, the said Ministers returned, not affecting any thing.

Saturday, 17 Dec.

This day according to Order of Parliament, the said *James Naylor* was conveyed from Newgate to the Old Exchange, where he stood in the Pillory from twelve till two of the Clock: After which, he was bored through the Tongue with an hot Iron, and stigmatized on the Forehead with the Letter **B**. which Execution being done, he was conveyed back to Newgate.

This is observable, That Mr. *Rich*, formerly a Merchant, was on the Pillory most part of the time that *Nylor* suffered, and held him by the hand while his Tongue was bored, and his Forehead stigmatized.

(c)

From *Bristol, Saturday* 17 *January*.

This day the order of the Parliament was executed here upon *James Nailor*, in a manner as is described by the following order.

Mr. *Roach*,

> *Cause* James Nailor *to ride in at Lawfords-gate upon a horse bare ridged, with his face backward, from thence along Winestreet to the Tolzey, thence down High street over the Bridge, and out of Racklygate; there let him alight, and bring him into St. Thomas-street, and cause him to be stript and made fast to the Cart-horse; and there in the Market first whipped, from thence to the foot of the Bridge there whipt, thence to the end of the Bridge there whipt, thence to the middle of High-street there whipt, thence to the Tolzey their whipt, thence to the middle of Broadstreet there whipt, and then turn into Tailors-hall, thence release him from the Cart-horse, and let him put on his cloathes, and carry him from thence to Newgate by Tower-lane the back way.*

There did ride before him bearheaded, *Michael Stamper*, singing most part of the way, and several other friends, men and women; the men went bare headed by him, and *Robert Rich* (late Merchant of *London*) rode by him bare headed and singing, till he came to Redcliff gate, and there the Magistrate sent their officers, and brought him back on horse-back to the Tolzey, all which way he rode, singing very loud, where the magistrate were met.

Document III.15

The Savoy Declaration, 1658

A suggestion that representatives of the Congregational churches should meet in conference to draw up a statement of their faith was mooted in July 1658 and approved by Oliver Cromwell. The arrangements were entrusted to the elders of the churches in and about London and they nominated George Griffiths, preacher at the Charterhouse, to convene the representatives. They gathered at the Palace of the Savoy on 29 September 1658. About 200 men, mostly laymen, attended representing between 100 and 120 churches. A committee composed of Thomas Goodwin, Philip Nye, William Bridge, William Greenhill, Joseph Caryl and John Owen was nominated to draw up a draft confession of faith for the consideration of the conference. The conference completed its deliberations on 12 October. The Confession agreed in the main with the theology of the Westminster Confession but not with its ideas of church government and so, appended to the confession proper was a section, reproduced above, which described the church order of the Congregationalists. It long remained the definitive expression of their convictions on that topic. For a full account, v., A. G. Matthews, *The Savoy Declaration, of Faith and Order, 1658* (London, 1959). See also R. W. Dale, *History of English Congregationalism* (London, 1907), 381–6; Peter Toon, *God's Statesman: The Life and Work of John Owen* (Exeter, 1971), 103–6. For George Griffiths (1619–1702), v., A. G. Matthews, *Calamy Revised* (Oxford, 1934) and Richard L. Greaves, *Saints and Rebels* (Mercer University Press, 1985), chapter 3.

The text is reproduced from *A Declaration of the Faith and Order Owned and practised in the Congregational Churches of England; Agreed upon and consented unto By their ELDERS and MESSENGERS in Their Meeting at the Savoy, October 12, 1658* (London, 1659), 54–64. Paragraph XIV refers to those who were appointed by the Commissioners for the Approbation of Public Preachers ('The Triers') to parishes.

Of the Institution of Churches and the Order appointed in them by Jesus Christ

I. By the appointment of the Father, all Power for the Calling, Institution, Order, or Government of the Church, is invested in a Supreme and Soveraign maner, in the Lord Jesus Christ, as King and Head thereof.

II. In the execution of this Power wherewith he is so entrusted, the Lord Jesus calleth out of the World unto Communion with himself, those that are given unto him by his Father, that they may walk before him in all the ways of obedience, which he prescribeth to them in his Word.

III. Those thus called (through the Ministery of the Word by his Spirit) he commandeth to walk together in particular Societies or Churches, for their mutual edification, and the due performance of that publique Worship, which he requireth of them in this world.

IV. To each of these Churches thus gathered, according unto his minde declared in his Word, he hath given all that Power and Authority, which is any way needfull for their carrying on that Order in Worship and Discipline, which he hath instituted for them to observe, with Commands and Rules, for the due and right exerting and executing of that Power.

V. These particular Churches thus appointed by the Authority of Christ, and intrusted with power from him for the ends before expressed, are each of them as unto those ends, the seat of that Power which he is pleased to communicate to his Saints or Subjects in this world, so that as such they receive it immediately from himself.

VI. Besides these particular Churches, there is not instituted by Christ any Church more extensive or Catholique, entrusted with power for the administration of his Ordinances, or the execution of any authority in his name.

VII. A particular Church gathered and compleated according to the minde of Christ, consists of Officers and Members: The Lord Christ having given to his called ones (united, according to his appointment, in Church-order) Liberty and Power to choose Persons fitted by the holy Ghost for that purpose, to be over them and to minister to them in the Lord.

VII [sic]. The Members of these Churches are Saints by Calling, visibly manifesting and evidencing (in and by their profession and walking) their Obedience unto that Call of Christ, who being further known to each other by their confession of the Faith wrought in them by the power of God, declared by themselves, or otherwise manifested, do willingly consent, to walk together, according to the appointment of Christ, giving up themselves to the Lord, and to one another by the will of God, in professed subjection to the Ordinances of the Gospel.

IX. The Officers appointed by Christ to be chosen and set apart by the Church so called, and gathered, for the peculiar administration of Ordinances, and execution of Power or Duty which he intrusts them with, or calls them to, to be continued to the end of the world, are Pastors, Teachers, Elders, and Deacons.

X. Churches thus gathered and assembling for the Worship of God, are thereby visible and publique, and their Assemblies (in what place soever they are, according as they have liberty or opportunity) are therefore Church or Publique Assemblies.

XI. The way appointed by Christ for the calling of any person, fitted and gifted by the holy Ghost, unto the Office of Pastor Teacher or Elder in a Church, is that he be chosen thereunto by the common suffrage of the Church itself, and solemnly set apart by Fasting and Prayer, with Imposition of Hands of the Eldership of that Church, if there be any before constituted therein: And of a Deacon, that he be chosen by the like suffrage, and set apart by Prayer, and the like Imposition of Hands.

XII. The Essence of this call of a Pastor Teacher or Elder unto Office, consists in the Election of the Church, together with his acceptation of it, and separation *by Fasting and Prayer*: And those who are so chosen, though not set apart by Imposition of Hands, are rightly constituted Ministers of Jesus Christ, in whose Name and Authority they exercise the Ministery to them so committed. The Calling of Deacons consisteth in the like Election and acceptation, with separation *by Prayer.*

XIII. Although it be incumbent on the Pastors and Teachers of the Churches to be instant in Preaching the Word, by way of Office; yet the work of Preaching the Word is not so peculiarly confined to them, but that others also gifted and fitted by the holy Ghost for it, and approved (being by lawful ways and means in the Providence of God called thereunto) may publiquely, ordinarily and constantly perform it; so that they give themselves up thereunto.

XIV. However, they who are ingaged in the work of Publique Preaching, and enjoy the Publique Maintenance upon that account, are not thereby obliged to dispense the Seals to any other then such as (being Saints by Calling, and gathered according to the Order of the Gospel) they stand related to, as Pastors or Teachers; yet ought they not to neglect others living within their Parochial Bounds, but besides their constant publique Preaching to them, they ought to enquire after their profiting by the Word, instructing them in, and pressing upon them (whether young or old) the great Doctrines of the Gospel, even personally and particularly, so far as their strength and time will admit.

XV. Ordination alone without the Election or precedent consent of the Church, by those who formerly have been Ordained by vertue of that Power they have received by their Ordination, doth not constitute any person a Church Officer, or communicate Office-power unto him.

XVI. A Church furnished with Officers (according to the minde of Christ) hath full power to administer all his Ordinances; and where there is want of any one or more Officers required, that Officer or those which are in the Church, may administer all the Ordinances proper to their particular Duty and Offices; but where there are no teaching Officers, none may administer the Seals, nor can the Church authorize any so to do.

XVII. In the carrying on of Church-administrations, no person ought to be added to the Church, but by the consent of the Church it self; that so love (without dissimulation) may be preserved between all the Members thereof.

XVIII. Whereas the Lord Jesus Christ hath appointed and instituted as a means of Edification, that those who walk not according to the Rules and Laws appointed by him (in respect of Faith and Life, so that just offence doth arise to the Church thereby) be censured in his Name and Authority: Every Church hath Power in it self to exercise and execute all those Censures appointed by him, in the way and Order prescribed in the Gospel.

XIX. The Censures so appointed by Christ, are Admonition and Excommunication; and whereas some offences are or may be known onely to some, it is appointed by Christ, that those to whom they are so known, do first admonish the offender in private; in publique offences where any sin, before all; or in case of non-amendment upon private admonition, the offence being related to the Church, and the offender not manifesting his repentance, he is to be duely admonished in the Name of Christ by the whole Church, by the Ministery of the Elders of the Church; and if this Censure prevail not for his repentance, then he is to be cast out by Excommunication with the consent of the Church.

XX. As all Believers are bound to joyn themselves to particular Churches, when and where they have opportunity so to do, so none are to be admitted unto the Priviledges of the Churches, who do not submit themselves to the Rule of Christ in the Censures of the Government of them.

XXI. This being the way prescribed by Christ in case of offence, no Church-members upon any offences taken by them, having performed their duty required of them in this matter, ought to disturb any Church-order, or absent themselves from the publique Assemblies or the Administration of any Ordinances upon that pretence, but to wait upon Christ in the further proceeding of the Church.

XXII. The Power of Censures being seated by Christ in a particular Church, is to be exercised onely towards particular Members of each Church respectively as such; and there is no power given by him unto any Synods or Ecclesiastical Assemblies to Excommunicate, or by their publique Edicts to threaten Excommunication, or other Church-censures against Churches, Magistrates, or their people upon any account; no man being obnoxious to that Censure, but upon his personal miscarriage, as a Member of a particular Church.

XXIII. Although the Church is a Society of men, assembling for the celebration of the Ordinances according to the appointment of Christ, yet every Society assembling for that end or purpose, upon the account of cohabitation within any civil Precincts or Bounds, is not thereby constituted a Church; seeing there may be wanting among them, what is essentially required thereunto; and therefore a Believer living with others in such a Precinct, may joyn himself with any Church for his edification.

XXIV. For the avoiding of differences that may otherwise arise, for the greater Solemnity in the Celebration of the Ordinances of Christ, and the opening a way for the larger usefulness of the Gifts and Graces of the holy Ghost; Saints living in one City or Town, or within such distances as that they may conveniently assemble for divine Worship, ought rather to joyn in one Church for their mutual strengthning and edification, then to set up many distinct Societies.

XXV. As all Churches, and all the Members of them are bound to pray continually for the good or prosperity of all the Churches of Christ in all places, and upon all occasions to further it; (Every one within the bounds of their Places and Callings, in the exercise of their Gifts and Graces) So the Churches themselves (when planted by the providence of God, so as they may have opportunity and advantage for it) ought to hold communion amongst themselves for their peace, increase of love, and mutual edification.

XXVI. In cases of difficulties or differences, either in point of Doctrine or in Administrations, wherein either the Churches in general are concerned, or any one Church, in their Peace, Union, and Edification, or any Member or Members of any Church are injured in, or by any proceeding in Censures, not agreeable to Truth and Order: it is according to the minde of Christ, that many Churches holding communion together, do by their Messengers meet in a Synod or Councel, to consider and give their advice in, or about that matter in difference, to be reported to all the Churches concerned: Howbeit these Synods so assembled are not entrusted with any Church-Power, properly so called, or with any Jurisdiction over the Churches themselves, to exercise any Censures over any Churches or Persons, or to impose their determinations on the Churches or Officers.

XXVII. Besides these occasional Synods or Councels, there are not instituted by Christ any stated Synods in a fixed Combination of Churches, or their Officers, in lesser or greater Assemblies: nor are there any Synods appointed by Christ in a way of Subordination to one another.

XXVIII. Persons that are joyned in Church-fellowship, ought not lightly or without just cause to withdraw themselves from the communion of the Church whereunto they are joyned: Nevertheless, where any person cannot continue in any Church without his sin, either for want of the Administration of any Ordinances instituted by Christ, or by his being deprived of his due Priviledges, or compelled to anything in practice not warranted by the Word, or in case of Persecution, or upon the account of conveniency of habitation; he consulting with the Church, or the Officer or Officers thereof, may peaceably depart from the communion of the Church, wherewith he hath so walked, to joyn himself with some other Church, where he may enjoy the Ordinances in the purity of the same, for his edification and consolation.

XXIX. Such reforming Churches as consist of persons sound in the Faith, and of conversation becoming the Gospel, ought not to refuse the communion of each other, so far as may consist with their own Principles respectively, though they walk not in all things according to the same Rules of Church-Order.

XXX. Churches gathered and walking according to the minde of Christ, judging other Churches (though less pure) to be true Churches, may receive unto occasional communion with them, such Members of those Churches as are credibly testified to be godly, and to live without offence.

PART IV

PERSECUTION, 1660–1689

Document IV.1

Early Persecution of Quakers

The persecution that occurred during the years after the Restoration was less of a shock to Quakers than to other dissenting groups. They had been accustomed to defying the law since George Fox's first imprisonment in Nottingham in 1649 (v., NJ 41–3). Reports of meetings broken up, assaults by members of the public, arrests, trials, and imprisonments are the stuff of Quaker correspondence and pamphlets throughout the Interregnum. The following excerpt provides an example. It is taken from what may be the earliest of the Quaker 'sufferings' pamphlets, designed to justify the actions of Quakers and attract public sympathy. It was written by Richard Hubberthorne, a former army captain who joined with Fox in 1652 and it described the treatment of Elizabeth Leavens and Elizabeth Fletcher at Oxford in 1654.

The tract is entitled, *A true Testimony of the zeal of Oxford professors and University men, who for zeal do persecute the servants of the living God* (1654). The Vice-Chancellor of the University of Oxford since 26 September 1652 was Dr John Owen. It shows how the Quakers were already forging a theology of suffering, the 'daily cross' and the 'cross to the will', so that through unity with the experience of Christ, suffering comes to be seen as a necessary part of the process of salvation. The result was, that by the time of the Clarendon Code, Quakers were well placed to withstand the experiences of the years following, when four hundred Quakers died in prison and several thousand more were crippled in health or fortune. For a fuller account of early Quaker reaction to persecution, v., Rosemary Moore, *The Light in Their Consciences: Early Quakers in Britain 1644–1666* (University Park, PA, 2000), pp 155–63 and 185–92. For Quakers during the Restoration period v. SPQ and *The History of the Life of Thomas Ellwood, Written by Himself* (1st edn, London, 1714; new edn, ed. Rosemary Moore, Altamira, 2004).

[p. 1] A Brief and true testimony to all the people, of the unjust and unlawful proceedings of those called justices in *Oxford*, against two Northern women, who in obedience to the Lord, came to *Oxford*, upon the 20 of the fourth Moneth, who several daies as they were moved of the Lord, passed through the streets, colledges and steeple-houses, declaring the word of the Lord freely. And upon the 15 day being the first day of the week, were moved to go to a steeple-house & when the Priest had done, one of the women began to speak in answer to what was delivered, and in exhortation to the people. Then two of the justices cried out, *Take her away, carry her to prison*; and they took them away, and carried them to a prison called Buckerdo where onely fellons and persons are committed for murder and other hainous offences, and secured ...

[p. 2] And this is to be observed as a true testimony of these two servants of the Lord, that they did neither beg nor steal, neither did they wrong nor violence to any man; they coveted no mans silver, gold nor apparel; but because they obeyed the word of the Lord, and did his work faithfully speaking the word of the Lord in boldness against the deceits of the Priests and people, in the streets, in the market-place, in the synagogues, and in the colledges, clearing and discharging their consciences, in the Lords work and service, freely administering that which they had freely received from the Lord, of whom they do receive their reward; for their reward is with them, and the presence of the Lord God doth accompany them, and for their obedience to the Lord, they receive the shame of the world, as ever the servants of the Lord did, who were mocked, buffetted and shamefully used, being tied together at *Johns* Colledge and pumped, and kicked and buffetted, and thurst into a pool called Gileses pool, so that they went into a remote place, to wash the dirt off their cloathes.

And here both Magistrates, and Schollars, and they who pretend to be Ministers of the Gospel, are the chiefest actors in this persecution, and so do make themselves manifest to be in the same generation of the Scribes, and Pharisees, and hypocrites who were ever persecutors of the righteous seed, whomever it hath brought forth: and so they fill up the measure of their fathers iniquities.

[p. 3] Again, as concerning the Justices being assembled, the Vice-chancellour being the chief actor in this persecution, said, *That they blasphemed the name of God, and did abuse the Spirit of God, and dishonour the grace of Christ*, and asked the women, *Whether they did read the Scriptures*, they answered, *Yea, they did*; then they asked them, *Whether they were not to be obedient to the power of the Magistrate*, they answered, *They were obedient to the power of God, and to the power as it was of God, their souls were subject unto it for conscience sake.*

Well, said the Vice-chancellor, *you prophane the word of God, and I fear you know not God, though you so much speak of him*. And then they concluded, that there was matter enough for their commitment and punishment, and wished the women to withdraw; Consenting, that a paper should be drawn up for their being whipped out of the City ...

... And the next morning their wills were performed, though with much unwillingness in the executioner. Many other particulars might be mentioned of their sufferings, afflictions and patience, under reproachings, revilings, slanders and false accusations cast upon them, which is the portion of the righteous in the world, as Christ said, *Blessed are you when men shall revile you, and persecute and speak all manner of evil against you falsly, for my names sake: rejoyce and be exceeding glad, for great is your reward in heaven, for so persecuted they the Prophets that were before you*. Mat.5.11.12.

Document IV.2

Consolation in Prison

Humphrey Smith was a former parish minister turned Quaker and possibly one of the rare Quakers who actually sought martyrdom. He was imprisoned with several others in vile conditions in Winchester, released shortly before the Restoration, and died in 1662 during a second imprisonment in Winchester. While in prison he contributed to a continuous stream of pamphlets.

The following document is extracted from Humphrey Smith, *The Sounding Voyce of the Dread of God's Mighty Power* (London, 1658), pp. 6–8. It exemplifies the way in which apocalyptic imagery is combined with a sense of the presence of the Lord. For Humphrey Smith, as for all Quakers, the Kingdom of God was present as well as future.

For behold the Lord is with us, the Shout of a King is among us, the Lord whose name is holy is come, he hath uttered his voice from Heaven, and now the Nations of the earth are angry, but the Lord will reign in righteousness, and all his enemies shall be astonished at his presence, and his adversaries shall be amazed for ever, their hearts shall be turned as a stone within them, and men shall be at their wits end, for fear and for looking after those things which shall come upon the earth, and all them whose names are written in it, their wisdome shall not preserve them, their understandings shall not defend them, neither shall all their subtilty cover them from the Light, their nakedness shall appear to their everlasting shame, and the prisoners of hope shall rejoyce over them for ever more.

For behold I say your day is come, wherein you shall bow down under the prisoners, and fall under the slain, according to the words of the spirit of prophecy, *Isaiah* 10.4. and the slain over you shall rejoyce for ever more, having the high prayses of God in their mouths, and the sword of the spirit in their hearts, with which they shall cut in pieces and pierce in sunder, the bowels of all flesh, and it shall be as chaff before them, and the strength thereof as the passing away of the morning cloud, and in the strength of the most high, shall the army of the *Lyon of the tribe of Judah*, go on and prosper, even as *Kings*, whose armies are swift to the battel, their faces are as an Adamant, and their countenances fierce, and terrible, the sound of their voice is dreadful, and the noise of their appearance astonisheth the Heathen, the earth before them is full of its fruit, behind them its a desolate wilderness, they spare not the ancient, nor the honourable, neither have they respect to the persons of men; they even smile at destruction when it's coming, and they are prepared for all your oppressions.

Wherefore now gather your selves together, O ye potsheards of the earth, and stand up all you that thirst for blood, assemble your selves together all ye persecutors, let your counsels come up from hell, and let the depth of the powers of darkness shew forth it selfe in the utmost of its strength, and with it combine ye all together, and stand up in the power of your King, which is the Angell of the *bottomless pit*, who is head among (in) and over all you who thirsteth for the blood of the innocent. Now come and draw near in the very height of your Fathers wrath, and behold we meet you in the infiniteness of our Fathers love, and stand you together in the depth of your secret subtilty, and behold we abide in the pure wisdome of the most High. Stand ye up for the glory and honour of the world, and we abide faithful for the glory of the Lord our maker.

And this I say plainly unto you, that your long tyranny will never weary out the patience we have received, neither can you inflict more punishment then the Lord hath enabled us to bear; and as your wrath is increased, our humility is increased much more; and as you are filled, and moved with envy, we are much more filled and overcome with the power of the Fathers life; and though you contrive wayes to ensnare the innocent, we take no thought aforehand to deliver our selves, for selfe we have denyed, and we have given up our bodies and souls a living sacrifice unto God, to do or suffer his will: And him that kills the body we feare not, much lesse those that can but whip or imprison but for a few moneths; for our life you cannot reach, neither can you disturb their rest whom the Lord hath crowned with honour, who out of the world are redeemed and bought with the price of blood most precious, but are become his, to follow him whither ever he lead them, though it be through tryals, great tribulations, bonds and long imprisonments, these things cannot move them who are brought to rest in the deserts, and sleep in the woods; Yea, and there is none can make them afraid with all their threats, unrighteous Laws, bonds, Bridewells, long unjust imprisonments, or death it self.

And this honour hath the Saints, and herein do they rejoyce for evermore, in that they are counted worthy to suffer for his Names sake, who was made perfect through sufferings, and thereby overcame all the powers of Darknesse, whereby *Principalities and powers are spoiled for ever, and through sufferings are we made more then conquerours over all our enemies*, whose day will have an end, whose cruelty will cease, whose tyranny will be rewarded upon their own heads, and their memoriall will rot for ever; but the faithfulnesse of the faithfull shall never be taken from him, nor the innocency of the harmlesse shall never be forgotten, neither shall they ever want strength to stand in the day of battell, nor courage and boldnesse to endure, when the enemies of the Lord ariseth up in opposition against the brightnesse of the rising of the power of the Lamb of God, who is come to take away the sin of the world, even him who is the Light, and the Heir, against whom with one consent, the Rulers of the earth, the Hireling Priests, with all the prophane, and unclean, and all them of all opinions in the world, are joyning together in one combination, as with one minde conspiring in their enmity, to slay, and murther the Heir that is now come to make an end of sin, who saith, *I am the Light*.

H.S.

Document IV.3

The Quaker Peace Testimony

After the restoration of the King in 1660, the returning Cavaliers feared a Puritan uprising and were especially wary of the more extreme groups, Baptists, Fifth Monarchists and Quakers. In this difficult situation Quakers tried to show their loyalty but the Fifth Monarchist rising in January 1661 gave the authorities a pretext to take repressive action. On 10 January a proclamation was issued prohibiting meetings of Baptists, Fifth Monarchists and Quakers. Within a few weeks over four thousand had been arrested, and many meetings were entirely denuded of men Friends. The following declaration was an attempt to dissociate Friends from the Fifth Monarchy plot. The problem was that Quakers were known to have been supporters of the previous government. Many Quakers had served in the parliamentary armies, and some had served in the militias raised during 1659. The assertion in the text, that Quakers had never taken part in wars, was something of a compromise with the truth, and all concerned must have known this. It was true, however, that Quakers had never taken up arms against the government in power, that Fox had consistently advised his followers to take no part in civil disturbances, that Quakers did not resist arrest or mob attacks, and that some Quakers had already reached a pacifist position. The form of government of the country, Quakers believed, was a matter for God to decide.

The following is from the *Declaration from the Harmless and Innocent People of God called Quakers, against all Plotters and Fighters in the World* (January 1661).

For the removing of the Ground of Jealousie and Suspicion from both Magistrates and People in the Kingdoms concerning Wars and Fightings.

And also something in Answer to that Clause of the King's Late Proclamation, which mentions the Quakers, to clear them from the Plot and Fighting, which therein is mentioned, and for the clearing their innocency.

This Declaration was given unto the King, upon the 21 day of the 11th Month 1660 [i.e., 21 January 1661]

Our Principle is, and our Practices have always been, to seek peace and ensue it, and to follow after righteousness, and the knowledge of God, seeking the Good and Well-fare, and doing that which tends to the peace of All. Wee know that Warres and Fightings proceed from the Lusts of men, as James 4:1, 2, 3, out of which Lusts the Lord hath redeemed us; And so out of [p. 2] the Occasion of War; the Occasion of which War, and the War it self (wherein envious men, who are lovers of themselves more than lovers of God, lust, kil, & desire to have mens lives or estates) ariseth from the lust; All bloody Principles & Practices we (as to our own particular) do utterly deny, with all outward Wars, and Strife, and Fightings with outward Weapons, for any end, or under any pretence whatsoever, and this is our Testimony to the whole World.

And whereas it is objected;

But although you now say, *That you cannot Fight, nor take up Arms at all; yet if the Spirit do move you, then you will change your Principle, and then you will sell your Coat, and buy a Sword, and Fight for the Kingdom of Christ.*

Answer, As for this, we say to you, that Christ said to *Peter, Put up thy Sword in his place*: Though he had said before, he that had no Sword, might sel his Coat and buy one (to the fulfilling of the Law and Scripture) yet after when he had bid him put it up, he said, *He that taketh the Sword, shall perish with the Sword* ...

That Spirit of Christ by which we are guided, is not changeable, so as once to command us from a thing as evil, & again to move unto it; And we do certainly know, and so testifie to the World, that the Spirit of Christ, which leads us into all Truth, will never move us to fight and war against any man with outward Weapons, neither for the Kingdom of Christ, nor for the Kingdoms of this World ...

[p. 3] So we, whom the Lord hath called into the obedience of his Truth, *have denyed Wars and Fightings*, and cannot again any more learn it: And this is a certain Testimony unto all the World, of the truth of our hearts in this particular, That as God perswadeth every man's heart to believe, so they may receive it; For we have not (as some others) gone about cunningly with devised Fables: Nor have we ever denyed in Practice what we have profess'd in Principle, but in sincerity and truth, and by the Word of God have we laboured to be made manifest unto all men; that both we and our waye might be witnessed in the hearts of all people: And whereas all manner of Evil hath been falsly spoken of us, We hereby speake forth the plain Truth of our hearts, to take away the occasion of that offence, that so we being innocent, may not suffer for other mens offences, nor be made a prey upon by the wills of men, for that of which we were never guilty; but in the uprightnesse of our hearts, we may, under the Power ordained of God, for the punishment of evil-doers, and for the praise of them that [p. 4] do well, live a peaceable and godly life, in all godliness and honesty; for although we have alwayes suffer'd, and do now more abundantly suffer, yet we know that it's for righteousness sake ...

[p. 5] Therefore consider these things, ye men of Understanding: For Plotters, Raisers of Insurrections, Tumultuous ones, and Fighters, running with Swords, Clubs, Staves and Pistols one against another, We say, These are of the World, and hath its foundation from this Unrighteous World; from the foundation of which the Lamb hath been slain, which Lamb hath redeemed us from this unrighteous world; And we are not of it, but are Heirs of a world in which there is no End, and of a Kingdom where no corruptible thing enters: And our Weapons *are spiritual* and *not Carnal,* yet *Mighty through God, to the plucking down of the strongholds of sin & Satan,* who is Author of *Wars, Fighting, Murder* and *Plots*; and our *Swords* are broken into *Plow-shares,* and *Spears* into *Pruning-hooks,* as Prophesied of in *Micah* 4. Therefore we cannot learn War any more, neither rise up against Nation or Kingdom with outward Weapons: though you have numbered us among the Transgressors and Plotters, the Lord knows our Innocency herein, and will plead our Cause with all Men and People upon Earth, at the day of their Judgment, when all men shall have a reward according to their works.

Therefore *in love* we warn you for your Souls good, *not to wrong the Innocent* nor the Babes of Christ, which hee hath in his Hand, which he tenders as the Apple of his eye ...

[p. 6] ... If you Oppress us as they did the Children of *Israel* in *Egypt*; and if you Oppress us as they did when *Christ* was born, & as they did the Christians in the Primitive times, we can say, *The Lord forgive you*; & leave the Lord to deal with you, and not Revenge our selves. And if you say as the Council said to *Peter* and *John, You must speak no more in that Name*; and if you serve us as they served the *Three Children,* spoken of in *Daniel,* God is the same as ever he was, that lives for ever and ever, who hath the Innocent in his Arms.

Oh Friends! offend not the Lord, and his *Little Ones*; neither afflict his People; But consider, and be moderate, and do not run hastily into things, but mind, and consider *Mercy, Justice,* and *Judgment*; that is the way for you to prosper, and get the favour of the Lord. Our Meetings were stopped and broken up in the daies of *Oliver,* in pretence of Plotting against him; and in the daies of the *Parliament,* and *Committee of Safety,* wee were looked upon as Plotters to bring in KING CHARLES; and now we are called Plotters against KING CHARLES. Oh that men should lose their Reason, and go contrary to their own Conscience, knowing that we have suffered all things, and have been accounted Plotters all along, though we have declared against them both by word of mouth and Printing, and are clear from any such things, though we have suffered all along because we would not take up Carnal Weapons to fight withall against any; and are thus made a prey upon, because we are the Innocent Lambs of Christ, and cannot avenge our selves. These things are left upon your Hearts to consider. But we are out of all those things, in the patience of the Saints, and we know, that as Christ said, *He that takes the Sword shall perish with the Sword*, Mat.26.52.Revel.23.10.

This is given forth from the People called Quakers, to satisfie the King *and His* Council, *and all those that have Jealousie concerning Us, that all occasion of Suspition may be taken away, and our Innocency cleared.*

[p. 7] Given forth under our Names, & in the behalf of the whole body of Elect People of God, who are called *Quakers*.

George Fox	Gerrard Roberts	Henry Fell
Rich. Hubberthorn	John Balcon	John Hinde
John Stubbs	Leonard Fell	John Furley, jun
Francis Howgill	Samuel Fisher	Thomas Moor

Document IV.4

The Ejected Ministers Bid Farewell, 1662

When the Act of Uniformity came into force on St Bartholomew's Day 1662, those ministers who were unable to conform with the stipulations of the Act and had not already left their parishes had to depart. Their 'Farewell Sermons' provide an insight into what those men had to say to their flocks before parting with them. They had a difficult task to perform. They had to justify their Nonconformity and that meant suggesting their disapproval of the legislation and of the authorities that had promoted it. On the other hand they wished to prepare their congregations for the uncertain future that faced them. A number of themes recur in the sermons. They contain much by the way of consolation and warnings against contemporary evils. There is no mistaking the high regard they had for their ministry and the pain they suffered by being deprived of it. But they insist that their consciences compelled them to make what was a real sacrifice and so naturally there are some moving passages in the sermons. Those represented in the following extracts were all Presbyterians and reluctant Nonconformists. Many of them raise the question why God should have permitted the churches to suffer through being deprived of so many ministers. Several take the view that sin and the lack of moral reformation in the churches themselves were at least part of the explanation. The quotations are taken from *A Compleat Collection of Farewell Sermons ... Revised and Corrected from many Faults of former Editions: and now Collected into one entire Volume, more perfect then any other extant, containing 42 Sermons ... London 1663*. The copy used here is not as perfect as the title-page suggests. Page numbers do not appear until page 113.

(a) This sermon was delivered by Edmund Calamy (1600–66) 'the elder', the grandfather of Edmund Calamy (1671–1732), the historian of the Great Ejection. He was elected rector of St Mary Aldermanbury, London, 27 May 1639 and was there until ejected in 1662. That was also where he delivered the sermon and his critical remarks have to do with the parishioners there, v., DNB, CR, and James Reid, *Memoirs ... of those Eminent Divines who Convened in the ... Assembly at*

Westminster (London, 1811), I, 165–89 (reprinted by Banner of Truth, 1982). He refers to his predecessors. Thomas Taylor, D.D. (1576–1633), was there from 22 January 1625 to about 1630, v., DNB, and John Stoughton, D.D., was at Aldermanbury from 1632 until his death. He was buried 9 May 1639, v., B. Brook, *The Lives of the Puritans* (London, 1813), III, 527. Traditionally it took seven years to complete an apprenticeship and Calamy uses the term for the time spent by him and his predecessors in the parish.

(b) Thomas Manton (1620–77) was the ejected rector of St Paul's, Covent Garden, London. Like Edmund Calamy he was one of the most distinguished leaders of the Presbyterians, v., DNB, CR.

(c) Thomas Case (1598–1682) was ejected in 1660 from the Rectory of St Giles in the Fields, London, v., DNB, CR, James Reid, *Memoirs of ... Eminent Divines*, I, 204–18.

(d) William Jenkyn (1612–85) was vicar of Christ Church, London, ejected in 1662, v., DNB, CR. The sermon is a detailed exposition of the theme that Christian worship is not confined to consecrated buildings, a fitting theme in view of the fact that he, together with many of his congregation, would before long have to worship outside the parish churches. In the above quotation the salient points of his argument have been selected. There is a good summary of the sermon in Samuel Palmer, *The Nonconformist's Memorial* (2nd edn, London, 1802), I, 114.

(e) Thomas Jacomb (1622–87) was the rector of St Martin's, Ludgate, London, and was ejected in 1662, see DNB, CR. The duty to which he refers in the first sentence is refusing to conform with the Church of England.

(f, g) Dr William Bates (1625–99) was vicar of St Dunstan's in the West, London, and was ejected in 1662. He was one of the most distinguished of Presbyterian leaders. Calamy (*An Account of the Ministers ...* (London, 1713), II, 49) says of him, 'He was generally reputed one of the best Orators of the Age'. See also DNB, CR.

(h) William Beerman or Berman (died 1700) was ejected from the chaplaincy of St Thomas's Hospital, Southwark, Surrey, in 1662, v., CR.

(i) Daniel Bull (died 1698) was rector of Stoke Newington, Middlesex, ejected in 1660, see CR.

(a) 'Mr. Calamys Sermon, Preached, *August* 17. 1662'. The text was 2 Sam. 24: 14 – 'And David said unto God, I am in a great strait, let us fall now into the hand of the Lord (for his mercies are great) and let me not fall into the hand of men'

[p. 3] There are straits suffered for God and a good Conscience, *Heb*.11.36, 37. those Martyrs there were driven to great straits: but these were straits for God and a good Conscience, and these straits were the Saints greatest enlargements, they were so sweetned to them by the consolations and supportations of Gods Spirit; a Prison was a Paradise to them, *Heb*.10.34. they look joyfully at the spoiling of their goods, *Acts* 5.41. *They departed from the presence of the Council, rejoycing that they were counted worthy to suffer shame for his Name.* Straits for a good conscience are greatest enlargements; therefore St. *Paul* glorieth in this strait ...

[p. 5] Doth sin bring Nations and Persons into external, internal, and eternal straits? then this sadly reproves those that chuse to commit sin to avoid perplexity. There are thousands in *England* guilty of this, that to avoid poverty, will lye, cheat and couzen, and to gain an estate will sell God and a good conscience, and to avoid loss of estate and imprisonment, will do any thing; they will be sure to be of that Religion which is uppermost, be it what it will ... Consider it is sin onely that makes trouble deserve the name of trouble; for when we suffer for Gods sake, or a good Conscience, these troubles are so sweetned by the consolations of Heaven, that they are no troubles at all: therefore in Queen *Maries* days the Martyrs wrote to their friends out of prison, *If you knew the comforts we have in prison, you would wish to be with us. I am in prison before I am in prison*, saith Mr. *Sanders*.

[p. 8] Take heed of prophaning the Christian Sabbath which is much prophaned every where; a day that Christ by his resurrection from the dead hath consecrated to be kept holy to God: Certainly if the Jewes were so severely punished for breaking the Sabbath, which was set apart in memory of the Creation, surely God will severely punish those that break the Sabbath, set apart in memory of Christs Resurrection ...

[p. 8] If sin bringeth a Nation into marvellous labyrinths, learn what great cause we have to fear that *God* should bring this *Nation* into great distress, because of the great *abominations* are committed in the midst of it: Our King and Sovereign was in great strait in the daies of his banishment, but God hath delivered him. God hath delivered this *Nation* out of great straits; but alas, we requite God evil for good, and in stead of repenting of old sins, we commit new sins. I am told there are new Oaths invented, Oaths not fit to be named in any place, much less here: Certainly the drunkenness and adultery, the oppression and injustice, the bribery and Sabbath-breaking, the vain and wicked swearing and forswearing this Nation is guilty of, must of necessity provoke God to say of us as he did of them in *Jer*.15.29. *Shall I not visit for these things, saith the Lord?* shall not my soul be avenged on such a Nation as this? God will not only punish us, but be avenged on us. There is no way to avoid a National Desolation, but by a National Reformation.

[pp. 8–9] Learn what cause you of this Congregation and Parish, what cause you have to expect that *God* should bring you into great straits, because of your great *unthankfulness* and *unfruitfulness* under the means of Grace, you that have so long enjoyed the Gospel; you have had the *Gospel* in this place in great abundance; Dr. *Taylor* he served an Apprentice in this place; Dr. *Stoughton* served another Apprenticeship, and I, through Divine Mercy, have served three Apprenticeships, and another almost among you; you have had the Spirit of God seven and thirty years in the faithful Ministry of the Word, knocking at the door of your hearts, but many of you have hardened your hearts. Are there not some of you, I only put the question, that begin to loath the Manna of your Souls, and to look back towards *Egypt* again? Are there not some of you have itching ears, and would fain have Preachers that would feed you with dainty phrases, and begin not to care for a Minister that unrips your Consciences, speaks to your hearts and souls, and would force you into Heaven by frightening you out of your sins? Are there not some of you, that by often hearing Sermons, are become Sermon-proof, that know how to sleep and scoff away Sermons? I would be glad to say, that there are but few such; but the Lord knoweth there are too too many that by long preaching, get little good by preaching, insomuch that I have often said it, and say it now again, there is hardly any way to raise the price of the Gospel-Ministry, but by the want of it: And that I may not flatter you, you have not profited under the means you have enjoyed, therefore you may justly expect God may bring you into a strait, and take away the Gospel from you: God may justly take away your Ministers by death, or other ways ...

(b) 'Dr. Manton's Sermon'. 'Preached on August 17.1662'. His text was Hebrews 12: 1 – 'Seeing we are encompassed with so great a cloud of witnesses, let us lay aside every weight ...'

[pp. 13–14] [The witnesses] are propounded to us, not for their words only, and for their *profession*, but for their *deeds*, for their bitter *sufferings*; and they abundantly manifest to us, that there is nothing *impossible* in our duty, or any thing so difficult but may be *overcome* through *Christs* strength enabling us: They all had the same nature we have; they were of the like passion with us, *flesh* and *blood* as we are, of the same *relations* and *concernments* and then on the *other side*, we have the same *cause* with them, the same *recompence* of reward to *encourage* us, the same *God* and *Saviour* to recompence us; he suffered for us as well as for them; therefore we should follow in their steps, and hold fast our confidence to the end, for they have shewed us, that poverty, reproaches, death it self, and all those things that would look harsh, and with a ghastly aspect upon the eyes of the *world*, are no such *evils*, but that a *Believer* may rejoyce in them, and triumph over them. I say, they have shewed the blandishments of the world have not such a charm, but they may be renounced without any loss of considerable joy and contentment, and that the duties of Christianity are not so hard, but that a little waiting upon God will bring in grace enough to perform them; and therefore saith the Apostle, *Seeing we have a cloud of witnesses, let us lay aside, &c.*

(c) 'Mr *Case*'s Sermon'. 'Preached August 17.1662'. His text was Rev. 2:5 – 'Remember therefore from whence thou art fallen, and repent, and do the first works ...'

[p. 41] Sin is departure from God, Repentance a coming back again to God ... My Brethren, we have no great cause to boast of *Englands first love*: Never so good as it should be, yet many can remember when *England* hath been much better than it is.

Time was, when Doctrines have been more sound, Discipline more exercised for the suppressing of sin and prophanness, Ordinances kept mor pure from sinful mixtures: when *London* kept Sabbaths better than now, honoured them that were set over her for their works sake; would have thought nothing too good for a faithful Minister: when Christians loved one another with a dear, hearty, fervent love: when there was less complement, but more real love and affection among Christians: when Christians improved their meeting, converse, Christian Conference, and other soul duties to better purpose than now: not to foolish disputations, or wanton sensual excess, but to their mutual edification: when they improved their times for comparing their evidences, communicating their experiences, and building up one another in their most holy faith: when there was more industry in Professors than now, to bring in Converts, when private Christians thought it their duty to be subservient to the work of their Ministers, to bring in others to Christ, especially their family.

[p. 42] Time was, when more care of the truly godly poor; when error was more odious; when Popery was more hated than now; when the name of a tolleration would have made Christians to have trembled; when Christians were better acquainted with their Bibles: when more time spent in secret Prayer: when more tender of one anothers names and honours, would heal one anothers reputations, and would spread the lap of charity over those mis-reports and scandals that might be cast upon them ... Oh do you not only [see] *your first works*, but our *fore-fathers first works*: be as zealous for God and his truths, as tender, mutually careful of another as they.

(d) 'Mr. *Jenkyn*'s Afternoon Sermon'. '*Preached* August 17. 1662'. The text was Exod. 3: 2, 3, 4, 5 – 'And the Angel of the Lord appeared unto him in a flame of fire out of the midest of a bush ... And he said, Draw not nigh hither: put off thy shoes from off thy feet, for the place where thou standest is holy ground'

[pp. 64–75] *Put off thy shoes* ... The reason by which this is back't, *Because the place whereon Moses did stand, was holy ground*. The meaning I take to be this, it is holy in regard of that visible and miraculous token, symbol, and sign of his presence, that is here discovered in this place; not because the place was (as I do not understand how any place is) of its own nature holy; but God did testifie, that the place being the place of his special presence, had thereby a holiness; there being now a sign given by God to *Moses*, that he was extraordinarily and miraculously there ...

The holiness of a place doth consist in the separation thereof, the setting it apart, the distinction and discrimination in the way of some excellent pre-eminence, or the exalting of it before and above all other places. Thus the holiness of places is taken in Scripture, *Exod*.30.31.37.38 ... Hence a thing is said to be unholy in Scipture, when it is common, is not separated and set apart to holy employments and services; and from everything that is of civil concernment ...

The extraordinary presence of God was by his miraculous *apparitions* discovering himself by some miraculous token, vision, sign, or manifestation of his presence, as now here in this *burning, and not consuming Bush*; here was a miraculous token of God's presence ... And remember this place now, of Gods extraordinary manifestation of himself in the *Bush*, was holy for that time, and no longer, wherein he did manifest himself ...

It is not now in the times of the Gospel in any mans power to set apart a place for Religious duties, so as that it should be unlawful upon a due *occasion* to use it for civil employments, or that it should be always unlawful to alienate to other uses, besides those uses that are divine: the Bread and Wine sanctified by *Gods* own *institution*, by the Minister, after the publick use and *administration* of them in the Ordinance, are not *now holy*, but they may be eaten in a civil use and way as our *ordinary* and *common food* ... And so the *common* Utensils, as the Cup, and the like, when they are come to be old, they may be used for other employments, without fear of sin ...

That no place is now in the time of Gospel hath such an holiness either from Institution or Use, as to sanctifie or make more acceptable or effectual the Services therein performed: This is not in the time of the Gospel; God is present at places of Religious performances, not with respect unto the place, but the performance by him instituted and enjoyned; and therefore he doth not say, *Where two or three are met together, I will be in the midst of that place*, but *among them*. God will be present in the place for the Duties sake, not among them for the Places sake. Prayers and other Duties in the Ceremonial Law were regarded for the Places sake, but now we must abhor this piece of Judaism: For a man to set a place apart by Consecration, that this place makes the Duty any thing the more excellent, or acceptable to God, this is to make the Traditions of men equal to the Institution of God ... Our Churches and Meeting-places, are not holy (if they be holy at all) without relation to the Duties performed, but our Duties are holy without relation to the Church or the Place. *None* but God can Consecrate a place to be an effectual means of Worship ...

That there is no place so holy as to exclude another place from being as holy in a way of proper sanctity & holiness ... God now makes not one place properly more holy then another; and there is not now properly any Religious difference of places. We have not now the Precept of God to sanctifie and separate one place from another, to prefer one place before another; we have not now the miraculous Presence of God, his appearing as at the Bush. God hath not given us under the Gospel those Symboles of his standing Presence and Residency, as by the *Ark*, and *Mercy-seat*, and *Altar* of old, he gave unto *his people*. And as for his Ordinances, if they make a place holy in regard of performance of Duty to God there, and his spiritual presence in that place, then my Parlour, Chamber or Closet, are holy, where I use to pray, and where God doth afford his assisting blessing, and comforting presence. So that if you make the spiritual presence of God to make a thing holy, in regard of Gods spiritual presence going along with those services, then your Houses are holy, and the Field is holy where you walk when you meditate, and praying by the River side makes it holy ... If this be so, that there is no holiness in places, then first of all, be the more encouraged to serve God in your families, in those places where God hath set you, where God is as well pleased with your service as in publick places ... Love the holiness of the living Members, be not so much in love with the holiness of wood and timber, bricks and stones, but wherever you see the Image of Christ, be in love with that soul; wherever the presence of God shines, do thou say, Oh! my soul, delight to come into the company of these men; *The righteous is more excellent then his neighbour*. If there be heaven upon earth, it is in the company of godly men ...

(e) 'Dr. *Jacomb*'s Forenoon Sermon'. '*Preached* August 17. 1662'. The text was John 8: 29 – And he that sent me, is with me: the Father hath not left me alone: for I do alwayes those things that please him' [p. 115] Is this pleasing of God, a duty of so great importance and benefit? then be tender and charitable in judging of those that differ from you and others, upon this account, because they dare not displease God. I may in this caution, aim at my self and others of my brethren in the work of our Ministry: but I am not here at present to take my last farewel; I hope I may have a little further opportunity of speaking to you: but if not, let me require this of you, to passe a charitable interpretation upon our laying down the exercise of our Ministry: there is a greater Judge than you, must judge us all at the great day: and to this Judge we can appeal before Angels and men, that it is not this thing, or that thing, that puts us upon this dissent, but it is conscience toward God, and fear of offending him. I censure none that differ from me, as though they displease God: but yet, as to my self, should I do thus and thus, I should certainly violate the peace of my own conscience, and offend God, which I must not do, no, not to secure my Ministry; though that either is, or ought to be, dearer to me than my very life: and how dear it is, God only knoweth. Do not add affliction to affliction, be not uncharitable in judging of us, as if through pride, faction, obstinacy, or devotednesse to a party, or which is worse than all, in opposition to Authority we do dissent; the Judge of all hearts knows it is not so: but it is meerly from those apprehensions which after prayer, and the use of all means do yet continue; that doing thus and thus, we should displease God: therefore deal charitably with us, in this day of our affliction: If we be mistaken, I pray God to convince us: if others be mistaken, whether in a publick or private capacity, I pray God in mercy convince them; but however things go, God will make good this truth to us; in this work he will not leave us, and our Father will not leave us alone; for it is the unfeigned desire of our soul, in all things to please God.

(f) '*Dr. Bates*'s Forenoon Sermon. *August.* 17.1662'. The text was Heb. 13: 20, 21 – 'Now the God of Peace that brought again from the dead our Lord Jesus, that great shepherd of the sheep, through the blood of the everlasting Covenant ...'

[pp. 120–2] He is the God of peace, as with respect to the bloud of Christ, which is the purchase of peace; so with respect to the Covenant which is made between God and us, [*Through the bloud of the everlasting Covenant,*] there are three sorts of Covenants amongst men; some are *Covenants* of *Friendship* and *Amity*, some are *Covenants* of *Trade* and *Commerce*, and some are *Covenants* of *Assistance* and *Help*. Now all these qualifications meet in this Covenant which is made between God and Believers: it is a Covenant of *Peace* and *Friendship*, for now we stand upon termes of amity with God. Those who were strangers and enemies are now reconciled. And there is between God and us perfect peace; there is a League (as the Scripture speaks) between God and the Creature. It is the Covenant of Trade, there is now a way opened to Heaven, we may now ascend to God in duties of holinesse, and God descends to us by the excitations of his grace and influences of joy. And 'tis a Covenant of Assistance, for he promises not only to give us the reward of the Covenant, but to secure unto us the condition, he promises to enable us to discharge the condition of Faith and Repentance. Now upon this account of that Covenant which is founded in the blood of Christ, he is the *God of Peace* to his people.

1. *Use* is by way of *Conviction*. This may discover to us how distant their temper is from God, who are enemies to peace. We unman our selves; we unchristian our selves so far as we are opposite to this blessed temper of Peace. Certainly as disturbed water cannot make any reflection unto us of that face that looks into it; so when our spirits are disturbed by animosities, exasperations, heats and divisions, 'tis impossible for us to see the Image of God, as he is the God of Peace. And certainly there is no more dolefull consideration in the World than this, That man whom God made so sociable a creature, who hath all the engagements and endearments laid upon him, which may cause him to live in peace and gentlenesse towards those who are of the same nature with him; yet that in fiercenesse of our hearts, should exceed those of the most savage creatures. Man comes into the World naked, and altogether unarmed, as if he were designed for the Picture of Peace: but could you look into the hearts of men, you would find there such tumults, such divisions, such seeds of enmity against their fellow-creatures, that Tygres and Lyons are calm and peaceable in comparison of them. 'Tis very strange to consider, that when promises are made to bury all differences as rubbish under the foundation, that nevertheless the great work of many persons should be onely to revive those former animosities, to make those exasperations fresh and keen upon their own spirits; but is this to imitate the God of Peace? These to promote divisions and disturbances amongst us, cloath their enemies with the Livery of shame and reproach, that so they may be baited by their Fury, that make it their design to represent that Party which they think is dissonant from them, with the most odious appearances (you know this is the old Art) and those showers of calumnies which are in the World, they usually precede the storm of persecution. The Devil was first a Lyar, and then a Murtherer; and those who are of this seed, they follow his Art. In the Primitive times, all the Persecutions of the Heathens arose from the reproaches of Christians: so it is now. It is an easie thing to blast the name of those persons, who are design'd for ruine. But if the contending parties would consider, (If I may call one Party contending, which is onely liable to Penalties, and is resolved to bear them patiently) how unlike this is to that God of peace, methinks it should allay the rancour that is in mens spirits, and make an atonement between all the differences and divisions that is amongst them.

(g) 'Dr. *Bates*'s Afternoon Sermon' on the same text

I know you expect I should say something as to my Non-conformity. I shall only say thus much, It is neither fancy, faction, nor humour, that makes me not to comply, but meerly for fear of offending God. And if after the best means used for my illumination, as prayer to God, discourse, study, I am not able to be satisfied concerning the lawfulness of what is required, if it be my unhappiness to be in errour, surely *Men* will have no reason to be angry with me in this World, and I hope God will pardon me in the next.

(h) 'Mr. *Beerman*'s Farewel Sermon'. Text: Acts 20: 17–38

[p. 311] Lay up for suffering times; there are few of you I believe are so bad husbands, but will lay up for a rainy day, I mean against a time of sickness comes, wherein you will be unable to work; are you thus careful to maintain your bodies? and will you be careless of your souls? O be careful to provide for stormy weather; you have winter garments for your bodies to preserve them from cold, oh let patience be your winter garment, to preserve & keep your selves warm in afflictions; I know that he that will live godly in Christ Jesus shall suffer persecution, and that through tribulations and sufferings we must enter the Kingdom of Heaven; shall I not then provide for them? But you may say, What, doth persecution attend the godly? A man may escape them, as well as suffer them? Put case afflictions should not come, thou wilt be never the worse for being provided for them; For he that is fit to dye, is fit to live; & that man that is fit to suffer affliction is fit to live without them. It was *Paul*'s Exhortation to the *Ephesians*, 6.10. *Finally, my Brethren, put on the whole Armour of God, that ye may be able to withstand the wiles of the Devil.* And it is wisdom in a man, to provide for a misery before it come ...

(i) 'Mr. Bull *of* Newington-Green *his* Farewel-Sermon *in the Afternoon*'. Text: Acts 20:32

[p. 408] And truly, my dearly beloved in the Lord, this is my great work now, when I am dying to you as to my publick Preaching: My beloved, I am very sensible that it is a very sad & solemn thing for a Minister to be rent from a People that he loves as his own Soul, that he hath laboured among; for to bid adieu to those solemn meetings, wherein I have preach'd to you, wherein we have mingled our sighes and our tears before the Lord, wherein we have rejoyced and set down before the Lord at his Table; now to think that I must minister with you and for you no more in these Ordinances, me thinks it is a heart-breaking consideration, to think that I am now dying in this congregation, to think that I am now dying whilest I am preaching; but this is my comfort under these sad thoughts, that I can *commit you to God, and to the Word of his grace, to one that is able to keep you, and to build you up, and to give them an inheritance among them that are sanctified*. Like a dying Father, I can commend you to the care of such a Friend, infinitely able to supply all that I could not do for you.

Document IV.5

Philip Henry's Diary

Henry was dispossessed of the curacy of Worthenbury, Bangor-on-Dee, Flints., on 24 October 1661 by Henry Bridgeman (1615–82), the vicar of the parish. His diary over the preceding weeks reveals his anxieties. For Philip Henry (1631–96), v., S. Palmer,

The Nonconformist's Memorial (2nd edn, London, 1802), III, 483–90; M.H.Lee, *Diaries and Letters of Philip Henry* (London, 1882); DNB; DWB; and bibliography appended to these works. One further snippet of information may be added. In October 1660 Henry was presented at the Great Sessions for not reading the Book of Common Prayer since 24 June 1660 (NLW, MS. Wales 4, 986/1; Wales 4, 986/2). The people whom he mentions were: Daniel Matthews, his father-in-law (but whom he describes simply as 'father' in the diary), died on 17 January 1667 and was buried at Hanmer Parish Church; Daniel's daughter, Katherine, was born 25 March 1629 and died 25 May 1707 and married Philip Henry on 26 April 1660. Sir Thomas Hanmer (d. 1678) was a luke-warm royalist (v., DWB, s.n. 'Hanmer', and Sir John Hanmer, *Occasional Notes ... for a Memorial of the Parish of Hanmer in Flintshire* (Westminster, 1871)); Richard Steele (d. 16 November 1692, aged 64) was the ejected vicar of Hanmer (v., E. Calamy, *An Account of the Ministers ...* (London, 1713), II, 708–9); William Bruce was the ejected curate of Marbury, Whitchurch (v., CR); Lieut. Ralph Weld, a Presbyterian, was churchwarden at Wrexham Parish Church and left Henry a legacy of £5 (v., A. N. Palmer, *A History of the Older Nonconformity of Wrexham* (Wrexham, 1888), 7 and *History of the Parish Church of Wrexham* (Wrexham, 1886), 87, n. 16); John Hanmer was a signatory of *The Word for God* and Puritan incumbent of Llanfihangel y Creuddyn, Cardiganshire, which he lost in 1658 for an unknown reason (v., Thomas Richards, *Religious Developments in Wales* (London, 1923), 224; Dr Henry Bridgeman (1615–82), dean of Chester from 13 July 1660 and bishop of Sodor and Man, 1671 (v., DNB); Richard Taylor (d. 1697), ejected from Holt (v., *Y Cofiadur*, 31 (1962, 82–3); John Adams (d. 1670), ejected between October 1661 and August 1662, (v., CR); Richard Hilton was Henry's successor; Brian Walton (1600?–61) was consecrated bishop of Chester on 2 October 1660 and died 29 November 1661 (v., DNB); Edward Bold was presented to Hawarden, 30 November 1646, and died in 1655 (v., Richards, *Developments*, 480); for Judge John Puleston (1583?–1659), v., DWB, s.n. 'Puleston (Family)'; John Broster was ejected from Penley before October 1660 but conformed later (v., *Y Cofiadur*, 31 (1962), 13.

23 [August 1661] Two great concernm^{ts} of mine are now upon ye wheel, one in reference to my mayntenance for time past, the other in ref. to my Continuance for time to come, lord, bee my Friend in both, but of the two rather in the later.

24. This day compleats the thirtieth year of my Age; so old & no older Alexander was when hee had conquer'd ye great world, & I have not yet conquer'd the little world, myself – so old Christ was w^n hee began to preach, & according to ye present face of th. I am now as if I had done preaching, many of greater grace & gifts then I, are layd aside already, and when my turn comes, I know not, the will of ye lord bee done, hee can doe his work without us.

25. Common-prayer tendered, God knows how loth I am to goe off my station, but I must not sin agt. my conscience. many hearers from Wrexham, a welch-man sent to Bangor to read Common-prayer.

27. I went to Whitch. & thence to Ash where I stay'd all night & was much made of, Offence taken at Mr. Hanmer saying more y^{en} needed about Conformity, hee shall bee Lot's wife to mee.

28. I cal'd at Brunnington in my return home, my father seemes to have little care of us or our Concernments, God grant wee may never stand in need of him.

29. Mr. Bruce after great professions, and high expressions to ye contrary, I heare is reordayned, hath subscrib'd & reads – wherefore let him that thinkes hee stands, take heed lest hee fall – I conceive want & Freinds were urgent with him, which are trying, lord keep mee in the critical timee – Marg^t the daughter of Richard ye Clerck, sick, I pray'd for her & by her, but shee hardly understood mee through extremity. I know not how to deal with persons in sickness, lord help mee.

31. Studying day, peace without disturbance, health without Sicknes, and many many mercyes vouchsafed, blessed bee ye name of ye lord.

24. Sister Mary went to Chester to a Shirurgion, having a sore foot bitten with a leech. [24 follows 31 in the MS.]

September 3. The Clerk's daughter buryed. They first carry'd her into ye Church, whereuon I went away, judging it my duty not to Countenance them in superstitious vanityes, afterw, y^ey bury'd her, then I spake to ye people, witnessing agt w^t they had done, Those that were present, were divided, pro & con, the refuse, rabble for it, the sober serious persons of ye place agt it, it raysd a great dust for ye time, & it may bee I shall hear of it again, but my own heart condemns mee not.

4. Mr. Thomas from Tilstock, Mr. Ralph Weld from Wrexham came to see mee. Mr. Bridg & Mr. Hanmer were on y^eir way but fearing where no fear was, return'd again.

7. I met uncle Burroughs at Brunnington who gave me some light ref. to my suit, tis seldom I goe from home on Saturday, but my work, blessed bee God, was in some good forwardnes before. About this time Mr.John Puleston dy'd having wasted away his body upon his lusts, lord, let those that remayn behind take warning. hee left Edw. his heir.

8. This morning I verily thought, I should have been hindred from preaching but was not, the lord heard prayers. Dr. Bridgman sent mee a prohibition from ye Chancelour, to peruse, upon complaint from Sr Tho. Hanmer, ye fanatiques from Wrexham flockt hither, but twas not publisht, Mr. Taylor hindred at Holt, Mr. Adams at Penley, lord, think of ye vineyard. They took ye Cushion from mee but ye Pulpit was left, blessed bee God.

10. I was at Chester, confer'd with D^r Br [idgman], gave him what light I could touching Worthenb[ury] affayres hoping it may bee a meanes to keep him from agreeing wth Mr. P[uleston] there being possibility nay probability of recovering the Tithes another way with the house & £250. left by will for the finishing of it for I well know w^n y^ey agree it must bee upon condition of my removal, which I am labouring agt if possible, to prevent it, not for my own but Worthenb. sake. After I was gone Sr Tho. Hanmer & Mr. P. came & with Mr. Harper, y^ey concluded, as I heard afterw. that D^r Br. should remove mee by ye 1st of Novemb, next & that hee should have all ye Tithes to Bangor to him & his successors, & mutual bonds were given of £500. for p.formance of Articles. Mr. P. promising withal, that whatsoever his father had done for ye church besides, by will or otherw. hee would confirm & make good for which no thankes to him if done before – Thus hath D^r Br. rendered mee evil for good, lord, lay it not to his Charge.

11. Dr Bryan Walton B^p came to Chester.

12. Family humiliation.

16. I went to Chester where I tarry'd 4 dayes, it being assize week hoping for a tryal with Mr. P. but miss'd of it, tis ye first time I ever went to law, wherein though I know noth. by mysf. yet am I not thereby justify'd.

16. [sic]. The sermon before the Judges full of bitternes, from Gen. 49.5.7. the charge full of meeknes & moderation comparatively.

19. D^r Br. first acquainted mee of his agreem^t with Mr. P. wch though it troubled mee for ye present yet upon second thoughts I blessed God for ye good wch I am perswaded hee will fetch to mee out of it in the issue – Amen, so bee it.

20, 21. Cold & Tooth-ake caught at Chester, yet assisted in Study, blessed bee God.

22. Mr. Taylor restor'd to Holt by^e B^p who barkes not bec. hee cannot bite – lord, stir up thy strength & come & help us, in vain is Salvation hoped for from ye hills & from ye mountaynes.

Bishops restor'd by proclamation in Scotland, contrary to the solemn league & Covenant, as the Scots say: the lord is Judge.

23. I went to Bronnington wth my dearest, my Fathers countenance is not towards us. I pray God wee may bee in nothing wanting in our Duty to him, & let the lord work his will with us.

24, 25. I was not well of ye cold, sickness doth not, as it should, make mee more fervent & earnest but rather more remiss in secret dutyes, ye reason is, tis not extremity, lord, sanctify every twig of thy rod, and let all th. work together for my spiritual & eternal advantage.

26, 27. Somewhat better, blessed bee God. I count it a great mercy, that w^n the sun sets, there is a moon to rise to p.form duty in the Family.

An order was brought to mee to bee publisht inhibiting Strangers from coming hither to church, but I publisht it not, lord provide for poor Congregations, that are as sheep without a shepheard.

30. Upon this day 8. year, I came first to Emeral, since which time I have past through variety of providences, both mercyes & crosses, wherewith the lord hath exercised mee. Many dangers I have been deliver'd from, both in my inward & outward man, and many Comforts & benefits I have receiv'd and enjoy'd, several wayes, but my returns have not been answerable, father forgive mee, and lay not my sin, my sin to my charge – A falling out in London for precedency betw. French & Spanyards, some kild, more wounded , – 4. I borrowed £10. of Mr. Steel for ye charges of my suit, which I repay'd *Oct*. 17.

October 1. Mr. Tho. Bold, son to Mr. Bold late of Hard. came to see mee, to w^m I gave the best directions I could in his studyes & desire of God that hee may rise up in his Fathers place, a useful, faithful, instrum^t in ye house of God in his generation.

2. I went to Wrexham, heard of ye death of Mr. Vaughan of Cludyatt, a great & rich man, but a leper, & his name will rott.

4. I went to Chester, took a copy of the articles betw. Dr. Br. & Mr. Pu. which it may bee may stand mee in some stead hereafter. Hee hath merely betrayed mee, lord lay it not to his charge, I searcht in ye office after a presentm^t this last Assize

but there was none of mee but of Mr. Steel y^er was for not reading the book of Common Prayer.

7. Mr. Adams of Penley came to see mee, God hath done well for that poor place, imploying first Mr. Broster & now him amongst them, I hope not in vayn

8. I preacht the third donative sermon of Mr. Broughton, for which I received ten Shillings – Text. Luk. 19.41. when hee was come near hee beheld the City and wept over it – It is a grief of heart to J.X^t to see the misery and danger of poor impenitent sinners.

10. Wee kept a day of Private prayer and humiliation in the family, & the lord was with us – this Confession much affected mee, that things are not so amongst us As they should bee amongst those that are the Relations of a minister of J.X^t. lord, pardon & grant for time to come it may bee better.

14. D^r Br. was at Worthenb. saw the house, gave mee fair words, but intends my removal to gratify Mr. Pu. malice & his own profit, now ye lord the God of the Spirits of all flesh get a man over the Congregation.

15. Upon ye evening of this day, Dr. Bernard, Parson of Whitchurch, dyed, it seemes suddenly, the lord provide for that people

17. I was cited to appear at ye B^ps court as upon this day, but went not; my fault was hindring the publishing of the Deans Order for hindring Strangers, if I had hindred it, it had been a small fault, but I did not, only refused to publ. it my self.

19. Day of preparation for the sacrament I preacht from 2 Chr. 30.18 &c. the good lord pardon – full of feares, lest wee bee hindered, & lest someth. fall betw. the cup and the lip, for our adversaryes bite the lip at us.

20. Through the good hand of our God upon us wee have this day enjoyd one sweet sacrament more – They did all ye hindrance they could, bringing a Corps to bee bury^ed just after the sermon, the grave near ye very place where the Communion table should have stood, & after all a Quaker, brother to the party bury'd, spoke, saying, holy men of God never us'd to preach by the hour-glass & more to that purp. which was a design from Satan to discompose us, but notwithst. afterwa. wee proceeded & had liberty, blessed bee God – ye young man bury'd was son to Tho. Andrewes, servant to Sr John Hanmer, who upon this day fortnight was at Worthhenb. Church, this day sennight at Worthenb. Alehouse & this day in his grave, hee dy'd suddenly – Robert Yale presented hims^f to ye Sacramen [sic] but was not with mee before, yet I gave it to him, in regard hee hath been a Communicant at Bangor with Mr. Fogg & I believe hath knowl: &c.

21. I was not well in ye evening of this day, & thought, it may bee tis death

22. At Bangor I had a discharge from D^r Br. after ye next Sabbath, I spake with Sr Tho, Hanmer about my charge in ye Militia, tis no matter how little I deal in ye world, for I know not how. the lord make mee wise for heaven wch is ye best wisedom.

23. I went to Whitch, with my dear, where wee discharg'd our scores, visited o^r friends & return'd in safety, blessed bee God.

24. D^r Br. came to Worthenb. sent for mee to ye Governo^rs & before a Rable there again repeated & read over my discharge, the circumst. whereof, place, maner, witnesses somew^t griev'd mee, hee cal'd it peevishnes, I justify not mys^f.

lord lay not my sin to my charge, nor his sin to his

25. I heard, Sr Tho. Hanmer was fallen sick. rejoice not w^n thine enemy falleth

26. help vouchsafed in study, to God bee Glory.

27. Farewel-sermons – Text Phil. 1.27 my desire was to profit rather y^{en} to affect. it fell out, wee just finisht ye Catechism this day – ye lord ye God of ye spirits of all flesh, set a man over ye Congregation – I trust twill turn to ye futherance of ye Gosp.

28. Mr. Pu. warn'd mee out of ye house, I took time to consider.

29. Several were with mee to Advise about Com. Pr. – lord, shew thy people what thy will is.

30. I visited Richard Griffith, Clerk, sick, but could fasten noth. on him to doe him good.

31. Colkins – alias, ignes fatui.

November 1. I went to Chester, Chiefly to advise about my lease, Mr. Ratcl. thinkes it will not hold. if I am legally discharg'd from Worthenb. to advise also about coming to hear Common Prayer. A new snare is layd for y^{os} few Minist^{rs} y^t remayn in places & are faithful, y^{ey} are requir'd to publish an Act, wherein ye Covenant is declar'd an unlawful Oath & ye long Parliam^t nullify'd, wch many stick at, lord, break snares.

2. I return'd home, Mr. Hilton my successo^r with mee, endeavouring to possess him with right thoughts of his work here – this morning, ye old Clerk dy'd, mee thinks tis somew^t remarkable y^t hee & I should have our dismission together, only hee by death & I in another way.

3. Mr. Hilton preacht, well – read Com.Pr. which was bad, bury'd after ye mode which was worse – I think wee ought in our Place to witness agt. y^{es} Corrup. but not theref. to separate from Gods publique worship ...

Document IV.6

Robert Collins: Prepare for Suffering

The preacher was Robert Collins (1633–98), rector of Talaton, Devon, ejected in 1660 when the sequestered rector was restored. For an account of his own sufferings under persecution, v., Calamy, *An Account of the Ministers* ..., 2 vols (London, 1713), and for further personal details, v., C.R.

This extract is from *A Compleat Collection of Farewel Sermons* (London, 1663), 277–8.

Arm your selves with Resolutions to suffer for the faith of the Gospel, and for the wayes of Jesus Christ; As you should love the truth above your lives, so labour to be made willing for to part with life, estate, liberty, any thing for to keep the wayes of Jesus Christ. It is not the honour of the Gospel of Christ to hear Christians to break out into murmurings, passions, discontents, contentions that are carnal and sinful; your work is, humbly, meekly, and patiently to lie under the hands of God, and under the hand of man too; that becomes Christians. Suffering is that that will restore the glory of Religion, that will keep the truth delivered to you, that will honour the Cause of Christ best of all: ... You have the glorious commendation of the Lord Jesus Christ upon this account, that he gave a free and full account of the Doctrine of his Father, and of his glorious person, before *Pontius Pilate*, a bloudy Persecutor. It was not by saying to his Disciples *Fight*, nor by saying *My Kingdom is not of this world*, but he gave a glorious confession before the face of *Pilate*, of the righteousness of his Truth, Doctrine, Gospel, and of his Person. Fear to ensnare the freedom of the Truth with your own Liberty; do not ensnare it to your own lusts, not to the will of any man; Oh, that we could study, and improve these Scriptures more! it would make us fear God more, and man less. This is that that would make us to say, as holy *David* did, *Psal.* 119.161. *Princes have persecuted me without a cause, but my heart standeth in awe of thy word*: for he that hath the most fear on you, and upon you, you will be more afraid to fall into his hands. It is a childish thing for a Christian to tread down the belief of any Doctrine, or practise any Worship for fear of man, who hath no more power to hurt us, than we give him our selves by our fear; *Fear not him that can but kill the body, &c*. It was the way of Gods people formerly, that they came to divide between duty commanded by God, and commanded by man. You may read in all the dayes of Antichrists persecution, from the beginning they came to divide in matter of obedience to God and his truth; and worship and obedience to man. Christians! nothing but a suffering spirit will help you to this, for there is no other way of Obedience in this case to Authority, but to suffer under it Meekly, Patiently, as Lambs: This made the three children to divide between the command of the King, and the command of God: What sayes *Nebuchadnezzar*? *Every knee that bowes not, shall be cast into the Furnace:* Very well. *As for that matter*, say they, *O King, we are not careful to answer thee; for we will not bow down, &c*. What, will they not obey him? Yet they will obey him by suffering, as becomes Christians, and is the example of Christ; as if they should say, truly we are terrified with the burning Furnace, but we are terrified with Hell too; We are terrified by the threats of the great King, and we are likewise terrified with the threats of the great God: He is able to deliver us out of your torments: You are not able to deliver us from his torments: So in the Case of *Daniel*: Arm your selves with this Resolution of suffering, and lying down patiently and meekly under those things that you cannot do, so that God may be honoured by your holy resolution upon this account: For truly you never do contend successfully for the Faith of the Gospel, till you contend by suffering; for it is said, They overcame by the blood of the Lamb: You never make Religion your business, till the World see you can let such great things goe, as Life, Estate, Liberty, to keep it: Then Wisdom is justified of her Children. You never glorifie the truths of God so much by practice, or writing, as by suffering for them. Those glorious truths against Popish Justification, mixing of Works and Faith, *Transubstantiation*, *Purgatory*, *Idol-worship*, against all those things that were super added, contrary to Gods Justification, there is such a glory upon the truths, that it is hard for the Popish power ever to darken them again, because we see them written in the honourable and blessed scarrs of the Witnesses, and burnings of those glorious Martyrs. If you would take one another by the hand, when God takes away our faithful Guides, and say, Brethren, Sisters, Friends, come let us hold together; there's no way in the world to hold on together like suffering; for the Gospel really would get more advantage by the holy, humble sufferings of one gracious Saint, meerly for the word of righteousness, then by ten thousand Arguments used against Hereticks, and false worship ...

Document IV.7

Joseph Alleine: Be Resolute!

This extract is from the 'Christian Letters', pp. 8–9, appended (with separate paging) to *The Life and Death of that Excellent Minister of Christ Mr. Joseph Alleine* (London, 1672). He was indicted at the Quarter Sessions, 14 July 1663, and continued in prison until 20 May 1664. For Alleine (1634–68), assistant at St Mary Magdalene, Taunton, ejected in 1660, v., also CR.

To my dearly beloved the Flock of Christ in Taunton, Grace and Peace

... Now, Brethren, is the time when the Lord is like to put you upon trial; now is the hour of temptation come. Oh! be faithful to Christ to the death, and he shall give you a Crown of life...

Let not, my dear Brethren, let not the present Tribulations or those imending, move you. This is the way of the Kingdom: Persecution is one of your Land-marks: Self denial and taking up the Cross is your A B C of Religion; you have learnt nothing that have not begun at Christs-Cross. Brethren, the Cross of Christ is your Crown; the reproach of Christ is your riches; the shame of Christ is your glory; the damage attending strict and holy diligence, your gr eatest advantage; Sensible you should be of what is coming, but not discouraged; humbled, but not dismayed; having your hearts broken, and yet your spirits unbroken; humble your selves mightily under the mighty hand of God; but fear not the face of man: may you ever be low in humility, but high in courage: little in your own apprehensions of your selves, but great in holy fortitude, resolution and holy magnanimity, lying in the dust before your God, yet triumphing in faith and hope, and boldness and confidence over all the power of the enemies. Approve your selves as good Souldiers of Jesus Christ, with *No Armour*, but that of righteousness; *No weapons* but strong crying and tears; looking for no Victory but that of Faith; nor hoping to overcome, but by patience.

Share my loves among you, and continue your earnest prayers for me, and be you assured that I am and shall be through Grace, a willing thankful Servant of your Souls concernments.

From the common Gaole *Joseph Alein*
May 28, 1663

Document IV.8

Calamy's Sufferers

The following examples of Nonconformist sufferings during the period of persecution are selected from Edmund Calamy's book, *An Account of the Ministers, Lecturers, Masters and Fellows of Colleges and Schoolmasters, who were Ejected or Silenced after the Restoration in 1660. By, or before the Act of Uniformity* (2nd edn, London, 1713), II. The extracts describe the cases of the following: (a) Robert Atkins (d. 28 March 1685, aged 59), rector of St John's, Exeter; deprived by bishop's sentence, 23 September 1662; (b) George Hughes (d. 3 July 1667), vicar of St Andrew's, Plymouth; ejected in August 1662 as related below; (c) Robert Collins (1633–6 March 1698), rector of Talaton, Devon; ejected 1660; (d) Humphrey Philips (died 'very aged' on 27 March 1707); ejected as an assistant at Sherburne, Dorset, after previously losing his fellowship at Magdalen College, Oxford, in 1660; (e) Samuel Shaw (c. 1637–96), rector of Long Whatton, Leics.; ejected 1661; and (f) Thomas Worts (d. March 1697), rector of Banningham, Norfolk; ejected 1660. More information about the men mentioned is to be found under their names in A. G. Matthews, *Calamy Revised* (Oxford, 1934). For Thomas Lamplugh, bishop of Exeter 1676–88, and John Greville (1628–1701), created earl of Bath on 20 April 1661 and appointed governor of Plymouth the following month, v., DNB. For Obadiah Hughes (1639–24 January 1705), Nicholas Sherwill (d. 1696), Samuel Martyn (d. 1693), v., Matthews, *Calamy Revised*.

(a) Robert Atkins

Some of the Magistrates of the City of *Exon* [Exeter], who were very severe against other Dissenting Ministers, yet favour'd and conniv'd at him. Three meetings were taken in his House, the Names of many taken; yet neither he nor the House Fin'd. One Mayor and Justice who were far more Busy than their Brethren, Fin'd his House Twenty Pounds, (tho' the People were not found in his, but in a Neighbour's House) Hereupon they came and broke up his Doors, to Distrain for the Fine: But finding his Books, and best Goods remov'd, they seiz'd on him, who was very ill of the Gout; brought him down from his warm Chamber in a Chair into his Court; expos'd him for some Hours to the cold Air, (by which his Health was much impair'd,) and made his *Mittimus*, to send him to Prison, for this Fine. Of all the great Multitude which were gather'd about his House upon this Occasion, the Mayor and Justice could not either by Promises or Threats, get any to carry him to Prison. At length some of his Friends paid his Fine ... One of his Hearers was Prosecuted in the Spiritual Court for having his Child Baptiz'd by a Nonconformist. When Dr. *Lamplugh*, late Archbishop of *York*, then Bishop of *Exon*, understood that Mr. *Atkins* had Baptiz'd it; he put a stop to the Proceedings of the Court, dismiss'd the Man without paying any Costs, and spake very honourably of Mr. *Atkins*, for his Learning and Moderation. [p. 216]

(b) George Hughes

After a long Calm he had enjoy'd for 18 Years, Commissioners came down to

Plymouth in *August*, 1662, and after they had put out all the Magistrates of the Town except one, the same Day summon'd Mr. *Hughes* before them, and told him, *he was dismiss'd from his Ministry at* Plymouth. Not content to let him die with his Brethren on the fatal *Bartholomew*, they silenc'd him a week before. He continu'd in the Town after his Ejectment, which could not be born where he was so much esteem'd, and therefore he was summon'd with his Assistant and Brother-in-law Mr. *Thomas Martin*, his Son Mr. *Obadiah Hughes*, and Mr. *Nicholas Sherwill*, to appear before the *Earl of Bath*, Governor of *Plymouth*. However they were not suffer'd to see the Earl, but committed by the Deputy-Lieutenants of the County, tho' nothing was objected against them. Mr. *Hughes* senior and Mr. *Martin* were sent with two Files of Musqueteers to St. *Nicholas* Island. Mr. *Hughes* junior, Mr. *Sherwill*, and others were confin'd at *Plymouth*. The latter were first set at Liberty, but on condition they should not return to *Plymouth* without leave of the *Earl* of *Bath*, or his Deputy. The old Gentleman and Mr. *Martin* remain'd in the Island 9 Months, till at length his Health being much impair'd, and his Legs grown black and swoln, and an incurable Dropsy and Scurvy contracted, (which was occasion'd as is suppos'd by the Saltness of the Air,) he was offer'd his Liberty upon Condition of giving Security of £2000 not to live within 20 Miles of *Plymouth*. Which was accordingly done by his Friends without his Knowledge. Whereupon he retir'd to *King's-bridge* in *Devonshire*. There he still continu'd in great Weakness to study hard, and spend his Time in private Devotion, and most holy Counsels and Conferences with the many pious Friends that came to visit him ... [pp. 224–5]

(c) Robert Collins

After his Ejectment, he liv'd at *Ottery St. Mary*, about 3 Miles off, where he had an Estate of about £100 *per An.* upon which he subsisted very comfortably. He was much respected by the good People of the Town and the Places adjacent; who usually attended on his Ministry in the publick Church, and were now desirous to have the Benefit of his Labours in a more private Way. He preach'd therefore to such as desir'd his Assistance in his own House, between the Forenoon and Afternoon Service; and usually with his own Family attended the publick Worship in the Afternoon. He liv'd very peaceably till the Conventicle Act took Place: But then his House was on the Lord's Day surrounded with the Officers and the vilest Rabble of the Town; who not daring to break open the Doors, till they had got a Warrant from a neighbouring Justice, they kept the Congregation Prisoners till Night when the Warrant came. When the Doors were open'd the People were uncivilly treated by the Gentlemen, and the Rabble that attended them. Getting the Names of whom they pleas'd, and taking some into Custody, Warrants were issued out for levying £20 on Mr. *Collins* for Preaching, and £20 for his House, and 5*s*. on each of the Hearers, tho' there was no Proof that there was any Preaching or Praying at all; And tho' they fin'd Mr. *Collins* £20 for his House, yet it deserves a Remark that there was no Person found there, but in a neighbour's House adjoining. After this follow'd breaking open of Houses and Shops, taking away

Goods and Wares, forcing open Gates and breaking Bars, and driving off Cattle, and exposing them to Sale, for the raising of the Fines, which was an affecting Sight. Many were depriv'd of what they could but ill spare from their numerous and necessitous Families. Sometime after this, upon a Lord's Day, in which not so much as any Prayers were read in the publick Church, Mr. *Collins* open'd his Doors to all Comers, that as many as his House would well contain might have an Opportunity of worshipping God, at a Time when they could not do it any where else. Within a few Days, a Justice of the Neighbourhood sent for two poor Men who had been at the Meeting, to come to his House, and requir'd them to inform him who preach'd, and what were the Names of the Hearers. They desir'd to be excused: But he threaten'd them with the Goal [sic], and order'd their *Mittimus* to be made; which so affrighted them, that they told all that they knew; declaring at the same Time their Dissatisfaction at the Constraint which they were under. Mr. *Collins* was hereupon fin'd £40 for himself, and £40 for his House; and his Hearers 10*s*. and 5*s*. a-piece, at their pleasure; and Warrants were issu'd out accordingly, and many Goods were distrain'd; some of which were never redeem'd: And no account was given to the Crown, but what was rais'd, was profusely spent in their Clubs. While the Money lasted, the Meeting was undisturb'd: But when the Stock was out, they again surrounded Mr.*Collins's* House on the Lord's Day, and broke open the Doors, and offer'd many Abuses; and took the Names of the Persons present. At the next Quarter-Sessions they indicted Mr. *Collins*; and about 30 of his principal Hearers for a Riot. They hereupon applying to Council, were advis'd to get a *Certiorari*, to remove the Cause, which was accordingly done: But when it was produc'd at an Adjournment of the Quarter-Sessions, and read, it was found to be Dated the 32nd Day of the Month, and therfore thrown aside; and all the Persons concern'd who were order'd to be present, were commanded to be taken into Custody. But they could seize upon only one, the rest making their Escape. Another *Certiorari* was procur'd afterwards, and so the Cause was remov'd to an higher Court; where after a great deal of Money spent, the Busniess was quash'd, and the poor People deliver'd to their great Joy. However the Neighbouring Gentlemen still went on to attack the Meeting, but were often disappointed. For the People were either separated before they came, or so dispers'd that they could not find them. Whereupon they reso[l]v'd to take up Mr. *Collins*, and send him to Prison, upon the Act of 23 *Eliz.* for £20 a Month, for not coming to Church. A Warrant was accordingly granted, which the Constables resolv'd to execute at the Funeral of one Mrs. *Wyat*, a Relation of Mr.*Collins's*, concluding that he would be there. He was there according to their Expectation, and as the Corpse went along by the High-Constable's Door, in whose House the Petty Constables were met, they spy'd him, and flew upon him like so many Tygers, and carry'd him away, tho' £1000 Bail was offer'd for him. They kept him *in salva Custodia* several Days, and then carry'd him before the Justices, who met on purpose, and they sent him to the high Goal at *Exon*, whither more than an Hundred of his Hearers accompany'd him on Horseback; and he was confin'd 6 Months. 'Tis observable that the High-Constable, in whose House the Petty Constables met, was then at *Exon*: And on the very Day Mr. *Collins* was seiz'd, was taken sick, and dy'd on the Lord's Day following. This was the more taken Notice of, because he was one of the greatest Enemies that Dissenters had in the Town. And yet the poor People were presented at almost every Quarter-Sessions, Privy-Sessions, or Monthly Meeting of the Justices, for many Years together. Some were prosecuted on the Act for £20 a Month, and others excommunicated, to their great Charge and Damage: And they could have no settled Rest till the Toleration.' [pp. 251–2]

(d) Humphrey Philips

'Being turn'd out by the [University] Visitors after the Restauration, he retir'd to *Sherborn*, where he had been Two Years before Assistant to Mr. *Bampfield*. There he was useful to many, and very successful till the *Uniformity Act* took place on *Bartholomew*-day; and then both Mr. *Bampfield* and he preach'd their Farewel Sermons, and the Place was a *Bochim*. However, they did not leave their People, but preach'd to such as would hear them in an House, till they were apprehended and sent to an Inn, which was made a Prison for them and Twenty of their principal Hearers; which put them to a considerable Charge. They were bound over to the next Quarter-Sessions, and to their good Behaviour in the meantime. When they understood that the good Behaviour was dsign'd to be an Obligation not to Preach, they openly renounc'd it, and went on with their Work. Being at Liberty, they went to Mr. *Thomas Bampfield*'s at *Dunkerton* near *Bath*, where they preach'd at first to a small Number, but it increas'd gradually. They were often threatned. but not discourag'd. After some time Mr. *Francis Bampfield* was apprehended in *Dorsetshire*, and sent to *Dorchester* Goal, where he continu'd Nine Years. Mr. *Thomas Bampfield*, and Mr. *Philips* now his Chaplain, were also sent to *Ilchester* Goal. Mr. *Bampfield* return'd Home in a Months time; but Mr. *Philips*, after Eleven Months Confinement, was brought from Prison in the depth of Winter, and a snowy Time, to the Assizes at *Wells*, where he met with hard Usage, being put into a Chamber like *Noah's Ark*, full of all sorts of Creatures, and put into a Bed with the *Bridewell*-Keeper, where the Sheets were wet, and clung to his Flesh. The Justice who committed him, gave him hard Language: But the Judge discharg'd him; he having satisfy'd the Law. Whilst he was in Prison, there was another Disturbance at Mr. *Thomas Bampfield*'s by one of *Bath*, who searching after his Inkhorn to take Names, having a Pistol in his Pocket ready cockt, shot himself in the Thigh, which endanger'd his Life, and made him miserable all his Days. Mr. *Philips* having his Liberty, went over to Holland ... Upon his return to *England*, he went back again to *Dunkerton*, where he continu'd to Preach with good Success, tho' he met with great Difficulties, especially from Mr. *Bampfield* and his Brother, who espous'd the *Seventh-day-Sabbath* ... [pp. 259–61]

(e) Samuel Shaw

'I have known him ... spend part of many Days and Nights too in Religious Exercises, when the times were so dangerous that it would hazard an Imprisonment, not to be drunk or be in a Bawdy-House or Tavern, but to be worshipping GOD with five or six People, like minded with himself. I have sometimes been in his Company for a whole Night together, when we have been fain to steal to the place in the Dark, stop out the Light, and stop in the Voice, by cloathing, and fast closing the Windows, till the first Day break down the Chimney has given us notice to be gone ...' [p. 435 – part of a letter by an unknown correspondent printed by Calamy]

(f) Thomas Worts

'A great Sufferer for Nonconformity, and a very worthy Man. He was imprison'd by a Writ *de excommunicato capiendo*, taken out *Nov.* 15. 1664; and continued in the Common Goal till *Sept.* 3. 1665, when the Plague was at the Height in *London*. He was made close Prisoner till *November* the 9th, not knowing by whose Order, or for what additional Offence. On *Feb.* 2. he with Six more, was put into the Castle [at Norwich], in a Hole in the Wall, over an Arch, on the *West* Side of the Castle, which had neither Door, Window, nor Chimney. There was Room in a Corner for one Truckle-Bed; the rest lay in Hammocks. The Hole had three Wickets into the Felons Yard, one of which must be open Night and Day, lest they should have been stifled in the Night with the Steam of the Charcoal. For Five Weeks the Door below (for the Hole is about 40 Steps high, up a narrow Passage in the Wall) was kept lock'd Night and Day. The Keeper usually went away about Four of the Clock, with the Key to a Neighbour Village, about a Mile and a half Distance from the head Goaler's House, and return'd not till about Eight in the Morning, in whose Absence none could come to them, whatever Occasion there might be. During those five Weeks, they were not permitted so much as to come out into the Yard. If a Prisoner's Wife came to see him, he was call'd down to the Door, and the Keeper would set his Back against one Side of the Door, and his Foot against the other, and so the Husband and Wife might only see and speak with each other. They had Leave to run up and down Stairs as oft as they would, which was instead of a Walk or Gallery for five Weeks Time. Their Maid was not allow'd to come up with their Provision. After the five Weeks, these Persons were permitted to go into the Castle-Yard, during the Time of their Continuance there, which was about Two Months: And then they were remov'd to another Prison. They were wonderfully preserv'd this Year from the Contagion, which the Arrows of the Almighty fell mortally very near them, on one Side and another, there being only a Lane between, so that they could both hear and see some that were shut up, crying for Bread, and were themselves shut up also, and could not flee, save only to their strong Tower, *the Name of the Lord*, where they found Safety and Peace ... Yet were they preserv'd in that nasty Hole, at whose Wickets came in the odious excrementitious smells of the common Yard of the Felons ... Mr.*Worts* continu'd a Prisoner Seven Years.' [pp. 481–2]

Document IV.9

Persecution and Toleration

From *The Sufferers-Catechism* (1664). There are 44 pages in the book. It bears no name of author nor place of publication but Edward Bagshaw in *The Life and Death of Mr. Vavasor Powell* (London, 1671), 120 attributes it to Powell. He wrote it in Southsea Prison where he and Nathaniel Rich (d. 1701, v., DNB) had been confined since September 1662. It illustrates quite vividly how the experience of persecution compelled a change of conviction about toleration. In his *Christ and Moses Excellency* (1650), 179–80, Powell had written, 'The Churches, and Saints of Christ, doe not hold, nor grant a Generall Tolleration ... therefore let them [the Presbyterians] not father that *falshood* upon *Independents* (so called) that they are for a Tolleration of all *Sects* and *Opinions*, whereas they plead onely for such as are truely consciencious ...'. Those that stray from the paths of orthodoxy are to be excommunicated from the churches and left 'to the Civill Magistrate'. The appreciative references to Barrow, Greenwood and Penry are rare in later Puritan literature. As a native of Radnorshire, Powell would doubtless have a special interest in Penry. Henry Barrow and John Greenwood were executed at Tyburn on 6 April 1593 (v., DNB, s.n., Barrow, Henry) but John Penry was executed at St Thomas a Watering in south London on 29 May 1593 (v., William Pierce, *John Penry* (London, 1923), 480. The place is identified by Peter Heylin in *Aerius Redivivus: A History of the Presbyterians* (Oxford, 1670), 325). See also, R. Tudur Jones, 'The Sufferings of Vavasor' in Mansel John (ed.), *Welsh Baptist Studies* (Cardiff: South Wales Baptist College, 1976), 77–91.

[p. 3] Quest. 7. *Why are all the godly to expect sufferings and persecutions?*
Because it is one of the wayes that God hath appointed to do them good by; it is food to feed them; a school to teach them; water to cleanse them; fire to purify them; a hedge, and a wall, to keep them from their sins; and a means to help them to be partakers of his holiness ...

[p.5] Quest. 15. *Is it the revealed will of God the Father, and of Christ, that any should be persecuted or destroyed, for Religion or Conscience sake?*
Answ. No surely. See *Job.* 19.22.28, *Psal.* 69.25 and 109.16. *Mat.* 7.12. *Acts* 7.52.

Quest 16. *How doth that further appear?*
Answ. 1. Because it is contrary to the nature and behaviour of God and Christ, who are gracious, merciful, patient, and long-suffering to the worst of men, much more to the Righteous, *Job* 33.24.25 [p. 6] *Jonah* 4.2. *Mat.* 5.45. *Luke* 6.35.36. *Rom.* 2.4. I *Tim*.2.4.
2. Because it is contrary to the end of Christs coming into the world, who came to save mens lives, and not to destroy them, *Luke* 9.56. I *Tim*.1.13.
3. Because persecution for Religion is a sin, therefore it is contrary, and not according to the revealed will of God; See *Mat.* 5.12. *Luke* 11.9. I *Cor* 15.49. *Gal* 1.12. I *Tim* 1.13.

4. Because that persecuting the Saints and Servants of God, and of Christ, for Religion, is to persecute God and Christ himself, 2 *Kings* 19.6. *Psal.* 83.5 & 21.11. *Isa.* 37.28. *Ezek.* 35.13. *Zech.* 2.8. *Acts* 9.5. I *Cor.* 8.12. 2 *Cor.* 1.5. *Col.* 1.24.

5. Because Christ hath commanded, that the Tares should grow together in the field (or World) with the Wheat, until the Harvest. *Mat.* 13.30.

6. Because it is contrary to the Law of nature to do to others what we would not have them do to us, *Mat.* 7.12. *Luke* 6.35.

7. Because it doth arrogate a judicial power over the Consciences of men, which is peculiar to Christ alone, and in that sense Saints are the Subjects of Christ only ...

8. Because it is a destructive principle to humane society; for by the same Rule one power or authority may persecute those that will not conform to their Laws; another of contrary judgement may as well persecute them; as *Indians the Turks, and They Christians*; and so among *Christians, Papists Protestants*, and *Protestants Papists*.

9. Because it is a breech of the Law of Love, which commands men to love their Neighbours as themselves ...

10. Because it is the Lord alone that must perswade men to be of the true Religion (if they be in errour) and satisfie doubtful Consciences ...

11. Because every man is to give an account to God for himself, and for his own actions, and not for anothers ...

12. Because to persecute, is to beat their fellow-servants, which Christ doth utterly disallow of ... [p. 7]

13. Because it is the will of Christ, that the Rulers of this World shall be subject to him, and his Kingdome, in spiritual things; and that his people should be obedient to them in all lawful civil things ...

14. Because it is a mark of *Antichrist*, and of the *Whore*, to persecute; and one of the sins for which they are to be destroyed, *Rev.* 13.15, 16 and 18.6, 24.

15. If it be lawful by God's Word to punish for matters of Religion and Conscience, then it is necessary to shew out of the same word, what sorts of erroneous persons are to be punished, and if they do that, and begin with the right persons (which are Idolaters and false Worshipers) then their hands may be first against themselves, and their own friends, and so have enough to do at home.

[p. 11; Why did the people of God suffer in the past?]

For witnessing against the *Bishops*, the *National Church* of *England*, and Ceremonies; as *Greenwood, Barrow, Penry*; and others in Queen Elizabeths dayes.

[pp. 14–15; Among the false charges against the persecuted is the following:]

6. That in their provate Meetings (which they call Conventicles) they did use to put out the Candles, and to commit Adultery, Incest, and other wicked things; and the accusation is above 1500 years old ... and to this day the black-mouth-lying-Devil and his seed, spits out this old stinking falsehood and slander ...

[p. 23; When is it right to escape from prison when committed by lawful authority? Some have escaped in times past.]

The same did one Mr. *Penry* (a Welsh-Minister) in Queen *Elizabeths* dayes, being apprehended by a Pursevant, he desired leave first to pray, which wrought such conviction upon the Pursevant, that he went away to look for others, and left him in his Chamber, giving him an opportunity to escape, but he durst not; but soon after he (and two others) were hanged at *Tybourn*, *viz*. Mr. *Barow* and Mr. *Greenwood*. for witnessing against the Prelates, and their Superstition ...

[p. 25; Suffering 'is the Saints high-way to Heaven']
Christians should be encouraged to suffer because of the Reward, Recompence and Glory, which they shall receive after their sufferings; yea, the more they suffer, the greater will their rewards be ... Is not communion with God the Father, Jesus Christ, and Spirit, and fellowship with an innumerable company of Saints and Angels; Is not a Crown, a Kingdom, a World, a Paradise, Heaven, unspeakable Joy, unconceiveable Pleasures, and unimaginable, unexpressible, everlasting and eternal Glory ... worth the suffering for, or the leaving of a little wordly dust and dirt; undergoing a few months or years imprisonment, or banishment: or a few hours (or perhaps minutes) torment and punishment upon our corrupt flesh and bones?

[pp. 29–30] Quest. 35. What are the duties of suffering Christians towards those that persecute them?
Answ. 1. To love them ... with a love of pitty, and good will to their souls and bodies.
2. To bless them ...
3. To pray for them ...
4. To bear with them patiently, without reviling, reproaching, or threatening them ...
5. To do what good they can unto them ... and especially to their souls, by seeking their conversion.
6. To give them the respect that is due to them according to their Places and Offices ...
7. Not to intend or take revenge upon them, if they are able...
Lastly, To forgive them (as far as they are able) especially if they acknowledge their faults.

[p. 36] Quest. 41. *What are the duties of Christians that do not suffer ... towards those that do?*
Answ. 1. To sympathize with them, and have a fellow-feeling of their sufferings, as members of the same Body, though not of the same visible Congregation, or just of the same Judgement ...

[pp. 38–9; The authorities ought not to persecute:]
Because by your Persecution you encreased the number of Christians ... they grow like the *Camomile*, the more they are trampled upon ...

Document IV.10

The Declaration of Indulgence, 1672

It was not for nothing that Charles had insisted in Clause XVIII of the Conventicle Act 1670 upon his royal supremacy in ecclesiastical affairs. Although his tactics during the years after his restoration were often tortuous, the evidence is strong that he was no persecutor. Several times during those years he had sought to modify the severity of the penal code but without success. With the 1672 Indulgence he took the opportunity to have his own way in the matter of suspending its stipulations. But of course he acted without the consent of Parliament. When that body met on 3 February 1673 its members were furious in their criticism of the King's use of the royal prerogative. In view of such opposition Charles broke the Great Seal on the Declaration on Friday, 7 March 1673. The Indulgence had lasted just one year. But it was a very significant year in the history of Nonconformity. The records produced by the Indulgence revealed the resilience of Nonconformity as well as the failure of persecution to uproot it, as the King admitted. For discussions of its significance, v., in addition to works mentioned below, M. R. Watts, *The Dissenters* (Oxford, 1978), I, 247–50; R. W. Dale, *History of English Congregationalism* (London, 1907), 436–40; R. Tudur Jones, *Congregationalism in England* (London, 1907), 90–4.

The extract is taken from E. Cardwell, *Documentary Annals of the Reformed Church of England* (Oxford, 1839), II, 282–6. It is reproduced in full in Thomas Richards, *Wales under the Indulgence* (London, 1928), 69–71, and A. Browning, *English Historical Documents, 1660–1714* (London, 1953), 387–8. The original is in *State Papers Domestic*, Charles II, vol. 304, no. 1. The voluminous materials produced by the process of applying for licences, both for meeting-places and preachers, and the details of all the licences granted, have been published in full by G. Lyon Turner in his *Original Records of Early Nonconformity under Persecution and Indulgence* (London, 1911, 1914), vol. I, Text; vol. II, Summaries; vol. III, Historical and Expository. See also Frank Bate, *The Declaration of Indulgence (1672): A Study in the Rise of Organised Dissent* (London, 1908).

His Majesty's Declaration to all his Loving Subjects

CHARLES R.

Our care and endeavours for the preservation of the rights and interests of the Church have been sufficiently manifested to the world by the whole course of our government since our happy restoration, and by the many and frequent ways of coercion that we have used for reducing all erring or dissenting persons, and for composing the unhappy differences in matters of religion which we found among our subjects upon our return. But it being evident by the sad experience of twelve years that there is very little fruit of all those forcible courses, we think ourself obliged to make use of that supreme power in ecclesiastical matters which is not only inherent in us but hath been declared and recognized to be so by several statutes and Acts of Parliament ...

And in the first place, we declare our express resolution, meaning and intention to be that the Church of England be preserved and remain entire in its doctrine, discipline and government as now it stands established by law; and that this be taken to be, as it is, the basis, rule and standard of the general and public worship of God ... And further we declare that no person shall be capable of holding any benefice, living or ecclesiastical dignity or preferment of any kind in this our kingdom of England who is not exactly conformable.

We do in the next place declare our will and pleasure to be that the execution of all and all manner of penal laws in matters ecclesiastical, against whatsoever sort of nonconformists or recusants, be immediately suspended, and they are hereby suspended; and all judges, judges of assize and gaol delivery, sheriffs, justices of the peace, mayors, bailiffs and other officers whatsoever, whether ecclesiastical or civil, are to take notice of it, and pay due obedience thereunto.

And that there may be no pretence for any of our subjects to continue their illegal meetings and conventicles, we do declare that we shall from time to time allow a sufficient number of places, as they shall be desired, in all parts of this our kingdom for the use of such as do not conform to the Church of England, to meet and assemble in order to their public worship and devotion, which places shall be open and free to all persons. But to prevent such disorders and inconveniences as may happen by this our indulgence, if not duly regulated, and that they may be the better protected by the civil magistrate, our express will and pleasure is that none of our subjects do presume to meet in any place until such place be allowed and the teacher of that congregation be approved by us.

And lest any should apprehend that this restriction should make our said allowance and approbation difficult to be obtained, we do further declare that this our indulgence, as to the allowance of the public places of worship and approbation of the teachers, shall extend to all sorts of nonconformists and recusants except the recusants of the Roman Catholic religion, to whom we shall in no wise allow public places of worship, but only indulge them their share in the common exemption from the execution of the penal laws, and the exercise of their worship in their private houses only.

And if after this our clemency and indulgence any of our subjects shall presume to abuse this liberty, and shall preach seditiously, or to the derogation of the doctrine, discipline or government of the established Church, or shall meet in places not allowed by us, we do hereby give them warning, and declare we will proceed against them with all imaginable severity. And we will let them see we can be as severe to punish such offenders, when so justly provoked, as we are indulgent to truly tender consciences.

Given at our court at Whitehall,
this 15th day of March,
in the four and twentieth year of our reign.

Document IV.11

1672 Indulgence: Petition and Licence

See G. Lyon Turner, *Original Records* (London, 1911), I, 244. Not all applications were couched in such fulsome terms. Indeed there were many applications submitted through agents who applied for batches of them simultaneously. The abbreviations have been extended but the spelling is unchanged.

The licence granted to Jenkyn (b) is an example of a 'general licence' since he was allowed to preach in any licensed place of worship. Some 'teachers' were permitted to preach only at a specified place or places. For Henry Bennet, 1st earl of Arlington (1618–85), one of King Charles's closest associates, v., DNB. For Jenkyn, ejected vicar of Christ Church, London, who died in 1685, v., CR.

(a) An Example of a Petition for Licences

To the dread Soveraigne Charles the Second by the grace of God King of England Scotland France and Ireland defender of the faith &c

The humble petition of your Majesties Faithfull Subjects in your Citty of Bristoll.

Most humbly sheweth
That with many others of your Majesties true hearted, non-conforming Subjects in England, who in every corner of the Land, doe sing for Joy of heart, wee also some of your Majesties most Faithfull Subjects in Bristoll in the name of many more of our Neighbours doe rise up, and call your Majestie blessed for your unparalelled grace expressed in your declaration of Indulgence to us.

Humbly prayeing your Majestie for the benefit of this gracious Indulgence in your city of Bristoll, and that the house of Mr John Loyde, lyeing on St. James Back in the said Citty may be allowed to Mr John Weekes of the Presbiterian perswasion, whom we have chosen for our Teacher there; for which your Royall grace as wee shall every way be obliged to acquit our selves with such moderation, fidelity, and peaceablenes as never to give your Majestie any cause of offence, soe wee shall continue to pray for your Majesties prosperity in length of dayes, and life for ever more.

John Tucker	Rich. Payne
Michaell Pope	Hugh Whyte
William Salmon	William Willoughby

(b) An Example of a Licence Granted to a Minister

CHARLES &c.
To all Mayors, Bailiffs, Constables & other Our Officers, & Ministers Civill and Military whom it may Concerne, Greeting. In pursuance of Our Declaration of the 15 March 1671/2 Wee doe hereby permit & licence Wm Jenkyn to bee a Teacher

of the Congregation allowed by Us in a Howse or Chamber in Horne Alley in Aldersgate Street London for the use of such as doe not conforme to the Church of England, who are of the Perswasion commonly called Presbyterien. With further licence & permission to him the said Wm Jenkin to teach in any other place licenced by Us according to Our said Declaration. Given at Our Court at Whitehall the 2^d day of Aprill in the 24th yeare of Our Reigne 1672.

By His Maties Command
Arlington

(c) An Example of a Licence Granted for a Place of Worship

CHARLES &c. To all Mayors, Bailiffs, Constables & other Our Officers & Ministers Civill & Military, whom it may concerne, Greeting. In pursuance of Our Declaration of the 15 of March 1671/2 Wee have allowed & Wee hereby allow of a Howse or Chamber in Horn Alley in Aldersgate Street London to be a place for the use of such as doe not conform to the Church of England who are of the Perswasion commonly called Presbyterien to meet & assemble in, in order to their Publick Worship & devotion. And all & singular Our Officers & Ministers Ecclesiasticall, Civill and Military, whom it may concerne, are to take due notice hereof, And they & every of them are hereby strictly charged & required to hinder any Tumult or Disturbance, & to protect them in their said Meetings & Assemblies. Given at &c the 2^d day of Aprill in the 24th yeare of Our Reigne 1672.

By his Maties Command
Arlington

Document IV.12

John Milton: True Religion and Toleration

OF TRUE RELIGION, HÆRESIE, SCHISM, TOLERATION was published in March or April 1673. It is printed, with full annotations, in D. M. Wolfe (ed.), *Complete Prose Works of John Milton* (New Haven, 1982), VIII, 408–40. The page numbers in the above excerpts refer to this reprint. It appeared at a dramatic juncture in religious history. The King's Declaration of Indulgence, suspending the penal laws against Nonconformists, was issued on 15 March 1672. He had done this without the endorsement of Parliament. When it did meet on 4 February 1673 it was not disposed to look favourably on this royal usurpation of its authority in ecclesiastical matters. On 10 February it declared that only by an Act of Parliament could penal laws in matters ecclesiastical be suspended. On 8 March the Declaration was withdrawn. Although the Commons passed an act to remove the penalties for Protestant Nonconformity, it was badly mauled in the Lords and never became law. Unhappily, on 12 March 'An Act for preventing dangers that may happen by Popish Recusants' – usually known as the Test Act – was passed and had the effect of limiting the rights of Nonconformists to contend for public office. This was the political background of Milton's tract *On True Religion*. In it Milton presents the bare minimum of the

Protestant argument for toleration. His polemic against Roman Catholicism was in tune with the anti-Catholic agitation that sprang up with the publication of the King's Declaration of Indulgence. The Declaration did allow Catholic worship in the private houses and that was sufficient to spark off the protests.

[p. 419] True Religion is the true Worship and Service of God, learnt and believed from the Word of God only. No Man or Angel can know how God would be worshipt and serv'd, unless God reveal it: He hath Reveal'd and taught it us in the holy Scriptures by inspir'd Ministers, and in the Gospel by his own Son and his Apostles, with strictest command to reject all other traditions or additions whatsoever ... With good and Religious Reason therefore all Protestant Churches with one consent, and particularly the Church of *England* in Her thirty nine Articles, artic. 6*th*, 19*th*, 20*th*, 21*st* [p. 420] and elsewhere, maintain these two points, as the main Principles of true Religion; that the Rule of true Religion is the Word of God only: and that their Faith ought not to be an implicit faith, that is, to believe, though as the Church believes, against or without express authority of Scripture. And if all Protestants as universally as they hold these two Principles, so attentively and Religiously would observe them, they would avoid and cut off many Debates and Contentions, Schisms and Persecutions, which too oft have been among them, and more firmly unite against the common adversary. For hence it directly follows, that no true Protestant [p. 421] can persecute, or not tolerate his fellow Protestant, though dissenting from him in some opinions, but he must flatly deny and Renounce these two main Principles, whereon true Religion is founded; while he compels his Brother from that which he believes as the manifest word of God, to an implicit faith (which he himself condemns) to the endangering of his Brothers soul, whether by rash belief, or outward Conformity, for *whatsoever is not of Faith, is Sin*.

I will now briefly show what is false Religion or Heresie, which will be done easily: for of contraries the definitions must be contrary. Heresie therefore is a Religion taken up and believ'd from the Traditions of men, and additions to the word of God. Whence also it follows clearly, that of all known Sects, or pretended Religions at this day in Christendom, Popery is the only or the greatest Heresie: and he who is so forward to brand all others for Hereticks, the obstinate Papist, the only Heretick ...

[p. 422] Sects may be in a true Church as well as in a false, when men follow Doctrin too much for the Teachers sake, whom they think almost infallible; and this becomes, through Infirmity, implicit Faith; and the name Sectary pertains to such a Disciple.

Schism is a rent or division in the Church, when it comes to the separating of Congregations; and may also happen to a true Church, as well as to a false; yet in the true needs not tend to the breaking of Communion; if they can agree in the right administration of that wherein they Communicate, keeping their other Opinions to themselves, not being destructive to Faith. The Pharisees and Saduces were two Sects, yet both met together in [p. 423] their common worship of God at *Jerusalem*. But here the Papist will angrily demand, What! Are Lutherans,

Calvinists, Anabaptists, Socinians, Arminians, no Hereticks? I answer, all these may have some errors, but are no Hereticks. Heresie is in the Will and choice profestly against Scripture; error is against the Will, in misunderstanding the Scripture after all sincere endeavours to understand rightly: Hence it was said well by one of the Ancients: 'Err I may, but a Heretick I will not be'. It is a humane frailty to err, and no man is infallible here on earth. But so long as all these profess to set the Word of God only before them as the Rule of faith and obedience; and use all diligence and sincerity of heart, by reading, by learning, by study, by prayer for Illumination of the holy Spirit, to understand the Rule and obey it, they have done [p. 424] what man can do; God will assuredly pardon them, as he did the friends of *Job*, good and pious men, though much mistaken, as there appears, in some points of Doctrin. But some will say, with Christians it is otherwise, whom God hath promis'd by his Spirit to teach all things. True, all things absolutely necessary to salvation: But the hottest disputes among Protestants calmly and charitably enquir'd into, will be found less then such. The Lutheran holds Consubstantiation; an error indeed, but not mortal. The Calvinist is taxt with Predestination, and to make God the Author of sin; not with any dishonourable thought of God, but it may be over zealously asserting his absolute power, not without plea of Scripture. The Anabaptisis accus'd of Denying Infants their right to Baptism: again they say, they deny nothing but what the Scripture denies them. The Arian and Socinian are charg'd to dispute against the Trinity: they affirm to believe the Father, Son, Holy Ghost, according to Scripture, and the Apostolic Creed; as for terms of Trinity, Triniunity, Coessentiality, Tri [p. 425] personality, and the like, they reject them as Scholastic Notions, not to be found in Scripture, which by a general Protestant Maxim is plain and perspicuous abundantly to explain its own meaning in the properest words, belonging to so high a Matter and so necessary to be known; a mystery indeed in their Sophistic Subtilties, but in Scripture a plain Doctrin. Their other Opinions are of less Moment. They dispute the satisfaction of Christ, or rather the word *Satisfaction* as not Scriptural: but they acknowledge him both God and their Saviour. The *Arminian* lastly is condemn'd for setting up free will against free grace; but that Imputation he disclaims in all his writings, and grounds himself largely upon [p. 426] Scripture only. It cannot be deny'd, that the Authors or late Revivers of all these Sects or Opinions, were Learned, Worthy, Zealous and Religious Men, as appears by their lives written, and the same of their many Eminent and Learned followers, perfect and powerful in the Scriptures, holy and unblameable in their lives: and it cannot be imagin'd that God would desert such painful and zealous labourers in his Church, and ofttimes great sufferers for their Conscience, to damnable Errors & a Reprobate sense, who had so often implor'd the assistance of his Spirit; but rather, having made no man Infallible, that he hath pardon'd their errors, and accepts their Pious endeavours, sincerely searching all things according to the rule of Scripture, with such guidance and direction as they can obtain of God by Prayer. What Protestant then who himself maintains the same Principles, and disavowes all implicit Faith, would persecute, and not rather charitably tolerate, such man as these, unless he mean to abjure the Principles of his own Religion? If it be askt how far they should be tolerated? I answer doubtless equally, as being all Protestants; that is on all occasions to give account of their Faith, either by Arguing, Preaching in their several Assemblies, Publick writing, and the freedom of Printing. For if the *French* and *Polonian* Protestants enjoy all this liberty among Papists, much more may a Protestant justly expect it among [p. 427] Protestants; and yet some times here among us, the one persecutes the other upon every slight Pretence.

But he is wont to say, he enjoyns only things indifferent. Let [p. 428] them be still; who gave him authority to change their nature by enjoyning them? If by his own Principles, as is prov'd, he ought to tolerate controverted points of Doctrine not slightly grounded on Scripture, much more ought he not to impose things indifferent without Scripture. In Religion nothing is indifferent, but, if it come once to be Impos'd, is either a command or a Prohibition, and so consequently an addition to the word of God, which he professes to disallow. Besides, how unequal, how uncharitable must it needs be, to Impose that which his conscience cannot urge him to impose, upon him whose conscience forbids him to obey? What can it be but love of contention for things not necessary to be done, to molest the conscience of his Brother, who holds them necessary not to be done? To conclude, let such a one but call to mind his own Principles above mention'd, and he must necessarily grant, that neither can he impose, nor the other believe or obey, ought in Religion, but from the word of God only ...

[p. 429] Let us now enquire whether Popery be tolerable or no. Popery is a double thing to deal with, and claims a twofold Power, Ecclesiastical, and Political, both usurpt, and the one supporting the other.

But Ecclesiastical is ever pretended to Political. The Pope by this mixt faculty, pretends right to Kingdoms and States, and especially to this of *England*, Thrones and Unthrones Kings, and absolves the people from their obedience to them; sometimes interdicts to whole Nations the Publick worship of God, shutting up their Churches: and was wont to dreign away the greatest part of the wealth of this then miserable Land, as part of his Patrimony, to maintain the Pride and Luxury of his Court and Prelates: and [p. 430] now since, through the infinite mercy and favour of God, we have shaken off his *Babylonish* Yoke, hath not ceas'd by his Spyes and Agents, Bulls and Emissaries, once to destroy both King and Parliament, perpetually to seduce, corrupt, and pervert as many as they can of the People ... As for tolerating the exercise of their Religion, supposing their State activities not to be dangerous, I answer, that Toleration is either public or private; and the exercise of their Religion, as far as it is idolatrous, can be tolerated neither way: not publicly, without grievous and unsufferable scandal giv'n to all consciencious Beholders; not privately, without great offence to God, declar'd against all kind of Idolatry, though secret ...

[p. 431] Having shown thus, that Popery, as being Idolatrous, is not to be tolerated either in Public or in Private; it must be now thought how to remove it and hinder the growth thereof ... Are we to punish them by corporal punishment, or fines in their Estates, upon account of their Religion? I suppose it stands not with the Clemency of the Gospel, more then what appertains to the security of the State:

But first we must remove their Idolatry, and all the furniture thereof, whether Idols, or the Mass wherein [p. 432] they adore their God under Bread and Wine ... Let them bound their disputations on the Scripture only, and an ordinary Protestant, well read in the Bible, may turn and wind their Doctors ...

[p. 433] The next means to hinder the growth of Popery will be to read duly and diligently the Holy Scriptures ...

[p. 438] The last means to avoid Popery, is to amend our lives: it is a general complaint that this Nation of late years, is grown more numerously and excessively vitious then heretofore; Pride, Luxury, Drunkenness, Whoredom, Cursing, Swearing, bold and open Atheism every where abounding: Where these grow, no wonder if [p.439] Popery grows a pace ...

[p. 440] Let us therefore using this last means, last here spoken of, but first to be done, amend our lives with all speed; least through impenitency we run into that stupidly, which we now seek all means so warily to avoid, the worst of superstitions, and the heaviest of all Gods Judgements, Popery.

Document IV.13

The Bristol Baptists

The records preserved by the Broadmead Baptist Church, Bristol, provide the fullest account of the life, organisation and trials of a seventeenth-century Dissenting congregation. The records were prepared by Edward Terrill between 1672 and 1678. On 6 April 1666 Terrill, a schoolmaster, was set apart by 'fasting and prayer' as a ruling elder in the church. He died in 1685. The material was edited by Edward Bean Underhill (1813–1901; for whom v., DNB) and published by the Hanserd Knollys Society (which he founded) under the title *The Records of a Church of Christ, Meeting in Broadmead Bristol 1640–1687* (London, 1847) – usually referred to as 'The Broadmead Records'. The numbers appended to the following selections refer to the pages in this volume. New edn, Roger Hayden, *The Records of a Church of Christ in Bristol, 1640–1687* (Bristol, 1974).

The Records list ten persecutions, a number reminiscent of the ten persecutions suffered by the early Church according to the scheme popularised by the early fifth-century historian Orosius. According to the Records the tenth persecution occurred [p. 431] in 1681. In fact, as Terrill's account shows, the congregation suffered incessant harassment from January 1660 to July 1686 but the persistence of the authorities, civil and ecclesiastical, was matched by the steadfastness of the church members. Extract (a) opens with a reference to the second Conventicle Act and the 'Fourth Persecution' refers to the first Conventicle Act of 1664.

Extract (b): For Guy Carleton (1598?–1685), bishop of Bristol, 1671, and of Chichester from 1678, v., DNB. For John Thompson (d. 4 March 1675), John Weeks (d. November 1698, aged 65), and William Troughton (d. 1689), ejected from St Martin's Salisbury in 1660, v., A. G. Matthews, *Calamy Revised* (Oxford, 1934). Thomas Hardcastle, the minister of Broadmead, died in October 1677. For Andrew Gifford, v., J. Ivimey, *A History of the English Baptists* (London, 1811–30), I, 412–14; II, 541–52.

(a)

[pp. 104–5] On the 10th of the third month [May], 1670, the act against conventicles commenced, which was the forfeiture of twenty pounds to be levied on every one that preached, for any one offence, and twenty pounds for the house or ground where we met; and five shillings the first time, and ten shillings every time after the first conviction for the hearers; to be levied by distress upon the persons convicted, their goods and chattels. Which persecution was general over the church in the nation, especially where any in office was willing to trouble, because there was £100 fine upon the justice of the peace, who, upon information brought before him, would not prosecute.

Which trouble was our seventh persecution in Bristol since king Charles II returned:-

The first was in Sir Henry Creswick's year, 1660, [when] our persecutions began.

The second persecution was in Alderman Cale's mayoralty, anno 1661, when about a month our pastor was imprisoned.

The third was by the deputy lieutenants: began 26th October, anno 1662.

The fourth persecution, like a violent storm, began upon us in the beginning of Sir John Knight's mayoralty; and in the third month following, the act to banish us came forth.

The fifth persecution was by Alderman Lawford, in his year, 1664; both these coming together were very heavy upon us, for their continuance.

The sixth persecution arose in Sir Thomas Langton's year, anno 1666; so that

This, our seventh persecution, in Sir Robert Yeamen's year, began tenth day, third month, 1670.

(b) [pp. 214–16]

OUR EIGHTH PERSECUTION. ANNO 1674.

About this time, in this eighth month, October, 1674, began our eighth persecution in this city; for a little before this, in the seventh month last past, a new bishop, one Guy Carleton, being come to Bristol to settle here, who being though aged and grey, a violent man against good people that separated from that which he called the church: for he had been formerly a captain in King Charles I.'s army, against the parliament: and had been out of the nation with this King, Charles II. in his exile. And now being made a lord bishop of Bristol, he resolved to destroy all our meetings and said he would not leave the track of a meeting in Bristol; but make us all come to church, as he called it.

Now in those few years, last past, of our peace, it had pleased the Lord to give such a breathing and liberty to his people, that those whose hearts were drawn forth to separate from the world's worship, as many were, and by our last persecution being driven out into the fields, many were convinced and converted, and from thence cleaved to us. And all professors had got several distinct meetings, by themselves, according to their several apprehensions and light received. So that there were now six separate churches settled in this city; viz., three baptized congregations, two independent congregations, and one presbyterian congregation: viz., Mr. Hardcastle's, being our meeting, most part baptized; Mr. Gifford's, all baptized; and Mr. Kitchen's, all baptized And Mr. Thompson's and Mr. Troughton's congregations, were independents; and Mr. Weeks's congregation were presbyterians ... [pp. 213–14]

Thus the Lord having settled us for several years before, in order, as armies with banners: yet but little flocks of kids, in comparison with the multitudes from the many synagogues of the Philistines of our days. Their Goliath, Guy, the bishop, being come, and he having now got a mayor, within a month after he came, fit for his purpose – one greatly in his favour, Ralph Ollive by name, a vintner, and a great drinker, a man given to much wine, – being now newly elected and sworn, that would do what the bishop would have him.

And not only were these two ... bad instruments risen up, as formidable enemies against us; but the Lord suffered to be raised up another wicked instrument to be a scourge and trial to us, his poor people ... Which third and pestilent adversary against us, which did the drudgery of the work for them, was one John Hellier, an attorney at law of this city, and had been bred up here. And he was one very crafty and subtle in the law, that, through craft prospering in his hand, had gotten an estate of about £200 per annum ... This John Hellier [was] now living in James's parish, where three of the great meetings were ... and this year he was made churchwarden of his parish, as they call it. All which strengthened him against us; for thereby, as his fig-leaf, he laboured to cover himself, pretending what he did against us was in persuance of his duty: that he might not break his oath, as he said. So he came with his man to our meetings, and turned informer, and gave informations against our three meetings in said parish; namely, Mr. Weeks's, Mr. Hardcastle's, and Mr. Gifford's. And the bishop also sent three, and sometimes more, of his own clergy; namely parson Pledwell of Peter's, Heath of Austin's, and Godwin of Philip's, that would come up in our meetings, in the midst of the sermon, and stay some time, and take notice of as many as they could know: then go to the mayor, and give information against us. Thus when they should be preaching to their own flocks in their parishes, they left them, and would so audaciously come to devour us, in the attire of foolish shepherds, but inwardly were ravening wolves ...

[pp. 222–5] Then upon the 14th day of the said 12th month, Feb. 1674–5, the next Lord's Day following Mr. Thompson's commitment, the mayor, Ralph Ollive, with Alderman Hicks and Alderman Lawford, and the mayor's serjeants, came to Mr. Weeks's meeting, and to our meeting; and they finding Mr. Hardcastle preaching, as also Mr. Weeks, they carried them both away, and committed them to the custody of a chief constable until the morrow ...

Now, three of our ministers being imprisoned, some of each congregation of the brethren met together to consult how to carry on our meetings, that we might keep to our duty, and edify one another now our pastors were gone ... And ... we concluded this: to come and assemble together, and for one to pray and read a chapter, and then sing a psalm, and after conclude with prayer: and so two brethren to carry on the meeting one day, and two another: for a while, to try what they would do with us. So we did, and ordered one of the doors of our meeting place to be made fast, and all to come in at one, but open it when we go forth: and to appoint some youth, or two of them, to be out at the door, every meeting, to watch when Hellier, or other informers or officers, were coming: and so to come in, one of them, and give us notice thereof. Also some of the hearers, women and sisters, would sit and crowd in the stairs, when we did begin the meeting with any exercise, that so the informers might not too suddenly come in upon us; by reason of which they were prevented divers times.

Upon the 21st day of 12th month, Feb. 1674, being the next Lord's day after our pastor was imprisoned, Hellier comes about to our meetings with his man and officers. In the morning [he] goes to Mr. Gifford's, and finds him preaching; which he informs the mayor thereof, for his conviction, that if they catch him after that day of his conviction in the corporation, they might imprison him, as the other ministers. In the afternoon he goes to Mr. Weeks's, and carries away divers to prison; then comes to our meeting, and finding that door we come in to be, with people and women in the stairs, so thronged that they could not get in; though they did hale several, and pulled Mrs. Bush down stairs, yet could not get up through them:- then they went to the other door, and broke it open; and then they rushed in upon us that way, and took observations of the names of them they counted chief, and carried Sam. Tipton and Mr. Joseph White, whom they struck very violently, and bound them over to answer for meeting.

Upon the 28th of the 12th month, 1674 [i.e., 28 February 1675], the informers came to our meetings again. And at brother Gifford's meeting, Hellier, with the officers, finds him preaching again; and now having a warrant for him, they carry him away before the mayor, who binds him to appear the next day; which being the 1st of March ... the mayor commits Mr. Gifford to prison, to the three ministers before, for six months.

But one of the ministers, namely, Mr. Thompson, who was first imprisoned, was very sick when he came in, and although divers persons of note in this city, in the compassion of their hearts for this sick minister, did go to the mayor and sheriffs, and to Sir John Knight, to get leave that he might be permitted to go home; but they could not prevail. And his physician [Dr Chauncey] interceded that he might be removed out of that stinking prison, to some convenient house for air, and to administer somewhat more conveniently to him, and he showed the danger of his condition; yet, notwithstanding, they hardened their hearts, and would not grant it, because the bishop would not give leave.

So that upon the 4th of March 1674–5, following, at twelve of the clock in the night, Mr. Thompson, the said imprisoned minister for Jesus Christ, he departed this life, in Newgate prison. He was a corpulent, tall, big man: having lain in prison but about three weeks and two days; of that he was sick about one week. Wherefore, being gross [they] could not keep him; so that the next day, being the 5th of March, he was honourably interred at Phillip's; being carried from the prison to his grave, and was accompanied with all sort of professors, except quakers, insomuch that the like funeral, for number, had not been seen in Bristol in the memory of this generation; being judged by some to be not less than five thousand people of all sorts: which made the adversaries admire ...

[pp. 225–6] Now all the foresaid churches, our ministers being taken from us, one dead, and the rest imprisoned – and we feared their death likewise in such a bad prison – and we being pursued closely every meeting ... we considered which way to maintain our meetings, by preserving our speakers.

In order to which, at our own meeting, to prevent spies that might come in the room as hearers: ... we contrived a curtain, to be hung in the meeting place, that did inclose as much room as above fifty might sit within it; and among those men, he that preached should stand; that so, if any informer was privately in the room as a hearer, he might hear him that spake, but could not see him, and thereby not know him. And there were brethren without the curtain, that would hinder any from going within the curtain, that they did not know to be friends: and so let whoso would come into our meeting to hear, without the curtain. And when our company and time were come to begin the meeting, we drew the curtain, and filled up the stairs with women and maids that sat in it, that the informers could not quickly run up.

And when we had notice that the informers, or officers, were coming, we caused the minister, or brother that preached, to forbear, and sit down. Then we drew back the curtain, laying the whole room open, that they might see us all. And so all the people begin to sing a psalm, that, at the beginning of the meeting, we did always name what psalm we would sing, if the informers, or the mayor or his officers come in. Thus still when they came in we were singing, [so] that they could not find any one preaching, but all singing. And, at our meeting, we ordered it so, that none read the psalm after the first line, but every one brought their bibles, and so read for themselves: that they might not lay hold of any one for preaching, or as much as reading the psalm, and so to imprison any more for that, as they had our ministers ...

Document IV.14

Richard Baxter Rebuts Slanders

Peter Gunning (1614–84) became bishop of Chichester in 1669 and was translated to Ely in 1675 where he died.

The offer of the bishopric of Hereford to Richard Baxter (1615–91) is recounted in *Reliquiae Baxterianae*, 281–3. His letter to the Earl of Clarendon, 1 November 1660, declining the offer is printed in Francis John (ed.), *An Excerpt from* Reliquiae Baxterianae (London, 1910), 165–8.

From Matthew Sylvester, *Reliquiae Baxterianae* (London, 1696), III, 104–6.

§ 235. About the beginning of May [1673] in my Walk in the Fields, I met with Dr. *Gunning*, now Bishop of *Chichester* ... and at his Invitation went after to his Lodgings, to pursue our begun Discourse: which he vehemently professed that he was sure, that it was not Conscience that kept us from Conformity but meerly to keep up our Reputation with the People, and we desired alterations for no other ends; and that we lost nothing by our Nonconformity, but were fed as full, and lived as much to the Pleasure of the Flesh in Plenty, as the Conformists did: And let me know what odious thoughts he had of his poor Brethren, upon Grounds so notoriously false, that I thought few Men who lived in *England* could have been so ignorant of such matters of Fact. But alas, what is there so false and odious which exasperated factions, malicious Minds will not believe and say of others? And what Evidence so notorious which they will not out-face? I told him that he was a stranger to the Men he talked of; that those of my Acquaintance (whom he confessed to be far more than of his) were generally the most Conscionable Men that I could find on Earth: That he might easily know Reputation could not be the thing which made them suffer so much Affliction; because 1. many of them were young men, not pre-engaged in point of Reputation to any side. 2. He knew that we lost, by our Nonconformity, that Worldly Honour, which we were as capable of as he and others: We did not so vilifie the King, Parliament, Lords, Bishops, Knights, and Gentry, who were most against us, as to think it a place of Worldly Honour to be vilified by them, and called Rogues, and sent to the common Goals [sic] among Rogues, and branded to the World, as we are in the *Oxford Act* of Confinement, and banished five Miles from Cities and Corporations: Our Consciences would not allow us to say, that he, and such as he, who were *Clergy-Lords* and Parliament-Barons did conform out of Pride or Love of Reputation; and which was the liker to a reasonable Conjecture? That he should be moved by Pride who chuseth the way of worldly Wealth and Domination and Honour, giving Laws to his Brethren, and vilifying them, and trampling on them at his Pleasure, as on a company of contemned, scorned Wretches; or they that chuse the way of this Contempt and Scorn with Poverty and Corporal Distress? Whose honour is it that such Men seek? You account their Followers the refuse of the World as you do them. And if they themselves think better of them, yet they will know that they are mostly of the meaner sort, and that poor Men have little to spare for others; and we are not so sordidly dis-ingenious as not to be sensible that to be beholden to poor Men that want themselves, for our daily Bread, is not the work of Pride, but putteth our *Humility* to it to the utmost. It's foolish Pride, which chuseth the hatred and scorn of the Great Men of the World, instead of Dignities and Honour, and chuseth to suffer Scorn and Imprisonment among poor Men, to whom we must be beholden for a beggarly Sustenance.

And as for the *Plenty* and fullness which they upbraid us with, it telleth us that there is nothing so immodest and unreasonable which some Mens Malice will not say. Do they not know into what Poverty *London* is brought by the late Fire, and want of Trade? And what Complaints do fill all the Land? And how close-handed almost all Men are that are themselves in want? And Ministers are not so impudent as to turn Beggers without Shame? I had but a few days before had Letters of a worthy Minister, who, with his Wife and six Children, had many Years had seldom another food than brown, Rye Bread and Water, and was then turned out of his House, and had none to go to: And of another that was fain to spin for his Living: And abundance I know that have Families, and nothing, or next to nothing of their own, and live in exceeding want upon the poor Drops of Charity which they stoop to receive from a few mean People. And if there be here and there a rich man that is Charitable, he hath so many to relieve, that each one can have but a small share. Indeed, about a dozen or twenty Ministers about *London*, who stuck to the people in the devouring Plague, or in other times of Distress, and feared no Sufferings, have so many People adhering to them, as keep them from Beggery, or great want; and you judge of all the rest by these, when almost all the rest through *England*, who have not something of their own to live upon, do suffer so much as their Scorners will scarce believe. It is no easie thing to have the Landlord call for Rent, and the Baker, the Brewer, the Butcher, the Taylor, the Draper, the Shoemaker, and many others call for Money, and Wife and Children call for Meat and Drink, and Cloathes, and a Minister to have no Answer for them, but *I have none*. And the Bishop had the less modesty in standing confidently to my Face of his certainty of our *losing nothing by our Nonconformity*, when he himself knew that I was offered a Bishoprick in 1660 and he got not his Bishoprick, (for all his extraordinary way of Merit) till about 1671, or 1672: and I had not a Groat of the Ecclesiastical Maintenance since the King came in; nor, to my best remembrance, ever received more then the four Pound even now mentioned, as a Salary for Preaching these Eleven Years, nor any way for Preaching the Sum of eight Pound in all those Years: Yea, on this occasion, I will not think it vain to say, that all that I remember that ever I received as gifts of Bounty from any whatsoever since I was silenced (till after *An*. 1672) amount not in the whole to 20*l*. besides ten Pound *per Annum* which I received from Serjeant *Fountain* till he died, and when I was in Prison, twenty pieces from Sir *John Bernard*, ten from the Countess of *Exeter*, and five from Alderman *Bard*, and no more, which just paid the Lawyers, and my Prison Charge (but the expenses of removing my Habitation was greater:) And had the Bishop's Family no more than this? In sum, I told the Bishop that he, that cried out so vehemently against schism, had got the Spirit of a Sectary: and as those that by Prisons and other sufferings were too much exasperated against the Bishops, could hardly think or speak well of them, so his cross Interests had so notoriously spoiled him of his Charity, that he had plainly the same temper with the bitterest of the Sectaries, whom he so much reviled ...

Document IV.15

Doing Penance

Nonconformists feared and hated the Ecclesiastical Courts. Thomas Gwyn was the squire of Pant-y-cored in the parish of Garthbrengi in Breconshire and within the diocese of St David's. In 1685 he was cited into the Consistory Court of the Archdeaconry of Brecon and found guilty of absenting himself from his parish church and attending Dissenting meetings. He was condemned to do public penance and on

24 July 1685 he entered a bond in the sum of £100, payable to the bishop, to fulfil the promises he made in his confession. In order to illustrate what such a punishment involved, a description of the ceremony as practised in that archdeaconry is provided. It occurred in 1678 and the offender, Morgan Lloyd, lived in the parish of Talgarth.

The following quotations come from the Brecon Consistory Court Act Books. They are in the National Library of Wales, Aberystwyth, in the Church in Wales collection, SD/CCB/10 and SD/CCB/G. For a masterly description of the procedures used in the Consistory Courts, v., W.T.Morgan's article, 'The Consistory Courts in the Diocese of St. David's, 1660–1858', *Journal of the Historical Society of the Church in Wales*, VII (1957), 5–24. For a similar treatment of procedures in the spiritual courts of York and examples of the types of documents issued by them, v., J. S. Purvis, *An Introduction to Ecclesiastical Records* (London, 1953), 64–95. It is not known whether Thomas Gwyn did present himself for the humiliating ceremony. There was provision in the Consistory records for sentence to be pronounced in the offender's parish church in his absence. For further discussion of the operation of the Ecclesiastical Courts in the Diocese of St David's, v., R. Tudur Jones, 'Religion in Post-Restoration Brecknockshire 1660–1688', *Brycheiniog*, VIII (1962), 11–66.

(a) Thomas Gwyn's Confession

I Thomas Gwyn of Gartbrengy, gent, doe Acknowledge that I have contrary to the lawes of God And of this Church And realm of England for these many yeares absented my selfe from the Church and the Communion thereof And frequented Conventicles and private meetings to the great danger of my owne soule and evill example of others for which I am most hartyly greived And doe most humbly beseech God almighty to pardon my sinns therein And intreat all good Christians to pray for me and I doe most sincerely promise to conforme to the doctrine and discipline of the Church of England as now by law established to frequent my parish Church and therein behave myself decently and receive the most holy communion According to the liturgie And perform all other dutyes as required by the canons of the Church and lawes of the realme.

14 July 1685. Thomas Gwyn'

(b) Morgan Lloyd's Sentence of the Court

That the said Morgan Lloyd shall on sundaie being the 10th of November instant, present himselfe and be receaved in the Church porch of Talgarth aforesaid by the church wardens of the said parishe and there by the Apparitor of this Court be vested with a white sheet and a white wand be put into his hand, be conducted at the beginning of Divine Service by the said Apparitor with his staffe of office goeing before him and the churchwardens assisting to the first step going up to the Comunion Table, there stand still after the reading of the Nicene Creede, with his face towards the congregacon, where the Preist that officiates that day shall first audibly and distinctly read the sentence given against him in this Court, and in English or Welsh explaine or interpret the same soe that people may understand the cause of this pennance enjoyned and be hereby warned not to offend in the like kind ... The said Criminal shall upon his knees repeat the words following after the Preist with an audible voyce, Soe that the people may hear and understand him ... [Then follows his confession.]

Document IV.16

Episcopal Attitudes

(a) William Lloyd of St. Asaph to William Sancroft, archbishop of Canterbury, 24 November 1682

William Lloyd (1627–1717) was bishop of Bangor from 1680 to 1692 when he was translated to Lichfield and in 1700 he moved to the diocese of Worcester (for his career, v., A. Tindal Hart, *William Lloyd* (London, 1952), DNB and DWB). He was somewhat enigmatic in his attitude to the repression of Dissent. During his first Episcopal Visitation he invited leading Dissenters to discuss their standpoint with him at Llanfyllin on 22 September 1681 and the debate continued for two days. Subsequently he discussed theology at considerable length with the Quaker Richard Davies (1635–1708) and intervened to suspend his prosecution in the church court (v., *An Account of the Convincement, Exercises, Services, and Travels ... of Richard Davies* (London, 1710), 207–9; Hart, *William Lloyd*, 43; D. R. Thomas, *The History of the Diocese of St. Asaph*, 3 vols (Oswestry, 1906–13), I, 125–6). Four days after the Llanfyllin debate he met the Presbyterians at Oswestry and the bishop's dignity and patience during the discussion made a favourable impression on Philip Henry (J. B. Williams (ed.), *The Life of the Reverend Philip Henry* (London, 1825), 153) and similarly Henry impressed the bishop who said of Henry that 'he did not look upon him as Schismatic, but only as a Separatist, and, if he were in his diocese, he did not question but he should find some way to make him useful' (ibid., 156). Lloyd was especially concerned with the activities of the Dissenters in Wrexham. The following documents illustrate the bishop's ambivalent attitude towards them and raises difficult questions about his dual policy of urging repression and promoting discussion with Dissenters.

The document is in the Bodleian Library, Tanner MS. cxlvi, 33–33v.

For Vavasor Powell (1617–70), see the Welsh biography by R. Tudur Jones, *Vavasor Powell* (Swansea, 1971). His widow was Katherine, the fifth daughter and tenth child of Colonel Gilbert Gerrard of Crewood, Chester, and Anna, the daughter of William Brettargh of Brettargh Holt, Lancashire. Her sister Anna was married to Thomas Hardcastle, the minister of Broadmead Baptist Church, Bristol. The man described by the bishop as 'one Evans' was John Evans (1628–1700) who became minister to the Independent congregation at Wrexham in 1668, v., DWB; A. N. Palmer, *A History of the Older Nonconformity of Wrexham* (Wrexham, 1888; reprinted Wrexham, 1988). John and Katherine were the parents of the Presbyterian minister Dr John Evans (c. 1680–1730), best known to historians for the 'Lists' of Nonconformist congregations which he compiled between 1717 and 1729, for whom v., DNB and DWB. For the location of Brynyffynnon, v., A. N. Palmer, *The History of the Town of Wrexham* (Wrexham, 1893). For Edgebury, v., DWB, s.n., 'Edisbury

(Family)'. Sir William Williams (1634–1700) was elected Speaker of the House of Commons in 1680 and 1681. For his tortuous career, v., DNB; DWB. William Lloyd's predecessor at St Asaph was Isaac Barrow who occupied the see from March 1669 to his death on 24 June 1680 (v., D.R.Thomas, *A History of the Diocese of St. Asaph* (Oswestry, 1870), 228–9). The excerpt illustrates how troublesome it was for a bishop to compel the secular authorities to act in support of the church courts. In a letter to Sancroft, 21 January 1683, William Lloyd describes in detail the legal procedures involved, Tanner MS. cxlvi, 30–31v.

I am very much Troubled for the poor Souls at Wrexham in my Diocese. They were horribly poisoned by one Vavasor Powell in the late wretched times. The widow of Vavasor maried one Evans who succeeds the other in his principles. This man (I may adde, & this woman) keep a conventicle still at Brynyffynon a house they rent of m^r Williams the late Speaker ... Before all this in my Predecessor's time he had been denounced Excommunicate. I now signified him into the Chancery, & got a writ against him from thence, which was subsigned by the Judge of Assize, (as all such writs must be in this Country) at the last Lent-Assizes for Denbighshire. Ever since this writ has layn in the hands of the high-Sheriff Mr Joshua Edgebury, the unworthy brother of the worthy Dr. Edgebury, or in the hands of his Undersheriff unexecuted. And so Evans keeps his Conventicle still, & the sheriff knows it, for he lives in the same Parish. I writt to the Justices of the Peace at their Sessions, after Christmas last, to desire them to execute the Laws in this Case. But neither have they done any thing, not that they are disaffected to the Church, but they are so divided among themselves that they cannot agree to any Public business.

(b) William Lloyd of St Asaph to William Sancroft, archbishop of Canterbury, 21 December 1682

There is some obscurity about the bishop's references to the incumbents of Wrexham. William Smith came there not later than 1664 and he was buried at Wrexham on 2 December 1684 (A. N. Palmer, *History of the Parish Church of Wrexham* (Wrexham, 1886), 66). So the old vicar was alive when Lloyd wrote his letter although he writes as though he were dead. He was followed by Peter Wynne who was buried on 11 November 1686. The records of the parish are vague about the curates. Richard Jones died in 1678 and the next curate recorded was Ellis Lewis in 1686 (ibid., 76). Sir George Jeffreys (1648–89) was the notorious Judge Jeffreys. He was the son of John Jeffreys of Acton. He was made judge of the Chester circuit in 1680 (v., DNB). At the time of William Lloyd's request he was of the 'court party' and had fits of leniency towards Dissenters. His nephew was Griffith Jeffreys of Acton, high sheriff of Denbighshire in 1683. (For the pedigree of the Jeffreys of Acton, v., A. N. Palmer, *History of the Thirteen Country Townships of the Old Parish of Wrexham* (Wrexham, 1903), between pages 168–9.) For further information about the conferences with the conventiclers at Wrexham, v., T. Richards, *Wales under the Penal Code* (London, 1925), 40–5.

I was never so much concerned as I am now for suppressing of that impudent

Conventicle at Wrexham. For while the old Vicar lived that was past doing any service & never came within the Church for a twelve-month together nor any for him but a Curat the cheapest he could get & one that I should have proceeded against as a Scandalous man if I could have found any proof of any one thing of many that were alledged against him by common Fame, all that time I thought it not worth the while to do my utmost to keep the people from meeting at their Conventicle, when if that had been obteind, I could not hope to bring them to Church. But yet I did write to the Justices at their Quarter-Sessions to desire them to use their Authority according to Law, & I signifyd the Teacher & took out a writ against him, & put it in the Sheriffs hands as I acquainted your Grace in a former Letter [reference to letter of 24 November 1682, Tanner MS. cxlvi, 33–33v]. All this having proved ineffectual for the breaking of the Conventicle I am now for using all the power I can to get it done. For now I have left them no Excuse for not coming to Church. Tho as yet I have found no Vicar to my minde I have removed the old Curate & put in 2 very good men to supply both for Vicar & Curate. There are 2 good Sermons every Sunday & prayers twice a day all the week, & all Offices performd there as well as in any Country Church that I know. Besides that at my last being at Wrexham where I stayed from the 7th till the 13th instant, I conferd with divers of the Conventiclers in private, & I had 2 public Conferences with them all-together (for by taking out Writts against some that were Refractory I have brought all the rest to obey my Citations as often as I think fit to call them together) where before a hundred other persons each time, I heard & answerd all they had to say for their separation; and as I am sure all others were fully satisfied, so I believ there was not one of the Conventiclers but was convinced they had not one Text of Scripture on their side. I desired them to take time till the 12th of the next moneth when I intend God willing to be with them again; because they were still referring me to books I desired them to consult their Books & their Authors & to furnish themselves with Arguments against that time, & if they could bring their Teachers to manage them for them to whom I promised a truce on that Condition. They were every face that I saw of them so extremely cast down, that I know they were ashamed of their Cause, & I believ would forsake it if they were not held Together by mutuall Compacts, & those would seem to be dissolv'd if they were hinder'd from meeting at their Conventicle. It is now if ever in the power of Sir George Jeffreys to hinder them because his Nephew is high Sheriff of that County & both he and his under-sheriff live in that parish. Perhaps the sheriff cannot do it without the Justices of peace because against him they are protected on Sundays, & the Teacher may hide himself all the week. This I hear the last Sheriff has to say for himself. But Sir George knows what may be done by Law & by whom: & as he has the greatest power over the sheriff, so the Lord President has the like or more over the Justices. I beseech your Grace to use your Interest with either or with both of them to get the business done. For this is a Season for it. The Quarter-sessions will be at Wrexham on the 11th of the next month.

I beg this withall that when you speak to either of them, you would be pleasd not to mention this Letter, nor to seem to do it at my solicitation. For I am very well, for ought I know, with the Judge & with my Lord President. And since every man expects to be owned in this place, they may perhaps take it ill of me that I do not write to themselves. Your Grace is knowne very well to minde the good of the Church in every part of your province; & it will not seem strange to them if upon the information which they know I gave you before, your Grace thinks fit to minde them again, & to continu your Application to them till you hear that we are rid of this Conventicle. But if your Grace shall think fit to have me write to either of them or both I will do it when you please to give me your direction.

I pray for the long continuance of your Grace's good health & prosperity & humbly craving your blessing take leav.

My good Lord. Your Graces most obliged & most obedient Son & Servant, W.Asaph.

(c) William Lloyd, bishop of St Asaph, to Commisary John Edwards, 17 July 1683

> In the 'damnable conspiracy' referred to in this extract was the Rye House Plot to assassinate the King which was divulged on 12 June 1683 and which seemed to implicate Dissenters. William Lloyd's excited response to the news is obvious from the strong words of his letter. His biographer describes this as a letter of 'a very frightened man' (Tindal Hart, *William Lloyd* (London, 1952), 48) and suggests that it represents a change of attitude towards the Dissenters. It is true that leading Dissenters had taken a generous view of the Bishop's dealing with them. Charles Owen, the brother and biographer of James Owen (1654–1706) – 'Owen the preacher' in the above quotation – describes Lloyd as 'That excellent and Learned Prelate, being a declared Enemy to Persecution, studied to reduce the Dissenters in his Diocess, by mild and Christian Methods ...' (Charles Owen, *Some Account of the Life ... Of ... James Owen* (London, 1709), 29) and Philip Henry's son, Matthew, writes of him, 'That learned bishop ... set himself with vigour to reduce dissenters ... with the *cords of a man* ... and to endeavour their conviction by discourse' (J. B. Williams (ed.), *Life of Philip Henry* (London, 1825), 152). But the letters quoted above suggest that they had mis-read the bishop's character. He was sanguine about the impact his arguments were making on the resolution of the Dissenters but at no time did he abandon the conviction that compulsion would have to be used if argument failed. Walter Griffith (d. 1702), 'mercer' and banker of Llanfyllin, was a prominent member of the Independent Church in the town and his name, together with that of his wife, appears frequently in the Montgomery Gaol Files (*Cofiadur*, 31 (1961), 14–15). His wife was Mary, the sister of Thomas Edwards (1649–1700) of Rhual, Flints., a member of the Independent Church at Wrexham and the author of the High Calvinist book *The Paraselene Dismantled of her Cloud* (1699). Philip Henry wrote a touching letter to William Lloyd, 25 March 1682, pleading for leniency towards Walter Griffith and others (M. H. Lee, *Letters and Diaries of Philip Henry* (London, 1882), 337–8). 'Llangallyn' in the excerpt should be 'Llangollen'.
> The extract is in the Lloyd-Baker MSS, Hardwicke Court, Gloucester.

Let Owen the preacher and all the rest at Oswestry that were formerly decreed be now published, and in short every protestant-dissenter (as those bloody wretches are pleased to call themselves) that is decreed and not yet published ... And get the

Sheriffs to do their duties. For 'tis visible that all this while we have been treating with these Sectaries, it has been God's wonderful providence that when they mustered in their conventicles they had not come out to cut our throats. Pray let Walter Gryffith of Llanfyllin, Roger Williams of Llangallyn [sic] and any other whom you think likeliest to have been in the damnable conspiracy, be recommended to the Sheriff's especial care that they may be forthcoming in case there be anything discovered against them.

(d)

James Owen was the one who supplied Calamy with information about those ejected in 1662 from the parishes of Wales. How times had changed! Lloyd was playing a formative part in the initiation of the Glorious Revolution. He was one of the seven bishops put on trial at the King's Bench on 29 June 1688 for the petition which he had presented to King James II in protest against the order to read his Second Declaration of Indulgence in all the churches and it was a matter of urgency to secure the support of Dissenters. But the promise at the end of the quotation was only very partially fulfilled. The extract is from E. Calamy, *Continuation* (London, 1727), 'Dedication', xxi.

Then and about that time [i.e., June 1688] did Dr. Lloyd, Bp. of St. Asaph, passing through Oswestry in Salop, send for Mr James Owen the Dissenting Minister of that Town and enter into great Freedom in conversing with him, about the great danger of the Protestant Religion. He ventured to acquaint him with the secret (till then unknown to him) of the invitation sent to the Prince of Orange, by many Lords & Gentlemen, of which he owned himself to be one. And he freely expressed his Hope, that the Protestant Dissenters would readily concur for promoting the Common Interest: Adding these remarkable Words: You and we are Brethren: We have indeed been angry Brethren, but we have seen our folly: and are resolved if ever we have it in our power again, to shew that we will treat you as Brethren.

Document IV.17

The Trial of Richard Baxter

George Jeffreys (1648–89) was appointed Chief Justice on 29 September 1683, despite the fact that Charles II said of him that he had 'no learning, no sense, no manners, and more impudence than ten carted street-walkers'. He presided over Titus Oates's trial in May 1685. Jeffreys is best known for the 'Bloody Assizes' which began on 24 August 1685 after the failure of the Duke of Monmouth's invasion. 'As a criminal judge he was undoubtedly the worst that ever disgraced the bench'. See DNB and H. Montgomery Hyde, *Judge Jeffreys* (London, 1940). For Titus Oates (1649–1705) and the Popish Plot, v., DNB; Jane Lane, *Titus Oates* (1949), John Pollock, *The Popish Plot* (London, 1903) and Malcolm V. Hay, *The Jesuits and the Popish Plot* (London, 1934). For Sir Roger L'Estrange (1616–1704), Tory pamphleteer and bitter opponent of Nonconformists, v., DNB. William Bates, D.D. (1625–99), was a leading Presbyterian who was ejected from St Dunstan's-in-the-West, London. He declined the Deanery of Lichfield and Coventry but with Baxter and others was a participant in the various conversations about comprehension. When he died he was minister of the Presbyterian Church at Hackney. For Bates, v., DNB and CR. Richard Wallop (1616–97), later a judge, defended Titus Oates as well as Baxter. 'He was constantly incurring the displeasure of Judge Jeffreys who never lost an opportunity to browbeat him' – so DNB. Sir John Rotherham (1630–96?) became a judge in 1688 and was a consistent hater of episcopacy, v., DNB. Sir Henry Ash(h)urst (v., DNB) came of a staunchly Presbyterian family. His father, Henry Ash(h)urst (1614?–80) was a wealthy London draper and friendly with Philip and Matthew Henry and John Eliot (1604–90), the 'Indian Apostle' (v., DNB). He was Treasurer of the Society for the Propagation of the Gospel. Baxter preached his funeral sermon. For further comment on Baxter's trial, v., G. F. Nuttall, *Richard Baxter* (London, 1965), 109–11 and F. J. Powicke, *The Reverend Richard Baxter under the Cross* (London, 1927), 143ff. Powicke also prints the letter written by Archbishop Tillotson to Matthew Sylvester, 3 February 1692, encouraging him to proceed with the biography of Baxter and in which he refers to the trial and says that there was 'nothing more honourable than when the Rev. Baxter stood at bay, berogued, abused, despised; never more great than then' (ibid., 291–5).

The following account is in Edmund Calamy, *An Abridgement of Mr. Baxter's History of his Life and Times. With An Account of the Ministers, &c. who were Ejected after the Restauration of King Charles II*, 2 vols (London, 1713), I, 368–72. The original spelling, punctuation and italics have been retained.

On the 28th of *February* [1685], Mr. Baxter was Committed to the *King's-Bench* Prison, by my Lord Chief Justice *Jefferies's* Warrant, for his Paraphrase on the New Testament, Printed a little before; which was call'd a Scandalous and Seditious Book against the Government. On the 6th of *May*, which was the first Day of the Term, he appear'd in *Westminster* Hall, and an Information was ordered to be drawn against him. *May* the 14th, he Pleaded not Guilty to the Information. *May* the 18th, he being much Indispos'd, mov'd that he might have farther Time given him for his Tryal, but it was deny'd him. He mov'd for it by his Council: but *Jeffereys* cries out in a Passion, *I will not give him a Minutes Time more to save his Life. We have had* (says he) *to do with other sorts of Persons, but now we have a Saint to deal with; and I know how to deal with Saints as well as Sinners. Yonder* (says he) *stands* OATS *in the Pillory* (as he actually did at that very Time in the New Palace-Yard;) *and he says he suffers for the Truth, and so says* Baxter; *but if* Baxter *did but stand on the other side of the Pillory with him, I would say Two of the greatest Rogues and Rascals in the Kingdom stood there*. On *May* the 30th, in the Afternoon, He was brought to his Tryal, before the Lord Chief Justice *Jefferys* at *Guild-hall*. Sir *Henry Ashhurst*, who could not forsake his own, and his Fathers Friend, stood by him all the while. Mr. *Baxter* came first into Court, and with all the Marks of Serenity and Composure, waited for the coming of the Lord Chief Justice, who appear'd quickly after with great Indignation in his Face. He no sooner sate down, than a short Cause was Call'd and Try'd: After which the Clerk began to read the Title of another Cause. *You Blockhead you* (says *Jefferys*) *the next*

Cause is between RICHARD BAXTER *and the King.* Upon which Mr. *Baxter's* Cause was Call'd. The Passages mentioned in the Information, were his Paraphrase on *Mat.* 5. 19. *Mark* 9. 39. *Mark* 11.31. *Mark* 12. 38, 39, 40. *Luke* 10. 2. *John* 11. 57. and *Acts* 15.2. These Passages were pickt out by Sir *Roger L'Estrange*, and some of his Companions. And a certain noted Clergy-man (who shall be nameless) put into the Hands of his Enemies some Accusations out of *Rom.* 13.&c. as against the King, to touch his Life, but no use was made of them. The great Charge was, that in these several Passages he reflected on the Prelates of the Church of *England*, and so was guilty of Sedition, &c. The King's Councel open'd the Information at Large with its Aggravations. Mr. *Wallop*, Mr. *Williams*, Mr. *Rotherham*, Mr. *Atwood*, and Mr. *Phipps*, were Mr. *Baxter's* Counsel, and had been feed by Sir *Henry Ashhurst*. Mr. *Wallop* said, that he conceiv'd the Matter depending being a Point of Doctrine, it ought to be referr'd to the Bishop his Ordinary: But if not, he humbly conceiv'd the Doctrine was innocent and justifiable, setting aside the Innuendo's, for which there was no Colour, there being no Antecedent to refer them to (*i.e.* no Bishop or Clergy of the Church of *England* nam'd). He said the Book accus'd, *i.e.* the Comment on the New testament, contained many Eternal Truths: But they who drew the Information were the Libellers, in applying to the Prelates of the Church of *England*, those severe Things which were written concerning some Prelates, who deserv'd the Characters which he gave. My Lord (says he) I humbly conceive the Bishops Mr. *Baxter* speaks of, as your Lordship if you have read Church History must confess, were the Plagues of the Church, and of the World. Mr. *Wallop*, says the Lord Chief Justice, 'I observe you are in all these dirty Causes: And were it not for you Gentlemen of the Long Robe, who should have more Wit and Honesty, that support and hold up these Factious Knaves by the *Chin*, we should not be in the Pass we are'. My Lord, says Mr. *Wallop*, I Humbly conceive, that the Passages accus'd are natural Deductions from the Text. 'You humbly conceive, *says* JEFFERYS, and I humbly conceive: Swear him, Swear him'. My Lord, says he, under Favour, I am Counsel for the Defendant, and if I understand either *Latin* or *English*, the Information now bro't against Mr. *Baxter* upon such a slight Ground is a greater Reflection upon the Church of *England*, than any Thing contain'd in the Book he's accus'd for. Says *Jeffreys* to him, 'Sometimes you humbly conceive, and sometimes you are very Positive: You talk of your Skill in Church History, and of your Understanding *Latin* and *English:* I think I understand something of them as well as you; but in short must tell you, that if you don't understand your Duty better, I shall teach it you'. Upon which Mr. *Wallop* sate down.

Mr. *Rotherham* urg'd that if Mr. *Baxter's* Book had sharp Reflections upon the Church of *Rome* by Name, but spoke well of the Prelates of the Church of *England*, it was to be presum'd that the sharp Reflections were intended only against the Prelates of the Church of *Rome*. The Lord Chief Justice said, *Baxter* was *an Enemy to the Name and Thing, the Office and Persons of Bishops. Rotherham* added, that *Baxter* frequently attended Divine Service, went to the Sacrament, and perswaded others to do so too, as was certainly and publickly known; and had in the very Book so charged, spoken very moderately and honourably of the Bishops of the Church of *England*. Mr.*Baxter* added, my Lord, I have been so moderate with Respect to the Church of *England*, that I have incurr'd the censure of many of the Dissenters upon that Account. 'BAXTER for Bishops, *says JEFFERYS*. That's a merry Conceit indeed. Turn to it, Turn to it'. Upon this *Rotherham* turn'd to a Place, where 'tis said, 'That great Respect is due to those truly call'd to be Bishops among us: *Or to that Purpose*: Ay, *saith* Jeffreys, This is your *Presbyterian Cant*; truly call'd to be Bishops: *That is himself and such Rascals, call'd to be Bishops of* Kidderminster, *and other such Places*. Bishops set apart by such Factious, Sniveling *Presbyterians* as himself: A *Kidderminster* Bishop he means. According to the Saying of a Late Learned Author: and every Parish shall maintain, a Tithe Pig Metropolitan. *Mr.* Baxter *beginning to speak again: says he to him, Richard, Richard*, dost thou think we'll hear thee Poison the Court &c. thou hast written Books eno' to load a Cart, every one as full of Sedition (I might say Treason) as an Egg is full of Meat. Hadst thou been whipp'd out of thy Writing Trade Forty Years ago, it had been happy, Thou pretendest to be a Preacher of the Gospel of Peace, and thou hast one foot in the Grave: 'tis Time for thee to begin to think what Account thou intendest to give, But leave thee to thyself, and I see thou'lt go on as thou hast begun, but by the Grace of God, I'll look after thee. I know thou hast a mighty Party, and I see a great many of the Brotherhood in Corners, waiting to see what will become of their mighty Donne, and a Doctor of the Party (*looking to Dr. Bates*) at your Elbow, but by the Grace of Almighty God, I'll *Crush you all*'...

[Then Atwood and Baxter himself sought to bring some reasonableness into the case but to no avail.]

... At length the Chief Justice summ'd up the Matter in a long and fulsome Harangue, 'tis notoriously known (*says he*) that there has been a Design to ruin the King and Nation. The Old Game has been renewed: And this has been the main Incendiary. He's as modest now as can be: But Time was, when no Man was so ready *at Bind your King's in Chains, and your Nobles in Fetters of Iron: And to your Tents O Israel. Gentlemen, for God's sake don't let us be gull'd twice in an Age, &c* ...

... The Jury immediately laid their Heads together at the Bar, and found him *Guilty* ...

... On *June* the 29th following, He had Judgment given against him. He was fin'd 500 Marks; to lie in Prison till he paid it: and be bound to his good Behaviour for seven Years ...

PART V

ASPECTS OF NONCONFORMIST EXPERIENCE

Document V.1

Preaching

For Nonconformists, as for Puritans generally, preaching was the divine ordinance which brought about he conversion of sinners and the edification of the church. An astonishing number of sermons were delivered and published during the seventeenth century and congregations listened avidly to them, even though some of them were very lengthy. It was natural therefore that the purpose of preaching should be explained with great care and the necessity for it insisted upon.

Extract (a) is from *The Fountain Opened* (1638) by Richard Sibbes as printed in A. B. Grosart (ed.), *The Complete Works of Richard Sibbes, D.D.* (Edinburgh, 1863), V, 505–7. For Sibbes (1577–1635), v., 'Memoir' in vol. I of the *Complete Works* and DNB. Although not a Nonconformist, his influence upon many Nonconformists was immense. For the nature and significance of Puritan preaching, v., Peter Lewis, *The Genius of Puritanism* (Haywards Heath: Carey Publications, 1977) and Horton Davies, *The Worship of the English Puritans* (Westminster: Dare Press, 1948), chap. XI.

Extract (b) is from Walter Cradock, *Gospel-libertie* (London, 1648), 28. For Cradock (1606?–59), v., DWB; G. F. Nuttall, 'Walter Cradock (1606?–1659): The Man and His Message', in *The Puritan Spirit: Essays and Addresses* (London, 1967) and *The Welsh Saints* (Cardiff, 1957), chap. 2.

Extract (c) is from Thomas Goodwin, *Works* (Edinburgh, 1865), XI, 364–5. For Goodwin (1600–80), President of Magdalen College, Oxford, from 1650 to the Restoration, v., 'Memoir' by Robert Halley, prefixed to W*orks* (1861), II and DNB.

(a)
It is not sufficient that physic be provided; but there must be an application of it. It is not sufficient that there is a treasure; but there must be a digging of it out. It is not sufficient that there be a candle or light; but there must be a holding out of the light for the good and use of others ... It is not sufficient that there be a box of ointment, but the box must be opened, that the whole house may be filled with the smell ...

To preach is to open the mystery of Christ, to open whatsoever is in Christ; to break open the box that the savour may be perceived of all. To open Christ's natures and person what it is; to open the offices of Christ: first, he was a prophet to teach, wherefore he came into the world; that he was a priest, offering the Sacrifice of himself; and then after he had offered his sacrifice as a priest, then he was a king ...

But it is not sufficient to preach Christ, to lay open all this in the view of others; but in the opening of them, there must be application of them to the use of God's people, that they may see their interest in them; and there must be an alluring of them, for to preach is to woo. The preachers are *paranymphi*, the friends of the bridegroom, that are to procure the marriage between Christ and his church; therefore, they are not only to lay open the riches of the husband, Christ, but likewise to entreat for a marriage, and to use all the gifts and parts that God hath given them, to bring Christ and his church together.

And because people are in a contrary state to Christ, 'to preach Christ', is even to begin with the law, to discover to people their estate by nature. A man can never preach the gospel that makes not way for the gospel, by shewing and convincing people that they are out of Christ. Who will marry with Christ, but those that know their own beggary and misery out of Christ? ... What need a Saviour, unless we were lost? What need Christ to be wisdom to us, if we were not fools in ourselves? What need Christ be sanctification to us, if we were not defiled in ourselves? What need he be redemption, if we were not lost and sold in ourselves to Satan, and under his bondage? ... In a word, being to bring Christ and the church together, our aim must be, to persuade pople to come out of their estate they are in, to come and take Christ ... Therefore the gospel is promulgated in a sweet manner ... The law comes with 'Cursed, cursed'; but now in the gospel Christ is preached with sweet alluring ... This is the manner of the dispensation in the gospel, even to beg people that they would be good to their own souls. Christ, as it were, became a beggar himself, and the great God of heaven and earth begs our love, that we so care for our own souls that we would be reconciled unto him ... He himself becomes a beseecher of reconciliation, as if he were the party that had offended. This is the manner of the publication of the gospel ...

(b)
[Jesus Christ] sends us not to hire servants ... we are not sent to get *Gally-slaves* to the Oares, or a Beare to the stake; but he sends us to wooe you as spouses, to marrie you to Christ: and in wooing there must not be *harsh* dealing: and when a man hath wooed and got a wife she must be kindly used ...

(c)
See here the necessity of this ordinance [i.e., preaching], so as to attend upon it, waiting upon God in the dispensation of it for the conversion of thy soul. 'A necessity lies upon me,' says Paul, 'to preach the gospel'. Now that necessity of his duty was founded upjn another necessity, namely, that it was a means to save the souls of men whom God had committed unto him. As for such as already converted, I shall not need to urge upon them the necessity of this ordinance, they have one within who will do it ... If they should want a few meals of their appointed food, there is a new creature within them would cry for bread ... Now, for such as are not yet converted, le me ask them but this one question, Do you think salvation necessary? Yes; then so is this, *necessitate medii*; for (says the apostle) it is 'the power of God unto salvation.' But you will say, God's power can save me by other means, if he will. I deny it not; but see what James says: James i.18, 'Of his own will begat he us with the word of truth'. He that out of his good pleasure begets us, our of the same free will hath chosen this means, even the word of truth, to do it by ... But you will say, as Rom. x., 'Have we not all heard?' I have heard sermons enough already, if they would do me any good. Yes (God be thanked), 'their sound is gone into all the world.' But let me ask you another question, which the apostle asks in the former words, Have all you that have heard obeyed the gospel? Hast thou had faith wrought? has thy heart and life been

changed as yet by this word heard? ... And if thou be one of the menbers yet unchanged, thou hast as much need to attend to the word as if thou hadst never heard it, that so thou mayest escape that damnation and fiery vengeance that will befall them who 'obey not the gospel of Jesus Christ,' 2 Thess. i. 8 ...

Document V.2

John Cotton: Conversion

Quoted from Samuel Clarke, *A Collection of the Lives of Ten Eminent Divines* (London, 1662), 57–8. For William Perkins (1558-1602), v., Introduction by Ian Breward to Breward (ed.), *The Work of William Perkins* (Sutton Courtenay Reformation Classics 3, Abingdon, 1970). The precise date of his death was 22 October 1602. For 'Sibs', i.e., Richard Sibbes (1577–1635), v., 'Memoir' by A. B. Grosart in *The Complete Works of Richard Sibbes, D.D.* (Edinburgh, 1862), I and DNB. For John Cotton (1584–1652) v., DNB and A. Johnson (ed.), *Dictionary of American Biography*, 22 vols (New York, 1928–37). For the significance of his influence on Congregationalism, v., G. F. Nuttall, *Visible Saints* (Oxford, 1957), 14–17.

The manner of his Conversion, according to his own relation was thus. During his residence in the University, God began to work upon him by the Ministery of Mr. *William Perkins* of blessed memory: But the motions, and stirrings of his heart which then were, he suppressed, thinking that if he should trouble himself with matters of Religion, according to the light he had then received, it would be an hinderance to him in his Studies, which then he had much addicted himself unto. Therefore he was willing to silence those suggestions, and in ward Callings which he had from Gods Spirit, and did wittingly defer the prosecution of that work until afterwards. At length, as he was walking in the fields, he heard the Bell tolling for Mr. *Perkins*, who lay a dying, whereupon he was secretly glad in his heart, that he should now be rid of him, who had (as he said) laid siege to, and beleaguered his heart. This became matter of much affliction to him afterwards, God keeping it upon his Spirit, with the aggravation of it, and making it an effectual means of convincing, and humbling him in the fight, and sense of the natural enmity that is in mans nature against God. Afterwards hearing Dr. *Sibs* (then Mr. *Sibs*) preaching a Sermon about Regeneration wherein he shewed, First, what Regeneration was not, and so opening the state of a meer Civil man, Mr. *Cotton* saw his own condition fully discovered, which (through Gods mercy) did drive him to a stand, as plainly seeing himself, destitute of true Grace, all his false hopes, and grounds now failing him: and so he lay for a long time, in an uncomfortable despairing way: and of all other things this was his heaviest burden, that he had wittingly withstood the means, and offers of Grace and mercy which he found had been tendered to him; thus he continued till it pleased God to let in a word of Faith into his heart, and to cause him to look unto Christ for his healing, which word also was dispensed unto him by the same Doctor *Sibs*, which begat in him a singular, and constant love to the said Doctor, of whom he was also answerably loved.

Document V.3

John Bunyan: Temptations and Conversion

This extract is from John Bunyan, *Grace abounding to the Chief of Sinners*. The first edition was published in 1666. For a detailed account of the various editions and a discussion of the characteristics of the Puritan spiritual autobiography see Roger Sharrock's Introduction to his edition of the text in *John Bunyan Grace Abounding to the Chief of Sinners* (Oxford, 1962). For Bunyan, v., John Brown, *John Bunyan (1628–1688): His Life, Times, and Work* (tercentenary edn, London, 1928) and Richard Greaves (ed.), *John Bunyan* (Courtenay Studies 2, Abingdon: Sutton Courtenay, 1969) and the books and articles mentioned in it; Christopher Hill, *A Turbulent, Seditious and Factious People: John Bunyan and his Church* (Oxford, 1989); Michael A. Mullett, *John Bunyan in Context* (Keele, 1996).

183. Now the most free, and full, and gracious words of the Gospel were the greatest torment to me; yea, nothing so afflicted me as the thoughts of Jesus Christ: for the remembrance of a Saviour, because I had cast him off, brought both the villany of my sin, and my loss by it to my mind. Nothing did twinge my Conscience like this. Every time that I thought of the Lord Jesus, of his Grace, Love, Goodness, Kindness, Gentleness, Meekness, Death, Blood, Promises and blessed Exhortations, Comforts and Consolations, it went to my Soul like a Sword; for still, unto these my considerations of the Lord Jesus, these thoughts would make place for themselves in my heart; *Ay, This is the Jesus, the loving Saviour, the Son of God, whom thou hast parted with, whom you slighted, despised, and abused. This is the* only *Redeemer, the* only *one that could so love sinners as to wash them from their sins in his own precious Blood: but you have no part nor lot in this Jesus, you have put him away from you, you have said in your heart,* Let him go if he will. *Now, therefore, you are severed from him. Behold, then, his Goodness, but you yourself be no partaker of it.* O thought I, what have I lost! What have I parted with! What have I dis-inherited my poor Soul of! Oh! 'tis sad to be destroyed by the grace and mercy of God; to have the Lamb, the Saviour, turn Lyon and Destroyer, *Rev.* 6. I also trembled, as I have said, at the sight of the Saints of God, especially at those that greatly loved him, and that made it their business to walk continually with him in this world: for they did both in their words, their carriages, and all their expressions of tenderness and fear to sin against their precious Saviour, condemn, lay guilt upon, and also add continual affliction and shame unto my soul. *The dread of man was upon me, and I trembled at God's* Samuels, I *Sam.* 16.4.

184. Now, also, the Tempter began afresh to mock my soul another way, saying, That Christ, indeed, did pity my case, and was sorry for my loss, but forasmuch as I had sinned, and transgressed as I had done, he could by no means help me, nor

save me from what I feared; for my sin was not of the nature of theirs, for whom he bled and died, neither was it counted with those that were laid to his charge when he hanged on the tree; therefore unless he should come down from Heaven, and die anew for this sin, though indeed he did greatly pity me, yet I could have no benefit of him. These things may seem ridiculous to others, even as ridiculous as they are in themselves, but to me they were most tormenting cogitations; every of them augmented my misery, that Jesus Christ should have so much love as to pity me when he could not help me; nor did I think that the reason why he could not help me was because his Merits were weak, or his Grace and Salvation spent on them already, but because his faithfulness to his threatning would not let him extend his mercy to me. Besides, I thought, as I have already hinted, that my sin was not within the bounds of that pardon that was wrapped up in a promise; and if not, then I knew assuredly, that it was more easie for Heaven and Earth to pass away than for me to have Eternal Life. So that the ground of all these fears of mine did arise from a stedfast belief that I had of the stability of the holy Word of God, and, also, from my being misinformed of the nature of my sin.

185. But O how this would add to my affliction, to conceit that I should be guilty of such a sin, for which he did not die! These thoughts would so confound me, and imprison me, and tie me up from Faith, that I knew not what to do: but Oh thought I, that he would come down again, O that the work of Mans Redemption was yet to be done by Christ; how would I pray him, and intreat him to count and reckon this sin amongst the rest for which he died! But this Scripture would strike me down, as dead, *Christ being raised from the dead, dieth no more: Death hath no more dominion over him*, Rom. 6.9.

186. Thus, by the strange and unusual assaults of the tempter, was my Soul, like a broken Vessel, driven, as with the Winds, and tossed sometimes head-long into dispair; sometimes upon the Covenant of works, and sometimes to wish that the new Covenant, and the conditions thereof, might, so far forth as I thought myself concerned, be turned another way, and changed. But in all these, I was but as those that jostle against the Rocks; more broken, scattered, and rent. Oh, the unthought of imaginations, frights, fears, and terrors that are affected by a throrow application of guilt, yielding to desperation! This is the man that hath his dwelling among the Tombs with the dead; that is always crying out, and cutting himself with stones, Mark 5.2–5. But I say, all in vain; desperation will not comfort him, the old Covenant will not save him. Nay, Heaven and Earth shall pass away before one jot or tittle of the Word and Law of Grace shall fall or be removed: this I saw, this I felt, and under this I groaned ...

[...]

229. But one day, as I was passing in the field, and that too with some dashes on my Conscience, fearing lest yet all was not right, suddenly this sentence fell upon my Soul, *Thy righteousness is in Heaven*; and methought withall, I saw with the eyes of my Soul Jesus Christ at Gods right hand, there, I say, as my Righteousness; so that wherever I was, or whatever I was doing, God could not say of me, *He wants my Righteousness*, for that was just before him. I also saw moreover, that it was not my good frame of Heart that made my Righteousness

better, nor yet my bad frame that made my Righteousness worse: for my Righteousness was Jesus Christ himself, *the same yesterday, and to-day, and for ever*, Heb. 13.8.

230. Now did my chains fall off my Legs indeed, I was loosed from my affliction and irons, my temptations also fled away: so that from that time those dreadful Scriptures of God left off to trouble me; now went I also home rejoycing, for the grace and love of God: So when I came home, I looked to see if I could find that Sentence, *Thy Righteousness is in Heaven*, but could not find such a Saying, wherefore my Heart began to sink again, onely that was brought to my remembrance, *He of God is made unto us Wisdom, Righteousness, Sanctificatiion, and Redemption*; by this word I saw the other Sentence true, I Cor.1.30.

231. For by this Scripture, I saw that the Man Christ Jesus, as he is distinct from us, as touching his bodily presence, so he is our Righteousness and Sanctification before God: here therefore I lived, for some time, very sweetly at peace with God thorow Christ; O methought Christ! Christ! there was nothing but Christ that was before my eyes: I was not onely for looking upon this and the other benefit of Christ apart, as of his Blood, Burial, or Resurrection, but considered him as a whole Christ! As he in whom all these, and all his other Vertues, Relations, Offices, and Operations met together, and that as he sat on the right hand of God in Heaven.

232. 'Twas glorious to me to see his exaltation, and the worth and prevalence of all his benefits, and that because of this; Now I could look from my self to him, and should reckon that all those Graces of God that now were green in me, were yet but like those crack'd-Groats and Four-pence-half-pennies that rich men carry in their Purses, when their Gold is in their Trunks at home: O I saw my Gold was in my Trunk at home! In Christ my Lord and Saviour! Now Christ was all; all my Wisdom, all my Righteousness, all my Sanctification, and all my Redemption ...

Document V.4

Morgan Llwyd: Conversion

This extract is from *Llyfr y Tri Aderyn* in (T. E. Ellis (ed.), *Gweithiau Morgan Llwyd* (Bangor, 1899), I, 258–61. The original is in Welsh.

The book is cast in the form of a conversation between three birds – the Eagle representing the State, the Raven the Church of England and the Dove the true Christian. Although the above speech is by the Dove and addressed to the Eagle in the dialogue, it is very obviously a piece of autobiography. It also shows vividly the close connection in the minds of so many Puritans between personal conversion and literary activity. Llwyd, however, is anxious not only because he fears that his literary work may be inspired by selfish ambition but also because the allusive and allegorical style of his writing may cause more confusion than enlightenment. In fact, the main title of his book is 'A Mystery for some to understand and for others to mock'. At several points Llwyd's experiences converge with those of the Quakers, as will be seen in the document that follows. He did not himself become a Quaker but shared with them a profound interest in the complexities of the spiritual life and the need for sincerity and release from formalism. There is a considerable body of writing in Welsh about Llwyd and his work as befits one who was a master of prose writing. Of these productions, the most significant are E.Lewis Evans, *Morgan Llwyd* (Liverpool, 1930), Hugh Bevan, *Morgan Llwyd y Llenor* (i.e., M.Ll. the Writer) (Cardiff, 1954) and Goronwy Wyn Owen, *Morgan Llwyd* (Caernarfon, 1992). For treatments in English, v., G. F. Nuttall, *The Welsh Saints 1640–1660* (Cardiff, 1957); M. Wynn Thomas, *Morgan Llwyd* (Writers of Wales Series, Cardiff, 1984); Meic Stephens (ed.), *The Oxford Companion to the Literature of Wales* (Oxford, 1986) and R. Tudur Jones, 'The Healing Herb and the Rose of Love', in R. Buick Knox (ed.), *Reformation, Conformity and Dissent* (Epworth, 1977).

Dove: ... By nature I was dead and, when I saw that, I tried to live. But I could not until everything in and around me had become dead to me. Then nature lost its hold on me and at that moment I caught hold of the Creator or rather He took hold of me. Previously I heard sermons but did not listen. I said prayers but I was not praying. I sang psalms but my heart was dumb. I partook of the sacrament but saw not the body of the Lord. I talked and said many things but not really from my heart – until the rose blossomed in me.

After all the agitation an end had to come at last before a beginning and I had to die before the grain of wheat grew through my soil. Sin revived and killed me. God was offended and frowned from the throne of my conscience while the Devil was smiling and laughing at me and shouting within me, 'Ho, ho, the bird is mine! It is surely in the trap. His mind is in three iron fetters, held fast in his own will and in the spirit of the great world and he is under God's displeasure as I am'. I feared too that it would be impossible to break those three fetters and gain my freedom. The hounds of Satan also followed the scent after me. The country's mockers made fun of me. And when the Hunter saw that I did not care what the world and its hounds said, he provoked the children of the Kingdom and some of the King's children (as it were) to scold, dishearten and hinder me and to cool my zeal. When this also failed the enemy roused all the roots of hell within me to be angry, unclean, cruel, worldly, surly, downcast, full of vain thoughts. This made me sorry to live and afraid to die because there was no sin that I saw in the worst of men that did not try to raise its head in my heart. Heaven had abandoned me and hell drew closer. God's angels became strangers and images of creatures appeared. I saw that I had fallen amongst merciless spiritual thieves between Jerusalem and Jericho until the glorious Samaritan, the heavenly Redeemer, came to me and raised me up. I say all this for your sake so that if you ever come to be in these crises due to sin, do not give way to despair and worldly grief and do not thrash about like a sheep in briers but stay quiet by the roadside. The Redeemer will come by and set you free. If not, should your end come, let it be in his arms as you rest on his word and promise. If you follow this advice, you shall live in the spirit of strength, love and moderation.

I had it in my heart to write to you to warn you in perfect love but the Serpent came and sought to hinder my pen. It spat its poison at me, whispering like this, 'It is self that has put you to work. You write too obscurely; no one can understand you until the fog rises. You do not understand yourself. Let alone! Men have knowledge enough if they only acted upon it. There are already too many books in the world. As your only reward, you will be abandoned like an owl in wasteland, as a pelican, yes, like an idiot or one of the vain philosophers who seek by the light of nature to know the Godhead in the natural world. Have you ever seen the Lord? Have you heard God Himself? Hide away in some hole and give over writing. God's day has dawned. Leave everyone alone and be comfortable in your conscience. Rejoice! Eat your food with a light heart. Stroll about and take your pleasure as you see almost everyone else doing and your days may be long on earth.'

This is how the cunning dragon spoke to me and this is how it sought to deceive me. This is how it did its worst to hinder my thinking, to seal my lips and to paralyse my hand. And if the Serpent had its way I would not be allowed to write this nor you to read it. But the Dove came and helped and assisted me by saying, 'Carry on! Every servant must exercise his talent, no matter what people say. If not, woe is that servant. It is not self that motivates you here but true love towards God and also faithful love towards Wales. It is of no profit to you nor to anyone else if you waste your time in unbelief and unfruitfulness. Some will gain understanding despite the fog and darkness. Yes, although your flesh does not comprehend what the Holy Spirit in you is writing, there is a spiritual element that does (Is. 29.18). There are not many Welsh books in Wales since the papers of the Britons of yore were burnt. And (says God) my people in Wales are destroyed for lack of knowledge (Hos. 4.6) and, as for you, it matters not what disrespect you suffer in the flesh' ...

Document V.5

Quaker Convincements

Quaker conversions, or 'convincements', to use George Fox's term, often followed the pattern of a serious, religious childhood, with increasing personal concern and unhappiness about sin, then a failure to find any satisfaction in any kind of church and a final acute struggle before accepting the Quaker faith. The progression can be traced in the early pages of Fox's *Journal* (NJ 1–11) though he did not tell such a clear story as some of his followers. The experiences of Richard Farnworth and Isaac Penington are summarised here.

Extract (a) is from R. Farnworth, *The Heart Opened by Christ* (London, 1654). Richard Farnworth (1627?–66), from Tickhill near Doncaster, was one of the most prolific early Quaker authors. The religious experience he describes took place before George Fox arrived in that area. One point of special interest is the detailed contrast which Farnworth draws between the Quaker standpoint and the practices of the parish church which at that time was Presbyterian. The book was a contribution to the debate on the authentication of ministers of religion occasioned by the setting up of the Commissioners for the Approbation of Publique Ministers (the 'Triers') in March 1654. For accounts of typical Quaker convincements, v., EQW 155–60, the story of Richard Hubberthorne extracted from Swarthmore mss. iv. 4 and iii. 1, letters from Hubberthorne to Fox written in the summer of 1652, at the height of his personal crisis, and from R. Hubberthorne, *A True Testimony of Obedience in the Heavenly Call* (London, 1654), 1–2; also EQW 167–79, extracted from Francis Howgill, *The Inheritance of Jacob* (London, 1656). See also R. Davies, *An Account of the Convincement, Exercises, Services, and Travels of that Ancient Servant of the Lord Richard Davies* (London, 1710).

Extract (b) is from the 'Preface' and 'Description of Babylon' in Isaac Penington, *Babylon the Great Described* (London, 1659), *Works* vol. 1, 135–8. Isaac Penington (1616–79) was the son of Sir Isaac Penington, Lord Mayor of London, representative of the City of London in the Long Parliament and a member of Cromwell's Council of State. Penington junior's spiritual pilgrimage took him first from the Independents to the Seekers. Although not at first impressed by the Quakers whom he met in London, at one of their meetings in 1658 he felt 'the power of the most High amongst them'. 'I felt the dead quickened', he wrote, 'the seed raised, insomuch as my heart ... said "This is he, there is no other, this is he whom I have waited for and often sought after from my childhood ..."' (Thomas Ellwood's 'Testimony' prefacing Penington's collected *Works*, first pub. 1681, new edn Glenside, Pa, 1995–7, also online at the Quaker Heritage Press website.) Extract (b) is an earlier account of this experience v., EQW 230 and R. Melvin Keiser and Rosemary Moore, *Knowing the Mystery of Life Within: Selected Writings of Isaac Penington in their Historical and Theological Context* (London, 2005). Penington suffered much for his Quakerism during the period after the Restoration.

(a) Richard Farnworth

[p. 1] The Condition of a troubled Soul that could find no rest, peace, comfort, nor staisfaction in any thing below the Divine Power and glory of God, breaking forth and appearing through several operations and manifestations, by the blessed Spirit of the Lord Jesus, the Saviour of the Soul.

About the 16 year of the age of my natural life, the Lord did begin to work under a cloud, and let me see the vanity that I lived in, and wrought me into some inward trouble of mind, and I seeing that the wrath of God was revealed against sin in me, knew not what to do to satisfie his Justice that was offended; but by consulting with mine own heart, and carnal reason together, set on some self-acting, to seek for life, peace, comfort, and satisfaction to my soul, and so concluded in my self, that reading, hearing of Sermons, and prayer, was the way and means to appease the wrath of God, and to attain to salvation, believing in the Declaration of the Scriptures, and Christ dying at *Jerusalem*, to satisfie the infinite Justice which was offended by me a sinfull creature; and so betook my self to read often, and pray often, at set times, and to hear Sermons often, that it became customary, and I left off my sports and pleasures, looking upon them all to be vain and heathenish, and became very strict in observing [p. 2] what the Priests did press me unto, and read three times a day, and prayed as often, and several times in the night, and rose out of bed to pray upon my bare knees, because *David* prayed several times in the night, and what I did, it was from imitation of others, knowing no better way then at that present, but as the Priests taught me, who themselves were never taught of God ...

And all this while I was but carnal and earthly, knowing nothing of the new birth, and the resurrection of the just, but walked on in an outward profession, believing all to be true that the Priests told me, and was very zealous for them at that time, and was Catechized by them, observed to do as they gave me directions, and would gladly do what was and might make most for the glory of God, and as they told me, that the Steeplehouse was the Church and House of God, I did then believe them, and as they told me that Sprinkling Infants was one of the Sealing Ordinances; and that which they called a Sacrament, was another; I gave credit to what they said, and was mighty zealous for those traditions three or four years; and I did then loath all open prophaneness, and sports, and pleasures, and Idle and vain company, and grew solid and serious in my way, desiring of the Lord to instruct me and teach me his mind and will, that I might do what he made known unto me, out of the integrity of mine heart, and being strict in hearing, reading and praying, I was reproached by the rude people, and [p. 3] called a Puritan, Roundhead, and the like, and so rejoyced in that, calling it the Cross of Christ; but the Cross of Christ is a mystery.

And about the 20 year, or 21 of my age, I began to question many things that I had been so zealous for; and something rose up in my spirit to work me into an examination of my way and worship that I then lived in, and made me restless in my spirit, and set me on searching the Scriptures very diligently, and by the light of God in my conscience, and the Scriptures together testifying, I came to see that the Steeplehouse was not a Church, nor the house of God, as they had told me; and I believed that prayer was more acceptable in that house then in any other place, till the Lord convinced me of that error received by tradition from the Priests; for I was made to see by the breakings forth of the light of God in my spirit, that the Steeplehouse was no Church, for the Scripture saith, that Christ came to redeem his Church with his blood, and not that Stonehouse; and that the Church of Christ was made all of living stones, elect and pretious, and there is not one living stone in that; and although there were a Temple commanded to be built by *Solomon*, and that was but a figure for the time present, till Christ came to put an end to the Covenant outwardly, Temple, and Sacrifices, that were then offered up; and Christ said, that there should not be one stone left upon another in that Temple that was at *Jerusalem*, and there were never any other commanded to be builded; and now there are many Idols Temples which are no Churches, for the Church is in God the Father of our Lord Jesus Christ, as *Paul* and *Silvanus* writ to the Thessalonians, and the Church of Christ were of one heart, and one mind; but now in the English Churches, or people that assemble together in the Idols Temple, they are of confusion, one saying one thing, and another saying another, both Priests and people divided. But in the Church of Christ there is true unity, and no jarring nor jangling; and the Saints their bodies are Temples for the holy Ghost to dwell in, as God hath said, 2 *Cor.* 6. 17, 18.

Then was I convinced by the light of Christ in my conscience, that the Priests were very formal in that which they called [p. 4] prayer, and that they kept a form of words, and knew beforehand what to speak, when to begin, and when to end ... till I was convinced that either to get prayers out of a book, or to pray by a book, was carnal and formal ... and as the light of God did arise in me, I could not be satisfied with such carnality, and so likewise their Preaching became but as the telling of a Tale ...

[p. 7] And before the time came that we were to go to eat bread and Wine, which they call a Sacrament, and Communion of Saints; but is not (I say before the time came that it was to be given, and I to receive it) there was great reasoning in me, and great preparation I made by reasoning and praying, and powring forth my complaint to the Lord to fit me, and prepare me, and make me worthy to partake of that Ordinance, and make me a fit Communicant, and the like; but after three or four weeks preparation, still I was not right in my self, and knew not what to do, whether to receive it or not; yet lest I should offend, I went, and when I was going, all the way I prayed, and pondered in my heart, and desired of the Lord to seal up assurance to my soul that day by the same; and when I was to receive [p. 8] the Cup into my hand, I trembled in my heart for fear, lest I should be unworthy; and after I had received the bit and the sup, I sat pondering of it in my heart, and waited in expectation in my self, to receive some divine operation, and spiritual change, and to receive assurance of the pardon of sin; but none came in: But the thoughts of my heart did exceedingly trouble me, and *Judas* was brought into my remembrance, how that Satan entred after that he had received the sop: and then great questioning and reasoning did arise in me, whether I were of the number of Gods Elect, yea or no, and great fear came upon me, and I went home, and prayed to the Lord, and cryed and prayed a week or two before I was cleared, and so it wrought for good, for I saw then by the light of God in my conscience, that it was not the body and bloud of Christ, but a carnal invention ... and so was I made to see the error of the Priests in that thing, and that theirs was but a sacrificing to Devils, and not to God, as the Gentiles did, so doe they, I *Cor.* 10. 20, 21 ...

[p. 9] For a year, or very nigh, I was full of trouble, and did see into the deceits of Priests, but looked that some of them should be right, and went from one to another ... and I saw them to be confused in their sayings, one saying one thing, and another saying another ... which did exceedingly trouble me, for in hearing them as the pure seed of God sprung in me, and groaned for deliverance, never a Priest that ever I heard or met with, could deliver, nor direct me where to wait till deliverance came, but drove me further off, for when all duties and performances failed, and death passed upon them that I neither found life in hearing, reading nor prayer, but was ... disquieted and did mourn, and I lamented, but no eye pittied, for ... instead of healing they wounded, and set me to act and do in my will, as I had done, and bad me repent, and believe, and the like, but never told me, neither how to repent nor believe by experience ...

[p. 11] So I was made to deny the priests and their way of worship, and deny all that I had gathered together under them, and wait upon God for teaching, counsel, and direction in all things, according to his promise, which he hath [p. 12] fulfilled; and in waiting upon the Lord, in the light of the spirit of truth I found much inward peace, joy, comfort, and satisfaction to my soul, and the righteous law of the spirit of life set up within, convincing of sin, and the righteous judgement of God, condemning all unrighteousnesse, as the light and law of the spirit of life in Christ Jesus did discover it in me, and the eternal word and power of God were preached in me by Christ Jesus, my Lord, which power did shake the earth, sea, and dry land, and did overturn the mountains by the roots, and put darkness to an end in me, so that the true light of the glory of God in the face of Jesus Christ, doth now shine in my soul, and the heavenly treasure doth dwell in an earthen vessel, as the Apostle did witnesse, 2 *Cor.* 4. 6,7.

And ... Christ is our bread of life, and water of life, and feedeth our souls with the refreshing mercies of his eternal love, so that we having received the promise of the Father, which is the spirit of his Son, crying *Abba*, Father, in our hearts, guiding and leading us into all truth, that we are made to exalt and set forth Jesus Christ to be the everlasting Minister of the new Covenant, and his Gospel is free, and he Preacheth glad tidings to our souls, and giveth good gifts to our souls, and we are made to cry, *Hosanna* to the highest, praises, praises be to our God and Saviour, the Lord God and his Son, and the holy Ghost the Comforter, whom the [p. 13] world knoweth not, nor the priests and Clergy-men, with all their high notions, and guilded pretences, cannot find out ... I deny all that are hirelings, and teach for Tythes, gifts and rewards ...

(b) Isaac Penington
[p. 135] There hath been in me a zeal for God from my childhood, and a most earnest search into the Scriptures (which my soul deeply relished, and my heart honored and loved, and still doth) for the revelation of the mind and will of God. Two things did I earnestly search and beg for: the one was for the discovery of the outward way of worship; the other for the inward life, virtue, and power, which I looked upon the outward as the proper means to lead me to. At the beginning of the troubles in these nations, there was a lively stirring in me, and a hope that God was bringing forth somewhat. I likewise felt the same stirring in many others, at which my heart was rejoiced, and with which my soul was refreshed; but I found it soon begin to flag and wither, which forced me to retire, and to separate from that where I found the life and power dying and decaying. In my separation the Lord was with me; my soul remembereth it right well; and he had [p. 136] regard to the simplicity, honesty, and integrity of my heart, which he himself had kindled in me. And though I fell too soon into a way of church-fellowship and ordinances; yet he had regard to me, and pitied me, and refreshed my life even there. But at length and the form overgrew us, and the sweet and precious life in us began to die. Then the Lord found out another way to refresh us (namely, by a sensible relating of our conditions, and of his dealings with us, and workings in us), which was very sweet and precious at first; but the enemy crept in there also. Out of this state I never made any change; but here the hand of the Lord fell upon me, striking at my very root, breaking all my life in sunder, and trampling my crown in the dust. Then I became a man of sorrows (being stripped of all my life, faith, hope, joy, comfort, in one day) not knowing which way to look, nor what to desire. Sometimes there were breathings stirring in me, but they were presently judged; sometimes a little glance of refreshment from a scripture presented to me; but suddenly taken away, and my death and darkness increased thereby. Then should I wish, Oh that I might appear before his throne! for surely my conscience is clear in his sight, and I have

not wickedly departed from my God, but was broken in pieces by his hand, even while my soul was earnestly seeking after him. Oh how my soul did mourn, to see how I was fit to be made a prey to every ravening spirit! and many did seek to devour me, but the hand of the Lord was with me, preserving me, though I knew it not. And though I was wholly broken, and desolate of all that I had called, or could call, knowledge (insomuch that I could not call any thing either good or evil), yet the Lord, by a secret instinct, preserved me exceedingly out of that which was evil, and kept my heart secretly panting after the fountain and well-spring of good. Yea, when I was at length (through deep despair of ever meeting with God any more in this life) captivated by the world, and betrayed by the love of it (which at last rose up in me, and gained upon me, by persuading me that my present estate and condition did require the free use of it, and the enjoyment of all it could afford), yet the Lord followed me, and often was I visited with secret loathings of the world, and turnings from it, and pantings after the spring of my life: but these were dreaded by me, and suddenly quenched by the [p. 137] evil part, for fear of that misery and unutterable anguish which I had felt hereby; the remembrance whereof was fresh in me.

In this my courting of the world, and estrangement from the life, the reasoning part (which the Lord had been long battering, and had laid very low) gathered strength in me; and I began to grow wise again, and able to judge of the things of God, and to hope and wait for some great appearance, wherein at length I might be visited, and meet with that which I so vehemently desired, and stood in such need of. Thereby the enemy deeply deceived me, pleasing me herewith, and keeping me hereby from unity with that which alone was able to give me the sight of him, whenever he should appear. And in this fleshly wisdom I judged and despised the true life in others; as weak, low, and not able to bring them to that which I stood in need of, and waited for. Yea, the more I considered and reasoned in my mind, and the more I conversed with them (hoping thereby to find some clear ground either of owning or turning from them), and further off still was I; till at length the Lord powerfully touched, and raised up the life in me (which by all these reasonings and consultations, all this while, I slew); and then by degrees (waiting upon that), I saw, I felt, I tasted, I handled, as the Lord pleased to open to me here, that which was shut out from me in my narrowest search and closest reasonings. Thus the Jew in me was cast off, and the Gentile called: but who can read this? I am sure the eye of man's religious wisdom cannot.

Hereby my eyes have been opened, and I have seen the fetters, whereby I have been held captive from my life all my days: yea, many of the streets and chambers of Babylon hath mine eye beheld (in the pure life), wherein the witch dwells which enchanteth from the life: yea, I have heard the tongue of the false prophet, which speaketh so like the true prophet, as no flesh can discern or distinguish between them: yea, I have seen the dragon in the temple, worshipped there for God, by the strictest sort of professors. And now, in tender bowels, in the true light of life, from the pure movings of the eternal spirit (as the Lord pleaseth to guide and direct) do I come forth to visit my poor fellow-creatures and captives in Babylon. And what I have seen and known, I testify for the relief of others, that, if it [p. 138] be possible (by the mercy and good hand of God), they may escape that misery wherewith my poor soul hath been overwhelmed, and may come out of that filthy, abominable city which God is making desolate; where the pure life, the conquering faith, the suffering love, the purifying hope, the putting off of the body of sin, the putting on the living garment, is not and cannot be witnessed, but men are only dreaming of these things in Babylon; where all the satisfaction they have, is from the pleasure of their dream; but when they awake they will find leanness, and penury, and nakedness upon their souls ...

Babylon is the spiritual fabric of iniquity; the mystical great city of the great king of darkness; built in imitation of Sion, painted just like Sion, that it might be taken for Sion, and be worshipped there, instead of the true, eternal, ever-living God, and King of Sion.

Document V.6

The Joy of the Spiritual Marriage

This extract is from Thomas Goodwin, *Of the Object and Acts of Justifying Faith* in *Works* (1864), VIII, 398–401. For Goodwin (1600–80), President of Magdalen College, Oxford, 1650–60, v., 'Memoir' by Robert Halley in Thomas Goodwin, *Works* (Edinburgh, 1865), II; C.R. and DNB.

For our communion is with God, and with his Son, Jesus Christ. Our communion is with God, who, as the Father of spirits, is the fountain and centre of our souls, and they cannot have any rest or complacent satisfaction but in the bosom of this their Father ... Our communion is also with Christ.

Then also the union, on which this our communion is founded, is of all other the closest, which by the help of faith in the understanding, and of love in the will, joins God and the soul into one spirit. For there are two arms of the soul wherewith we embrace God, the understanding, and will; and there are also two hands in believers, adjoined to those arms, faith and love, by which we lay hold on God, and embrace him.

(1) Faith, as it always unites us unto Christ, so sometimes it is strengthened and elevated by a light flowing from above, and makes us to rejoice with joy unspeakable: I Pet. i.8 ... This heavenly light, with which faith sometimes shines, is not a dry light, but drops with honey, and bedews the soul with the most delicious sweetness. What doth Philip pray for? John xiv.8, 'Philip saith unto him, Lord, shew us the Father, and it sufficeth us;' it was sufficient to satisfy him, what Christ promised, ver.21, 'He that hath my commandments, and keepeth them, he it is that loveth me; and he that loveth me shall be loved of my Father, and I will love him, and will manifest myself to him:' which he often performs, and sometimes illuminates the mind with light, which doth not only shew him conspicuous to be seen, but which doth exhibit him present to the soul in the most real and intimate presence, whence ariseth the most real and closest union and communion, and also the highest and most glorious joy ...

(2) I now come to consider the second bond of communion, and the other cause of this 'joy in the Holy Ghost', which is the conjugal union of the will to God in the bonds of love. For as soon as that threefold aspect of the Trinity [i.e., communion with Father, Son and Holy Ghost] ... hath shined in the soul, she kindles with an heavenly flame, and a reciprocal love to God ariseth in her; for the love of God manifested to her, doth as with a fan make this flame of divine love to break forth. And hence the holy soul doth triumph, and is sweetly delighted, for that great conjunction of these two loves, both of that which flows from God to us, and that which is in us infused, never falls out, but it brings jointly with it an august and solemn jubilee in the heart ...

Nor is the joy of a Christian yet in its height and splendour, for the soul doth not only perceive that she is loved again by her beloved, but that she is most closely united with him, and that she enjoys her beloved, which union Christ himself makes; and as the enjoyment of him is the blessed fruit of that union, so he is the efficient of it too.

First, The soul is united to Christ, for being allured by the sight of the divine excellencies, and powerfully drawn by his love, as with a magnetic force, she goes out of herself, and most earnestly desires union with God; this she breathes after with so great a vehemence, as she doth not only desire to be united to Christ, but to be melted, to be transformed into him, as much as his being her absent bridegroom will admit; she reposeth and layeth close herself in the most inward bowels of his love. for whoever loves God is said to abide, and to dwell in God, I John iv.15, 16.

Secondly, And behold now how good and pleasant it is, for God and the soul, as husband and wife, to dwell together in unity; and not only to cohabit, but to rejoice in one another: Isa. lxii. 5, 'For as a young man marrieth a virgin, so shall thy sons marry thee; and as the bridegroom rejoiceth over the bride, so shall thy God rejoice over thee.' Cant. i. 2, 'Let him kiss me with the kisses of his mouth, for thy love is better than wine.' And behold how Christ dismisseth his spouse filled with himself, and full of joy; for what virtue and efficacy must there be in the kisses of his mouth, whose lips breathe life, Gen. ii. 7 ... Nor doth Christ only give the kisses of his mouth, but the entire possession of himself, so that the soul takes hold on, and possesseth whole God, wholly as her own, so as it is free for her to enjoy all the sweetness of God (if it were possible to an infinity), and to draw out and taste all the pleasures which can be drawn from Christ, even to eternity.

Document V.7

John Owen: Union with Christ

This extract is from *Of Communion with God the Father, Son, and Holy Ghost* (1657), reproduced in W. H. Goold (ed.), *The Works of John Owen, D.D.* (Edinburgh, 1862), II. The page numbers in the extract refer to this edition. There is an excellent summary of the book in Sinclair B. Ferguson, *John Owen on the Christian Life*

(Edinburgh, 1987), 74–98. For Owen (1616–83), v., Peter Toon, *God's Statesman: The Life and Work of John Owen* (Exeter, 1971).

[p. 54] the next thing that comes under consideration is, the *way* whereby we hold communion with the Lord Christ ... Now, this the Scripture manifests to be by the way of *conjugal relation*. He is married unto us, and we unto him; which spiritual relation is attended with suitable conjugal affections. And this gives us fellowship with him as to his personal excellencies ... So Isa. liv, 5, 'Thy Maker is thine husband; the LORD of hosts is his name; and thy Redeemer the Holy One of Israel; The God of the whole earth shall he be called.' This is yielded as the reason why the church shall not be ashamed nor confounded in the midst of her troubles and trials – she is married unto her Maker, and her Redeemer is her husband ...

[p. 55] And it is the main design of the ministry of the gospel, to prevail with men to give themselves unto the Lord Christ, as he reveals his kindness in this engagement ... And this is a *relation* wherein the Lord Jesus is exceedingly delighted, and inviteth others to behold him in this his glory ... The day of his espousals, of taking poor sinful souls into his bosom, is the day of the gladness of his heart ...

[p. 56] The time of his taking the church unto himself is the day of his marriage; and the church is his bride, his wife, Rev. xix. 7,8 ... Christ makes himself over to the soul, to be his, as to all love, care, and tenderness of a husband; and the soul gives up itself wholly unto the Lord Christ, to be his, as to all loving, tender obedience ... Christ gives himself to the *soul*, with all his *excellencies*, righteousness, preciousness, graces, and eminencies, to be its Saviour, head, and husband, for ever to dwell with it in this holy relation ...

[p. 57] On the part of the *saints*, it is their *free, willing consent* to receive, embrace, and submit unto the Lord Jesus, as their husband, Lord, Saviour, – to abide with him, subject their souls unto him, and to be ruled by him for ever.

Document V.8

George Fox: 'According to the Spirit I Am the Son of God'

A reader of Fox's *Journal* or his collected *Epistles* is barely aware of the extremes of behaviour and beliefs described in *Querers and Quakers* (v. Document III.8). Fox's collected works were smoothed down by careful editing to suit the taste of the end of the century. The next extract is an early epistle of Fox which was not included in the collected edition, although at least two manuscript versions survive. Note the address to Friends 'raised to discerning'. This is one of a number of indications that there were various strata among Quakers and that newcomers to Quakerism were not expected to absorb the full teaching immediately. Spelling modernized.

The text is that of Swarthmore MS. ii. 55, with spelling and where possible punctuation modernised; also in Caton mss. ii. 48–9, in Friends' House, London. For a full introduction to this epistle v., H. Larry Ingle, 'George Fox as Enthusiast', JFHS, 55 (1983–9), 265–9.

According to the spirit I am the son of God and according to the flesh I am the seed of Abraham, which seed is Christ, which seed is but one in all his saints, and the promise is to the seed, which seed is not many but one, which seed is Christ and Christ in you. The mystery which has been hid from ages, but now is made manifest, which seed though there be ten thousand, yet are all one, which seed bruises the serpents head; & the serpent speaks in all in the first nature and is the head; upon the seed if the serpent is cursed with the seed of the Woman the seed of the woman [Gen. 3: 15] is head and speaks. And male and female come to the beginning, and Christ is all and in all, and the promise of God here is fulfilled; According to the spirit I am the son of God before Abraham was, before Jerusalem was, the same which does descend, the same does ascend and all the promises of God are yea come out of time from God, into time, so that which is captivated in the earth in time, and to it the seed which is Christ, they are all yea and a man fetches up out of him, where there is no time; all that can perceive this are happy and blest who have ears to hear, blessed are your ears, who have eyes to see blessed are your eyes, and blessed is he that receives the truth, in the love of God and walks in it up to God; The blessing is upon Abraham and his seed, blessing I will bless thee and multiplying I will multiply thy seed, and blessed is he that blesses thee and cursed is he that curses thee. To the seed all Nations shall bow where it is carried up into power, and will not bow to the devil, if he would give it all the glory of the world, but tramples upon all, and worships no god but the living God, though there be many gods in the world. Every form and Nation has a god, but it will worship none of these gods, but tramples upon them all. Every carnal heart who loves the wages of unrighteousness, who has a god as Balaam had, but was slain with the seed, the seed of God where it is raised up by the same spirit that raised up Jesus Christ who are brought from the dead, reign over all the world, and comprehend all the world have the same mind that was in Christ Jesus, the same spirit that raised Christ Jesus and he that has not is none of his, but he that has comprehends all Nations, languages, kindreds and tongues, and all Babylons ways, and all the Mystery of Iniquity, and the master of harlots, and all manner of colours, which no beast has, this seed where it is redeemed, it comes out of kindreds and they be all one if ten thousand, out of all Nations God is pure who hath spoken it, and as many as received the word, I say unto you, you are gods, as it is written in your law, and the scriptures cannot be broken, and he that denies the word of God breaks scriptures. Now wait all to have these things fulfilled in you, if it be never so little a measure wait in it, that ye may grow up to a perfect man in Christ Jesus, there is a feeding upon the milk of the word, before you come to the word.

    Let a copy of this be sent to Margaret Fell & every other friends that are raised to a discerning

Document V.9

James Nayler: Union with Christ

This extract is from James Nayler, *Love to the Lost* (London, 1656). For Nayler see III.14. The page numbers refer to the original edition. The possibility of complete union with Christ was a tenet of Quakerism from the beginning and many of their contemporaries considered, not without some justification, that Quakers took this belief to the point of blasphemy. The following extract is the chapter concerning Christ Jesus. Note the emphasis on the eternal, spiritual Christ. Quakers always had a problem in reconciling their experience of the living Christ with the human life of the man, Jesus, and his work on earth. Note also the last three paragraphs on freedom from sin. Quakers meant this actually and literally. Some critics thought their claims were impossible. As one of them put it, 'Some of them affirmes, that they are come up to so much perfection, that they have not had an ill thought nor spoken an ill word, for two years together' (Francis Harris, *Queries Proposed to the Quakers* (London, 1656), 22). But Quakers were utterly serious about the obligation to express in daily life the practical consequences of living in the light of Christ and were severe on those of their adherents who failed to live up to the required standards.

Concerning Christ Jesus

[p. 54] This is he whom the world much talk of, but few there be that know him, though it be He by whom all things were made, who is the Life of all Creatures, the Beginning of all Creatures who was before all, a King, of whose Dominion there is no end ...

And this is He who is the Light of the world, and lighteth every man that comes into the world; who stands at the door and knocks, and if any hear his voice and open, he will come in and sup with him; and such know him, and he knows them who hear his voice, by which they are quickned out of the trespasses and sins, and the Seed of God raised out of death; but where Death reigns, Christ is rejected, and the wisdome by which he should be known is foolishnesse.

So if you desire to know him who is not of this world, but who is before the world was, a Witnesse against all the worlds wayes and wickednesse, then [p. 55] minde the light in you which thus witnesseth; for as Christ is, so is his light that leads to him; for that which bears testimony against the world, is not of the world, even as he is not of the world, and so leads out of the world, to him who is not known in the world: for the world by wisdome knows him not. And as thou follows the light out of the world, thou wilt come to see the seed, which by the worlds wisdom and glory is crucified; to which seed are all the Promises, and wherein is all the knowledge of God and Christ: and as that Seed is raised, therein is the Father revealed, and his Power and God-head, in his Son Jesus Christ, which in him dwells, and without him is not revealed, but being known is Life Eternal, and Eternal Power, and Eternal Glory, and Riches, made manifest in the Light: for as you know this Seed raised by the same Spirit, that raised Jesus Christ from the death; So shall you see him to whom all Power and Judgement is committed in

Heaven and Earth: of whom it is said, When he bringeth his onely begotten Son into the world, let all the Angels worship him; who maketh his Angels Spirits, and his Ministers a flame of fire; whose Flesh is the Life of Men, and his Light is as a Law that goeth forth, whereby man is led to his food, and the Sons of men sees out of darknesse; and this is he who cannot be limitted, nor his person restrained in one place, who filleth Heaven and Earth with his presence, and appeareth at his pleasure to his own; (though the wise of the world knows him not, and therefore limit him above the Stars) who dwelleth in the bodies of his Saints; But as for the Reprobates, they know him not so, who have put the good day far from them, and hate reproof, that they may spend their dayes in folly, and feed themselves with the wind, and fill their hearts with carnal delights. When the hearts of the Children of light are established with grace, yet these will be disputing about the body of Christ; but the body of sin rules in them, whereby they are darkned and become heart-blind, past feeling the measure of *God*, whose hearts are overcharged with surfeiting, and cares of the world, and their minds corrupted with earthly things.

To such I say, Cease your imaginations, as to find out what Christ is in that state, for he alone reveals himselfe in spirit, to such as wait in the light, and love that which is pure; to such his appearance is as the Sun, whose rising is not by the will of Man, but for his appearing all the world must wait, to be refreshed with the beams of his Glory, and to all who ar yet in the night, shall he appear, if you look towards the place of his rising, which is not, Lo here, Lo there; but within you in your hearts: and all who are come to the sure word of Prophesie, as to a light that shines in a dark place, to which you do well to take heed, till the day dawn, and the day starre arise in your hearts, you shall see the Sun arise where the day star appears in your hearts, if in the light you waite that shines in the darknesse: and you shall feel the vertue and life of him, and receive thereof to live in the same with him: and you shall see him as he is, and knoiw him to be the Sun of Righteousnesse, whose arising is, with healing in his wings, and whose breaking forth is upon all his enemies which over the seed hath raigned; whose spiritual weapons are mighty through *God* to the pulling down strong holds, casting down imaginations, and [p. 56] every high thing that exalteth it self against the Knowledge of God, and bringing into captivity every thought to the obedience of himselfe, and having in readinesse to revenge all disobedience when your obedience is fulfilled.

And thus the Saints know the Son, with his Light, his Power and Dominion over all things in Heaven and in Earth; who rules in righteousness in the hearts of his people, trampling down Satan under their feet, which Sonne of God Hypocrites call Lord, Lord, but the Devil they serve and obey, and though such have got the words of Lord, and Christ, and Jesus, yet they know not his light, his power, his kingdome, and dominion, over sin and the Divel in them, to set them free therefrom, by his light and life ...

Nay it is manifest amongst you, that the Name Jesus which gives the Saints victory over sin, you know not; Who have it in words, and therewith make a cover for your sin, your pride, lust and excesse. What covetousnesse, and all manner of unrighteousnesse is covered over with a profession of the Name of Christ, which redeems from those things all that knows him ...

But who sayes they know Christ, and are redeemed; and commits sin, not keeping his commands, is a lyar: and so abides not in the truth, and anointing: and so is of the Divel, and not of Christ; for he that abides in Christ, sins not: For the Name of Jesus Christ is power over all sin, as it is known, and the Creature baptized into it by faith. So all that know Christ, know the seed, the promise, the Word of Life, the Covenant, the Heritage, the righteousnesse, the kingdom, the power, the glory which is not of this world, and the Father of all: which you that commits sin have not seen. Neither can any say that Jesus is Lord but by the Spirit; so you whose knowledge is without, another Lord rules within.

Document V.10

A Puritan Soldier at Home

Lieut.-Col. John Hutchinson (1615–64), of Owthorpe, Nottinghamshire, was a distinguished parliamentary soldier and served as parliamentary governor of the town and castle of Nottingham during the Civil Wars. He was elected MP for Nottingham in 1646. At first he sided with the Independents but later, under the influence of his wife, he became a Baptist. He was a member of the first two Councils of State under the Commonwealth but retired into private life in 1653 due, not least, to disillusion with the policies of Cromwell. He signed the King's death sentence but was not excepted from the Act of Indemnity. He was, however, constantly under suspicion, was arrested and died of fever at Sandown Castle, 11 September 1664.

The following extract is the description of him by his wife, Lucy, from her autobiography prefixed to her *Memoirs of the Life of Colonel Hutchinson*, written between 1664 and 1667 but not published until 1806. Lucy (born in 1620), was the daughter of Sir Allen Apsley, Lieutenant of the Tower of London. She had received an excellent education and was proficient in French and Latin and acquired some knowledge also of Greek and Hebrew. Her account of her husband is unique in Puritan literature. It provides an intimate and touching portrait of him. She makes no attempt to hide the fact that he was her hero. The picture of him and his family goes a long way towards correcting the misleading caricatures of the Puritans – especially well-to-do Puritans – that have dominated people's imagination. She died at an unknown date after 1675. For John and Lucy Hutchinson, see C. H. Firth's article in DNB with a full bibliography.

[The first section is entitled, 'His Description'. After a detailed account of his physical characteristics, she goes on:]

he was quick in his pace and turns, nimble and active and graceful in all his motions; he was apt for any bodily exercise, and any that he did became him; he could dance admirably well, but neither in youth nor riper years made any practice of it; he had skill in fencing, such as became a gentleman; he had a great love of music, and often diverted himself with a viol, on which he played masterly; and he had an exact ear and judgment in other music; he shot excellently in bows and guns, and much used them for his exercise; he had great judgment in paintings, graving, sculpture, and all liberal arts, and had many curiosities of value in all kinds; he took great delight in perspective glasses, and for his other rarities was not so much affected with the antiquity as the merit of the work; he took much pleasure in improvement of grounds, in planting groves, and walks, and fruit-trees, in opening springs and making fish-ponds; of country recreations he loved none but hawking, and in that was very eager and much delighted for the time he used it, but soon left it off; he was wonderfully neat, cleanly, and genteel in his habit, and had a very good fancy in it, but he left off very early the wearing of anything that was costly, yet in his plainest negligent habit appeared very much a gentleman; he had more address than force of body, yet the courage of his soul so supplied his members that he never wanted strength when he found occasion to employ it; his conversation was very pleasant, for he was naturally cheerful, had a ready wit and apprehension; he was eager in everything he did, earnest in dispute, but withal very rational, so that he was seldom overcome; everything that it was necessary for him to do he did with delight, free and unconstrained; he hated ceremonious compliment, but yet had a natural civility and complaisance to all people ...

[The next section bears the title, 'His Virtues'.]

in the head of all his virtues I shall set that which was the head and spring of them all, his Christianity ... By Christianity I intend that universal habit of grace which is wrought in a soul by the regenerating Spirit of God, whereby the whole creature is resigned up into the divine will and love, and all its actions directed to the obedience and glory of its Maker, As soon as he had improved his natural understanding with the acquisition of learning, the first studies in which he exercised himself were the principles of religion, and the first knowledge he laboured for was a knowledge of God, which by a diligent examination of the Scripture, and the several doctrines of great men pretending that ground, he at length obtained. Afterwards, when he had laid a sure and orthodox foundation in the doctrine of the free grace of God given us by Jesus Chgrist, he began to survey the superstructures, and to discover much of the hay and stubble of men's inventions in God's worship, which his spirit burned up in the day of their trial. His faith being established in the truth, he was full of love to God and all his saints. He hated persecution for religion, and was always a champion for all religious people against all their great oppressors ...

Document V.11

Thomas Goodwin: *The Heart of Christ*

In 1642 Thomas Goodwin published *Christ set Forth in his Death, Resurrection, Ascension, Sitting on Gods right hand, Intercession* and appended to it a 'treatise', with a separate title-page, *The Heart of Christ in Heaven, Towards Sinners on Earth*.

In its opening paragraph he refers to the former work.

The Heart of Christ in Heaven is sometimes described as a 'classic' and not without justification. It represents an aspect of Puritan spiritual experience that helps to explain the attraction of Puritan preaching. The emphasis on divine grace and mercy was a constant theme and is expressed here by Goodwin in a striking and uncommon way. A writer in the *Edinburgh Review* (January 1874) sought to connect Goodwin's exposition of the 'Heart of Christ' with the Roman Catholic devotion to the Sacred Heart, a suggestion already made by Lemontey, *Œuvres* (1831), VII, 443 and v., T. Wenzelburger in *Unsere Zeit* (15 November 1873) for an early German translation of Goodwin's book. In fact the devotion to the Sacred Heart had begun in the Middle Ages. For its development, v., ODCC, art. 'Sacred Heart'.

For Thomas Goodwin (1600–80), v., *Works* (1861), vol. 2, i–lxxv; DNB and CR. He was one of the Dissenting Brethren at the Westminster Assembly, President of Magdalen College, Oxford, from 1650 to the Restoration, one of the leading figures at the Savoy Conference of 1658 and a prominent Nonconformist after the Restoration.

[pp. 1–3] Having set forth our Lord and Saviour JESUS CHRIST in all those great and most solemne actions of his, his *Obedience* unto *death*, his *Resurrection, Ascension into heaven*, his *sitting at Gods right hand*, and *Intercession* for us ... I shall now annexe (as next in order, and homogeneall thereunto) this Discourse that follows, which layes open *The HEART* of Christ, as now he is in heaven, sitting at Gods right hand, and interceding for us; *How* it is *affected*, and *graciously disposed* towards sinners on earth that doe come to him; how willing to receive them; how ready to entertaine them; how tender to pity them in all their infirmities, both sinnes and miseries. The scope and use whereof will be this, To hearten and encourage Beleevers to come more boldly unto the Throne of Grace, unto such a Saviour and High-priest, when they shall know how sweetly and tenderly his heart (though he is now in glory) is inclined towards them; and so to remove that great stone of stumbling which we meet with, (and yet lyeth unseen) in the thoughts of men in the way to faith, that Christ being now absent, and withall exalted to so high and infinite a distance of glory, as to *sit at Gods right hand, &c.* they therefore cannot tell how to come to treat with him about their salvation so freely, and with the hopefulnesse to obtaine, as those poore sinners did, who were here on earth with him: Had our lot been (think they) but to have conversed with him (in the dayes of his flesh) as *Mary*, and *Peter*, and his other Disciples did here below, wee could have thought to have beene bold with him, and have been familiar with him, and to have had any thing at his hands; For they beheld him afore them, a man like unto themselves, and he was full of meeknesse, and gentlenesse, he being then himselfe made sinne, and sensible of all sorts of miseries; but now he is gone into a farre countrey, and hath put on glory and immortality, and how his heart may be altered thereby we know not. The drift of this Discourse is therefore to ascertaine poore soules, that his *Heart* (in respect of pity and compassion) remains the same it was on earth; that he intercedes there with the same heart he did here below; and that he is as meek, as gentle, as easie to be entreated, as tender in his bowels; so that they may deale with him as fairely about the great matter of their salvation, and as hopefully, and upon as easie tearmes obtaine it of him, as they might if they had beene on earth with him, and be as familiar with him in all their requests, as bold with him in all their needs: then which nothing can be more for the comfort and encouragement of those, who have given over all other lives but that of faith, and whose soules pursue after strong and entire communication with their Saviour Christ.

[pp. 11–13] But certainly, no loving Husband ever endeavoured more to satisfie the heart of his Spouse during his absence, then Christ doth his Disciples hearts, and in them , all Beleevers:..First, he lets them see what his heart would be unto them, and how mindfull when in heaven, by that *businesse* which he professeth hee went thither to performe for them: concerning which, observe first, that he lovingly acquainted them with it afore-hand what it is, which argued care and tendernesse, as from an husband unto a wife it doth; And withall, how plain heartedly doth he speak, as one that would not hide any thing from them? *Ioh.* 16.7. *I tell you the truth* of it, (sayes he) *it is expedient* (and expedient) *for you* [sic], *that I goe away.* And secondly, he tels them, it is wholly for them and their happinesse; *I goe to send you a Comforter*, whilst you are in this world, & *to prepare a place for you*, (*Iohn* 14.2) when you shall goe out of this world: *There are many mansions in my Fathers house*, and I goe to take them up for you, & to keep your places for you till you come. And there againe, how openly and candidly doth he speak to them? *If it had beene otherwise*, (sayes he) *I would have told you*: You may beleeve me, I would not deceive you for all the glory in that place to which I am agoing. Whom would not this opennesse and nakednesse of heart perswade? But then thirdly, the *businesse* it selfe being such as is so much for us and our happinesse; how much more doth that argue it? And indeed, Christ himselfe doth fetch from thence an argument of the continuance of his love to them. So *ver.* 3. *If I goe to prepare a place for you*, (if that be my errand) then doubt not of my love when I am there; All the glory of the place shall never make me forget my businesse. When he was on earth, he forgot none of the businesse for which he came into the World: Shall *I not doe my Fathers businesse?* (sayd he, when he was a child) yes, and he did it to the utmost, by *fulfilling all righteousnesse*. Surely therefore he will not forget any of that businesse which he is to do in heaven, it being the more pleasant work by far. And ... *He is entred as a Fore-runner*, an Harbinger, to take up places there for us, and if he could forget us, yet our names are all written in heaven round about him, & are continually afore his eyes written there, not onely by Gods election, so *Heb.* 12.23. *ye are come to mount Sion, and to the heavenly Ierusalem, and to the Church of the first-borne (which are written in heaven;) and to Iesus, and to the bloud of sprinkling, &c.* but Christ himselfe scores them up anew with his bloud, over every mansion there, which he takes up for any. Yea, he carryeth their names written in his heart, as the High-priest did the names of the ten Tribes on his breast, when he entred the Holy of Holies. He sits in heaven to see to it, that none other should take their roomes over their heads, (as we say). And therefore, I *Pet.* I.4. Salvation is said to *be reserved in Heaven for them*, that is, kept on purpose for them by Jesus Christ ...

[pp. 14–15] ... Then ... to manifest his mindfulnesse of them, and of all beleevers else, when he should be in glory, he tels them that when he hath dispatched that busines for them, and made Heaven ready for them, and all the elect that are to come, that then he meanes to come again to them ... He condescends to the very laws of the Bridegrrooms; (for notwithstanding all his greatnesse, no Lover shall put him down in any expression of true love). It is the manner of Bridegrooms, when they have made all ready in their Fathers house, then to come themselves and fetch their Brides, and not to send for them by others, because it is a time of love, Love decends, better then ascends; and so doth the love of Christ, who indeed is Love it self, & therefore comes down to us himself: *I will come again and receive you unto my self*, (sayes Christ) *that so where I am, you may be also*. That last part of his speech gives the reason of it, and withall bewrayes his entire affection; It is as if he had said, The truth is, I cannot live without you; I shall never be quiet till I have you where I am, that so we may never part againe, (that is the reason of it,) Heaven shall not hold me, nor my Fathers company, if I have not you with me, my heart is so set upon you: And if I have any glory, you shall have part of it. So *ver.* 19. *Because I live, you shall live also*. It is a reason, and it is halfe an oath besides; *As I live* is Gods oath; *Because I live* sayes Christ; He pawnes his life upon it, and desires to live upon no other tearms ...

[pp. 16–17] ... what his heart would be towards them in his absence, he expresseth by the carefull provision hee makes, and the order hee takes for their comfort in his absence. *Ioh.* 16.18. *I will not leave you as Orphanes*, (so the word is). I will not leave you like father-lesse and friendlesse children at sixes and sevens. My Father and I have but one onely friend who lyes in the bosome of us both, and proceedeth from us both, the holy Ghost, and in the meane time I will send him to you. Doing herein as a loving Husband useth to doe in his absence, even commit his Wife to the dearest friend he hath; so doth Christ ... And *Chap.* 16.7. he saith, *I will send him to you*. Who,

First, shall be a better Comforter unto you than I am to be in this kind of dispensation, (which whilst I am on earth, I am bound up towards you in) ... who by reason of his office, will comfort you better then I should doe with my bodily presence ...

And yet secondly, all the comfort he shall speak to you all that while will be but from the expression of my heart towards you: For as he comes not of himselfe, but *I must send him*, (*Ioh.* 16.7). so *he will speake nothing of himselfe*, but *whatsoever he shall heare, that will he speake*, (*ver.* 13). And *ver.* 14. he sayes, *He shall receive of mine, and shall shew it unto you*. Him therefore shall I send on purpose to be in my roome, and to execute my place to you my Bride, Spouse, and he shall tell you (if you will listen to him, and not grieve him) nothing but stories of my love ...

[Having analysed the doctrine in the light of numerous scriptural passages, Goodwin draws the discussion to a close as follows:]

[pp. 139–40] As the Doctrine delivered is a *comfort*, so the greatest *motive* against sinne; and perswasive unto obedience ... You know not by sinning what blowes you give the heart of Christ: If no more but that his joy is the lesse in you, it should move you, as it useth to do those that are ingenuous. And take this one incentive to obedience, that if he retaine the same heart and mind for mercy towards you which he had here on earth: Then to answer his love, endeavour you to have the same heart towards him on earth, which you hope to have in heaven; and as you daily pray, *Thy will be done on earth as it is in heaven.*

In all miseries and distresses you may be sure to know where to have a friend to help you and pity you, even in heaven, CHRIST; one whose nature, office, interest, relation, all, doe engage him to your succour; you will finde men, even friends, to be oftentimes unto you unreasonable, and their bowels in many cases shut up towards you. Well, say to them all, If you will not pittie me, *Choose, I know one that will,* one in heaven, whose *heart is touched with the feeling of all my infirmities,* and I will goe and bemoane my selfe to him. *Come boldly ... even with open mouth*, to lay your complaints, and *you shall find grace and mercy to helpe in time of need.* Men love to see themselves pitied by friends, though they cannot *help them*: Christ can and will doe both.

Document V.12

John Owen: The Presence of Christ

The following extract is from *Of Spiritual Gifts*, in W. H. Goold (ed.), *The Works of John Owen, D.D.* (Edinburgh, 1852), IV, 499–500.

The Lord Jesus Christ hath faithfully promised to be present with his church 'unto the end of the world.' It is his temple and his tabernacle, wherein he will dwell and walk continually. And this presence of Christ is what makes the church to be what it is, – a congregation essentially distinct from all other societies and assemblies of men ...

Let men be formed into what order you please, according unto any outward rules and measures that are either given in the Scripture or found out by themselves, let them derive power and authority by what claim soever they shall think fit, yet if Christ be not present with them, they are no church, nor can all the powers under heaven make them so to be. And when any church loseth the especial presence of Christ, it ceaseth so to be ...

And those churches do exceedingly mistake their interest who are solicitous about other things, but make little inquiry after the evidences of the presence of Christ among them. Some walk as if they supposed they had him sure enough, as it were, immured in their walls, whilst they keep up the name of a church, and an outward order that pleaseth and advantageth themselves. But outward order, be it what it will, is so far from being the only evidence of the presence of Christ in a church, that when it is alone, or when it is principally required, it is none at all ...

Document V.13

The Glory of Silent Meetings

Quakers disapproved of set, prearranged sermons. Some Quakers did preach at length, and even published collections of sermons, but they were supposedly extempore and taken down in shorthand. In a Quaker meeting for worship there would be a good deal of silence, in which the bulk of the spoken ministry would be delivered by regular ministers, though anyone who felt truly moved could contribute to the ministry. Two discussions of Quaker worship follow.

Extract (a): Alexander Parker to Friends, 14 January 1661, *A Manifestation of Divine Love*, from pp. 15–19. Publishers old-style date 1660. Parker (1628–89) was a friend of George Fox living in London. This is part of a long epistle of general advice to Friends and was written during a time of great political upheaval and uncertainty. Page numbering is from the version in LEF.

Extract (b): George Keith, *The Benefit, Advantage and Glory of Silent Meetings* (London, 1670). Keith (1638–1716), one of the greatest intellectuals among seventeenth-century Quakers, was a friend of the Quaker theologian Robert Barclay. For Barclay, v. VI.18. Keith finally left the Quakers and was ordained in the Church of England and became one of the first missionaries sent to America by the Society for the Propagation of the Gospel.

(a)
[p. 365] So Friends, when you come together to wait upon God, come orderly in the fear of God: the first that enters into the place of your meeting, be not careless, nor wander up and down, either in body or mind; but innocently sit down in some place, and turn in thy mind to the light, and wait upon God singly, as if none were present but the Lord; and here thou art strong. Then the next that comes in, let them in simplicity of heart, sit down and turn in to the same light, and wait in the Spirit: and so all the rest coming in, in the fear of the Lord, sit down in pure stillness and silence of all flesh, and wait in the light; a few that are thus gathered by the arm of the Lord into the unity of the Spirit; this is a sweet and precious meeting, where all meet with the Lord ...

Those that are brought to a pure, still waiting upon God in the Spirit, are come nearer to the [p. 366] Lord than words are: for God is a Spirit, and in the Spirit is he worshipped; so that my soul hath dear union with you, who purely wait upon God in the Spirit, though not a word be spoken to the hearing of the outward ear. And here is the true feeding in the Spirit; and all who thus meet together to wait upon the Lord, shall renew their strength daily. In such a meeting, where the presence and power of God is felt, there will be an unwillingness to part asunder, being ready to say in yourselves, it is good to be here: and this is the end of all words and writings, to bring people to the eternal living Word. So, all dear hearts, when you come together to wait upon God, come singly and purely; that your meetings together may be for the better, and not for the worse.

And if any be moved to speak words, wait low in the pure fear, to know the mind of the Spirit, where and to whom they are to be spoken ... If any be moved to speak, see that they speak in the power; and when the power is still, be ye still ...

And all who speak of the movings of the Lord, I lay it as a charge upon you, to beware of abusing the power of God, in acting a wrong thing under pretence of being moved by the Lord; for the pure power may move, and then the enemy (who goes about like a roaring lion, seeking whom he may devour,) he may present a wrong thing to the view of the understanding; and here is a danger of abusing the power, acting that which the true power condemns, and yet pretending that the power moves to it; this is a double sin. Therefore, let every one patiently wait, and not be hasty to run in the dark; but keep low in the true fear, that the understanding may be opened to know the mind of [p. 367] the Spirit; and then as the Spirit moves and leads, it is good to follow its leadings; for such are led into all truth ... Thus, my Friends, as you keep close to the Lord, and to the guidance of his good Spirit, ye shall not do amiss; but in all your services and performances in the worship of God, ye shall be a good savour unto the Lord; and the Lord will accept of your services, and bless and honour your assemblies with his presence and power.

(b)
[p. 14] Now among divers great and blessed advantages and benefits, which they who came to be convinced did find, in the sitting down together to wait in silence, there were some that in the silence, their minds being turned towards the light and life of God, which had appeared to them, they came to find there minds stayed therein, and thereby, for a great and mighty power broke forth, in the light, unto which their minds were turned and did gather their minds into it more and more, whereby they came to know a being planted and grounded, and rooted and setled and established in the truth, and in the light, and life, and spirit, and power thereof, and so they came to be gathered out of the tossings, and waverings of mind, and out of the incumbrances and wandrings into stability and steddiness in the truth, which was even as to be delivered from a stormy and tempestuous Sea, and brought to dry land, and thus also they came to be gathered out of their own thoughts and imaginations and uncertain conjectures, and guessings concerning the things of God, and religion, into the clear and certain manifestation of truth, by which also they came to receive an inward discerning, so as to distinguish, and [p. 15] make a difference infalliby betwixt things and things in them, as to see and know and feel what was of God, and what was not of him, but of man or of Satan, and so as they waited in this silence, their minds being turned towards the Lord, they could discern the right and wrong spirit, and the work and motion of each, and came to see, what was to be kept and spared, and what was to be denied, what was to be preserved alive, and cherished and nourished, and what was to be slain, and famished and starved, and so in the silence they came to find the pure judgement of the Lord, to pass over and through all in them, as the refiners fire, which purifieth the Gold and Silver, but consumeth the dross and maketh a clear separation, and the power of the Lord God was found and felt to work mightily in them, for the breaking down and killing, and consuming and destroying every evil thing and work, which had place in them, and removing and taking out of the way, whatever, clouded, or vailed, or burthened the pure life to arise and shine forth, and so the mountains which were raised over the seed and burthened it, came to be

shaken, yea the Earth and Heavens, (by which these bodily quakings and tremblings did also seize upon divers, and from this the Name *Quakers* was in scorn cast upon friends) that the mountain of the Lord might be raised up a top of them all, and so through the mighty workings of Gods power, which was revealed in the light to which their minds was turned, in silence, they came to be brought out of the mixture wherein they stood formerly into a clearness and soundness of condition in the truth, both as to spirit and judgement, in their own particulars, and so they came to a clear and sound understanding of the things of God, and of Truth, and Religion, and the way of worship, and to have clear and sound thoughts and apprehensions of them, which did purely and clearly arise in the light, in which their minds became stayed, and so in due time a pure and clear ministration in words was given unto many of them, so that they preached pure and sound and clear Doctrine, in a pure and clear manifestation of life unto which pure ministration many came to be brought, who had a ministration formerly among people of divers sects, and opinions which stood in the mixture aforesaid, that was not clear grain and food, and therefore hurt both themselves and others, but being gathered together unto this pure ministration (which they received, by sitting down to wait upon the Lord to learn together in silence with all subjection, the pure and clear and perfect Knowledge of things) they came both to be saved themselves, and to be made instrumentall to save others.

Document V.14

Jeremiah Burroughs: The Principles of Worship

The following extract is from Jeremiah Burroughs, *Gospel-Worship* (London, 1650), 8–11. For Burroughs (or Burroughes, 1599–1646), v., DNB. He was a Congregationalist and one of the 'Dissenting Brethren' in the Westminster Assembly of Divines. The quotation comes from the first sermon in the book, its text being Levit. 10: 3. The word 'will-worship' occurs frequently in Nonconformist polemical writing. Burroughs explains its meaning in this passage. The word 'nice' bears the meaning 'fastidious' in the passage. These sermons were taken down as they were delivered, according to the preface 'To the Reader', and it adds that the book 'riseth not up to that exactness and perfection as might have been in them [the sermons] had he publisht them himself'. For the topic in general, v., Horton Davies, *The Worship of the English Puritans* (Westminster: Dacre Press, 1948).

That in Gods Worship there must be nothing tendered up to God but what he hath commanded, whatsoever we meddle with in the Worship *of God, it must be what we have a Warrant for out of the Word of God.*

Hence I say, that all things in Gods worship must have a warrant out of Gods word, must be commanded. It's not enough that it is not forbidden: I beseech you observe it: it is not enough that a thing is not forbidden, and what hurt is there in it? But it must be commanded: I confess in matters that are Civil and Natural, there this may be enough; If it be but according to the rules of prudence, and not forbidden in the word; we may make use of this in Civil and Natural things. But now when we come to matters of Religion, and the Worship of God, we must either have a command, or somewhat out of Gods Word by some Consequence drawn from some command wherein God manifests his will; either a direct command, or by comparing one thing with another, or drawing consequences plainly from the Words. We must have a warrant for the *Worship of God* ... It's true there are some things in the *Worship of God* that are Natural and Civil helps, and there we need not have a Command: As for instance; when we come to *worship God*, the Congregation meets, they must have a convenient place to keep the air and weather from them: now this is but a natural help, and so far as I Use the place of Worship as a natural help, I need have no Command. But if I will put any thing in a *Place* beyond what it hath in its own nature, There I must look for a Command. For if I account one place more *Holy* than another; or to think that God should accept of worship in one place rather than in another: This is to raise it above what it is in its own Nature. So that when any creature is raised in a Religious way, above what it hath in it by *Nature*; if I have not Scripture to warrant me I am therein superstitious. It's a very useful rule for to help you: If any Creature that you make any use of in a way of Religion beyond what it hath in its own *Nature*, if you have not some warrant from the *Word of God* (whatever specious shew there may be in it) it is *Superstition* ...

And so for garments, to use those that are decent, the light of reason is enough: but if I wil put any thing upon them beyond what there is in them in their own nature, as heretofore in a Surplis, what, Had that any more decency in it's own nature, but only mans *Institution*? Now when man shall put a Religious respect upon a thing, by vertue of his own Institution when he hath not a warrant from God; Here's superstition! we must all be *willing* worshipers, but not *Wil-*worshipers; We must come freely to worship God; but we must not worship God according to our own wills, and therefore what ever we do in the Worship of God, if we have not a warrant for it, when this is said, *Who requireth this at your hands*? It will stop our mouthes another day: In *Matthew* 15.9. *In vain do they worship me, teaching for Doctrine the Commandements of men. In vain*: it is a *vain* thing to Worship God, when there is nothing but a Commandement of man for this Worship ... How many things have there been in the Worship of God that you can shew no warrant for? A great many things meerly mens inventions, however they are now cast out, because Authority would have it so; but you ought to be humbled before God for all your Will-worship, for all your yielding, to any thing in the Worship of God, that was *taught by the precepts of men* ...

... *In the matters of Worship God stands upon little things*: Such things as seem to be very small and little to us, yet God stands much upon them in the matter of Worship. for there is nothing wherein the Prerogative of God doth more appear than in Worship: as Princes, they stand much upon their Prerogatives: Now God hath written the Law of natural Worship in our hearts, as that we should love God, fear God, trust in God, and pray to God; this God hath written in our hearts: But there are other things in the Worship of God that are not written in our hearts, that only depend upon the Will of God revealed in his Word, which were no duties except they were revealed in his Word. And these are of such a nature as we can see no reason for but only this, because God will have them ... Let us learn to make conscience of little things in the Worship of God, and not to think, O how nice such are, and how precise and nice in such small things! Thou doest not understand the nature of Divine Worship if so be thou art not nice about it; God is nice and stands upon little things in the matter of his Worship ...

Document V.15

Bedford Church Book

The minutes of the Church were not regularly kept. The following are a selection of entries to illustrate various aspects of the business transacted at church meetings. The first entry comes three weeks after John Bunyan had accepted the pastorate. It is dated 10 February 1672.

The extracts show with what care discipline was exercised, both in receiving members and in admonishing offenders. The last paragraph provides an example of a letter transferring a member from one church to another. 'Brother Jesse' was Henry Jessey (1601–63). He had adopted Baptist principles and was baptised on profession of faith in June 1645. He was an Open Communion Baptist, as was Bunyan. According to CHST, V, 251 he attended the ministries of Thomas Goodwin and John Owen. For Jessey, v., DNB and CR. The extracts are from John Brown, *John Bunyan* (3rd edn, London, 1885), 247–9, 312–13.

It was agreed upon that the 16th of this instant should be set apart for seeking God by prayer with fasting for our children and carnall relations, and for the tempted and afflicted, and for the Lord's blessing upon ye ministery; and that there be in each part of the congregation, viz.: as well at Hanes and Gamlinghay as here, not only at the time aforementioned, but monethly, one day in a moneth observed.

25th of the 4th moneth [25 June 1672]: It was ordered that a brief confession of faith bee drawne up by the elders and gifted brethren of the congregation against the next meeting, that after the Churches approbation thereof it may be propounded to all that shall hereafter give up themselves to ye Lord and to us by the will of God, and their unfeigned consent thereto required. There was also appointed a meeting for prayer for our children and relations.

[The following entries are in John Bunyan's handwriting.]

Gamlinghay, the 31st of the 8th moneth [31 October 1672]: The desire of Sister Behemont to walke in fellowship with us was propounded and [she] was received at the next Church meeting.

At a full assembly of the Congregation was with joynt consent of the whole body, cast out of the Church, John Rush, of Bedford, for being drunk after a very beastly and filthy maner, that is above the ordenery rate of drunkerds, for he could not be carried home from the Swan to his own house without the help of no less than three persons who, when they had brought him home, could not present him as one alive to his familie he was so dead drunke. This assembly of the Church was held on the 25th day of the second month.

1674. A Church meeting was holden at Bedford the 10th of the 2nd month [10 April], to pray God to bless admonition upon four in the congregation that had transgressed.

At the same meeting also, the Church waas told that our Sister Landy had bin admonished for withdrawing communion againe, for countenancing Card-play, and for deceiving the Church with her former seeming repentance. At the same meeting the Church was told that our Sister Elizabeth Maxey had bin admonished for disobedience to her parents, to witt, for calling her father lier, and for wicked carriages to her mother.

On the 7th of the 3rd month [7 May 1674] was a meeting of the Congregation holden at Cotten End, wher was a relation made of severall acts of the Church, there also our Brother Nehemiah Coxe did publickly make an acknowledgment of several miscaridges by him committed, and delivered his repentance for the same; and because he had bin faulty in such things heretofore, therefore it was desired by some of the Brethren: That the form of his submitting should be presented to us in writeing, which it accordingly was, and was as followeth: Whereas several words and practises have bin uttered and performed by me that might justly be construed to have a tendencie to make rents and devisions in the congregation I doe declare myselfe unfeignedly repentant and sorry for the same. Ne. Coxe.

At the same meeting, singing of Psalmes was propounded to the Congregatiion, also that the Congregation at Hitchin intreated that the Church would consent to give up our Brother Wilson to them to be chosen to office by them

At a Church meeting holden at Gamblingay the 18th of the 3rd month [18 May 1674] was our Sister Landey withdrawn from. The causes were for that she had withdrawn communion from the saints, had dispised gifts in the Church, had taught her children to play at cards, and remained impenitent after several admonitions.

At a Church meeting holden at Bedford the 29th of the 3rd moneth [29 May 1674] ... Ordered that a letter be sent to that Church of whom Brother Jesse once was pastor, to know whether it be their Church principle still to hold communion with saints as saints, though differing in judgment about watter Baptizm, that we may better know what to doe as to our Sister Martha Cumberland as to her joyning with them or not. At the same time, John Overhand was mentioned to be joyned in fellowship with us, but considering that upon several accounts his life of profession hath not bin accompanied with that holyness as becomes the gospel it was concluded in the negative.

The 7th of the 12th month 1676 [7 February 1677]. The Church of Christ in and about Bedford to the Church of Christ in and about Braintree, sendeth greeting. Holy and beloved, we fellow heires with you of the grace of life having considered your request concerning our honnered and beloved brother Samuel Hensman ...

doe as before God and the Elect Angels grant and give up to you our elect brother to be receaued by you in the Lord, and to be nourished in the church at Braintree with you as one that is dear to the Father and our Lord Jesus Christ. And this we the willinger doe because as we are informed conserneing you beloved, you are not ridged [i.e., rigid] in your principles, but are for communyon with saints as saints; and have been taught by the word to receaue the brotherhood because they are beloued and receauved of the Father and the Sonne to whose grace we commend you with the brother of late a member with us; but bow one of you. Grace be with you all. John Bunyan, Sam. ffenn, &c.

Document V.16

Richard Baxter: Faith and Love

These two extracts are a very small sample of Richard Baxter's extensive pastoral writings. They reflect his intense concern about people's spiritual health. Geoffrey F. Nuttall quotes Baxter's statement that 'personal Conference with every one about the State of their own Souls, together with Catechizing' of all the things he did at Kidderminster 'yielded me most comfort in the practice of it' (*Richard Baxter* (London, 1965), 57.)

Extract (a) is from *Directions and Persuasions to a Sound Conversion* (1658) in W. Orme (ed.), *Works* (London, 1830), VIII, 268–9.

Extract (b) is from *The Character of a Sound, Confirmed Christian* (1669) in W. Orme (ed.), *Works* (London, 1830), VIII, 390.

(a)
To receive Christ, is not only ... to receive his doctrine, though it is certain that his doctrine must be received, and the rest is implied in this. But when the understanding receiveth the Gospel by assent, the will also accepteth or receiveth Christ as he is offered, by consent; and both these together are the receiving of Christ; that is, the true justifying faith of God's elect. It is not therefore a physical, passive reception, as wood receiveth the fire, and as our souls receive the graces of the Spirit; but it is a moral reception, or reputative, which is active and metaphorical. This will be better understood when the object is considered, which is, 'Christ Jesus the Lord'. To receive Christ as Christ, or the anointed Messias, and as the Saviour and our Lord, is to believe that he is such, and to consent that he be such to us, and to trust in him, and resign ourselves to him as such. The relation we do indeed receive by a proper passive reception. I mean our relation of being redeemed members, subjects, disciples of this Christ. but the person of Christ we only receive by such an active, moral, reputative reception, as a servant by consent receives a master, a patient by consent receives a physician, a wife by consent receives a husband, and as a scholar or pupil by consent receives a teacher or tutor, or the subjects by consent receives a sovereign. So that it is the same thing that is called, 'receiving Jesus the Lord,' and, 'believing in him,' as it is expounded, John i. 12.

Aspects of Nonconformist Experience

(b)
A Christian indeed doth love God in these three gradations: he loveth him much for his mercy to himself, and for that goodness which consisteth in benignity to himself; but he loveth him more for his mercy to the church, and for that goodness which consisteth in his benignity to the church. But he loveth him most of all for his infinite perfections and essential excellencies; his infinite power, and wisdom, and goodness, simply in himself considered. For he knoweth that love to himself obligeth him to returns of love; especially differencing, saving grace: and he knoweth that the souls of millions are more worth incomparably than his own, and that God may be much more honoured by them, than by him alone; and therefore he knoweth that the mercy to many is greater mercy, and a greater demonstration of the goodness of God, and therefore doth render him more amiable to man; Rom. ix. 3. And yet he knoweth that essential perfection and goodness of God, as simply in himself and for himself, is much more amiable than his benignity to the creature; and that he that is the first efficient, must needs be the ultimate, final cause of all things; and that God is not finally for the creature, but the creature for God, (for all that he needeth it not) 'For of him, and through him, and to him are all things;' Rom. xi. 36. And as he is infinitely better than ourselves, so he is to be better loved than ourselves ...

Document V.17

Samuel Fisher: A Prophetic Call

Except in connection with conversion experiences, and in their calls to particular acts of service, the religious experiences recorded by Quakers were generally corporate and associated with the meetings for worship. Reliance on individual religious experience, unchecked by reference to the corporate authority of the meeting and its elders, was not encouraged; the first Quakers had a great deal of trouble with individuals whose 'light' led them to extravagant behaviour, and the bad publicity following the Nayler affair (v. III.14) gave a warning to Fox and other Quaker leaders that extreme individualism must not be tolerated. Moreover, Quakers were dubious about religious experience because it did not necessarily lead to life in the light of Christ; Fox, as well as leaving the regular preachers, had also left 'those called the most experienced people' before discovering that Christ alone could 'speak to his condition' (NJ 11).

Therefore, if the word 'mysticism' is used in connection with Quakers, it is necessary to be clear about the sense of the word. Fox, in his way, was a mystic, and so were other Quakers, in the sense that they had powerful religious experiences, but their mystical experience tended to be like that of Amos: 'The Lord took me from following the flock, and the Lord said unto me, "Go, prophesy unto my people Israel"'(Amos 7: 15). The call could be an extremely uncomfortable experience, and the Quaker concerned might be most reluctant to obey it.

The following extract is from Samuel Fisher, *The Scorned Quakers True and Honest Account* (London, 1656).

Samuel Fisher (1605–65) was a considerable scholar, well known as a powerful disputant, who had held a parish lectureship in Kent before becoming a Baptist minister. He turned Quaker in 1654, and was a leading Quaker author and minister until his death in the London plague in 1665. His major theological work was *Rusticos ad Academicos* (1660), an attack on the teaching of John Owen and other eminent theologians. This is his account of his call to address Cromwell.

Following this episode Fisher was seized again and prevented from speaking, so he published the substance of his message as a book, which was a call to members of the government to repent for its persecution of Quakers, and a warning that great people should not seek their own personal advantage, or the Lord would surely punish them.

The scorned Quakers true and honest account, both why and what he should have spoken (as to the sum and substance thereof) by commission from God, but that he had not permission from men, in the Painted Chamber on the 17th day of the 7th month 1656, before the Protector and Parliament ...

On the 22nd day of the 6th month 1656, it being two days after the general election of Members of Parliament for the several counties of the nation, the word of the Lord came to me, even to me, Samuel Fisher, at my own outward being at Lydd in Kent, saying, 'Go thou to the Protector and to the Parliament, when they shall be met together in the Painted Chamber at Westminster, on the day appointed for the first sitting of the Parliament, and there speak among them what I shall bid thee, even the words that I shall in the mean time put into thy mind, and at that time into thy mouth;' which motion, (howbeit at that present time I was still and quiet, and not unwilling of the Lord's will were he to continue it upon me, but sweetly satisfied within me to obey it), yet was afterwards at sundry times (even so often as flesh and blood drew me to consult with it) attended with no small commotion in my mind, and being often held under a sense of the tediousness and the terribleness of so great and weighty a service, which the carnal part that ever opposes and (till it be subdued) oppresses the pure, and did still represent of dangerous consequence to me, as to the outward ... . Nevertheless being called of the Lord to seek his face yet further, even seven or eight days together with fasting, tears and supplications for the full clearing of his mind unto me in that matter, and his strengthening of me to it, in case he would not excuse me in it, nor send his message by the mouth of any other beside myself (than whom (O Lord, thou knowest) I thought a more unworthy one could not be singled out, among all thy saints that are employed publicly about thy service) ... . On the ninth day waiting upon God after the receiving of something for the sustenance of my outward, I was also more than ordinarily sustained in my inward man; Yea, the Lord not only put it out of doubt, and perfectly sealed it up to me, that I must go ... and removed all my fears of the frowns of mans face, and counter pleaded all my pleas to him that I should not speak for fear, that they would not hear me ... without any more gainsaying, or giving any heed to flesh, and blood, I from thenceforth concluded unalterably to be there, and accordingly was there at the time appointed, and began to speak so soon as I could get conveniency of a standing, after the Protector had done his speech ... .

[Other members of the audience held him and prevented him from speaking until the Protector was leaving.]

But the word of the Lord burning then as a fire in my bowels; so that I could not but speak, whether I should be heard yea, or nay, for I was weary with forbearing, and it forced me to crowd in and stand between two of them, that stood before me on a form, and so I spoke whether they would or no ...

Document V.18

George Fox: The Care of Souls

George Fox's epistles are a magnificent collection of pastoral writing. They were published in 1698, and make up volumes VII and VIII in his collected *Works*. Unfortunately there is no modern critical edition, although there are several collections of extracts in print, a good introductory collection being Cecil W. Sharman (ed.), *No More but My Love: Letters of George Fox* (London: Quaker Home Service, 1980). The epistle reproduced here is one of a few for which the original manuscript survives, probably written from a shorthand record of one of Fox's addresses to general meetings in the autumn of 1656 when he was trying to repair the damage done by Nayler's defection (v. III.14). It was heavily edited before printing, and while some of the editorial alterations were merely intended to smooth a rough text, and to make a spoken address more suitable for reading, Fox's theology was also softened. Derogatory references to human kings, whose reigns Fox compared unfavourably with the kingship of Christ, were removed, necessitating the rewriting of a large section in the middle of the epistle. Emphasis on the reign of Christ as king was not very common in Quaker writings, certainly not in those intended for publication, because of the risk of confusion with Fifth Monarchists.

This epistle, no. 131 (*Works*, VII.126–9), dealt with all kinds of matters connected with the practicalities of being a Quaker, and it is here reproduced from the original manuscript of 1656: Swarthmore MSS., 2.95. The spelling and punctuation have been modernized.

Friends every where, dwell in the power of the Lord God, which is without end, in which you may all have unity. And take heed of striving about earthly things and about the earth that is the unredeemed, out if it up to God, out of the paradise and the garden but that with the wisdom you may come to order the creatures by which they were made and created, and by it yourselves governed. After that riches do increase, take heed of setting your hearts upon it, lest it become a curse and a plague unto you. For when you were faithful at the first, the world would refrain from you, and not have commerce with you; but after, when they see you were faithful and steadfast in the thing that is righteous and just, then they came to have commerce and trade with you the more, because they know you will not cozen them, nor cheat them: then you come to have more trading, double than ever you had, and more than the world. Then is the danger and temptation to you, drawing your minds into it and ploying them with it; so that you can hardly do any thing to the service of God, but there will be crying, my business, my business; and so your minds will go into the things, and not over the thing; and so therein you do not come into the image of God, in which is dominion. And so there, when your minds is got into riches, and cumbered you go back into that which you were before; and then the Lord God will cross you, and stop you by sea and land, and take your goods from you, that your minds should not be cumbered and the customers; then that mind that is in it will fret, that is out of the power of God.

And all Friends, take heed of jars and strife, for that is it which will eat out the good in you; therefore let it not lodge in your bosoms, lest it eat out the good in you, and you come to suffer in your own particulars. Therefore dwell in the love and life, and the power and the seed of God, which is the honourable state. And all that speaks abroad, see that you be in the life, and power, and seed of God, that will edify the body, and not with the brittle, peevish, hasty, fretful mind that which knocks down, that must speak which edifies the body in love. And all take heed of vain words, and tattling which are idle words, but every where stop such; that love may continue in the body, and that the seed may spread over all, that unity may be kept. And all Friends every where, if Friends be poor, and in want, or in prison, that you may in wisdom relieve and cherish such. And all Friends every where, stop the deceit, which would devour and destroy, which is out of the truth, and the wisdom; which must be limited, that transgressed the spirit of God. For since the days of the apostles, the true church hath been in the wilderness, and the beast, false prophet, antichrist, and false church have ruled and reigned: amongst whom have been the many names and horns and Kings and Emperors amongst Christians, which have professed themselves to be Elders Presbyterians. Amongst this eldership have they had outward and earthly Kings who have got up since the days of the apostles amongst whom was Christ who ended all king Solomon's reign and David's among the Jews outward, and so come to Christ who was the true Christians' King. Jesus was their King by whom all things were made and they had no earthly king. And when the Christians went from the apostles into the world, and got up earthly kings amongst them, and many heads, when they went from the seed of God in themselves, in the male and in the female, then they lost their king which is the head, and so whoever goes from the seed of God in himself and sets up other heads, then they lose the one head which is Christ Jesus; and then comes to be covered and the seed loaden as a cart with sheaves; and then they break into many heads when they go from the seed in the male and in the female, which is one head, and then comes up Kings and Emperors and all fighting about earthly things, and warrings with carnal weapons about earthly things, and self-interest, and man's honour and titles, the church and religion and worship and ministry, that have been since the days of the apostles, and since the fall. The Jews did kill with the sword the heathen, and one another with the outward carnal weapons and the outward King among them, but Christ Jesus, the prince of life, who ends with the sword and fulfils the law, and ends the outward Jews' types, figures, and shadows, and ordinances and carnal weapons, who is the king of the whole earth, who comes to save men's lives, yet slays and 'kills with the sword of the spirit, which be the word of his mouth.' And the apostles, who followed Christ, they wrestled not with flesh and blood; so all, who come to winess Christ to reign and to rule, (who is the prince of life, that saves men's lives,) and follow him, do not wrestle with flesh and blood to destroy men's lives. And here comes the wisdom to be known, that is from above, that is pure and gentle, and easy to be entreated, that is not sensual, carnal, and devilish. So in the time of the law among the Jews there was fighting outwardly; but in the time of Christ, when Christ came to end the law, they were to love enemies, and not to kill them; and pray for persecutors, and not kill them, and love them that hate them, and not kill them. But in the times since the days of the apostles, in the apostate christians' time, they are houghting [?huffing] up and they are crying up the outward sword again; and this is the Dragon's and the Beast's power, the prince of death, which hath reigned since the apostles' days. But who come to follow Christ, they come to reign over all these fighting Christians with carnal weapons, that are out of the truth and got up since the days of the apostles ... So keep your meetings, particular and general, in the power of the Lord God, and dwell in the life, and power, and wisdom of the Lord, that all uncleanness whatsoever may by the power of the Lord be brought down and rooted out ... And all Friends every where, take heed of printing any thing more than you are required of the Lord God. And all Friends every where, take heed of wandering up and down about needless occasions, for there is danger of getting into the careless words, and out of seriousness, and weightiness, and savouriness. And all Friends every where, take heed of wronging the world, or any one, in bargains, or overreaching them; but dwell in the sweet cool power of the Lord God, and in righteousness, that it may run down; and that will keep you low. And all Friends every where, take heed of slothfulness and sleeping in your meetings; for in so doing you may be bad examples to others. And all take heed of wandering up and down, and going anyway, but as you are moved of the Lord God, as to speak, or any other; for travelling is dangerous to lift up and to go amongst settled meetings ... Therefore let all live in the seed, and wisdom, and fear, and consider, before they utter, that the life be up; whereby all may be settled, and they themselves washed and dwell in the seed, that you may all come to know Christ's reign. And them that are moved to record them that are born or die, and them that are joined together by the Lord, they may [do] so that all may be done by the power of the Lord God, it is done and nothing out of it: and in that you will all have unity in the record of life and know it to record all things that you do and act, whereby the power of God and the seed of God may come up, which is the heir of the blessing and of the promise; that you may come to know the place where there is no curse, and the Lamb's power, throne, life, and dominion. And in the wisdom of God all dwell, that to him you may be a sweet savour, and a blessing in the hearts of all people; that nothing may rule nor reign amongst you, but the seed itself, and the life of God.

Let this be read in your meetings. G.F.

Document V.19

Morgan Llwyd: True Justice

The following extract is from Morgan Llwyd, *Llyfr y Tri Aderyn* (Book of the Three Birds), in T. E. Ellis (ed.), *Gweithiau Morgan Llwyd* (Bangor, 1899), I, 237–9. There is a rather old-fashioned English translation of the book by L. J. Parry in *Transactions of the National Eisteddfod of Wales, Llandudno, 1896* (Liverpool, 1898), 195–274. See also Geraint H. Jenkins, *Protestant Dissenters in Wales, 1639–1689* (Cardiff, 1992).

Expect justice not from men but from God and without a doubt you shall get it. The time is very near when everyone will get his due. The injustice that others do to you is but as a fleabite compared with the tyranny you impose on your own soul. Remember that above all before you go to law. How beastly intolerant many people are! So ready to sue; so unready for the gospel that teaches us to give our cloak to him who steals our coat before quarreling. It is better to suffer the greatest injury than to engage in the least quarrel. Rather be like a mute lamb under the hand of the shearer and a deaf and dumb innocent amongst his accusers.

Woe be to you, lawyers. There is a law that shall consume you. Woe to the contentious in a country; they are the firebrands of hell. Woe to you, murderous physicians. Many a groan has ascended against you. Woe to you, oppressors, who swallow wealth. You will have to spew it all out together with your own blood. Woe to you, the gentry with your evil examples, dragging the poor after you to destruction. How will you render an account for your poor tenants? What will become of you when every high thing shall be cut down and burnt? Woe be to every large tree and every small tree that does not bring forth good fruit. The fire has been kindled in Wales. The door of your forest (Oh, country of today's Britons) is open to the conflagration. The axe is poised at your root. If you do not now bring forth good fruit, you shall be cut off and cease to be a people. And woe to you, wastrels, who spend your time, your health, your money and your eternal minds on vanity. Woe to you, ignorant labourer. All your work is nothing but digging the earth and nurturing it and driving animals on the mountain. They suffer being driven by you and because of that they are witnesses against you. Woe be to you, cunning and wicked reader, who searches books to find faults or pictures. Truth will discover your faults and judge you. Woe be to you, hypocrite, who fears the face of man. You do not fear sinning in secret but you will be judged in the open. Woe be to you, nimble, lazy beggar, that will not work for anyone's benefit. You desire not such benefit and such benefit you shall lose. Woe be to you, sleepy conscience, which (like a dumb dog) betrays its master; a long time howling awaits you. Woe be to you who hasten to join the mob (agile in spirit) to eat the sugar of carnal lust in the devil's race and carousing in your souls. Soon enough you will not have a drop of water to cool the tip of your tongue. Woe be to you, evil gentlefolk, who lick the sweat of the poor and force your tenants to groan as you break their bones. Your day of reckoning is coming quickly without tarrying. Woe to you, mute priests, who love foxes that bark at the sheep, – bitter, blind dogs, proud, lazy, rapacious, snarling, sleepy, ashy, and stinking. You will all be cast out of the Church. And woe be to you, the ancient inhabitants of Wales, that still have not been awakened.

But blessed are you who yearn for God. You will be filled by Him. Blessed are you, the constantly faithful and diligent; your work will be blessed. Blessed are those who pray with sincerity, they will always be heard. Blessed are those who deny themselves; God will not deny them. Blessed are those who truly sow God's wheat; they shall enjoy a spiritual harvest. Blessed are the spiritual ones; God's secret is theirs. Blessed are the watchful; the Devil will not get hold of them. Blessed are those who wait expectantly; Jesus Christ will visit them. Blessed are they who suffer for the Lamb; they shall reign with Him ... And (in a word) blessed is the one who is born again. He has been born to inherit all things. God will be his Father and he a dear child of God. The Lamb will be his light and he will be a light in the Lord ...

Document V.20

John Bunyan: The Final Triumph

For a text carefully collating the additions in the various early editions of *Pilgrim's Progress*, together with a detailed introduction, v., J. B. Wharey (ed.), *The Pilgrim's Progress* (2nd edn, revised by Roger Sharrock, London, 1960). See also John Brown, *John Bunyan* (London, 1885; London, 1928); W. Y. Tindall, *John Bunyan: Mechanick Preacher* (New York, 1934); Henri Talon, *John Bunyan: The Man and His Works*, trans. Barbara Wall (London, 1951); Roger Sharrock, *John Bunyan* (London, 1954); U. M. Kaufmann, *The Pilgrim's Progress and Traditions of Puritan Meditation* (New Haven, Conn., 1966); R. L. Greaves (ed.), *John Bunyan* (Abingdon: Courtney Studies, 1969); E. Beatrice Batson, *John Bunyan: Allegory and Imagination* (London: 1984); Christopher Hill, *A Turbulent, Seditious, and Factious People* (Oxford, 1988; the American edition, 1989, is entitled *A Tinker and a Poor Man*); N. H. Keeble, *The Literary Culture of Nonconformity in Later Seventeenth-Century England* (Leicester, 1987); chap. 6 in John R. Knott, *Discourses of Martyrdom in English Literature 1563–1694* (Cambridge, 1993).

When Days, had many of them passed away: Mr. *Dispondencie* was sent for. For a *Post* was come, and brought this Message to him; *Trembling Man, These are to summon thee to he ready with thy King, by the next Lords Day, to shout for Joy for thy Deliverance from all thy Doubtings*

And said the Messenger, That my Message is true, take this for a Proof. So he gave him *The Grashopper to be a Burthen unto him*. Now Mr. *Dispondencie's* Daughter, whose Name was *Much-a-fraid*, said, when she heard what was done, that she would go with her Father. Then Mr. *Dispondencie* said to his Friends; My self and my Daughter, you know what we have been, and how troublesomly we have behaved our selves in every Company. My Will and my Daughters is, that our *Disponds*, and slavish Fears, be by no man ever received, from the day of our

Departure, for ever; For I know that after my Death they will offer themselves to others. For, to be plain with you, they are *Ghosts*, the which we entertained when we first began to be Pilgrims, and could never shake them off after. And they will walk about and seek Entertainment of the Pilgrims, but for our Sakes, shut ye the Doors upon them.

When the time was come for them to depart, they went to the Brink of the *River*. The last Words of Mr. *Dispondencie*, were, *Farewel Night, welcome Day*. His Daughter went thorow the River singing, but none could understand what she said.

Then it came to pass, a while after, that there was a *Post* in the Town that enquired for Mr. *Honest*. So he came to the House where he was, and delivered to his Hand these Lines: *Thou art Commanded to be ready against this Day seven Night, to present thy self before thy Lord, at his Fathers House*. And for a Token that my Message is true, *All thy Daughters of Musick shall be brought low*. Then Mr. *Honest* called for his Friends, and said unto them, I Die, but shall make no Will. As for my Honesty, it shall go with me; let him that comes after be told of this. When the Day that he was to be gone, was come, he addressed himself to go over the *River*. Now the *River* at that time overflowed the Banks in some places. But Mr. *Honest* in his Life time had spoken to one *Good-conscience* to meet him there, the which he also did, and lent him his Hand, and so helped him over. The last Words of Mr. *Honest* were, *Grace Reigns*. So he left the World.

After this it was noised abroad that Mr. *Valiant-for-truth* was taken with a Summons, by the same *Post* as the other; and had this for a Token that the Summons was true, *That his Pitcher was broken at the Fountain*. When he understood it, he called for his Friends, and told them of it. Then said he, I am going to my Fathers, and tho with great Difficulty I am got hither, yet now I do not repent me of all the Trouble I have been at to arrive where I am. *My Sword*, I give to him that shall succeed me in my Pilgrimage, and my *Courage* and *Skill*, to him that can get it. *My Marks* and *Scarrs* I carry with me, to be a witness for me, that I have fought his Battels, who now will be my Rewarder. When the Day that he must go hence, was come, many accompanied him to the River side, into which, as he went, he said, *Death, where is thy Sting?* And as he went down deeper, he said, *Grave **where is** thy Victory? So* he passed over, and the Trumpets sounded for him on the other side.

Then there came forth a Summons for Mr. *Standfast*, (This Mr. *Stand-fast*, was he that the rest of the Pilgrims found upon his Knees in the *inchanted* Ground.) For the *Post* brought it him open in his Hands. The Contents whereof were, *That he must prepare for a change of Life, for his Master was not willing that he should be so far from him any longer*. At this Mr. *Stand-fast* was put into a Muse; Nay, said the Messenger, you need not doubt of the truth of my Message; for here is a Token of the Truth thereof, *Thy Wheel is broken at the Cistern*. Then he called to him Mr. *Great-heart*, who was their Guide, and said unto him, Sir, Altho it was not my hap to be much in your good Company in the Days of my Pilgrimage, yet since the time I knew you, you have been profitable to me. When I came from home, I left behind me a Wife, and five small Children. Let me entreat you, at your Return (for I know that you will go, and return to your Masters House, in Hopes that you may yet be a Conductor to more of the Holy Pilgrims,) that you send to my Family, and let them be acquainted with all that hath, and shall happen unto me. Tell them moreover, of my happy Arrival to this Place, and of the present late blessed Condition that I am in. Tell them also of *Christian*, and of *Christiana* his Wife, and how *She* and her Children came after her Husband. Tell them also of what a happy End she made, and whither she is gone. I have little or nothing to send to my Family, except it be Prayers, and Tears for them; of which it will suffice, if thou acquaint them, if paradventure they may prevail. When Mr. *Standfast* had thus set things in order, and the time being come for him to hast him away; he also went down to the River. Now there was a great Calm at that time in the River, wherefore Mr. *Stand-fast*, when he was about half way in, he stood a while and talked to his Companions that had waited upon him thither. And he said,

This River has been a Terror to many, yea the thoughts of it also have often frighted me. But now methinks I stand easie, my Foot is fixed upon that, upon which the Feet of the Priests that bare the Ark of the Covenant stood while *Israel* went over this *Jordan*. The Waters indeed are to the Palate bitter, and to the Stomack cold; yet the thoughts of what I am going to, and of the Conduct that waits for me on the other side, doth lie as a glowing Coal at my Heart.

I see my self now at the *end* of my Journey, my *toilsom* Days are ended. I am going now to see *that* Head that was Crowned with Thorns, and *that* Face that was spit upon, for me.

I have formerly lived by Hear-say, and Faith, but now I go where I shall live by sight, and shall be with him, in whose Company I delight my self.

I have loved to hear my Lord spoken of, and wherever I have seen the print of his Shooe in the Earth, there I have coveted to set my Foot too.

His Name has been to me as a *Civit-Box*, yea sweeter then all Perfumes. His Voice to me has been most sweet, and his Countenance, I have more desired then they that have most desired the Light of the Sun. His Word I did use to gather for my Food, and for Antidotes against my Faintings. He has held me, and I have kept me from mine Iniquities: Yea, my Steps hath he strengthened in his Way.

Now while he was thus in Discourse his Countenance changed, his *strong men* bowed under him, and after he had said, *Take me, for I come unto thee*, he ceased to be seen of them.

But glorious it was, to see how the open Region was filled with Horses and Chariots, with Trumpeters and Pipers, with Singers, and Players on stringed Instruments, to welcome the Pilgrims as they went up and followed one another in at the beautiful Gate of the City.

As for *Christian's* Children, the four Boys that *Christiana* brought with her, with their Wives and Children, I did not stay where I was, till they were gone over. Also since I came away, I heard one say, that they were yet alive, and so would be for the Increase of the Church in that Place where they were for a time.

Shall it be my Lot to go that way again, I may give those that desire it, an Account of what I here am silent about; mean time I bid my Reader *Adieu*.

FINIS

PART VI

A THEOLOGICAL MISCELLANY

Document VI.1

The Baptist Confession of Faith, 1677, 1688

CHAP. XXVI.

Of the Church.

The following is the section on the Church in the confession that was agreed upon by representatives of the Particular Baptist Churches of England and Wales in 1677 and reaffirmed in 1688. It was entitled *Confession of Faith Put forth by the Elders and Brethren Of many Congregations of Christians (baptized upon Profession of their Faith) in London and the Country*. In the Introduction, 'To the Judicious and Impartial Reader', the reasons for publishing it are explained. They found 'no defect' in the Westminster Confession nor in the Savoy Declaration and so, the authors say, 'we did readily conclude it best to retain the same order in our present Confession'. They add that they made 'use of the very same words with them both, in those articles (which are very many) wherein our faith and doctrine is the same with theirs. And this we did, the more abundantly to manifest our consent with both, in all the fundamental articles of the Christian religion, as also with many others whose orthodox confessions have been published to the world'. There was then an ecumenical motive operating here. Persecution had brought Presbyterians, Congregationalists and Baptists closer together and this confession is an expression of that common mind. In this selection, the strictly theological sections have been omitted and those that express the convictions that were unique to the Baptists have been reproduced. The age of persecution ended with the passing of the Toleration Act in May 1689. A general assembly of the representatives of 107 Particular Baptist congregations in England and Wales met in London from 3 to 12 September 1689 and approved the Confession of 1677, a second edition of which had been published in 1688.

The original spelling has been retained. For this and other Baptist confessions, v., W.L.Lumpkin, *Baptist Confessions of Faith* (Philadelphia, 1959).

1. The Catholick or universal Church, which (with respect to internal work of the Spirit, and truth of grace) may be called invisible, consists of the whole number of the Elect, that have been, are, or shall be gathered into one, under Christ the head thereof; and is the spouse, the body, the fulness of him that filleth all in all.

2. All persons throughout the world, professing the faith of the Gospel, and obedience unto God by Christ, according unto it; not destroying their own profession by any Errors everting the foundation, or unholyness of conversation, are and may be called visible Saints; and of such ought all particular Congregations to be constituted.

3. The purest Churches under heaven are subject to mixture, and error; and som have so degenerated as to become no Churches of Christ, but Synagogues of Satan; nevertheless Christ always hath had, and ever shall have a Kingdome, in this world, to the end thereof, of such as believe in him, and make profession of his Name.

4. The Lord Jesus Christ is the Head of the Church, in whom by the

appointment of the Father, all power for the calling, institution, order, or Government of the Church, is invested in a supream & soveraigne manner, neither can the Pope of *Rome* in any sense be head thereof, but is that Antichrist, that Man of sin, and Son of perdition, that exalteth himself in the Church against Christ, and all that is called God; whom the Lord shall destroy with the brightness of his coming.

5. In the execution of this power wherewith he is so intrusted, the Lord Jesus calleth out of the World unto himself, through the Ministry of his word, by his Spirit, those that are given unto him by his Father; that they may walk before him in all the ways of obedience, which he prescribeth to them in his Word. Those thus called he commandeth to walk together in particular societies, or Churches, for their mutual edification; and the due performance of that publick worship, which he requireth of them in the World.

6. The Members of these Churches are Saints by calling, visibly manifesting and evidencing (in and by their profession and walking) their obedience unto that call of Christ, and do willingly consent to walk together according to the appointment of Christ, giving up themselves, to the Lord & one to another by the will of God, in professed subjection to the Ordinances of the Gospel.

7. To each of these Churches thus gathered, according to his mind, declared in his word, he hath given all that power and authority, which is any way needfull, for their carrying on that order in worship, and discipline, which he hath instituted for them to observe; with commands, and rules for the due and right exerting, and executing of that power.

8. A particular Church gathered, and compleatly Organized, according to the mind of Christ, consists of Officers, and Members; And the Officers appointed by *Christ* to be chosen and set apart by the Church (so called and gathered) for the peculiar Administration of Ordinances, and Execution of Power, or Duty, which he intrusts them with, or calls them to, to be continued to the end of the World, are Bishops or Elders and Deacons.

9. The way appointed by *Christ* for the Calling of any person, fitted, and gifted by the Holy *Spirit*, unto the Office of Bishop, or Elder, in a Church, is, that he be chosen thereunto by the common suffrage of the Church it self; and Solemnly set apart by Fasting and Prayer, with imposition of hands of the Eldership of the Church, if there be any before Constituted therein; And of a Deacon that he be chosen by the like suffrage, and set apart by Prayer, and the like Imposition of hands.

10. The work of Pastors being constantly to attend the Service of *Christ*, in his Churches, in the Ministry of the Word, and Prayer, with watching for their Souls, as they that must give an account to him; it is incumbent on the Churches to whom they Minister, not only to give them all due respect, but also to communicate to them of all their good things according to their ability, so as they may have a comfortable supply, without being themselves entangled in Secular Affairs; and may also be capable of exercising Hospitality towards others, and this is required by the Law of Nature and by the Express order of our Lord Jesus, who hath ordained that they that preach the Gospel, should live of the Gospel.

11. Although it be incumbent on the Bishops or Pastors of the Churches to be instant in Preaching the Word, by way of Office; yet the work of Preaching the Word, is not so peculiarly confined to them; but that others also gifted, and fitted by the Holy *Spirit* for it, and approved, and called by the *Church*, may and ought to perform it.

12. As all Believers are bound to joyn themselves to particular *Churches*, when and where they have opportunity so to do; So all that are admitted unto the priviledges of a *Church*, are also under the Censures and Government thereof, according to the Rule of *Christ*.

13. No Church-members upon any offence taken by them, having performed their Duty required of them towards the person they are offended at, ought to disturb any *Church* order, or absent themselves from the Assemblies of the *Church*, or Administration of any Ordinances, upon the account of such offence at any of their fellowmembers; but to wait upon *Christ*, in the further proceeding of the *Church*.

14. As each *Church*, and all the Members of it, are bound to pray continually, for the good and prosperity of all the *Churches* of *Christ*, in all places; and upon all occasions to further it (every one within the bounds of their places, and callings, in the Exercise of their Gifts and Graces) so the *Churches* (when planted by the providence of God so as they may injoy opportunity and advantage for it) ought to hold communion amongst themselves for their peace, increase of love, and mutual edification.

15. In cases of difficulties or differences, either in point of Doctrine, or Administration; wherein either the Churches in general are concerned, or any one Church in their peace, union, and edification; or any member, or members, of any Church are injured, in or by any proceedings in censures not agreeable to truth, and order: it is according to the mind of Christ, that many Churches holding communion together, do by their messengers meet to consider, and give their advice in, or about that matter in difference, to be reported to all the Churches concerned; howbeit these messengers assembled, are not entrusted with any Church-power properly so called; or with any jurisdiction over the Churches themselves, to exercise any censures either over any Churches, or Persons: or to impose their determination on the Churches, or Officers.

CHAP. XXVII.

On the Communion of Saints.

I. All *Saints* that are united to Jesus Christ their *Head*, by his Spirit, and Faith; although they are not made thereby one person with him, have fellowship in his Graces, sufferings, death, resurrection, and glory; and being united to one another in love, they have communion in each others gifts, and graces; and obliged to the performance of such duties, publick and private, in an orderly way, as do conduce to their mutual good, both in the inward and outward man.

2. *Saints* by profession are bound to maintain an holy fellowship and communion in the worship of God, and in performing such other spiritual services, as tend to their mutual edification, as also in relieving each other in outward things according to their several abilities, and necessities; which communion, according to the rule of the Gospel, though especially to be exercised by them, in the relations wherein they stand, whether in families, or Churches; yet as God offereth opportunity is to be extended to all the houshold of faith, even all those who in every place call upon the name of the Lord Jesus; nevertheless their communion one with another as *Saints*, doth not take away or infringe the title or propriety, which each man hath in his goods and possessions.

CHAP. XXVIII.

Of Baptism and the
Lords Supper.

I. Baptism and the Lords Supper are ordinances of positive, and sovereign institution; appointed by the Lord Jesus the only Law-giver, to be continued in his Church to the end of the world.

2. These holy appointments are to be administered by those only, who are qualified and thereunto called according to the commission of Christ.

CHAP. XXIX.

Of Baptism.

I. Baptism is an Ordinance of the New Testament, ordained by Jesus Christ, to be unto the party Baptized, a sign of his fellowship with him, in his death, and resurrection; of his being engrafted into him; of remission of sins; and of his giving up unto God through Jesus Christ, to live and walk in newness of Life.

2. Those who do actually profess repentance towards *God*, faith in, and obedience, to our Lord Jesus, are the only proper subjects of this ordinance.

3. The outward element to be used in this ordinance is water, wherein the party is to be baptized, in the name of the Father, and of the Son, and of the Holy Spirit.

4. Immersion, or dipping of the person in water, is necessary to the due administration of this ordinance.

CHAP. XXX.

Of the Lords Supper.

1. THE Supper of the Lord Jesus, was instituted by him, the same night wherein he was betrayed, to be observed in his Churches unto the end of the world, for the perpetual remembrance, and shewing forth the sacrifice in his death confirmation of the faith of believers in all the benefits thereof, their spiritual nourishment, and

growth in him, their further ingagement in, and to, all duties which they owe unto him; and to be a bond and pledge of their communion with him, and with each other.

2. In this ordinance Christ is not offered up to his Father, nor any real sacrifice made at all, for remission of sin of the quick or dead; but only a memorial of that one offering up of himself, by himself, upon the crosse, once for all; and a spiritual oblation of all possible praise unto God for the same; so that the Popish sacrifice of the Mass (as they call it) is most abominable, injurious to Christs own only sacrifice, the alone propitiation for all the sins of the Elect.

3. The Lord Jesus hath in this Ordinance, appointed his Ministers to Pray, and bless the Elements of Bread and Wine, and thereby to set them apart from a common to an holy use, and to take and break the Bread; to take the Cup, and (they communicating also themselves) to give both to the Communicants.

4. The denyal of the Cup to the people, worshiping the Elements, the lifting them up, or carrying them about for adoration, and reserving them for any pretended religious use, are all contrary to the nature of this Ordinance, and to the institution of Christ.

5. The outward Elements in this Ordinance, duely set apart to the uses ordained by Christ, have such relation to him crucified, as that truely, although in terms used figuratively, they are sometimes called by the name of the things they represent, to wit body and Blood of Christ; albeit in substance, and nature, they still remain truly, and only Bread, and Wine, as they were before.

6. That doctrine which maintains a change of the substance of Bread and Wine, into the substance of Christs body and blood (commonly called Transubstantiation) by consecration of a Priest, or by any other way, is repugnant not to Scripture alone, but even to common sense and reason; overthroweth the nature of the ordinance, and hath been and is the cause of manifold superstitions, yea, of gross Idolatries.

7. Worthy receivers, outwardly partaking of the visible Elements in this Ordinance, do then also inwardly by faith, really and indeed, yet not carnally, and corporally, but spiritually receive, and feed upon Christ crucified & all the benefits of his death: the Body and Blood of *Christ*, being then not corporally, or carnally, but spiritually present to the faith of Believers, in that Ordinance, as the Elements themselves are to their outward senses.

8. All ignorant and ungodly persons, as they are unfit to enjoy communion with *Christ*; so are they unworthy of the Lords Table; and cannot without great sin against him, while they remain such, partake of these holy mysteries, or be admitted thereunto: yea whosoever shall receive unworthily are guilty of the Body and Blood of the Lord, eating and drinking judgment to themselves.

Document VI.2

William Dell: Church, Holy Spirit and Learning

For Dell (d. 5 November 1669), v., DNB and CR where A. G. Matthews says, 'He is now regarded as in advance of his times.' His writings give lucid and persuasive expression to the radical views characteristic of the 'spiritual authors' of the Commonwealth era.

Extract (a) is from Dell's *The Way of True Peace and Unity In the True Church of Christ* (London, 1651) in *Several Sermons and Discourses of William Dell* (London, 1709), 185–90, 210–11, 233–4, 258–65.

Extract (b) is from *Christ's Spirit a Christian's Strength* (London, 1651), in *Several Sermons and Discourses of William Dell* (London, 1709), 10–11, 18–19, 20–1.

Extract (c) is from *Right Reformation ... In a Sermon Preached to the Honourable House of Commons, on Wednesday November 25th, 1646* (London, 1651), in *Several Sermons and Discourses of William Dell* (London, 1709), 150–2. For severe criticism of Dell's views on this topic, v., Samuel Rutherford, *A Survey of the Spirituall Antichrist, Opening the secrets of Familisme and Antinomianism ... In Two Parts* (London, 1648), chap. LXXXIV, pp. 187–219.

Extract (d) is from *The Stumbling-Stone* (London, 1651) in *Several Sermons and Discourses of William Dell* (London, 1709), 402–4. In 'To the Reader', Dell says, 'Here I present thee with this *Discourse*, which met with such notable Opposition and Contradiction from the *University* of *Cambridge*, to whom it was delivered, and also from such of the *Town* then present, who are *baptized* into the University spirit ... '

(a) The Right Church

The Right Church is not the whole multitude of the People, whether good or bad, that joyn together in an outward Form or Way of Worship; for in this Church there are *Whoremongers, Idolaters, Thieves, Murderers*, and all sorts of wicked and unbelieving Persons, which are so far from being the Church of Christ, that they are the very Synagogue of Satan, and Children of the Devil ... But the Church I shall speak of, is the true Church of the New Testament, which I say is not any outward or visible Society, gathered together into the consent or use of outward things, Forms, Ceremonies, Worship, as the Churches of Men are; neither is it known by seeing, or feeling, or the help of any outward Sense, as the Society of Mercers, or Drapers, or the like; but it is a Spiritual and Invisible Fellowship, gathered together in the unity of Faith, Hope, and Love, and so into the unity of the Son, and of the Father by the Spirit; wherefore it is wholly hid from carnal eyes, neither hath the World any knowledge or judgment of it.

This true Church is the Communion of Saints, which is the Communion Believers have with one another; not in the things of the World, or in the things of Men, but in the things of God; for as Believers have their union in the Son, and in the Father, so in them also they have their Communion; and the Communion they have with one another in God, cannot be in their own things, but in Gods things, even in his Light, Life, Righteousness, Wisdom, Truth, Love, Power, Peace, Joy,

&c. This is the true Communion of Saints, and this Communion of Saints is the true Church of God.

Now this true Church of God, differs from the Churches of Men, in very many particulars, as follows.

1. Members come unto the Churches of men, either of their own minds, or else by the perswasion, or by the forcing of others; and so, but after the will of man; but none come to this true Church but from the drawing of God the Father and his own calling, according to his own purpose.

2. In the Churches of men; members are admitted through an outward confession of doctrine; but none are admitted into this true Church, but through a new birth from God and his Spirit ...

3. In the Churches of men there are more wicked than righteous; but in this true Church of Christ the people are all righteous, not one excepted ...

4. In the Churches of men, the people for the most part, are only taught of men, who are their heads and leaders, and whose Judgments they depend on, and follow in all things; but in the right Church, the people are *all taught of God* ...

5. In the *Churches of men*, the greatest part are *hated* and *rejected of God*, as being *strangers* and enemies to Christ; but in the true Church all the members are dear to God, as Christ is dear ...

7. The Churches of men are all of them more or less the habitation of Antichrist, who (as *Paul* saith, 2 *Thes*. 2.4.) *as God sitteth in the Temple of God*, that is, not the true Temple of God, but in the Churches of Men, which arrogate to themselves that name and title, *shewing himself that he is God*: For Antichrist always dwells there, where men have a *form of godliness, denying the power*; but the true Church is *built together*, to be the *habitation of God in the Spirit, Ephes*. 2.22 ...

8. The Churches of men are as large as men will make them; for they that have chief power in these Churches, interesting themselves in worldly Magistrates, through their favour and help, make their Churches as large as the Magistrates Dominions ... But the true Church, which is the Kingdom of the Son, is only the preparation of the Fathers Kingdom, and so will admit no more into it, than the Fathers Kingdom will admit into it; the Sons Kingdom and the Fathers Kingdom being of like latitude and extent ... Now from hence these three things are evident.

1. That the Kingdoms of *England, Scotland*, &c are not the *Church*, but the *World*, as well as the Kingdoms of *France, Spain, Hungary*, &c. but in all these, and all other Kingdoms, the Faithful who are taken into union and communion with *Christ*, and with one another in him, they are the Church, and not the Kingdoms themselves.
2. In particular Assemblies, whether *Parochial, Congregational*, all the *Company* that meet together ther Bodily, and have outward communion in outward Ordinances, are not the Church; but those among all these, that meet together in one Faith and Spirit, in one Christ and God.
3. That it belongs not to Magistrates and Worldly Powers, to say, which is the Church, and which is not the Church; who do belong to it, and who do

not; but it belongs to Christ only to point out his own Church, seeing he only knows it, and it only stands by his Election and Collection, and not by mans.

9. The Churches of men knit themselves together into such Societies, by some outward Covenant or Agreement among themselves: But the true Church is knit into their Society amongst themselves, by being first knit unto Christ their Head; and as soon as ever they are one with him, they are also one with another in him ... So that the true Church is a Spiritual Society, knit unto Christ by Faith, and knit to one another in Christ, by the Spirit and Love ...

[Four further contrasts follow. Then the nature of the unity of the true church is discussed on the basis of Ephes. 4: 4–6.]

Now they break this bond, of the Churches Unity, that either make themselves, or others Lords over the Church, besides Christ, and parcel out this one Kingdom of the Son to many Lords, to the great dishonour of Christ, and disunion of the Church.

The Pope was the first that professed himself to be the general Master in the whole Church of God: and after the Pope, a general Councel took this honour to it self; and by degrees this last became as hard, yea, a harder taskmaster to the Church, than the former. After, when particular Kingdoms fell off from the Pope and his Antichristian Church, the mistery of iniquity, was not by this means wholly dissolved; but only was contracted and brought into a less compass; for then the Archbishop made himself general master of the Church in each particular Kingdom, as the Pope before had done in all; and after the Archbishop rises up a National Assembly, as the General Councel after the Pope; and each of these in their courses, usurp Lordship over the Church of Christ, to the sad dissolution of its unity.

Most evident then it is, that during the time of the Apostasie, the Church hath been most miserably Lorded even amongst us; for the Priest he Lorded it over the People, the Arch-deacon over the Priest, the Dean over the Arch-deacon, the Bishop over the Dean, and the Arch-bishop over the Bishop; under which woful bondage the Church cried out, as Isa.26. *O Lord our God, other Lords besides thee have had dominion over us*. And is this bondage of the Church now eased, by calling off those strange Lords? Yea, do not men rather seek to encreace it, by setting yet stranger over it, whose names are so full of mistery, that the common People cannot understand them? for now they would have the Classical Presbytery set over the Congregational, and the Provincial over the Classical, and the National over the Provincial; for so it is Voted [in the Westminster Assembly of Divines], THAT IT IS LAWFULL AND AGREEABLE TO THE WORD OF GOD, THAT THERE BE A SUBORDINATION OF CONGREGATIONAL, CLASSICAL PROVINCIAL AND NATIONAL ASSEMBLIES FOR THE GOVERNMENT OF THE CHURCH: Now here is mistery, and nothing but a certain rising up into the old Power, under a new name.

... Now if this might be brought about, which they design, the Church would be so far from being eased of its strange Lords that it should have them exceedingly multiplyed; for what is a National Assembly, but an Archbishop multiplied? and what a Provincial Assembly, but a Bishop multiplied? And a Classical, but a Dean and Arch-deacon multiplied? And thus the former Lords being removed, they would in their stead, cause the Church to swarm with Classical, Provincial and National Lords, and would by no means suffer Christs own Kingdom to return to its own Lordship and Dominion ...

[The power of the Keys.] These Keys appertain not only to greater *Congregations* of Christians, but to the very least Communion of Saints, as Christ hath promised, *Where two or three are met together in my name, there am I present in the midst of them*: Where we see, that two or three, gathered together in Christ's name, have as much power as *Peter*, and all the Apostles; because Christ is equally present with these, as with those ...

More particularly, this true power, of the true Church, is ... Christs power in the Faithful, which is, the self same with Christs power in himself; and so ... It is not a power of violence, but a power of influence, even such a power as the Head hath over the Members, and the Soul over the Body; it is not coercive, but a perswasive Power, a Power that makes men willing, that are not willing, and doth not force the unwilling, against their wills ... This Power doth not make others Suffer, to enlarge the Church, but suffers it self, to bring this about; so Christ, as *Wickliff* saith through his poverty, humility and suffering injury and death, got unto him the Children of his Kingdom, and not by force; and the Martyrs enlarged the Church of Christ, by dying themselves.

[Among the rules by which the true Church may walk in the ways of peace are the following:]

1. The true Church is to preserve it self distinct from the world: and is neither to mingle it self with the world, nor to suffer the world to mingle it self with it ...

2. The Church being thus distinct from the world, is to be contended [sic, contented] with its own power, for its own affairs; and is not to introduce, or entertain any power in it, that is not of it. Wherefore, the true Church, being such a Kingdom as is not of this world, stands in need of no worldly power ...

The Third Rule is, Not to bring or force men into the *Church*, against their wills. The Kingdoms of the World are unquiet, because many that are unwilling are under those Regiments, but *Christs Kingdom* is therefore quiet, because all the *People* in it are willing, and none of them forced in, but all are perswaded ...

The fourth Rule is, To make void the distinction of *Clergy* and *Laity* among *Christians*; For the *Clergy* or Ecclesiastical men have all along, under the reign of *Anti-Christ*, distinguished themselves from other Christians, whom they called the *Laity*; and have made up a distinct or several Kingdom among themselves; and separated themselves from the Lay in all things; and called themselves by the name of the *Church*; and reckoned other Christians but as common and unclean, in respect of themselves. Whereas in the true Church of *Christ* there are no distinctions, nor sects, nor difference of persons; no *Clergy*, or *Laity*; no *Ecclesiastical*, or *Temporal*; but they are all, as *Peter* describes them, I *Pet*.2.9.

A chosen generation, a royall Priesthood, a holy Nation, a peculiar People, to shew forth the virtues of him that called them out of darkness into his marvelous light. And so all Christians, through the Baptism of the Spirit, are made *Priests* alike unto God: and every one hath right and power alike, to speak the word; and so there is among them no *Clergy* or *Laity*, but the *Ministers* are such who are chosen by Christians, from among themselves, to speak the word to all, in the name and right of all; and they have no right or authority at all to this office, but by the consent of the *Church*. And so *Presbyters* and Bishops, or (which is all one) *Elders* and *Overseers* in the *Church*, differ nothing from other *Christians*, but only in the office of the word, which is commited to them by the *Church*; as an *Alderman* or *Common Councel* man in the City differs nothing from the rest of the *Citizens*, but only in their *Office*, which they have not of themselves neither, but by the Cities choice ...

(b) The Power of the Spirit

By *Nature*, we are all without *strength*, weak, impotent Creatures, utterly *unable* to do any thing that is *truly* and *spiritually* righteous and good ... But when we receive the *Spirit*, we receive *power*; for power is an inseparable adjunct of the *Spirit*, as *weakness* is of *flesh*; yea the *Spirit it self* which is given us, is power ... The *Spirit* is power *essentially* in it self; for it is *one* God with the *Father* and the *Son*, co-essential. co-equal, co-eternal; and so as *Christ* is the power of God, so also is the *spirit*, the power of God; yea the *spirit* is the *God* of power, as well as the *power* of God. The *Spirit*, is power *operatively* in us, by being in us.

[He then analyses the operations of the Holy Spirit in us. A Spirit of Knowledge, of Power, of Wisdom, of Faith, of Righteousness, of Fear of the Lord and of Love and Unity. On this last topic he writes,]

The Holy Spirit is a Spirit of Power in us by being in us a Spirit of Love and Unity. The Holy Spirit, is a Spirit of Love and Unity in the Godhead; for the Father loves the Son, with the Spirit; and the Son loves the Father with the Spirit; and the Father is one with the Son in the Spirit; and the Son is one with the Father in the Spirit ... Now what the Spirit is in the Godhead, he is the same in the Church of God, which is the true Temple and Habitation of the Godhead, and that is, a Spirit of Love and Unity: For why is there such constant Love and Unity between the members of the same body, but because one Spirit runs through them all? and so there is such constant love and unity between all Believers, because one Holy Spirit runs through them all ...

There is a necessity of this Power of the Spirit for Ministers ... For if they have not this power of the Holy Spirit, they have no power at all. For Christ sent them, only as his Father sent him; and so Christ never gave unto them any Earthly or Humane or Secular Power, no Power of Swords or Prisons, no Power of outward constraint and violence. Christ gave them no such outward and worldly Power, for the inlargement of his Kingdom, as not being at all suitable to it. For his Kingdom is Spiritual, and what can Carnal Power do in a Spiritual Kingdom?

(c) Right Reformation

Forceable Reformation, is unbeseeming the *Gospel*; for the Gospel, is the *Gospel of peace*, and not of force and fury. *Civil Ecclesiastical Reformation* reforms by breathing out *Threatnings*, *Punishments*, *Prisons*, *Fire*, and *Death*; but the Gospel by *Preaching Peace*. And therefore it is most unbeseeming the Gospel, to do any thing rashly and violently, for the advancement thereof; for the *Gospel of Peace*, is not to be advanced by violence; and therefore *violent Reformers*, live in contradiction to the *Gospel of Peace*, and cannot be reckoned Christians, but Enemies to Christianity; sith Christianity doth all by the Power of the Anointing; but Antichristianity, doth all by the Power of the World ...

(d) Criticism of the Universities

By the *foolishness of preaching*, that is, by the *Word of Faith* out of the mouth of *Babes* and *Sucklings*, which the *World* reckons, *foolishness*; by this alone, doth God bring about the *Salvation* of the Elect.

Now at these things how grievously are the *Worldly-wise*, and deep learned ones (as they esteem themselves) offended? that Gods Spirit alone should be sufficient Unction for the Ministry of the *New Testament*, and that God should on set purpose lay aside the Wise and Prudent men, and choose *babes*, and out of their mouth ordain his great strength to set up Christs Kingdom in the world, and to destroy *Antichrists*? Yea this Doctrine will chiefly offend the *University*.

For you will say; *if this be so*, What need is there then of our *Philosophy*, and of our *Arts* and *Sciences* to the *Ministry* of the New Testament? ... And what need is there of our *Scarlet*, and *Tippets*? And what need is there of our *Hoods* and *Caps*, &c. If the *Unction* of the *Spirit* alone be sufficient for the right *Ministry*, and Christ do perfect his praise by the *mouths of babes and Sucklings*, then what need is there of all these things?

I *Answer, No need at all*, as to *Christs Kingdom*, and the *Ministry* of that: For it is one of the *grossest errors* that ever reigned under *Antichrists* Kingdom, to affirm that *Universities are the fountain of the Ministers of the Gospel*, which do only proceed out of *Christs flock* ...

Now if any say, *This Doctrine being commonly taught and received, will throw down the Universities*.

I *Answer*. If the *Universities* will stand upon an *Humane* and *Civil account*, as *Schools* of good *Learning* for the instructing and educating Youth in the knowledge of the *Tongues*, and of the *liberal Arts and Sciences*, thereby to make them useful and serviceable to the Commonwealth, if they will stand upon this account, which is the surest and safest Account they can stand on, and will be content to shake hands with their *Ecclesiastical* and *Antichristian Interest*, then let them stand, during the good Pleasure of God; but if they will still exalt themselves above themselves, and place themselves on Christs very *Throne*, as *if they had ascended upon high to lead captivity captive, and to give gifts to men for the work of the Ministry*, and so will presume to darken the Glory of *Jesus Christ* and his true

Ministry which he sends forth, as his *Father* sent *Him*, then let them in the name of Christ descend into that darkness out of which they first sprang, that the *Glory* of Christ may fill the World.

Document VI.3

Morgan Llwyd: Be Nonconformists!

The following extract is from *Llyfr y Tri Aderyn* (Book of the Three Birds), in T. E. Ellis (ed.), *Gweithiau Morgan Llwyd o Wynedd*, (Works) (Bangor, 1899), I, 206. This book was published in 1653. At that time Llwyd was a stern critic of Cromwell and later of his Protectorate but on 24 December 1656 he was approved by the Triers as minister at Wrexham where he served until his death in June 1659. The above extract illustrates his sympathy with some at least of William Dell's convictions, v., previous document.

Eagle: Some say that the Church is the Ark and there are learned godly men who think so.

Dove: Head and body are one. Branches and roots are one. Husband and wife are one and so are spirit and soul, the fuel and the fire. He who sanctifies is one with him who is sanctified. And Christ and his Church are one – it is flesh of his flesh, spirit of his spirit. He who is in Christ is also in the true Church. Eve was drawn from Adam and the Church from Christ and Christ from the flesh of the Church and the Church again from the Spirit of Christ. Many people speak of many different kinds of churches for the whole world is God's house and Hell itself will be filled because He dwells through all things. The parish churches are but empty barns; many a parish church is like a goat pound or a sheepfold. Other churches consist of men who are like those animals of Jacob's – speckled, spotted and ringstraked (Gen. 30). So far few speak the pure language of Israel. There is amongst us the speech of two nations (as Nehemiah says, Neh. 13. 24), the upper lip is Israel, the lower lip is Ashdod. The people are in Babel. The churches let in water and their beams are rotting. Some (certainly) are as golden candlesticks, others of brass, others of lead and yet they are all candlesticks. Some are queens (Song of Solomon 6. 8) and some are concubines (Gal. 4. 30) but only a few remain in the house with the Son of God. And so there is no church but the spiritual, no spirit but the Second Adam, no temple of God except man's pure mind, no lasting temple for man but the Almighty and the Lamb. no unity except the unity of the Eternal Spirit, no singing, no communion, no unity, no prayer, no membership in any church unless the Spirit of the Head rules with power. They profess that they know God but in their actions they deny that God has loved them and sees them and will judge them. Therefore flee out of yourself and from the old parochial palaces and from the old rotting churches lest they fall on you and lest you fall under them into the grave and the pit.

Document VI.4

Regeneration

The following extract is from Thomas Cole, *A Discourse of Regeneration, Faith and Repentance. Preached at the Merchants-Lecture in Broad-street* (London, 1689). For Cole (1627?–97), v., CR and DNB.

Thomas Cole's text is John 3: 3, 'Jesus answered and said unto him' (that is, Nicodemus), 'Except a man be born again, he cannot see the kingdom of God'.

[p. 2] The text speaks of a Nativity, or first Original of a Christian, and derives his Descent from the Holy Spirit; that is very high; we may look for something extraordinary in such a Birth, which is here called *Regeneration*, or our being born again, or a second time. This is a great Mystery, and cannot be understood, till it is in some measure felt. *Regeneration* is not a Notion, but a Nature; not a mere empty Speculation floating in the Brain, but an inward living Principle rooted in the Heart: I am not speaking of things without you, at a distance from you, that [p. 3] are foreign and extrinsical to your souls, but of that which is essential to the Being and Constitution of a Christian as such; you are not only Auditors this day, but each of you the subject of my present Discourse; I am not only speaking to you, but of you; 'tis what you are, or are not, in the inward state of your souls, that I am now enquiring after ...

[p. 8] That we might the better understand the Nature of *Regeneration*, let us consider the several Names given it in Scripture; *Regeneration*, *Renovation*, *New Creation* [p. 9] *Conversion*, are Synonimous terms in Scripture, and do all signify the same thing, do all imply the Corruption of Mans Nature, that produceth nothing but what is like it self; how specious soever it may seem to be, 'tis but Flesh; therefore all fleshly Wisdom, Beauty and Glory, must be mortified and abolished; the Scripture calls for a new Birth, a new Creation after the Image of God, that Man may be enabled to do good ...

Regeneration is of a larger Extent and Signification than Justification and Sanctification; 'tis initially all that belongs to a state of Grace ...

[p. 10] Therefore I shall describe *Regeneration* or at large define it thus, *viz*.

'Tis a wonderful work of God, begetting the Elect again unto himself, by implant- [p. 11] ing them into Christ, from whom they derive a spiritual being, and in whom they live spiritually for ever and ever; growing up daily into his likeness, till they come to the stature of a perfect man in him.

In *Regeneration* there is a supernatural form of true holiness impressed upon the Soul, that the preternatural form of sin and ungodliness brought in by the Devil, may be abolished; nothing that is physically natural, is abolished by *Regeneration*, which takes not away any natural faculty or affection of the Soul, only sets them upon right Objects. *Regeneration* produces a new spiritual being in the Soul, draws the Image of God upon the heart, sets the Soul into a holy order and rectitude; when the natural faculties of the rational Soul are brought under the power of supernatural Principles, that man is regenerated.

Regeneration implies the beginning of the new Life, or new Creature; birth is the beginning of life; *we are born of God, John* 1.13. This is caused by God's quickening of us, *Eph.* 2.5. in and through our union to Christ by faith, who is our life, a quickening Spirit in us, and to us, I *Cor.* 15.45. They who are born of God, are not still-born, but born alive, quickened by the Spirit of Christ.

[p. 12] This new life appears most in the Will, by its real tendency towards God, *Phil*.2.13. Where you see the will of a man turned to God and Christ, you may be confident God hath been at work in that Soul ...

[p. 13] In *Regeneration* there is a power put into a man to believe and repent, which are acts of the new Creature; so that a man must first be a new Creature; and that which makes him so, is *Regeneration*; before that, an unregenerate person is called an old man, the old man is distinct from our selves as men; we must distinguish between the corruption of humane Nature, and humane [p. 14] Nature it self, which *Regeneration* does not destroy, but perfect; it implies a change of state, and a change of nature, the foundation of both is laid in our *Regeneration*, by virtue of our incorporation into Christ *who is made unto us righteousness and sanctification*; the efficacy of his Blood and Spirit does reach our Souls, being one with him; we die with him, and rise with him, are discharged from sin upon the account of his Satisfaction, and are raised up unto newness of life by vertue of his Resurrection.

Document VI.5

Faith and Justification

The following extract is from *The Whole Works of the Reverend John Flavel* (4th edn, London, 1740), I, 274–5 from Sermon IV on John 6: 44. For Flavel (1630?–91), v., 'Life' prefixed to this volume and DNB.

By saving Faith, Christ is said to *dwell in our Hearts*, Eph. iii.17. but it is neither by *Assent*, nor by *Assurance*, but by *Acceptance*, and receiving him that he dwells in our Hearts; not by *Assent*, for then he would dwell in the Unregenerate; nor by *Assurance*, for he must dwell in our Hearts before we can be assured of it: Therefore it is by Acceptance ...

By Faith we are justified, *Rom.* v.1 ... The Scripture ascribes great Difficulties to that Faith by which we are saved, as being most cross and opposite to the corrupt Nature of Man; but of all the Acts of Faith, none is clogged with like Difficulties, or conflicts with greater Oppositions than the receiving Act doth ...

What shall I say of Faith? It is the *Bond* of Union; the *Instrument* of Justification; the *Spring* of spiritual Peace and Joy; the *Means* of spiritual Life and Subsistence; And therefore the great *Scope* and *Drift* of the Gospel; which aims at, and presseth nothing more, than to bring Men and Women to believe ...

It is the Instrument of our Justification, *Rom*. v.1. 'Till Christ be received ... we are in our Sins; under Guilt and Condemnation; but when Faith comes, then comes

Freedom: *By him all that believe are justified from all Things*, Acts xiii.38. Rom. viii.1. For it apprehends or receives the pure and perfect Righteousness of the Lord Jesus, wherein the Soul, how guilty and sinful soever it be in it self, stands faultless, and spotless, before the Presence of God: All Obligations to Punishment, are, upon believing, immediately dissolved: A full and final Pardon sealed. O precious Faith! Who can sufficiently value it ...

And I find four Opinions about the Interest of Faith in our Justification: Some will have it to justify us *formally*, not relatively; (i.e., upon the Account of its own intrinsical Value and Worth; and this is the *Popish* Sense of Justification by Faith. Some affirm, that though Faith be not our perfect legal Righteousness, considered as a Work of ours, yet the *Act* of believing is imputed to us for Righteousness (*i.e.*) God graciously accepts it instead of perfect legal Righteousness and so, in his Esteem, it is our evangelical Righteousness. And this is the *Arminian* Sense of Justification by Faith.

Some there are also, even among our Reformed Divines, that contend that Faith justifies and saves us, as it is the Condition of the new Covenant. And lastly, Others will have it to justify us as an *Instrument* apprehending or receiving the Righteousness of Christ; with which Opinion I must join; When I consider my Text calls it *receiving of Christ* ...

Document VI.6

Sanctification

The following extract is from John Owen, *A Discourse Concerning the Holy Spirit* (London, 1674) in *The Works of John Owen*, ed. W. H. Goold (Edinburgh: Banner of Truth, 1977), III. The page numbers in the extract refer to this edition.

Dr John Owen is expounding 1 Thes. 5: 23, 'And the very God of peace sanctify you wholly; and let your whole spirit and soul and body be preserved blameless unto the coming of our Lord Jesus Christ' and has the following comments amongst others.

[p. 367] And in this place, – 1. The *author* of our sanctification, who only is so, is asserted to be 'God.' He is the eternal spring and only fountain of all holiness; there is nothing of it in any creature but [p. 368] what is directly and immediately from him; there was not in our first creation. He made us in his own image. And to suppose that we can now sanctify or make ourselves holy is proudly to renounce and cast off our principal dependence upon him. We may as wisely and rationally contend that we have not our *being* and our lives from God, as that we have not our *holiness* from him, when we have any. Hereunto are the proud opinions of educing a holiness out of the principles of nature to be reduced. I know all men will pretend that holiness is from God; it was never denied by Pelagius himself: but many with him, would have it to be from God in a way of *nature*, and not in any way of *especial grace*. It is this latter way that we plead for ... 2. And, therefore, is he that is the author of our sanctification so emphatically here expressed ... 'Even God himself.' If he doth it not, none other can do it; it is no otherwise to be wrought nor effected. There is no other way whereby it may be brought about, nor doth it fall under the power or efficacy of any means absolutely whatever, but it must be wrought by God himself. He doth it of himself, from his own grace; by himself, or his own power; for himself, or his own glory ...

[p. 369] God, even God himself, the God of peace, is the author of our holiness ... And he is here said to sanctify us ... 'universally and completely', carrying on the work until it comes to perfection: for two things are intended in that expression:- First, That our *whole nature* is the subject of this work, and not any one faculty or part of it. Second, That as the work itself is sincere and universal, communicating all parts of real holiness unto our whole nature, so it is carried on to *completeness* and perfection ...

Wherefore,

Sanctification, as here described, *is the immediate work of God by his Spirit upon our whole nature, proceeding from the peace made for us by Jesus Christ, whereby, being changed into his likeness, we are kept entirely in peace with God, and are preserved unblameable, or in a state of gracious acceptation with him, according to the terms of the Covenant, unto the end.*

Document VI.7

Heaven

The quotations come from Christopher Love, *Heavens Glory, Hells Terror* (London, 1653), 93–4, 96–9. The original spelling and punctuation have been retained. This is within a series of sermons on Col. 3: 4, *When Christ who is our life shall appear, then shall we also appear with him in glory*. The book was published after Love's death and the address 'To the Christian Reader', testifying that the sermons were accurately reproduced from his notes, is signed by Edmund Calamy, Simeon Ashe, Jeremiah Whitaker, William Taylor and Allen Geare. For Love (1618–51), v., DNB. The sermons were preached at his church, Lawrence Jury, London. 'Mausoleus Tomb' is a reference to the memorial of white marble, designed by Phythias, and built by Artemisia c. 353 BC, for her dead husband, Mausolus, satrap of Caria. Fragments of it are now in the British Museum. It was one of the seven wonders of the ancient world.

When a mortal man speaks any thing of that eternall blessedness of the Saints in glory, he doth but as much as if a blind man should dispute about the light which he never saw, and so cannot distinctly speak any thing concerning it. We shall know more then either the Scripture doth speak, or your hearts can conceive. So that I may break out into that extasie the Apostle doth, I Cor.2.9. *Neither eye hath seen, nor ear hath heard, nor can it ever enter into the heart of man to conceive, what God hath prepared for them that love him.* The eye hath seen many admirable things in nature, it hath seen mountains of Crystall, and Rocks of Diamonds, it hath seen mines of Gold, and coasts of Pearl, spicy islands ... the eye hath seen ... the

Pyramides of Ægypt, the Temple of *Diana*, *Mauseolus* Tomb, which by Geographers are made the wonders of the world; and yet the eye that hath seen so many wonders in the world, could never pry into the glories of heaven. *Neither hath the ear heard*: The ear of man hath heard the most delightfull and ravishing melodies, and yet that singing & melodious musick that shal be in glory, the ear never heard it ...

First, the soul shall be freed from all things that may any way make it miserable. And there are three things that will make the soul miserable, Sin, the causes of sin, and the punishment or effects of sin ...

I now come to the positive endowments the soul shal enjoy when it appears in glory with Jesus Christ: These I shall reduce to three heads, first, there shall be a beatificall vision of God, secondly, a reall enjoyment of God: thirdly, there shall be perfection of al graces ...

First, there shal be a beatificall vision of God, Mat.5.8 *Blessed are the pure in heart, for they shall see God*. So I John 3.2. *When he shal appear, we shall see him as he is*: Here we see onely what he is not; God we see is not an unjust God, and he is not a weak, nor is he an unwise God: but then we shall see him as he is. So *Job* 19.26, 27. *I know that my Redeemer liveth, and that he shall stand upon the earth at the last day, and with these eyes I shall see God &c* ... Now if you ask, What is it to see God ... I answer, seeing of God implies two things.

1. It implies to have a reall enjoyment of the favour and love of God to you in Christ ...

2. A perfect knowledge of God in his nature. And that is the chief importance of this word, *seeing of God*; not as if we should see his divine essence with bodily eyes: for bodily eyes are not capable of seeing the divine essence of God; but to see God with the eye of the minde, you shall see God with more perfect knowledge then now you see. Now you know him but darkly, see God but in a glass, know God but as a Riddle, the Trinity of persons in the Godhead, and the unity of both natures in Christ, these are riddles to flesh and blood; but when you are in glory, you shal know God more perfectly, and have a perfect apprehension (though not comprehension) of the Nature, Atributes, and majesty of God ...

[Second], Because sight without fruition gives little comfort; therefore there shal be a reall enjoyment and fruition of God: you shall enjoy God so far as your natures are capable. As now you are bespangled with a divine nature, yet you have some blots and blurres upon you, by reason of sin in you; but then shall all those blots be wip't away, & you shal have the divine nature shining forth gloriously in you. Here you have an enjoyment of God, it's true, but first you enjoy God mediatly by ordinances, but then you shall enjoy God immediatly face to face, I Cor.13.10. 2. You enjoy God in measure, there is but a little enjoyment of God here, but there you shall enjoy God above measure; here you have the fulness of a bucket, there you shall have the fulness of an Ocean. 3. Here you enjoy God by fits and starts, you have many interruptions in your way; now you lose God, then you find him in an ordinance; but in glory you shall enjoy God without intermission or cessation at all ... 4. Here you have God in expectation, but there you shall have him in possession.

There shall be a perfection of all grace when once you come into this place of glory: here you have perseverance in grace, but not perfection: I Cor.13.9. *We know but in part, but when that which is perfect is come, then that which is imperfect shall be done away.* Here your graces are not compleat, but when once you are in heaven, all your imperfections shall be made perfect. And amongst the perfection of your graces, there are three eminent graces that shall gloriously shine in heaven. The grace of *Love*, the grace of *Knowledge*, and the grace of *Joy* ...

First, the grace of *Love*, when all other gifts and miracles fail, the grace of *Love* shall be perfected. And (as *Anselm* saith) they shall love God more then themselves, and one another as well as themselves, your love then shall run in one channel. Here you divide your love between God and man, between God and your comforts, God and your estate; but then all your love shal center in God.

Secondly, your *Knowledge* likewise: Here you know in *part*, but in an imperfect glass, but then you shall know God as he is; and see all those rayes of glory and majesty, which now your dim eye cannot behold. And then thirdly, your joy and delight in God, that grace shal wonderfully shine in heaven; and for all the sorrows and sighings you have had for sinne upon earth, your joy shall be greater in singing *Hallelujah's* to your God in heaven, This shall be the great happiness of all you that are the Elect of God.

Document VI.8

Hell

After preaching his series of ten sermons on the glories of heaven, Christopher Love went on to preach seven sermons on the terrors of hell. In the first sermon he explains why he thought it necessary to handle this theme. It throws an unexpected light on the place given to the subject in Puritan preaching. The text of the sermons was Matthew 10: 28, 'But rather fear him which is able to destroy both body and soul in hell.'

The extracts are from Christopher Love, *Hells Terror: Or, A Treatise of the Torments of the Damned* (London, 1653), 6–11, 103. This work was issued together with *Heavens Glory* but with a separate title-page. 'Mr Bolton' was Robert Bolton (1572–1631) and the reference is to his book, published posthumously, *The Foure Last Things: Death, Judgment, Hell and Heaven* (London, 1632); for Bolton, v., DNB.

First, I handle it now, because I have so largly handled the glory of the Elect in heaven, for the comfort of the godly: now I shall speak of the Torments of hell for the punishment of the wicked, that so if the glory of the Elect have not allured your affections, the hearing of the Torment of the damned in hell might startle your Consciences, and awaken you out of your securities.

Secondly, I handle it, lest any of you should grow secure and presumptuous, in nourishing ungrounded hopes of glory, expecting to be in glory with Jesus Christ upon the former Sermons; lest you should thus vainly hope, I deemd it meet to conjoyne this subject with it, that so you might be equally poysed from presumption on the one hand, and despair on the other.

Thirdly, Because it is a Doctrine so little preacht, and so little writ of in these days; I know but onely one Book in English writ upon this subject, by Mr *Bolton*; and very few in Latin: and therefore being so usefull a subject, usefull for the wicked and usefull for the godly; and yet so little handled, and now a days much cried down, and cried against this reason; also put me upon this Doctrine.

[Perhaps the punctuation in the last sentence is wrongly printed and the sentence should read, 'and cried against, this reason also put me upon'.]

Fourthly, I handle this Doctrine, because I am perswaded, did many men know distinctly the torments of hell, they would never walk in a way of sin, that leads to hell as they doe ... Did men but know that they who live and die unrepenting, lie burning in their lusts, shall one day burn in fire; did they but know that they that can swallow bowls of wine, and drink to excess, they shall one day drink draughts of brimstone in hell: did men but know that they that grind their Teeth through hatred and indignation against the godly here, shall one day gnash their Teeth in hell hereafter ... did men but know this Doctrine well, they would not be so profane, and sinfully wicked as they are now a days ...

Now, There are two Objections, why men should not preach upon such a subject as this is.

I. Some will say, This is Legall preaching, To cast flashes of hell fire about the Congregation; this is not to preach the gospell, but the Law: to take off this therefore, I shall speak four things by way of Answer.

    1. Surely, Jesus Christ was no legall preacher, yet he preacht this Doctrine, for these are Christs own words [in the text]; and therefore preaching of hell and the Torments thereof, cannot justly be call'd legall preaching, because Jesus Christ, the Minister of the new Covenant, he was the person that most of all preacht of hel ...

    2. It is the great policie of the Divell to nuzzle men in securitie in their sins; to have all soul searching preaching, and sin reproving preaching ... call'd legal preaching ...

    3. If preaching of Terrour be legal preaching, then the Law was more preacht in the new Testament then ever it was under the old ...

    4. Whereas it is said, that preaching of terrour is legall preaching; I say this, that Sermons of terrour have done more good upon unconverted souls, then Sermons of comfort ever have done; Sermons of hel may keep many out of hell ...

[II]. But it may be some men will object and say, indeed preaching of hell, it is lawfull, but preaching of Christs love, and preaching of free grace, they are more winning subjects, and they are Doctrines more to build upon; and Doctrines more to refresh and clear the hearts of the people of God ...

[He makes five points in reply. The fifth begins with the following words:]

Those men that have cried so much to have preaching upon strains of love, and of free grace, I am sure, as some manage the matter, they have hardened more souls, then ever they have converted by those Sermons. For my part, Beloved, I know not one man that hath been converted by these new teachers, that pretend more light then their Brethren, and pretend to hold forth Christ more clearly then their Brethren. I do not see holiness shining in their lives above others, Whereas I am sure, those that did preach mixt doctrine, sometimes fear, and sometimes love, sometimes strains of wrath, sometimes of grace, these did most work upon the Consciences of their hearers ...

[In the following sermons Love discusses in great detail the questions people ask about hell, whether it exists, why the majority of the human race will be consigned to it, how the doctrine can be reconciled with God's justice and mercy, what is the precise nature of the torments that the damned will suffer. Here he discusses hell fire.]

Is it so, that there shall be fire in hell? then here see the justice and righteous Judgment of God, that God will punish your bodies, that have been instruments of sin, as well as your souls. God will not onely punish your souls with a worm of Conscience, but God will punish your bodies with fire also. Your eyes, that have been eyes of uncleanness, those very eyes shall be inflamed with fire. Your mouths that have taken down drink with excess, shall then take down fire and shovels of brimstone in abundance. Your members, that have been members of uncleanness burning in lust, shall one day burn in the fire of hell, and this body of yours that hath been an instrument of sin, this body by the just hand of God shall be a body burning in hell. And now, O see then, whether the pleasures of sin, that come by the body, can be equivalent to the torments of this fire ... And thus I confess it hath been a dismal subject I have been preaching upon. Yet peradventure God may bless it to some. Some are wrought upon with love, some won with fear ...

Document VI.9

Walter Cradock: Gospel Liberty

The text was 1 Cor. 10: 23: 'All things are lawful for me, but all things are not expedient'. See Walter Cradock, *Gospel-libertie* (London, 1648). Prefixed to the book is an 'Epistolar [sic] Preface' by Nathanael Homes, 'From my Study at *Mary Stainings, London*. July 10, 1648'. Homes (1599–1678) established an Independent congregation at London at the end of 1643. He was ejected from St Mary Staining in 1662, v., CR, DNB and S. Palmer, *The Nonconformist's Memorial* (2nd edn, London, 1802).

[p. 39] *Saints in the new Testament in point of lawfulnes, are not so strictly bound, as the Saints were under the old Testament.*
[p. 40] ... But I see the devill gets much advantage by nick-names, by calling men *Presbyterians*, and *Antinomians*, and *Anabaptists* and I know not what; therefore I beseech you beware, how you use those names, (though I say not it is

A Theological Miscellany

unlawfull) yet there be mistakes, (let us call them as gently as we can) that are generally among us, either
> On the left hand, or On the right.
> And both are to be reproved from this doctrine.

On the left hand, I mean those that make every thing lawfull, and would have no *band*, nor *tie* (as it were) they would make the way wider than Christ hath made it; they would make a greater *latitude* than God hath made. Now I say, these all come to be reproved, from this word ALL in the text [1 Cor. 10: 23]: for I shewed that by the word *all* is not meant *all* things in a universsallity, that I may be any thing, I may be a *drunkard* and be a *Christian*, I may be a *swearer*, and be a *Christian*, I may doe what I list, and yet be a *Christian*: but ... by *all things* is meant many things, & those that take it universally will doe nothing. Therefore on the left hand I say, these doe mistake; and of these there be three sorts, all godly Christians I hope they are ...

There are one sort of people among us, (you have a name for them, but I will not use it) that doe apprehend so much beautie, and loveliness in *spirituall* things, in grace, and the worke of the Spirit, in the person, and excellencies of Christ, and the like [p. 41] that they looke upon the externall manner of Gods worship, or government as a smal contemptible thing, with a disdainfull eye. Beloved, I make not men of straw to speak to: but I know many godly people that hold so, that say it is ridiculous, and they care not which way the Church of God be ordered, or governed, because the Kingdome of God consists in *righteousness, and peace, and joy in the holy Ghost*; And they smile to see contentions between *Presbyterians* and others and think that these are too mean, and too low things for Saints to looke after. Give me leave to tell you my thoughts, I confesse as I conceive that of all others, this is the least error, yet it is an error, and mistake: for though it be true that spirituall things are the maine, and other things are but little to be regarded in comparison, under the new Testament; yet I may say of outward things as farre as Christ hath enjoyn'd them, as Christ saith of tything *mint*, and *annise*, when he speaks of *righteousness, These things ought yee to have done: but the other you ought not to have left undone*. So this is the maine worke for a Christian to doe, and it is blessed to see a Saint make that his maine studie. But if God makes lawes, and give commands about externall things, outward things, I must not neglect that neither. It is (as one observes) as with the Saints and the world, they both see the misery: but the Saints begin to studie the causes of contention; and the old saying is, happy is he that knows the causes. One maine cause of contention among us is, God comes now with more light than wee had before; we have more, and more; but this light is not a full light, I mean thus, this light comes, and shines but in part of the will of God to us: that is, [p. 42] we see part of the will of God, and part wee see not, and while we learne one part, we forget another part of the will of God. And this is ordinary among Christians, while they learne *faith* and *justification*, they forget *puritie*, and *holines*; while they learne *Church-discipline* they forget godliness; while they learne holines within, they forget obedience without.

The knowledge of heavenly things comes into the soules of people now a dayes, as the Sun shines on the earth; How is that? You know when the Sun shines in our horizon, it doth not shine to the other end of the world, it is night with them when it is day with us; So, when the light shewes one thing, another truth is lost; And this is the reason of division, light is come, but it is not a full light, it reveales not all the will of God, but teacheth one, one thing, and another, another. Wee see not all together. This is one thing wherein men mistake; though I much commend them for their prizing of spirituall things, yet if their be a real command of God in outward things I humbly beseech you that you would not disdaine and despite it. That is all I have to say to them.

There are a second sort of people that mistake on the left hand, and make the rule wyder than it is; those that goe farther than those; that is, that doe not only slight, external worship and government &c. As farre as God hath laid it downe but breake downe the pales, even to the morall law of God, and think that the way is now so wide that even the ten commandements, that the *morall law* it self is done away; there are some conceive so. But concerning that I think there is no subject that I could prove more [p. 43] fully, with stronger arguments, yet I will not trouble you nor my self now; and I shewed before how Christ came not to destroy the *morall law*; neither for that use that *Paul* makes of it, to *reveale sin*, to make us *esteeme of Christ*, or to be a light, the Spirit being within: for they are not contradictorie as some simply think and speak; but the Spirit within, and the law without is a lanthorne. Only the damnation is gone: but there are other motives to obey it; *heaven and earth shall passe, but the law of God shall not passe.* So now you see two sorts. And I hope, if there be any such here that they will also take their shares: for if every one would here with humilitie and take his part I hope there would soone be an end of most of our contentions.

The third sort goe farther than those on the left hand, they make it so broad this *all things are lawfull.* That not only in point of goverment, or of the morall law (for those that hold against the morrall law they hold that we ought to doe the things, but not upon the same motives; they hold that we are not to be whoremongers, and drunkards, &c.) but the third sort say, if we worship God in our *spirits* it is no matter what we doe with our *bodies*, we may worship God in our *spirits*, and goe to *masse*, and doe any thing, the bodie is but as a toole in a carpenters hand.

It is not worth the while to confute those, I could give many reasons to the contrary. Christ hath *redeemed soul*, and *bodie*, therfore we must *gloryfie God* in both. And you know the *soule* and *bodie* that goe on in sin shall be damned the one and the other: therefore the *bodie* hath need to looke to it as well as the soul. And we are commanded to beare witnes to the [p. 44] truth of God, how can we doe it if the *bodie* may doe any thing? we need never suffer persecution, as all that are in Christ must; if I will be content to serve Christ in my soule only, I will not suffer persecution, I will goe to masse, *and sweare*, and be *drunk &c.* Againe, we are called to be *like Christ* and he was holie *in soule, and bodie;* how can we be *like* him if we will be holie in our souls only and not in our bodies? Nay it is impossible: for *out of the abundance of the heart the mouth speaketh:* that is, if the soule be holie, the bodie will be so too: if there be *wickednes in* the *heart* there must be wickednes in the *bodie*, and if there *be holines* in the *soul*, there will be also *in the bodie.* If any hold an opinion to make contention by it, let them take it as an admonition from the Lord to consider what they do.Thus you se[e] the errors on the left hand. As I desire power of the Lord to tell yon what [I] think, so I desire that you would indeavour to understand.

The errours on the right hand are contrarie to this, when as Paule saith *All things are lawfull* as the one makes it universall *that every thing is* lawfull, so the other makes *nothing* lawfull almost. My meaning is this; they on the right hand having an *old Testament s*pirit (mark that word, for from thence is the contention) having a spirit not suitable to the new Testament; though (mistake me not) they differ but in degrees cheifly, and principally; they make *lawes* and *ties*, and *bonds*, and *knotts*, and *knacks* and many ridiculous things to tie, and bind themselves, where Christ Jesus in the new testament hath not bound them; and hence comes chiefly the contentions, and controversies of these times betweene two sorts of people; you know who they are.

[p. 45] What is *an old Testament spirit?*
I speake not to make the breach wider; but desire that it may be healed: therfore I say that you may take notice of it, & take heed of it, *an old Testament spirit* is this, that there is in both a disposition to make a curious externall peice of *government*; as curious, nay say they, why not more curious than *Moses* made in the *Old*? I say, in externall things. And out of this principle every one will have his brat, and straine and squeeze the Scripture one this way, and another that, and make fine peices that will never stand ...

Document VI.10

John Biddle: Against the Trinity

Extract (a) is selected from the Preface to Biddle's *Confession of Faith Touching the Holy Trinity* (London, 1648, reprinted in London in 1691 together with some of his other writings, including his earlier tract *Twelve Arguments against the Deity of the Holy Spirit* (London, 1647)).

Extract (b) is from a letter which Biddle wrote from prison to Sir Henry Vane, on 1 April 1647. For Henry Vane (1613–62), MP for Hull, governor of Massachusetts 1636–7 and leading parliamentarian, v., C. H. Firth in DNB and Violet Rowe, *Sir Henry Vane the Younger* (London, 1970). For John Biddle (1615–62), the 'Father of English Unitarianism', v., J.Toulmin, *A Review of the Life ... of John Biddle* (London, 1791); DNB and ODCC. He was the most notable and articulate of the seventeenth-century Socinians. He graduated from Magdalen Hall, Oxford, in 1638 and later kept a school at Gloucester. The MS. of his *Twelve Arguments* was seized in 1645 and when published in 1647 was ordered to be burned by the public hangman. He suffered imprisonment from time to time, was exiled to the Isles of Scilly in 1655, and eventually died in prison. He was much influenced by the Polish Socinians, some of whose writings he translated and published, including a version of the Racovian Catechism (Polish version, 1605; Latin in 1611, Biddle's in 1652) which was based on work done by Faustus Socinus. Some of his writings were published after his death in the 'Unitarian Tracts', sponsored by the Socinian Thomas Firmin. For Socinus (1539–1604), v., ODCC; and for Firmin (1632–97), v., DNB, A. Gordon, *Addresses:*

Biographical and Historical (London, 1922), 92–119, and his article in DNB. For the violent verbal attacks on antitrinitarians by Thomas 'Gangraena' Edwards and others, v., M. R. Watts, *The Dissenters* (Oxford, 1978), I, and H. J. McLachlan, *Socinianism in Seventeenth Century England* (Oxford, 1951), 149–62.

(a)
Though we might justly renew the old complaint, that truth is a stranger in the earth, even in respect of sundry things exceedingly important for the good of human society, yet shall we find, upon a diligent examination of the matter, that this wayfaring condition of truth hath in nothing more disclosed itself than in the knowledge of the true God. For to omit the sudden and general revolt of the nations to idolatry, how unstable and fleeting was this knowledge even in Israel itself, though God had chosen that nation above all others to be his people ... But not only the history of by-past ages, but even the experience of our own times abundantly showeth how deeply Christians themselves are guilty of making a defection from the true God, being so thickened on their lees, that (did we not look unto the mighty power of God, who alone doeth wondrous works) we should conceive it utterly impossible to clarify them from the filth of superstition. For though Luther and Calvin deserve much praise for the pains they took in cleansing our religion from sundry idolatrous pollutions, yet are the dregs still left behind. I mean the gross opinion touching three Persons in God. Which error not only made the way for those pollutions, but, lying at the bottom, corrupteth almost our whole religion. For firstly, it introduceth three Gods and so subverteth the unity of God, so frequently inculcated in Scripture. Neither is it enough to say with Athanasius, that though the Father be God, the Son God, the Holy Spirit God, yet there are not three Gods, but one God. For who is there (if at least he dare make use of reason in his religion) who seeth not that it is as ridiculous as if one should say, Peter is an Apostle, James an Apostle, John an Apostle, yet there are not three Apostles, but one Apostle? ...

Secondly, this tenet of three Persons in God hindereth us from praying according to the prescript of the Gospel. For how can any man pray to God through his Son Jesus Christ, as the Gospel directeth us, if God be not the Father only? Did God consist of three Persons, would it not, when we invocate God, be all one as if we should say: O Father, Son and Holy Spirit, give me what I ask through thy Son Jesus Christ; and so Christ be the Son not only of the Father, but also of the Holy Spirit – yea of himself? ...

The assertion of three Persons in God also thwarteth the common notion that all men have of God, namely that God is the First Cause of all things, he only being of himself, and all others from him ... Herein is the great fault of Christians. Turning quickly aside from the straight and easy way of believing in God, set down in Scripture, and (according to the inbred curiosity of men) hunting after obscurities, they have, by the cunning of Satan, lost themselves in the endless mazes of error and superstition, erecting a new Babel, confounding the pure and plain language of the Holy Spirit with their Modalities, eternal generations and Processions, Incarnations, Hypostatical Unions and the like monstrous terms, more fit for conjurers than for Christians.

(b)

For my own particular, after a long and impartial enquiry of the truth in this controversy, and after much earnest calling upon God to give unto me the spirit of wisdom and revelation in the knowledge of him, I find myself obliged, both by the principles of Scripture and of Reason, to embrace the opinion I now hold forth, and as much as in me lieth, to endeavour that the honour of Almighty God be not transferred to another ... What shall befall me in pursuance of this work, I refer to the disposal of the all-wise God, whose glory is dearer to me not only than my liberty, but also than my whole life.

Document VI.11

Stephen Nye: Unitarianism

The following is an extract from *A Brief History of the Unitarians, also called Socinians – In Four Letters, Addressed to a Friend* (2nd edn, London, 1691); the First Letter, pp. 3–6, 8–9. The tract was first published in 1687. The 'Friend' was Thomas Firmin. Stephen Nye (c. 1648–1719) was the grandson of Philip Nye (1596?–1672), a leading Independent. Stephen was the rector of Little Hormead, Herts., from March 1679 until his death. The historical section of the tract, though reasonably accurate, is in fact extremely brief and the publication consists mainly of a polemical presentation, based primarily on Scripture, of the case against the doctrine of the Trinity. Nye exemplifies the influence of Socinianism within the Church of England but he showed no inclination to separate from it. In later life he became less radical. For his influence on Firmin and Biddle, v., Alexander Gordon's article on him in DNB.

Sir,

In answer to yours, demanding a brief Account of the *Unitarians*, called also *Socinians*, their Doctrine concerning God (in which they differ from other Christians the *Remonstrants* professedly agreeing with them in other points of Faith and Doctrine) and the Defence which they usually make of their Heresy. They are called *Socinians* from *F. Socinus*, an Italian Nobleman, and the principal Writer of their Party. They affirm, God is only One Person, not Three. They make our Lord Christ to be the Messenger, Servant, and Creature of God; they confess he is also the Son of God, because he was begotten on blessed *Mary* by the Spirit or Power of God, *Luke* 1.35. But they deny, that he or any other Person but *the Father* (the God and Father of the said Lord Jesus Christ) is God Almighty and Eternal. The Holy Ghost, or Spirit, according to them, is the Power and Inspiration of God, *Luke* 1.35.

That the Lord Christ was a Man, the Son, Prophet, Messenger, Minister, Servant, and Creature of God; not himself God, is proved, they think, by these Arguments:-

[Twelve arguments are presented, each followed by the relevant scriptural quotations, with references.]

Protestant Nonconformist Texts 1

1. If our Lord Christ were himself God, there could be no person greater than He; none that might be called His Head or his God; none that could in any respect command him. But the Holy Scriptures teach that *the Father* is greater than Christ; is the Head, and the God of Christ; and gave commandments to him, what he should Say, and what he should do.

[The texts quoted: John 14: 28; 1 Cor. 11: 3; John 20: 17, 12: 49, 14: 31.]

2. If our Lord Christ were indeed God, it could not without Blasphemy be (absolutely and without Restriction) affirmed of him, that he was the Creature, Possession, the Servant, and Subject of God; or that for his Obedience he was rewarded and advanced by God. But the inspired Authors of Holy Scripture do say that the Son our Lord Christ is the Creature of God, the Possession of God, the Servant of God; was obedient to God, and for that cause by him rewarded and exalted; also that when God shall have subjected all men to his Son our Lord Christ; yet even then shall he remain subject to God.

[Col. 1: 15; Heb. 3: 1, 2; 1 Cor. 3: 23; Mat. 12: 17, 18; Phil. 2: 8, 9; 1 Cor. 15: 28.]

3. He that is true God, is not the Minister, or Priest of any other Person or Persons; he neither doth nor will (being himself Omnipotent and All-Sufficient) mediate or interceed with any whomsoever, for his Servants and People. But 'tis certain, that our Lord Christ is the Minister, and Mediator of God and Men; a Priest that appeareath in the Presence of God, and intercedeth with him for Men.

[Heb. 8: 6; 1 Tim. 2: 5; Heb. 2: 17, 9: 24, 7: 25.]

4. Almighty God doth all things in his own Name, and by his own Authority; he ever doth his own Will, and seeketh his own Glory; for he declares himself to be the prime Object of Faith and Worship, and pronounces all Doctrines and Religions to be vain which proceed not from him alone. But in our Lord Christ all things are contrary; for he declares, that he came not into the World of his own Name or Authority, or to do his own Will, or seek his own Glory, or propound himself the principal Object of our Faith or Worship, or to publish a Doctrine of his own.

[John 17: 28, 5: 43, 8: 42, 5: 30, 8: 50, 12: 44; Phil. 2: 11; John 7: 16.]

5. God was always most wise, never ignorant of any thing; he needeth not the concurrence of any other Person, to assure him that he judgeth right. He needeth not to be tried by Temptation. And as he is infinitely Great, so he is no less Good. But the Sacred Writers do not speak of the Lord Christ after this Tenor. They say of him, that he increased in Wisdom; that he professed himself ignorant of some things; that he ascribed the certainty and infallibility of his own Judgment to the Father's Presence in him; that he was tried by great Temptations, being thereto exposed by the Holy Ghost; that he refused to be called Good, on this account, that only God is Good.

[Luke 2: 52; Mark 13: 32; Mat. 24: 36; John 11: 34, 8: 16; Mat. 4: 1; Luke 18: 19.]

6. God giveth what and to whom himself pleaseth; he needs not the Aid of any other; he intreateth not for his People, much less for himself; he cannot die, and he deriveth his Power from none but himself. But 'tis certain that the Lord Christ could not himself, without the previous Ordination of his Father, confer the prime Dignities of Heaven, or of the Church; he placed his Safety on his Father's Presence and Help; He prayed often and fervently to the Father. After his

Resurrection he received of *Another* that great Power which he now enjoyeth; but so, that the Father reserveth to himself some principal Regalities.
[Mat. 20: 23; John 8: 29; Luke 22: 42; Heb. 5: 7; John 17: 20; Ephes. 1: 19, 20; Mat. 28: 18; Acts 1: 7.]

7. The Lord Christ is in Holy Scripture described to be the Son of God and the Image of God (Luke 1.35, John 3.16, Col.1.15). 'Tis (say the *Socinians*) as impossible that the Son or Image of the one true God, should himself be that one true God, as that the Son should be the Father, or the Image that Thing whose Image it is; which they take to be simply impossible and contradictory to commonsense, which Religion came not to destroy, but to improve.

8. Our Lord Christ is by the sacred Writers so *distinguished from* and *opposed to* God, that it amounts to as much as an express denial that he is God. Nothing that is God can be distinguished from or opposed to God; for Distinction and Opposition suppose Diversity.
[Cor. 15: 28; Phil. 2: 11; Rom. 16: 27; 1 Tim. 2: 5; Luke 18: 19.]

9. Very many Texts directly affirm, That only *the Father* is God.
[John 17: 1, 3: 1; 1 Cor. 8: 6; Heb. 1: 2; Eph. 4: 4–6; 1 Cor. 15: 24; James 3: 9; Rom. 15: 6.]

10. If the Lord Christ were indeed God as well as Man, or (as *Trinitarians* speak) *God the Son* incarnate in an Humane Nature; it had been altogether superfluous to give the Holy Spirit to his said Humane Nature, as Director and Guide. For what other help could that Nature need, which was one Person with (as they speak) *God the Son*; and in which *God the Son* did Personally dwell?
[Luke 4: 1; Acts 1: 2, 10: 38.]

11. Had the Lord Christ been (as *Trinitarians* speak) *God the Son* joined to an Humane Nature; he could not have ascribed his miraculous Works to the Holy Ghost, or to the Father dwelling in him; but to the Son, dwelling in him and united to him; much less could he so expressly deny that himself was at all the Author of them.
[John 5: 30, 14: 10; Mat. 12: 28; Acts 2: 22.]

12. Had our Lord been more than a Man, the Prophecies of the Old Testament, in which he is promised, would not describe him *Barely* as the Seed of the Woman; the Seed of *Abraham*; a Prophet like unto Moses; the Servant and Missionary of God, on whom God's Spirit should rest.
[Gen. 3: 15, 2: 18; Deut. 18: 18, 'interpreted of Christ in the New Testament'; John 1: 45; Acts 3; 22, 7: 37; Isaiah 42: 1, 'interpreted of Christ'; Mat. 12: 17, 18.]

[This opening section of the First Letter is followed by a similar section designed to show, in seven arguments, that 'the Holy Ghost or Spirit and the Power of God are spoken of as one and the same thing'. Argument 5 is of special interest, in that it seeks to demonstrate the extent to which the Apostles' Creed does not support the notion of the divinity of either Son or Spirit.]

If the compilers of this Creed had believed that either the Son or the Spirit is God, 'tis unaccountable that they should take no notice of it in a Creed, and such a Creed as was purposely drawn up to represent the Essential and Necessary Articles of the

Christian Religion. If a *Socinian*, say they, were to make a Confession of his Faith, he would do it in no other Words but these of the Apostles, and on the contrary, no *Trinitarian*, after having decribed *the Father* by all the Characters of God (saying he is *God* Almighty and *Maker of Heaven and Earth*) would fail to mention the Divinity of the Son and Holy Spirit. Whence we must needs infer that the Compilers of this Creed believed as the *Socinians*, not as the *Trinitarians* believe concerning God, our Lord Christ, and the Holy Spirit.

[The seventh and final argument of this section reads as follows:]

To conclude; Theirs (they say) is an accountable and a reasonable Faith; but that of the *Trinitarians* is absurd, and contrary both to reason and to *Itself*; and therefore not only false but *impossible*. For you say, they teach, that there are Three *Almighty most Good and most Wise* Persons, and yet but One God; as if every *Almighty most Wise and Good* Person were not God, a most perfect God; and consequently Three such Persons, Three Gods. You add yet more absurdly, that there are Three Persons who are *severally and each of them* true God, and yet there is but One true God. This is *an Error in counting* or numbering, which, when stood in, is of all otyers the most brutal and inexcusable: and *not to discern it, is not to be a Man*. But we would not, say they, trouble ourselves at the Nonsense of this Doctrine, if it did not impose false Gods on us; by advancing Two to be Gods who are not so; and rob also the One true God of the Honour due to him, and of which heis jealous.

This, Sir, is the doctrine of the *Unitarians*, more commonly called *Socinians*, concerning Almighty God, and these are their arguments.

[The 'brief and fair Deduction of their History' follows.]

Document VI.12

Henry Hedworth v. William Penn

For a full account of the life and writings of Hedworth (1626–1705), v., H. J. McLachlan, *Socinianism in Seventeenth Century England* (Oxford, 1951), 298–316. He was one of the leading Socinians of his day but since all his writings were originally published anonymously, he was for long unknown to the historians of Antitrinitarianism. He was certainly the 'Gentleman, a Person of excellent Learning and Worth' whose letter was published at the end of Stephen Nye's *Brief History of the Unitarians called also Socinians* (1687) (v., the previous document). His friends took great care to conceal his identity and most of his extant letters are usually signed simply with the initials 'H.H.'. He appears to have been a well-educated gentleman of independent means. He probably fought in the parliamentary army in the civil wars. Having visited the Netherlands, where he met Dutch Remonstrants and Antitrinitarian refugees, he became an enthusiastic Socinian and an amateur theologian of no mean ability, a disciple of John Biddle and associate of Thomas Firmin.

He was a vigorous defender of toleration but he is now known to have been the

A Theological Miscellany

author of some tracts attacking the Quakers. That brought him into controversy with William Penn (1644–1718) (for whom, v., DNB and NIDCC). Penn's *Sandy Foundation Shaken* (London, 1668) attacked some orthodox doctrines, including that of the Trinity. The printer was arrested and confined to the Tower and Penn published *Innocency with her Open Face* (London, 1669), asserting his orthodoxy. This apparent equivocation moved Hedworth to publish anonymously *The Spirit of the Quakers Tried* (London, 1672) attacking the views of the Quakers in general and in particular George Fox's use of Scripture in *The Great Mistery of the Great Whore* (London, 1659). Penn replied with *The Spirit of Truth Vindicated* ([London], 1672), a long and learned disquisition with numerous references to the early church Fathers, accusing his opponent of Socinianism and extreme Antitrinitarianism. This is what provoked Hedworth to publish *Controversie Ended* (London, 1673) from which the following extract is taken. Finally, Penn replied in *A Winding Sheet for Controversie Ended* (London, 1672). This concluding tract reveals that Penn knew the identity of his opponent. It includes a strong personal attack on him and also on Thomas Firmin. Although much of the controversy can now be 'consigned to the limbo of theological debate', as McLachlan says, it is still not without significance – especially as *Controversie Ended* provides the first example of the use of the word 'Unitarian' in English. The following extract is reproduced not so much because of its criticisms of Quakerism but because its clear echoes of *The Racovian Catechism* and its obvious anxiety to play down any suggestion of heterodoxy are typical of Socinian apologetic.

The following is from Henry Hedworth, *Controversie Ended* (London, 1673), 53–7.

Nevertheless because Mr. P[enn] has made it his great study to render me & consequently what I have said (though 'tis inconsequent enough) odious and detestable, under the name of *Socinian*, *Bidlean* and the like, and although I wrote nothing but what was approved by men of learning and piety, and strangers to me, and (for ought I know) to all my Friends: I will therefore present to the readers a short account of these men's opinions concerning Christ, who for distinction sake call themselves *Unitarians*, being so called in those places,[1] where by the Laws of the Country they have equal liberty of Religion with other men, or because they own but one Person, and one Substance or Essence of the most High and independent God, and to distinguish them from other Christians that hold Three Persons, and one Essence of God, and are therefore denominated *Trinitarians*.

I say therefore, that they are very zealous Assertors of the Unity of God, and that is the reason (as they solemnly profess) why they cannot allow three Persons in the God-head, because they think that it destroys his Unity or Oneness; and I have showed that the *Quakers* (W[illiam]. P[enn] especially) do also disallow them. Notwithstanding the *Quakers*, according to their equivocating manner, can call God the Father by the name of Christ, and the other cannot, I know not that they differ in one little tittle more concerning the one God.

But concerning the one Mediator between God and Men, the Man Christ Jesus, I *Tim* 2.5. the *Unitarians* willingly and heartily acknowledge, that he was for-ordain'd before the foundation of the World, I *Pet* 1.20[2] that he was born of the Virgin *Mary*, by the coming of the Holy Ghost upon her, and the power of the most High overshadowing her, *Luke* 1.35. and there he is called (IS) the Son of God;

likewise that he, and no man but he, ascended into heaven, and descended thence, *John* 3.13.³ being sanctified and sent into the World, into which he came, not to do his own Will, but the Will of him that sent him, *John* 6.30. that by reason of this mission and sanctification, he did, whilst he was here in earth, deservedly challenge the name of *God*, or the *Son of God*, *John* 10.34, 35, 36. in a far more excellent sense than either the Magistrates among the Jews, that were called gods, and Sons of the Most High, *Psal*.82.1, 6. Or Moses, who was God to *Pharaoh*, Exod.7.1. and also to his Brother *Aaron*, Exod.4.16. or than any Angel, who in the Dispensation of the Law, did represent God, and was therefore called by his Name, *Acts* 7.35. *Exod*.23.20. *Gal*.3.19. see *Jud*.13.22. And that as there was but one God then, so there is but one God now, notwithstanding that Jesus is *God over all*. Unto which glorious and supreme Dominion, next to the most High God himself, Jesus did attain, by doing the Will of God fully and perfectly on Earth, the perfection of which obedience was, that *being*, as it is said, *in the form of God, he thought it not robbery* [or a prey] *to be equal with God, but made himself of no reputation* &c and *became obedient unto Death, even the death of the Cross. Wherefore God also hath highly exalted him, and hath given him a Name which is above every Name, that at the Name of Jesus every knee should bow, – and that every tongue should confess that Jesus is Lord, to the glory of God the Father*, Phil.2.6, 7.8, 9, 10, 11. *That God hath made that same Jesus, whom ye* [the Jews] *have crucified, both Lord and Christ*, Acts 2.26. *Him hath God exalted with his right hand to be a Prince and a Saviour*, Acts 5.31. *God raised him from the dead, and set him at his own right hand, in the heavenly places, far above all principality and power*, &c. For by God's exalting Jesus, and setting him at his right hand, they understand that this same Man Jesus, that was crucified and raised from the dead, was also taken up in the sight of the Apostles into Heaven, a Cloud receiving him out of their sight, *Acts* 1.9. And that he is there, having not now a Body of Flesh and Blood, (for *flesh and blood cannot inherit the Kingdom of God*, I Cor.15. 50.) but an heavenly, spiritual, incorruptible and glorious body of a Man, the like whereof all the Saints shall have in the Resurrection, when the Man Jesus shall descend from Heaven to judge the World; that in the meantime he sits at God's right hand, that is, he has all power in Heaven and Earth committed to him, and reigns over Men and Angels, as will appear by comparing I *Cor*.15.25. with *Psal*.110.1. They believe that the Father hath committed all judgment unto the Son; that all men should honour the Son, even as they honour the Father. John 5.23. Therefore they worship Christ, and call upon him as their Lord, their King, their great High-Priest, their God, that searcheth their hearts, and is perfectly able to save them that come unto God by him. And they say, it's no wonder, that they honour Christ as God, whilst they acknowledge God his Father to be above him, forasmuch as the Author to the Hebrews doth the same. (*Heb*.1.8.9.) ... Finally, *When all things shall be subdued under him* [this man Jesus], *then shall the Son also himself be subject to him that put all things under him, that God may be all in all*, I Cor.15.28.

Now I know not anything of all that I have said concerning the Manhood, Resurrection, and Exaltation of Jesus, wherein the *Trinitarians* and *Unitarians* do not agree. The only Point of difference between them is this: Whether this

Dominion, Power and Glory, which are conferred upon the Man Jesus, be conferred upon him by assuming him into a personal Union with God, so that the Man and a Person of God make one individual Person; or whether they be conferred upon him by God's communicating to him such Supernatural and Divine Power as he never communicated, nor ever will to any Man or Angel, and greater than that which God himself cannot bestow. The first the *Trinitarians* hold, the latter the *Unitarians*. Herein they both agree, That the Man Jesus is really invested with this Power. But for the *Quakers*, I have showed that they really deny this Person, this Man Jesus, and consequently all that power and glory which he is invested with. So that all that they talk of him, and all their contention for him, is mere equivocation ... And now let the World judge, whether I did not use a soft expression, when I said that some Doctrines of the *Quakers* did render them very dishonourable and dangerous to Christian Religion. If the Deists in *France* should once get the *Quakers* knack of equivocating, and meaning by Jesus Christ, when they speak of him, nothing but God, then what havoc might they make of Christian Religion?

Notes

1. This is obviously a reference to Transylvania, where the 'Unitarian Religion' established by the radical Reformer Francis David (c. 1510–79) had been given official recognition. The Polish Socinians of the Minor Reformed Church (otherwise known as the Polish Brethren) also rejected the doctrine of the Trinity. For this reaon, they were invariably designated 'Arians' by their Catholic opponents, a charge they themselves rigorously repudiated. The name 'Unitarian' was never used in Poland, but by 1665, when the refugee Socinians in Amsterdam were publishing their massive edition of the collected writings of Faustus Socinus and his disciples, they were beginning to describe themselves as 'the Polish Brethren whom people call Unitarians' – as the full Latin title of the work indicates, *Bibliotheca Fratrum Polonorum Quos Unitarios Vocant*.
2. The idea of the pre-existence of Christ, though a distinguishing characteristic of post-Reformation Arianism, was in fact rejected by many of the early Unitarians, and it was because of this that the Polish Brethren denied that they were Arians.
3. It looks as if Hedworth had accepted the strange notion that at the outset of Christ's ministry, and not simply after his death and resurrection, he had been taken up into heaven to enable him to receive his divine commission from God. This curious belief in an early Ascension, followed by a return to earth, which was based on an idiosyncratic interpretation of some Johannine texts, was certainly characteristic of the original Socinians.

Document VI.13

The Quakers' Gospel Order

Quakers soon became aware of the need for a rudimentary organisation to arrange meetings and care for people in need, and since their doctrine of the church differed significantly from that of other Puritans, its development provides a distinct variation on the theme of Nonconformist church government. The conception of the light of Christ in the conscience as an all-sufficient guide caused complications. It was not possible that it should say different things to different people, yet in practice there were differences and they had to be reconciled. Before long Friends developed a system of discipline by regular meetings of responsible Friends, and these meetings also dealt with the problems of Friends in need. The following extracts illustrate some of the developments. V. BQ, SPQ and Moore, *The Light in Their Consciences* for further details.

(a) The Epistle of the Elders of Balby, 1656.
This extract is a slightly abbreviated form of the resolutions of a meeting in the autumn of 1656, consisting of representatives from the churches in Yorkshire, Lincolnshire, Nottingham and Derbyshire, the original Quaker heartland. Fox had 'ordered' them to meet at Balby, near Doncaster, 'to consider of such things as might be propounded unto them, and to enquire into the cause and matter of disorder if any be'. The Nayler affair (v. III.14) had caused Friends to concentrate on matters of church order and discipline. From the copy in the Lancashire Records Office, Preston, FRM 1/39. For modern Quaker use of this paper, v., *Quaker Faith and Practice* (London, 1994) 1.01.

(b) Edward Burrough on the London Men's Meeting, 1662.
This extract comes from the John Penington ms, 4.29–34, full text in LEF 287–310. As the Quaker movement grew and became centred in London, it was no longer possible to administer it from Swarthmoor and from 1656 onwards the central organisation was in the hands of leading London men Friends who met regularly to deal with church business. In 1662, at the outset of the worst persecution and a few months before his own death in Newgate, Edward Burrough, George Fox's chief assistant after the disgrace of Nayler (v. III.14) wrote a lengthy paper about the development of Quaker work in London, the origins and composition of the Men's Meeting and how it should conduct its business.

(c) Fox on Monthly and Quarterly Meetings, about 1669.
The practice of holding regular meetings for business, which was described above and in Extract (a), was probably widespread among Quakers by the later 1650s. In 1657 Fox began the work of superimposing a county organisation onto these, usually monthly, meetings in order to facilitate the collating of information about the persecution of Quakers, and also as a means of collecting funds. The intense persecution of the early Restoration years prevented any further development of the organisation, but when circumstances eased during the later 1660s, Fox set up a system of regular Monthly and Quarterly meetings all over the country. He had not completely thought out the details at this stage, so his instructions were frequently revised during the next few years. The extract that follows comes from a mixed collection of instructions put together as Epistle 264 (*Works* VII).

A Theological Miscellany

(d) Developing the National Organisation.

Control of publications issued in the name of Quakers was an important part of Fox's new organisational and disciplinary system and in 1673 the Second Day Morning Meeting, a committee of leading, mainly London, men Friends was set up for this purpose. The final form of the national annual meeting (soon known as the Yearly Meeting) took longer to develop. A national gathering, the first since before the Restoration, was held in 1668, and during the next ten years various different arrangements were tried. This extract is from a copy in the Southwark Meeting record book in Friends House Library, also LEF 326-7, and describes the arrangements as they stood in 1673.

(e) Setting up the Meeting for Sufferings, 1676.

Continuing persecution convinced some Friends that it was possible to do more to challenge legal decisions, and to do this they set up a special committee, called the Meeting for Sufferings, which drew representatives from all Quarterly Meetings and met during the London law terms. After much discussion the arrangements for the composition and work of this committee were finalised at a meeting in June 1676. The extract comes from the record of this meeting and is from LEF 346-53; Leek MSS. 91-4; Book of Cases 1-2, in Friends House Library.

For a study of the involvement of Quakers with the law, v., C. W. Horle, *The Quakers and the English Legal System 1660-1688* (Philadelphia, 1988), 173-7 for the setting up and early work of the Meeting for Sufferings. See also *Quaker Faith and Practice* (London, 1994), chap. 7, for its contemporary functions.

(f) Sarah Fell and the Women's Quarterly Meeting, 1681.

During the 1670s Fox and Margaret Fell, now his wife, encouraged the development of women's business meetings parallel to those of the men. The first of these meetings was probably that started in London about 1657-8, and its main function was to care for Friends in need. Some Friends did not welcome the extension of the women's meetings, especially when their duties were extended to vetting the suitability of couples applying for marriage. Many men objected to appearing before the women's meeting for this purpose. See Christine Trevett, Trevett Christine, *Women and Quakerism in the Seventeenth Century* (York, 1991, 78-86); R. Melvin Keiser and Rosemary Moore, *Knowing the Mystery of Life Within: Selected Writngs of Isaac Penington in their Historical and Theological Context* (London, 2005, 107-13). Clare J. L. Martin, 'Tradition versus Innovation: the Hat, Wilkinson-Storey and Keithian controversies' (*Quaker Studies* 8/1, Sept. 2003) 13-14; Gareth Shaw, 'The Inferior Parts of the Body: the development and role of women's meetings in the early Quaker movement' (*Quaker Studies* 9/2 March 2005), 191-203.

This extract comes from a letter, (Thirnbeck mss 15, in Friends House, London, published in the *Journal of the Friends Historical Society* vol. 9 (1912) 135-7). It was written by Sarah Fell to her sisters, a few days before her marriage. Spelling is modernised. Sarah was the most able of Margaret Fell's daughters, and was in charge of the household management. Her account book, published, ed. Norman Penney, *The Household Account Book of Sarah Fell* (Cambridge, 1920), is a valuable historical resource.

(a)

The Elders and Brethren send unto the Brethren in the north these necessary things following; to which, if in the light you wait, to be kept in obedience, you shall do well. Fare well.

1. That the particular meetings, by all the Children of Light, be duly kept and observed, where they be already settled, every First-day of the week; except they be moved to other places. And that general meetings be kept in order and sweet in the life of God, on some other day of the week than on the First-day, unless there be a moving to the contrary: that so in the light and life, the meetings may be kept, to the praise of God.

2. That care be taken, that as any are brought into the truth, meetings be in such places amongst them, as may be for the most convenience of all, without respect of persons: and that hands be laid on none suddenly, lest the truth suffer.

3. That if any person draw back from meetings, and walk disorderly, some go to speak to such as draw back; to exhort and admonish such with a tender, meek spirit, whom they find negligent or disorderly. And if any, after admonition, do persist in the thing not good, let them again be admonished and reproved before two or three witnesses; that by the mouth of two or three witnesses, every thing may be established. And if still they persevere in them, then let the thing be declared to the church: and when the church hath reproved them for their disorderly walking, and admonished them in the tender and meek spirit, and they do not reform, then let their names and the causes, and such as can justly testify the truth therein, and their answers be sent in writing to some whom the Lord hath raised up in the power of his Spirit to be fathers, his children to gather in the light, that the thing may be known to the body; and with the consent of the whole body, the thing may be determined in the light.

4. That as any are moved by the Lord to speak the word of the Lord at such meetings, that it be done in faithfulness, without adding or diminishing. And if at such meetings, any thing at any time be otherwise spoken by any out of the light, whereby the seed of God cometh to be burthened; let the person or persons in whom the seed of God is burthened, speak in the light (as of the Lord they are moved,) in meekness and godly fear, to him; but let it be done in private, betwixt them two, or before two or three witnesses, and not in the public meetings, except there be a special moving so to do.

5. That collections be timely made for the poor, (that are so indeed,) as they are moved, according to order, for relief of prisoners, and other necessary uses, as need shall require: and all moneys so collected, an account thereof to be taken ...

6. That care be taken for the families and goods of such as are called forth into the ministry, or are imprisoned for the truth's sake ...

7. That as any are moved of the Lord in his Light to take a brother or sister in marriage, marriage being honorable in all, and the bed undefiled, let it be made known to the children of light, especially to those of the meeting of which the parties are members ... That there may be a record in writing (witnessing the day, place, and year, of such things) kept within [that meeting] of which one or both of them are members ...

8. That a record be kept in every meeting of the births of the children of such who are members of that meeting, and of the burials of the dead who die in the Lord …

9. That husbands and wives dwell together according to knowledge, as being heirs together of the grace of life; that children obey their parents in the Lord; and that parents provoke not their children to wrath …

10. That servants be obedient to them that are their masters in the flesh, in things that are good, in singleness of heart …

11. That care be taken that none who are servants depart from their masters, but as they both do see in the light …

12. That the necessities of the poor, widows and fatherless, may be truly supplied, and that such as are able to work, and do not, may be admonished: and if, after admonition, they refuse to work, then let them not eat …

13. That care be taken, that as any are called before outward powers of the nation, that in the light, obedience to the Lord be given.

14. That if any be called to serve the commonwealth in any public service, which is for the public wealth and good, that with cheerfulness it be undertaken …

15. That all Friends that have callings and trades, do labour in the thing that is good, in faithfulness and uprightness; and keep to their yea and nay in all their communications …

16. That no one speak evil of another, neither judge one against another …

17. That none be busy bodies in other's matters but each one to bear another's burdens, and so fulfil the law of Christ..

18. That Christian moderation be used towards all men …

19. That Elders made by the holy Ghost, feed the flock of God, taking the oversight thereof willingly, not by constraint, but of a willing mind; neither as lords over God's heritage, but as examples to the flock of Christ.

20. That the younger submit themselves to the elder …

> Given forth at a general meeting of friends in truth at Balby in Yorkshire in the 9th month 1656. From the Spirit of truth to the children of light, in the light to walk; that all in order may be kept in obedience; that he may be glorified, who is worthy over all and blessed for ever. Amen.
> Richard Farnsworth, William Dewsbury and others

Dearly beloved friends, these things we do not lay upon you, as a Rule or Form to walk by, but that all with the measure of Light which is pure and holy, may be guided, and so in the Light walking and abiding, these may be fulfilled in the spirit, not from the Letter, for the Letter killeth but the Spirit giveth Life.

(b)
We therefore, in the name, power and wisdom of the Lord Jesus Christ, as we were endued with the same, and as he had given us power and authority so to do, for the furtherance of the gospel and the prosperity of the work of the Lord, committed to our charge, did by virtue of the same, ordain and appoint, that the men Friends of the City, or the ancientest of them in the truth, (not excluding any,) should meet

together at the Bull and Mouth or elsewhere, once in the fortnight, or once a month, as they in the wisdom of God should find it necessary, for the management of truth's affairs ...

[Burrough then gave instructions for the continued operation of the meeting.]

First, that the meeting do consist of just and righteous men, all believing in the truth, and walking in the same, men of sound principles and judgment in the truth of Christ, of good and blameless conversation amongst men ... the meeting not limited to a number of persons, but freedom for all Friends in Truth, none excepted ... But if any person out of the truth and of another spirit, contrary to the faith of Christ professed and practised by Friends, come to the meeting, such are not members thereof ...

Secondly, that the meeting be kept once a-week or fourteen days, as service and truth's necessities do require, as the Friends see cause when and where to appoint it: and being orderly come together, not to spend time with needless, unnecessary and fruitless discourses; but to proceed in the wisdom of God, in such things as may upon occasion be moved amongst you, for the service of truth and good order of the body; to hear and consider, and if possible to determine the same in justice and truth, not in the way of the world, as a worldly assembly of men, by hot contests, by seeking to outspeak and over-reach one another in discourse, as if it were controversy between party and party ... But in the wisdom, love and fellowship of God, in gravity, patience, meekness, in unity and concord ...

Thirdly – And if at any time, any matter or occasion shall be presented to the meeting, which is doubtful or difficult ... the judgement be suspended ... till more Friends that are anciently grown in the truth have the understanding of the matter ...

Fourthly – But if at any time, any strife or division shall happen to fall out amongst Friends ... concerning any outward things, as bargains, debts or the like [the meeting is to make enquiries and attempt a settlement] ... that the body may be preserved in love and peace together ...

Fifthly – That cognizance shall be taken, and all records faithfully kept of all births, marriages and burials ... That marriages particularly, be carefully ordered in the wisdom of God..

Sixthly – That especial care be taken concerning provision for the poor that believe and profess the truth ...

Seventhly – That care be taken in the meeting of men, for the collecting and preserving all Friends sufferings ...

Written, as moved of the Lord, in the ninth year of the publishing of truth in this City, and is to be presented to the meeting of men to be read amongst them in the fear of the Lord.

By one that from the beginning has travailed in the work of the Lord in this city, 1662. Edward Burrough

(c)
Now concerning them that do go to the Quarterly Meeting, they must be substantial

Friends, that can give a testimony of your suffering, and how things are among you in every particular meeting. So that none that are raw or weak, that are not able to give a testimony of the affairs of the church and truth, may go on behalf of the particular [local] meetings to the Quarterly Meetings, but may be nursed up in your Monthly Meetings, and there fitted for the Lord's service. So that two may go one time from every particular meeting, and two another time, or as it is ordered in your Monthly Meetings. So that some may go from all your meetings, that make up your Monthly Meeting; for the Quarterly Meeting should be made up of weighty, seasoned, and substantial Friends, that understand the business of the church; for no unruly and unseasoned persons should come there, nor indeed into the Monthly Meetings, but who are single-hearted, seasoned and honest.

And if anyone should speak or tattle any thing out of your Monthly or Quarterly Meetings, to the blemishing or defaming of any person or the meetings, such are to be brought to judgement and condemnation; (for it breaks the privilege and order of your christian society in your meetings) so that all may be kept and preserved in the power of theLord, and in his spirit, love and unity.

And therefore keep your meetings solid and sober, and let the authority of your men's and women's meetings be in the power of God; for every heir of the power has the right to that authority, and in it keep the King of kings' and Lord of lords' peace in his church.

(d)
At a General Meeting of Friends, for managing the public affairs of Truth throughout the Nation, held in Devonshire House, London, 29th of 3rd Month, 1672.

It is concluded, agreed, and assented unto, by Friends then present, that for the better ordering, managing, and regulating of the public affairs of Friends relating to the Truth and the service thereof, there be a General Meeting of Friends held at London, once a year, in the week called Whitsun-week, to consist of six Friends for the city of London, three for the city of Bristol, two for the town of Colchester, and one or two from each and every of the counties of England and Wales respectively. That the Quarterly Meetings in London, Bristol, Colchester, and all and every counties of England and Wales respectively, at their Quarterly Meetings immediately preceding the said week called Whitsun-week in every year, do take care to nominate the number of Friends aforesaid, to be present at the General Meeting aforesaid; there to advise about the managing of the public affairs of Friends throughout the nation ...

(e)
[Those present are listed, then the record continues:] At a meeting of aforesaid Friends and others, assembled upon account of Sufferings, held at James Claypoole's, the 12th day of the 4th mo.1676.

Agreed as followeth:

1. – That the whole Friends appointed for the Meeting of Sufferings, do all meet the Fifth day next preceding every term.

2. – That one-fourth part of the Friends of this meeting, be nominated and appointed to meet weekly, every Fifth day, at or before the 11th hour in the forenoon, as a weekly Meeting for Sufferings; leaving a liberty to any other faithful Friend concerned to meet with them: which said Friends so appointed, are to continue as the Meeting for Sufferings, until the Fifth day next before the next ensuing term; and then a new choice to be made, one other fourth part of the Friends appointed for Sufferings, to attend the next ensuing quarter, weekly as aforesaid; and so for every Fifth day next preceding each term, a new choice and appointment of other Friends, to attend the service of Sufferings as aforesaid.

> The list of appointees follows and paragraph 3 instructs those who are unable to attend a meeting to give notice of their inability. Paragraph 4 instructs Ellis Hookes (who was the Friend's clerk and the first to hold paid executive office amongst British Friends) to convey the present resolutions to correspondents in the various counties of England and Wales so that 'country Friends may henceforward understand Friends' care and order therein, and direct their letters to the persons here appointed'.

5. – That only the present sufferings, wherein the Friends in the counties expect some relief or redress, be sent to the Friends of London before nominated to assist the Friends in the country; and that such sufferings as are collected and intended to be recorded, be as formerly sent to Ellis Hookes.

> Further instructions about conveying information and providing speedy replies follow in paragraphs six to ten. The final paragraph reads:

11. – And further, that Friends be careful to draw up their sufferings full and short, according to former directions; it being the intention of Friends here, once a month, to publish in print half a sheet or a sheet, of the most remarkable and grievous sufferings; to the end cruelty may not be acted in a corner, and not be known.

(f)
                 Instructions. How you may order the
                 business in the Quarterly Women's
                 Meeting Book, as follows:-

When the meeting is; what business as passes the meeting, and is to be recorded in the book: you must have a sheet of paper and write it there first in the time of the meeting, while matters are in discourse, for then things are the freshest upon the mind, and words will rise most suitably to answer the matter in hand. And at leisure it may be written fair in the book, observing my way and method, that I have used formerly. But the first business that is to be done, is, to call over the meetings, and see that there be some women from every particular [local] meeting in the county; and in the beginning of the book, you will find all the meetings written down, by name, one after the other, by which you may call them over in order, as they are set in the book. And if there be any meeting that there is no women from, that must be taken notice of, what meeting it is that neglects, and enquiry made into the cause of their neglect, and if it be such as requires it, they should be reproved for their slackness, and desired to more care for the future.

At the meeting which is in the seventh month every year, enquiry must be made, how it is with the women, in every particular meeting in the county, as to the clearness of their testimonies against tithes, and the unrighteous demands touching the priests' wages and steeplehouse repairs, etc., at which meeting an account is to be brought from every particular meeting in the county. ...

And if there be any paper of condemnation brought from any that have fallen into transgression, if the matter be recorded in the book, and discoursed on at the meeting, let such paper be fixed to the book. ...

What good papers or epistles, of my Father [ie George Fox, now married to Margaret Fell] or other Friends, as comes to you, may be read in the meetings, from time to time, as there is occasion. There are some loose in the book, that have been read formerly...I have often had it in my mind to record some of them in the book, but had so much business etc. that I could not get it done, but would desire you, that it be not neglected much longer.

This in short is what is in my mind at present, and it's my belief and confidence that the Lord God, who supplies all his people, will fit and furnish you to perform and manage this his work and service, as there shall be a necessity, unto whom I commit you for strength, wisdom and counsel, to whom be praises for evermore.

The 5th of 3rd month 1681.   S. F.

For my dear Sisters Mary Lower, Susannah Fell and Rachel Fell,
These

Document VI.14

Early Quaker Theology

Extract (a) is from Richard Farnworth, *A Brief Discovery of the Kingdom of Antichrist* (London, 1653), 21–2. The biblical references in the margin are significant. They are: Rev. 19: 12–16; Rev. 19: 18–21; Mal. 4: 2–3; Zech. 13; Rev. 11: 15. For further treatment of eschatology, v., B. W. Ball, *A Great Expectation: Eschatological Thought in English Protestantism to 1660* (Leiden, 1975); Christopher Hill, *Antichrist in Seventeenth-Century England* (London, 1971); Peter Toon (ed.), *Puritans, the Millenium, and the Future of Israel* (Cambridge and London, 1970), especially T. L. Underwood, 'Early Quaker Eschatology'; B. S. Capp, *The Fifth Monarchy Men* (London, 1972); *Past and Present*, no. 52 (August 1971), 106–17, no. 55 (May 1972), 68–70 and no. 57 (November 1972) for the debate between Capp and Lamont about the nature and extent of millenarianism; Iain H. Murray, *The Puritan Hope* (Edinburgh: Banner of Truth, 1975). For comments on the relationship between millenarianism and Quakerism in the Welsh context, v., G. F. Nuttall, *The Welsh Saints, 1640–1660* (Cardiff, 1957), chap. IV, 'The Impact of Quakerism'.

Quakers were not, technically, millenarian if that word be used in its exact sense to refer to the thousand-year reign of Christ before the final judgement. They generally described the coming end of the age in terms of Old Testament prophecy combined with the less explicit texts from the Book of Revelation and they were rarely interested in the exact fulfilment of obscure prophecies. But it is not possible to draw a clear line between the Quaker and Fifth Monarchist teaching of 1653 for both emphasised the part that the saints would play in the establishment of the kingdom upon earth. The passage quoted is typical of a number of apocalyptic passages in Quaker tracts, especially those dating from 1653 and early 1654. After the Restoration, tracts of this nature dwindled and finally disappeared.

Theological debate and dispute, in the middle of the seventeenth century, was more like a popular sport than anything else. Sometimes a disputation would be a set public debate before an audience and would afterwards be written up and published. Or it might be a literary debate. The Quakers were enthusiastic debaters in both modes. Bunyan debated with Burrough at Bedford on 23 May 1656 and afterwards published *Some Gospel Truths Opened* (London, 1656) in which he criticised the spiritualising of Christ by Quakers and emphasised in reply the human nature of Christ in unity with his divine Nature. Burrough replied with *The True Faith of the Gospel of Peace* (London, 1656). Although there is much personal abuse in it, it does present the essence of early Quaker Christology. Extract (b), from pp. 3 and 26–7, quotes a part of it. Burrough states Bunyan's questions and then replies to them. Bunyan replied with *A Vindication of a Book Called Some Gospel Truths Opened* (1657) to which Burrough responded with *Truth (Strongest of All) Witnessed Forth* (London, 1657). For a full discussion of the debate v. Lawrence S. Kuenning "The Bunyan-Burrough Debate of 1656–7 analyzed using a computer hypertext', PhD Thesis, Westminster, PA, 2000, on line at www.qhpress.org/texts

(a) Eschatology

Rejoyce ye Saints and righteous ones, the Lord is Judge, Lawgiver and King, and he will save you out of the paw of the Lion and the paw of the Bear, and set you free from slavish feare: wo to the wicked, it shall be ill with them: though the Beast make war with the Saints, yet be of good chear, the Saints shall overcome, the man that sits upon the white Horse with his sharp sword shall prevaile and get the victory, and deliver out of the paw of the Lion: Prophet, proud Priest, Formalist, self-conceited Pharisee, covetous Professor, Hypocrite, and Dissembler, shall all fall together, the Beast, and the 24 Elders, Antichrist, and all his upholders must be cut off, and fall down before the power of God, in his poor despised people, the wicked shall be as a shell under the soals of their feet.

The Kingdomes of the world must bee the Kingdomes of the Lord, and of his Christ, and the earth shall be full of the knowledge of the Lord, and every man shall sit under his owne Vine, and under his owne Fig tree, and none shall make him afraid, *then shall there be Judges as at the first, and Counsellors as at the beginning and* Sion *shall be redeemed with Iudgement, and her converts with righteousnesse, and the destruction of the transgressors, and of the sinners shall be together, and they that forsake the Lord shall be consumed,* Isa. I. 26, 27, 28.

Seek peace, seek righteousness, if so be that ye may be hid in the day of the Lords wrath.

A Theological Miscellany

(b) John Bunyan versus Edward Burrough
[Burrough states Bunyan's first question thus:]
1 *Qu*. If thou saiest that every man hath a measure of the Spirit of Christ within him, why say the Scriptures that *Some are sensuall, having not the spirit*, and Christ saith, *The world cannot receive it*? John 14.

Answ. Some men are sensuall, and have not the Spirit because they receive it not, and some cannot receive it, because they believe not in him from whence it comes, yet is the measure of the Spirit given unto every man to profit withall, as the Scripture saith. And it is given to within him, to reprove him of sin, but few doth receive it; and when thou can learn to distinguish between a thing being given, and a receiving of such a thing, then thou may be answered in thyself. It is one thing in god to give the Spirit, and another thing in the creature to receive it. He gives it to many that receive it not, to follow it, and to be guided by it. Thus far I answer, and let them that are led with a spirit of delusion, answer thee further.

[Burrough states Bunyan's second question thus:] What is the Church of God redeemed by from under the Law, is it something that is done within them, or by something done without them? If it be redeemed by something that worketh in them, then why did the man Christ Jesus hang upon the Crosse in Mount *Calvery*, and without the Gates of *Jerusalem*, for the sins of his people, and why doe the Scriptures say that through this man is preached unto us the forgivenesse of sins? &c

Answ. The Church of God is redeemed by Christ Jesus which is revealed within all that believe, and Christ Jesus wrought in them mightily, and it was he that wrought in them to will and to doe, this is plain according to Scripture. And the man Christ Jesus hanged upon the Crosse on Mount *Calvery*, because they wickedly judged him to be a blasphemer, and through their envy persecuted him to death, because he bore witnesse against them; and as in their account he died, and hanged upon the Crosse for an evill doer, and this is one ground (at least) why he hang'd upon the Crosse, and the Scriptures say that *through this man is Preached the forgivenesse of sins, beause there is no other that can forgive sin, nor the blood of any other thing that can take away sin* but the blood of God, ...

3 *Qu*. What Scripture have you to prove that Christ is or was crucified within you, risen within you, ascended within you?

Answ. There is no Scriptures that mentions any one of our particular names, and thy Query is raised from thy understanding of us, so I judge; but Christ is within us, that we dare not deny, and he is the Lamb that was slain in the streets of the great City, which is spiritually called *Sodom* and *Ægypt*, (mind spiritually) and he is now risen, and ascended, this we know through faith in his Name, and I leave thee to receive a fuller answer from them that are led with a Spirit of delusion (if they will give it thee.)

4 *Qu*. Is that very man that was crucified on Mount *Calvery*, between two Thieves, whose Name is Jesus the Son of *Mary*, is he the very Christ of God, yea or nay?

Answ. Yea he is the very Christ of God, which was before the world was, by whom the world was made, who was made manifest from *Mary's* womb, and was persecuted to death by the Scribes, and Pharisees in whose steps thou treads in asking subtill queryes to insnare the Innocent, as they did, read thy example, and thy selfe to be an Enemy to the Christ of God.

5 *Qu*. Is that very Man with that very body within you yea or nay?

Answ. The very Christ of God is within us, we dare not deny him, and we are Members of his body, and of his flesh, and of his bone as the *Ephesians* were, they that are led by a spirit of delusion shall answere the rest of this query, if they will.

6 *Qu*. Was that very Jesus that was borne of the Virgin *Mary*, a reall Man of flesh and bones, after his resurrection from the dead, out of *Josephs* Sepulchre yea or nay; for the Scripture saith he was, and if so, then did that Man, goe away from his Disciples, and not into them in his body, as the Scriptures declare, or did he with that body of flesh goe into his Disciples, as some fond dreamers thinke?

Answ. What the Scriptures speakes of Christ we owne to be truth, and ownes him to be what the Scriptures speakes of him and all Mens imaginations of him we deny, and their false interpretations of the Scripture concerning him and let the fond dreamers who are in their thoughts be reprooved, for wee dare owne nothing to be truth, but what the Spirit of the Lord beares witnesse of according to the Scripture, and thus farre I answere in behalfe of the Quakers; let them who are led with the spirit of delusion answere, the rest which concerns themselves ...

[One further question of Bunyan's is answered and that is followed by a series of counter-questions.]

Document VI.15

The Baptists and Total Immersion

The following is from the Gould Manuscript in Regents Park College, Oxford, 'A Repository of Divers Historical Matters relating to the English Antipedobaptits. Collected from Original papers of Faithful Extracts [by Benjamin Stinton] – Anno 1712' – Number 2, the so-called Kiffin Manuscript. Printed in EED, II, 302–3. For details of the persons named and an examination of the Gould Manuscript, v., EED, I, 326–56.

1633 Sundry of ye Church whereof Mr Iacob & Mr Iohn Lathorp had been Pastors, being dissatisfyed wth ye Churches owning of English Parishes to be true Churches desired dismission & Ioyned togeather among themselves, as Mr Henry Parker, Mr Tho. Shepard Mr Sam^{ll} Eaton, Marke Luker, & others wth whom Ioyned Mr Wm Kiffen.

1638 Mr Tho: Wilson, Mr Pen, & H. Pen, & 3 more being convinced that Baptism was not for Infants, but professed Believers joyned wth M^r Io: Spilsbury ye Churches favour being desired therein.

1640 3^d Mo: The Church became two by mutuall consent just half being wth

Mr P. Barebone, & ye other halfe with Mr H. Jessey Mr Richard Blunt wth him being convinced of Baptism y^t also it ought to be by diping ye Body into ye Water, resembling Burial & riseing again, 2 Col: 2. 12. Rom: 6. 4 had sober conferance about in ye Church, & wth some of the forenamed who also ware so convinced: And after Prayer & conferance about their so enjoying it, none haveing then so so [sic] practised in England to professed Believers, & hearing that some in ye Nether Lands had so practised they agreed & sent over Mr Richard Blunt (who understood Dutch) wth Letters of Commendation, who was kindly accepted there, & returned wth Letters from them Io: Batte a Teacher there, & from that Church to such as sent him.

1641 They proceed on therein, viz, Those Persons y^t ware persuaded Baptism should be by dipping ye Body had mett in two Companies, & did intend so to meet after this, all these agreed to proceed alike togeather. And then Manifesting (not by any formal Words a Covenant) wch word was scrupled by some of them, but by mutual desires & agreement each testified:

Those two Companyes did set apart one to Baptize the rest; So it was solemnly performed by them.

Mr Blunt Baptized Mr Blacklock, y^t was a Teacher amongst them, & Mr Blunt being Baptized, he & Mr Blacklock Baptized ye rest of their friends that ware so minded, & many being added to them they increased much ...

Document VI.16

Walter Cradock: The Simplicity of the Gospel

This extract is from *Divine Drops Distilled* (London, 1650), 212–13. The sermons contained in this book were taken down and edited by Thomas Shelton (1601–50?) who also wote a pleasing preface. Shelton was a zealous Puritan but is best known for his systems of shorthand, one of which was used by Samuel Pepys in his diary, v., DNB.

We speak much of *reformation*, and it is to be *desired*; but among other *errours* in *Religion* this is one: many think that the *main point* in Religion is the *setting up* of *government*; whereas our *main reformation* is in *pulling down*, and not in *setting up*: for we have a world of *institutions* set up that will never hold. And among those *latter institutions* that good people have *set up*, I believe that there are not many will *hold*: but these will, the *Doctrine of Christ crucified*, and the *pouring out of Gods spirit*. And as many as tend to this, and *flow* from this, without scruple I think we may *die* for them. But when our *Bibles* have gone through the hands of *Papists* so many *hundred yeers*, when a man shall come *die* for it, he is afraid that such a thing may be *crept into the text*, & a thousand such thoughts of *Athiesme* will come upon a man: but when a man can say, this is *Christ crucified*, and *Christ pouring out of his spirit*, let the *particles* and the *words* run as they will, this is the *maine* that will hold.

As the *Gospell* was *intended*, and *designed* for *simple men* more then *others*, so (with reverence) the *Gospell* is a more *simple, plain thing* then most men in the world conceive. The *Gospell* needs not the thousand part of the *distinctions*, and *definitions*, that the *schoolmen* have, and that men *multiply*. It is a *simple story* concerning *Christ crucified*, and how the *Holy Ghost was poured upon men*, and this was *preached* by *fishermen as God gave them utterance*, and it was *prophesied* of before.

If *Religion* be a simple thing, taught by *fisher-men* with *the pouring out of* the *Spirit*, then there need not all those *disputes* concerning the *Arts*, &c. For my part I think *learning* to be a very good thing to perfect a mans *naturalls*: but I think on the other side that a man that *savingly*, and *clearly* knows *Christ crucified*, and the *pouring out of the spirit*, he is the fittest man in the *world* to be a preacher.

We should *know* things a thousand fold *better*, and *clearer* then we do, if we would *judg* of things as *God judgeth* of them; if we would use the *language* of the *Scripture*, and the *notions* of the *holy spirit* in the *Scripture*. If we would know a *Saint* from a *sinner* ... a man that is the *Lords*, and another that is not, this is the *maine* way, the *chief essentiall* difference, the one hath the *spirit*, the other *hath not*. It is not so much whether yonder man *pray*, or *fast*, or *preach*, or *repeat*, or whether he doth many good *outward morall things*, but whether he hath the *spirit of God*; though it be now *almost* a *ridiculous thing* to *name* the *spirit of God*. We should I say *distinguish man* from *man* by the *spirit*.

And *labour* in a *speciall manner* to assure our *selves* that we have the *spirit of God*. We should not *rest* in this, that I have left *such sins*, or I do *such duties*, but go on still, till I come up to this, that with *all humility*, and *thankfulnesse* I may say, *God hath given to me of his holy spirit*, the *spirit* of *Jesus Christ dwells in my heart* ...

Document VI.17

William Penn: Quaker Theology for the Non-Quaker

William Penn (1644–1718), son of Admiral Sir William Penn, turned Quaker as a young man and became one of the leading Quakers of the later seventeenth century. A prolific author on theological and political subjects, he is noted outside Quakerism for his position as a defendant in the Bushel trial of 1670 which established the principle that English juries need not accept the instructions of the judge, and also as the founder of Pennsylvania, which he established by a grant from King Charles II in repayment of a debt to his father. Of the enormous literature on Penn, see especially Richard and Mary M. Dunn, eds. *The World of William Penn* (Philadelphia, 1986). Penn had a good knowledge of the Fathers as well as the Bible, and was a keen controversialist. The following extract comes from *Wisdom Justified of her Children from the Ignorance and Calumny of H. Hallywell* ... published in 1673. The book was addressed 'To the Justices of the Peace in the County of Sussex', and the introduction, about half of which is reproduced here, is a statement of Quaker faith that is expressed in such a way as to accommodate Quaker theology, so far as possible, to the intended readers, and suited to the taste of the later seventeenth century. After an explanation of his reasons for writing, he continued:-

Therefore I beseech you, to whom this discourse is more particularly dedicated, to consider of us, not by tradition, education, religions established by human laws, or imperial decrees; but by that understanding which this 'Immortal law and everlasting foundation of virtue' as Heathen Plutarch calls it, will afford you to judge us by.

It has been man's venturing to wade into the holy scriptures without this divine principle, that has caused so many fearful miscarriages about religion. Something in man prompts him to religion; but man, being not wholly guided by that which so inspires him with religious desires, hastily spoils all with the intermixture of his own fantasies and conceits; and because he is assured that what first inclined him was right, he sticks not to style his own inventions orthodox; and then, impatient of contradiction, with a fury as great as his ignorance, endeavours the overthrow of whatever stands in his way, and refuses to receive his mark in his forehead, or his right hand. This has occasioned so much trumpery in religion; ceremonies, show and mere formality, have swallowed up the greatest part of it: now were men brought to God's heavenly gift in themselves, it would reclaim and leaven the mind, chain the affections, and bring religion into holy and self-denying living, and erect an holy regimen in the heart and soul, by which the heavenly image would be renewed, and man become as one born again; without which translation, there can be no entering into God's heavenly kingdom.

This the first Protestants made to be the reason of their revolt from Rome; for though it is true, that they charged the Papists with making God's tradition (the holy scriptures) void by their numerous dark traditions; yet that which begot that holy loathing of Rome's superstitions, idolatries, and will-worship, was God's grace in their hearts; and their best argument against Rome was this, 'The Scripture which I believe from the testimony of God in me, and which I can only understand from the illumination thereof, owns no such thing, and therefore I reject it'....

I omit to mention a whole cloud of witnesses, because I intend not to dwell here, only this would I be at, and I entreat you all to weigh it, whether any thing can give to understand aright, and enable to practice those things of God, which it is necessary for man both to know and to do, but God's light, grace, or word in the heart: what else can give us to relish the divine authority of the scriptures themselves, or to believe the things treated therein to be undeniable truths? ...

Thus, God, who made heaven and earth, knows, we came to receive that knowledge of him, which we now expose ourselves to all hardships to maintain.

We professed God; but, like our neighbours, in works we denied him. We worshipped him after man's conceivings; insomuch that I may say, we worshipped the unknown God in a false way. No doubt but we were stocked with the common talk of religion; but the cross of Christ we were strangers to. His blood we extolled, whilst by wicked works we trod it underfoot: and believed ourselves saved by it, who were uncleansed from sin. The whole end of his coming we esteemed the top of all love; but never knew enough of it, truly kindled in our hearts, where by to work such faith and resignation as could give us victory over the world. Thus were we, Jews-like, children of God, whilst we crucified the Son of God; and of the seed of Abraham, whilst the serpent's seed reigned; heirs of the kingdom, yet not born again; free, yet the bondslaves of vanity. O! at this time of day it was that God found us out, and broke in upon our souls with his righteous judgements for sin, and laid judgement on the line, and righteousness to the plummet, within us; the book of conscience was opened, and great fear surprised us, and deep sorrow fell upon us, which brought that sudden and strange change, that made us both the derision of profane, and wonder of sober men....

Having thus been made sensible of the terrors of the Lord for sin, and being brought into a true understanding of that religion and worship which most please God, some of us were constrained, and in conscience bound, to go forth into the world, and publish these tidings of judgement for sin, and conversion through righteousness, wrought by the mighty power of God in the conscience, that all might be awakened to try their works, whether they were of God or men; or whether they had been doing their own wills or the will of God; so that they might be brought to experience God to be a God nigh at hand, reconciled in Christ, blotting out sin, and renewing a right spirit within; by which their religion might no longer stand in the traditions of men, or on the education of parents, but upon the convictions and operations of God's grace in the conscience. And thus is all that Christ did without, brought nigh and home to the very soul. The seed of the woman is known to bruise the head of the serpent; Christ, the Light and Lamb that taketh away the sins of the world, not only to take away the sins of the past through remission, but cleanse from the nature, root and ground of sin by his holy blood, which sprinkles all consciences that wait and walk in the light (the just man's path) from dead works, to serve the living God in uprightness for ever.

For this cause are we brought out into the world; and behold the vessel we are embarked in, our lading, and the country we make for; the vessel, truth; the lading, faith and good works; our souls, the passengers; and the country, the land of everlasting rest.

This I could not but present you with, that no endeavours of our enemies may be able to lodge a false character of us and our principles with you.

Document VI.18

Robert Barclay: *The Possibility and Necessity of ... Immediate Revelation*

The most famous Quaker theologian was Robert Barclay (1648–90) a Scot who, having studied with Jesuits in Paris, went to Aberdeen University and was convinced as a Friend in 1666. Related through his mother to the British royal family, he, like Penn, was a friend of the Duke of York and was appointed a member of the Scots Privy Council in 1679. His best-known work, *An Apology for the True Christian Divinity* was published, in Latin, in 1676, with an English version in 1678 (new edn, ed. Peter D. Sippel, Glenside, PA, 2002, on line at www.qhpress.org/texts). It is an attempt to expound Quakerism as a rational body of thought, compatible with the Cartesian philosophy of the day, and it is still normative for much Quaker theological thinking.

At the time he was writing the *Apology*, Barclay and his friend George Keith were in correspondence with a Dutch barrister named Adriaan van Paets, from Rotterdam, a well known member of the Dutch Collegiant church who had written a paper against the possibility of continuing revelation. Barclay wrote him a lengthy refutation which is, as it happens, an excellent summary of Barclay's theological ideas. The original was, naturally, in Latin, and was not published at the time, but in 1686 Barclay translated it into English and prepared it for publication. However, for some reason it was not put into print until thirteen years after Barclay's death, when it was issued under the title *The Possibility and Necessity of the Inward and Immediate Revelation of the Spirit of God* (London, 1703). The abridged version which follows was kindly prepared by Dr Hugh Pyper.

The Possibility and Necessity of the Inward and Immediate Revelation of the Spirit of God, Towards the Foundation and ground of True Faith, Proved, in a Letter writ in *Latin to* the *Heer Paets; and* now also put into *English*
by Robert Barclay

First published 1686.

London, Re-Printed and Sold by *T. Sowle,* in *White-Hart-Court* in *Gracious-street,* 1703

... that the whole matter may be the more clearly understood, it will be fit in the first place, to propose thy Argument, whereby thou opposest the *Immediate Revelation of GOD* in the Saints, thence concluding thou hast fully overturned the Foundation of the People called *Quakers*. Which Argument of thine is,

That since (as thou judgest) the Being and Substance of the Christian Religion consisteth in the Knowledge of, and Faith concerning the Birth, Life, Death, Resurrection and Ascension of Christi Jesus, Thou considerest the substance of the Christian Faith as a contingent Truth, which contingent Truth is matter of fact: whence thou reasonest. *That matter of fact cannot be known but by the relation of another, or by the perception of the outward Senses: Because there are naturally in our Souls no* Ideas *of contingent Truths, such as are concerning necessary Truths:* to wit. *That GOD is, and that the whole is greater that the part; And since it may without absurdity be said , that GOD cannot make a contingent Truth to become a necessary Truth, neither can GOD reveal contingent Truths or matters of Fact, but as contingent Truths are revealed; But matters of Fact are not revealed but by the outward Senses:* From whence thou concludest, *That Men are not even obliged to believe GOD producing any Revelation in the Soul concerning matter of Fact, whether of a thing done or to be done, unless there be added some Miracles obvious to the outward Senses, by which the Soul may be ascertained that that Revelation cometh from God:* And this thou endeavourest also to prove from the Scripture, *Rom. 10.* where the Apostle saith, *Faith cometh by hearing:* And because the Apostle speaketh afterwards of those who were sent in the plural number: Thence thou concludest, *That to be spoken of outward Preaching by the Ministry of Men:* And since the Apostle uses a Question, saying. *How shall they believe unless they hear?* Thou gatherest from the Induction and Connexion of the Text, that the Apostle treats only *of outward hearing; thence concluding, that without outward hearing, faith cannot be produced:* And therefore, that there can *be no Immediate Revelation by the simple Operation of the Spirit in the Mind,* unless there be somewhat proposed to the *Outward Senses.*

Before I proceed to a direct Answer to this Argument, some things are necessary to be premised,

First then, that it is falsely supposed, that the Essence of the Christian Religion consists in the Historical Faith and Knowledge of the *Birth, Death, Life, Resurrection and Ascension of Christ.* That Faith and Knowledge is indeed a part of the Christian Religion, But not such an *Essential* Part, as that without which a Christian Faith cannot consist, but an *Integral* Part, which goes to the compleating of the Christian Religion, as the Hands or Feet of a Man are Integral Parts of a Man, without which nevertheless a Man may exist, but not an intire and compleat Man.

Secondly, If by *Immediate Revelation,* be understood such a revelation of GOD as begets in our Souls an historical Faith and Knowledge of the Birth of Christ in the Flesh, without the means of the holy Scripture, we do not contend for such a Revelation as commonly given or to be expected by us or any other Christians, for albeit many other Evangelical truths be manifested to us by the immediate Manifestation of God, not using the Scripture as the means; yet the Historical Knowledge of Christ is not commonly manifested to us, nor to any others, but by the Holy Scripture as the means, and that by way of a *Material Object* to produce that sight, while the Light of the Sun concurs as the *formal Object* of that vision or sight: So that when we Livingly and Spiritually know the History of the Birth of Christ in the Flesh, the *Inward Revelation* or *Illumination* of GOD, which is like the Sun's Light, proceeding from the *Divine Sun,* doth shine into the Eye of the Mind and by *Its* Influence moves the Mind to assent to the Historical Truth of CHRIST's Birth, Life &c. in the Reading or Hearing the Scripture, or meditating therein.

Thirdly, Nevertheless we do firmly assert, that GOD can most easily, clearly and certainly manifest to our minds the Historical Truth of CHRIST's Birth &c. when it so pleaseth Him, even without the Scripture, or any other outward mean. And because this Argument seems to be formed against the possibility of such a Revelation, therefore I shall proceed to discuss it. But first, thou may'st mind that the Prophets who foretold CHRIST'S *coming in the Flesh,* and *being to be born of a Virgin, and afterwards to suffer Death,* did know these Truths of Fact, by the *Inward Inspiration* of GOD, without Outward Means, for which, see *I Pet.* 1.10,11. Now that which hath been, may be.

Fourthly, this Argument doth at most conclude, that we cannot know *Naturally* any Truth of Fact, but by the relation of another without us, or by the perception of the outward Senses, Because there are *naturally* in our Minds no *Ideas* concerning contingent Truths (and every Truth of Fact is a contingent Truth) as there are of necessary Truths. This then proveth that we cannot *naturally* know any contingent Truth but by the relation of another, or perception of the outward Senses: but that hindreth not, but we may know a contingent Truth by a *supernatural Knowledge*, GOD supplying the place of an outward Relator, who is so true that he may be and ought to be believed, sith God is the fountain of Truth.

Fifthly, when GOD doth make known unto Men any matter of Fact by Divine immediate Revelation or Inspiration, GOD speaking as to the Ear of the Heart of the inward Man, or as by his Finger writing it therein. Two things are to be considered in such an *Immediate Revelation.*

1. To *Materiale,* the matter of Fact or thing revealed, which is contingent.

2. To *Formate,* The Form or Mode, how the Revelation is made, which Form is an inward, Divine and *supernatural Revelation,* which is the Voice or Speech of God, inwardly speaking to the ear of the inward Man or Mind of Man, or a Divine Writing, supernaturally imprinted therein. Now as to the *Material* Part, or the thing and matter revealed, this is indeed a contingent Truth, and of it self is not manifest to the Mind, but because of the Form, that is, because of the *Divine Mode* and *supernatural* inward Operation, the matter is known to be true: for that Divine and Supernatural Inward Operation, which the Mind doth feel and perceive in it self, is the Voice of GOD speaking unto Man, which by its *Nature* and *specifick Property,* is as clearly distinguished and understood to be the Voice of GOD, as the Voice of *Peter* and *James* is known to be the Voice of such Men: for every Being, as a being, is knowable and that by its own specifick Nature or Property proceeding from its Nature, and hath its proper *Idea* by which it's distinguishable from every other thing, if so be its *Idea* be stirred up in us, and clearly proposed to us.

Sixthly, Now as some Beings are *Natural,* some *Supernatural,* so some *Ideas* are natural, some Supernatural: And as when any *natural Idea* is excited in us, we clearly know it. So also, when a *supernatural Idea* is raised, we clearly know that whereof it is the *Idea:* but the Voice of GOD speaking to the Mind of Man, is a supernatural Being, and stirreth up in us a *supernatural Idea,* by which we clearly know that inward Voice to be the Voice of GOD, and not the Voice or Operation of another, or of any evil Spirit, or Angel, because none of these has a *supernatural Idea,* as the Voice of GOD, and his Divine Operation hath; for it is full of Vigour, Virtue, and Divine Glory, as saith the *Psalmist,* who had often experience of it, and we also in our measures are Witnesses thereof, for the Voice of GOD is known to be his by its Divine Virtue.

Seventhly, the Senses are either *Outward* or *Inward,* and the *Inward Senses* are either *Natural* or *Supernatural:* We have an Example of the Inward Natural Sense in being Angred or Pacified, in Love and Hatred, or when we perceive and discern any Natural Truth (such as the Natural Maxims, to wit. *That the whole is greater than the part:* or when we deduce any Conclusion by the strength of Natural reason, that Percepton also in a larger Sense may be called an *inward Sense.* But an Example of an *inward supernatural Sense* is, when the Heart or Soul of a pious Man feels in it self *Divine Motions, Influences, and Operations,* which sometimes are as the Voice or Speech of GOD, sometimes as a most pleasant and glorious Illustration or visible Object to the inward Eye, sometimes as a most sweet Savour or Taste, sometimes as a Heavenly and Divine Warmness, or (so to speak) melting of the Soul in the Love of GOD. Moreover, this *Divine and supernatural Sense,* divinely raised up in the Mind of Man, doth so evidently and clearly perswade the Understanding to assent to the thing revealed, that there is no need of an outward Miracle, for this Assent is not because of the thing it self, but because of the Revelation proposing it, which is the Voice of GOD: for when the Voice of GOD is heard in the Soul, the Soul doth as certainly conclude the truth of that Voice, as the truth of GOD's Being, from whom it proceeds.

These things being thus premised, I now proceed to a direct Answer: For what is said, that GOD cannot make a contingent Truth to become a necessary Truth. I agree: But, when any *Contingent Truth* is manifest to us by the *Immediate Revelation* of GOD, there is in it two things to be considered, to wit, the thing revealed which is *Contingent,* and the Revelation it self, which upon the Supposition that it is a Divine Revelation, *is no Contingent Truth,* but a most *Necessary Truth.* And this all Mankind will say. That this Proposition, *Every divine Revelation is necessarily true,* is as clear and evident as that Proposition, *That every Whole is greater that its Part*.

But thou wilt say. How knowest thou that a *Divine Revelation* is a *Divine Revelation*? I answer, How knowest thou that a Whole is a Whole, and a Part is a Part? Thou wilt say, By the *natural Idea* excited in me of a Whole and of a Part. I answer again, Even so, a Divine Revelation is known to be such by a *Supernatural Idea* of Divine Revelation stirred up in us and that by a Divine Motion or *Supernatural* Operation. But it is no wonder that Men, who have no Experience of *Supernatural Ideas,* or at least do not heed them, do deny them; which is as if a Man naturally blind, denied Light or Colours; or a deaf Man, Sounds, because they experience them not. Therefore we cannot dissemble that we feel a fervent Zeal, even Divinely kindled in us against such an absurd Opinion, as affirms. *That God cannot ascertain us of his Will in any contingent Truth, but by proposing it to the outward Senses*. This Opinion does in a manner turn Men into Brutes as if Man were not to believe his GOD, unless he propose what is to be believed to the outward Senses, which the Beasts have in common with us; yea, it derogates from GOD's Power, and imputes Weakness to him, as if he could not do that which not only both good and evil Angels can do, but which the meanest Creatures can do, and the most unsensible: As for instance, the Heat of the Fire, the Coldness of the Air, and Water worketh upon us; yea, if a Pin prick us we feel it, and that by the outward Sense; because the Objects are outward and carnal. But since GOD is a most Pure and Glorious Spirit, when he operateth in the Innermost Parts of our Minds by his Will; shall not He and his Will be clearly felt according to his Nature? That is, by a *Spiritual and supernatural Sense;* For as the Nature of GOD is, so is the Nature of his Will, to wit, purely Spiritual; and therefore requireth a *Spiritual Sense* to discern it; which *Spiritual Sense,* when it is raised up in us by a Divine Operation, doth as clearly and certainly know the Voice or Revelation of the Will of GOD, concerning any thing which GOD is pleased to reveal, however *Contingent,* as the outward Sense knows, and perceives the *Outward Object,* and it is no less absurd to require of GOD, who is a most pure Spirit, to manifest his Will to Men by the outward Senses, else not to be credited; As to require us to see Sounds, and hear Light and Colours. For as the Objects of the outward Senses are

A Theological Miscellany

not to be confounded, but every Object is to have its proper Sense: So must we judge of inward and spiritual Objects, which have their proper *Sense,* whereby they are to be perceived. And tell me how God doth manifest his Will concerning matters of Fact, when he sends his Angels to Men, since Angels (as is commonly received) have not outward Senses, or at least not so gross ones as ours are? Yea, when Men die, and appear before the Tribunal of GOD, whether unto eternal Life or Death, how can they know this, having laid down their Bodies, and therewith their outward Senses? And nevertheless this Truth of GOD is *a Truth of Fact,* as is the historical Truth of Christ's Birth in the Flesh. And, which is yet more near, how do good and holy Men, even in this Life, most certainly know that they are in Favour and Grace with GOD? No *outward Revelation* doth make this known unto them, but *the Spirit* (as saith the Apostle) *beareth witness with our Spirits, that we are the Children of GOD.* For the meer Testimony of a humane Conscience, without the inward Testimony of the holy Spirit, cannot beget in us a firm and immoveable Testimony of our Sonship, because the Heart of Man is deceitful; and if the Testimony thereof were true, at most it is but a humane Testimony, which begetteth in us only an humane Faith: But that Faith by which holy Men believe they are the Sons of GOD, is a *Divine Faith,* which leans upon a *Divine Testimony* of the holy Spirit, witnessing in them that they are the Sons of GOD. Moreover, when a good Man feels in himself that undeclarable Joy of the holy Spirit, concerning which the holy Scripture speaks, and which is the common privilege of the Saints, how or whence feels he this Joy? Truly this Argument concludes no less against *this heavenly spiritual Joy* which is begotten in the Souls of the Saints by the holy Spirit, than it does against the immediate Revelation of GOD; for there is *no natural Idea* in Men of this spiritual Joy; else meer natural Men, yea, such as are prophane and ungodly, would feel it as much as the Godly: but because it is *a Supernatural thing,* therefore it can have *no true Idea,* but what is Supernatural. Moreover, whence is it that prophane Men feel sometimes in themselves the Wrath of GOD as Fire, when all things, as to the outward, go as prosperously with them as with the Godly, and oftentimes more prosperously? For there is *no natural Idea* in Men of this inward Wrath of GOD: There is also an inward Grief oftentimes raised up in wicked Men from the sense of this Wrath of GOD, which very much vexeth and tormenteth their minds; and nevertheless this Grief hath *no natural Idea* in us: For oftentimes wicked Men feel not this Sorrow, for GOD sometimes is, as it were, silent, while the Wicked sin, as in *Psalm* 50.

All which do most clearly demonstrate that there are in Men *Supernatural Ideas* of Supernatural Beings; which *Ideas* are nevertheless not perceived by us, unless they be stirred up by some *Supernatural Operation* of GOD, which raiseth up in us *Supernatural and Spiritual Senses,* which by their Nature are as distinguishable from the natural Senses, whether inward or outward, as the natural Senses are distinguishable one from another by their specifick Difference. Of which Spiritual Senses the Scripture speaks frequently. [...] Yea, it is the Promise of the Gospel, that *the Glory of GOD shall be seen of holy Men;* such as are clean of Heart, even in this Life ...

For this argument seemeth to do no less Injury to the Saints, than to rob them of this most glorious Treasure, both in this Life and that to come; For there is in us *no Natural Idea* of this Divine Glory, as there is not of GOD himself, which is any ways proportionable unto so great Happiness, which the Scripture so much declareth of, by which the Godly are rewarded, partly in this Life, and plenarily in that which is to come. We confess indeed, there is in all Men, as well the Godly as the Ungodly, some sort of *Idea of* GOD, *as of a most perfect Being;* and that therefore this Proposition, *There existeth a most perfect Being,* doth as clearly appear to humane Understanding as that *the whole is greater than the part*; And therefore this Proposition, *That a most perfect Being existeth,* ought to be numbred among the Principles that of themselves are manifest; *But this Idea* of GOD is as manifest to Ungodly as to Godly Men, yea, is as clearly perceived by the Devil, as by the most holy Angels, for all the Devils know that GOD is; yet how blind is the Devil, and all wicked men, as to the Vision of GOD, which is the chief Reward of the Saints.

There is then either *no such Vision of GOD,* neither in this Life nor in that to come, or there is a *Supernatural Idea of GOD in us,* by which we are made capable of this Vision: Which *Supernatural Idea of GOD,* differeth much from that *Natural Idea of GOD,* which *Cartesius* and his Followers so much talk of, (albeit others, long before *Cartesius,* did observe this *Natural Idea of GOD,* and spoke of it) But the Happiness of the Saints consists not in contemplating *this Natural Idea of GOD*; Else the Wicked would be as happy as the Godly, yea the very Devil as the most holy Angel, Since as is said both the Devil, and most wicked Men, do as clearly perceive this *Natural Idea of GOD* as the most holy Men or Angels.

If the Scriptures then be true, there is in Men a *Supernatural Idea of GOD,* which altogether differs from this natural *Idea,* I say, in *all Men*; Because all Men are capable of Salvation; and consequently, of injoyning this Divine Vision: Now this Capacity consisteth herein, that they have such a *Supernatural Idea* in themselves: For if there were no such *Idea* in them, it were impossible they should know God: *For whatsoever is clearly and Distinctly known, is known by its proper Idea,* neither can it otherways be clearly and distinctly known; For the *Ideas* of all things are Divinely planted in our Souls; for they are not begotten in us by outward Objects or outward Causes, (as the better Philosophy teacheth) but only are by these outward things excited or stirred up: and this is true, not only in *Supernatural Ideas of GOD,* and things Divine, and in *Natural Ideas* of the natural Principles of humane Understanding, and Conclusions thence deduced by the strength of humane Reason, but even in the *Ideas* of outward Objects, whch are perceived by the outward Senses; As that noble Christian Philosopher *Boetius* hath well observed, to which also the *Cartesian Philosophy* agreeth: for when I see an outward Object, whether it be a Man, or Horse, or Bird, the outward Object does not treat in my eye, or yet in my mind, the *Idea* of those things: for the outward Object does nothing but imprint in our sensible Organs a Corporal motion: Now there is nothing in a Corporal motion that can form in us the *Ideas* of these things; for all *Ideas* are of a spiritual Nature: Now nothing that is Corporal can produce that which is Spiritual, because the less excellent cannot produce the more excellent; Else the Effect would exceed its Cause, which is against all sound

Reason, that it should bring forth what were of a higher and more excellent kind. Therefore all *Ideas,* whether *of Natural or Spiritual things,* are Divinely implanted in our Minds; which nevertheless do not always appear, but sometimes appear, and sometimes are as it were hid in us, and sometimes are stirred up in us by Causes outward or inward, and again do as it were sleep and shun our Observation, and seem not to be otherways distinguished by our Minds, but as Thoughts and Perceptions of the Mind from the Mind it self. That is, as the *Mode* from the *Subject,* or as a Bodily Motion from the Body whereof it is the Motion; *For as is the Relation of a Bodily Motion to a Body, so is the Relation of a Thought or Perception of the Mind to the Mind.* In this nevertheless they differ, that the Mind can move it self, and operate in it self, which a Body cannot do: But as a Body can be moved by another; So also can the Mind, after its manner, be moved by another; and that both by outward and inward Causes: But chiefly by God himself, in whose hand all Souls and Creatures are. But of these things there is enough said at present, and I hope, I have not thus far impertinently Philosophized.

PART VII

POETRY

Document VII.1

John Milton: On the New Forcers of Conscience

For a fully annotated version of this poem, v., J. Carey and A. Fowler, *The Poems of John Milton* (London and Harlow, 1980), 295–8. It was probably written in August 1646.

Under the Long Parliament

Because you have thrown off your prelate lord[1]
And with stiff vows renounced his liturgy[2]
To seize the widowed whore plurality
From them whose sin ye envied, not abhorred,
Dare ye for this adjure the civil sword
To force our consciences that Christ set free,
And ride us with a classic[3] hierarchy
Taught ye by mere A.S.[4] and Rutherford?[5]
Men whose life, learning, faith and pure intent
Would have been held in high esteem with Paul.
Must now be named and printed heretics
By shallow Edwards[6] and Scotch What-d'ye call:[7]
But we do hope to find out all your tricks.
Your plots and packing worse than those of Trent:[8]
    That so the Parliament
May with their wholesome and preventive shears
Clip your phylacteries, though baulk your ears,[9]
    And succour out just fears.
When they shall read this clearly in your charge
New Presbyter is but Old Priest writ large.[10]

Notes

1. Episcopacy was formally abolished by decree in September 1646.
2. By an ordinance of January 1645 Parliament had adopted the *Directory for Public Worship* as a replacement for the *Book of Common Prayer*.
3. A barbed reference to the 'classis', the first-level district assembly in the hierarchy of Presbyterianism.
4. 'A.S.' was Adam Stewart, a Scottish Professor of Philosophy at Leiden, who replied to Thomas Goodwin's *Apologeticall Narration* (London, 1643) with his *Some Observations* (London, 1643).
5. Samuel Rutherford (1600–61), Professor of Divinity at St Andrews and one of Scotland's greatest theologians, was one of the four Scots Commissioners at the Westminster Assembly, v., Nigel M. de S. Cameron (ed.), *Dictionary of Scottish Church History and Theology* (Edinburgh, 1993), 735–6.
6. Thomas Edwards (1599–1647), a vehement advocate of strict Presbyterianism and the author of *Gangraena* which contained an attack on Milton's teaching about divorce.

7. Almost certainly a reference to Robert Baillie (1599–1662), Professor of Divinity and Principal of the University of Glasgow and one of the Scottish Commissioners at the Westminster Assembly, v., Nigel M. de S. Cameron (ed.), *Dictionary of Scottish Church History* (Edinburgh, 1993), 51.
8. 'Trent' is a reference to the Council of Trent (1545–63) which formulated the principles of the Catholic Reformation.
9. In 1634 William Prynne (1600–69) was condemned by the Court of Star Chamber to lose his ears and in 1637 after another court action he was condemned to lose what remained of them. Henry Burton (1578–1648) suffered the same punishment in 1636 and John Bastwick (1593–1654) in 1637. That was in addition to huge fines and perpetual imprisonment. For all three, v., DNB.
10. Apart from the obvious meaning, Milton is at the same time indulging in a learned witticism. 'Priest' is a contracted form of the Latin 'presbyter', so 'presbyter' is etymologically 'priest' expanded.

Document VII.2

John Milton: Sonnet XV, On the Late Massacre in Piedmont

This celebrated sonnet was written, probably in May 1655, in protest against the persecution of the Waldenses, which was also the occasion of a public condemnation by Cromwell, who commissioned Milton to write a formal letter of protest in Latin on 25 May to various heads of state and an address to be delivered to Charles Emmanuel II, the Duke of Savoy. He had sent an army under the Marquis of Pianozza to expel the Waldenses (or Vaudois) from the villages of Torre Pellice and San Giovanni. These were not in the area in which they had been granted the right to reside by the Duke of Savoy in 1561. The massacre happened on 24 April 1655 and the Vaudois estimated that 1,712 men, women and children had been killed. The Vaudois had their rights of residence restored to them by a peace treaty on 18 August.

For a fully annotated version of the poem, v., J. Carey and A. Fowler, *The Poems of John Milton* (London and Harlow, 1980), 411–12.

> Avenge, O Lord thy slaughter'd saints, whose bones
>   Lie scatter'd on the Alpine mountains cold;
>   Even them who kept thy truth so pure of old,
> When all our fathers worship'd stocks and stones,
>
> Forget not: in thy book record their groans
>   Who were thy sheep and in their ancient fold
>   Slain by the bloody Piedmontese, that roll'd
> Mother and infants down their rocks.[1] Their moans
>
> The vales redoubled to the hills, and they
>   To heaven. Their martyr'd blood and ashes sow
> O'er all the Italian fields[2] where still doth sway

Poetry

> The triple tyrant:³ that from these may grow
> A hundredfold, who having learnt thy way
> Early may fly the Babylonian woe.⁴

Notes

1. This grim atrocity was apparently a notorious feature of the massacre. Mothers and their babies were indeed flung down the mountain sides.
2. An appropriate reference to Tertullian's famous observation, 'The blood of the martyrs is the seed of the Church', in his Apologeticus, 1.
3. The 'triple tyrant' is the Pope, whose tiara is surmounted by three crowns.
4. All the original Reformers, taking their cue from Revelation 17 and 18, used the name Babylon as a term of abuse for the Church of Rome.

Document VII.3

John Milton: 'Lycidas'

'Lycidas', which has been described as perhaps the most famous Threnody in the English language, was Milton's contribution to a memorial volume to his friend Edward King. It appeared as the last of thirteen English poems in *Obsequies to the Memory of Mr. Edward King* (Cambridge, 1638) and was composed in November 1637. King was drowned in a shipwreck off the coast of north Wales, 10 August 1637. Milton and King were both members of Christ's College, Cambridge, but the closeness of their friendship has often been questioned. It is perhaps significant that the elegy was the response to a request rather than an expression of personal grief, and there are those who see the whole poem, with its elaborate classical and pagan imagery, as a veiled attack on the Church of England into which King hoped to be ordained – the 'fatal and perfidious bark' which caused his death. This view is certainly supported by the heading which Milton himself added to the elegy in the later edition of 1645, 'In this Monody the Author bewails a learned Friend ... and by occasion foretells the ruin of the corrupted Clergy, then in their height.' The attack on the 'corrupt clergy' is nowhere clearer or more pointed than in the following extract.

For Edward King (1612–37), v., DNB; and for a fully annotated version of the poem, v., J. Carey and A. Fowler, *The Poems of John Milton* (London and Harlow, 1980), 411–12.

[Lines 108–51]

> Last came, and last did go,
> The pilot of the Galilean lake;¹
> Two massy keys he bore of metals twain
> (The golden opes, the iron shuts amain);
> He shook his mitred locks, and stern bespake,
> How well I could have spared for thee, young swain,
> Enow of such as for their bellies' sake

Creep and intrude and climb into the fold?
Of other care they little reckoning make
Than how to scramble at the shearers' feast,
And shove away the worthy bidden guest;
Blind mouths! that scarce themselves know how to hold
A sheep-hook, or have learn'd aught else the least
That to the faithful herdsman's art belongs!
What recks it them?[2] What need they? They are sped;
And when they list, their lean and flashy songs
Grate on their scrannel[3] pipes of wretched straw;
The hungry sheep look up and are not fed,
But swoll'n with wind, and the rank mist they draw,
Rot inwardly and foul contagion spread;
Besides what the grim wolf[4] with privy paw
Daily devours apace and nothing said:[5]
But that the two-handed engine[6] at the door,
Stands ready to smite once, and smite no more.

Notes

1. The 'Galilean pilot' would appear to be an obvious reference to the Apostle Peter, the former Galilean fisherman, traditionally regarded (on the basis of Matthew 16: 28–9) as the head of the Church and the holder of the keys of the Kingdom. But an ingenious alternative suggestion is that Milton might have been thinking of Christ Himself, the Good Shepherd, who could in a sense be called a 'Galilean pilot' (v., Mark 6: 45–52), and who, according to Revelation 1: 18, is 'the holder of the keys of hell and death'.
2. 'What business is it of theirs?'
3. This is the first appearance of the word. The OED suggests that its meaning is 'thin'.
4. The 'grim wolf' is clearly the Church of Rome, working in secret to make converts.
5. 'Nothing said' presumably refers to the absence of any protest on the part of the clergy of the Established Church.
6. The true meaning of the 'two-handed engine' has been hotly debated. Suggestions have included the Old and New Testaments, the Law and the Gospel, and the two Houses of Parliament. But the most likely explanation is that it is a reference to the executioner's axe, which required two hands to wield it. Milton may have afterwards believed that the execution of Archbishop Laud in 1645 was symbolic of the 'ruin of the corrupt clergy' which he claimed to have predicted.

Document VII.4

John Milton: Psalm LXXXIV and Psalm VIII

In April 1648 John Milton translated Psalms lxxx–lxxxviii although they were not published until 1673. D. Masson, *Life of John Milton*, 7 vols (London, 1881), I, 243 surmises that Milton was inspired to attempt the translation when the Commons and the Lords disagreed about the best version of the metrical psalms to be adopted by the newly reformed Church of England, the former preferring that of Francis Rous and the latter that of William Barton. The second psalm quoted above comes from his translations of Psalms i–viii, composed in 1653 and also published in 1673. This collection is of literary interest because each of the eight psalms is composed in a different metre. Both psalms are included here, not only because they exemplify the genius of the greatest of Puritan poets, but because the psalms were so very significant in Nonconformist spirituality and worship. For a fully annotated edition of Milton's poetical works, v., J. Carey and A. Fowler, *The Poems of John Milton* (2nd edn, London and Harlow, 1980). For Milton's place in the history of hymnody, v., article 'Psalters, English' in John Julian, *Dictionary of Hymnology* (London, 1907).

(a) Psalm LXXXIV

1. How lovely are thy dwellings fair
    O Lord of Hosts, how dear
   The *pleasant* tabernacles are!
    Where thou dost dwell so near.
2. My soul doth long and almost die
    Thy courts O Lord to see,
   My heart and flesh aloud do cry,
    O living God, for thee.
3. There even the sparrow *freed from wrong*
    Hath found a house of *rest*,
   The swallow there, to lay her young
    Hath built her *brooding* nest,
   Even by thy altars Lord of Hosts
    They find their safe abode,
   And home they fly from round the coasts
    Toward thee, my King, my God,
4. Happy, who in thy house reside
    Where thee they ever praise,
5. Happy, whose strength in thee doth bide,
    And in their hearts thy ways.
6. They pass through Baca's *thirsty* vale,
    That dry and barren ground
   As through a fruitful wat'ry dale
    Where springs and showers abound.
7. They journey on from strength to strength,
    With joy and gladsome cheer
   Till all before *our* God *at length*
    In Sion do appear.
8. Lord God of Hosts hear *now* my prayer
    O Jacob's God give ear,
9. Thou God our shield look on the face
    Of thy anointed *dear*.

10. For one day in thy courts *to be*
     Is better, *and more blest*
   Than in the *joys of vanity*,
     A thousand days *at best*.
   I in the temple of my God
     Had rather keep a door,
   Than dwell in tents, *and rich abode*
     With sin *for evermore*.
11. For God the Lord both sun and shield
     Gives grace and glory *bright*,
   No good from them shall be withheld
     Whose ways are just and right.
12. Lord God of Hosts *that reign'st on high*,
     That man is *truly* blest,
   Who *only* on thee doth rely,
     And in thee only rest.

(b) Psalm VIII

August 14, 1653

O Jehovah our Lord how wondrous great
   And glorious is thy name through all the earth!
So as above the heavens thy praise to set
   Out of the tender mouths of latest birth,

Out of the mouths of babes and sucklings thou
   Hast founded strength because of all thy foes
To stint the enemy, and slack the avenger's brow
   That bends his rage thy providence to oppose.

When I behold the heavens, thy fingers' art,
   The moon and stars which thou so bright hast set,
In the pure firmament, then saith my heart,
   O what is man that thou rememberest yet,

And think'st upon him; or of man begot
   That him thou visit'st and of him art found?
Scarce to be less than gods, thou mad'st his lot,
   With honour and with state thou hast him crowned.

O'er the works of thy hand thou mad'st him lord,
   Thou hast put all under his lordly feet,
All flocks and herds, by thy commanding word,
   All beasts that in the field or forest meet,

Poetry

Fowl of the heavens, and fish that through the wet
   Sea-paths in shoals do slide. And know no dearth.
   O Jehovah our Lord how wondrous great
And glorious is thy name through all the earth.

Document VII.5

Morgan Llwyd: A Hymn

The following poem is in T. E. Ellis (ed.), *Gweithiau Morgan Llwyd* (Bangor, 1899), 71–2.

'MY GOD THOU COVEREST THYSELF'

1. My God thou coverest thy selfe
     As with a robe of light
  All things are of and unto thee.
     To thee bee praise and might.

2. Lord, thou art strong and wise of heart
     and infinitly high
  Thou dost despise the lofty ones
     and all mens reines dost try.

3. How precious is thy kindnesse lord!
     How excellent thy grace!
  How stedfast is thy covenant!
     How beautifull thy face!

4. The fountaine of eternall light
     doth ever flow from thee.
  And in thy light and thine alone
     thy blessed light wee see.

5. How great and wondrous are thy workes!
     they make a mighty sound
  How just and true are all thy wayes!
     in all the nations round.

6. The kingdomes all as potters clay,
     thou mouldest at thy will.
  Thy promises and our requests
     thou dost at once fulfill.

7. The kingdomes of this world become
    the kingdomes of our lord
  and of his Christ, and hee must raigne
    To him lett all accord.

8. wee give thee thanks, Almighty lord
    and blessed soveraigne
  which art and wast, and art to come
    and dost begin to raigne.

9. The depths and secretts of thy will
    thou hidest from the wise
  and dost reveale them unto Babes
    whom knowing men despise.

Document VII.6

A Fifth Monarchy Hymn

'Mr. Powell's hymn at Christ Church, Dec. 18,' [1653].

This appeared originally in the *Scout*, 27 January–3 February 1653/4 and is quoted in Alexander Griffith, *Strena Vavasoriensis* (London, 1654), 24. It shows how hymn-singing, as opposed to metrical psalm-singing, was beginning to emerge at least in the more enthusiastic Nonconformist services. Examples of Vavasor Powell's poetry can be found in E. Bagshaw, *The Life and Death of Mr. Vavasor Powell* (London, 1671), 95–105, and appended to his *Bird in the Cage Chirping* (London, 1661) there is a version of *Lamentations* 'in meeter', pp. 1–25, and 'A True Christian's Pilgrimage', pp. 26–46, and also in *Three Hymns, or Certain Excellent new Psalms* (London, 1650).

    To Christ our king, let us praise sing,
    Who is our Saviour dear,
    Who is our Protector and our Rock,
    Who will come and soon appear.

    To humble his, and try their hearts,
    And make them clean and pure
    To set his Kingdom upon Earth
    Which ever shall endure.

    His Saints shall reign with him on earth
    And great ones then shall bow;
    The battle and the Battle ax
    And men of war shall know.

Poetry

That he will arise, and he will rule,
And their power will fall,
And Christ our great Commander, He
Shall be our General.

Hast Lord, come quickly down,
Thy Saints do wait and pray
And men would faign. if they knew how
Thy Prophets kill and slay.

But they shall live, and eke stand up
And give their testimonmy
Against the Monarchs of the Earth
That sit and reign on high

Document VII.7

Two Quaker Poems

Early Quakers disapproved of most aspects of contemporary popular culture, and before 1661 they published very little verse. Then during the next few years some thirty Quaker authors published their poems. The impetus was, probably, partly the example of John Perrot, a popular Quaker preacher who published a considerable amount of poetry, and partly that verse was found to be a useful means of expression at a time of persecution. Perrot quarrelled with George Fox, and Quakers published little more poetry until late in the century. These two poems both appeared in 1662. The first, by Richard Greenway from Blackfriars, was printed in a collection of short, mostly apocalyptic, papers entitled *An Alarm from the Holy Mountain*. The second was by William Bayly, a shipmaster originally from Poole. It appeared in a similar collection of short papers called *A Message sent forth from the Risen Seed of God*. See Luella Wright, *The Literary Life of Early Friends*, Columbia University Press, 1932; Rosemary Moore, 'Seventeenth Century Published Quaker Verse', (*Quaker Studies* 9/1, Sept 2004) 5–16. For Perrot, v., Kenneth L. Carroll, *John Perrot, Early Quaker schismatic* (London, 1970); Nigel Smith, 'Exporting Enthusiasm: John Perrot and the Quaker Epic' in Thomas Healy and Jonathan Sawday, eds, *Literature and the English Civil War* (Cambridge, 1990); Clare J. L. Martin, 'Tradition versus Innovation: the Hat, Wilkinson-Storey and Keithian Controversies' (*Quaker Studies* 8/1, Sept. 2003), 5–11.

(a) By Richard Greenway
Pro. 29 and 19, *where there is no vison the people perish; And thus saith the* Lord Joel 2 and 28, *I will pour out my spirit upon all flesh, and your Sons and your Daughters shall Prophesy, and your Old men shall dream dreams, and your young men shall see Visions.*

Awake Awake Oh Arme of God thou that hast cut the Whore,
And wound the Dragon and the Beast they they may rise no more;
Thy Lambs and Babes do praise thy name and call thee ever blest,
For when the Wolves would them devour'd thou wast their fould of rest,
When as the roaring Beasts of the field did seek them to devour,
Thou didst appear for them, and was their strength and Tower.

The wicked were swelling like the Sea, and foaming as the flood,
But thou hast stopped them by thy arm, and rebuk'd them by thy word,
Eternal is thy truth O God, blessed are all that do the same,
They have a strength to flye unto; they know thy holy Name,
Which in the earthly darkness yet lyes hid, and long time so hath been,
But in thy light and day that's bright, it is and hath been seen;

To the confounding of all lyes, and such as Truth oppose,
For he is risen that wil plead its cause against his foes,
Since it is so let all know Truth is strongest of all,
And when the lofty have done all they can, like Cedars they must fall,
Unto the Earth as void of breath, any longer to contend
Against the strong and powerful Rock, that never will have end.

Then God's word that is a sword the Wicked for to slay,
It will be well for all that in it dwell, in this his mighty day,
They that thereof possessors are will feel a strength and stay,
When as the wicked shall be tost like Chaffe that's driven away,
Which into th'fire at last will come to be consum'd with heat,
Therefore let all in time Repent before it be to late.

(b) By William Bayly

>Seek not by Laws, made in man's will
>The blood of Innocents to spill
>For if you do, the Law of God
>Within your heart, shall be the Rod
>Which shall you smite, with stroaks full soar
>And you Condemn, for evermore
>For your decrees, which are unjust
>They shall not stand; Gods Counsel must.
>Professions, words and prayers long,
>>He hath no pleasure in
>
>Without the life of righteousness,
>All Scarifice [sic] is sin
>The day is broke, and God's just stroake
>>On Hypocrites must come,
>
>Their many words and Carnal swords
>Can't save them from their doom,
>>>>Amen.

PART VIII

THE DAWN OF TOLERATION

Document VIII. 1

The Toleration Act, 1689: An Act for exempting their Majesties' Protestant Subjects dissenting from the Church of England from the Penalties of certain Laws

The Toleration Bill was brought into the House of Lords on 28 February 1689 and passed both Houses without difficulty. It received the royal assent on 24 May. The three articles mentioned in clause VIII, which Dissenters were exempted from subscribing, were (34) *Of the Traditions of the Church*, (35) *Of the Homilies*, and (36) *Of Consecration of Bishops and Ministers*. Unitarians were excluded from the benefits of the Act since it says explicitly that nothing in it 'shall be construed to give, in any case, benefit or advantage to any person that shall deny the doctrine of the Blessed Trinity' (clause XVII). In 1697 an Act was passed which made the denial of the Trinity a penal offence, punishable on a second conviction, with three years' imprisonment (9 and 10 William III, cap 35). Roman Catholics were also excluded from the benefits of the Act.

This Act, I Gul. & Mar., cap 18, is in R. Drayton (ed.), *Statutes of the Realm* (London, 1819), VI, 74–6 and in George Gould (ed.), *Documents Relating to the Act of Uniformity* (London, n.d., but 1862), 507–16 and in part in A. Browning (ed.), *English Historical Documents, 1660–1714* (London, 1953), 400–3.

Forasmuch as some ease to scrupulous consciences in the exercise of religion may be an effectual means to unite their Majesties' Protestant subjects in interest and affection,

II. Be it enacted ... that [the Acts now in force against Nonconformity], nor any other law or statute of this realm made against papists or popish recusants, except the [First Test Act, 1673], and except also [The Second Test Act, 1678], shall be construed to extend to any person or persons dissenting from the Church of England that shall take the oaths mentioned in [the Act legalizing the Convention, 1689], and shall make and subscribe the declaration mentioned in [the Second Test Act, 1678] which oaths and declaration the justices of peace at the general sessions of the peace to be held for the county or place where such person shall live are hereby required to tender and administer to such persons as shall offer themselves to take, make and subscribe the same, and thereof to keep a register; and likewise none of the persons aforesaid shall give or pay, as any fee or reward, to any officer or officers belonging to the court aforesaid, above the sum of sixpence, nor that more than once for his or their entry of his taking the said oaths, and making and subscribing the said declarations; nor above the further sum of sixpence for any certificate of the same to be made out and signed by the officer or officers of the said court ...

V. Provided always, and be it enacted ... that if any assembly of persons dissenting from the Church of England shall be had in any place for religious worship with the doors locked, barred or bolted during any time of such meeting together, all and every person or persons that shall come to and be at such meeting shall not receive any benefit from this law, but be liable to all the pains and penalties of all the aforesaid laws recited in this Act for such their meeting, notwithstanding his taking the oaths and his making and subscribing the declaration aforesaid.

VI. Provided always, that nothing herein contained shall be construed to exempt any of the persons aforesaid from paying of tithes or other parochial duties, or any other duties to the church or minister, nor from any prosecution in any ecclesiastical court or elsewhere for the same ...

VIII. And be it further enacted ... that no person dissenting from the Church of England in Holy Orders or pretended Holy Orders or pretending to Holy Orders, nor any preacher or teacher of any congregation of dissenting Protestants, that shall make and subscribe the declaration aforesaid, and take the said oaths at the general or quarter-sessions of the peace to be held for the county, town, parts or division where such person lives (which court is hereby empowered to administer the same), and shall also declare his approbation of and subscribe the articles of religion mentioned in the statute made in the thirteeth year of the reign of the late Queen Elizabeth, except the thirty-fourth, thirty-fifth and thirty-sixth, and these words of the twentieth article, viz., 'the Church hath power to decree rites or ceremonies, and authority in controversies of faith, and yet', shall be liable to any of the pains or penalties mentioned in an Act made in the seventeenth year of the reign of King Charles the Second entitled, An Act for restraining nonconformists from inhabiting corporations, nor the penalties mentioned in the aforesaid Act made in the two and twentieth year of his late Majesty's reign, for or by reason of such persons preaching at any meeting for the exercise of religion, nor to the penalty of one hundred pounds mentioned in an Act made in the thirteenth and fourteenth of King Charles the Second entitled, An Act for the uniformity of public prayers and administration of sacraments and other rites and ceremonies, and for establishing the form of making, ordaining and consecrating of bishops, priests and deacons in the Church of England, for officiating in any congregation for the exercise of religion permitted and allowed by this Act.

IX. Provided always, that the making and subscribing the said declaration, and the taking the said oaths, and making the declaration of approbation and subscription to the said articles, in manner as aforesaid, by every respective person or persons herein before mentioned, at such general or quarter sessions of the peace, as aforesaid, shall be then and there entred of record in the said court, for which sixpence shall be paid to the clerk of the peace, and no more; provided that such person shall not at any time preach in any place, but with the doors not locked, barred, or bolted, as aforesaid.

X. And whereas some dissenting Protestants scruple the baptizing of infants, be it enacted ... that every person in pretended Holy Orders, or pretending to Holy Orders, or preacher or teacher, that shall subscribe the aforesaid articles of religion except before excepted, and also except part of the seven and twentieth article touching infant baptism, and shall take the said oaths and make and subscribe the declaration aforesaid in manner aforesaid, every such person shall enjoy all the privileges, benefits and advantages which any other dissenting minister as aforesaid might have or enjoy by virtue of this Act.

XI. And be it further enacted ... that every teacher or preacher in holy orders, or pretended holy orders, that is a minister, preacher, or teacher of a [dissenting] congregation ... shall be thenceforth exempted from serving upon any jury, or from being chosen or appointed to bear the office of churchwarden, overseer of the poor, or any parochial or ward office, or other office in any hundred of any shire, city, town, parish, division, or wapentake.

XII. And be it further enacted ... that every justice of the peace may at any time hereafter require any person that goes to any meeting for exercise of religion, to make and subscribe the declaration aforesaid, and also to take the said oaths or declaration of fidelity hereinafter mentioned, in case such person scruples the taking of an oath, and upon refusal thereof, such justice of the peace is hereby required to commit such person to prison without bail or mainprize, and to certify the name of such person to the next general or quarter sessions of the peace to be held for that county, city, town, part or division where such person then resides ... and he shall be taken thenceforth ... for a popish recusant convict ...

XIII. And whereas there are certain other persons, dissenting from the Church of England, who scruple the taking of any oath, be it enacted ... that every such person shall make and subscribe the aforesaid declaration, and also this declaration of fidelity following, viz.:

I, A.B., do sincerely promise and solemnly declare before God and the world, that I will be true and faithful to King William and Queen Mary; and I do solemnly profess and declare, that I do from my heart abhor, detest, and renounce, as impious and heretical, that damnable doctrine and position, that princes excommunicated or deprived by the pope, or any authority of the see of Rome, may be deposed or murdered by their subjects, or any other whatsoever. And I do declare, that no foreign prince, person, prelate, state, or potenate hath, or ought to have, any power, jurisdiction, superiority, pre-eminence, or authority ecclesiastical or spiritual within this realm.

And shall subscribe a profession of their Christian belief in these words:

I, A.B., profess faith in God the Father, and in Jesus Christ, his Eternal Son, the true God, and in the Holy Spirit, one God, blessed for evermore; and do acknowledge the Holy Scriptures of the Old and New Testament to be given by divine inspiration.

Which declaration and subscription shall be made and entred of record at the general quarter sessions of the peace for the county, city, or place where every such person shall reside ...

XVI. Provided always ... that all the laws made and provided for the frequenting of divine service on the Lord's Day ... shall be still in force.

XVII. Provided always ... that neither this act, nor any clause, article or thing herein contained, shall extend ... to any papist or popish recusant whatsoever or any person that shall deny, in his preaching or writing, the doctrine of the blessed Trinity, as it is declared in the aforesaid articles of religion.

XVIII. Provided always, and be it enacted ... that if any person or persons, at any time after the tenth day of June, do and shall willingly and of purpose, maliciously or contemptuously come into any cathedral or parish church, chapel, or other congregation permitted by this Act, and disquiet or disturb the same, or misuse any preacher or teacher, such person or persons, upon proof thereof before any justice of the peace ... shall find two sureties, to be bound in the penal sum of fifty pounds, and in default of such sureties, shall be committed to prison, there to remain till the next general or quarter sessions.

XIX. Provided always, that no congregation or assembly for religious worship shall be permitted or allowed by this act, until the place of such meeting shall be certified to the bishop of the diocese, or to the archdeacon ... or to the justices of the peace ... and registered in the said bishop's or archdeacon's court respectively, or recorded at the said general or quarter sessions; the register, or clerk of the peace whereof respectively, is hereby required to register the same, and to give certificate thereof to such person as shall demand the same, for which there shall be no greater fee nor reward taken, than the sum of sixpence.

Document VIII.2

The Happy Union, 1691

Persecution had drawn the different Nonconformist churches closer together. Open Baptists, Independents and Presbyterians had co-operated in worship and ministry in many places. In church organisation it was difficult to distinguish between a Congregational and a Presbyterian Church since persecution had effectively destroyed the Presbyterian system of synods and church courts. Richard Baxter's attempts to bring the two bodies together in 1668–9 had failed (v., M. Sylvester, *Reliquiae Baxterianae* (London, 1696), III, 69) but by 1689 the time seemed opportune to try again. In the summer of 1690 representatives of the two persuasions set up the Common Fund to relieve the poverty of ministers who had suffered privation in the previous years. But many prominent leaders believed that a yet closer union might be possible. The moving spirit was John Howe and in consultation with John Faldo he formulated some heads of agreement to present to a conference consisting of six Congregationalists and six Presbyterians. Faldo died on 7 February 1691 and Howe revised his proposals and the new *Heads of Agreement* were signed by almost all the Presbyterian and Congregational ministers on 6 March 1691. The following extract presents the main points of the *Heads of Agreement Assented to by the United Ministers in and about London, formerly Called Presbyterian and Congregational* (London, 1691), 16 pp. The spelling has been modernised. It is also reproduced in CHST, VIII, 38ff. and Iain Murray, *The Reformation of the Church* (Edinburgh: Banner of Truth, 1965). See also Williston Walker, *The Creeds and Platforms of Congregationalism* (New York, 1893; reprinted Boston, 1960).

The Happy Union was formally inaugurated at the Stepney Meeting-house on 6 April 1691 where the minister, Matthew Mead (d. 16 October 1699, for whom v., CR and DNB), preached on the theme 'Two Sticks made One' on the basis of Ezek. 37: 19. But the Union did not remain happy for long. Some leading Congregational ministers refused to sign the Agreement. Acute doctrinal differences erupted over the remarkable ministry of Richard Davis (1658–1714) of Rothwell (for whom v., Matthias Maurice, *Monuments of Mercy* (London, 1729), 58–120 and DWB). For details of the creation of the Happy Union and the subsequent controversy that brought about its demise, v., R. Tudur Jones, *Congregationalism in England* (London, 1962), 112–18. For the Common Fund, v., Alexander Gordon, *Freedom after Ejection* (Manchester, 1917). For further comment, see E. Calamy, *An Abridgement Of Mr. Baxter's History* ... (London, 1713), I, 476–83; J. Toulmin, *An Historical View* ... (London, 1814), 100–5; R. W. Dale, *History of English Congregationalism* (London, 1907), 474–9; and M. R. Watts, *The Dissenters* (Oxford, 1978), 295–7.

The Heads of Agreement

Preface

Endeavours for an agreement among Christians, will be grievous to none who desire the flourishing state of Christianity itself. The success of these attempts among us, must be ascribed to a presence of God so signal, as not to be concealed; and seems a hopeful pledge of further blessings.

[After rehearsing the various considerations that inspired the promoters of the scheme, the Preface says:]

Therefore it is incumbent on us, to forbear condemning and disputing those different sentiments and practices we have expressly allowed for: To reduce all distinguishing names, to that of United Brethren: to admit no uncharitable jealousies, or censorious speeches; much less any debates as to which party seems most favoured by this agreement ...

The following Heads of Agreement have been resolved upon, by the united ministers in and about London, formerly called Presbyterian and Congregational; not as a measure of any national constitution, but for the preservation of order in our congregations that cannot come up to the common rule by law established.

I. Of Churches and Church-Members

1. We acknowledge our Lord Jesus Christ to have one Catholic Church, or Kingdom, comprehending all that are united to him, whether in heaven or earth. And do conceive the whole multitude of visible believers, and their infant seed (commonly called the Catholic visible Church) to belong to Christ's spiritual kingdom in this world: but for the notion of a Catholic visible Church here, as it signifies its having been collected into any formed society, under any visible human head on earth, whether one person singly, or many collectively, we, with the rest of Protestants, unanimously disclaim it.

2. We agree, that particular societies of visible saints, who under Christ their Head are statedly joined together, for ordinary communion with one another in all the ordinances of Christ, are particular churches, and are to be owned by each other

as instituted Churches of Christ, though differing in apprehensions and practice in some lesser things.

3. That none shall be admitted as members, in order to communion in all the special ordinances of the Gospel, but such persons as are knowing and sound in the fundamental doctrines of the Christian religion, without scandal in their lives; and, to a judgment regulated by the Word of God, are persons of visible godliness and honesty; credibly professing cordial subjection to Jesus Christ ...

6. That each particular church hath right to choose their own officers; and, being furnished with such as are duly qualified and ordained according to the gospel rule, hath authority from Christ for exercising government, and of enjoying all the ordinances of worship within itself.

7. In the administration of church power, it belongs to the pastors and other elders of every particular church (if such there be) to rule and govern: and to the brotherhood to consent, according to the rule of the Gospel.

[Two other clauses follow.]

II. Of the Ministry

1. We agree, that the ministerial office is instituted by Jesus Christ, for the gathering, guiding, edifying, and governing of the Church; and to continue to the end of the world.

> Clause 2 emphasises the need for ministers to be qualified for their work while clause 3 says that only those called by a particular church should be ordained.

4. That in so great and weighty a matter as the calling and choosing a pastor, we judge it ordinarily requisite, that every such church consult and advise with the pastors of neighbouring congregations.

5. That after such advice, the person consulted about, being chosen by the brotherhood of that particular church over which he is to be set, and he accepting, be duly ordained and set apart to his office over them; wherein it is ordinarily requisite, that the pastors of neighbouring congregations concur with the preaching elders, if such there be.

[Clauses 6 and 7 deal with further details about ordination and the qualifications of those to be ordained.]

III. Of Censures

[The discipline of offenders is to be administered by the individual church in accordance with Mat. 18: 15, 16, 17 first privately and in cases of impenitence culminating in excommunication.]

IV. Of Communion of Churches

1. We agree, that particular churches ought not to walk so distinct and separate

from each other, as not to have care and tenderness towards one another. But their pastors ought to have frequent meetings together, that by mutual advice, support, encouragement, and brotherly intercourse, they may strengthen the hearts and hands of each other in the ways of the Lord.

2. That none of our churches should be subordinate to one another; each being endued with equality of power from Jesus Christ. And that none of the said particular churches, their officer, or officers, shall exercise any power, or have any superiority over any other church, or their officers.

3. That known members of particular churches, constituted as aforesaid, may have occasional communion with one another in the ordinances of the Gospel, viz., the Word, prayer, sacraments, singing psalms, dispensed according to the mind of Christ: Unless that church with which they desire communion, hath any just exception against them ...

5. That one church ought not to blame the proceedings of another, until it hath heard what that church charged, its elders, or messengers, can say in vindication of themselves from any charge of irregular or injurious proceedings ...

V. Of Deacons and Ruling Elders

We agree, The office of deacon is of divine appointment, and that it belongs to their office to receive, lay out, and distribute the church's stock to its proper uses, by the direction of the pastor, and the brethren if need be. And whereas divers are of opinion, that there is also the office of ruling elders, who labour not in the Word and doctrine; and others think otherwise; we agree, that this difference make no breach among us.

VI. Of Occasional Meetings of Ministers, &c

1. We agree, that in order to concord, and in any other weighty and difficult cases, it is needful, and according to the mind of Christ, that the ministers of several churches be consulted and advised with, about such matters.

[Two clauses follow giving further details.]

VII. Of our Demeanour towards the Civil Magistrate

1. We do reckon ourselves obliged continually to pray for God's protection, guidance, and blessing upon the rulers set over us.

[Two clauses follow.]

VIII. Of a Confession of Faith

As to what pertains to soundness of judgement in matters of faith, we esteem it sufficient that a church acknowledge the Scriptures to be the Word of God, the perfect and only rule of faith and practice; and own either the doctrinal part of those commonly called the Articles of the Church of England, or the Confession, or Catechisms, Shorter or Larger, compiled by the Assembly at Westminster, or the Confession agreed on at the Savoy, to be agreeable to the said rule.

IX. Of our Duty and Deportment towards them that are not in Communion with us

1. We judge it our duty to bear a Christian respect to all Christians, according to their several ranks and stations, that are not of our persuasion or communion.

2. As for such as may be ignorant of the principles of the Christian religion, or of vicious conversation, we shall in our respective places, as they give us opportunity, endeavour to explain to them the doctrine of life and salvation, and to our uttermost persuade them to be reconciled to God.

[Two further clauses complete the document.]

Document VIII.3

Quakers and the Trinity

The provisions of the Toleration Act were only available to Trinitarian bodies, posing a problem for Quakers who would not agree to express their faith in a set form of words in non-Biblical language. (It can still cause difficulties. Special arrangements to accommodate churches that are non-credal on principle have been set up as part of the CCBI and other ecumenical structures.)

Since the government wished to include the Quakers under the Act, and since most Quakers also wished to take advantage of it, it was a matter of agreeing a form of words, and this was done, largely by making use of the spurious Trinitarian insertion in 1 John 5:7–8. (See *SPQ* p 156 and note), for Quakers had always declared that they believed in Father, Son and Spirit, and that their objection to the doctrine of the Trinity was that it used terminology, the words 'Trinity' and 'Person', that are not in the Bible. However, doubts about Quaker orthodoxy were still widespread, and an anonymous anti-Trinitarian pamphlet, *A Dialogue by way of Question and Answer concerning the Deity*, popularly supposed to have been written by a Quaker, was distributed to Members of Parliament. It was proved ultimately to be the work of William Freke (1662–1744), who was fined £500 for publishing an `infamous libel.' (DNB), but meanwhile it required an answer. The following extract is taken from a broadside, *The Christian Faith and Profession of the People commonly called Quakers*, published about the end of 1693. It carried the signatures of eighteen leading Quakers, the first being George Whitehead (1636?–1723), originally from Westmorland but now a prosperous London grocer, who was the acknowledged Quaker leader at the turn of the century, when Fox and Barclay were dead and Penn was in financial and political trouble.

Whereas we have often been Misrepresented, and Unjustly Branded with Denying and Opposing the Divinity or Deity of our Blessed Lord and Saviour Jesus Christ, the Son of the Living God; as also His Humanity or Manhood; and we understanding that a late Occasion is taken by means of a Pamphlet ... to renew such Misrepresentation against us as being our Principle, which we solemnly, and in the Fear of Almighty God, do Disown and Testify against, as a false Aspersion cast upon us.

For,

1. The said Pamphlet is none of ours, nor owned by us, nor do we know who is the Author of it.

2. Wherein it Opposes the Divinity or Deity of the Son of God, it is absolutely contrary to our Faith, Principle and Profession.

3. That Profession of our Christian Belief and Profession of Faith, *In God the Father, and Jesus Christ his Son, and in the Holy Spirit, as being one God blessed for ever more*; And our Acknowledging *The Holy Scriptures of the Old and New Testaments to be given by Divine Inspiration*: We stand by this Profession as stedfastly Believing and Owning it, as 'tis Incerted in the Act of *Parliament* ... Entitled, *An Act for Exempting their Majesties Protestant Subjects Dissenting from the* Church of England, *from the Penalties of certain Laws*; Divers Members in the Present *Parliament* may please to remember, that we publickly Owned the said Profession and Belief *before a Grand Committee in the Parliament House*.

Many of our Books also do clearly Evince and Declare our sincere Belief and Confession of Jesus Christ, the Son of the Living God, both as he is true God and perfect Man.

1. As being the Word that was with God, and was God, by which all things were made, that were made, *John* 1. 1, 3.

2. As in him was that Life, which Life was the Light of Men, *John* 1. 4.

3. As being that true Light, which Enlightens every Man that comes into the World, *John* 1. 9.

4. That the Father, the Son, and Holy Spirit; or the Father, the Word, and Holy Ghost: are One in Being, not Divided, tho as such distinguished in Scriptures, I *John* 5.7.

5. That the Eternal (Heb.2. 16) Word, or Son of God (I *Cor.* 15. 3) took Flesh, and according to the Flesh came of the Seed of (I *Cor.* 15. 3) *Abraham*, & (*Mat.* 2. 1) *David*, and (*Mat.* 2. 1) was Born of the *Virgin Mary* (*Rom.*5. 8) at *Bethlehem* in *Judea*; Was Crucified and (*Rom.* 4. 25) Died for our Sins, and (*Rom.* 1. 4) Rose again for our Justification; And declared to be the Son of God with Power, according to the Spirit of Holiness, by the Resurrection from the Dead.

6. That the same Christ is also Testified to be God over all Blessed for ever, *Rom* 9. 5. The true God and Eternal Life, I *John* 5. 10. The Great Mystery of Godliness: God manifest in Flesh, Justified in Spirit, seen of Angels, &c. I *Tim.* 3. 16.

These with many other Testimonies of Holy Scripture we Sincerely Believe and Profess, for the Divinity and Humanity (or Manhood) of our Blessed Lord and Saviour Jesus Christ, the Son of the Living God, in Opposition to all Reproaches, Misrepresentations and false Reports to the contrary. Signed On Behalf of the People commonly called Quakers. ...

Select Bibliography

This bibliography is restricted to printed books. References to specialist articles and manuscript sources will be found in the annotations appended to the individual documents. There is a convenient bibliography to Puritan works in general together with a copious topical index to their contents in Robert P. Martin, *A Guide to the Puritans* (Banner of Truth, 1997). In the following list the place of publication is London unless stated otherwise.

Ashley, M.P., *John Wildman, Plotter and Postmaster* (1947).
Bailey, Richard, *New Light on George Fox and Early Quakerism* (San Francisco, 1992).
Ball, B.W., *A Great Expectation: Eschatological Thought in English Protestantism to 1660* (Leiden, 1975).
Barbour, H. (ed.), *William Penn on Religion and Ethics* (Studies in American Religion, 52, Lewiston and Queenstown Lampeter, 1991).
Barbour, H. and Roberts, A., *Early Quaker Writings* (Grand Rapids, 1973; reprinted 2002).
Barbour, Hugh, *The Quakers in Puritan England* (Yale, 1964, 1985).
Barclay, A.R. (ed.), *Letters of Early Friends* (1841).
Barclay, Robert (of Reigate), *The Inner Life of the Religious Societies of the Commonwealth* (1879).
Barclay, Robert, *An Apology for the True Christian Divinity* (1676; new edn, ed. Peter D. Sippel, Glenside, Pa., 2002).
Barker, W.S., *Puritan Profiles* (Mentor, 1996).
Bate, F., *The Declaration of Indulgence (1672): A Study in the Rise of Organised Dissent* (1908).
Bauman, R., *Let Your Words be Few: Symbolism and Silence among Seventeenth-Century Quakers* (Cambridge, 1983).
Besse, J. (ed.), *An Abstract of the Sufferings of the Quakers* (1733–8).
Bevan, H., *Morgan Llwyd y Llenor* (Cardiff, 1954).
Birkel, M.L. and Newman, J.W. (eds), *The Lamb's War* (Richmond, 1992).
Bittle, W., *James Nayler, 1618–1660* (Richmond, 1986).
Braithwaite, W.C., *The Beginnings of Quakerism* (1st edn, 1912; 2nd revised edn, Cambridge, 1955).
Braithwaite, W.C., *The Second Period of Quakerism* (1st edn, 1919; 2nd revised edn, Cambridge, 1961).
Brook, B., *The Lives of the Puritans* (3 vols, 1813).
Brook, V.J.K., *Matthew Parker* (Oxford, 1962).
Brown, J., *John Bunyan (1628–1688): His Life, Times, and Work* (tercentenary edn, 1928).

Brown, L.F., *The Political Activities of the Baptists and Fifth Monarchy Men in England during the Interregnum* (1912; reissued New York, 1965).

Browning, A. (ed.), *English Historical Documents 1660–1714*, VIII (1953).

Burgess, W.H., *John Robinson* (1920).

Burgess, W.H., *John Smith, the Se-Baptist, Thomas Helwys, and the First Baptist Church in England* (1911).

Burrage, C., *Early English Dissenters* (2 vols, Cambridge, 1912).

Cadbury, H.J., *George Fox's 'Book of Miracles'* (Cambridge, 1948; new edn, Philadelphia and London, 2000).

Cadbury, H.J., *The Annual Catalogue of George Fox Papers, Compiled in 1694–1697* (Philadelphia, 1939).

Calamy, E., *An Abridgement of Mr.Baxter's History of His Life and Times* (2 vols, 1713).

Calamy, E., *An Account of the Ministers, Lecturers, Masters and Fellows of Colleges and Schoolmasters, who Were Ejected or Silenced after the Restoration in 1660 ...* (2 vols, 1713).

Capp, B.S., *The Fifth Monarchy Men* (London, 1972).

E. Cardwell, *Documentary Annals of the Reformed Church of England* (2 vols, Oxford, 1839).

Carlson, L.H., *Martin Marprelate, Gentleman Master Job Throckmorton Laid Open in His Colors* (San Marino, 1981).

Carlson, L.H. (ed.), *The Writings of Henry Barrow* (vol. 3 in *Elizabethan Nonconformist Texts*, 1962).

Carruthers, S.W., *The Everyday Work of the Westminster Assembly* (Philadelphia, 1943).

Clark, H.W., *History of English Nonconformity*, I (1911).

Cole, Thomas, *A Discourse of Regeneration* (1689).

Collinson, P., *Archbishop Grindal 1519–1583* (1979).

Collinson, P., *The Elizabethan Puritan Movement* (1982).

Corns, T.N. and Loewenstein, D. (eds), *The Emergence of Quaker Writing: Dissenting Literature in Seventeenth-Century England* (1995).

Cradock, W., *Divine Drops Distilled* (1650).

Cradock, Walter, *Gospel-libertie* (1648).

Cressy, David and Ferrell, Lori Anne, *Religion and Society in Early Modern England: A Sourcebook* (New York and Abingdon, 2nd edn, 2005).

Cross, F.L. (ed.), *The Oxford Dictionary of the Christian Church* (1st edn, 1958).

Dale, R.W., *History of English Congregationalism* (1907).

Damrosch Leo, *The Sorrows of the Quaker Jesus: James Nayler and the Puritan Crackdown on the Free Spirit* (Harvard, 1996).

Davies, Adrian, *The Quakers in English Society 1655–1725* (Oxford, 2000).

Davies, Horton, *The Worship of the English Puritans* (Westminster: Dacre Press, 1948).

Davies, J.H. (ed.), *Gweithiau Morgan Llwyd* II (Bangor, 1908).

Douglas, J.D. (ed.), *The New International Dictionary of the Christian Church* (Exeter, 1974).

Dunn, R. and Dunn, Mary M. (eds), *The World of William Penn* (Philadelphia, 1986).
Ellis, T.E. (ed.), *Gweithiau Morgan Llwyd*, I (Bangor, 1899).
Ellwood, Thomas, *History of the Life of Thomas Ellwood, Written by Himself* (1st edn, London, 1714; new edn, ed. Rosemary Moore, Walnut Creek, 2004).
Endy, Melvin B., Jr, *William Penn and Early Quakerism* (Princeton, 1973).
Epistles from the Yearly Meeting of Friends in London, 1681–1857 (2 vols, 1858).
Evans, E. Lewis, *Morgan Llwyd* (Liverpool, 1930).
The Examinations of Henry Barrow, John Greenwood and John Penrie (n.p., n.d.).
Fell, Sarah, *The Household Account Book of Sarah Fell* (ed., N. Penney, Cambridge, 1920).
Fox, George, *The Journal of George Fox* (ed. Norman Penney, 2 vols, Cambridge, 1911).
Fox, George, *The Journal of George Fox* (ed. John Nickalls, Cambridge, 1952).
Fox, George, *The Journal* (ed. Nigel Smith, London, 1998).
Fox, George, *The Works of George Fox* (8 vols, Philadelphia, 1831; reprinted, 1990, ed. T.H.S. Walker).
Frere, W.H. and Douglas, C.E., *Puritan Manifestoes* (1954).
Garman, M., Applegate, J., Benefiel, M. and Meredith, D., *Hidden in Plain Sight: Quaker Women's Writings, 1650–1700* (Wallingford, Pa., 1996).
Gee, H., and Hardy, W.J., *Documents Illustrative of English Church History* (1896).
Glines, Elsa F., *Undaunted Zeal: The Letters of Margaret Fell* (Richmond, Ind., 2003).
Goold, W.H. (ed.), *The Works of John Owen, D.D.* (24 vols, Edinburgh, 1850–3; Banner of Truth reprint, 16 vols, 1965).
Gordon, A., *Addresses: Biographical and Historical* (1922).
Gould, George (ed.), *Documents Relating to the Act of Uniformity* (London, n.d., but 1862).
Greaves, R. (ed.), *John Bunyan* (Sutton Courtenay, 1969).
Greaves, R.L., *Saints and Rebels* (Mercer University Press, 1985).
Grieve, A.J. (ed.), *An Aequity of an Humble Supplication by John Penry* (facsimile edn, 1905).
Griffith, A., *Strena Vavasoriensis* (1654)0.
Grosart, A.B. (ed.), *The Complete Works of Richard Sibbes* (7 vols, Edinburgh, 1862–4).
Gwyn, Douglas, *Seekers Found,* (Wallingford, Pa., 2000).
Haller, W., *Liberty and Reformation in the Puritan Revolution* (3rd edn, 1967).
Hardacre, P.H., *The Royalists during the Puritan Revolution* (The Hague, 1956).
Harding, T. (ed. and trans.), *The Decades of Henry Bullinger* (Cambridge: Parker Society, 4 vols, 1849–52).
Hart, A. Tindal, *William Lloyd 1627–1717* (1952).
Hasler, P.W. (ed.), *The History of Parliament: The House of Commons, 1558–1603*, II (3 vols, HMSO, 1981).
Helwys, Thomas, *The Mistery of Iniquity* (facsimile edn by Baptist Historical Society, 1935).

Select Bibliography

Hill, C., *A Turbulent, Seditious, and Factious People: John Bunyan and his Church* (Oxford, 1988).
Hill, C., *Puritanism and Revolution* (1958).
Hill, C., *The World Turned Upside Down* (Penguin, 1975).
Hooker, Richard, *Works* (ed., J. Keble; revised by R.W. Church and F. Paget, Oxford, 1888).
Horle, Craig W., *The Quakers and the English Legal System* (Philadelphia, 1988).
Ingle, Larry, *First among Friends: George Fox and the Creation of Quakerism* (New York and Oxford, 1994).
Ivimey, J., *A History of the English Baptists* (1811–30).
Jacob, Henry, *The True Beginning and Institution of Christ's True Visible or Ministeriall Church* (Leiden, 1610).
John, Mansel (ed.) *Welsh Baptist Studies* (South Wales Baptist College, 1976).
Jones, R.Tudur, *Vavasor Powell* (Swansea, 1971).
Jordan, W.K., *The Development of Religious Toleration in England* (4 vols, 1932, 1936, 1938, 1940).
Kaufmann, U.M., *The Pilgrim's Progress and Traditions in Puritan Meditation* (New Haven, Conn., 1966).
Keiser, R. Melvin and Moore, Rosemary, *Knowing the Mystery of Life Within: Selected Writings of Isaac Penington in their Historical and Theological Context* (London, 2005)..
Knappen, M.M., *Tudor Puritanism* (3rd edn, 1970).
Knott, J.R., *Discourses of Martyrdom in English Literature, 1563–1694* (Cambridge, 1993).
Knox, R. Buick, *Reformation, Conformity and Dissent* (Epworth, 1977).
Kunze, Bonnelyn, *Margaret Fell and the Rise of Quakerism* (Stanford and London, 1993).
Lee, M.H., *Diaries and Letters of Philip Henry* (1882).
Lewis, P., *The Genius of Puritanism* (2nd edn, Haywards Heath, Carey Publications, 1979).
Lloyd, A., *Quaker Social History 1669–1738* (1950).
Lumpkin, W.L., *Baptist Confessions of Faith* (Philadelphia, 1959).
Mack, Phyllis, *Visionary Women: Ecstatic Prophecy in Seventeenth-Century England* (Berkeley, Calif., 1992).
McGinn, D.J., *John Penry and the Marprelate Controversy* (Rutgers University, 1966).
McGregor, J.F. and Reay, B., *Radical Religion in the English Revolution* (Oxford, 1984).
McKim, D.K. (ed.), *Encyclopedia of the Reformed Faith* (Edinburgh, 1992).
McLachlan, H.J. *Socinianism in Seventeenth Century England* (Oxford, 1951).
Marsh, Christopher W., *The Family of Love in English Society, 1530–1630* (Cambridge, 1994).
Matthews, A.G. (ed.), *Calamy Revised* (Oxford, 1934).
Miller, J.C. (ed.), *The Works of Thomas Goodwin, D.D.* (12 vols, Edinburgh, 1861–6).

Select Bibliography

Miller, Perry, *Orthodoxy in Massachusetts 1630–50* (Cambridge, Mass., 1933).
Moore, Rosemary, *The Light in Their Consciences: Early Quakers in Britain 1644–1666* (University Park, Pa., 2000)..
Morgan, N., *Lancashire Quakers and the English Revolution* (1985).
Mullett, Michael A., *John Bunyan in Context* (Keele, 1996).
Murray, I.H. *The Puritan Hope* (Edinburgh: Banner of Truth, 1975).
Nicholson, W. (ed.), *The Remains of Edmund Grindal* (Cambridge: Parker Society, 1842–3).
Nightingale, B., *The Ejected of 1662 in Cumberland and Westmoreland* (2 vols, Manchester, 1911).
Nuttall, G.F., *The Holy Spirit in Puritan Faith and Experience* (Oxford, 1941; reprinted with new introduction by Peter Lake, Chicago, 1992).
Nuttall, G.F., *Richard Baxter* (1965).
Nuttall, G.F., *The Puritan Spirit* (1967).
Nuttall, G.F., *The Welsh Saints, 1640–1660* (Cardiff, 1957).
Nuttall, G.F., *Visible Saints* (Oxford, 1957).
Nuttall, *James Nayler: A Fresh Approach* (Friends' Historical Society, 1954).
Owen, G.W., *Morgan Llwyd* (Caernarfon, 1992).
Paas, S., *De Gemeenschap der Heiligen* (Uitgeverij Boekencentrum, Zoetermeer, 1995).
Packer, J.I., *Among God's Giants* (Kingsway, 1991).
Palmer, A.N., *History of the Older Nonconformity of Wrexham* (Wrexham, 1888; reprinted Wrexham, 1988).
Palmer, A.N., *History of the Parish Church of Wrexham* (Wrexham, 1886) .
Palmer, S., *The Nonconformist's Memorial* (3 vols, 2nd edn, 1802).
Peel, A., *The First Congregational Churches* (Cambridge, 1920).
Peel, A., *The Seconde Parte of a Register* (Cambridge, 1915).
Peel, A. and Carlson, L.H. (eds), *The Writings of Robert Harrison and Robert Browne* (vol. 2 in Elizabethan Nonconformist Texts, 1953).
Peters, Kate, *Print Culture and the Early Quakers* (Cambridge, 2005).
Penington, Isaac, *The Works of the Long Mournful and Sorely-Distressed Isaac Penington* (1st edn, 2 vols, London, 1681; *The Works of Isaac Penington: A Minister of the Gospel in the Society of Friends, Including His Collected Letters*, ed. Licia Kuenning, 4 vols and supplement, Glenside, Pa., 1995–7).
Penington, Mary, *Experiences in the Life of Mary Penington*, ed. Gil Skidmore (1992).
Penny, William, *Selected Works* (5 vols, 1782).
Pierce, W., *An Historical Introduction to the Marprelate Tracts* (1908).
Pierce, W., *John Penry, His Life, Times and Writings* (1923).
Pierce, W. (ed.), *The Marprelate Tracts, 1588, 1589* (1911).
Pollock, J., *The Popish Plot* (1903; Cambridge, 1944).
Powicke, F.J., *A Life of the Reverend Richard Baxter 1615–91* (2 vols, 1924–7).
Powicke, F.J., *Henry Barrow, Separatist* (1900).
Powicke, F.J., *The Reverend Richard Baxter under the Cross (1662–1691)* (1927).
Quaker Faith and Practice: The book of Christian Discipline of the Yearly Meeting

of the Religious Society of Friends (Quakers) in Britain (1994).
Reid, James, M*emoirs of the Lives and Writings of those eminent Divines who convened in the ... Assembly at Westminster* (vol. I, 1811; vol. II, 1815; one-volume reprint in 1982).
Richards, T., *Puritan Movement in Wales, 1639 to 1653* (1920).
Richards, T., *Religious Developments in Wales, 1654–1662* (1923).
Richards, T., *Wales under the Indulgence* (1928).
Richards, T., *Wales under the Penal Code* (1925).
Robinson, H. (ed.) *The Zurich Letters* (2 vols, Cambridge: Parker Society, 1842–5).
Rogers, P.G., *The Fifth Monarchy Men* (Oxford, 1966).
Rordorf, W., *Sunday* (trans. A.A.K. Graham, 1968).
Ross, Isabel, *Margaret Fell, Mother of Quakerism* (1949).
Rowse, A.L., *Ralegh and the Throckmortons* (1962).
Sharrock, Roger, *John Bunyan* (1954).
Simmons, R.C. (ed.), *English Puritanisme* (facsimile edn, Farnborough, 1972).
Smith, Nigel, *Perfection Proclaimed: Language and Literature in English Radical Religion 1640–1660* (Oxford, 1989).
Statutes at Large (1786).
The Statutes: Third Revised Edition (1950).
Stephens, M., *The Oxford Companion to the Literature of Wales* (Oxford, 1986).
Stow, J., *A Survey of London* (1603; 2 vols, ed. C.L. Kingsford (Oxford, 1971).
Strype, J., *Life and Acts of Matthew Parker* (1711).
Sylvester, M., *Reliquiae Baxterianae* (1696).
Thomas, M. Wynn, *Morgan Llwyd* (Writers of Wales Series, Cardiff, 1984).
Tindall, W.Y., *John Bunyan: Meckanick Preacher* (New York, 1934).
Toon, P., *God's Statesman: The Life and Work of John Owen* (Exeter, 1971).
Trevett, Christine, *Women and Quakerism in the Seventeenth Century* (York, 1991).
Trevett, Christine, *Quaker Women Prophets in England and Wales 1650–1700* (New York, 2000)..
Turner, G. Lyon, *Original Records of Early Nonconformity under Persecution and Indulgence* (3 vols, 1911, 1914).
Underhill, E.B., *The Records of a Church of Christ, Meeting in Broadmead Bristol 1640–1687* (Hanserd Knollys Society, 1847).
Underwood, Ted Leroy, *Primitivism, Radicalism, and the Lamb's War: the Baptist-Quaker Conflict in Seventeenth-Century England* (New York, 1997).
Usher, R.G., *The Presbyterian Movement in the Reign of Queen Elizabeth* (Camden Society, 1905).
Usher, R.G., *The Rise and Fall of the High Commission* (Oxford, 1913).
Vann, R.T., *The Social Development of English Quakerism 1655–1755* (Harvard, 1969).
Warfield, B.B., *The Westminster Assembly and Its Work* (New York, 1931).
Watkins, Owen C., *The Puritan Experience* (London, 1972).
Watts, M.R., *The Dissenters*, I (Oxford, 1978).

Wharey, J.B. (ed.), *The Pilgrim's Progress* (1928; 2nd edn, revised by R.Sharrock, 1960).
White, B.R., *The English Separatist Tradition* (Oxford, 1971).
Whitley, W.T., *A Baptist Bibliography* I (1916–22).
Whitley, W.T., *The Works of John Smyth* (2 vols, 1915).
Williams, D., *John Penry: Three Treatises Concerning Wales* (Cardiff, 1960).
Williams, Glanmor, *Welsh Reformation Essays* (Cardiff, 1967).
Wolfe, D.M. (ed.), *The Complete Works of John Milton* (1953).

Index of Persons

Adams, John 244–5, 247
Agricola, Julius 141, 145
Ainsworth, Henry 124
Alleine, Joseph 250
Alured, Matthew 193
Ames, William 3, 109, 113
Andrewes, Lancelot 103
Aquinas, Thomas 136
Arber, E. 118
Aretino, Pietro 144
Aristotle 75
Arlington (Earl) 262
Arminius 137, 144
Ashe, Simeon 344
Ashley, M.P. 193
Ashurst, Henry 279–80
Atkins, Robert 251
Audland, John 202, 211–12
Augustine, St. 203
Aylmer, John 87–9, 97–8

Bacon, Agnes 118
Bacon, Francis 138
Bacon, Nicholas 118
Bagshaw, Edward 256, 292
Bailly (ie), Robert 118, 386
Ball, B.W. 367
Bancroft, Richard 3, 55–67
Barclay, Robert 310, 374–81, 404
Barebone, Praise-God 371
Barker, Robert 55, 61
Barlow, William 103
Barrow, Henry 3, 67–86, 118, 120, 124, 205, 256–8
Barrow, Isaac 275
Barton, William 389
Bastwick, John 386
Bate, Francis 259
Bates, William 236, 241–2, 279
Batte, John 371
Bauthumley, Jacob 198
Baxter, Richard 9, 13, 15, 270–2, 278–81, 316–17, 400

Bayly, William 333–4(b)
Baynes, Paul 113
Bedell, Henry 33
Beerman, William 236, 243
Bernard, John 272
Berry James 192
Bevan, Hugh 291
Biddle, John 11, 351–3, 356
Bilson, Thomas 103
Bishop, George 211
Bittle, William 217
Blacklock, S. 371
Blinman, Richard 131–2
Blunt, Richard 371
Boehme, Jakob 202
Bold, Edward 244, 246
Bolton, Robert 346
Bonner, Edmund 33
Boteler, Philip 62
Boweland, Thomas 23, 32, 34
Bownde, Nicholas 125
Boyle, Mr/Master 90
Bradney, Joseph 131
Bradshaw, William 109–13
Braithwaite W.C. 213, 217
Braudel, F.P. 15
Brenner, Y.S. 15
Breward, Ian 287
Bridge, William 9, 130, 151–64, 221–5
Bridgeman, Henry 243–7
Bridges, John 87, 103, 107
Brook, Benjamin 165
Broster, John 244, 247
Brown, James 191
Brown, John 288
Brown, L.F. 193
Browne, Anthony 62
Browne, Dorothy 62
Browne, J. 130
Browne, Phillip 55
Browne, Robert 3, 55–67
Browning, A. 259, 397
Bruce, J. 32

Bruce, William 244–5
Bryan, Francis 144
Bull, Daniel 236, 243
Bullinger, Henry 19–22, 165
Bunyan, John 7, 9, 12, 14, 288–90, 314, 323–5, 367–70
Burgess, Cornelius 165, 190
Burgess, W.H. 118, 132
Burrage, C. 33–5, 62, 91, 118, 132
Burrough, Edward 211, 360, 363(b)–4, 367–70
Burroughes, Jeremiah 9, 152–64, 312–14
Burton, Henry 386
Bushel, Edward 372
Byfield, Adoniram 165, 190

Calamy, Edmund (the elder) 235–8, 344
Calamy, Edmund (the younger) 14, 16, 244, 248, 251, 278–81, 401
Cale, Alderman 267
Calvert, Giles 211, 216
Calvin, John 141–2, 165
Cameron, Nigel M. de S. 385–6
Camm, John 211–12
Capp, B.S. 193, 367
Cardwell, E. 53, 259
Carey, J. 385–9
Carleton, Guy 266–7
Carlson, Leland H. 55, 63, 67, 72, 87, 118, 124
Carroll, Kenneth L. 393
Carruthers S.W. 165
Carter, William 151
Cartwright, Thomas 1–3, 109
Caryl, John 217, 221–5
Caryl, Joseph 12
Case, Thomas 236, 238
Chadderton, Laurence 103
Charles Emmanuel II of Savoy 386
Charles I (King) 2, 7, 10, 125–127
Charles II (King) 2, 12, 15, 213, 233–4, 259–60, 267, 278, 372
Cheynell, Francis 154
Cicero 75
Clarendon (Earl), 270
Clark, H.W. 151
Clarke, Samuel 287
Clarkson, Laurence 11
Claypoole, James 365

Clement of Alexandria 136, 144
Cole, Mary 215–16
Cole, Thomas 341–2
Collins, Robert 248–50, 252–4
Collinson, P. 32, 36, 109, 125
Constantine (Emperor) 4
Cooper, Thomas 87, 97–8
Coppe, Abiezer 11
Cosin, Richard 99–100
Cotton, John 3, 128–9, 287–8
Cotton, Priscilla 215–16
Coverdale, Miles 25, 32
Cox, Richard 62
Cradock, Walter 14, 285–6(b), 348–51, 371–2
Creswick, Henry 267
Cromwell, Oliver 9–10, 12, 192–3, 211, 304, 318, 340, 386

Dale, R.W. 35, 63, 89, 113, 221, 259, 401
Damp, Christopher 113
Damrosch, Leo 217
Davies, Horton 33, 285, 312
Davies, Richard 76, 274, 293
Davis, J.C. 198
Davis, Richard 401
Deacon, John 217
Dell, William 11, 334–40
Dewsbury, William 363
Dexter, H.M. 118
Dexter, M. 118
Donne Lee, Edward 97, 100
Douglas, C.E. 37
Dove, John 103
Drayton, R. 397
Dudley, Ambrose 118
Dudley, Robert 118
Dumouriez, Maréchal 16
Dunn, Mary M. 372
Dunn, Richard 372
Durie, John 11

Eaton, Samuel 370
Edgbury, Joshua 275
Edward VI (King) 108
Edwards, John 277
Edwards, Thomas 10, 352, 385
Egerton, Stephen 103
Elizabeth I (Queen) 1–2, 7, 19, 45–7, 53–4

Index of Persons

Ellis, T.E. 322, 340, 391
Ellwood, Thomas 229, 293
Elton, G.R. 15, 46, 53, 97
Epiphanius 136, 144
Erbury, Dorcas 217, 219
Erbury, William 11, 128
Eusebius 13, 136, 144
Evans, E. Lewis 291
Evans, John 274–5
Ewens, Thomas 211
Exeter, Countess of 272
Eyre, John 130

Faldo, John 400
Farmer, Ralph 211
Farnworth, Richard 363, 367
Feake, Christopher 192
Fell, Henry 235
Fell, Leonard 235
Fell, Margaret 213–15, 301, 361
Fell, Sarah 360, 366(f)–7
Fell, Susannah 367
Fell, Thomas 213
Ferguson, Sinclair B. 299
Field, John 2, 37–41
Field, Richard 103
Firmin, Thomas 351, 353, 356–7
Firth, C.H. 304, 351
Fisher, Samuel 235, 317–19
Fitz, Richard 3, 33–37
Flavel, John 342–3
Fletcher H. 144
Fletcher, Elizabeth 229
Fowler, A. 385–9
Fowler, Giles 34
Fox, George 11, 201, 202, 205–10, 213, 217, 229, 233, 235, 292–3, 310, 317, 319–21, 357, 360–1, 364(e)–5, 393, 404
Foxe, John 13, 149
Freke, William 404
Frere, W.H. 37
Frewen, Accepted 13
Fuller, Thomas 103–9
Furly, John 235

Gardiner, S.R. 16, 193
Garment, Joshua 199–200
Geare, Alan 344

Gee, H. 149
George, Timothy 118
Giffard, George, 72
Gifford, Andrew 266, 268–9
Glines, Elsa F. 213
Goodman, Gabriel 23–32
Goodwin, Thomas 9, 12, 15, 128, 151–64, 285–7(c), 305–9, 385
Goodwin, William 221–5
Goold, W.H. 15, 299, 309, 343
Gordon, Alexander 351, 353, 401
Gouge, William 12
Gould, George 397
Greaves, Richard L. 217, 288, 323
Greenham, M. 56, 59, 62
Greenhill, William 151, 221–5
Greenway, Richard 393–4
Greenwood, John 3, 4, 72, 124, 256–8
Grell, O.P. 132
Grenville, John 252
Greville, Robert 145
Grieve, A.J. 91
Griffith, Alexander 392
Griffith, George 217, 221
Griffith, Walter 277–8
Grindal, Edmund 2–3, 22–33, 45–53, 107
Grosart, A.B. 285–7
Gunning, Peter 270–2
Gwyn, Thomas 272–4

Haller, William 151
Halley, Robert 285, 298
Hallywell, H. 372
Halsey, Mary 191
Hanmer, John 244–8
Hanmer, Thomas 244–8
Hardacre, P.H. 15
Hardcastle, Thomas 266, 268, 274
Hardy, W.J. 149
Harris, Francis 302
Harris, William 200
Harrison, Robert 3, 55, 63
Harrison, William 55
Hart, A. Tindal 264, 277
Hasler, P.W. 100
Hawkins, Robert, 23–32
Hay, Malcolm V. 278
Hayden, Roger 266
Haygood, Elizabeth 199

Healy, Thomas 393
Hedworth, Henry 356–9
Hellier, John 268–9
Helwys, Thomas 116, 132–4
Henry, Philip 243–8, 274
Herle, Charles 151, 165, 190
Hetherington William 165
Hicks, Alderman 267
Higginson, Francis 202
Hildersham, Arthur 103
Hill, Christopher 198, 288, 323, 367
Hollister, Denys 211
Homes, Nathanael 348
Hooker, Robert 5
Hooper, John 30, 33
Hooton, Elizabeth 201–2
Hooton, Oliver 201–2
Hopkins, S.V. 15
Horle, C.W. 361
Howe, John 12, 15
Howe, John 400
Howgill, Francis 202, 211, 235
Hubbert, Thomas 100
Hubberthorne, Richard 201, 229, 235, 292–3
Hughes, George 251–2
Hughes, Obadiah 252
Hughes, Stephen 14
Humphrey, Laurence 20–1, 23, 33
Huss, John 142, 144
Hutchinson, John 304–5
Hutchinson, Lucy 304–5
Hutter, Jakob 203
Hyde, H. Montgomery 278

Ingle, H. Larry 213, 300
Ireland, James, 23–32
Irenaeus 136
Israel, J. 132
Ivimey, J. 16, 266

Jackson, B., 53
Jacob, Henry 4, 113–16, 370
Jacomb, Thomas 236, 240–1
James I, (King) 1, 2, 15, 103, 106–9
James II (Duke of York) 374
Jeffreys, George 275–6, 278–81
Jenkins, Geraint H. 322
Jenkyn, William 236, 239–40, 261–2

Jerome of Prague 142, 145
Jerome, St. 136, 144
Jessey, Henry 314, 371
John, E. Stanley 131
John, Francis 270
Johnson, A. 287
Johnson, Francis 4, 124
Jones, R. Tudur 73, 91, 192, 256, 259, 273–4, 291, 401
Jones, T.R. 118
Jordan, W.K. 132
Julian, John 389
Juxon, William 13

Kaufmann, U.M. 323
Keeble, N.H. 323
Keiser, R.Melvin 293, 361
Keith, George 310–2, 375
Kiffin, William 370
King, Edward 387
King, John 103
Kingsford, C.L. 32
Kitchen, Mr 268
Knappe, M.M. 33, 46, 62
Knewstubs John 103, 107
Knightley, Richard 87
Knott, John R. 16, 323
Knox, John 108, 138
Knox, R. Buick 291
Kuenning, Lawrence S. 368
Kunze, Bonnelyn 213

L'Estrange, Roger 279–80
Lamplugh, Thomas 251
Langton, Thomas 267
Laud, William 2, 6–7, 13, 388
Lawford, Alderman 267
Lawson, John 201, 209
Leavens, Elizabeth 229
Lee, Edward Donne (*see* Donne Lee)
Lee, M.H. 244, 277
Leith J.H. 165
Lémontey, Pierre Édouard 306
Lever, Thomas 19–20, 23
Lewin, William 99–100
Lewis, Peter 285
Lilburne, John 11
Lloyd, Morgan 273
Lloyd, William 274–8

Index of Persons

Loyde, John 261
Llwyd, Morgan 290–2, 322–3, 340, 391–2
Lockington, Mrs 200
Love, Christoher 344–8
Lower, Mary 367
Luker, Mark 370
Lumpkin, W.L. 116, 329
Luther, Martin 142

McGinn, Donald J. 87
McGregor, J.F. 198
McKim, J.K. 165
Mack, Phyllis 201, 215
McLachlan, H.J. 352, 356–7
Madox, Mr 89
Manners, Emily 201
Manton, Thomas 217, 236, 238
Marprelate, Martin 3, 87–90, 97
Marshall, Charles 211
Martin, Clare J.L. 361, 393
Martin, Roger 32
Martyn, Samuel 252
Mary of Guise 107
Mary Tudor, Queen, 19, 103, 108, 237
Mary, Queen of Scots 103, 108
Masson, D. 388
Matthew, Tobie 103
Matthews, A.G. 9–10, 16, 221, 251, 266, 334
Matthews, Daniel 244
Matthews, Katherine 244
Maurice, Matthew 401
Mausolus 344
Mead, Matthew 400
Melancthon, Philip 29
Miller, Perry 109
Milton, John 10, 14, 135–45, 149–50, 262–6, 385–91
Mitchell, A.F. 165
Monmouth, Duke of 278
Montanus 202
Moore, Rosemary 213, 217, 229, 293, 360–1, 393
Morecraft, Richard 23–33
Morgan, W.T. 15, 273
Morton, A.L. 198
Mozley, J.F. 32
Muggleton, Ludovicke 11
Mullett, Michael A. 288

Munday, Anthony 88
Murray, Ian H. 367, 400

Nayler, James 209, 216–20, 302, 317, 319, 360
Neal, Daniel 145
Nero (Emperor) 136
Newcomen, Matthew 10
Newman, Humphrey 88, 90
Nicholson, W. 46, 53
Nickalls, John L. 213
Nixon, William 23, 32
Nuttall, G.F. 109, 113, 118, 128, 201, 279, 285, 291, 367
Nye, Philip 8–9, 151–64, 217, 221–5, 353
Nye, Stephen 353–6

Oates, Titus 278
Okey, John 193
Ollive, Ralph 268
Orme, W. 316
Overall, John 103
Owen, Charles 277
Owen, James 277–8
Owen, John 1, 9, 12, 15, 221–5, 229–30, 299–300, 309, 318, 343–4

Paas, S. 73
Paets, Adriaan von 375
Pagitt, Ephraim 10, 201
Palmer, A.N. 244, 274–5
Palmer, Herbert 165, 190
Palmer, S. 243, 348
Parker, Alexander 310–11
Parker, Henry 370
Parker, Matthew 2, 22
Parker, Robert 113
Parker, W.R. 135, 149
Parry, L.J. 322
Partridge, Randall 34
Paul, R.S. 165
Paul, St. 143
Payne, Richard 261
Peel, A. 33, 37, 55, 63
Penington, Isaac 293, 296–8(b)
Penington, John 360
Penn, Admiral Sir William 372
Penn, William, jr 356–7, 372–4, 404
Penney, Norman 361

Penry, John 4, 7, 53, 87, 90–100, 118, 120, 205, 256–8
Pepys, Samuel 371
Perkins, William 287
Perowne, T.T. 32
Perrot, John 393
Petersson, R.T. 15
Petronius 136
Phelps Brown, E.H. 15
Philips, Humphrey 254
Pierce, William 87–8, 97, 100
Plato 137
Plomer, H.B. 216
Plooij, Daniel 118
Pollock, John 278
Pope, Michael 261
Powell, Vavasor 11, 192, 256–8, 274–5, 392–3
Powicke, F.J. 33, 72–3, 118, 279
Prynne, William 386
Puleston, John 244–8
Purvis, J.S. 273
Pyper, Hugh 375
Pythagoras 141

Rainolds (*see* Reynolds)
Reay, Barry 198
Rees, Abraham, 91
Reeve, John 11
Reid, James 151
Reid, John 235
Reynolds (Rainolds) John 103, 107–8
Rich, Nathaniel 256
Rich, Robert 217, 220
Richards, Thomas 16, 131, 192, 244, 259, 275
Ridley, Nicholas 30, 33
Roberts, Gerrard 235
Roberts, Thomas 63
Robins, Joan 199
Robins, John 199
Robinson, Henry 103
Robinson, John 4, 6, 116–18, 132
Roborough, Henry 165, 190
Rogers, H. 16
Rogers, P.G. 193
Roper, John 25
Rordorj, W. 125
Rotheram, John 279–81

Rous, Francis 389
Rowe, Violet, 351
Rowse, A.L. 87
Rutherford, Samuel 385

Salesbury, William 96
Saltmarsh, John 11
Sampson Thomas, 20–1, 23, 33
Sancroft, William 275
Sanders, Mr 237
Saunders, Thomas 193
Sawday, Jonathan 393
Sawrey, John 213
Schaff, Philip 165
Schwenkfeld, Kaspar von 202
Scotus, Duns 136
Sharman, Cecil W. 319
Sharpe, Henry 88, 90
Sharrock, Roger 323
Shaw, Gareth 361
Shaw, Samuel 254–5
Shelton, Thomas 371
Shepherd, Thomas 370
Sherwill, Nicholas 252
Sibbes, Richard 265–6
Sidney, Philip 145
Simmons, Martha 216–18
Simmons, R.C. 109
Simmons, Thomas 216, 218
Simpson, Sidrach 9, 151–64
Sippel, Peter D. 375
Sirlock, Ernest 135
Smith John 23–32
Smith, Humphrey 230–2
Smith, Nigel 198, 393
Smyth, John 4, 116–18, 132
Socinus, Faustus 351
Sparke, Thomas 103
Spenser, Edmund 136
Spilsbury, John 370
Spooner, F. 15
Stanhope, Edward 87
Stearns, R.P. 118
Stephens, Meic 291
Stewart, Adam 385
Stinton, Benjamin 370
Stoughton, John 236–7
Stranger, Hannah 217–19
Struthers, J.B. 165

Index of Persons

Strype, John, 19, 87
Stygold, Christopher, 130
Sylvester, Matthew 16, 400

Talon, Henry 322
Taylor, George 213–14
Taylor, Richard 244
Taylor, Roland 33
Taylor, Thomas 236
Taylor, William 344
Terrill, Edward 266–70
Tertullian 387
Theodoret 53
Thomas, D.R. 274–5
Thomas, M. Wynn 291
Thomason, George 10
Thompson, John 266–9
Throckmorton, Job 87, 97
Thurloe, John 211
Tindall, W.Y. 323
Toon, Peter 221, 300, 367
Toulmin, John 351
Tovey, Alan 73
Trevett, Christine 201, 215, 361
Troughton, William 266, 268
Tucker, John 261
Turner, G. Lyon 259, 261
Twisse, William 165
Tyacke, H. 132
Tynne, James 33

Underhill, E.B. 266
Underwood, T.L. 367
Usher, R.G. 97

Valentinus 203
Vane, Henry 8, 351

Wakefield, Gordon 135
Waldegrave, Robert 90
Walker, John 9
Walker, Williston 400
Wallop, Richard 279, 280

Walter, Henry 131
Walwyn, William 11
Warfield, B.B. 165
Watts, Michael R. 34–5, 62–3, 73, 97, 113, 116, 132, 151, 259, 352, 401
Watts, Trefor 131
Weeks, John 261, 266–9
Wenzelburger, T. 306
Wharey, J.B. 323
Whitaker, Jeremiah 344
Whitaker, W. 125
White, B.R. 32, 62–3, 118, 132
White, William 23–32
Whitehead, George 404
Whitgift, John 2–3, 19, 87, 97, 104
Whitley, Y.W. 116
Whyte, Hugh 261
Wickham, William 100
Wigston, Robert 88, 90
Wilcox, Thomas 2, 37, 42–4
Wildman John 193
Willans, Thomas, 213–14
William III (of Orange, and Mary) 1, 278, 397
Williams, David 87, 91
Williams, G.F. 203
Williams, Glanmor 87, 90
Williams, J.B. 274, 277
Williams, William 275
Wilson, J. Dover 88
Wilson, Thomas 370
Willoughby, William 261
Winstanley, Gerard 11
Wolfe, D.M. 262
Wood, Anthony 103
Worts, Thomas 255
Wright, Luella 393
Wroth, William 131
Wykeham, William (*see* Wickham)

Yeamen, Robert 267

Zwingli, Huldrych 19, 165

www.ingramcontent.com/pod-product-compliance
Lightning Source LLC
Chambersburg PA
CBHW081146290426
44108CB00018B/2454